A Long Time Burning

A LONG TIME BURNING

The History of Literary Censorship in England

DONALD THOMAS

Can Statutes keep the British Press in awe,
When that sells best, that's most
against the law?
James Bramston, *The Man of Taste* (1733)

FREDERICK A. PRAEGER, *Publishers*
New York · Washington

BOOKS THAT MATTER

Published in the United States of America in 1969
by Frederick A. Praeger, Inc., Publishers
111 Fourth Avenue, New York, N.Y. 10003

© *1969, in London, England, by Donald Thomas*

Library of Congress Catalog Card Number: 73–83392

174288

Printed in Great Britain

FOR CAROL

Contents

vii

Contents

List of Illustrations

(The following illustrations fall between pages 276–277)

1   'Aretine's Postures.' One of the *Sedici modi* engraved by Marcantonio Raimondi in 1524 from the work of Giulio Romano.

2   Frontispiece and title-page from *Harris's List of Covent-Garden Ladies* for 1793. James Roach and James Aitken were successfully prosecuted in 1794 for publishing this 'obscene libel'.

3   *The Brightest Star in the State . . . or . . . A Peep out of a Royal Window*. One of two prints for which the Constitutional Association prosecuted William Benbow in 1821, on the grounds that they libelled George IV. The case was eventually dropped.

4 and 5   *Mars, Venus and Vulcan*, and *Leda*. Frontispieces of William Benbow's *Rambler's Magazine: or, Fashionable Emporium of Polite Literature* for January and February 1822. The Society for the Suppression of Vice prosecuted Benbow on a charge of publishing these frontispieces, described as 'two obscene and indecent pictures representing the persons of men and women in most indecent postures attitudes and situations'. The jury acquitted him.

6   *The Guard of Honor*, illustrating a story of the same title, appeared in the *New London Rambler's Magazine* in 1829. John Duncombe was fined £50 and imprisoned for six months for publishing this and other material in the magazine. The indictment described the picture as 'representing a dog and the person of a woman partly naked in a most indecent posture and attitude'. There is some similarity to Fragonard's painting *La Gimblette*.

7 and 8   Cover and illustration from William Dugdale's magazine, *The Exquisite*, which he published as 'H. Smith' from 1842 to 1844.

9   One of the *Freethinker*'s 'Comic Bible Sketches'.

10   Public display—1870
    Charles Grieves, who had been Dugdale's printer, was sentenced to a year's hard labour in February 1870 for publishing the *Ferret*. Particular exception was taken to the cover of this second

Preface

The main problem in writing a history of literary censorship is to avoid writing the history of too many other things at the same time—and, on the other hand, not to confine the account to a mere chronicle of cases and statutes. Somewhere between the aridity of legal history and the evasiveness of generalisations about the 'spirit of the age' lies a middle path: this is the path which I have tried to follow. As a glance at the bibliography of this book will show, quite a number of writers have already described, in whole or in part, the impact of censorship on English literature and it seems only just that I should acknowledge my debt to them first of all. When I have been fortunate enough to discover new material of some importance, particularly with reference to censorship during the later eighteenth and earlier nineteenth centuries, I have incorporated this in my own account.

In the last chapters of the book I have tried to show what the term 'pornography' seems to imply, since it is one of the easiest words to use imprecisely and about as hard to define adequately as 'poetry' or 'beauty.' To most people, a book might be erotic without being necessarily pornographic, it might—as in the case of *Gulliver's Travels* or *Tristram Shandy*—be regarded by certain critics as obscene without being pornographic: if it were both erotic and obscene, it would generally be classified as pornography. This may be a useful enough working definition for such a term and my own interest in trying to expand it is literary rather than linguistic.

I cannot remember when I first considered the possibility of writing a history of censorship but I certainly rejected it at the time and now, in retrospect, I am thankful to Mr. Morris Ernst, the champion of *Ulysses* and *The Well of Loneliness* in the American courts, who persuaded me in the autumn of 1964 that the undertaking was well worthwhile. During my subsequent research I was made aware once more of the kindness and patience of so many librarians and keepers of records. Among those who are not normally thought of as keepers of records for this purpose, I owe most of my account of the Vizetelly prosecution of 1889 to Mr. Leslie Boyd, Clerk of the Central Criminal Court, and his staff who with, no doubt, many more urgent calls on their time found and produced for me the elusive documents relating to Vizetelly's trial. A great deal of my research was bound to involve access to books not generally available and I am grateful particularly to the staff of the British Museum and the Bodleian Library for making my work so easy in this respect. I should also like to express my thanks to Mr. John Saltmarsh, Acting Librarian of King's College, Cambridge; to the staff of the Public Record Office Repository at Ashridge; the Corporation of London Record Office; the Middlesex Record Office, and the Library of University College, Cardiff.

In the summer of 1967, at a time when documents in the Public Record Office were, in general, open to inspection after thirty years, I traced some of the material relating to press prosecutions of the 1930s to the Metropolitan Police file classified in the Public Record Office as Mepol. 3. This, however, was not to be opened until after a hundred years. It is perfectly reasonable that certain documents in such files should not be opened so long as the information in them might cause distress to innocent people. Perhaps a hundred years is the right period in these cases. What is quite unreasonable is that documents of legitimate public interest, like the Attorney-General's opinion on *Ulysses* in 1936, which was decisive in allowing the novel to circulate freely in England, should be closed until the third decade of the twenty-first century. The kindness and persistence of Mr. Ted Rowlands, M.P., who took up this point on my behalf with the Home Office, led to the eventual disclosure of the *Ulysses* opinion but other documents of this kind await either the twenty-first century or, let us hope, sensible reclassification.

To Professor Arthur Johnston of the University College of Wales, Aberystwyth, and to Professor Geoffrey Tillotson of Birkbeck College, University of London, I owe much of my interest in the literature of the eighteenth and nineteenth centuries and most of my knowledge of it. Throughout the writing of this book I have been deeply grateful for the advice and enthusiasm of Mr. Murray Mindlin, both during his editorship of the quarterly *Censorship* and afterwards. Some of the material relating to the Licensing System; *The School of Venus*; Leigh Hunt's *Examiner*, and the Vice Society, in the present book first made its appearance in the form of contributions to *Censorship*. My thanks are due as well to Mr. Robert Dumbleton, Mr. David Selbourne, and Mr. and Mrs. Alan Simons for drawing my attention to books and information which, left to myself, I should have missed. To Mr. Colin Franklin of Routledge and Kegan Paul I am grateful for his reading of the manuscript and his helpful comments on it. To my wife has fallen the task of acting as both critic and collaborator in putting the book together, while still managing to preserve that *hortus conclusus* in which work is both possible and congenial. I owe it to her that this book was written in three years rather than thirty.

I

The Fear of Literature

One of the most interesting revelations of a man's views on literary censorship is provided by the successive editions of David Hume's essay 'Of the Liberty of the Press', first published in *Essays Moral and Political* in 1741. He remarks that foreigners are justifiably surprised at the freedom which the British nation enjoys 'of communicating whatever we please to the Public, and of openly censuring every Measure entered into by the King or his Ministers'. Other nations, says Hume, enjoy no such privilege and the only reason for its existence in Britain is that the country is neither an absolute monarchy nor a complete democracy but one in which the forces of political power are balanced. This kind of judgment was to become a truism of British political thinking and Hume, in the first edition of his essay, concludes with one of those stirring perorations which we are well accustomed to in discussions of this sort.

'Tis seldom, that Liberty of any Kind is lost all at once. Slavery has so frightful an Aspect to Men accustom'd to Freedom, that it must steal in upon them by Degrees, and must disguise itself in a thousand Shapes, in order to be received. But if the Liberty of the Press ever be lost, it must be lost at once. The general Laws against Sedition and Libelling are at present as strong as they possibly can be made. Nothing can impose a farther Restraint, but either the clapping an IMPRIMATUR upon the Press, or the giving very large discretionary Powers to the Court to punish whatever displeases them. But these Concessions would be such a bare-fac'd Violation of Liberty, that they will probably be the last Efforts of a despotic Government. We may conclude, that the Liberty of *Britain* is gone for ever, when these Attempts shall succeed.[1]

There is nothing remarkable about such sentiments, unless perhaps we feel that what Hume sees as the spirit of freedom in 1741 is nothing more than a tolerance born of lassitude on the part of a Whig administration, drained of energy by its quarter of a century in office. But still, words like these are calculated to warm the heart of any believer in the freedom of the press, and so it may come as a surprise to find that the whole of this fervent conclusion to the essay 'Of the Liberty of the Press' was omitted when the eleventh edition of

[1] *Essays Moral and Political* (Edinburgh, 1741), pp. 17–18.

1

it was published in 1770. Worse than that, when the final version was published in 1777 (the year after Hume's death) the conclusion to this essay was replaced by a brief and devastating comment on press freedom in a society neither wholly democratic nor wholly monarchical.

It must however be allowed, that the unbounded liberty of the press, though it be difficult, perhaps impossible, to propose a suitable remedy for it, is one of the evils, attending those mixt forms of government.[1]

The liberty of the press, which had seemed so important in 1741, was now something which required 'a suitable remedy'. Of course, this hostility to the 'popular leaders' following the 'Wilkes and Liberty' riots of 1768 occurs elsewhere in Hume's later writings, and even in 1741 he confessed that he would rather 'see an absolute monarch than a republic in this island'. Yet the real explanation of the change in Hume's views on the press lies less in his own mental development than in the social and political history of the mid-eighteenth century. By 1777 the fears which a number of writers had expressed about the mob—Henry Fielding had described it with uneasy irony as the fourth estate of the realm—seemed to be well founded. To many people, violence and the defiance of authority had been characteristics of the mob since the seventeenth century, but the riots in support of Wilkes in 1768, the birth in 1769 of the Society for the Defence of the Bill of Rights, had for the first time given this starved, illiterate, and unenfranchised mass of humanity some kind of cohesion and political objective. Violence and defiance had been harnessed so that the mob was on its way to becoming 'the People'. The devastation of the Gordon riots in London in 1780 (when even Wilkes found himself defending the Bank of England against the insurgents), and the 'Church and King' riots in Birmigham eleven years later, tested the effectiveness of violence as a political weapon, while the revolution in France provided what seemed like the ultimate demonstration. Hume lived long enough to witness the first murmurings against monarchy and ministers, the first serious demands for electoral reform: freedom of the press might have been desirable enough under the benign incompetence of a declining Augustan administration, but it was quite another thing when exploited by those who had pledged themselves to bloody revolution and the overthrow of constitutional government. In 1741 the only alternative to the Whigs had been the Tories, who succeeded to power in any case two decades later: the alternatives by 1777 seemed much more likely to be con-

[1] *Essays and Treatises on Several Subjects* (London, 1777), I, 12.

stitution or revolution; law or anarchy. Even those who felt some sympathy with the demands of the revolutionaries in the years that followed remained advocates of censorship, for fear of the mob. In 1792, when Thomas Paine was prosecuted and convicted of seditious libel for publishing his *Rights of Man*, in which he attacked what he called 'The farce of monarchy and aristocracy', William Pitt, who was then Prime Minister, is reported to have said, 'Paine is no fool, he is perhaps right; but if I did what he wants, I should have thousands of bandits on my hands to-morrow and London burnt.' Men in Pitt's position may be prone to exaggerate such dangers, but he had cause to remember 'London burnt' twelve years earlier in the Gordon riots and there is no reason whatever to doubt that his fears were genuinely felt. Yet while he approved of the prosecution of Paine, Pitt made no attempt to suppress William Godwin's *Enquiry Concerning Political Justice* (1793), because it cost three guineas a copy and was therefore, he felt, unlikely to fall into the wrong hands.[1]

Whether or not a book became the subject of a criminal prosecution might depend on its intellectual pretensions as well as its retail price. For instance, the bluff, no-nonsense arguments of Thomas Paine's attacks on the Bible and the Christian religion in his *Age of Reason* (1793), and the same approach in Elihu Palmer's *Principles of Nature* (1801) led to a series of attempts by English courts to suppress these and similar publications. On the other hand, as the publishers of such books indignantly pointed out, no attempt was ever made to censor the far more intellectually powerful comments on Christianity in Hume's 'Essay on Miracles', which forms the tenth section of the *Enquiry Concerning the Human Understanding* (1748), or the notorious fifteenth and sixteenth chapters of Gibbon's *Decline and Fall of the Roman Empire* (1776–88). Censorship, in this respect, exists for the protection of the unsophisticated reader, who must be shielded not from the irony or the sophistries of Gibbon and Hume but from the cruder onslaughts of men like Paine and Palmer. To the Victorians, a generation or more later, the book which cast the most significant doubts on Christian belief was probably Strauss's *Leben Jesu*, which appeared in a translation by George Eliot in 1846. Yet however much Strauss might undermine the faith of certain churchmen of the more intellectual kind, his book was unlikely to be a favourite with the less-educated classes of society, so it is no surprise to find it escaped prosecution, while the anger of the law was reserved for such publications as the *Freethinker*'s 'Comic Bible Sketches' (1882), which could be understood by all but the feeble-minded and which,

[1] The first part of Paine's *Rights of Man* sold at 2*s*. 6*d*. and the second part at 3*s*.

though they might offend or amuse, seemed unlikely to persuade many readers to a new point of view.

The last quarter of the eighteenth century, with its development of popular education through the new Sunday schools and its system whereby those who had learnt to read would read aloud to those who had not, provoked a powerful demand for stricter moral censorship in literature. The desire to protect the lower orders—and children of all classes—was most fervent from then on in the case of literature regarded as obscene or even indecorous. When the poet Robert Montgomery (1807–55) wrote his verses 'On the Effects of Indiscriminate Novel Reading', he had a very clear idea of where the worst of these effects were to be found.

> E'en sluttish housemaids crib a farthing light,
> To whimper o'er the novel's page by night;
> And then, like heroines, scorning to be wed,
> Next night make John the hero of their bed.[1]

When Charles Bradlaugh and Annie Besant were prosecuted in 1877 for publishing Charles Knowlton's *Fruits of Philosophy*, one of the most widely circulated books on the subject of birth control to appear in the nineteenth century, the prosecution naturally maintained that once the fear of pregnancy was removed promiscuity was bound to follow. But who was going to be promiscuous? Certainly not those with the puritan earnestness of Bradlaugh and Mrs. Besant. One consideration, above all others, must have secured the book's conviction: the knowledge that, according to the Solicitor-General, if it were allowed to go free it would be 'permitted to circulate through all classes of society at 6*d*. a copy'.[2] The twentieth century has perpetuated this attitude towards obscene literature, or rather towards literature which is alleged to be obscene. In 1935, for example, Edward Charles's *The Sexual Impulse* was destroyed by order of the Westminster Police Court, the magistrate remarking that such a book was not 'fit and decent for people of the working class to read'.[3] In 1960, when Penguin Books were prosecuted for publishing D. H. Lawrence's *Lady Chatterley's Lover*, the opening address for the prosecution included a question to the jury which was worthy of Robert Montgomery. 'Is it a book that you would even wish your wife or your servants to read?'[4] And in 1964, when John Cleland's *Fanny Hill* was condemned by the Bow Street magistrate, much was

[1] Robert Montgomery, *Poetical Works* (London, 1836), p. 276.
[2] *The Times*, 19 June 1877.
[3] *The Times*, 17 October 1935.
[4] *The Trial of Lady Chatterley*, ed. C. H. Rolph (London, 1961), p. 17.

made of the fact that the book had been sold as a 3*s.* 6*d.* paperback at the Magic Shop in the Tottenham Court Road and was therefore available to the, presumably, rather unsophisticated reader who habitually bought his books from this type of shop. In 1966 when an application for a destruction order was brought before the Marlborough Street magistrate in respect of an American novel, *Last Exit to Brooklyn* by Hubert Selby, it was alleged that its price (30*s.*) did not put it beyond the reach of an adolescent who enjoyed an adequate rate of pocket-money.

It has always been the case that at least a small group of people has been privileged to read literature which may have been forbidden to the rest of its contemporaries or compatriots. Even in the sixteenth century, when the possession of certain books was a capital offence, Privy Counsellors were allowed to import seditious literature for their own perusal, and bishops might give permission to approved applicants to read books which were normally banned. Four centuries later the same principle seems to apply. On 18 September 1967 the *Daily Telegraph* reported that the Home Office had set up a library of obscene books for the use of Members of Parliament. No book would be admitted unless it had been successfully prosecuted under the Obscene Publications Act and use of the library would be strictly reserved for Members of Parliament. Where prohibited literature is concerned, there is no such thing as equality before the law. Since the eighteenth century books have been primarily censored not because they 'imagined' the death of the reigning sovereign or denied the doctrine of the Trinity—which would previously have been reason enough—but because of the effect which they might have on the newly literate or semi-literate masses. Even a book whose importance was recognised might have to be condemned: thus William Pitt allowed the reasonableness of Paine's case in *The Rights of Man* but was still relieved that the book should have been banned. At the other extreme, no one would suggest that the carefully catalogued and preserved collections of pornography in the British Museum or Bodleian libraries should be seized and destroyed by order of the courts, though we cannot allow the full text of *Fanny Hill* to be sold in the Tottenham Court Road. The potential readership of a book is, by the Obscene Publications Act of 1959, what determines its fate: at the very time when the case against Mayflower Books had been brought for publishing *Fanny Hill* at 3*s.* 6*d.*, a much older edition of the same novel was auctioned at Christie's without so much as a warrant being applied for.

Of course there is no precise point at which literary censorship began to take into account the emergence of a mass readership, it is, rather, an attitude which one can see developing throughout the eighteenth century. The Victorians, looking back from their own point of vantage, could put a much more precise date to the division between censorship as exercised in an almost static, feudal spirit, and censorship—or perhaps the lack of it—in a better-educated and more democratic society. This date was 1695, when the House of Commons refused to renew the Licensing Act by which virtually all books were required to be licensed before they could be published. This system of pre-censorship had been in force for most of the time since the introduction of printing into England by Caxton in 1476 and, naturally, the collapse of such a system seemed to Victorian observers to mark the great dawn of intellectual liberty.

By the cessation of those laws which restricted the liberty of printing, there was laid the foundation of that great Public Press, which, more than any other single cause, has diffused among the people a knowledge of their power and has thus, to an almost incredible extent, aided the progress of English civilisation.[1]

Such was the view of H. T. Buckle in his *History of Civilisation in England* (1857–61), while Lord Macaulay described the rejection of the licensing system as an event, 'which has done more for liberty and for civilisation than the Great Charter or the Bill of Rights'.[2] The Victorians had good reason to be sensitive about the political aspects of press freedom, since despite the 'triumph' of 1695, freedom of expression on political issues seemed to many of them to have been a very recently acquired privilege, something which had been wrested from George IV rather than from James II or William and Mary. Yet from the end of the seventeenth century until the middle of the nineteenth there had been a growing freedom of expression on political and religious issues, even though some of the more frightened—and therefore repressive—administrations had made full use of prosecutions for seditious or blasphemous libel to curb the most outspoken authors: such was the general Victorian opinion. Looking back from the mid-nineteenth century, Lord Macaulay remarked with satisfaction that 'the history of our country during the last hundred and sixty years is eminently the history of physical, of moral, and of intellectual improvement'.[3] And yet, as every historian of the period feels obliged to tell us, while the Victorian press was in so many respects more free than any of its predecessors, there were certain areas in which taboo, if not outright censorship, was stricter than it had ever been.

[1] H. T. Buckle, *History of Civilisation in England* (London, 1857–61), I, 353.
[2] T. B. Macaulay, *History of England* (London, 1849–61). IV, 540.
[3] *ibid.*, I, 3.

6

During a hundred and sixty years the liberty of our press has been constantly becoming more and more entire; and during those hundred and sixty years the restraint imposed on writers by the general feeling of readers has been constantly becoming more and more strict. At length even that class of works in which it was formerly thought that a voluptuous imagination was privileged to disport itself, love songs, comedies, novels, have become more decorous than the sermons of the seventeenth century. At this day foreigners, who dare not print a word reflecting on the government under which they live, are at a loss to understand how it happens that the freest press in Europe is the most prudish.[1]

Hardly had Macaulay written these words than 'the general feeling of readers' was reinforced by something stronger in the shape of Lord Campbell's Obscene Publications Act of 1857. Macaulay saw more clearly than many of his countrymen the realities of the Victorian situation, while the self-congratulation of many of his liberal contemporaries merely illustrates the fallacy of believing that because at any given time we may be free of the censorship which was familiar to an earlier generation we are therefore free of censorship altogether. The Obscene Publications Act of 1959 allows us to read *Lady Chatterley's Lover* while the Race Relations Act of 1965 makes the publication of racist literature a criminal offence. The relevant question at any stage of human history is not 'Does censorship exist?' but rather, 'Under what sort of censorship do we now live?'

[1] *ibid.*, IV, 607.

2

Censorship Before Publication: 1476–1695

It would have taken an act of extraordinary naïvete to believe that when the 'mystery' of printing was introduced into England in 1476 it would remain free from royal control or interest. When nine years later the crown passed to Henry VII he soon chose to assert his authority over the press and appointed Peter Actors as his stationer. Patents were granted to printers by the Crown and, in general, the printers showed no inclination to quarrel with the way in which their activities were regulated.[1] From the introduction of printing until the end of licensing in 1695 represents a distinct period of literary censorship in England, both as a time when literature was officially approved before publication and as an age in which censors could concentrate on the subject-matter of a book or pamphlet without having to consider whether or not it was safe to communicate such subject-matter to a mass readership. Naturally, this earliest form of literary censorship dealt almost entirely with the suppression of political opposition and religious dissension. From time to time there were short-lived efforts to prevent the publication of books on the grounds of their obscenity or lasciviousness but the real spur to this kind of censorship was the knowledge that such literature might get into the hands of the lower orders of society and would incite them to perform obscene or lascivious acts of the sort described in these books, a problem not much encountered until after 1695. Nonetheless, in the latter half of the seventeenth century there was some official recognition of the undesirability of obscene literature, even to the extent of prosecuting those who printed or sold it.

In the twentieth century there are still those who would advocate setting up an official committee or board of censors, perhaps made up of representatives of the book trade, who would examine books before publication and would, if they were approved, guarantee them immunity against subsequent prosecution. Generally speaking, this is the system which operated in England throughout the sixteenth and seventeenth centuries, backed by penalties which were, in the last resort, more savage than any which the twentieth century would tolerate.

[1] Actors was succeeded in 1501 by William Faques, who became 'printer to the King.'

Yet despite such penalties and the obvious determination of the authorities to enforce the pre-censorship of literature, the history of the period is the history of the ultimate ineffectiveness of such measures.

The dangers of a disaffected press grew more apparent as the troubles facing the Tudors at home and abroad increased in number and complexity. The licensing system was firmly established by a decree of Star Chamber, issued in the uneasy circumstances of 1538 and forbidding printers to issue any book in English, 'Onles vpon examination made by some of his gracis privie counsayle, or other suche as his highnes shall appoynte, they shall have lycense so to do.'[1] For the next eighteen years the administration of this literary censorship remained in the hands of the Privy Council until, in the reign of Queen Mary, it was decided to make the book trade its own censor, after the incorporation of the Company of Stationers in 1556. On the principle of setting a thief to catch a thief, the Stationers' Company (to which almost everyone engaged in the book trade was compelled to belong) was invested by the Crown with the power and the obligation of operating a censorship by examining and licensing books before publication. Inevitably, the Crown would still retain the ultimate power of dealing with seditious or heretical publications and it would exercise direct control over the grisly array of punishments prepared for the publishers of such literature. The granting of this charter to the Stationers' Company was described with a spirit of philistinism which made it quite clear that, on the part of the authorities, this was a recognition of the dangers of literature rather than of its usefulness or dignity: the aim was the suppression of what were specifically referred to as 'sediciosi et haeretici libri'.[2] The Master and the Wardens of the Stationers' Company were empowered to search for and destroy unlicensed books and unlicensed presses, as well as inflicting fines or short prison sentences on the culprits. The imposition of heavier penalties remained the prerogative of the Crown. A royal proclamation of 5 June 1558 condemned unlicensed books 'whereby not onely God is dishonored, but also an encoragemente geuen to disobey laweful princes and gouernors'.[3] The proclamation clearly shows the seriousness with which the problem of subversive and forbidden literature was regarded by the Tudor state and it contains a stern warning that 'whosoeuer shal after the proclaymyng hereof, be founde to haue any of the sayde wycked and seditious bokes, or

---

[1] 16 November 1538. Pollard and Redgrave *Short-Title Catalogue 1475-1640*, 7790.

[2] *Transcript of the Registers of the Company of Stationers* ed. E. Arber (London, 1875-94), I, xxviii.

[3] *ibid.*, I, 92.

finding them doo not forthwith burne the same, without showing or readynge the same to anye other person, shall in that case be reputed and taken for a rebell, and shall without delay be executed for that offence accordynge to th ordre of marshall law'.[1]

Queen Mary died soon after this last proclamation, and the Catholicism of her reign was replaced by the anti-Catholicism of Elizabeth. Many books approved during Mary's reign now changed places with those that had been condemned, yet however much the list of books to be suppressed might vary, the apparatus and philosophy of censorship was much the same in both reigns. Naturally the Elizabethan state strove to make the working of the censorship more efficient and on 10 November 1559, when the power of the Stationers' Company to regulate the book trade was confirmed, Elizabeth also issued a list of those who were empowered to license the publication of books. With few exceptions, this authority was limited to the Archbishops of Canterbury and York; the Bishop of London, and the Vice-Chancellors of Oxford and Cambridge. Each book, when licensed, was to be entered in the Stationers' Register and a fee paid to the Company. As in the reign of Mary, this system of censorship was backed up by threats of death for those who offended against it to the extent of possessing or circulating seditious literature. The severest penalties were associated with two categories of banned books, pro-Catholic literature, which was usually printed abroad, and Puritan literature, which was the work of printers in England. These two categories of books represented the two great imagined threats to political stability: the overthrow of the established order by foreign Catholic intervention, and its overthrow by Puritan subversion at home. So a proclamation of 1 March 1569 (when Catholicism rather than Puritanism still seemed the more immediate danger) referred to the presence in the country of certain seditious books published 'on the other syde of the sea,'[2] a reference to the activities of the Catholic exiles. Owners of such books were given twenty-eight days in which to surrender them to their bishops or ordinaries, though they would then be permitted to read them if they could persuade an archbishop or a bishop to give them special permission. (After a similar proclamation in 1573 relating to Puritan literature it appears that few, if any, books were handed in and it seems reasonable to suppose that those who possessed them may have regarded the prospect of handing them in as more dangerous than keeping them.) In July 1570 another proclamation contained the hardly necessary reminder that authors of seditious books could expect to be hanged, drawn, and quartered, if they were caught.

[1] *ibid.*, I, 92.   [2] *ibid.*, I, 430.

Four months later this penalty was also applied to anyone aiding or abetting the author of such a book. But threats of death and torture could make little difference to the activities of men like Robert Parsons or Edmund Campion, whose missionary zeal included acceptance of the fact that martyrdom for the Catholic faith might be their temporal reward. Under their supervision books like Campion's *Decem Rationes* and Parsons's *Brief discours contayning certayn reasons why Catholiques refuse to goe to church* were published. Apart from the more obvious dangers of operating a secret press in England, these Elizabethan Catholics faced considerable problems in finding an adequate supply of paper and type. As one might expect, the publications of such secret presses show typographical signs of having been produced under considerable technical handicaps. Campion was caught, tortured and executed, but despite some moments of extreme danger neither Parsons nor his press was ever apprehended.

As internal subversion replaced invasion from abroad as the greatest potential threat in many people's minds, the authorities began to concern themselves increasingly with the clandestine publications of the Puritan presses rather than with the work of men like Parsons. In a general attempt to check the flow of unlicensed literature, Star Chamber in 1586 prohibited all printing except at London, Oxford and Cambridge, where it might more easily be kept under supervision. No new presses were to be licensed without the explicit authority of either the Archbishop of Canterbury or the Bishop of London. Yet this stricter censorship was one of the contributory causes of the appearance in 1588–9 of the seven anti-episcopal satires, Presbyterian in sympathy, known as the 'Martin Marprelate' tracts. Under Archbishop Whitgift the censorship had grown more determined and in this case retribution was reasonably swift, even though there remains some doubt as to its accuracy. In September 1589 a secret report to Lord Burghley resulted in the naming of Robert Waldegrave and John Hodgkys—identified by the type used for printing the tracts—as the printers of the Martin Marprelate satires, and of two other men, Newman and Penrye, as the publishers. It was deduced from the handwriting and style that Penrye was the author, and he was subsequently executed. This deduction was, to say the least, incomplete, and it is more generally assumed that Job Throckmorton, who escaped punishment at the time, was the real author of the satires.

After the death of Elizabeth in 1603, the Stuarts inherited from the Tudors the system of censorship as part of the machinery of government. Growing hostility between the Crown and Parliament, as well as between the Puritans and the Church of England led to a number of skirmishes as the result of publications, which one side or the other objected to. The last major pronouncement on censorship before the Civil War was the *Decree of Starre-Chamber Concerning Printing* issued on 11 July 1637. In addition to the existing licensers, this decree conceded that law books might be licensed by Lords Chief Justice, histories by Principal Secretaries of State, and books on heraldry by the Earl Marshal. This was not so much a relaxation of censorship (1637 was no time for that) as a tacit admission that the growing number of books called for an increase in the number of licensers and that the whole licensing system was bound to get more and more unwieldy as the trade in books developed. In some respects the decree acknowledged an extension of censorship by providing that all imported books should be seized and not released until they had been examined by the Archbishop of Canterbury, or the Bishop of London, or the Master or Wardens of the Stationers' Company, or their representatives. The surprising thing is that so many of those in the early eighteenth century who wanted to reintroduce the system of pre-censorship by licensing, regarded this decree as a model document, oblivious of the way in which it had delegated authority so that the administration of the book trade was handed over to an ill-defined and therefore largely irresponsible bureaucracy.

With the abolition of the Court of Star Chamber in 1640 the literary censorship which it exercised was, in theory, removed. Of course, censorship during the Civil War would have been extremely difficult to operate. Some printers and booksellers went over to the side of Parliament, others fled with the King from London and set up elsewhere to distribute propaganda for the Royalist cause. Rival newsbooks, part news and part invective, appeared on either side. Parliament, however, tried to take the law into its own hands long before the war was over by deciding in 1643 to impose licensing on the press by its own authority, a measure which John Milton bitterly described as 'the immediate image of a Star Chamber decree.' In place of the licensers named in the decree of 1637, the Order of 1643 substituted no fewer then twenty-seven licensers, chosen from schoolmasters, ministers of religion, doctors, and others. As licensers they were probably no better and no worse than their predecessors had been but the sudden increase in their numbers did little to develop censorship as an effective political instrument.[1] Milton, certain in a time of uncertainty, ignored the decision of Parliament and issued his tract of 1643 on *The Doctrine and Discipline of Divorce* unlicensed and un-

[1] In 1588, by contrast, there had been eight principal licensers and four assistants. See *Records of the Stationers' Company 1576–1602*, ed. W. W. Greg and E. Boswell (London, 1930), pp. xlii–xliii.

12

registered. The tract itself naturally provoked controversy and condemnation of its author's views on divorce, but no questions were asked as to the legality of its publication. Milton followed it in 1644 with his *Areopagitica*, in which he attacked the whole system of licensing and urged the Long Parliament to reverse its decision of the previous year, but something more than Miltonic eloquence was needed to bring this about and the order of 1643 remained in force. Parliament was no less eager than Star Chamber to keep literature under its control and as early as 1640 a Parliamentary Committee had drawn up three categories of books. The first consisted of 'good and vendible books' like Walker's *Doctrine of the Sabbath*: the second category contained books fit only to be sold to selected readers, Thomas à Kempis's *Imitation of Christ* was cited as one of these; the third category was of books 'fit to be burnt' and these were briskly summed up as 'Missals, Primers and Offices of Our Lady.' Indeed, it seemed that, during the later years of the Commonwealth, Cromwell had really succeeded in bringing the press to heel but as George Wither pointed out in his poem *A Suddain Flash* (1657) this subservience on the part of the press was 'but a cunning dog trick, to deceive.'

Hardly was the Restoration of the monarchy and of Charles II accomplished in 1660 than, the Cromwellian apparatus of censorship being now defunct, Parliament was asked to enact a new law by which the press would once again be subject to pre-censorship by licensing. The first attempt to get this law through Parliament in 1661 was a fiasco because the Lords insisted that their homes should be exempt from search and the Commons, understandably irritated by this, rejected the entire bill.[1] But within a year the Licensing Act of 1662 had become law, embodying the main principles of the decree of 1637. In view of the recent English experience of Puritan government it is interesting that the Act of 1662 requires that books shall be licensed as containing nothing 'contrary to good life or good manners.' It is not clear whether this is meant to specify obscene literature but certainly the French description of obscene literature as 'contraire aux bonnes moeurs' was already in use at this time.

Roger L'Estrange was appointed surveyor of printing presses and

---

[1] The Stationers' Company had long since experienced the hostility of its members to search. 'Whereas vpon a Search by M[r] Butter, Mr. Waterson & Mr. Miller deputed by the wardens they came vnto the house of ffrancis Groue to Search for bookes vnlawfull & demanding his servant to show them his warehouse, he gave them very vnfitting words insomuch that they told him he deserued to be whipt at the hall w[ch] his Master hearing told them that the Wardens had as good kisse his breach.' *Records of the Court of the Stationers' Company 1602 to 1640*, ed. W. A. Jackson (London, 1957), p. 301.

licenser of the press: lists of licensed books, including reprints, were published in the *Term Catalogues*, which continued to appear as bibliographies of new publications even after the end of the censorship, concluding with a final number in 1711. The Licensing Act of 1662 ran until 1679 and the censorship which Milton had evaded in 1643 threatened the suppression of *Paradise Lost* in 1667. Thomas Tomkyns, chaplain to Archbishop Sheldon, advised a ban on the poem because its evidently anti-royalist author had the temerity to suggest in the first book of his epic that an eclipse of the sun

> with sudden fear of change
> Perplexes Monarchs.
> (11.598–599)

The Licensing Act of 1662 should have been renewed in 1679 but on 3 February that year Parliament was dissolved and in the small amount of parliamentary business carried out from then until the death of Charles II in 1685 its renewal was not included. From 1679 until 1685 the press was therefore 'free' in the sense that the system of pre-censorship by licensing had lapsed. But seditious, blasphemous, obscene, and defamatory publications were still punishable at common law, as a whole series of cases was to show. In his diary for 1680–1, for instance, Narcissus Luttrell describes ten prosecutions of publishers at common law for issuing seditious or blasphemous publications, and he indicates that these were by no means the only cases which had come to his attention. Quite apart from this, while the licensing laws were suspended there was an increase in the number and scale of actions for *scandalum magnatum*. This was an offence which had been recognised since the reign of Edward I, when it was designed to protect 'magnates' from the libels of lesser men. Star Chamber, which during its own lifetime had been empowered to deal with this offence had repeated the warning against publishing such libels. 'Let all men take heede how they complayne in wordes against any magistrate, for they are gods.'[1] Now, while the licensing laws were suspended, the Duke of York (who was to succeed his brother as James II in 1685) brought three separate actions for *scandalum magnatum* against Pilkington, Titus Oates, and Dutton Colt, who had been Member of Parliament for Leominster. In each case the Duke was awarded damages of £100,000. Similar actions were brought by men like the Earl of Danby, a former minister of Charles II, and the Earl of Macclesfield. Actions for personal libel

---

[1] Quoted in W. Holdsworth, *History of the English Law* (London, 1903–52), V, 209.

were at this time still the weapon of the wealthy or the politically powerful; libel actions among lesser men were not the fashion until the
nineteenth century.

When Parliament met again in 1685 it found the time to renew the
Licensing Act, which ran until 1693 and was then renewed until 1695.
But there were those to whom the experience of 1679–85 was evidence
enough that the press could be controlled by the existing laws, even
if pre-censorship were abolished. In 1679, when the Licensing Act was
renewed for the first time, Charles Blount (who was no friend to
censorship of any kind) argued this case in his *Just Vindication of
Learning*, pointing out the restraints of law to which an author would
still be subject if licensing were abolished.

As for example, if any Audacious Villain shall Publish Treason, he is
already lyable to suffer as a Traytor; or if he Writes Scandalous Reflections
upon the Government, I presume he is by the present Laws of the Land
subject to a Fine and Imprisonment. Again if he publishes any Atheism,
Heresie or Schism, he is lyable to an Excommunication, and to be proceeded against accordingly in the Spiritual Court: Or if in his Writing he
defames any particular person he is obnoxious to a *Scandala Magnatum* if
he be a Peer; and to an Action upon the Case for Slander, if he be a Com-
moner. And last of all for Popish Books, *Quaere* whether there be not
Statutes already in force for the abolishing them, made 3 and 4 of *Ed.* 6.[1]

As we shall see, this was only one of many arguments pressed upon
the Commons in 1695 for the abolition of the whole system of pre-
censorship by licensing. There was, however, another class of
literature apart from seditious, blasphemous or personal libel: it was
a class whose significance had grown appreciably since 1660, and which
was now to occupy an increasing proportion of the censors' time.

THE RECOGNITION OF OBSCENE LITERATURE

Although the crime of obscene libel was not fully recognised in
English law until the case brought against Edmund Curll in 1725, and
although the authorities in the sixteenth and seventeenth centuries
had far more reason to concern themselves with seditious or blasphemous publications than with obscene ones, certain publishers were
nevertheless condemned in the later seventeenth century for obscene
or lascivious books. Even in the sixteenth century, when the authorities saw no grounds for bothering themselves much about allegedly
obscene books, there was still pressure on them to take action of some
sort against this moral subversion. In 1580, for example, William
Lambard proposed, 'An acte to restrain licentious printing,' in which

[1] *A Just Vindication of Learning* (London, 1679), p. 17.

he condemned such books as 'set up an arte of making lasciuious vngodly love.' Yet even Lambard's motives were commercial as much as moral: he objected to erotic literature because it sold so well, 'to the manifest injurie of the godly learned, whose prayse woorthie endevours and wrytinges are thearfore the lesse read.'¹ He also objects to the manner in which these 'wanton woorkes' upset the balance of the nation's economy by their enormous consumption of paper, 'it selfe a forrein and chargeable comoditie'.² Despite complaints of this sort, the licensers authorised editions of Pietro Aretino's dialogues, the *Ragionamenti*, in 1588, and Jaggard's edition of the *Decameron* in 1620, the latter book destined to provoke a number of destruction orders from twentieth century magistrates. Perhaps it was easier for the authorities to tolerate such books at a time when the erotic or bawdy classics of European literature were not English nor, as a rule, available in English translations. So far as Lambard and his sympathisers were concerned, the worst was yet to come.

One curious case occurred during the reign of Elizabeth and is worth mentioning because it shows what is, to us, a somewhat unusual attitude on the part of the censors towards obscenity in literature. In 1599 the Archbishop of Canterbury and the Bishop of London ordered the burning of a number of books including Christopher Marlowe's translation of Ovid's *Elegies*, the poet's celebration of 'my lewd and loose behaviour,' whose motto might well be the line, 'And with your pastime let the bed-stead creake'.³ Any suggestion that the book was destroyed because of the amorous activities described in it is discounted when we realise that Marlowe's work was bound in the same volume as Sir John Davies's *Epigrammes*, a number of short, satirical poems whose style and subject-matter owed much to the epigrams of Martial. The list of books destroyed in 1599, as well as the instruction given for the future that 'noe *Satyres* or *Epigrams* be printed hereafter', suggests that Marlowe simply had the bad luck to be caught up in a campaign against personal denigration.⁴ Some of Sir John Davies's *Epigrammes* might qualify as bawdy, though not as erotic. He attacks his victims, giving them such Latin personae as Marcus, Flaccus, Rufus, Gella, or Lesbia, though sometimes, as in the case of Heywood, he retains a real name. Like Martial, his exposure of the embarrassments, vices, or sexual peculiarities of his subjects is insulting rather than titillatory. Here, for example, is one which stands as a worthy Elizabethan counterpart to the art of Martial.

¹ *Stationers' Register*, II, 751.
² *ibid.*, II, 751.
³ *The Works of Christopher Marlowe*, ed. A. H. Bullen (London, 1885), III, 208.
⁴ *Stationers' Register*, III, 677.

16

In Francum 33
WHEN *Francus* comes to sollace with his whore,
He sends for Rods & strips himselfe stark naked:
For his lust sleepes, and will not rise before,
By whipping of the wench it be awaked.
I enuie him not, but wish I had the powre,
To make my selfe his wench but one halfe houre.[1]

There is no reason to suppose that the subjects of the poems could not be readily enough identified by their contemporaries; and even if the scandal were relatively mild, the victim was unlikely to be best pleased by having it broadcast through the work of a well-known Elizabethan poet.

Yet though the Elizabethans might license translations of Ovid or William Aldington's translation of Apuleius's *The Golden Ass* (1566) and were certainly not disturbed by the mild indecency of squibs like Thomas Nashe's *Choice of Valentines, or Nashe his Dildo*, the censors of the seventeenth century were confronted by a more 'dangerous' type of literature which had its origin in Renaissance Italy, spread later to France, and was largely 'pornography' in the strict etymological sense of 'writing of whores'. Such publications certainly confirmed the moral prejudices of the Anglo-Saxons so far as their views on Italy were concerned. Even Thomas Nashe in *The Unfortunate Traveller* (1594) makes his hero, Jack of Wilton, describe Rome as 'The *Sodom of Italy*', and declare that it was from this sixteenth-century city of the plain that Englishmen had learnt, 'the art of atheisme, the art of epicurising, the art of whoring, the art of poysoning, the art of Sodomitrie'.[2] Had Nashe lived a hundred years later, he would have been able to add to this list the art of corrupting the minds of men and women by licentious and inflammatory literature.

The best-known author of erotic literature in the Europe of the late Renaissance was Pietro Aretino, largely as the result of work that was not his own. The celebrated piece of erotica known in England as 'Aretine's Postures' was principally a set of engravings by Marcantonio Raimondi of pictures by Giulio Romano, in which the various 'postures' of sexual intercourse were shown. Aretino's part in this venture was to contribute a series of poems, *Sonnetti Lussuriosi* (1527), to accompany these illustrations: the 'postures' themselves were not his. The book was condemned by the Pope when it first appeared, and the scandal attending its publication ensured that it would remain a firm favourite for some time to come. There was

---

[1] *The Complete Poems of Sir John Davies*, ed. A. B. Grosart (London, 1876), II, 31–32.
[2] *The Works of Thomas Nashe*, ed. R. B. McKerrow (Oxford, 1958), II, 301.

17

further free publicity for it when Aretino's works were condemned by the Council of Trent. By the end of the sixteenth century his fame had spread to England and in 1600 John Donne wrote to Sir Henry Wotton on the subject.

I am sory you should (with any great earnestnes) desyre any thing of P. Aretinus, not that he could infect; but that it seemes you are alredy infected with the common opinion of him: beleeve me he is much lesse than his fame and was too well payd by the Roman church in that coyne which he coveted most where his bookes were by the counsell of Trent forbidden which if they had beene permitted to have beene worne by all long ere this had beene worne out: his divinyty was but a sirrope to enwrapp his prophane bookes to get them passage, yet in these bookes which have devine titles there is least harme as in his letters most good: his others have no other singularyty in them but that they are forbidden.[1]

In *Ignatius his Conclave* (1611) Donne returns to Aretino, remarking that so far from describing any new form of sexual pleasure the pornographer has actually left out a number of those to be found in Greek and Latin authors. Yet however little he thought of Aretino, it is clear from his letter to Wotton that the 'Postures' were in demand by this time. Later references show that Aretino remained the great classic of pornography for most Englishmen throughout the seventeenth century. When *Rare Verities. The Cabinet of Venus Unlocked and her Secrets Laid Open* discussed what it rather circumspectly called 'pendulous venery' in 1657, its readers were advised to 'See more in *Aretine*'s Postures'.[2] If we can accept at face value a piece of dialogue between the old bawd, Mother Creswel, and her pupil Dorothea, in *The Whore's Rhetorick* (Adapted from Ferrante Pallavicino's *Retorica delle Puttane* of 1642) then 'Aretine's postures'—or at least most of them—were still in circulation in 1683.

M.c. Aretin's Figures have no place in my Rhetorick, and, I hope, will find no room in my Pupils apartment. They are calculated for a hot Region a little on this side *Sodom*, and are not necessary to be seen in any Northern Clime.
Dor. What do you mean by *Aretin*'s Figures?
M.c. Only, Child, Six and Thirty Geometrical Schemes which he drew for his own diversion.
Dor. What have I to do with those hard names, are those tame [sic] things to be had here?
M.c. Four and Twenty rough draughts may be had for money.[3]

[1] John Donne, *Complete Poetry and Selected Prose*, ed. John Hayward (London, 1949), p. 441.
[2] Sinibaldus, *Rare Verities* (London, 1658), p. 65.
[3] *The Whore's Rhetorick, Calculated to the Meridian of London* (London, 1683), p. 171.

Whatever the supply available in 1683, there had been a bad enough shortage—or perhaps a great enough demand—eight years earlier to induce the 'Gentlemen' of All Souls College, Oxford, to produce their own edition, using the university press in secret. The catastrophe which eventually overtook them was described in a letter from Humphrey Prideaux to John Ellis in January 1675.

The time that was chosen for the worke was the eveneing after 4, Mr. Dean after that time never useing to come to the theator; [where the press was housed] but last night, beeing imployed the other part of the day, he went not thither till the work was begun. How he took to find his press workeing at such an imployement I leave it to you to immagin. The prints and plates he hath seased, and threatens the owners of them with expulsion; and I think they would deserve it were they of any other colledge than All Souls, but there I will allow them to be vertuous that are bawdy only in pictures.[1]

What men like William Wilberforce, Thomas Bowdler, or Lord Campbell would have made of the remark, 'but there I will allow them to be vertuous that are bawdy only in pictures',—coming from a clergyman at that—is an interesting exercise in conjecture. Such tones of amused tolerance were to become increasingly rare during the next two centuries.

An adaptation of part of Aretino's *Ragionamenti* appeared in 1658 as *The Crafty Whore: or, The Misery and Iniquity of Bawdy Houses laid open* but before long it was France, rather than Italy, which supplied England with its most popular items of erotic literature. It is enough to name three of them. The most famous was undoubtedly Michel Millot's *L'Escole des Filles* published in Paris in 1655. We do not know when it first appeared in English, except that it was before 1688—possibly many years before. Nicholas Chorier's *L'Academie des Dames* (1680)—which had first appeared in Latin twenty years earlier as *Aloisiae Sigeae Toletanae Satyra Sodatica*—was also circulating in English by 1688. Jean Barrin's *Vénus dans le Cloître, ou la Religieuse en Chemise* was published in France in 1683 and an English translation was issued in the same year. All three books were to be the subjects of criminal prosecutions at one time or another.

In the Restoration period there was a great deal of bawdy literature produced by English writers but one cannot accurately call much of it erotic. An element which is rarely absent from obscene literature is the spirit of burlesque or parody. This may take the form of ridiculing certain respectable or romantic literary forms or, as in the nineteenth century, of ridiculing the generally accepted moral values of, say, family life. There is an anarchic quality in obscene writing (as there

[1] *Letters of Humphrey Prideaux to John Ellis* (Camden Society, 1875), p. 30.

19

is in satire) an urge to undermine what is intellectually or morally the accepted standard of the age. Charles Cotton's *Scarronides: or Virgil Travestie* (1664)— a very mild example—depends on Virgil's *Aeneid*. 'I sing the man, (read it who list,/A Trojan true as ever pist.)' Others, like *The Natural History of the Arbor Vitae* (c. 1709) with its self-conscious phallicism, depend on Homer. Such paradies as these were a derisive answer to Dryden's remark in the Dedication of his own translation of the *Aeneid* (1697) that 'A HEROIC POEM, truly such, is undoubtedly the greatest work which the soul of man is capable to perform.'[1] *Sodom: or, The Quintessence of Debauchery*, a scatological romp published in 1685 and attributed to the Earl of Rochester, mocks the literary and moral pretensions of Heroic Tragedy, while the answer to the poetry of platonic or over-romanticised love comes, for instance, in one of Rochester's songs of disillusionment.

> Against the Charmes our *Ballocks* have,
> How weak all humane skill is?
> Since they can make a *Man* a *Slave*,
> To such a *Bitch* as *Phillis*.

This song, though prosecutions were brought in 1693 and 1698 against publishers of the book containing it, seems unlikely to entice its readers into promiscuity and it ends on a note of revulsion.

> Bawdy in thoughts, precise in words,
> Ill natur'd, and a *Whore*,
> Her *Belly*, is a *Bag* of *T-rds*,
> And her *C——t*, a common shore.[2]

Pornography of the nineteenth and, particularly, the twentieth centuries has been far more concerned with deriding general moral values than with parodying specific pieces of literature. In the seventeenth and eighteenth centuries the element of direct parody is much more obvious. John Wilkes, or perhaps Thomas Potter, opened the *Essay on Woman* (1763) with the lines,

> Awake, my Fanny, leave all meaner things;
> This morn shall prove what rapture swiving brings!
> Let us (since life can little more supply
> Than just a few good fucks, and then we die)
> Expatiate free o'er that loved scene of man,
> A mighty maze, for mighty pricks to scan. . . .

because Pope had opened his *Essay on Man* in 1732 with the following lines.

[1] John Dryden, *Essays*, ed. W. P. Ker (Oxford, 1900), II, 154.
[2] *Poems on Several Occasions by the E. of R.* (Antwerp, 1680), pp. 73–74.

Awake, my St. John! leave all meaner things
To low ambition and the pride of Kings.
Let us (since life can little more supply
Than just to look about us and to die)
Expatiate free o'er all this scene of Man;
A mighty maze of walks without a plan.

While the output of allegedly obscene literature increased both in England and on the Continent, pressure grew among the Puritans and their sympathisers for its suppression. In 1640 the Puritans had organised a petition protesting against,

The swarming of lascivious, idle, and unprofitable books and Pamphlets, Play-Books, and Ballads, as namely *Ovid*s fits of Love; *the Parliament* of Women come out at the dissolving of the last *Parliament, Barnes* Poems, *Parkers* Ballads in disgrace of Religion, to the encrease of all Vice, and withdrawing of people from reading, studying, and hearing the word of God, and other good Books.[1]

Six years later *The Women's Parliament* was banned but under the Commonwealth such scurrilous periodicals as John Crouch's *Mercurius Democritis* were licensed without question. Ironically, it was not the Puritans but the Royalists who, in 1660, imprisoned Crouch and John Garfield, the publisher of *The Wandering Whore*, a paper of which four numbers had been issued.

Publishers of literature of doubtful moral tone certainly showed an increasing nervousness at the prospect of official action against them. *Rare Verities*, which was a translation of the *Geneanthropeia* of Sinibaldus published in Rome in 1642, is a case in point. When it appeared in 1657 its pseudo-scientific style was one obvious precaution against any steps that might be taken to bring the publisher to justice—though the relish with which the book discusses, for example, how females may change sex by a sufficient extension of the clitoris, says little for its claims to academic detachment. The translator argues uneasily in his preface that he might be regarded as a 'Capitall offender for Transcribing those things into English, which should have remained still in the obscurity of an unknown tongue,' but he protests that he is motivated only by a genuine, democratic desire to make such information available to all men and not to allow scholars to 'monopolize the trade of Drollery.'[2] Scholars, if they had their own way, would keep ordinary people in such total sexual ignorance that 'when they are married, they must be forced to come to them to be

---

[1] W. M. Clyde, *The Struggle for the Freedom of the Press from Caxton to Cromwell* (London, 1934), p. 54.
[2] *Rare Verities*, Sig. A5ʳ.–A5ᵛ.

taught the way of copulation.'[1] The ruse was successful and, apparently, no prosecution resulted. It is interesting, though, that when John Martin published his own translation of the same book in 1709 he was prosecuted but acquitted.[2]

The last quarter of the seventeenth century was a time of more frequent but still haphazard action against obscene literature. In 1677 a bookseller who had imported *L'Escole des Filles* and *Aloisiae Sigeae Toletanae Satyra Sodatica*—in their original French and Latin—from a bookseller in Amsterdam, had his shop closed by the licenser of the press, though only for a matter of hours. The fact that these books could have been imported without interference says little for the efficiency of those whose duty it was not to allow any books into the country without first examining them. But in any case the legality of the licenser's action against this bookseller in 1677 was strongly questioned.

Ultimately, the only place where legality could be defined was in the courts and certainly the situation, so far as the censors were concerned, was by no means clear. The Licensing Act of 1662 gave them a rather vague mandate to suppress indecent books but it neither gave very clear instructions as to the appropriate methods nor did it indicate which books were to be regarded as indecent. This situation was not resolved until well into the eighteenth century but, for the time being, confusion seems to have been worse confounded by the case of *The Whore's Rhetorick* in 1683. In April of that year John Wickens was sentenced at the Guildhall Sessions to pay a fine of forty shillings for publishing the book, not a great deal of money by comparison with fines imposed for publishing other types of illegal literature but nonetheless a clear indication of disapproval. Yet in the following February this same book, *The Whore's Rhetorick*, was approvingly listed with other publications in the official *Term Catalogue* for Hilary 168¾ and there seem to have been no further attempts to check its circulation.[3] There is another, though less cogent, anomaly in the case of *Venus in the Cloister: or, The Nun in her Smock*. This book was listed in the *Term Catalogue* for Easter 1683, yet it is the book which featured most prominently when Edmund Curll was prosecuted and convicted of the crime of obscene libel in 1725-8. By that time, however, there was less hesitation on the part of the censors in dealing with books of this kind.[4]

[1] *ibid.*, Sig. A6ʳ.   [2] P.R.O. K.B. 28/31/20.

[3] *The Term Catalogues*, ed. E. Arber (London, 1903), II, 62.

[4] Other literature advertised in the *Term Catalogues* included *The Nuns' Complaint against the Friars* (Easter, 1676); *The London Jilt; or, The Politick Whore* (Easter, 1683); *The Ten Pleasures of Marriage* (Trinity, 1683); *Eve Revived; or,*

Before the system of pre-censorship was finally abolished in 1695, the question of obscenity had been decided in the courts on a number of occasions, though not in the court of King's Bench. In 1688 the Stationers' Company sent the Messenger of the Press, Henry Hills, to investigate the state of the pornography trade in London, and to see what books he could manage to buy, presumably with a view to rounding up some of the pedlars of such publications. At the same time there were cases against three men at Guildhall Sessions. Benjamin Crayle was prosecuted for selling 'obscene and lascivious books,' including *The School of Venus*, which was the English translation of *L'Escole des Filles*; Francis Leach was arrested for publishing the Earl of Rochester's *Poems on Several Occasions*, and Joseph Streater was prosecuted for printing *The School of Venus* and a translation of Chorier's *L'Academie des Dames* under the title of *A Dialogue between a Married Lady and a Maid*. Streater was fined 40*s*. at Guildhall Quarter Sessions in April 1688 and Crayle was fined 20*s*. at the General Sessions in May. How much of a deterrent this was likely to be can be judged from the fact that copies of *The School of Venus* (which had by this time replaced 'Aretine's Postures' in general popularity) appear to have fetched anything from half-a-crown to six shillings, while even Rochester's poems would sell for a shilling or one and sixpence. In the case of Streater and Crayle the conviction was for *The School of Venus* and the indictment contained the passage objected to, which seems mild enough compared with certain other sections of the book.

Katy. Cousin, though your obligations are great, yet I poor wench have nothing but thanks to return you: but the postures you have informed me of I shall make use of as opportunity presents, so that my Gallant may perceive I love him.
Frank. 'Tis a comon fault among young people only to think of the present time, but they never consider how to make their pleasures durable and to continue for a long time.
Katy. Let me have your instructions, who are so great a mistress in the art of love.
Frank. But han't you had Mr. Roger's company lately?
Katy. Now and then I used to let him in and he lay with me, a whole night, which happiness I have been deprived of above this fortnight, for my mother's bed being removed out of her chamber (which is repairing) into mine, so that our designs tending that way have been frustrated ever since.

If the authorities thought that Streater and Crayle had learnt their

---

The Fair One Stark Naked (Michaelmas, 1683); *The Confessions of the New-Married Couple* (Michaelmas, 1683), and *The Amorous Abbess, or Love in a Nunnery* (Easter, 1684).

lessons, they were destined for a disappointment in the autumn of 1689, when both men were indicted for issuing *Sodom: or, The Quintessence of Debauchery.* The indictment against Crayle was signed by John Appleby and Robert Stephens, Messenger of the Press: the indictment against Streater, which is almost identical, was signed by these two and also by Crayle. Whether this was the result of some professional jealousy, or an attempt to turn king's evidence, it did him little good. Indeed, it was Crayle whom the authorities chose to use as an example. He found two colleagues to put up bail of £40 and £20 for him and was bound over to appear at the Guildhall Quarter Sessions on 10 January 1690. At his trial, before a jury, he was convicted, fined £20, instead of the 20s. in 1688, committed to prison, though subsequently released to be of good behaviour, and an inventory was taken of his goods. His trial was much less elaborate than that of Edmund Curll and no one thought it worth taking him before the court of King's Bench, yet the sentence imposed upon him clearly indicates that the authorities were disposed to take a serious view of obscene publications before the end of the seventeenth century. Crayle was not, of course, charged with 'obscene libel' since the phrase was not employed in such a case, the charge was that he had published 'librum flagitiosum et impudicum,' to which the full indictment added 'scandalosum' and 'lasciviosum.' The indictment also contains the eight lines from the play on which the prosecution was based, though, as in the case of *The School of Venus*, they are mild enough compared with what might have been chosen from the text. The speaker is Bolloxinion, King of Sodom.

> Thus in the zenith of my lust I reign;
> I eat to swive, and swive to eat again;
> Let other monarchs, who their sceptres bear
> To keep their subjects less in love than fear
> Be slaves to crowns, my nation shall be free;
> My pintle only shall my sceptre be,
> My laws shall act more pleasure than command,
> And with my prick I'll govern all the land.

The passage comes from the opening of the play, which is perhaps why it seemed logical to Crayle's prosecutors to cite it in the indictment. This was by no means the last that was to be heard of *Sodom* in the courts, nor of other works attributed to the late Earl of Rochester.[1]

It seems unlikely that nothing was used in evidence from either

---

[1] At Guildhall Quarter Sessions on 10 July 1693, Elizabeth Latham was fined five marks and committed to prison for publishing *Poems on Several Occasions by the E. of R.* The prosecution, brought by Robert Stephens, Messenger of the Press, was on the grounds of the book's lascivious and vicious qualities.

The School of Venus or *Sodom* beyond what was quoted in the indictment, since the extract from the dialogue between the two girls, at least, is no more obscene than a great deal of dialogue in Restoration comedy. The difficulty in trying to sum up the attitude of an age towards its literature is that there is rarely a single moral standard against which literature is judged, and in the second half of the seventeenth century the disparity between two such standards is particularly marked. On the one hand, there was a strong and growing literary ethic which was Puritan in nature: Puritan philosophy, in this respect, did not simply disapprove of literature which was obscene or erotic, it was basically a condemnation of all literature that was not in some way morally edifying or, in the words of the Puritan petition of 1640, tended to the 'withdrawing of people from reading, studying, and hearing the word of God, and other good Books'. Seventeenth-century puritanism, at its best, was later transmuted into the Victorian zeal for 'Good Books' or 'Great Books'. To the Puritan, of course, all fiction had been suspect, however innocent it might appear to be, and a great deal of poetry was to be condemned as well. Despite the indifference of the authorities—even in Cromwell's England—the Puritan campaign against immorality in literature had grown steadily from the inspiration of such works as Roger Ascham's *Schoolmaster* (1570) which attacked the 'bold bawdrye' of books like Malory's *Morte d'Arthur* or Painter's *Palace of Pleasure*, and which was followed by Stephen Gosson's *Schoole of Abuse* in 1579. By 1655 Henry Vaughan was prepared to put the matter very plainly in the preface to a new edition of his *Silex Scintillans*, showing, incidentally, that puritanism in such matters was not necessarily confined to those who might strictly be termed Puritans. Vaughan, one of the finest devotional poets in the language, turns to the danger of 'romances' or, as we should now call them, 'novels', and reminds his readers of the scriptural warnings against such immoral publications.

The most lascivious compositions of France and Italy are here naturalized and made English: and this, as it is sadly observed, with so much favour and success, that nothing takes—as they rightly phrase it—like a romance . . . If 'every idle word shall be accounted for', and if 'no corrupt communication should proceed out of our mouths', how desperate, I beseech you, is their condition, who all their lifetime, and out of mere design, study lascivious fictions: then carefully record and publish them, that instead of grace and life, they may minister sin and death unto their readers?[1]

Five years later Nathaniel Ingelo attacked the 'Lightness and Vanity' of fiction, demanding, 'Is there no joy but laughter? Doth nothing

---

[1] *Poems of Henry Vaughan Silurist*, ed. E. K. Chambers (London, n.d.), I, 3–4.

recreate but what is fabulous?'[1] The influence of such Puritan criticism outlived the seventeenth century, bequeathing to its successors—many of whom would never have regarded themselves as 'Puritan'—the belief that life was a serious business and that literature must therefore be an educative agent with no time for 'idle words' and with no right to deal in such worthless material as produced what George Eliot sternly reproved as 'the moral imbecility of an inward giggle'.[2] The Puritan attitude towards fiction endures quite clearly in a poem like Robert Montgomery's *Effects of Indiscriminate Novel Reading*, when he addresses the novelists themselves.

> In thy lewd leaves, how many pens have taught
> The filth of fancy and the lust of thought?[3]

It endures too in remarks like the *Evangelical Magazine*'s in 1793, 'Novels generally speaking, are instruments of abomination and ruin.'[4] Cultural puritanism was a powerful factor in the education of men like James Carlyle in the eighteenth century, according to his son, Thomas. 'Poetry, Fiction in general, he had universally seen treated as not only idle, but *false* and criminal.'[5] Only in the nineteenth century, when the work of novelists like George Eliot successfully incorporated the moral earnestness of the Puritan legacy, was this particular prejudice largely overcome.

Yet while the moral influence of puritanism, in this respect, attracted more and more supporters towards the end of the seventeenth century, there was another, co-existing attitude towards literature, an attitude which was non-committal, tolerant, and often amused by the material which scandalised the Puritans. One can detect this moral detachment, for instance, in Prideaux's letter about the printing of 'Aretine's Postures' at Oxford. Again, while Puritan susceptibilities might be offended even by the rather mild passage from *The School of Venus* quoted in the indictment of 1688, a man like Samuel Pepys—emphatically not a Puritan—reacted very differently, even to the more outspoken parts of the book, as he recalls in his diary for 1668.

13 Jan. Thence homeward by coach and stopped at Martin's, my bookseller, where I saw the French book which I did think to have had for my wife to translate, called *L'escholle des filles*, but when I came to look in it, it

---

[1] Nathaniel Ingelo, *Bentivolio and Urania* (London, 1660), Sig. D2ʳ.

[2] 'Debasing the Moral Currency', in *Impressions of Theophrastus Such* (London, 1901), p. 150.

[3] Robert Montgomery, *Poetical Works* (London, 1836), p. 276.

[4] I (1793), pp. 78–79.

[5] Thomas Carlyle, *Reminiscences* (London, 1881), I, 19.

is the most bawdy, lewd book that ever I saw, rather worse than *Putana errante*[1] so that I was ashamed of reading in it, and so away home. . . . . . . 8 Feb. Thence away to the Strand to my bookseller's, and there staid an hour, and bought the idle, rogueish book *L'escholle des filles*, which I have bought in plain binding, avoiding the buying of it better bound, because I resolve, as soon as I have read it, to burn it, that it may not stand in the list of books, nor among them, to disgrace them if it should be found.
9 Feb. (Lord's Day) Up, and at my chamber all the morning and the office doing business, and also reading a little of *L'Escholle des filles*, which is a mighty lewd book, but yet not amiss for a sober man once to read over to inform himself in the villainy of the world. . . . We sang until almost night, and drank mighty good store of wine, and then they parted, and I to my chamber, where I did read through *L'escholle des filles*, a lewd book, but what do no wrong once to read for information sake. . . . And after I had done it I burned it, that it might not be among my books to my shame.[2]

Neither this attitude nor the Puritan one is in itself typical of the later seventeenth century: the characteristic of that period of literary history is that the two attitudes should have stood against each other in the way that they did. The history of moral censorship is, in great part, the history of a conflict between two such views. Of course, in the later seventeenth century the Puritans may have appeared to be a defeated political and cultural minority: the works of Rochester were acceptable as an amusement for courtiers and gentlemen; 'Aretine's Postures' were unlikely to do much harm at All Souls; *The School of Venus* was safe enough reading for a man of the sophistication of Samuel Pepys. The small reading class of the seventeenth century might be, preponderantly, patrician and classically educated—and male. What would happen in another hundred years, when the benefits of spreading literacy had produced a much larger reading public, which was generally rather than classically educated, middle-class rather than patrician, and female rather than male? 'Obscenity in any Company is a rustick uncreditable Talent;' remarked Jeremy Collier in 1698, 'but among Women 'tis particularly rude.'[3] Would the successors of the Puritans still be a defeated minority when the great question was whether a particular book was fit to be read by a man's wife and daughters, even by his servants and the lower orders of society? In 1692, even before the end of the licensing system, the first Society for the Reformation of Manners was founded. The

[1] The authorship of this book is uncertain but it was possibly the work of Nicolo Franco.
[2] *The Diary of Samuel Pepys*, ed. H. B. Wheatley (London, 1952), VII, 261 and 290–1.
[3] Jeremy Collier, *Short View of the Immorality and Profaneness of the English Stage*, 3rd edn. (London, 1698), p. 7.

suppression of indecent literature was not among its stated aims, but anyone who supposed that manners could be reformed while the press was left unmolested was guilty of an optimism bordering on delusion.

THE END OF THE LICENSING SYSTEM

1695 saw the abolition of pre-censorship by licensing, an event which Macaulay was to describe as having done more for liberty and civilisation than either Magna Carta or the Bill of Rights. Yet despite the grandeur of the comparison, Macaulay was greatly disappointed by the way in which the decision of Parliament was taken. Here, surely, was the time and place for a great libertarian gesture, the final overthrow of tyranny should have been accompanied by a loud proclamation that the day of intellectual liberty had dawned after the long night of Stuart oppression. The British Parliament did no such honour to the new freedom. Instead, as Macaulay observed, 'The Licensing Act is condemned, not as a thing essentially evil but on account of the petty grievances, the exactions, the jobs, the commercial restrictions, the domiciliary visits which were incidental to it.'[1] So much for the dawn of intellectual liberty.

In 1695 a parliamentary committee had first of all recommended that the Licensing Act should again be renewed but on 11 February the Commons rejected this recommendation. The Lords, however, agreed with the Committee that the Act ought to be renewed, and they informed the Commons accordingly. The Commons then proposed a conference with the Lords and presented them with a list of reasons for not renewing the Act, a list composed by John Locke himself.[2] Now it may be that the Commons felt the Lords would be more impressed by a list of practical objections to the licensing system than by any sonorous plea for intellectual liberty, at all events the Lords gave way on the issue and the Licensing Act was allowed to lapse.

The Commons' objections to pre-censorship by licensing showed that whether or not any readers might have been depraved or corrupted by banned literature, the licensing system itself had certainly corrupted some of the censors. The Stationers' Company, instead of being merely the guardians of the book trade, were turning the censorship into a financial swindle. Officials of the Company were accused by the Commons of preventing the publication of 'innocent and useful Books' by others, so that they might later authorise 'what belongs to,

---

[1] *History of England*, IV, 541.
[2] Locke's arguments against the licensing system parallel those of the Commons. See John Locke, *Life and Letters*, ed. P. King (London, 1858), pp. 203–7.

and is the Labour and Right of, others', for publication by 'themselves and their Friends'.[1] Similar instances of corruption had been cited seventy years earlier by George Wither in *The Schollers Purgatory Discovered in the Stationers Common-wealth*. Of course, the Stationers' Company was responsible for inspecting and approving imported books but those officials on whom the responsibility devolved were booksellers themselves, in a very competitive trade. Quite apart from any pilfering that might take place, the temptation to bankrupt a rival sometimes proved too strong and the means were so easily available. The examination of the imported books would simply be postponed for so long that 'the Importer may be undone, by having so great a Part of his Stock lie dead; or the Books, if wet, may rot and perish'.[2] A more general cause of complaint was that no specific fee had been laid down for licensing a book, 'by colour whereof great oppression may be, and has been, practised'.[3] Finally, the Commons demanded why special provision should have been made in the Act of 1662 for John Streater, 'That he may print what he pleases, as if the Act had never been made; when the Commons see no cause to distinguish him from the rest of the Subjects of *England*.'[4] Despite the absence of grand libertarian pronouncements, there were enough suggestions of fraud, extortion, intimidation, and theft on the part of those responsible for enforcing the censorship to warrant the most careful investigation—if not the abolition—of controlling the press by licensing.

The overriding practical reason for abolishing the system was that it had never worked particularly well in any case. No arguments, however treasonable or heretical, were silenced by it, since no man who wished to publish them would be foolish enough to ask the permission of the licensers before doing so. (On the other hand there were cases of innocent books being licensed and then having their texts altered before they appeared.[5]) By accident or corruption certain notorious books of the period were licensed and in 1632 William Buckner had been fined £50 and committed to prison by Star Chamber for licensing *Histriomastix*. Unlicensed printing was sometimes difficult, even dangerous, but as the activities of both Catholics and Puritans showed, it was by no means impossible. Of course, the offenders might be caught and punished—after the publication of the book

---

[1] *Journals of the House of Commons*, XI, 306.
[2] *ibid.*, XI, 306.
[3] *ibid.*, XI, 306.
[4] *ibid.*, XI, 306.
[5] St. Francis de Sales', *Praxis Spiritualis: or, The Introduction to a Devout Life*, was burnt at Smithfield on the orders of Archbishop Laud because pro-Catholic material had been added after licensing.

in question—but whether their martyrdom did as much for the state as it did for their own cause is extremely doubtful. In the reign of Charles I, when judicial disfigurement rather than death was the punishment for seditious or blasphemous libel, the most hideous penalties were inflicted upon authors without deterring them from their purpose. William Prynne, for instance, was sentenced in 1632, for publishing his *Histriomastix*—'Women Actors notorious Whores' —to pay a fine of £5,000, to be imprisoned for life and to have both his ears cut off in the pillory. *Histriomastix* had appeared only a few weeks before the Queen took part in a pastoral at Somerset House. Undeterred by his punishment, Prynne continued to write on behalf of the Puritan cause from the Tower of London. In 1637, for seditious libels in his *News from Ipswich*, he was sentenced to pay a further fine, to lose the stumps of his ears, which Star Chamber was annoyed to find had been overlooked in 1632, and to be branded on both sides of his face with the letters 'S.L.' for 'Schismatical Libeller'. Even this failed to silence him. On this second occasion, one of Prynne's colleagues, Bastwick, suffered with him and was subsequently thrown into prison where, he was told, he would remain until such time as he recanted. That, said Bastwick, would not be until Doomsday, in the afternoon. A few years later John Lilburne was accused of sending between ten and twelve thousand seditious books into the country from Holland. He was fined £500, flogged, and pilloried. Even in the pillory his attacks on those who tried to silence the press were so vehement that he had to be gagged tightly enough to cause a haemorrhage.

At this particular period of English history a consistent censorship would, in any case, have been difficult to operate. For example, in 1546 all books by such Protestant authors as Tyndale and Coverdale were ordered to be destroyed. Then, at the accession of Edward VI in 1547 Tyndale and Coverdale were approved and it was the turn of Catholic authors to be banned. In 1553, with the accession of a Catholic Queen, the position was reversed and both Tyndale and Coverdale were among those authors to be banned once more. In 1558 the crown passed to the Protestant Elizabeth and there was yet another reversal of policy. These frequent upheavals must at least have ensured that most books were available to a reader at one time or another. A different kind of confusion existed in the reign of Charles I, when books like Manwaring's *Religion and Allegiance* (1627) or Richard Montague's *Appello Caesarem* (1625) were condemned by Parliament, although approved by the King, while others condemned by the Crown were approved by Parliament. In 1643 the power of licensing passed to Parliament, though there were still Royalist printers at large, but with the Restoration in 1660 certain approved and banned books changed places again. Indeed, in 1663 the printer John Twyn was executed for treason after producing the anti-royalist *Treatise of the Execution of Justice*. By 1695 the two-party system in Parliament was far enough developed for politicians to appreciate the danger of a censorship which would alter with every change in political fortunes. Of the Licensers of the Press since 1660, Sir Roger L'Estrange had been a Tory, his successor, James Fraser, was a Whig, and Edmund Bohun was a Tory. As Addison later pointed out, the danger of passing laws to censor the views of your political opponents was that the same laws would apply to you when you found yourself out of office.[1]

The experience of the thirty-five years between the Restoration and the end of licensing showed that the book trade had, literally, outgrown the system of censorship. In economic terms, it was a system designed to supervise the publication of a limited number of books, whose production gave employment to a reasonably small number of printers and publishers. Economically, the policies of censorship were restrictive, as, for example, the decree of 1586 which prohibited the setting up of any more presses, licensed or not, without very special permission. The absurdity of the situation was pointed out by Richard Atkyns in 1664.

There are at least 600 Booksellers that keep Shops in and about *London* and Two or three Thousand free of the Company of Stationers; the Licensed Books of the Kingdome cannot imploy one third part of them: What shall the rest do? I have heard some of them openly at the *Committee* of the *House of Commons* say, They will rather hang than starve; and that a man is not hang'd for stealing but being taken; *necessitas cogit ad turpia*.[2]

In the same year Roger L'Estrange assured the Privy Council that no less than 200,000 copies of seditious publications had been circulated in the first two years of the reign of Charles II, and Atkyns explains how the black market in prohibited books affected the ordinary purchaser.

An unlicensed Book bears Treble the price of another; and generally the more Scandalous a Book is, by so much the more dear. . . . I was lately in a Book-seller's Shop, where I saw a Book in *Quarto*, entituled, *Killing no Murder*, it had but eight Leaves in all, stitch't up without binding, he demanded 5*s.* for it, and would not take less: A Book of the same bigness Licensed would have cost but 4*d.* or 6*d.* at the most.[3]

---

[1] *Thoughts of a Tory Author concerning the Press* (London, 1712), p. 27.
[2] Richard Atkyns, *The Original and Growth of Printing* (London, 1664), p. 16.
[3] *ibid.*, pp. 16–17.

Killing no Murder had been published in Holland in 1657 by Colonels Selby and Titus after the failure of a plot against Cromwell's life. It was, in this sense, a justification of tyrannicide.[1]

It is no surprise to find Samuel Pepys among the customers for prohibited books, and to hear how six months after his encounter with *L'Escole des Filles* he set out to buy a copy of Hobbes's *Leviathan*, 'which is now mightily called for; and what was heretofore sold for 8s. I now give 24s. for, at the second hand, and is sold for 30s., it being a book the Bishops will not let be printed again'.[2] In this respect the book trade has changed little during the past three hundred years. The day after the condemnation of *Fanny Hill* at Bow Street in 1964 such copies of the paperback as had already been issued were offered for as much as £8 in Soho. When the successful case against *Last Exit to Brooklyn* was brought at Marlborough Street in 1966 its price in Soho doubled from 30s. to £3 at once: after the Old Bailey case in November 1967 the unofficial price was £5 to £6.

Not only was the seventeenth-century censorship quite unable to prevent a black market in illegal books, it soon faced the intimidating prospect of having to censor a newspaper industry as well. In 1680, during the suspension of the licensing system, the King's judges announced that the publication of any news—whether true or false— was to be illegal. Their announcement appeared in the *London Gazette* on 5 and 17 May, the *Gazette* being an official newspaper and the only one authorised. Shortly afterwards, Lord Chief Justice Scroggs in condemning *The Weekly Pacquet of Advice from Rome*, which like most periodical publications of the time contained virtually no news whatever, repeated the warning. 'And that is for a public notice to all people, and especially printers and booksellers, that they ought to print no book or pamphlet of news whatsoever without authority.'[3] There had been no shortage of 'news books' representing both sides of the question during the Civil War and as political unrest grew once more it was quite clear that newspapers were going to appear whether the authorities licensed them or not.

By 1695 all but the most dedicated supporters of the licensing system must have realised that nothing much was to be gained by its retention, and something to be lost—in the spirit of the times—by insisting on the necessity of an *imprimatur* with all its associations of

[1] L'Estrange believed it might be possible to control the size of the book-trade by buying out printers with money raised through fines for illegal publications. *Considerations and Proposals in Order to the Regulation of the Press* (London, 1663), Sig. a3ᵛ.
[2] *The Diary of Samuel Pepys*, VIII, 91.
[3] Henry Hallam, *The Constitutional History of England*, 5th edn. (London, 1846), II, 170.

intellectual tyranny which were regarded as alien both in terms of politics and religion. The practical objections to continuing such a system were overwhelming and, after all, those who believed in restraints imposed on the press had a very real consolation. There had been no licensing between 1679 and 1685, yet the common law had shown itself able enough to deal with sedition, blasphemy, and even obscenity. Why should the courts not be able to control the press in the same way if licensing were to be removed permanently? The ultimate powers of censorship had, in any case, always rested with the courts: it was not the Company of Stationers who had condemned men to the gallows or to physical mutilation. There was certainly no lack of laws and precedents which could be applied to the press and, if it became 'free' in 1695, its freedom would be of that relative kind so succinctly summed up by Lord Chief Justice Mansfield in 1784. 'To be free, is to live under a government by law. The *liberty of the press* consists in printing without any previous licence, subject to the consequences of law. The *licentiousness* of the press is *Pandora*'s box, the source of every evil.'[1] It was these 'consequences' which English literature was about to experience.

[1]   *v.* Dean of St. Asaph, 1784.

3

Enemies of the State: 1695–1760

THE UNREST OF THE AUGUSTANS

The danger of such unbounded liberty, and the danger of bounding it, have produced a problem in the science of government, which human understanding seems hitherto unable to solve. If nothing may be published but what civil authority shall have previously approved, power must always be the standard of truth; if every dreamer of innovations may propagate his projects, there can be no settlement; if every murmurer at government may diffuse discontent, there can be no peace; and if every sceptic in theology may teach his follies, there can be no religion. The remedy against these evils is to punish the authors; for it is yet allowed that every society may punish, though not prevent, the publication of opinions which that society shall think pernicious; but this punishment, though it may crush the author, promotes the book; and it seems not more reasonable to leave the right of printing unrestrained, because writers may afterwards be censured, than it would be to sleep with doors unbolted, because by our laws we can hang a thief.

Samuel Johnson, *Works of the Most Eminent English Poets* (1779–81)

Dr. Johnson's expression of disenchantment with the 'free' press is very nearly contemporary with David Hume's: Johnson looks back over the first century of that liberty which Milton had advocated so strongly and sees its rewards in terms of political instability and philosophical scepticism. Men were not wiser or nobler by virtue of such freedom as they were granted in 1695, indeed it was still far from self-evident to this Tory pessimist that the removal of licensing had conferred the least benefit on society. Of course, such views of literary censorship were by no means unchallenged, and there were many critics whose real objection to the removal of licensing was simply that it had made way for other methods by which successive governments might silence their political opponents. The only real tolerance was born of indifference, as soon as crisis followed torpor, booksellers and authors were among the first targets.

Political censorship is necessarily based on fear of what will happen if those whose work is censored get their way, or if they are effective in persuading a large number of readers to share their point of view. The nature of political censorship at any given time depends on the

34

censor's answer to the simple question, 'What are you afraid of?' If this question had been put in the opening years of the eighteenth century, the answer would almost certainly have been that there were two related fears. First of all, there was the fear of the enemy 'across the water', the fear that the deposed James II—and later his son— would be restored to the English throne by the force of foreign intervention, bringing with him a foreign political despotism and an alien religion: the fear of Jacobites and Catholics. The second fear was of the enemy at home, the fear that the authority of Parliament might be usurped, either from above or below: the fear of a particular administration that it might be overthrown, or its effectiveness undermined, even by an opposition in Parliament itself. Those who seemed most likely to challenge the authority or decisions of Parliament were as a rule close enough to Parliament for this second fear to be the fear of the enemy within. (The third and worst fear, fear of the enemy below—the mob—was reserved for a later period.)

That there might be a Jacobite *coup d'état* or invasion was naturally the more intense of the two fears and in 1707 the law was strengthened by making it high treason to assert the Pretender's claim to the throne, James II being dead by then. Yet though fear of the Jacobites was a useful stimulus to political vigilance, most of the moves against the press were prompted by Parliament's concern for its own authority. The last of the Licensing Acts had expired in the spring of 1695, at the end of the parliamentary session: no sooner had the next session begun in November than the Commons had set up a Committee of Privileges to inquire into 'the Authors and Dispersers of Libels, and scandalous Papers, upon Persons who have served as Members of Parliament'.[1] A bill for the regulation of the press was given a first reading and then dropped. In the spring of 1697, however, another bill to prevent the publication of news except by licence was brought in, as a result of an attack in the *Flying Post* on the financial stability of the Exchequer Bills. This new attempt at censorship was defeated on a second reading but the editor of the *Flying Post* was, nonetheless, arrested by order of the Commons. In December 1697 a third bill to regulate the press was introduced in the Commons but this failed as well. In 1698 and 1702 similar bills were introduced in the Lords but never became law.

The dilemma of the Commons, willing to exercise control over the press but well aware of the shortcomings of the licensing system, is clearly illustrated by the final and protracted debate on licensing between December 1703 and March 1704, caused by John Tutchin's attack on Parliament in his paper the *Observator*. A complaint was

[1] *Journals of the House of Commons*, XI, 336.

made about this publication in December, and in January the Solicitor-General presented a bill 'to prevent the Licentiousness of the Press'.[1] The bill reached its second reading and passed to the committee stage by a majority of 127 to 90. But the committee stage was protracted, a decision being postponed from week to week until Parliament adjourned in March. In October, when the next session began, the bill had been forgotten. It is not entirely without significance, in view of such hesitation on the part of the parliamentary committee, that during this stage of the bill a petition was presented to the House by the free workmen printers of the City of London. These petitioners reminded the Commons—if they needed a reminder —that 'since the Expiration of an Act made in the Fourteenth Year of the Reign of King *Charles* the Second (for preventing the printing seditious Books and Papers, and limiting the Number of Printers and Printing Presses) the Petitioners are become so numerous, that there is scarce Business enough for them all at present; and, if they are confined to licensing, most of them, and their Families, will be reduced to Want.'[2] To anyone who had much knowledge of the book trade before 1695, this could be taken as a polite warning to the Commons that if the attempt to re-introduce licensing should be successful, many printers would be economically obliged to return to unlicensed printing. It seems, from the outcome of the committee stage, that the Commons heeded the warning. (In December 1695 the printers had petitioned the Commons to control the numbers of masters and apprentices, explaining, 'there is not lawful Business for several Members of the said Trade; which has occasioned so many scandalous and seditious Libels of late'.[3])

While Parliament was hesitating between the shortcomings of licensing and the vexations of a 'licentious press', its members were bombarded by the salvos of a pamphlet war. The most vociferous of the pamphleteers were, as it happened, less concerned with the privileges of Parliament than with the effects which press freedom would have on the nation's religious beliefs. *A Letter to a Member of Parliament shewing that a Restraint on the Press is inconsistent with the Protestant Religion, and dangerous to the Liberties of the Nation* (1698) makes its point on the title-page. It was answered by such pamphlets as Francis Gregory's *Modest Plea for the due Regulation of the Press* in the same year and another letter to a Member of Parliament in the following year '*shewing the Necessity of Regulating the Press*'. It is worth recalling that 1698 was the year of the Blasphemy Act so that press freedom and religious orthodoxy were bound to be allied topics. So far as the religious issues were concerned it

[1] *ibid.*, XIV, 278.   [2] *ibid.*, XIV, 338.   [3] *ibid.*, XI, 354.

was the High Church party which favoured a system of licensing while its opponents argued for continued abolition. There is a certain irony in this since some of the most celebrated cases of the early eighteenth century—notably that of Dr. Sacheverell—were prosecutions of High Church publications.

However much the two factions might appeal to Members of Parliament, the attitude of the Commons was ultimately to be determined by more worldly and self-centred considerations. As the first years of the new press freedom passed and nothing was done to reverse the decision of 1695 the arguments against reversing it grew stronger. Whatever new form of censorship was introduced would have to be the work of Parliament: yet Defoe in his *Essay on the Regulation of the Press*; Matthew Tindal in *Reasons against Restraining the Press* (both published in 1704), and Addison in *Thoughts of a Tory Author Concerning the Press* (1712) all put forward the one proposition which no Member of Parliament could ignore. If any party, while in government, imposes a system of censorship on its opponents, it will itself suffer the effects of that censorship when it is in opposition. The High Church faction was learning much the same lesson, by experience, at the time that these pamphlets were published.

In 1712 the Tory administration, which had by then succeeded to power, was still toying with the idea of some kind of press censorship. In January of that year Queen Anne herself complained to Parliament that the laws were not strong enough to prevent the publication of 'false and scandalous libels', and that some action must be taken. Throughout the spring of 1712 the Tories considered the possibility of re-imposing the old-style censorship but finally rejected that much-canvassed proposal in favour of a Stamp Act. This Act was intended to discourage political opposition by imposing a stamp duty of a penny a sheet on newspapers and two shillings a sheet on one copy of each edition of a pamphlet which was more than half a sheet. The value of this new measure to the Tory government was extremely doubtful. 'As to the tax,' Addison forecast gloomily, 'those who are aggriev'd will not think much of paying it if their Case is worth it.'[1] To make matters worse, the Tories were soon out of office and destined for decades in opposition, thus becoming—as had been prophesied—the victims of the very system which they had devised for their own enemies. As a matter of fact, the worst offenders were the quickest to find a loophole in the new law. Though a tax was imposed on whole sheets, no tax had been specified for half sheets or for papers of such sizes as one and a half sheets (6 pages). After the Stamp Act had been

[1] *Thoughts of a Tory Author Concerning the Press*, p. 31.

in operation for several years, John Tolland recorded that a number of newspaper publishers were evading the tax by bringing out papers in these odd sizes.[1] Naturally, these were the very periodicals which it had been intended to suppress, their columns written principally by 'papists, nonjurors, or other disaffected persons'. It was not until 1725 that another Stamp Act put an end to this practice by imposing a tax of $\frac{1}{2}d.$ on every half sheet.

Whigs and Tories alike showed extreme willingness to impose some kind of censorship on the press but were unable to devise one which would be completely effective. So far as this goes, it is worth remembering that though they had political quarrels between themselves there were a great many authors and publishers whom they could regard as their common enemies. Indeed, the authority and power of Parliament was something in which they were ultimately bound to have an equal interest, and a great many seditious libels were devoted to challenging or undermining that authority. Yet no form of general censorship would deal effectively with such abuses and there was no alternative to dealing with individual cases as they arose, either by parliamentary action or through the courts of law.

THE ENEMY ACROSS THE WATER

'We labour under two mighty Evils;' said Reldresal to Gulliver, 'a violent Faction at home, and the Danger of an Invasion by a most potent Enemy from abroad.'[2] As in Lilliput, so in England, the fear of that 'most potent Enemy' persisted. Almost as soon as William and Mary were established on the English throne, following the 'Glorious Revolution' in 1689, it became illegal to assert the claims of the deposed James II or his descendants, though it was not made treasonable by statute until 1707. Two men, Newbolt and Butler, were convicted of high treason long before this for publishing the *Declaration* of James II to his subjects, and another publisher, Douglas, had been imprisoned in 1693 for issuing *The Jacobite's Principles Vindicated*. Though Newbolt and Butler were pardoned, the Jacobite printer William Anderton had been executed earlier that year for printing two pamphlets but the extent of his guilt is uncertain. In 1707 it seemed unlikely, whatever the charge brought against him, that a publisher would actually suffer the penalties of high treason simply for advocating the Jacobite claims, however strenuously. Nevertheless, Parliament and the courts showed themselves extremely sensitive to any argument which seemed to favour the claims of the

[1] B.M. Add. MS. 4295, f. 49.
[2] Jonathan Swift, *Gulliver's Travels* (London, 1726), I, 71.

Pretender. For instance, any book which maintained that the Crown of England must pass by strict hereditary succession was, logically, bound to imply support for the Pretender as son of James II rather than for William and Mary, son-in-law and daughter of the King, or for his younger daughter, Anne. A book like Harbin's *Hereditary Right of the Crown of England Asserted* might seem to have little to do with contemporary issues, since it was no more than a description of the order of succession to the English throne during the medieval and Tudor periods: the rest of its illustrative material was drawn from Roman and early Christian sources. But the implications were obvious enough to the government: if the hereditary right was maintained, then it was the Pretender, James Edward, who as James III had the only legitimate claim to be King of England. The book had already appeared when a man by the name of Hilkaiah Bedford was identified as the person who had delivered the manuscript to the printer and, though the proceedings against him were protracted, he was finally sentenced in 1714 by the Lord Chief Justice to three years' imprisonment, a fine of 1,000 marks (£666 13*s.* 4*d.*) and to find sureties of £5,000 for his good behaviour for the rest of his life. The real value of money in the early eighteenth century was quite ten times that of the mid-twentieth century, and though a man might be sentenced to only three years' imprisonment, it was a customary condition that he should be kept in prison indefinitely so long as any fines or sureties remained unpaid. As it happened, Bedford died in prison.

It is understandable that the Whigs and their sympathisers, even though they were out of office, became far more sensitive about the Jacobite problem as Queen Anne's life drew to its close, and it was by no means a settled question who was going to succeed her. By this time, the only surviving heir of James II was the Pretender, favoured by some of the Tories and abhorred by almost everyone else. The Whig party might no longer form the government but it had power enough, and sufficiently powerful supporters, to attempt the suppression of any publication which suggested that when Queen Anne died the Pretender must succeed. 'There are some,' said the Queen, 'who are arrived to that Height of Malice, as to insinuate, that the Protestant Succession in the House of *Hanover* is in Danger under My Government.'[1] One man who fell foul of this particular censorship was Daniel Defoe, certainly no Jacobite, though an employee of the Tory ministry in 1713 when he published three pamphlets concerning the question of succession to the throne: *What if the Queen should die?; Reasons against the Succession of the House of Hanover,* and *Some Advantages of the Pretender's Possessing the*

[1] *Journals of the House of Lords*, XIX, 625.

Crown of Great Britain. Needless to say, Defoe's championing of the Jacobite cause was pure irony, as a Dissenter he had no wish whatever to see James Edward crowned. But irony was no defence in a case of seditious libel, however often it might be employed in practice, and the official view of irony in Augustan literature was summed up in *A Digest of the Law Concerning Libels*, in 1765. 'It seems to be now agreed, that not only Scandal expressed in an open and direct Manner, but also such as is expressed in Irony amounts to a Libel.'[1] Defoe was accused by his enemies and arrested but, through the good offices of the ministry, whose paid servant he was, released on bail, while the ailing Queen was persuaded to pardon him even before the case could be tried.

In 1715 came the Jacobite invasion with the Pretender at its head and at once the censorship of any discussion of the claims of James Edward, sympathetic or not, became much stricter. By royal decree the clergy were forbidden to mention politics in their sermons and a schoolmaster named Bournois, who denied the right of George I to succeed to the English throne, died as a result of the flogging to which he was sentenced for his opinion. By this time, the Whigs having replaced the Tory administration, Sir Robert Walpole had become leader of the government and had begun to stir up that hostility from the press which was to endure for quarter of a century. It was disenchantment with Walpole and the Kings whom he served, rather than any positive enthusiasm for the Jacobite cause, from which James Edward had most to hope. In 1716, for instance, such short-lived journals as *Robin's Last Shift* and *The Shift Saved* began with a condemnation of the Pretender for the way in which he had deserted his defeated armies, describing the activities of those troops in terms that could hardly be regarded as admiring. But as the dislike of Walpole and his administration grew, as well as dislike of the Hanoverian George I, the tone of these journals became less hostile towards the Jacobites and their leader. In April 1716 *Robin's Last Shift* warned its readers that Walpole was the real enemy, since he was about to suspend Magna Carta, prolong the life of the present Parliament indefinitely, get rid of George I, and establish a republic under his own dictatorial rule.[2] The author, printer, and publisher of the paper were arrested, and *The Shift Saved*, a similar production, was also suppressed a few months later. It is not surprising that the lives of such papers should have been short, if colourful, but there were others which survived for a great deal longer and which main-

[1] *A Digest of the Law Concerning Libels*, 1765, p. 6.
[2] *Robin's Last Shift: or, Weekly Remarks and Political Reflections upon the most material News Foreign and Domestic*, Saturday 14 April 1716.

tained their support for the Jacobite cause. The most celebrated of these was *Mist's Weekly Journal*, the work of Nathaniel Mist who devoted himself to opposing Walpole and defending the Pretender's claims throughout the reign of George I, after which he withdrew to join other Jacobite exiles in France. But despite the scare of another invasion, the Jacobite cause was lost from this point onwards, even if the fear of the enemy across the water endured for many years after 1715. So far as the government was concerned, that fear was the result of the way in which the popularity of the German-speaking George I declined steadily, leaving no reserves of good will for his son George II. Many people who were not Jacobites had little love for the house of Hanover either. For ten years after the uprising of 1715 the Whig government kept a careful watch on anything that might be an expression of support for the Pretender and it can only have been their extreme nervousness about this which would explain a certain act of savagery, quite unparalleled in the history of eighteenth-century censorship.

In 1719 a pamphlet of a single sheet appeared with the title *Ex Ore Tuo Te Judico, Vox Populi Vox Dei*. It put forward the claims of the Pretender, his hereditary right to the throne and his personal qualities, suggesting that if the people only knew more about these qualities they would find James Edward an admirable ruler. The pamphlet also made a point of discounting the legend that the Pretender was not the legitimate son of James II. In June 1719 a nineteen-year-old printer, John Matthews, was arrested in the City of London and a copy of this libel, which was still technically treasonable by the Act of 1707, was found in his pocket. When his room was searched, two more half sheets were found, each containing the first half of the pamphlet, and one complete copy of it was found as well. Matthews did not know the name of the author, nor did he apparently realise the significance of the pamphlet, in which the Pretender was referred to as the 'Chevalier'. However, the half sheets found in his room were all the evidence needed to convict him: the authorities would hardly expect to find the type still set up since—apart from the obvious dangers—it was the general practice of eighteenth-century printers to disperse the type after printing off an impression and to compose it again if another impression were called for. Matthews was charged with treason. In vain, he pleaded his ignorance of the pamphlet's contents; in vain, his brother assured the Lord Chief Justice that no seditious literature had ever been printed in their house; in vain, Matthews's counsel pleaded the youth of the accused. Matthews was found guilty, according to the law of 1707, and hanged with all due ceremony. The comparative mildness of much of the pamphlet, the rigorous execution of the sentence, the ignorance and the youth of the condemned man, all indicate clearly the rigour with which the anti-Jacobite censorship was imposed in this case. The next year John Lowden was found guilty of publishing the same pamphlet: he was fined 50 marks (£33 6s. 8d.) and imprisoned for three months. There seems to be a grotesque anomaly in this, though one has to remember that in the case of Matthews the government must have felt that by apprehending the printer they had to deal with the source of treasonable material. Ten years after the execution of Matthews the Attorney-General was in favour of prosecuting another publisher for treason, and indeed this might have happened but that the man, Edward Farley, died in prison before the case could be heard.

In 1757 John Shebbeare, looking back at the period which followed the Jacobite invasion of 1715 and its failure, remarked that whatever dangers might have seemed at the time to threaten the House of Hanover and the Protestant succession, the settlement of 1714 'became more effectually fix'd, than a Length of Years could have established it without that Incident.'[1] As this realisation penetrated to the minds of government and as—despite all alarms and rumours—the Pretender seemed able to do little more than invite George I to abdicate and devote all his time to being Elector of Hanover, official concern over anti-Hanoverian, pro-Stuart propaganda began to subside. In 1728, nine years after the fate of John Matthews, the printer and publisher of *Mist's Weekly Journal* were tried and convicted on a charge of libelling the royal family in an article which could hardly be anything but pro-Jacobite to most readers. The article disguised George I as 'Meryweis,' George II as 'Esreff,' the Pretender as 'the Sophi,' and set the scene in 'Persia.' George II is declared to be illegitimate and a lecher, the first accusation was probably not true but the second was, and there is an appeal to other countries for their assistance in restoring 'the Sophi' to the throne of 'Persia.'[2] Such an article was criminal, it might technically have been treasonable, but as the fortunes of the Jacobites waned it was no longer a hanging matter.

There was one kind of censorship, associated with fear of the Jacobites, which dragged on throughout most of the eighteenth century: it remained a crime to libel the Glorious Revolution or the revolutionary settlement of 1689. John Shebbeare was convicted of this in 1758 for sneering at the 'malignant Star of *Hanoverian* Politics,'[3]

[1] *A Sixth Letter to the People of England on the Progress of the National Ruin* (London, 1757), p. 63.
[2] *Mist's Weekly Journal*, Saturday 24 August 1728.
[3] *A Sixth Letter to the People of England*, p. 58.

42

in his *Sixth Letter to the People of England* (1757), and Richard Nutt had been convicted on a similar charge in 1754 for a libel on the revolutionary settlement in the *London Evening Post* of 7–10 September 1754. Woodfall was fined for publishing such material in the *Public Advertiser* in 1774 and even at the separate trials of Thomas Paine and Jeremiah Samuel Jordan in 1792 (for publishing the *Rights of Man*) the antiquated charge was dredged up of 'vilifying the Glorious Revolution'.[1] Whatever importance the government may have attached to this 'crime' it seems that those responsible for carrying out the punishment saw good cause to be lenient as time went by. It is good to know that when Shebbeare was pilloried he was 'greatly favoured: instead of putting his head *in* the hole of the pillory in the usual mode, the upper board was raised as high as possible, and there fastened. Shebbeare stood upright, without ever bending his neck in the least; looking through the wide opening between the upper and lower boards.'[2]

These cases were, of course, exceptional and long before 1792— or even 1745—the lack of interest in pro-Jacobite literature, even among those whose duty it was to censor it, is evident enough. The invasion of 1745 may have given a lot of people a bad fright but both before and after it the probability of a successful attempt to restore the House of Stuart seemed remote indeed. The knowledge that the dispute, though it might go on for sixty years, would not go on for ever and could only end in victory for the Hanoverians, made indifference, if not leniency, possible. Far more important than the Jacobite question in most people's minds was the rift between George II and the opposition under the aegis of Frederick, Prince of Wales. When in 1751 the House of Commons condemned to the flames *Constitutional Queries, earnestly recommended to the serious considerations of every true Briton*, which compared the Duke of Cumberland to Richard III, they were not suppressing the work of an embittered Jacobite who remembered 'Butcher' Cumberland's 'pacification' of Scotland after the defeat of the Jacobites at Culloden, but the attacks of Lord Egmont and the opposition led by the Prince of Wales, Cumberland's own brother. The Jacobite dispute itself had roots in the past which made it increasingly irrelevant as an issue of practical politics, and the only real question was the rather limited academic one—to most Augustans —of strict hereditary succession.

THE ENEMY WITHIN

Though the threat from abroad and the invasions of 1715 and 1745,

[1] P.R.O. K.B. 28/362/1 and P.R.O. K.B. 28/363/1.
[2] *Biographical, Literary, and Political Anecdotes* (London, 1797), I, 375.

presented the most dramatic—and at times melodramatic—problem with which Augustan ministries had to deal, the major task of political censorship during this period was the more mundane one of preserving the authority of Parliament and, more specifically, of preserving the authority and power of one particular party within Parliament. As we have already seen, when licensing ended in 1695, the first move to restore it came from the House of Commons within six months of voting for its abolition. The Commons had fought hard to preserve their rights against the encroachment of the monarchy, and what had been won—in terms of respect as well as power—was not to be eroded by 'the Licentiousness of the Press.' The normal method of dealing with seditious libels was, of course, by prosecution in a court of law, but where the authority of Parliament was questioned, the Commons, and sometimes the Lords, took direct action against the offending authors or publishers. Indeed, after half a century of this, there were those in the book trade who wondered whether they had done more than to exchange the tyranny of absolute monarchy for the tyranny of elected representatives.

Even though Parliament abandoned the idea of restoring the licensing system, those outside Parliament who continued to advocate such a system justified it by the extreme contention that nowhere, outside the Lords and the Commons, need freedom of expression be allowed. 'Liberty and Freedom of Speech is that high Privilege which belongs only to the two Houses of Parliament,' said the anonymous author of *Arguments Relating to a Restraint upon the Press*, addressed to Members of Parliament during the press controversy of 1712.[1] One wonders whether he could have been a Member of Parliament himself. Power and respect, which parliamentary privilege represented were scupulously guarded against the malicious and subversive libels of an irresponsible press and long before 1712 the House of Commons had taken direct action in a number of cases. As early as 1703, when an article in the *Observator* attacked the attitude of the Commons towards religious nonconformity, the House responded by ordering the arrest of John How and Benjamin Bragg, the printer and publisher of the paper. Both claimed that the real villain was John Tutchin, who had written the piece, and eventually the Commons released them both.[2] Two months later, in February 1704, the *Observator* published another attack on the House, which Members alleged was a scandalous and seditious libel. This time the arrest of all three men was ordered but, having profited by their earlier experience, the trio absconded and, though a reward was offered for their

[1] *Arguments Relating to a Restraint upon the Press* (London, 1712), p. 21.
[2] *Journals of the House of Commons*, XIV, 248; 269–70.

capture, the only response was a letter from Tutchin to the Speaker of the House, stating his case and regretting that it was impossible for him to attend in person.[1]

Among other prosecutions instigated by Parliament at this time was that of Daniel Defoe for his *Shortest Way with Dissenters* (1702) but the House of Commons was no less ready to deal with its own Members. In March 1714 it voted by a large majority to expel Richard Steele for his pamphlet *The Crisis*, in which he suggested that the decision of who should succeed Queen Anne could not safely be left to a Tory ministry, and he added 'some seasonable remarks on the danger of a popish successor.' The Whigs in the House of Lords were annoyed by Steele's expulsion and when Swift produced a Tory reply to *The Crisis* in his *Public Spirit of the Whigs*, they offered a reward of £300 for the discovery of the author. The Tories might control the Commons but the Whigs could still speak for the Lords. However, as was so often the case when Swift was the culprit, the reward went unclaimed. John Asgill had the unusual distinction of being expelled from both the English and Irish Houses of Commons for a book on the possibility of avoiding death, in which he argued that 'Men may be Translated from Hence into Eternal Life without passing through Death.' As with so many discoverers of such wonders, he expected this process to occur in his own case, thus earning the soubriquet of 'Translated Asgill.'

Pamphleteers like Defoe and Tutchin were prosecuted through the instigation of Parliament; editors of periodicals like the *Flying Post*, the *News-Letter*, and *Mist's Weekly Journal* were arrested by order of Parliament, summoned to the bar of the House of Commons and made to ask for pardon on their knees. As a matter of fact, Nathaniel Mist was more than equal to the occasion. When he was summoned in this way in 1721 he refused to answer any question put to him on the grounds that he was facing a separate criminal charge in the courts for seditious libels published in his *Weekly Journal* and that he was not obliged to incriminate himself in the House of Commons beforehand. His plea was successful and, best of all, though the House committed him to Newgate, he was acquitted at his trial through lack of evidence. In 1739 Robert Dodsley, one of the most eminent publishers of the eighteenth century by virtue of his *Select Collection of Old Plays* (1744) and his *Collection of Poems by Several Hands* (1748–1758)—better known as 'Dodsley's Miscellany'—was imprisoned by the House of Lords for publishing Paul Whitehead's poem *Manners*, which attacked several Members of the House. The Lords would have preferred to deal with Whitehead himself but he

[1] *ibid.*, XIV, 336–7; 349.

had absconded from justice, leaving Dodsley as the sole target for their vengeance.

The Commons showed themselves even more sensitive than the Lords to any criticism which seemed to call in question their status and privileges. This sensitivity is well illustrated in its more absurd aspect by a story which Edward Gibbon tells of a sermon preached before the Commons in 1772, when those few Members who had bothered to attend appeared to be asleep. When the sermon was over, they roused themselves and passed the customary vote of thanks to its preacher. Not until the sermon appeared in print did they realise that it was a eulogy of what they, presumably, regarded as anti-Parliamentary Stuart despotism, and an expression of the pious hope that George III would continue to reflect and develop those autocratic qualities which had made Charles I so beloved. With farcical solemnity the aggrieved House proceeded to reverse its vote of thanks.

Even to report the proceedings of Parliament, without authority, was an infringment of privilege and therefore illegal. It was felt, apparently, that the less the nation knew of what went on inside Parliament the less criticism there would be. As early as 1698 the House of Lords summoned John Churchill before them and reprimanded him for publishing a far from popular work, *Cases in Parliament Resolved and Adjudged upon Petitions and Writs of Error*. Five years later the Commons went so far as to declare it a breach of privilege to publish the results of divisions taken in the House. Of course, the natural hostilities provoked by the two-party system in Parliament were far too intriguing for publishers not to issue some account of them and then take the consequences. *The Gentleman's Magazine* in 1736, and later on the *London Magazine*, published regular reports of parliamentary debates until, in 1747, both editors were called to account before the House of Lords. Even so, the practice of reporting 'Debates in the Senate of Great Lilliput' or the 'Proceedings of the Political Club' continued. Samuel Johnson himself wrote the parliamentary reports for the *Gentleman's Magazine* between 1740 and 1743.

How could the power of Parliament exercised directly over authors and publishers be controlled? Technically, there was little that courts of law could do, even if they had wanted to. If the Commons or the Lords condemned men for what they had written or published, there was virtually no appeal. As late as 1799 Benjamin Flower, printer of the *Cambridge Intelligencer*, had been fined £100 and imprisoned for six months by the House of Lords for a libel on one of its Members, the Bishop of Llandaff. Flower appealed to the court of King's Bench against this sentence but its judges ruled that they were powerless to vary it and, what was more, that a court could not even grant bail in such a case. Yet long before Flower's case Parliament, by the exercise of what many people regarded as a tyrannical and unjustifiable control over the press, was losing sympathy among those on whose support it ultimately relied. A good illustration of this is the case of a bookseller called William Owen. Owen published a book with the title *The Case of Alexander Murray Esq.*, in which he described how Murray had been committed to Newgate by the Commons in 1751 for contempt of the privileges of the House. When he was brought to the bar of the House, Murray was told to kneel and ask for pardon but his reply was that he was accustomed to kneel before Almighty God and before no one else. By the time that Murray's case came up again, Owen had published the book in question and the Commons ordered that it should be prosecuted. The passage in the book to which they objected, however, is one with which a great many people outside Parliament might have sympathised.

What shall distinguish Britons from those who groan under the most arbitrary governments, if subject to the like tyrannical acts of oppression? And what shall defend a free people from these, whenever their representatives shall think fit to constitute themselves their judges, and wantonly inflict the severest pains and penalties by virtue of their mere will and pleasure?[1]

When Owen was tried before Lord Chief Justice Lee on 6 July 1752, he was defended by Pratt, who as Chief Justice was later to give favourable decisions to Wilkes in actions brought as a result of the *North Briton* affair, and prosecuted by the Solicitor-General, Murray, who as Lord Mansfield came to be regarded as the arch-enemy of those who were campaigning for a freer press. In Owen's case, the jury heard the evidence, the passages objected to in the book were read, and after due retirement the foreman announced a verdict of 'Not Guilty.' Murray, as Solicitor-General, protested at this, feeling with some justification that the jury was biased in favour of the defendant and had returned a verdict which was not consistent with the evidence. Before accepting this verdict, the Lord Chief Justice put a question to the foreman of the jury. 'Do you think the evidence laid before you, of Owen's publishing the book by selling it, is not sufficient to convince you that the said Owen did sell the book?' The foreman considered the question, appeared to suspect a trap, and simply replied 'Not Guilty'.[2] It was one of the very few cases in which either House of Parliament failed to achieve its end in proceedings against a printer, publisher, or author. At the same time it was an

---

[1] *Cobbett's State Trials*, XVIII, 1218.   [2] *ibid.*, XVIII, 1228.

omen of the coming struggle and, particularly, of the part which juries were to play in the fight against political censorship by taking the law into their own hands.

A great deal of political censorship during the earlier eighteenth century was naturally devoted not to the protection of parliamentary privilege but to the maintenance of a particular ministry—Whig or Tory in turn—and its defence against all enemies whether in Parliament or outside. Of course, any apologist for one of the political parties would obviously claim that the press had been free when his side was in office and that it was only his opponents who were bent on stifling liberty of expression. The Tories, for example, during their long spell in opposition after Walpole's accession to power protested, with every reason, against the numerous individual acts of political censorship for which his administration was responsible. Yet when the Tories looked back at their own tenure of office between 1710 and 1714, by some most remarkable lapses of memory they viewed it as a golden age of press freedom. Comparing the years when the Tories were in office with those of Walpole's ministry, the author of *The Doctrine of Innuendo's Discuss'd; or, The Liberty of the Press maintain'd* remarked in 1731, 'Yet at that time there were not so many Prosecutions against Libellers and Pamphleteers as have been made since his *meek Administration*, neither were any Attempts made to invade the *Liberty of the Press*.'[1] If Walpole had launched more prosecutions of this kind, it was simply because he had been in office a great deal longer—certainly the records which survive show no greater persecution of literature, proportionately, under the Whigs than under the Tories. As for the Tories not having attempted to limit the liberty of the press, what else had the Stamp Act of 1712 and the bill introduced in the Commons to restore licensing been but attempts to impose such limitations? It is in no way cynical to believe that the two parties wanted the best of both worlds—freedom to criticise while in opposition and the effective suppression of seditious libels in office. The measures which an opposition denounced as a violation of liberty, it would have imposed on the other party without a second thought, had it been in a position to do so.

Many of those whom one would like to think of as advocates of press freedom, in this respect, were in fact keen to ensure that liberty of expression was granted only to those whose views could be approved by them. Daniel Defoe, who had reason enough at one time to regret the operation of this kind of political censorship, remarked, 'Governments will not be jested with, nor reflected upon,

[1] *The Doctrine of Innuendo's Discuss'd; or, The Liberty of the Press Maintain'd* (London, 1731), p. 16.

nor is it fit that they should always lye at the mercy of every pen.'[1]
Jonathan Swift, who on two occasions had a price on his own head
for what he had written—once for *The Public Spirit of the Whigs* and
once for the *Drapier's Letters*—complained to Stella in 1712 that,
'These devils in Grub Street rogues, that write the *Flying-Post* and
Medley in one paper, will not be quiet. They are always mauling
Lord Treasurer, Lord Bolingbroke and me. We have the dog under
prosecution, but Bolingbroke is not active enough. He is a Scotch
rogue, one Ridpath.'[2] Even when Bolingbroke became 'active' the
result must have been a disappointment to Swift. Ridpath was convicted after an eight-hour trial in February 1713 but when ordered to
appear for sentencing in May he disappeared and Bolingbroke's
offer of a reward of £100 for his discovery failed to unearth him.
Worse still, the authorities discovered that, through a procedural
error, the sum which had been named as Ridpath's bail was no
longer forfeit.

The literature of party political warfare, with which this type of
ministerial censorship was concerned, was not of the sort which deals
in questions of fundamental political principle. In this sense it differs
from the literature of the Jacobite controversy, where there was the
basic issue of hereditary succession, as it does from the political
literature which features increasingly in cases of censorship after 1760
and which deals with the doctrines of democracy, equality, and the
immediate question of representative government. To the Augustans,
it was the corruption or the incompetence of a ministry or of particular
ministers which was the most urgent and relevant issue.

Ministerial sensitivity to criticism became evident as soon as the
power of Parliament and the relative powerlessness of the monarchy
had been effectively established. One man who contrived to annoy both
the Commons as a whole and the ministry in particular at this stage
was the editor of the *Observator*, John Tutchin, whose brush with
the Commons I have already described. Tutchin was an extreme
'democrat,' to use a nearly anachronistic term, and was said to be
secretary of the Calves-Head Club, which met to celebrate the
anniversary of the execution of Charles I by singing profane songs.
In a number of articles in the *Observator* between 1702 and 1704 he
alleged that certain ministers were in the pay of the French King and
that, as the result of this or not, the ministry had been guilty of ap-
pointing and promoting men, who were totally incompetent, to
positions of responsibility in the British navy. As the case against him
was prepared, he demanded, 'There is a plot against the queen and
the whole nation; is it any wonder then, that there are plots against

[1] *The Review*, August 1704.   [2] *Journal to Stella*, 28 October 1712.

me?. . . I understand, I should have been prosecuted by bill the last sessions, but that the high-fliers did not like the jury; nay, they say they do not like the two sheriffs, because they will not pack juries to find innocent men guilty.'[1] After this final barb there was no question of letting Tutchin go free. He was tried and convicted for the seditious libels which he had published in the *Observator*. His political enemies seemed to be poised for the sweetest of revenges as they waited for him to be sentenced and then, as on two previous occasions, Tutchin eluded them, although this time his methods were irreproachably legal. He moved in arrest of judgment on the grounds that certain documents relating to the accusation against him had been incorrectly made out in a number of minor details and therefore the proceedings at his trial must be invalid. To the dismay of his accusers it proved to be so, and there was nothing for it but to quash the conviction and set Tutchin free.

Not all whom the ministry of the day chose to prosecute were as fortunate as Tutchin and even without going to the lengths of a prosecution the government had an apparatus of censorship at its disposal, which was a relic from the days of licensing. Secretaries of State kept a careful watch on the activities of the opposition press and issued warrants for the arrest of authors, publishers, or printers of allegedly seditious publications without necessarily intending that these arrests should lead to the culprit's appearance in a court of law. There was an obvious difficulty in tracking down, or even in identifying some of those against whom the warrants were issued, while in other cases they could not even be named but were referred to simply as 'the author' or 'the printer.' Yet Secretaries of State had at least the advantage of continuing to employ Messengers of the Press, who had been used to supervise printing while the Licensing Act was still in force. These Messengers acted as spies on behalf of the government and reported to the Secretary of State on the activities of certain publishers and printers. Robert Clare, who acted as Messenger of the Press for Robert Harley, was given the job of drawing up lists of pamphlets and periodicals in 1705 while his colleagues, including Robert Stephens and David Edwards, were employed to supply information of other kinds. Edwards had been the printer of a condemned pamphlet, *The Memorial of the Church of England*, which provoked a prosecution in 1706 and his defection to the government side may have been particularly useful to Harley.[2] Apart from their

[1] *Cobbett's State Trials*, XIV, 1099.
[2] An account of Robert Clare's activities will be found in Henry L. Snyder, 'The Reports of a Press Spy for Robert Harley: New Bibliographical Data for the Reign of Queen Anne,' *The Library*, 5th series XXII (1967), pp. 326–45.

duties as informers, the Messengers of the Press might, on occasion, prevent the publication or at least the circulation of a book or pamphlet by persuading the publisher to suppress it. At other times they were ordered to seize a printer's material or even to break up the type for a newspaper or pamphlet whose publication the government was anxious to prevent. Messengers of the Press had often been printers themselves before accepting employment from the Secretary of State. They showed no lack of enthusiasm for their new job, however, and there is a tone of complete dedication in Clare's words to Harley. 'I could heartily wish I had a Power to visit every Printing-house in Town, which I endeavour to do every Day; I doubt not (since I can read the Metal as well as the Print) but I should make such Discoveries as would be wel-pleasing to your Honour.'[1] This was written on 10 October 1705 but a week later Clare was already obliged to confess that his usefulness was diminishing, 'Persons beginning to be suspicious of me Abroad,' and finally he had to write to Harley begging for money, because he had lost his trade as a printer by working for the government, was distrusted by the book trade and had not 'a Shilling in the World.' Except for a few men like Robert Stephens, the office of Messenger of the Press must have been an unenviable and precarious means of earning a living.

Some warrants issued by Secretaries of State did not result in prosecutions, since the culprits could not be traced but in other cases where the offenders were discovered and the trial might have ended with a conviction, the nature of the publication was bound to be discussed in court. If it alleged ministerial corruption or incompetence, that would be discussed too. John Oldmixon in his *Memoirs of the Press, Historical and Political* throws new light on Swift's complaint to Stella about the government's reluctance to prosecute opposition journalists in 1712. Oldmixon was then editor of the *Medley*, one of the newspapers of which Swift had complained. According to Oldmixon, Harley, who was by then Earl of Oxford and Lord Treasurer in the Tory administration, took certain numbers of the *Medley* to the Attorney-General and demanded a prosecution of their publisher but the Attorney-General was shrewder in his appreciation than the Lord Treasurer.

The Attorney-General brought back the papers to Mr. Harley, and declared nothing could be made of what was said therein, for the Reflexions were not on particular Persons and Things, and he apprehended the reducing them to Particulars in *Westminster-Hall* [if the case should come to court] would not only be a forc'd and unparallel'd Innuendo, but would bring

---

[1] *The Library*, 5th series XXII, 334.

Matters into Proof which were better left, as they were, dark and doubtful.[1]

Oldmixon, of course, was a staunch Whig who enjoyed this kind of gossip about the Tory administration of 1710–14 but there is still good reason to suppose that the government's reputation might have suffered more from a thorough discussion of the alleged libels than it would have gained merely from the conviction of Oldmixon and his associates.

The principal censorship at the level of party politics in the first half of the eighteenth century was naturally that imposed by Walpole on his Tory opponents. The years following 1715 represented a period of low morale and considerable disarray for the Tory opposition: there were, of course, pro-Jacobite publications like *Mist's Weekly Journal* but an opposition press whose criticism was devoted to attacking the Whig ministry was not really in evidence until well after 1720. In 1722 came the first signs of revival when the *Freeholders' Journal* began to expose the scandals of the government-sponsored South Sea Company, whose shares, inflated to ten times their original price, were to bring ruin to many investors when the 'South Sea Bubble' was pricked. Accusing the ministry of a scheme 'founded upon Corruption and Fraud,' the *Journal* demanded, 'Did not the very Essence of your Scheme consist in raising *South-Sea Stock* above its natural value?. . . . A noble Scheme indeed, to Pay the national Debts, by enabling one Set of the Creditors to pick the Pockets of the other!'[2] This was too much for Walpole's administration to tolerate and a warrant was issued for the arrest of the printer and the publisher, indicating that battle had commenced between government and the opposition press.

By 1725 the Tory press had become troublesome enough for the Whig ministry to close the loophole in the Stamp Act of 1712 by imposing a duty of $\frac{1}{2}d.$ on every half sheet of a newspaper. But, as Addison had pointed out thirteen years earlier, it would take more than stamp duty to silence political opposition and in 1726 the most formidable of all the Tory opposition journals, the *Craftsman*, was founded by Bolingbroke, who had returned from exile in 1723, and the two Pulteneys. It was the *Craftsman* which in December 1726 claimed that no publications had provoked government action while the Tories held office, except Steele's pamphlet *The Crisis* and the preface to Fleetwood's *Sermons*. The truth, as we have seen, was that though the Tories had been responsible for far more censorship than that, the Whig administration which succeeded them had been equally

[1] *Memoirs of the Press, Historical and Political* (London, 1742), pp. 11–12.

[2] *The Supplement to the Freeholders' Journal of Wednesday, March 21*, Friday 23 March 1721 (i.e. 1722).

repressive. Indeed, after five years of publishing the *Craftsman* it seemed to its authors that they might have been in danger of their lives and 'it has been more owing to the Honesty of a *true English Jury*, than the Lenity of their Prosecutors, that they have not incurr'd the Fate of *Matthews*'.[1] Naturally, this accusation has all the animus of party politics but it was certainly true that the Whigs, if not going to the extreme of executing opposition journalists, were quite prepared to use such methods as would silence them without the disagreeable necessity of a trial by jury. Nathaniel Mist, for example, had his printing materials seized and detained in 1718 on the orders of the Secretary of State and in 1721 the type for a number of his *Weekly Journal* was broken up by the government's Messengers of the Press. In 1722, at the time of the 'South Sea Bubble' scandal the printing materials for the *Freeholders' Journal* were taken into custody. Whig Secretaries of State would also issue warrants for printers or publishers in respect of books which had not yet appeared but which could be referred to with complete confidence as 'a scandalous and seditious Libel, the Title of which is yet unknown,' or 'now in the press,' or 'printing in a clandestine manner'.[2] Under the circumstances it was hardly realistic of the Tories to boast of their own liberality while in office and certainly alarmist to suggest that their journalists were in danger of going to the gallows, but on other and more substantial grounds they had good reason to attack the press censorship which Walpole's ministry had imposed.

By the inevitable sequence of events those Tories who, like Jonathan Swift, had been so anxious to crush opposition libels when they were in office, now became libellers themselves—and very effective ones. By 1720 Swift, as an Irish patriot, was already in difficulties over press censorship. His *Proposal for the Universal Use of Irish Manufacture* attacked England's political and economic tyranny over Ireland, urged a boycott of English goods, and a ban by the Irish House of Commons on the import of English cloth. The political and economic implications of Swift's plea to the Irish people 'never to appear with one single *Shred* that comes from England,' were too strong for the ministry to ignore. Edward Waters, the printer, was duly prosecuted but acquitted at once by the Irish jury: Lord Chief Justice Whitshed tried to have their verdict overruled but without success. Two years later William Wood was granted a patent to supply copper coinage for Ireland. The Irish asked for coinage of a guaranteed value but Wood, who is said to have obtained his patent by

[1] *The Doctrine of Innuendo's Discuss'd*, pp. 14–15.
[2] *Copies Taken from the Records of the Court of King's-Bench at Westminster* (London, 1763), *passim*.

53

bribing a mistress of George I, saw no obligation to guarantee any such thing. In 1724 Swift published five *Drapier's Letters* to the people of Ireland, denouncing Wood as a 'Sharper' and the coinage as 'Wood's Brass': he advised Irishmen not to accept the coins as legal tender and bitterly denounced the status imposed upon the Irish people. 'Am I a *Free-Man* in *England*, and do I become a *Slave* in six Hours by crossing the Channel?'[1] As if this were not bad enough, the Whig censorship aimed to deny the Irish even the right of expressing their grievances.

For those who have used *Power* to cramp *Liberty*, have gone so far as to Resent even the *Liberty of Complaining*, altho' a Man upon the Rack was never known to be refused the Liberty of *Roaring* as loud as he thought fit.[2]

When the fourth *Letter* appeared on 13 October 1724, the Irish Privy Council met and a reward of £300 was offered for the discovery of the author. His identity must have been widely known—and known even by certain members of the Privy Council—but the reward went unclaimed. Harding, the printer of the *Letter*, was brought before a grand jury, to whom Swift at once addressed his *Seasonable Advice to the Grand Jury*. He had already admitted writing the *Drapier's Letters* but the temper of Ireland was such that the authorities appear to have decided that the risks involved in arresting him were greater than the dangers of letting him go free. When the grand jury was asked to present the new pamphlet, *Seasonable Advice*, as a seditious libel, it refused to do so. A second grand jury was then empanelled to consider the *Drapier's Letters*. Not only did the jurors refuse to sanction a prosecution of the *Letters*, they went on to demand the prosecution of anyone who should attempt to introduce 'Wood's Brass' into Ireland. In 1725 Wood surrendered his patent and Walpole showed no enthusiasm for finding another bidder.

On its own side of the Irish Channel, the Whig ministry did its best to control the outbursts of the Tory *Craftsman*, often the work of Bolingbroke himself, and of *Fog's Weekly Journal*, which succeeded *Mist's Weekly Journal* after the flight of Nathaniel Mist to France. There were other anti-Walpole periodicals appearing as well, like *Common Sense*, against which prosecutions had to be launched. Of course, trial by jury was far from being a reliable method of censorship so far as the ministry was concerned and had to be reinforced by other measures already mentioned. The uncertainties of censorship

[1] *The Drapier's Letters to the People of Ireland*, ed. Herbert Davis (Oxford, 1935), p. 40.
[2] *ibid.*, p. 79.

through criminal prosecution are well illustrated by two cases involving the printer of the *Craftsman*, Richard Francklin, in 1729 and 1731. I shall refer to another aspect of these cases later on but for present purposes it is interesting to see how they were 'organised', to put it no stronger than that. In the first trial a 'friendly' jury had been picked by Barber, later Tory Lord Mayor, and they naturally found Francklin not guilty. The government responded to this setback by passing the Juries Act of 1730 which, altered the powers of men like Barber, and Francklin was prosecuted again in 1731. This time the jury was of a very different complexion, it even included the father of Walpole's mistress, Maria Skerrett, and future father-in-law of the Whig leader. Francklin was found guilty without hesitation. He was imprisoned for a year, fined £100 and ordered to find sureties of £2,000 for his good behaviour for the next seven years. At this rate, printing the *Craftsman* was too expensive a luxury for Francklin to afford and he was succeeded by Haines, who was in turn prosecuted and convicted for one number of the paper in 1737. Whether or not the Whig censorship was more repressive than the Tories had been, it could, on occasion, produce more spectacular results.

As dissatisfaction with Walpole's administration increased among the Whigs themselves, so during the 1730s the opposition under the patronage of Frederick, Prince of Wales, numbered Whigs as well as Tories among its members. Walpole himself became conspicuously the target for satire in works of literature which were to prove more than merely ephemeral. He was portrayed as Macheath the highwayman in John Gay's *Beggar's Opera* in 1728 and, when his reign was already over, as Jonathan Wild, the pick-pocket, in Fielding's *Jonathan Wild*, published in 1743. Twice the attempt to ridicule him on the stage was thwarted. There had been some form of stage censorship, of course, long before the Licensing Act of 1737 required that all new plays should be approved by the Lord Chamberlain before they were performed. In the reign of Edward III the Master of the Revels had been given the task of supervising these 'entertainments' and it was his censorship which affected such plays as Shakespeare's *Richard II* with its 'abdication scene,' and *Henry IV*.[1] In the eighteenth century the power of theatrical censorship passed to the Lord Chamberlain and it was he who banned John Gay's *Polly*, written as a sequel to the *Beggar's Opera*. This was before the Licensing Act of 1737 and the precipitating cause of that Act was Henry Fielding's

---

[1] 'And if there by anything immodest or prophane in Plays, that may be easily remedied by the Master of the Revels; who according to ancient Constitution, ought to see that nothing be spoken, but what is fit to be heard. *Plain-Dealing: in Answer to Plain-English* (London, 1704), p. 11.

Pasquin and the *Historical Register for 1736*, in which Walpole was depicted handing out bribes on the stage. This new law did not give the Lord Chamberlain power over the theatre but merely confirmed the power he already had, and introduced a continuing system of pre-censorship of plays.

Despite all the fuss over the theatre in 1737, no attempt was made to suppress Fielding's attack on Walpole in *Jonathan Wild*, published six years later. The truth was that the reading public between 1740 and 1760 showed itself extremely apathetic towards issues of party politics. Walpole, the focus of so much Tory hostility, was gone and, although the Whig ministry dragged on, it became a 'broad-bottomed' ministry numbering members of both parties among its supporters. In 1751 came the death of the Prince of Wales, who was the hope of so many opponents of the government ten years earlier. During those years the main centre of interest had been the European and colonial wars in which the country had been involved, rather than domestic politics. In 1749 the political apathy was such that the *Gentleman's Magazine* decided to give up reporting parliamentary debates, remarking, in its Preface, 'Politics, which some years ago, took up a large field, is now reducible into a small compass; this topic having, from the memorable conduct of the most celebrated patriots, failed to engage attention.' So far as the ministers themselves were concerned, they could be reasonably sure that, if they were obliged to resign, their places would probably be taken by men whose views were not markedly dissimilar to their own. The situation was one in which apathy and tolerance born of apathy might easily have bred. It must, indeed, have seemed to David Hume that at last the British nation enjoyed the freedom of 'openly censuring every measure entered into by the King or his ministers.' The events of 1763 were to change all that.

FREEDOM IN ALLEGORY, IRONY, AND THE APPEAL TO POSTERITY

There is no need to read a great deal of Augustan literature to appreciate that the censorship of political opinion had its effect on authors and on literary styles. There were some men who published their work with great caution, or even decided not to risk publication during their own lifetimes. Walpole himself had written *A Short History of the Last Parliament* in 1713, when his own political future was far from certain, since he had been expelled from Parliament and imprisoned in the Tower only the year before. With some misgivings he published the book, though only after taking the extreme precaution of having the printing press set up in his own house. Other authors were less fortunate or, perhaps, less resolute, though lack of resolution seems a harsh judgment on Swift, who was never able to publish his *History of the Last Four Years of the Queen* during his own life. Friends advised against publication and the book appeared in the safer, more apathetic climate of 1758, by which time Swift had been dead for thirteen years. Yet even an author who believed that there was safety in keeping a manuscript unprinted might have pondered the case of Algernon Sidney and thought again. Sidney, a dedicated republican and grand-nephew of Sir Philip Sidney, had been tried and executed after the Rye House Plot of 1683, largely on the evidence of the manuscript of his *Discourses concerning Government* which lay in his desk. The book was finally published fifteen years later.

A possible defence against political censorship was the use of allegory although, as in the case of Swift's *Gulliver's Travels*, the allusions of the allegory might be so abstruse as to prevent not only prosecution but even straightforward interpretation. In this case, Swift went to considerable lengths to conceal the origins of the work, maintaining the pretence that the book, however fanciful, was the work of Lemuel Gulliver, and negotiations with the publisher, Benjamin Motte, were undertaken by Gulliver's 'cousin,' Richard Sympson. At last, according to Pope, Motte received the manuscript, 'he knew not from whence, nor from whom,' dropped at his house in the dark from a hackney coach. In the first book Flimnap evidently represents Walpole, the fate of Gulliver after the defeat of Blefescu parallels Bolingbroke's after the death of Queen Anne, Bolgolam represents the Earl of Nottingham: further interpretation is possible, though how far this accords with Swift's allegorical intention and how far with mere ingenuity on the part of the interpreter becomes increasingly doubtful.

As Swift remarked, 'people in power were very watchful over the press, and apt not only to interpret, but to punish every thing which looked like an *innuendo*'.[1] Naturally, the Tory opposition resented this and held that it was a clear breach of political freedom for the government to interfere even with allegorical writing: after all, how could the ministers be sure that they had interpreted the allegory correctly? This point was made at some length by the author of *The Doctrine of Innuendo's Discuss'd*.[2] Yet if a book like *Gulliver's Travels* escaped prosecution, probably because the political allegory

---

[1] *Gulliver's Travels* (London, 1954), p. 4. The remark occurs in 'A Letter from Captain Gulliver to his Cousin Sympson', first published in 1735.
[2] *The Doctrine of Innuendo's Discuss'd: or, The Liberty of the Press Maintain'd* (London, 1731), pp. 13–14.

is of minor importance in the book's claims on the reader's attention, the use of allegory as a vehicle for seditious libels was nonetheless an offence. This was clearly stated, at the time of the publication of *Gulliver's Travels*, in *State Law: or, The Doctrine of Libels Discussed and Examined.*

> Nothing then remains which may by any Possibility evade the Law but Writing in *Allegory*, or, as the Reporter says here, *Descriptions and Circumlocutions*. Let us examine then what Right has the allegorical Style to escape better than the rest? If a Man draws a Picture of another, and paints him in any shameful Posture, or ignominious Manner, 'tho no Name be to it; yet if the Piece be such, that the Person abused is known by it, the Painter is guilty of a Libel; what then should serve in Excuse for the allegorical Libeller? Abusive Allegory in Writing, has a very near Resemblance to this satyrical Kind of Painting: The Man that is painted with a Fool's Cap and Horns, is certainly abused; but, says the Painter, he is disguised, and how can you pretend to know him. This is the very Subterfuge of the Allegorist, and ought to have the same Answer; if it be the common Notion, that this Picture represents a certain Person, the Drawer is answerable for the Injury he suffers. They that give Birth to Slander, are justly punished for it.[1]

No minister of the Crown could have put the issue more favourably from the government's point of view, and it is not surprising to find that this particular publication is dedicated to Charles Talbot, the Solicitor-General.

The interpretation of the law in this case may not have interfered with Swift but it was certainly the interpretation accepted, for instance, when the use of allegory in *Mist's Weekly Journal* in 1728 led to the arrest of those responsible for its publication. It was no defence to say that the resemblance between George I and 'Meryweis,' or George II and 'Esreff' was either a coincidence or else the product of the prosecutor's imagination. Another allegorist less fortunate than Swift was Mary de la Rivière Manley, who in 1709 had published her *Secret Memoirs and Manners of Several Persons of Quality of both Sexes from the New Atlantis, an Island in the Mediterranean*. The novel was published anonymously and was carefully described on the title-page of the first volume as being 'written originally in Italian'. In the dedication, Mrs. Manley claimed that it had first been translated from Italian into French and thence into English. Soon, however, a key to each volume appeared, identifying the characters of the novel as men and women who were among the most eminent in recent English history. Of course, to many people such clues seemed quite unnecessary. The satire was on the whole pro-Tory and anti-

[1] *State Law: or, The Doctrine of Libels Discussed and Examined* [1729], p. 58.

Whig, and, since there was a Whig government in power at the time, little surprise was caused when Mrs. Manley was arrested. All the same, it was the nature of her allegations, rather than mere political bias, which made the novel such entertaining reading: one suspects that a large number of Whigs enjoyed it quite as much as many Tories. Mrs. Manley suggests that the Duke of Marlborough had prostituted the Duchess to Lord Godolphin, that his path to promotion lay through the bed of the Duchess of Cleveland, when mistress of Charles II, and that to save himself from her subsequent vengeance he had prostituted his sister to the King. She described Queen Anne and the Duchess of Marlborough, the 'she-favourite,' lamenting the death of King William 'over some Flasks of sparkling *Champaign*,' and accused the elderly Lord Torrington of taking his mistresses to sea disguised as boys, with the result that their piercing screams during battle made him panic and break off the action. Fortunately for Mrs. Manley the Tories came to power in 1710 and the case against her was, naturally, dropped. Indeed, her fortunes changed with dramatic improbability so that in 1711 she became editor of the *Examiner*, in succession to Swift, who recommended her a pension for her services to 'the cause', and described her to Stella as having 'very generous principles for one of her sort; and a great deal of good sense and invention'.[1]

Irony, like allegory, was not an automatic defence against prosecution, in law it was no defence at all. In the case of Dr. Browne, who was prosecuted in 1706 for *The Country Parson's Honest Advice to my Lord Keeper* it was ruled that irony is libellous if the jury so interprets it. Of course, the operation of political censorship was a sufficiently haphazard business for any author who combined a certain amount of luck in this respect with a really skilful use of irony to accomplish a great deal. Successful irony was bound to be something which could not be objected to on its face value and whose ironical intent it would be difficult or undesirable to demonstrate in a court. It was Defoe's misfortune, for example, in pamphlets like *Some Considerations of the Advantages of the Pretender's Possessing the Crown of Great Britain* to have written a pamphlet which was a seditious libel if taken at face value and acceptable only if read as a piece of irony. This was what got him into trouble and the pardon which then extricated him made specific mention of the fact that the Crown accepted the libels as 'ironical Writing.'

On the other hand, Swift and Pope were both capable of writing the kind of irony which would have put any prosecutor in an extremely difficult position. They had learnt from Defoe's experience.

[1] *Journal to Stella*, 28 January 1712.

There is a very careful use of irony in Pope's 'Epistle to Augustus,' from the *Imitations of Horace* (1737), dedicated to George II as patron of literature and the arts. This in itself was ironic, since it would be hard to imagine a king less interested in English literature than George II—an apt sovereign for Walpole, who was known to Swift as 'Bob, the poet's foe.' In the first couplet Pope congratulates the King on having thrown open the seas to all nations, hardly tactful at a time when this was precisely the complaint of those who witnessed with growing apprehension the audacity of the Spanish towards British shipping. Throughout the poem, Pope harps on the King's genius for keeping the peace, knowing quite well that there were more and more demands for some kind of military action to be taken in the face of Spain's provocations. It is easy to feel that any puzzlement or uncertainty on the part of Pope's readers must have given way to a broad grin by the third couplet with its apparently ludicrous flattery.

> How shall the Muse, from such a Monarch, steal
> An hour, and not defraud the Public Weal?

Much the same technique was used by Swift in his verses *On Poetry: A Rhapsody*, in which he eulogised Walpole ('Of Wit and Learning Chief Protector') as well as the King, in a metre and style too close to that of Samuel Butler's *Hudibras* for their comfort.

> Fair *Britain* in thy Monarch blest,
> Whose Virtues bear the strictest Test;
> Whom never *Faction* cou'd bespatter,
> Nor *Minister*, nor *Poet* flatter. . . .

If ever a king was bespattered by faction, it was George II, who was divided even from his own son by the rancour of party warfare but poets like Pope and Swift had put the authorities in an impossible position. Anyone who had undertaken a prosecution of either writer would have faced the unenviable duty of explaining, in one way or another, that the shortcomings or personal defects of George II and Walpole were so self-evident that any praise of their characters must be intended as irony. Of course, the government was not entirely bereft of the means for showing its displeasure: Samuel Johnson believed that in Pope's case 'His political partiality was too plainly shown',[1] and that when the poet Paul Whitehead and his publisher, Dodsley, were in trouble with the House of Lords in 1739, this was intended as an indirect warning to Pope himself. Whatever the intention of the House of Lords, Pope's literary career was virtually

[1] *Lives of the English Poets* (London, 1953), II, 193.

over by then and his immunity, like that of Swift, shows that though irony was not an absolute defence against persecution or intimidation, it could be used with such skill as to make public proceedings against its author virtually impossible.

CENSORSHIP AND THE PROCESS OF LAW

By no means all acts of political censorship in the earlier eighteenth century involved a criminal charge of seditious libel, yet it was increasingly in courts of law—and particularly in the court of King's Bench—that those whose publications had displeased the government were called to account. There is certainly justification for the view that in such cases the state began with an apparent advantage over the defendant. By a ruling of Lord Chief Justice Scroggs in 1680 the jurors in a libel case were allowed to return a verdict only on questions of fact and not on those of law. That is to say, if a man was accused of publishing a seditious libel, the jury had simply to decide if he was the person who had published it and if the passages in question meant what the indictment said that they meant—this would obviously be important in a case of allegorical writing. These were the questions of fact, on which a verdict of 'guilty' or 'not guilty' would be returned. The most important question of all, however, was whether the passages objected to in the indictment were a seditious libel, but this was a question of law with which the jury had no right to deal and which was to be decided by the judges. In the majority of cases the proof that the accused man had published the book or periodical in question was a mere formality: the real issue was whether or not the publication constituted a seditious libel. Yet this was the very issue on which a man could not appeal to the jury but had to submit to the judge's ruling, a judge who was often regarded as a creature of the ministry, or at least as one whose political impartiality might well be questioned. Despite a growing hostility, this interpretation of the law was upheld in the great majority of cases until Fox's Libel Act of 1792. Yet long before the law was altered by this statute a number of juries had themselves done their best to undermine the ruling of Scroggs and most of his successors by returning verdicts which were often in absolute contradiction to the facts proved in a case. For example, when Francklin, the printer of the *Craftsman*, was prosecuted in 1729, there was no doubt whatever that he had published the material in question. But this was a Tory jury which happened to be on Francklin's side and they acquitted him. Of course, the law relating to the selection of jurors was altered at once but the manner of Francklin's acquittal encouraged those who believed that juries

61

might force a change in the libel law by their verdicts. Pulteney celebrated the acquittal of Francklin, which had no doubt upset the Attorney-General, Sir Philip Yorke, in his ballad *The Honest Jury*.

> For Sir Philip well knows
> That his innuendos
> Will serve him no longer
> In verse or in prose,
> For twelve honest men have decided the cause,
> Who are judges alike of the facts and the laws.

But as Pulteney and those who shared his hopes were soon to discover, it was only in a very small number of cases for the time being that the jury took similar action. One such case, however, which I have already described and in which a verdict of 'not guilty' was returned in the face of the facts, was that of William Owen in 1752. The Solicitor-General, who prosecuted Owen, was William Murray, later Lord Chief Justice Mansfield, who on one occasion conveniently misquoted Pulteney's ballad from the bench in such a way as to reverse its meaning.

> For twelve honest men have decided the cause,
> Who are judges of facts, though not judges of laws.

Despite the inaccuracy, Mansfield's version perfectly sums up the attitude of the judicature towards cases of seditious libel during the greater part of the eighteenth century. It was not until after 1760 that juries, by returning verdicts that made nonsense of the evidence, rendered the law as interpreted by Mansfield and his colleagues almost unworkable.

4

Blasphemy in an Age of Reason

THE POLITICS OF RELIGION

In the fifty years following the revolution of 1689 there was a no-man's-land between politics and religion which was the scene of isolated but intense combat. To many people it would have been a relief to separate politics and religion, and after the revolution there was a demand in Parliament that it should be made a criminal offence for the clergy to introduce politics into their 'discourses'. The difficulty, of course, was to distinguish between what was political and what was theological in such a controversy. Before the revolution, for instance, the Reverend Samuel Johnson had been whipped from Newgate to Tyburn for publishing his *Humble and Hearty Address to all the English Protestants in the Present Army* (1686), which urged its readers, on theological grounds, not to fight for a Catholic King. Nonetheless, the political implications were momentous. After the revolution the mingling of politics and religion was no less inevitable. John Lowthorp was fined 500 marks (£333 6s. 8d.) in 1690 for publishing *A Letter to the Lord Bishop of Sarum*, warning his readers that 'unless they repent, and bring in King *James* again, they were all damned'.[1] Three years later the publisher of *A Letter to Dr. Tillotson* (who was then Archbishop of Canterbury) was fined £100 for attacking the religious principles of an Archbishop who could swear allegiance to King James II before the revolution and to the usurpers afterwards.

On the one hand the authorities had to deal with the Catholic threat, for political reasons as much as any others, and even in 1750 the Secretary of State was still issuing warrants for the arrest of authors, printers, and publishers of such Catholic devotional literature as the *Manual of Devout Prayers and Devotions* or *Morning and Night Prayers*. Saying of mass remained a felony if the culprit was a foreigner and high treason if he was a native. At the other extreme there had long been an army of Nonconformist martyrs who reminded the Church of England that it was supposed to believe that the Bible contained all things necessary for salvation. What excuse could there

---

[1] *Proceedings on the King and Queen's Commissions* [3–5 September 1690], p. 4.

be, in that case, for the interposition of priests between God and man, for a set form of prayers, 'vain Repetitions,' and 'Song-praying'? It was of little comfort to the authorities that these criticisms also challenged the authority and practice of the Church of Rome, for in matters of authority, as Richard Steele once observed, the only difference between the Roman and Anglican Churches was that the first claimed it was infallible and the second merely that it was always right. Before and after the revolution of 1689 the Nonconformists suffered for their criticisms of the Church. Delaune was convicted in 1683 for attacking Anglican ceremonial in his *Plea for Nonconformists* and two years later Richard Baxter was imprisoned and fined £500 for questioning the authority of the priesthood in his *Paraphrase on the New Testament*. It was at Baxter's trial that Judge Jeffreys, who was presiding, is reported to have entertained the court with an almost music-hall imitation of Baxter's style of praying, turning up his eyes, clasping his hands, and beginning to sing through his nose.

Even after the revolution and the end of licensing, prosecutions were brought against such tracts as Matthew Tindal's *Rights of the Christian Church* (1706), which put the Nonconformist case against the authority of priests, and Daniel Defoe stood in the pillory for his *Shortest Way with Dissenters* (1702). Yet politics could no more be kept out of religion than religion out of politics and the majority of cases in the opening years of the eighteenth century were not concerned with Nonconformists who had attacked the Church of England. The culprits now were High Churchmen who attacked their fellow Anglicans and the Whig party as a whole for selling out to the Nonconformists by granting toleration, for acting as a fifth column within the Church and preparing to subvert its basic beliefs. James Drake's *Memorial of the Church of England* (1705) was the first of a number of High Church pamphlets to be prosecuted but the case was put most succinctly by Ned Ward, editor of the *London Spy*, in his *Hudibras Redivivus*, in which he attacked the betrayal of religious truth for the sake of political popularity.

> For he that will oblige the Throng
> Must ne'er hold one Opinion long,
> But turn his Doctrine and his Creed
> As often as the Cause has need.[1]

At the beginning of the eighteenth century, said Ward, it was 'so very difficult for an honest Man to distinguish a howling Wolf, from a true Shepherd, or a modern Saint, from a Knavish Hypocrite'.[2] This poem

[1] *Hudibras Redivivus: or, A Burlesque Poem on the Times Part the First* (London, 1705), p. 9.
[2] *Hudibras Redivivus*, Part I, 2nd edn. (London, 1708), I, Sig. A3^r.

was prosecuted in 1706 and Ward, like Defoe, was condemned to the pillory. Unlike Defoe, no one brought him flowers and the crowd pelted him.

The most remarkable skirmish in the disputed ground between politics and religion was the prosecution of a High Church propagandist in 1710. This was the trial of Dr. Henry Sacheverell before the House of Lords for two sermons, in which he attacked not only the Nonconformists and their sympathisers but—so his accusers claimed—the sacrosanct revolutionary settlement of 1689. Sacheverell had preached the first sermon on *The Communication of Sin* at Derby in August 1709, and the second on *Perils Among False Brethren* at St. Paul's before the Lord Mayor and Aldermen on 5 November 1709. The first of these sermons was the occasion for a bitter attack on the Nonconformists and their allies for '*Wild, Latitudinarian, Extravagant Opinions* and *Bewitching False Doctrines*, the *Impudent Clamours*, the *Lying Misrepresentations*, the *Scandalous* and *False Libels*, upon both the *King* and the *Church*.' But in his second sermon Sacheverell went further than this and exposed those 'false brethren' who were not Nonconformists but all too often the holders of high office, and yet had determined to betray their Church and their beliefs. Among these he included Bishops Burnet and Hoadly, and it was no secret that the character of 'Volpone,' whom he held up to scorn and detestation, was in fact that of the Whig leader, Godolphin. Such men, Sacheverell claimed, would 'renounce their creed and read the Decalogue backward . . . fall down and worship the very Devil himself for the riches and honour of this world.' Allusions to the late King William III and to ministers of the Crown were not difficult to find. Moreover, by his assertion that the security of the government must require 'the steady belief of the subject's obedience to the supreme power in all things lawful,' and his insistence upon 'the utter illegality of any resistance upon any pretence whatsoever,' Sacheverell was understood to be condemning the deposition of James II.

Before long Sacheverell's name was notorious and, according to Burnet, 40,000 copies of the second sermon were sold, many of them no doubt bought for free distribution by High Church or Tory sympathisers. However, Parliament voted this second sermon a libel and Sacheverell was impeached before the House of Lords, during which proceeding he had no lack of support from men as able as Addison or Atterbury, the Bishop of Rochester who was exiled for Jacobite activities in 1723. At the same time the mob rioted to show its disapproval of the action taken against him. At his trial Sacheverell defended himself ably enough but disappointed a number of his supporters by claiming that the apparent allusions to Godolphin and others in the sermons had not been intended by him, and that when he attacked toleration he only meant the toleration of blasphemy and sedition. This was too much for one of his female admirers, who is reported to have cried out at this point, 'The greatest villain under the sun!' Sacheverell was convicted, which was a foregone conclusion, but only by a majority of 69 to 52, seven bishops voting for conviction and six for acquittal. His sentence was a mere three years' suspension from preaching and, of course, the sermon was condemned to the flames, though as in the case of most other libels it continued to circulate. To his supporters the outcome seemed almost like a victory, which they promptly celebrated by obliging Parliament to order the destruction of various Nonconformist or heretical publications. There is a story in *Nichols' Literary Anecdotes* which relates how, at the time of Sacheverell's trial the Rector of Whitechapel commissioned an altarpiece of the Last Supper, in which the figure of Judas Iscariot was a portrait of Kennett, the Dean of Peterborough, who had been one of Sacheverell's bitterest enemies throughout the whole affair.

HERETICS AND BLASPHEMERS

After one or two cases which had left the matter in some doubt, it was established at the trial of John Taylor in 1676 that blasphemy, including the denial of doctrine, was not a matter reserved for ecclesiastical jurisdiction but could be dealt with in the criminal courts. The substance of Chief Justice Hale's judgment on that occasion was that a crime against religion was also a crime against the state.

And Hale saith, that such kind of wicked blasphemous words were not only an offence to God and Religion, but a crime against the Laws, State and Government, and therefore punishable in this Court. For to say, Religion is a Cheat, is to dissolve all those Obligations whereby the Civil societies are preserved, and that Christianity is a parcel of the Laws of England and therefore to reproach the Christian religion is to speak in subversion of the law.[1]

This remained the law, and a century and a half later Justice Bayley, sentencing Susannah Wright for blasphemous libel in 1823, remarked, 'Christianity is parcel of the English law, and we cannot permit that point to be argued now'.[2] An attack on religion was as much an attack on the state as if the writer had chosen the monarch or his ministers for a target: the judiciary was thus relieved from the taxing

[1] 1 Vent. 293.   [2] *State Trials* (New Series), I, 1370 n.

intellectual obligation of judging blasphemy in terms of theology: blasphemy was subversive and could be condemned as such.

What, for practical purposes, would constitute blasphemy? The Toleration Act of 1689 and the Blasphemy Act of 1698 between them made this clear. The Toleration Act granted freedom of worship only within what we should now regard as a very narrow range: at one extreme, toleration was not extended to Roman Catholics, nor, at the other extreme, to any Nonconformist who denied the doctrine of the Trinity. A Nonconformist minister was obliged to profess belief in thirty-four of the thirty-nine Articles of Religion of the Church of England, and in the greater part of two more. Such qualifications made it impossible that any religious belief or observance which differed radically from that of the Anglican Church would be allowed. Then, three years after the last Licensing Act had expired, Parliament passed *An Act for the more effectual suppressing of Blasphemy and Profaneness*. It is not difficult to see in this Blasphemy Act a warning to certain publishers and authors not to overstep the limits of the freedom granted them by the abolition of licensing. Most of the crimes listed in the Act would have been crimes at common law in any case but here was an opportunity to issue a public warning. The Act insisted, as its own justification, that 'many persons have of late years openly avowed and published many blasphemous and impious opinions contrary to the doctrines and principles of the Christian Religion greatly tending to the dishonour of Almighty God and may prove destructive to the peace and welfare of this kingdom.' The Act specified the categories of blasphemy as denial of the divine nature of any one of the three Persons of the Trinity; the assertion that there are 'more gods than one'; the denial of the divine authority of the Bible, and apostasy from Christianity. A first conviction disabled the blasphemer in law, and made him incapable of holding any ecclesiastical, civil, or military appointment. A second conviction carried a sentence of three years' imprisonment. At least the penalties showed a growing leniency, since only half a century earlier there were still categories of blasphemy punishable by death.

The Act of 1698 covered most of the cases of blasphemy or profanity for the next two centuries, though false prophecy was also criminal and so—until 1843—was profanity on the stage. This last offence was one which much concerned the new Societies for the Reformation of Manners and it is not surprising that by 1702 prosecutions had been brought against actors. Two cases, involving Ben Jonson's *Volpone* and other plays, seem to have come to nothing, but, as the result of a third case, fines were imposed on a group of actors, including Thomas Betterton and Anne Bracegirdle, for—

among other things—using the name of God as an expletive. Two of the plays in question were Congreve's *Love for Love* and Vanbrugh's *Provok'd Wife*, these two dramatists having borne the brunt of Jeremy Collier's attack in his *Short View of the Immorality and Profaneness of the English Stage* in 1698. Most novelists of the eighteenth and nineteenth centuries were prudent enough to indicate expletives that might be considered profane by no more than a first and last letter, if as much as that, though in 1850 Charlotte Brontë condemned this reticence in her preface to Emily Brontë's novel *Wuthering Heights*.

False prophecy was a very rare crime indeed and the only case of real significance occurred in 1707. It involved a small Protestant sect led by a French expatriate, Elias Marion, whose speciality was prophetic trances during which he was much preoccupied with Babylon, the Whore of Babylon, and the coming destruction of God's enemies—who, by a happy coincidence, happened also to be the enemies of Elias Marion. The fall of Anti-Christ was prophesied for 1709 and the destruction of Rome by an earthquake eagerly anticipated. The little group made a number of English converts, including Sir Richard Bulkeley, whom Edmund Calamy described as 'very short and crooked, but fully expected, under this dispensation, to be made straight in a miraculous way, though he happened to die before the miracle was ever wrought upon him, to his no small mortification and disappointment'.[1] *The Prophetical Writings of Elias Marion . . . uttered by him in London under the Operation of the Spirit* was published in London, in French and English, in April 1707, and its unflattering references to the Church of England as well as the Church of Rome were clear enough. Marion and two of his followers were put on trial in the court of Queen's Bench in July. Prosecuting counsel waggishly asked a defence witness whether the accused had prophesied anything about the outcome of their trial, 'at which the People in the Court smiled,'—as well they might, since the three defendants were destined to pay a fine of twenty marks each and to appear in the pillory at both Charing Cross and the Royal Exchange.

THE BIBLE, THE TRINITY, AND THE REASONABLENESS OF CHRISTIANITY

At first sight it might seem that the earlier eighteenth century was not a time when much censorship of theological speculation would be

[1] Edmund Calamy, *An Historical Account of my Own Life* (London, 1829), II, 75.

necessary. There was a growing belief in the reasonableness of Christianity as the basis of its claim on the minds of men if not on their faith. Of course, God's gifts to men had always included reason as well as revelation but now it seemed as if revelation, including biblical revelation, might be almost superfluous. The fashionable theological view was that the truths of Christianity were virtually accessible to reason alone and, indeed, some of the biblical narratives might even be a little intellectually embarrassing. The less enthusiastic view was that such unfettered use of reason would lead first to a type of Christian deism and then to a second stage of deism which was not Christian at all. Between these two opinions moved writers like Locke, who could still unite reason and revelation in such books as *The Reasonableness of Christianity, as Delivered in the Scriptures* (1695) or Archbishop Tillotson who followed a middle course by urging *the unreasonableness of Atheism*, while conceding that the existence of God could not be '*Mathematically* demonstrable.'[1] But Samuel Clarke, whose thesis for his Doctorate of Divinity at Cambridge was that 'no article of Christian faith is opposed to right reason,' was prepared to do better than the Archbishop. In the Boyle lectures for 1704–5, he claimed that the 'One only Method or continued Thread of Arguing,' about the existence of God, 'should be as near the Mathematical, as the Nature of such a Discourse would allow'.[2] If the great pagans of the past had been alive in 1705 they would, according to Clarke, have been compelled to acknowledge God, not on biblical evidence, but on that of 'the *Late* Discoveries in Anatomy,' and 'the *Modern* Discoveries in Astronomy'.[3] Seventeenth-century theologians might have been perturbed by what they saw as a revival of atheistic materialism in the work of Hobbes or Descartes but this presented no problem to Clarke. Turning to Epicurus and Lucretius, he exclaimed, 'How would they have been ashamed, if they had lived in These Days'.[4]

So long as the growth of reasonableness cast no aspersions on the Bible or the Trinity, the authorities made no attempt to interfere with theological speculation. From time to time there were cases involving denial of the Trinity and there was, besides, a numerically insignificant sect of Unitarians who were left to their own devices for the most part. In 1710 Sir Isaac Newton's successor as Lucasian Professor at

---

[1] *The Works of the Most Reverend Dr. John Tillotson* (London, 1720), Sig. B^r & p. 18.
[2] Samuel Clarke, *A Discourse Concerning the Being and Attributes of God* (London, 1749), Sig. a4^r.
[3] *ibid.*, p. 111–112.
[4] *ibid.*, p. 112.

Cambridge, William Whiston, was the defendant in proceedings brought both in the University and in Convocation for what he had said and written about the Trinity. In his sermons and essays he was alleged to have advocated a belief in God the Father as the only God, and to have described the Athanasian creed as an unwarranted innovation. He was deprived of his professorship, and Convocation decided that rather than give a man of Whiston's intellectual calibre the chance to argue his heresies in open court, Tenison, the Archbishop of Canterbury should take the offending passages to the Queen and ask her, as head of the Church, to declare them contrary to doctrine. Unfortunately, Tenison was disabled at the time by an attack of gout and his deputy evidently made little impression on the Queen, since the declaration never materialised.

There were sophisticated arguments against the Trinity put by men like Whiston, and honest but rather dull ones which appeared in such publications as the elderly John Clendon's *Tractatus Philosophico-Theologicus de Persona, Or a Treatise of the Word Person* (1710). He was tried and condemned for this in 1710 but escaped punishment at the last moment when it was discovered that the indictment against him had been inaccurately copied out. There were also anti-Trinitarians whose style was one of forthright abuse. In 1720 three men, Hall, Warner, and Wilkins, were sent to prison for publishing *A Sober Reply to Mr Higgs' Merry Arguments, from the Light of Nature, for the Tritheistick Doctrine of the Trinity*. As a matter of fact, there was nothing sober at all about this publication and its author, Joseph Hall, conducted his argument with all the subtlety of a fair-ground bruiser. He accused believers in the Trinity of having gone 'a whoring after other Gods,' and he reduced the nuances of philosophic discussion to a matter of simple arithmetic. 'As I have learnt at the Writing-School, I will continue to assert, that once *One* is not *Three*, and *Three* times *One* are more than *One*.'[1] Despite his facetious disrespect for Trinitarian doctrine, and the consequently greater indignation of his prosecutors, Hall, by reducing the argument to the level of the 'Writing-School,' was a less dangerous opponent than either Whiston or Clendon.

There was nothing much new in these attacks on the Trinity, since Unitarianism had been a common enough belief in the seventeenth century. Its immediate origins then were in the work of Lelio Sozzini (known as 'Socinus',) and his nephew, who had published their beliefs in the *Confession of Rakow* in 1605. These early Unitarians claimed that there was no biblical authority whatever for believing in the Trinity and that the doctrine was a mere invention of the Church.

---

[1] *A Sober Reply to Mr. Higgs' Merry Arguments* (London, 1720), p. 12.

But to the Trinitarians there was biblical authority for it in such texts as 1 John v. 7, as Tillotson pointed out. 'St. *John* makes mention of the *Father*, the *Word*, and the *Spirit*, the *Unity* of these *Three* is likewise affirmed, *There are Three that bear record in Heaven, the Father, the Word, and the Spirit: and these Three are One.*'[1] If the Unitarians were to win the argument it would have to be through an attack on the Bible, or rather on the orthodox interpretation of it.

More than a century before the Oxford Movement had suggested the essentially Catholic nature of the Church of England, members of that Church, as well as Nonconformists, regarded themselves as unequivocally Protestant. The Protestant religion was, to most of them, the religion of the Bible, and the Bible (as the fifth of the Thirty-Nine Articles puts it) 'containeth all things necessary to salvation'. It was inevitable that the Blasphemy Act should have laid such emphasis on the criminality of denying the divine authority of the Scriptures. Certainly there were those in 1698 who had already seen possible dangers: five years earlier Thomas Burnet in his *Archaeologica Philosophica* had announced, as one detractor put it, that '*All the Books of* Moses *were nothing but* Supposes', in other words that such stories as the Fall remained credible only if given an allegorical interpretation. The same case was put within a year by Charles Blount in his *Oracles of Reason*. Blount might well have got himself prosecuted in the end, had not a hopeless passion for his dead wife's sister driven him to prove devotion by self-inflicted wounds, of which he died.

In an age devoted to 'reasonable' Christianity there was a greater willingness to remove certain intellectual embarrassments from the Bible: the double question was how many other 'embarrassments' would have to be removed before reasonable men felt comfortable again, and how far would the authorities allow this to go before censoring the process as blasphemous libel? No attempt was made to silence either Burnet or—in the short time available—Charles Blount. William Whiston, undaunted by his experiences in the Trinitarian controversy, was disturbed by the way in which Old Testament prophecy seemed often to be out of step with New Testament fulfilment. With considerable sophistication, he began from the assumption that the text of the Old Testament was corrupt and showed that, by rearranging the text, the prophecies and their fulfilment could be made to match more satisfactorily.[2] Anthony Collins, however, in his *Discourse of the Grounds and Reasons of the Christian Religion* (1724) suggested that the fault lay not in the text but in the prophecies themselves. The censors looked on and made no attempt to interfere in

---

[1] *Works*, p. 494.
[2] *An Essay towards Restoring the True Text of the Old Testament* (1722).

the discussion. Of course, the criticism and analysis of biblical prophecy, to say nothing of the textual criticism involved, was a specialised matter, far too technical to appeal to a mass audience. There was
no danger of nation-wide apostasy by thousands of innocents who
had succumbed to Whiston's bibliographical sleight of hand or
Collins's involved discussion. How much further could the argument
go before springing the censor's trap?

The answer to this question came in 1729 in the case of Thomas
Woolston, Fellow Emeritus of Sidney Sussex, Cambridge, who had
published his first *Discourse on the Miracles of Our Saviour* in 1727,
following this with five more discourses in the next two years. Unlike
Whiston and Collins, he found the evidence of Old Testament
prophecy completely convincing: his argument was that the Messiahship of Christ ought to be proved by such prophecies without introducing any of the New Testament miracles. These miracles were
to be understood, at the best, as allegorical and, at the worst, according to St. Augustine as *'such works as Jesus did'* which *'might be imputed to, and effected by magic art'*.[1] (At Woolston's trial the Attorney-
General pointed out that St. Augustine had never suggested that the
miracles of Jesus were a kind of sorcery: what he had actually said
was that *'Infidels might suggest such a Thing'*.)[2] Having dispensed
with the need for the New Testament miracles, to his own satisfaction
at least, Woolston went on to discredit the actual biblical accounts,
a process in which he could hardly have been accused of over-
sophistication. The narrative of the Gardarene swine, he insisted,
must be false because it is well-known that Jews do not eat pork,
and so there would have been no need to keep pigs in Palestine. No
one seems to have pointed out at the time that Palestine was not
inhabited exclusively by Jews and that the 'country of the Gadarenes'
had a large gentile population. It also seemed incredible to Woolston
that people would have been so heartless as to leave the madmen
living among the tombs and that, as a last resort, they should have
been put to death for their own and everyone else's good. Among
other miracles he dismisses the transfiguration as being the effect of
Jesus standing in strong sunlight, and the voice from the cloud as a
rather sophisticated piece of ventriloquism. For these and similar
suggestions he was sent to prison for a year and fined £25 on each of
four charges. Even in an age of reasonable Christianity, he had exceeded the limits of permitted speculation. Chief Justice Raymond
told the court, 'I would have it taken notice of, that we do not meddle
with differences of opinion, and that we interpose only where the very

---

[1] *A Discourse on the Miracles of Our Saviour* (1727), pp. 10–11.
[2] *An Account of the Trial of Thomas Woolston* (London, 1729), p. 3.

root of Christianity itself is felt to be struck at.'[1] Not only had Woolston's somewhat blunt axe struck at the root, he had wielded it in such a way that his intention was clear to even the less-sophisticated readers. The technique of Whiston's textual criticism of the Old Testament might signify little except to a small highly-educated group, but the consequences of doing away with the New Testament miracles would be evident to a much larger and more suggestible public—that was Woolston's real crime. He was dismissed as 'poor, mad Woolston', but there is enough rationality in his discourses to suggest that this was unjust. He belonged very much to the mental climate of the early eighteenth century, yet even so the argument often veers away from the question of whether the Bible is historically accurate to that of whether it is morally defensible. All too soon the discussion of religion in England was to be at the less intellectually taxing level of whether Christianity was ethically justifiable. Not only did this generate far more heat than light, it also provoked the censors a great deal more.

[1] Fitzg. 64 at 66.

5

Obscene Libel and the Reformation
of Manners

THE CRIME OF OBSCENE LIBEL

When the first Society for the Reformation of Manners was founded in 1692, the suppression of obscene literature was not among its declared aims, if only because many of those for whose morals it feared were illiterate. The theatre was a different matter and its moral, or immoral, influence affected those who could not read as much as those who could, so before long the Society was concerning itself actively with 'the execrable Impieties of our most scandalous *Play Houses*, those Nurseries of Vice and Prophaneness (whither our Nobility and Gentry are unhappily sent to learn their Accomplishments in their younger Years).'[1] If the Society devoted a great deal of its time to enforcing the laws against profanity and sabbath-breaking or drunkenness, there was no lack of those ever ready to remind it of the scandal of sexual immorality, as in Meriton's *Immorality, Debauchery, and Profaneness* (1698), or in Disney's *Essay upon the Execution of the Laws against Immorality and Profaneness* (1708), while preachers like William Bisset urged the members of the Church of England to forget their theological differences with puritan Nonconformity and join in the crusade for a national reformation.

You have suppress'd perhaps some hundreds of lewd Houses, and brought others into better order: So far is well: But still remember, there's Work enough cut out for you. There are two strong *Cittadels* that still hold out against you; I mean, those two famous *Academies* of Hell, those *Nurseries* of all Vice, those *incorrigible Brothels*, the two Play-houses; *where Satan's seat is*; where he keeps his *head-quarters*; whence he can at any time draw forth fresh Supplies, and form in a manner what Parties he pleases; and whence he sends out *Detachments* every *Campaign*, (or rather, to speak in the *Jesuit*'s Language, those famous *Comedians*) he makes his *Missions* every Summer to the two *Universities* to train up our Youth in *their* Liberal Arts and Sciences.[2]

[1] *An Account of the Progress of the Reformation of Manners*, 13th edn. (London, 1705), p. 23.
[2] William Bisset, *Plain English. A Sermon at St. Mary-le-Bow, for the Reformation of Manners*, 5th edn. (London, 1704), p. 19.

74

As I have already suggested, any publisher who believed that such reforming zeal would leave the press untouched, was living in a fool's paradise. The Societies for the Reformation of Manners existed to enforce laws rather than to press for new legislation, and it may be that when the Societies were founded there seemed little hope of being able to enforce any law against obscene literature: it was doubtful to many people whether such a law existed. But where there clearly was a law, as in the case of profanity uttered on the stage, the Societies were only too willing to take action.

The general idea of reforming the manners of the country was one which commanded widespread support, from monarchy and Parliament included, as a portent of growing civilisation and refinement. No one need read very far in contemporary accounts of seventeenth-century life to realise that behaviour left something to be desired even in high social or academic places. When, for instance, Anthony à Wood, the Oxford antiquarian, published his book of reminiscences *Athenae Oxoniensis* in 1691, the Master of Balliol, Dr. Roger Mander, proclaimed it a book 'not fit to wipe one's arse with'.[1] There was, it seemed to many people, room for improvement in the nation's manners. Addison and Steele were among those authors who supported this idea of a national reformation, which was in many respects more effectively accomplished than they would have believed possible, or indeed would have wished. By a nice irony, when Coleridge, in his periodical *The Friend*, was discussing the *Tatler* and the *Spectator* a century afterwards, he remarked, 'a man—I will not say of delicate mind and pure morals, but—of common good manners, who means to read an essay which he has opened upon at hazard in these volumes to a mixed company, will find it necessary to take a previous survey of its contents'.[2] There were a number of earnest Augustans upon whom the reformation of manners recoiled in much the same way. Yet the cause was an attractive one and by the time that the Societies issued their thirty-first report in 1726 they could claim that, 'the Streets are very much purged from the wretched Tribe of *Night-Walking Prostitutes*, and most *detestable Sodomites*', and they were also able to add as evidence of real achievement, 'The Total Number of Persons prosecuted by the *Societies* in or near *London* only, for *Debauchery* and *Prophaneness*, for thirty-four Years last past, are calculated at 91,899.'[3] Even as the report was being prepared, the publication of an

[1] *The Life and Times of Anthony à Wood*, ed. Llewelyn Powys (London, 1961), p. 331.

[2] S. T. Coleridge, *The Friend*, 4th edn. ed. H. N. Coleridge (London, 1844), III, 326.

[3] *The One and Thirtieth Account of the Progress Made in the Cities of London*

obscene libel was recognised by the King's Bench judges as an offence at common law.

The first case of this kind in the court of King's Bench—as opposed to lesser courts like the Guildhall Sessions—was that of Hill in 1698 for publishing Rochester's *Poems on Several Occasions*. Shortly before his death the Earl of Rochester had been reconciled to the Church, however improbably, and suffered pangs of conscience about some of his poems. 'It seems,' said Horace Walpole, 'his lordship, when dying, had ordered all his immoral writings to be burned. But the age was not without its Curls to preserve such treasures.'[1] Shortly after Rochester's death *Poems on Several Occasions* was published in an unauthorised edition and containing a great deal of more or less obscene material, not all of which had been written by Rochester. In the *London Gazette* of 22–25 November 1680 an advertisement appeared.

Whereas there is a Libel of lewd and scandalous Poems, lately printed, under the name of the Earl of Rochester, Whoever shall discover the Printer to Mr. *Thom L. Cary*, at the sign of the *Blew Bore* in *Cheap-Side London*, or to Mr. *Will Richards* at his house in *Bow-street Covent-Garden*, shall have 5l. reward.

When Hill was prosecuted in 1698, although the moral character of the *Poems* was objected to, it seems possible but not probable that this was a private prosecution brought by those who were anxious to maintain the image of Rochester as a death-bed penitent. It is certainly possible to identify Cary in the advertisement of 1680 as a relative of one of Rochester's executors and Richards as a publisher employed by him, so that the family was clearly concerned with the poet's posthumous reputation.[2] Unfortunately the case against Hill was inconclusive, he absconded from justice and was in due course outlawed, so that his case went by default.[3]

Other works were published during this period without being prosecuted at the time, though their publishers certainly showed considerable circumspection. In 1694, for example, William Burnaby published his translation of Petronius as *The Satyr of Titus Petronius*

---

[1] Gilbert Burnet, *Some Passages in the Life and Death of John Earl of Rochester* (London, 1820), p. 7.

[2] Philip Gray, 'Rochester's *Poems on Several Occasions*', *The Library*, 4th series, XIX (1938–9), 185–7.

[3] 2 Str. 790. [Elizabeth Latham had already been convicted for this book in 1693.]

---

and Westminster, By the Societies for Promoting a Reformation of Manners (London, 1726), pp. 2 and 5.

Arbiter, peremptorily rejecting the notion that such a book might corrupt its readers, 'nor is it possible that any ill Man can talk a good one into a new Frame or Composition.'[1] All the same, he wisely left certain sections of the book in Latin. (The first English edition of Petronius to encounter trouble was a much later translation, whose destruction was ordered at the Westminster Police Court in 1934.) Other translations from classical literature circulated without difficulty, including a four volume edition of Lucian, published in 1711, with an introduction taken from Dryden and including a work rarely seen in English, *The Ass*. This too escaped the notice of the reformers of manners, despite the narrator's cavortings with Palaestra, which would have done credit to *The School of Venus* itself. In about 1709 there appeared *The Cabinet of Love*, a collection of poems drawn from the supposititious works of Rochester and others, and including a long translation of Mersius (i.e. Chorier's *L'Academie des Dames*) under the title of *The Delights of Venus*. It is interesting as some indication of the growing zeal for reform, that though this little collection was published without interference during the earlier eighteenth century, there are successful prosecutions recorded against it in 1798 and 1809.[2]

When the first major attempt to deal with obscene literature came in 1707, the prosecutors found that even if the King's Bench judges had the power to deal with offenders, they showed a disinclination to exercise it. John Marshall was prosecuted for publishing Rochester's *Sodom: or, The Quintessence of Debauchery* and *The School of Love* (another translation of *L'Academie des Dames*), the passage objected to in the first being pure bawdy and that in the second describing advice to a girl on auto-erotic techniques. At the same time, James Read and Angell Carter were prosecuted for publishing a sequence of fifteen poems entitled *The Fifteen Plagues of a Maiden-Head*. Since publishers were being fined at Guildhall Sessions in the seventeenth century for publishing *Sodom* and translations of Chorier, these later cases might have been dealt with at the Sessions as well but were in fact transferred to the court of Queen's Bench, as though the magnitude of the crime had been recognised at last. Verdicts of guilty were returned in each case but Read moved in arrest of judgment on the grounds that obscene libel was not something with which the court had power to deal. Surprisingly, in view of later rulings, the court agreed with him. 'There are ecclesiastical courts,' said Lord Chief Justice Holt, 'why may not this be punished there? If we have no precedent we cannot punish. Shew me any precedent.'[3] Holt was

---

[1] *The Satyr of Titus Petronius Arbiter*, trans. William Burnaby (London, 1694), Sig. A7r.

[2] P.R.O., K.B. 28/387/2; K.B. 28/428/22.   [3] *State Trials*, XVII, 157n.

willing enough to admit that the poem 'tends to bawdry,' but, as Justice Powell pointed out, even Star Chamber had quashed an indictment because it was for 'matters of bawdry'. Powell's own view reflected the general attitude of the court towards pornography, an attitude which was to change radically in less than twenty years.

This is for printing bawdy stuff, that reflects on no person: and a libel must be against some particular person or persons, or against the government. It is stuff not fit to be mentioned publicly. If there is no remedy in the Spiritual court, it does not follow there must be a remedy here. . . . It tends to the corruption of manners but that is not sufficient for us to punish.[1]

The notion that the corruption of manners was not a punishable offence would seem increasingly absurd as the eighteenth century passed but for the time being the only course open to the prosecution —and a quite unrealistic one at this time—would have been to take the matter to an ecclesiastical court. When the case ended in 1708 the prosecution of Read had failed and so, in consequence, had those of Carter and Marshall. It is not generally made clear in accounts of this case that the specific passages from the *Fifteen Plagues of a Maiden-Head* cited in the indictment and, therefore, directly considered by the court were the whole of the sixth and fifteenth 'Plagues'. These are reprinted in the second half of the present book. In 1709 charges were brought against John Martin for publishing *Gonosolgium Novum* and against Thomas Harrison and Anne Croome for publishing 'a profane, lascivious and pernicious lampoon called 'The Works of the Right Honourable the Earle of Rochester and Roscommon with some Memoirs of the Earle of Rochester's Life by Monsieur St. Evremont'.[2] Martin was acquitted and the charges against the other two defendants appear to have been dropped.

In the case of Edmund Curll, the court of King's Bench reversed its earlier decisions, Holt and Powell having been replaced by then by judges of more decided views. Curll was not a popular man, either among many of his contemporaries in the book trade or with the authorities: his methods of doing business were regarded as decidedly shady, and he inspired such personal dislike in Alexander Pope that the poet went to the lengths of administering an emetic to him. The list of books which Curll published included many curious volumes on venereal disease, hermaphrodites, impotence, and sodomy. It was not in the least surprising that he should have added to this list in 1718 a translation of the work of Meibomius, a German author of the

---

[1] *ibid.*, XVII, 157.
[2] P.R.O., K.B. 28/31/20; K.B. 28/32/9; K.B. 33/24/95.

seventeenth century, *De Usu Flagrorum*, done into English from the Latin original as *A Treatise of the Use of Flogging in Venereal Affairs*: this was to feature in the trial seven years later, though Curll must have been counting on its title rather than on its contents to make it a best-seller. In 1724 Curll issued a second book for which he was to be prosecuted, a new English edition of *Venus in the Cloister: or, The Nun in her Smock*. When the case against him began in 1725, the court concerned itself principally with *Venus in the Cloister*, though Curll was indicted for publishing both books. To a modern reader of Meibomius, the *Treatise of the Use of Flogging* seems a notably dry and rather pedantic work, not at all the sort of thing that Curll might regard as a real money-spinner or the authorities might think worth prosecuting. Here, for instance, is the first passage in the book cited in the indictment.

Your Father has prov'd by many Examples, how much FLOGGING prevails in *Venereal Affairs*, which I have no occasion to respect, or offend the Ears by a second Reading, although I knew a Person at *Venice*, who could not be sollicited to a Love-Encounter, any way but by the Blows of his Mistress's Fist.[1]

Meibomius piles example upon example, from history, classical literature, and medical authorities like Galen and Hieronymous Mercurialis, each instance tending to show that there are people whose sexual desires can be stimulated by whipping. The tone of the book is, to say the least, detached and academic: even the passages quoted in the indictment seem curious rather than obscene, especially at a time in British history when, according to Ned Ward in his *London Spy*, parties of young gentlemen would make an excursion to witness the public judicial flogging of convicted prostitutes. If Curll could get away with *Venus in the Cloister*, he could certainly get away with Meibomius, which perhaps explains why so much emphasis was placed on the former book at his trial. The curious thing is that Curll's edition of Meibomius had been bound in a single volume with a second work of his, *A Treatise of Hermaphrodites*, and though the title of this is cited in the indictment, no passages are quoted from it. In retrospect, it seems that it might have provided the prosecution with more effective ammunition than Meibomius's book. The reader who made his way diligently through sixty-eight pages of Meibomius promptly entered a much less arid world, where he found Philetus, disguised as a ladies' maid, attempting to woo his beloved Theodora away from the lesbian embraces of Amaryllis. Thus disguised, he is

[1] John Henry Meibomius, *A Treatise of the Use of Flogging in Venereal Affairs* (London, 1718), p. 16.

welcomed by Theodora, who believes he is making use of a godemiche, ''till the moment of ejaculation, which was not usual with the same Instrument in her Embraces with Amaryllis: when this happen'd, she was prodigiously surpriz'd, and endeavouring to disengage her self from *Philetus*, he folded her more closely in his Arms, and in the greatest Transport told her, he was her constant Admirer *Philetus*'.[1] These actions of Philetus evidently carry conviction to the heart of Theodora and her vow of reformation is expressed in a short verse.

> The Shadow I'll no longer try,
> Or use the pleasing Toy;
> A sprightly Youth I can't defy,
> The Substance I'll enjoy.[2]

The fact that such passages as this do not appear in the indictment, while the rather unimpressive extracts from Meibomius do, may serve as a warning against believing that in this kind of case the argument was necessarily confined to the passages from the book which appeared in the indictment. When Rochester's *Sodom* was prosecuted, for instance, no more than a few lines appeared in the indictment but it is impossible not to believe that the prosecution objected to the whole play.[3] As for *Venus in the Cloister*, it is not hard to see why the passages which appear in the indictment were chosen and since, so far as I am aware, no account of Curll's trial has ever cited them, I take the opportunity of including them in the latter half of this book. They are, after all, the passages on which the law of obscene libel was finally decided.

With passages enthusiastically describing fornication and academic discussion of flagellation produced in evidence, the case against Curll was strong but by no means overwhelming. Had not Lord Chief Justice Holt said in 1708 that there was no remedy to be found against obscene libels, except possibly in the ecclesiastical courts? It was on this ruling of Holt's that Curll and his counsel pinned their hopes. There was no point in arguing that Curll was not responsible for the publications nor in discussing the subjective question of whether the books were obscene. (Though it happened that the judges themselves disagreed on this last point, as we shall soon see.) If only Holt's ruling of 1708 could be confirmed, then there was no case for Curll— or for any other publisher of obscene literature—to answer.

It was no great setback when, in November 1725, Curll was found guilty in the court of King's Bench of publishing the two books. This

[1] *A Treatise of Hermaphrodites* (London, 1718), p. 44.
[2] *ibid.*, p. 45.
[3] P.R.O., K.B. 28/24/8.

was a mere formality, simply a decision on the question of fact, of whether or not Curll had published the two books before the court. It was only after this decision that the real legal battle began. For more than another two years the argument continued intermittently before the King's Bench judges to determine whether the publication of obscene libel was a crime at all, and if it was, whether it was one which might be dealt with by a temporal court. Curll's counsel argued that 'In the reign of Charles 2, there was a filthy run of obscene writings, for which we meet with no prosecution in the temporal courts.'[1] As we have seen, this was not strictly speaking true because, although there had been no cases in King's Bench, there had been cases at sessions, such as the prosecution and conviction of John Wickens in 1683 for publishing *The Whore's Rhetorick*. Of course, the outcome of cases at sessions would not be important enough for general publication and certainly Lord Chief Justice Holt felt that the King's Bench judges lacked any precedent for dealing with such an offence. 'If we have no precedent we cannot punish.' In Curll's case, however, the Attorney-General managed to produce a precedent, though not one which most people would have thought of, and he chose much broader ground for his attack than Curll's counsel had chosen to defend. 'What I insist upon is, that this is an offence at common law, as it tends to corrupt the morals of the king's subjects and is against the peace of the king.'[2] Then the Attorney-General introduced the curious case of Sir Charles Sedley. In June 1663, Sir Charles Sedley, Lord Buckhurst, Sir Thomas Ogle, and a party of friends had been celebrating at the Cock in Bow-Street. Rather the worse for drink, they went out on to the balcony of the building and, according to Anthony à Wood, 'putting down their breeches they excrementized in the street: which being done, Sedley stripped himself naked, and with eloquence preached blasphemy to the people'.[3] The official account differs slightly from this, Sedley is alleged to have exposed himself naked on the balcony to begin with, 'and there did such things and spoke such words . . . as throwing down bottles (pissed in) *vi et armis* among the people'.[4] In either event, a riot broke out and the crowd below stormed the house. Sedley was tried and fined 2,000 marks (£1,333 6s 8d.) by the court 'not intending his ruin but his reformation', he was imprisoned for a week, and bound over to be of good behaviour for three years. Anthony à Wood and Samuel Johnson both put the fine at £500 and Wood adds that when Sedley heard the sentence pronounced, 'he made answer that he thought he was the first man that ever paid for shiting. Sir Robert Hyde asked

---

[1] *State Trials*, XVII, 153–4   [2] *ibid.*, XVII, 154.
[3] *ibid.*, XVII, 156.   [4] *ibid.*, XVII, 155.

him whether he ever read a book called "The Compleat Gentleman" &c.? To which Sir Charles made answer that, "set aside his lordship, he had read more books than himself".'[1] Both accounts go on to explain how two of Sedley's cronies 'borrowed' the money to pay his fine from Charles II himself. 'Mark the friendship of the dissolute', said Dr. Johnson in disgust.[2]

More than sixty years after these events, the Attorney-General reminded the court of King's Bench that in Sedley's case it had declared itself to be the *custos morum* of the King's subjects, the official guardian of public morals. According to the Attorney-General, Curll's action in publishing *Venus in the Cloister* was as much a threat to morality and a breach of the peace as Sedley's conduct had been. Regardless of the decision reached by the judges in Read's case in 1708, Curll's behaviour was a criminal matter with which the court must deal. Moreover, the Attorney-General then went on to explain that the term 'Libel' in the phrase 'Obscene Libel', had been misunderstood in 1708. 'Libel' in this sense did not mean that a person or a group of persons was supposed to have been defamed by the publication, it was simply the English equivalent of the Latin *libellus*, meaning 'a little book'. Hence, an obscene libel was an obscene little book, a description which adequately summed up a number of Curll's publications.

Three judges heard the case, Raymond, Fortescue, and Reynolds. Both Raymond and Reynolds accepted the Attorney-General's argument but Fortescue could not. 'I own this is a great offence,' he said, 'but I know of no law by which we can punish it'.[3] This was precisely the view taken by the judges in 1708. Later on, in his report of the case, Fortescue confesses that he even doubted whether *Venus in the Cloister* was, strictly speaking, an obscene book. 'And indeed I thought it rather to be published on Purpose to expose the *Romish* Priests, the Father Confessors, and Popish Religion.'[4] Anti-Catholic propaganda was always welcome in the 1720s when there were still fears of the restoration of the House of Stuart to the throne by foreign intervention. Certainly *Venus in the Cloister* is said to have had its origin in the French wars of religion, though in reading the whole book one cannot help feeling that the motives behind its composition were largely non-theological.

As Curll's case dragged on, the favourably-inclined Fortescue was replaced by another judge, Page, who shared the views held by Ray-

[1] *Life and Times of Anthony à Wood*, p. 133.
[2] *State Trials*, XVII, 156.
[3] *ibid.*, XVII, 159.
[4] John, Lord Fortescue, *Reports of Select Cases* (London, 1748), p. 100.

mond and Reynolds, so that in 1728 the verdict against the bookseller was unanimously upheld. Curll had not made things any easier for himself by publishing during the course of his trial *The Memoirs of John Ker*. John Ker had been a government spy during the reign of Queen Anne and had met Curll while they were both in prison. Many people in positions of influence would have preferred for political and personal reasons, that Ker's memoirs should have remained unpublished and with their appearance in print whatever leniency Curll had once hoped for could be discounted, in fact a new charge was brought against him on account of their publication. Curll, having no doubt added to the number of his enemies in high places, was sentenced in February 1728. He was fined 25 marks (£16 13*s* 4*d*.) each for publishing *Venus in the Cloister* and Meibomius's *Treatise of the Use of Flogging*. On the later charge, relating to Ker's *Memoirs*, he was fined 20 marks (£13 6*s*. 8*d*.) and sentenced to be pilloried. Considering the money which Curll must have made out of his more notorious best-sellers, the fines for the two obscene libels were by no means ruinous. On the other hand, to a man with as many enemies as Curll, the pillory might be a serious and even a fatal business. Yet Curll was not without his fair share of ingenuity or low cunning, and it is not really surprising to find that the official account of his appearance in the pillory is strident with indignation.

This Edmund Curll stood in the pillory at Charing-Cross, but was not pelted, or used ill; for being an artful, cunning (though wicked) fellow, he had contrived to have printed papers dispersed all about Charing-Cross, telling the people, he stood there for vindicating the memory of queen Anne: which had such an effect on the mob, that it would have been dangerous even to have spoken against him: and when he was taken down out of the pillory, the mob carried him off, as it were in triumph, to a neighbouring tavern.[1]

According to the official morality of the time, any steps which a man might take to avoid having his head cracked open by a well-aimed brick, while fastened in the pillory, showed a deplorable lack of sportsmanship.

I have discussed Curll's case at some length because it is the case on which the English law of obscene libel was based. For more than two centuries, until the Obscene Publications Act of 1959, it remained an essential part of the law controlling the press. It seems odd, in view of the verdict, that Curll should have continued to advertise copies of *Venus in the Cloister* until 1735, though no action was taken against him. Perhaps this was only a publicity measure and, on

[1] *State Trials*, XVII, 160.

inquiry, the book might have been 'out of stock', but there is no doubt that after his trial there was considerable public interest in it. Another edition was being printed by John Leake in 1745 but the authorities discovered this and managed to suppress it before it could be put on sale. In 1740–1 Samuel Richardson published the four volumes of *Pamela: or, Virtue Rewarded* and Henry Fielding followed this in 1741 with his burlesque, *Shamela*. The virtuous Pamela's reading is confined to such literature as is pious and edifying but pride of place among the treasures of Shamela's library goes to no other volume than *Venus in the Cloister*. It hardly sounds as if the book had become unobtainable.

A final point about Curll's case, which is worth comment, is that the court decided that for a book to be condemned as an obscene libel it did not have to libel an individual in the more usual sense of the word. This was usually but not invariably true. For instance, in 1813 Robert Holloway, a printer, was convicted of an obscene libel on James Stewart, *alias* Moggy Stewart, in the second edition of *The Phoenix of Sodom: or, The Vere Street Coterie*, after the trial and conviction of a number of men for homosexual offences. Stewart was not guilty, despite the imputations in Holloway's pamphlet, and was therefore the victim of an obscene libel, for which Holloway was sentenced to eighteen months' imprisonment.[1] The number of such cases is small and they occur in the late eighteenth and early nineteenth centuries.

In 1738 the Societies for the Reformation of Manners went out of business, at least for the time being, but apart from any success which they had met with in their own declared spheres of interest, the Societies had done their bit to create a climate of moral opinion in which the government itself was willing to continue and even intensify the campaign against obscene literature. In April 1745, Lord Harrington, Secretary of State, issued warrants for the arrest of the author, publishers, and printer of *A Compleat Sett of Charts of the Coasts of Merryland* and *Aretinus Redivivus: or, The Lady's Academy*. The first of these, of which no copy survives, was a set of allegedly obscene prints describing the female anatomy in some detail: the second was yet another translation of Chorier's *L'Academie des Dames*. Several publishers and booksellers were arrested, some of them prosecuted and convicted, others released when they had surrendered their stocks. Not only *Merryland* and *Aretinus Redivivus* were involved in these cases but another old favourite, *The School of Venus*, as well. Four years later the appearance of John Cleland's *Memoirs of a Woman of Pleasure* was greeted by a warrant from the Secretary of State for the

[1] P.R.O., K.B. 28/445/10.

arrest of the author, publishers, and printer. In the following year, 1750, an abridgment of the same book under the title *Fanny Hill* met with the same treatment. Although, it seems, prosecutions of this sort tend to be arbitrary and to come in groups, there was no question by this time of the growing sympathy shown by the administration towards the reformation of literature. If authors and publishers could not carry out this reformation for themselves, it would be imposed upon them by outside pressure. Of course, the measures taken by the authorities were no more effective in the long term than they had ever been. *Fanny Hill* was in no danger of disappearing as the result of government action in 1749 and 1750. There were, as we shall see, a considerable number of cases in which Cleland's book featured and, indeed, by 1757 another bookseller by the name of Drybutter had been prosecuted and sentenced to the pillory for selling copies of it. Possibly the case against him was one of the results of the warrant issued in 1755 by the Secretary of State for the arrest of possessors of 'lewd and infamous Books and Prints'.[1] Nor was *The School of Venus* suppressed by these measures, since the same translation of it which had been prosecuted in 1745 was still circulating—and still being prosecuted—more than forty years later.[2] Nonetheless, the crusade against immoral literature had begun and its aims were no longer confined to bringing to justice a particular book or even a particular man like Edmund Curll, with whom many people had scores to settle. The warrant of September 1755 suggests a much more general campaign against obscene books and prints. Whatever the intentions of its original sponsors may have been, the movement for the reformation of manners had reached the press by the middle of the eighteenth century.

THE REFORMATION OF LITERATURE

Writing to George Cheyne about the progress of *Pamela* in 1741, Samuel Richardson remarked, 'I am endeavouring to write a Story, which shall catch young and airy Minds, and when Passions run high in them, to shew how they may be directed to laudable Meanings and Purposes, in order to decry such Novels and Romances, as have a Tendency to inflame and corrupt.'[3] Cheyne himself had written to Richardson, 'You ought to avoid Fondling and Gallantry, Tender

[1] *Copies Taken from the Records of the Court of King's Bench at Westminster*, 24 September 1755.
[2] P.R.O., K.B. 28/347/5 (1788).
[3] Samuel Richardson, *Selected Letters*, ed. John Carroll (Oxford, 1964), pp. 46–47.

Expressions not becoming the Character of Wisdom, Piety and conjugal Chastity especially in the Sex.'[1] Not every novelist in the mid-eighteenth century was as preoccupied as Richardson with the extent to which the general run of novels or 'romances' would debauch the minds of their readers, especially when those readers were young and female—and even, perhaps, of the servant class. In that non-industrial age, and indeed until well into the nineteenth century, servants made up the bulk of the lower orders of society, yet not every critic would have believed, like Richardson, that the works of Swift and Pope had better be burnt or that Sterne's *Tristram Shandy* was a catalogue of 'uncommon indecencies' whose author had destroyed his own character as a clergyman by printing 'such gross and vulgar tales, as no decent mind can endure without extreme disgust'.[2] Not every acquaintance would have remarked of Henry Fielding,

I could not help telling his sister, that I was equally surprised at and concerned for his continued lowness. Had your brother, said I, been born in a stable, or been a runner at a sponging house, we should have thought him a genius, and wished he had had the advantage of a liberal education, and of being admitted into good company; but it is beyond my conception, that a man of family, and who had some learning, and who really is a writer, should descend so excessively low, in all his pieces.[3]

And this was prompted not by *Joseph Andrews* nor by *Tom Jones* but by Fielding's last and most restrained novel *Amelia*, published in December 1751.

Fielding and Richardson show clearly in their different manners what had happened to the descendants of the puritans and non-puritans of the seventeenth century. Puritanism had become the cry for a reformation of manners, no longer confined to Puritans in the political or theological sense and, therefore, a much more powerful force. The non-puritans, like Pepys or Humphrey Prideaux, who had observed the peccadilloes of the human race with a detached and tolerant amusement, were now becoming the defeated minority. In many ways Fielding is a backward-looking novelist whose readership, ideally, would have been composed of such men. One does not have to read a novel like *Tom Jones* for very long to appreciate its appeal to an audience which is male and classically educated—to the reading public of the seventeenth century. In the mid-eighteenth century it was not Fielding but Richardson who was the 'new' type of novelist, concerned with a domestic, middle-class, and predominantly feminine world. In the eyes of the new moralists, like Richardson, Fielding's work was 'coarse' or 'low', he was not refined enough to linger,

[1] *ibid.*, p. 46n.   [2] *ibid.*, pp. 57 and 341–2.   [3] *ibid.*, pp. 198–9.

as Richardson did, on such incidents as Pamela's 'inward' shame on being presented with a gift of underwear by Mr. B.[1] On the other hand, Richardson and those who shared his views on the morality of literature, would have regarded with disgust such passages as that in *Tom Jones*, following the argument between Tom and Squire Western over Sophia.

'I wull have Satisfaction o' thee,' answered the Squire, 'so doff thy Clothes *At unt* half a Man, and I'll lick thee as well as wast ever licked in thy Life.' He then bespattered the Youth with Abundance of that Language, which passes between Country Gentlemen who embrace opposite Sides of the Question; with frequent Applications to him to salute that Part which is generally introduced into all Controversies that arise among the lower Orders of the *English* Gentry at Horse-races, Cock-matches, and other public Places. Allusions to this Part are likewise often made for the Sake of the Jest. And here, I believe, the Wit is generally misunderstood. In Reality, it lies in desiring another to kiss your A—— for having just before threatened to kick his: For I have observed very accurately, that no one ever desires you to kick that which belongs to himself, nor offers to kiss this Part in another.

It may likewise seem surprizing, that in the many thousand kind Invitations of this Sort, which every one who hath conversed with Country Gentlemen, must have heard, no one, I believe, hath ever seen a single Instance where the Desire hath been complied with. A great Instance of their Want of Politeness: For in Town, nothing can be more common than for the finest Gentlemen to perform this Ceremony every Day to their Superiors, without having that Favour once requested of them.[2]

There was no way of bridging the gulf between the strong, commonsense morality of Fielding's novels and the new domestic politeness of Richardson and his followers. Yet it was Richardson who, in the changed circumstances of the mid-eighteenth century was bound to set the style which lesser men imitated, though by a neat twist of fate *Pamela: or, Virtue Rewarded* was one of the only two English novels of the century to be listed in the *Index Librorum Prohibitorum* of the Roman Church. No less a critic than Samuel Johnson added his support to the new attitude towards literature, remarking of novels like *Tom Jones* in 1750, 'These books are written chiefly to the young, the ignorant, and the idle. . . . The highest degree of reverence should be paid to youth . . . nothing indecent should be suffered to approach their eyes or ears.'[3]

It is in the middle of the eighteenth century rather than at the beginning of the nineteenth that a new urge for purity and moral

[1] *Pamela*, Letter VII. (London, 1741), I, 12–13.
[2] *Tom Jones*, Bk. VI, ch. 9. (London, 1749), II, 287–8.
[3] *The Rambler*, No. 4. Saturday 31 March 1750.

reformation spreads through English literature. There are new classes of readers to be protected from a fate worse than illiteracy: women, children, and servants. A few children's books, as distinct from school books, are recorded between 1680 and 1740 but after 1740 they appear in much greater numbers. Yet, even so, quite a lot of reading-matter for children consisted of adult books either adapted (as in the case of *Robinson Crusoe* and *Gulliver's Travels*) or in their original form. In this second category lurked appalling moral dangers. From about 1760, with the development of the circulating libraries, the popular novel became an industry, and a glance at the catalogues of publishers like the Minerva Press shows clearly that, at this level, fiction was written mainly by women, about women, for women. At a higher level, Fanny Burney, Maria Edgeworth, and Ann Radcliffe illustrate the same phenomenon. Yet fiction, and indeed popular literature as a whole, had given rise to considerable concern by the middle of the century. In May 1753, for example, *The World* remarked disapprovingly of novels, 'The thing I chiefly find fault with is their extreme indecency. There are certain vices which the vulgar call fun, and the people of fashion gallantry; but the middle rank, and those of the gentry who continue to go to church, still stigmatize them by the opprobrious names of fornication and adultery.'[1] The same writer was disturbed to see, 'The most absurd ballads in the streets, without the least glimmering of meaning, recommend themselves every day both to the great and small vulgar only by obscene expressions.'[2] The same magazine, more than a year later, in July 1754, was still harping on the moral danger of 'putting Romances into the hands of young Ladies'.[3] Another periodical of the time, John Hawkesworth's *Adventurer*, warned its readers in December 1752 of the perils of fiction which was not written for a specific moral purpose, 'fiction, the power of which is not less to do evil than good'.[4] Before long the critics of immorality in literature were in full cry and they had long ceased to be regarded as an extreme or puritan minority, they numbered Richardson, Johnson, Hawkesworth and, in 1760, Lyttelton (whom Pope and Thomson admired and to whom Fielding had dedicated *Tom Jones*) joined in the general condemnation by remarking ironically in his *Dialogues of the Dead*, 'By the commerce of the world, men might learn much of what they get from books; but the poor women, who in their early youth are confined and restrained, if it were not for the friendly assistance of books, would remain long in an insipid purity

[1] *The World*, No. 19. Thursday 10 May 1753.
[2] *loc. cit.*
[3] No. 79. Thursday 4 July 1754.
[4] *The Adventurer*, No. 16. 30 December 1752.

of mind, with a discouraging reserve of behaviour.'[1] Then, in a more serious tone, Lyttelton adds, 'but I am concerned for the women who are betrayed into these dangerous studies'.[2]

Richardson was not alone, even in his dislike of writers of the stature of Swift or Fielding: the 'lowness' or coarseness which he found in Fielding's work was apparent to the majority of reviewers by the time that the last novel, *Amelia*, appeared in 1751. Swift's reputation too went through a careful and hostile examination. In the twenty-second of the *Dialogues of the Dead* Lyttelton makes Rabelais say of Swift's style, 'If the garb which it wore was not as *mean*, I am certain it was sometimes as *dirty* as mine.' In 1752 the Earl of Orrery in his *Remarks on the Life and Writings of Dr. Jonathan Swift* had already passed similar judgment on *Gulliver's Travels*. 'Sometimes it degenerates into filth. True humour ought to be kept up with decency, and dignity, or it loses every tincture of entertainment. Descriptions that shock our delicacy cannot have the least good effect upon our minds. They offend us and we fly precipitately from the sight. We cannot stay long enough to examine whether wit, sense, or morality, may be couched under such odious appearances.'[3]

Such opinions in themselves were not new—the novel or 'romance' had long been suspect for aesthetic as well as moral reasons—what was new was the number and influence of the opinions. The amused, tolerant, worldly urbanity of men like Humphrey Prideaux had given way before the new seriousness in literature, a seriousness which reflected the evangelical fervour of the new Wesleyan movement and its counterpart in the Church of England, gathering strength under the leadership of men who prepared the way for William Wilberforce and the Proclamation Society. Small wonder that there were no successors to Fielding or Smollett but many who in one respect or another tried to ape Richardson.

The new morality in literature, as elsewhere, was predominantly the morality of the middle class. As the *World* explained, sexual misdemeanours might be 'fun' to the lower orders and 'gallantry' to the leaders of fashion but to the 'middle rank' they were no more than fornication or adultery. In February 1755 the same periodical delivered the final judgment of that 'middle rank' on the aristocrat or gallant.

No vices or immoralities whatever blast this fashionable character; but rather, on the contrary, dignify and adorn it: and what should banish a man

---

[1] Dialogue, XXVIII.   [2] *ibid.*
[3] *Remarks on the Life and Writings of Dr. Jonathan Swift*, 2nd edn. (Dublin, 1752), p. 154.

from all society, recommends him in general to the best. He may with great honour, starve the tradesmen, who by their industry supply not only his wants, but his luxury. He may debauch his friend's wife, daughter, or sister; he may, in short, undoubtedly gratify every appetite, passion, and interest, and scatter desolation round him, if he be but ready for single combat, and a scrupulous observer of all the moral obligations of a gamester.[1]

No longer was such a man to set the moral standards of society, either in literature or elsewhere. Yet the power which the middle rank acquired in matters of literary taste would necessarily be employed far more in governing the 'vulgar' than in attempting the moral reclamation of 'people of fashion'. It was high time for the middle-classes to ask themslves, 'Would you want your servants to read this book?' In Richardson's novel *Pamela*, for instance, it is not so much the reformation of the rakish Mr. B. but the preservation of a servant girl's chastity which is the principal concern of the book. It is not hard to see why the novel should have had such a success, why it should have been eagerly recommended from the pulpit, it must have seemed the perfect moral tract for servants and employers alike, well-laced with warnings against reading the wrong sort of fiction.

As literacy spreads, the anxiety of paterfamilias for the chastity of his wife and daughters, or the morals of his servants, finds expression in the growing belief that erotic literature is almost always and necessarily corrupting, though he may not have been corrupted by it himself. Moreover, with the spread of literacy the area of literature considered to be dangerous was to grow as well. By the early nineteenth century it included, in Coleridge's view, even parts of the *Tatler* and the *Spectator*, and, in the view of Thomas Bowdler, quite a lot of Shakespeare. Even Samuel Richardson himself, the great moral reformer of English fiction in the eighteenth century, is described by Thackeray in *The Virginians* (1857–9) as a novelist now 'hidden behind locks and wires', an author to make 'pretty little maidens blush'.[2]

---

[1] No. 112. 20 February 1755.

[2] *The Works of William Makepeace Thackeray* (London, 1896), VIII, 242. [*The Virginians*, Chap. 26.] Thackeray introduces Richardson and Samuel Johnson as characters in his novel.

'Mr. Johnson stood, hat in hand, during the whole time of his conversation with Dr. Gilbert; who made many flattering and benedictory remarks to Mr. Richardson, declaring that he was the supporter of virtue, the preacher of sound morals, the mainstay of religion, of all which points the honest printer himself was perfectly convinced.

'Do not let any young lady trip to her grandpapa's bookcase in consequence of this eulogium, and rashly take down "Clarissa" from the shelf. She would not care to read the volumes, over which her pretty ancestresses wept and thrilled a hundred years ago; which were commended by divines from pulpits and belauded all

If we would explain how the alleged sexual frankness and permissiveness of the eighteenth century gave way to the reputed repression of the nineteenth, we should look a little more closely at the eighteenth in case, perhaps, it was neither as frank nor as permissive as its popular image would suggest. Certainly the eighteenth century had its fair share of fornicators and adulterers whose escapades were mirrored in literature but in both centuries there was a strong tone of moral earnestness in the discussion of sexual matters. The eighteenth century had its would-be Casanovas but—particularly in the latter half of the century—for every would-be Casanova there was a would-be Wesley or Wilberforce. The major campaigns, by way of prosecution, against obscenity and even indelicacy in literature are not really evident much before the beginning of the nineteenth century but the will to launch such campaigns goes far back into the eighteenth.

Europe over. I wonder, are our women more virtuous than their grandmothers, or only more squeamish?' *loc. cit.*

In Chapter 23 Thackeray has already hinted at the answer to this last question. 'The Lamberts were not squeamish; and laughed over pages of Mr. Fielding, and cried over volumes of Mr. Richardson, containing jokes and incidents which would make Mrs. Grundy's hair stand on end.' *Works*, VIII, 213.

6

Liberty *versus* Licentiousness: 1760–1792

THE SIGNIFICANCE OF THE WILKES AFFAIR

Never has the history of literary censorship been so involved in the events of one man's life as it was in those of John Wilkes's during the years 1763–9. The story of Wilkes and the way in which he dominated the political literature of the time has been told too often to need exhaustive repetition here, but the significance of his case can hardly be overestimated. 'Junius' put the point as well as anyone when in 1769 he described the fundamental and irretrievable mistakes made by the government in punishing Wilkes for publishing the *North Briton* No. 45—not to mention the *Essay on Woman*—and in their determination to keep Wilkes out of Parliament, once he had been expelled, despite the wishes of the majority of his constituents. 'Not contented with making Mr. Wilkes a man of importance, they have judiciously transferred the question, from the rights and interests of one man to the most important rights and interests of the people.'[1]

At the beginning of 1763 Wilkes was Member of Parliament for Aylesbury and editor of the *North Briton*, a periodical hostile to the new Tory administration under Lord Bute, and given to anti-ministerial attacks which were in themselves neither uncommon nor remarkable. In a comparatively short time, the fate of Wilkes and his paper had created a substantial body of opinion which was not merely hostile to Bute's administration, but which regarded the freedom of the press from political restraint as an end worth fighting for in itself. This was hardly a view which would have commended itself either to Defoe or to Swift, at least so long as their own party was in power. As Swift had warned in his *History of the Last Four Years of the Queen*, 'A particular person may, with more safety, despise the opinion of the vulgar, because it does a wise man no real harm or good, but the administration a great deal.'[2] Swift would have clung to this opinion still more tenaciously had he known the new political ideals which the 'vulgar' demanded the right to canvass during the reign of George III.

[1] *The Letters of Junius* (London, 1890), p. 216 [19 December 1769]. Junius had earlier suggested that Wilkes 'if not persecuted, will soon be forgotten', p. 158 (24 April 1769).
[2] *History of the Last Four Years of the Queen* (London, 1758), p. 245.

The case of John Wilkes began with one man's criticism of a specific aspect of ministerial conduct and ended in a much more general questioning of the whole legal and philosophical basis of British parliamentary government. '*The liberty of the press*,' wrote Wilkes, when the *North Briton* was founded in June 1762, 'is the birthright of a Briton, and is justly esteemed the firmest bulwark of the liberties of this country'.[1] Yet despite the fine resonance of such proclamations, neither Wilkes nor his ministerial opponents could have foreseen quite how far this belief was going to lead them.

Wilkes had published a number of attacks on ministers but none as bold as the denunciation of the King's Speech on the Peace of Paris, which had concluded the war with France and Spain, and which, incidentally, seemed likely to strengthen Bute's control of the government at home. Wilkes's outburst appeared in the *North Briton* No. 45 on 23 April 1763. He attacked the ministry for deserting its allies and, acknowledging that the King was only the mouthpiece of the ministry in this matter, he described the speech from the throne as 'the most abandoned instance of ministerial effrontery ever attempted to be imposed on mankind'.[2] As for Bute himself, Wilkes looked forward with relish to his dismissal from office.

In vain will such a minister or the foul dregs of his power, the tools of corruption and despotism, preach up in *the speech that spirit of concord, and that obedience to the laws, which is essential to good order*. They have sent the *spirit of discord* through the land, and I will prophesy, that it will never be extinguished, but by the extinction of their power.[3]

And if Wilkes had been able to convince his readers so far that he meant no disrespect to the Crown or to George III himself, even this was undone in the three sentences that followed.

A despotic minster will always endeavour to dazzle his prince with high-flown ideas of the *prerogative* and *honour* of the *crown*, which the minister will make a parade of *firmly maintaining*. I wish as much as any man in the kingdom to see *the honour of the crown maintained* in a manner truly becoming *Royalty*. I lament to see it sunk even to prostitution.[4]

Such an attack could not have been allowed to pass unchallenged, even by a more tolerant administration than Bute's and there followed five years of legal and parliamentary manoeuvring to bring Wilkes to justice. When he was first arrested, he argued successfully in the court of Common Pleas that the warrant was defective and that, in any case, as a Member of Parliament, he was immune from arrest. Moreover, a

[1] *The North Briton*, No. I, Saturday 5 June 1762.
[2] *The North Briton*, No. XLV, Saturday 23 April 1763.
[3] *ibid.*   [4] *ibid.*

jury awarded him £1,000 in damages against the Under-Secretary of State who was responsible for the way in which Wilkes's house had been searched. But in the autumn of 1763 the House of Commons voted the *North Briton* No. 45 to be a seditious libel and ordered it to be burnt by the common hangman. When this was attempted at the Royal Exchange on 3 December, Wilkes's supporters incited the mob to riot, making the execution of the Commons' orders virtually impossible and enlisting popular support on the side of Wilkes so effectively that, as Junius observed six years later, 'even his vices plead for him'.[1] Mobs had been persuaded to riot many times before on behalf of various political figures who were in trouble but the mob of the 1760s was to show more than a temporary allegiance to the cause of Wilkes and 'liberty'. The Commons charged Wilkes with being the author of the article and ordered him to appear before the House on 8 December but Wilkes had meanwhile been wounded in a duel with Samuel Martin, subsequently paid £41,000 from the Civil List for 'secret and special service'. Wounded but mobile, Wilkes left for Paris, from where he wrote to the Commons explaining that he was too ill to make the return journey. In January 1764, despite all the efforts of his supporters, Wilkes was expelled from the House of Commons and in February he was found guilty in the court of King's Bench of publishing the *North Briton* No. 45, though of course he was tried in his absence. In the following November, when there was still no sign of him, Lord Chief Justice Mansfield pronounced sentence of outlawry upon him. Mansfield, as Lord Chief Justice, was to be intimately concerned with questions of the liberty—or, to his mind, the licentiousness—of the press.

Wilkes returned uninvited from exile in 1768 and stood for election to Parliament as Member for the City of London, only to come bottom of the poll. In March he stood for Middlesex and was elected. Mansfield cancelled the outlawry on the grounds of an error in the writ and Wilkes was arrested to face another trial for publishing a seditious libel in the *North Briton* and a libel that was both blasphemous and obscene in the *Essay on Woman*. Though Thomas Potter, rather than Wilkes, is generally thought to have written the *Essay on Woman*, Wilkes was responsible for its publication in an edition of twelve copies. One copy of this fell into the hands of government sympathisers and was read aloud to the House of Lords in the autumn of 1763, by Lord Sandwich, so that its impiety and obscenity might be apparent to the legislature. Lord Lyttelton tried to put a stop to the reading but their lordships urged Sandwich on to the end. Now, in 1768, Wilkes was charged with publishing this parody as

[1] *Letters of Junius*, p. 152 [10 April 1769],

well as with publishing the *North Briton*. He was found guilty on both charges, fined £500 and sentenced to ten months' imprisonment for publishing the *North Briton* No. 45, and fined £500 and sentenced to a further twelve months' imprisonment for publishing the *Essay on Woman*. But the mob, which had rioted on his behalf in the autumn of 1763 was not going to let him down. His supporters, who included 6,000 weavers from Spitalfields, began a riot outside the prison in St. George's Fields, where they were met by pro-government demonstrators. In the ensuing fracas one of Wilkes's sympathisers was killed by a government supporter, M'Quirke, who was convicted of the murder but then promptly pardoned by the ministry. The Secretary of State, Lord Weymouth, in a letter to the Chairman of the Lambeth Quarter Sessions offered to use troops to suppress any further demonstrations of this sort against the government. Wilkes managed to get hold of a copy of Lord Weymouth's letter and published it with suitable comments. The House of Commons, condemning this as another of his libels, declared that his election as Member of Parliament for the county of Middlesex was invalid. Three times in 1769 Wilkes was elected for Middlesex until, on the last occasion, the Commons declared that the winner was his opponent, Colonel Luttrell, who had polled 269 votes against Wilkes's 1,143. In January 1769, while still in prison, Wilkes had been elected an Alderman of the City of London. He was elected Lord Mayor in 1774 and returned to Parliament in the following year, this time without any questions being asked as to whether or not his election was valid. By 1780 he achieved such improbable respectability as to be fighting with the authorities against the mob during the Gordon riots of that year.

Yet though Wilkes and the mob parted company—or at least sympathies—the controversy surrounding him had popularised the notion of 'liberty' and, more specifically, had raised the question of whether Parliament was as representative of the wishes of the electorate—to say nothing of the unenfranchised majority—as it ought to be. This question more than any other determined the nature of political censorship for over sixty years. Even before the Wilkes affair was concluded, the opposition to the ministry and even to the existing form of parliamentary government showed signs of becoming organised and coherent in a more popular form than at any previous time. The Society for the Defence of the Bill of Rights was, of course, dedicated to the cause of Wilkes when it was founded in 1769 but before long Wilkes had no further need of it, and it became the first of a number of similar organisations which were to act as a focus of anti-government opinion for more than half a century. Among the general demands of this first society was the establishment of the rights of juries to decide what was libellous or seditious. A growing number of people had become aware of how courts of law conducted such cases, since by this time newspapers were taking a significant interest in judicial proceedings.

The two most important factors determining the nature of literary censorship during the last forty years of the eighteenth century were the growing fear of political revolution and the increasing literacy of the masses, which made the communication of revolutionary ideas possible over a whole country or even a whole continent. The government feared that the mob would be first of all 'educated' and next informed of its political 'rights'. Even while the struggle between Wilkes and the ministry was unresolved the first Sunday school had been set up, offering general as well as religious instruction to those whose only access to education might be such weekly classes. Within another fifteen or twenty years these schools became widespread and just as Sunday was the only day of the week when the mass of the people had the opportunity to attend any sort of school, so it was the one day when they had the leisure to gather political information. During the last twenty years of the eighteenth century the Sunday newspaper made its appearance, much to the discomfiture of those who feared its dangerous, radical tendency and of those who merely regarded the publication of newspapers on Sunday as a form of Sabbath breaking. It was this Sabbath breaking, as well as the democratic and seditious tendencies of such papers that led, for example, to Lord Belgrave's bill in 1799 for the suppression of the sale and circulation of newspapers on the Lord's Day. Although this bill had the keen support of evangelicals like William Wilberforce, it was defeated on a second reading in the Lords by 40 votes to 26 and though Lord Kenyon revived the idea twenty years later, during the spate of prosecutions for seditious libel, when the unpopularity of the Prince Regent and the anti-reform ministry was at its height, by then the Sunday press was too firmly established to be rooted out in this manner.

By the second half of the eighteenth century, propagandists for parliamentary reform or even for wholesale revolution were no longer dependent on the London book trade for the dissemination of their ideas, although they made good use of it. By the middle of the century there were printers in Birmingham, Manchester, Liverpool, Leeds, and in many other towns which seemed of little importance at the time but were to be of considerable significance in the opening decades of the nineteenth century. The imposition of a political pre-censorship on the press (which was still being suggested in some

96

quarters) might theoretically have been possible in these circumstances but the practical task would have been a formidable one for any government to face. Quite apart from anything else, the use of new, portable presses in the early nineteenth century would have made the process of tracking down illicit printing infinitely more difficult. Yet there were voices urgently prophesying sedition and revolution, while lamenting the influence exerted by a press tainted with republicanism and democracy. As early as 1738 Parliament had been warned about the power of the press and its possible dangers.

The stuff which our weekly papers are filled with is received with greater reverence than acts of parliament; and the sentiments of one of these scribblers have more weight with the multitude than the opinion of the best politician in the kingdom.[1]

How much more significant were these words to seem half a century later when the 'multitude' included so many of the mob, either by virtue of their newly-acquired literacy or merely by their attendance at meetings and reading rooms where the inflammatory opinions of the Sunday journalists and others were read aloud for the benefit of those who could not yet read for themselves.

Whether or not Wilkes had published the *North Briton* there would have been Sunday schools, and whether or not he had been expelled from Parliament and imprisoned there would have been Sunday newspapers. Even the Society for the Defence of the Bill of Rights functioned quite adequately without the impetus of Wilkes's grievances. Yet the Wilkes affair, by providing a rallying point for anti-government feeling, gave a new coherence to the expression of radical opinions. In 1768 the mob shouted for Wilkes and liberty; the significance of Wilkes is that long after they had forgotten him they remembered liberty.

THE NEW VIOLENCE OF POLITICAL LIBELS

Nowhere was the lack of restraint in political libels more evident than in the abrasive style of insult perfected by Junius in his attacks on monarch, ministers, and public figures in general. These attacks appeared in the *Public Advertiser* between 1769 and 1771, including scathing denunciations of Grafton (as Prime Minister), Lord North, the Duke of Bedford (known as the negotiator of the Peace of Paris and as the Duke who had been horsewhipped on the racecourse at Lichfield by a disgruntled lawyer), Lord Chief Justice Mansfield, and even George III himself. Despite all efforts to establish the identity of

[1] *Parliamentary History*, X, 448.

Junius he was, and is, unknown. The authorship of the letters has been variously attributed to eminent contemporaries, including Wilkes, Burke, Gibbon, Chatham, and Shelburne. It seems probable from the knowledge shown of the War Office and the Secretary of State's Office that the author was Philip Francis, who had been a clerk in both. The coincidence of Junius's silences and Francis's absences from London, as well as the evidence of the handwriting, lend some support to this hypothesis. It should be said, though, that Woodfall, the publisher of the *Public Advertiser* denied this identification emphatically.

Junius's pursuit of Grafton was merciless: commenting on the fact that the first Duke of Grafton was an illegitimate son of Charles II, he remarks,

Charles the First lived and died a hypocrite. Charles the Second was a hypocrite of another sort, and should have died upon the same scaffold. At the distance of a century, we see their different characters happily revived and blended in your Grace. Sullen and severe without religion, profligate without gaiety, you live like Charles the Second, without being an amiable companion, and, for ought I know, may die as his father did, without the reputation of a martyr.[1]

In a subsequent letter to Grafton, Junius alludes to the prosecution brought against Vaughan for trying to buy an office of the Crown, something which Grafton was accustomed to sell to others.

By laying in a moderate stock of reputation, you undoubtedly meant to provide for the future necessities of your character, that with an honourable resistance upon record, you might safely indulge your genius, and yield to a favourite inclination with security. But you have discovered your purposes too soon; and, instead of the modest reserve of virtue, have shown us the termagant chastity of a prude, who gratifies her passions with distinction, and prosecutes one lover for a rape, while she solicits the lewd embraces of another.[2]

Junius's prime concern was not with the profundities of political philosophy and, in this respect, his style of abuse has more in common with Swift's than with Wilkes's. Yet the violence of his attacks owes much to the new mood of discontent and shows how intense was the dislike which the Tory administrations of Lord Bute and his successors had managed to engender, and how the would-be revolutionaries must have been convinced that compromise with such an administration would be out of the question. Even after Grafton was defeated and forced to resign, Junius showed him no mercy. 'If I were person-

[1] *Letters of Junius*, p. 159 [30 May 1769].
[2] *ibid.*, p. 210 [29 November 1769].

ally your enemy, I might pity and forgive you,' began Junius's letter of 14 February 1770, 'You have every claim to compassion, that can arise from misery and distress. The condition you are reduced to would disarm a private enemy of his resentment, and leave no consolation to the most vindictive spirit, but that such an object, as you are, would disgrace the dignity of revenge.'[1]

Yet Junius, it seemed, had gone too far in the letter which he addressed to the King himself on 19 December 1769.

From one false step you have been betrayed into another, and as the cause was unworthy of you, your ministers were determined that the prudence of the execution should correspond with the wisdom and dignity of the design. They have reduced you to the necessity of chusing out of a variety of difficulties;—to a situation so unhappy, that you can neither do wrong without ruin, nor right without affliction.[2]

The letter goes on to anticipate the King's deposition and warns him that when this takes place it will be of no use for him to seek refuge in Ireland, which his government has 'uniformly plundered and oppressed.' As for the American colonies, even though the prospect of independence may make them more tolerant, they will hardly be able to face the prospect of another monarch. Junius ends with a reference to the despotism of the Stuarts, adding, 'The prince who imitates their conduct should be warned by their example; and while he plumes himself upon the security of his title to the crown, should remember that, as it was acquired by one revolution, it may be lost by another.'[3]

Five hundred extra copies of the *Public Advertiser* were printed, so great was the anticipated demand for Junius's letter, but even then the paper was sold out within a few hours. This shortage of copies was to have an important consequence when the prosecutions began. Individual ministers might feel that the ignominy of enduring Junius's attacks was preferable to the ignominy of having one's name bandied about in a court of law but this libel on the King could hardly be ignored. Since it was impossible to identify Junius, a prosecution was brought against Woodfall, publisher of the *Public Advertiser*, and against John Almon who reprinted the libel in the *London Museum*. Almon was convicted and fined ten marks (£6 13s. 4d.) some time before Mansfield heard the case against Woodfall in June 1770. In Woodfall's case the jury was out for four hours and then returned the curious verdict of 'guilty of printing and publishing only'. This appeared to be a meaningless decision and could be interpreted only as a sign of growing unwillingness on the part of jurors to leave the

[1] *ibid.*, p. 222.　　[2] *ibid.*, p. 216.　　[3] *ibid.*, pp. 221–2.

final decision in political trials in the hands of the judiciary. When the case was argued further before the judges of King's Bench in November, they concluded that it was impossible to say what the verdict meant, and ordered a new trial. This proved impossible. During the earlier trial a copy of the *Public Advertiser*, containing the allegedly seditious libel, had been passed to the jury for their inspection. Apparently unnoticed by anyone, the foreman of the jury had pocketed this so that when the second trial began the Attorney-General was obliged to confess that he had no copy of the original letter by which to prove the fact of publication. There was nothing for it but to drop the case against Woodfall. After this second trial, the government brought a prosecution against John Miller who, like Almon, had reprinted Junius's letter to the King but, despite the clearest evidence that Miller had published the letter, the jury acquitted him.

Junius himself, though unable to take part directly in any of these cases, was by no means silent during the prosecutions of 1770. On 14 November that year he addressed himself to the trial judge in Woodfall's case, Lord Chief Justice Mansfield.

You will not question my veracity, when I assure you that it has not been owing to any particular respect for your person that I have abstained from you so long. Besides the distress and danger with which the press is threatened, when your Lordship is party, and the party is to be judge, I confess I have been deterred by the difficulty of the task. Our language has no term of reproach, the mind has no idea of detestation, which has not already been happily applied to you, and exhausted.[1]

Junius goes on to denounce Mansfield's attempts to restrict the powers of the jury in libel cases so that the liberty of the press shall be undermined. The prosecutions brought against Woodfall and Almon are condemned as contradicting 'the highest legal authorities, as well as the plainest dictates of reason'.[2] And in case Mansfield should be left with any illusions about his gifts as a lawyer, Junius adds, 'No learned man, even among your own tribe, thinks you qualified to preside in a court of common law'.[3]

'THE RIDICULOUS CLAIMS OF AMERICAN USURPATION'

The echoes of 'Wilkes and Liberty' carried further than many people at the time either believed or wished to believe. When Samuel Johnson in his pamphlet *The Patriot* (published at the time of the general election of 1774) remarked, 'Quebec is on the other side of the

---

[1] *ibid.*, pp. 244–5.   [2] *ibid.*, p. 249.   [3] *ibid.*, p. 252.

Atlantic, at too great a distance, to do much good or harm to the European world,' he was being unduly sanguine, though it was not from Quebec or Canada that the immediate influence was to be felt.[1] Indeed, Johnson shows in this same pamphlet (and in 1775 in *Taxation no Tyranny*) that it was the American colonists who caused him the most concern. He condemns the disaffected Americans in terms of eighteenth-century colonialism.

That man therefore is no patriot who justifies the ridiculous claims of American usurpation; who endeavours to deprive the nation of its natural and lawful authority over its own colonies; those colonies, which were settled under English protection; were constituted by an English charter, and have been defended by English arms.

To suppose, that by sending out a colony, the nation established an independent power; that when, by indulgence and favour, emigrants are become rich, they shall not contribute to their own defence, but at their own pleasure; and that they shall not be included, like millions of their fellow-subjects, in the general system of representation; involves such an accumulation of absurdity, as nothing but the shew of patriotism could palliate.

He that accepts protection, stipulates obedience. We have always protected the Americans; we may, therefore, subject them to government.[2]

The heresy of American political beliefs implied worse things even than the loss of the colonies and it was a heresy whose roots went back long before the first shots of the Revolutionary War were fired at Concord in April 1775. John Adams, who was to succeed Washington as President of the United States believed that the real revolution was the one which took place in the minds of the American colonists, and that was accomplished before 1775. 'Liberty' had been a popular cause on both sides of the Atlantic during the 1760s and while the British administration tried to silence the criticism of men like Wilkes or Junius at home, a careful watch had to be kept on any expression of sympathy for the Americans and—worse still—on any attempt to introduce revolutionary ideas from America.

One of the earliest expressions of such sympathy with the American colonists occurs in Junius's letter to the King, for which, as we have just seen, three men were prosecuted and one convicted.

They consider you as united with your servants against America, and know how to distinguish the sovereign and a venal Parliament, on one side, from the real sentiments of the English people on the other. Looking forward to independence, they might possibly receive you for their King, but, if ever you retire to America, be assured they will give you such a covenant to

---

[1] *The Patriot. Addressed to the Electors of Great Britain* (London, 1774), p. 11.
[2] *ibid.*, pp. 22–23.

digest, as the presbytery of Scotland would have been ashamed to offer to Charles the Second. They left their native land in search of freedom, and found it in a desert. Divided as they are into a thousand forms of policy and religion, there is one point in which they all agree: they equally detest the pageantry of a king and the supercilious hypocrisy of a bishop.[1]

Of course, Junius's offence in this passage—or one of his offences—was that he saw the Americans as not merely entitled to freedom but to independence as well. He goes further in this respect than, for example, Edmund Burke and further than John Horne Tooke who was prosecuted for another pro-American seditious libel but who nevertheless continued to regard the colonists as 'fellow-subjects'—as Samuel Johnson had done—and as 'Englishmen'. Horne Tooke had been one of the founders of the Society for the Defence of the Bill of Rights and was associated with its successor, the Constitutional Society, or the Society for Constitutional Information. Nearly two months after the outbreak of the Revolutionary War, the Constitutional Society met at the King's Arms Tavern on 7 June 1775. Horne Tooke's crime was to publish an account of that meeting, an account which, according to the prosecution, amounted to a seditious libel.

At a special meeting this day of several members of the Constitutional Society, during an adjournment, a gentleman proposed that a subscription should be immediately entered into by such of the members present who might approve the purpose, for raising the sum of 100 l. to be applied to the relief of the widows, orphans, and aged parents of our beloved American fellow-subjects, who, faithful to the character of Englishmen, preferring death to slavery, were for that reason only inhumanly murdered by the king's troops at or near Lexington and Concord, in the province of Massachusets.[2]

Horne Tooke was not brought to trial until 4 July 1777, before the ubiquitous Lord Chief Justice Mansfield at Guildhall. The prosecution was conducted for the government by Thurlow, the Attorney-General. Horne Tooke caused some consternation at first by announcing that the star witness for the defence would be none other than Thurlow himself. Mansfield hastily ruled that none of the rather contentious questions which Horne Tooke proposed to put to the Attorney-General was relevant. The prosecution had been brought by the Attorney-General on an *ex officio* information (which made it unnecessary for a grand jury to sanction the indictment) and the trial was before a special jury. (Special juries were not chosen from the ordinary lists of jurors but from lists made up principally of government employees or the more substantial men of business.)

[1] *The Letters of Junius*, pp. 217–18.   [2] *State Trials*, XX, 653.

In cases of this kind the Attorney-General was entitled to file an *ex officio* information against the defendant, and to have the case heard by a special jury, who would be more likely to sympathise with the government's case than an ordinary jury might be. Horne Tooke conducted his own defence but to no avail. The special jury found him guilty without hesitation and Lord Mansfield then sentenced him to a year's imprisonment and a fine of £200, as well as stipulating that before being released after his prison sentence he must find sureties totalling £800 for his good behaviour for three years. Sympathising with the American rebels had become a serious and expensive matter.

Had the government's problem merely been one of preventing the publication of material sympathetic to the rebellion in America, then that problem would have resolved itself with the granting of independence in 1783. There would still have been the novel and disagreeable experience of fighting a war to which a large proportion of the country was opposed as a matter of political principle but, nonetheless, the internal and external conflicts would have ended in 1783. Yet so far as political censorship was concerned, America independent remained as dangerous as America colonised. The United States, for a number of years before the French Revolution, seemed to be an inspiration and example to would-be republicans and revolutionaries in England, the 'fellow-subjects' of Englishmen having overthrown the tyranny of monarch and constitution, replaced this with the promise of a democratic republic. The task of censorship became one of checking the flow of ideas from west to east across the Atlantic, rather than stemming the tide of sympathy from east to west. A great deal of this censorship was devoted to the works of one man, Thomas Paine, both as a political and a theological writer. *The Rights of Man* and works like *A Letter Addressed to the Addressers on the late Proclamation* were to be among the most-prosecuted seditious libels during the last, troubled decade of the eighteenth century. In the first quarter of the nineteenth century Paine's *Age of Reason* and another American book, Elihu Palmer's *Principles of Nature* appeared more often in the courts than any other books had done in cases of blasphemous libel. As we shall see, popular political and theological controversy in England was soon to owe to America the kind of debt that more self-consciously intellectual discussion owed to Germany.

PARLIAMENT AND THE PRESS

While the ministers of George III were fighting their battles against Wilkes and his supporters at home and the American colonists abroad, Parliament itself was trying hard to assert, for almost the last time, the absolute sovereignty of its privileges in the face of press intrusion or disrespectful comment. The theory still survived that only by preserving a degree of secrecy with regard to its proceedings and thus insulating itself to some extent against the climate of popular opinion could Parliament carry out its functions adequately. The last attempt to maintain this secrecy came in 1771, when the House of Commons ordered that summonses should be issued for the publishers of the *Gazetteer*, the *Middlesex Journal*, and the *Evening Post*. These three had published accounts of proceedings in the House and, since this could still be regarded as a breach of privilege, they were summoned to give an account of their actions. But the authorities of the City of London (including Wilkes) who had supported these papers in their attempt to publicise the affairs of Parliament, continued to support Miller, the publisher of the *Evening Post*, when he failed to answer the summons of the Commons and a warrant was issued for his arrest. They refused to acknowledge the power of warrants issued by the Commons, and Wilkes, as a magistrate, arrested the Messenger of the House, and obliged the Members to put up the bail for his release. Brass Crosby, the Lord Mayor, and one of his Aldermen were then arrested by order of the Commons and committed to the Tower by a majority of 202 to 39. But Wilkes refused to accept any summons not made out to him as Member of Parliament for Middlesex and, since this was still a matter in dispute, the Commons reluctantly abandoned the case against him. The Commons were not without their supporters: George III himself had written to Lord North suggesting the undesirability of making the proceedings of Parliament public, but on the other hand there were now a number of societies for 'political information' who were prepared to make it their business to see that what went on inside Parliament was generally known. In any case, it was hardly likely that, as the communication of news through the growing newspaper industry attracted more and more readers, the proceedings of Parliament could have been restricted in this way for much longer. The final recognition of public interest and the right of the public to know what was happening in the legislature came in 1774 when Luke Hansard published the first official report of parliamentary proceedings.

Yet though the proceedings of Parliament might now be a matter of public knowledge, they were not to be the subject of unrestrained comment. For example, in 1789 a bookseller named John Stockdale (described in his obituary in the *Gentleman's Magazine* of 1815 as being of 'much eccentricity of conduct, and great coarseness of manners')[1] published *A Review of the Principal Charges against*

---

[1] *Gentleman's Magazine*, LXXXV, 649.

Warren Hastings, Esquire, Late Governor of Bengal. This was an attack by a Scottish clergyman, Logan, on the impeachment of Warren Hastings by the House of Commons, demanding 'What credit can we give to multiplied and accumulated charges, when we find that they originate from misrepresentation and falsehood?'[1] The impeachment itself dragged on until Hastings's acquittal in 1795 but the Commons hastily voted Stockdale's publication a seditious libel and he was duly prosecuted. He was most ably defended by Thomas Erskine, one of the greatest advocates of that or any other age: indeed, more than Erskine's skill was involved in this case, since he was to play a significant part in the campaign to destroy this type of political censorship. He claimed that the Attorney-General had quoted the allegedly libellous passages out of context. It was, of course, the normal practice for the prosecution to include in the indictment only those passages said to be libellous, but Erskine made this sound almost like a conspiracy to pervert justice.

The Attorney General on the principle of the present proceeding against this pamphlet, might indict the publisher of the bible for blasphemously denying the existence of heaven, in printing
"There is no God."[2]

Whatever the House of Commons might think of Stockdale's pamphlet, the jury needed no further convincing and promptly found the publisher not guilty. In this case they had been invited to curtail the right of the individual to criticise the proceedings of Parliament and they had declined to do so. The final comment on this may be left to the *Public Advertiser*, which published *Four Letters on the Subject of Mr. Stockdale's Trial* during the following year: the time when Parliament condemned publications simply by voting them criminal was not quite over but no longer did its Members entrust the punishment of the offender to a court of law.

Those who know anything of the House of Commons, or of any other public body in this or in any kingdom, need not be told how easy it is to carry a question, in which their privileges or dignity are stated to be involved. It is not, therefore, surprising that the Commons, *nemine contradicente*, voted *that* to be a gross libel, which twelve dispassionate gentlemen, upon their oaths, have declared *not to be one*; but it is a very nice question, and ought to be well considered, and will, I dare say, be well considered in future by the Member who shall propose it, whether a few detached sentences in an ingenious work, ought to be selected in order to institute a prosecution upon, in this free and enlightened age.[3]

The Whole Proceedings on the Trial of John Stockdale (London, 1790), p. 24.
[2]*ibid.*, pp. 40–41.
[3]*Four Letters on the Subject of Mr. Stockdale's Trial* (London, 1790), p. 8.

MEASURES TO CONTROL THE PRESS

To some observers at least the *Public Advertiser's* reference to 'this free and enlightened age' must have sounded like rather heavy irony. In 1768 the author of *Considerations on Proceedings by Information and Attachment* claimed confidently that ministers themselves were now seriously considering whether the political influence of the press might not be curbed by some form of pre-censorship, rather like the system which had been abandoned in 1695. The writer of the pamphlet indicates that such a possibility had been widely canvassed but he gives no specific details, adding only,

The prosecuting spirit of the times will not permit me to speak with that unreserved freedom which my inclination would prompt me to: a freedom which would render me obnoxious to those dreadful thunderbolts of ministerial vengeance, which it is my wish to have condemned as abhorrent to every idea of constitutional liberty.[1]

Whatever the difficulties in the way of imposing a new licensing system on the press, the ministry certainly appeared to be resorting to methods for dealing with publishers and booksellers which were at least repressive, if not unconstitutional. Such methods might be used to imprison a man or bring him to financial ruin without ever letting the case go before a jury. Indeed, one of the consequences of the case against Wilkes was the fate of William Bingley, who had continued to print the *North Briton* after the turmoil of 1763. In 1768 Bingley was summoned to show reason why a writ of attachment for contempt should not be issued against him for his activities in this respect. He was allowed bail, however, and then summoned before the court of King's Bench in the autumn. Here he was to be interrogated but, to the chagrin of his judges, Bingley refused to answer the questions put to him, on the grounds that his rights as a citizen entitled him to a trial by jury and that any attempt to deal with him otherwise was utterly unconstitutional. He was released briefly and then imprisoned in February 1769 for his refusal to answer these 'interrogatories', which was judged to be contempt of court. He remained in prison until May 1770, when the Attorney-General announced in the court of King's Bench that he had decided, after all, not to proceed further with the original writ of attachment, and Bingley was thereupon released. He alleged that he had been kept in prison for two years altogether, without ever being brought to trial, and what made matters worse was that Wilkes, in whose interest he was acting the

[1] *Considerations on Proceedings by Information and Attachment* (London, 1768), p. 2.

role of martyr, had refused all his appeals for financial help. It is a sad but, perhaps, not surprising reflection on human nature that so many crusaders against the power of official censorship appear in a rather less sympathetic light in their commercial and other dealings with lesser men.

There was a second case in 1768, not dissimilar to that of Bingley, involving John Almon who had published *A Letter Concerning Libels*, in which he attacked the prosecution of Wilkes and, in particular, the conduct of Lord Chief Justice Mansfield. Almon was summoned before the court of King's Bench by a writ of attachment to show cause why he should not be condemned for contempt of court. There was no question of his being tried by a jury. The case began but then was allowed to drag on so that as the author of *Considerations on Proceedings by Information and Attachment* put it, 'The poor publisher must have been put to a great expense to shew cause, without ever having the satisfaction to have it determined. It still hangs like a mill-stone over his head, ready to fall upon him and crush him to atoms'.[1] Such methods of inflicting financial hardship on publishers or of keeping penalties suspended over them to ensure their political subservience were to become rather popular with ministries of the late eighteenth and early nineteenth centuries.

But, of course, even if a case of seditious libel came before a jury, the government still had the great theoretical advantages of being able to choose a special jury, and of having the issue of whether or not the publication was libellous decided by the judge. This second advantage was lost by the reforms included in the Libel Act of 1792. Considering the demands for stricter political censorship which were voiced in the years immediately following the Act, this reform was accomplished only just in time. The events leading up to it are worth consideration.

PRESS FREEDOM AND THE RIGHTS OF JURIES

Whatever jurors in seditious libel cases may have thought themselves, there was no lack of general agitation for a reform of the law so that the right to decide what was libellous should be taken from the judges, and particularly from men like Lord Chief Justice Mansfield. The Society for the Defence of the Bill of Rights had made this reform one of its aims at its foundation in 1769. In the *Public Advertiser* in 1770 and outside it in 1771 'Phileleutherus Anglicanus' campaigned for a reform of the law, alleging that as things stood it was all too easy for the authorities to bring a prosecution against a

---

[1] *ibid.*, p. 38.

bookseller as 'an Opportunity taken to revenge some old Grudge for a former Publication'.[1] Similar assertions appeared in 1770 in such pamphlets as *A Dialogue between a Country Farmer and a Juryman on the Subject of Libels*, whose title-page bore the inscription 'The Liberty of the Press, and the Rights of Jurymen, are the Bulwark of the English Constitution'.

Whether the activities of Wilkes, on one side, rather than those of Mansfield, on the other, contributed the greater impetus to the demands for reform is a delicately-balanced question. Certainly, Mansfield as a jurist had his admirers and liked to regard himself as the Maecenas of contemporary literature but his attitude towards the liberty—or the 'licentiousness' as he preferred to call it—of the press, was one of sceptical hostility. In due course Lord Kenyon succeeded him as Lord Chief Justice but the reformers still showed no sign of mitigating their demands for a change in the libel law. In 1791, for instance, when reform of the law seemed at last to be coming, there appeared a pamphlet dedicated to Charles James Fox, *Areopagitica: An Essay on the Liberty of the Press*, which accused the executive of having exercised its authority *'in the double capacity of Judge and jury'*, and whose author thundered, *'The law, in cases of criminal prosecution for libel, is immoral, unconstitutional, and subversive of liberty, and the ends of public justice.'*[2]

Yet pamphleteering alone might not have been enough to alter the law so that publishers and authors stood a better chance of acquittal in political prosecutions than they did when left to the mercies of such men as Mansfield and Kenyon. By far the most impressive of the arguments for reform was the one presented by the behaviour of the juries themselves when, as in Woodfall's case in 1770, they returned such hopeless verdicts as 'guilty of printing and publishing only'. That was all they were required to find him guilty of, but the word 'only' made nonsense of the verdict. Such was the agitation over Woodfall's case, in the press and elsewhere, that in March 1771 Dowdeswell, with the support of Burke, introduced a Bill in the House of Commons which would have given juries the right to decide on whether a publication constituted a libel or not. The government did not commit itself officially to either side during the debate but the motion was nonetheless defeated by 218 to 72. It was to take more than the demonstration of the jurors in Woodfall's case to sway the House of Commons.

If one case more than any other could have persuaded Parliament

---

[1] *A Summary of the Law of Libel* (London, 1771), p. 32.

[2] *Areopagitica: An Essay on the Liberty of the Press* (London, 1791), pp. 65 and 67.

of the futility of continuing with the present law in the face of opposition from juries, it was probably the prosecution of William Shipley, Dean of St. Asaph, at the Shropshire Summer Assizes in 1784, when Erskine was the counsel for the defence.

Shipley's brother-in-law, Sir William Jones, had written *A Dialogue between a Gentleman and a Farmer* in 1783, describing it as 'a vehicle for explaining to common capacities the great principles of society and government, and for showing the defects in the representation of the people in the British Parliament.' The Dean was so impressed by his brother-in-law's pamphlet that he arranged for its publication by a Welsh Reform Society in 1784. The implications of the pamphlet are clear enough from the following passage, in which the gentleman and the farmer discuss a village club, using this as an analogy to parliamentary democracy. The farmer explains that '*The master for each night is chosen by all the company present the week before.*'

G. *What should you do, if any member were to insist on becoming perpetual master and on altering your rules at his arbitrary will and pleasure?*
F. *We should expel him.*
G. *What, if he were to bring a serjeant's guard when the militia are quartered in your neighbourhood, and insist upon your obeying him?*
F. *We would resist if we could: if not, the society would be broken up.*
G. *Suppose that, with his serjeant's guard, he were to take the money out of the box, or out of your pockets?*
F. *Would not that be a robbery?*
G. *I am seeking information from you. How should you act upon such an occasion?*
F. *We should submit, perhaps, at that time; but should afterwards try to apprehend the robbers.*
G. *What if you could not apprehend them?*
F. *We might kill them, I should think: and if the King would not pardon us, God would.*[1]

The prosecution was not brought by the Attorney-General but by Fitzmaurice, brother of Lord Lansdowne, and juries, on the whole, showed less sympathy towards private prosecutions. Erskine, in his defence of Shipley, pointed out that if this publication was a seditious libel then so was the Bill of Rights: as for the Glorious Revolution of 1689, it must have been a 'wicked rebellion,' and the existing government must logically be regarded as 'a traitorous conspiracy against the hereditary monarchy of England'.[2] Yet, more significant than this, Erskine began to attack the customary interpretation of the law of libel, almost inviting the jury to disregard it.

[1] *The Speeches of the Hon. Thomas Erskine* (London, 1810), I, 142–3.
[2] *ibid.*, I, 152.

But, if *you* are only to find the *fact of publishing*, which is not even disputed; and the Judge is to tell you, that the matter of libel being on the record, *he shall shut himself up in silence, and give no opinion at all as to the libellous and seditious tendency of the paper, and yet shall nevertheless expect you to affix the epithet of* GUILTY *to the publication of a thing, the* GUILT *of which* YOU *are forbid, and* HE *refuses to examine;*—miserable indeed is the condition into which we are fallen.[1]

Erskine can hardly have endeared himself to Buller, the assize judge, by these remarks but worse was to follow.

In his summing up, Buller informed the jury that it was the prosecution, not the defence, who had interpreted the law correctly. The only question for them to decide was whether or not the Dean of St. Asaph was guilty of publishing the pamphlet as alleged: it was not for them to decide whether the contents amounted to a seditious libel. That, he told them, was the law, 'and it has been so held for considerably more than a century past.'[2] The jury retired and came back into court after only half an hour. What followed is worth quoting verbatim, since the dialogue shows the state to which the law of libel, as interpreted by Mansfield and Buller, had been reduced: it also helps to explain why those who might otherwise have resisted any change in the law withdrew their opposition to Fox's Libel Bill eight years later. This was how the three-cornered argument went between Buller, Erskine, and the jury.

Clerk. Gentlemen of the jury, do you find the defendant guilty or not guilty?
Foreman. Guilty of publishing only.
Erskine. You find him guilty of publishing only?
A Juror. Guilty only of publishing.
Buller J. I believe that is a verdict not quite correct. You must explain that one way or the other. The indictment has stated that G means 'gentleman;' F 'farmer;' *the King*, 'the King of Great Britain.'
Juror. We have no doubt about that.
Buller J. If you find him guilty of publishing, you must not say the word 'only.'
Erskine. By that they mean to find there was no sedition.
Juror. We only find him guilty of publishing. We do not find anything else.
Erskine. I beg your Lordship's pardon, with great submission, I am sure I mean nothing that is irregular. I understand they say, 'We only find him guilty of publishing.'
Juror. Certainly that is all we do find.
Buller J. If you only attend to what is said, there is no question or doubt.
Erskine. Gentlemen, I desire to know whether you mean the word 'only' to stand in your verdict?

[1] *ibid.*, I, 198.   [2] *ibid.*, I, 218.

Juryman. Certainly.

Buller J. Gentlemen, if you add the word 'only' it will be negativing the innuendoes.

Erskine. I desire your Lordship sitting here as judge to record the verdict as given by the jury.

Buller J. You say that he is guilty of publishing the pamphlet, and that the meaning of the innuendoes is as stated in the indictment.

Juror. Certainly.

Erskine. Is the word 'only' to stand part of the verdict?

Juror. Certainly.

Erskine. Then I insist it shall be recorded.

Buller J. Then the verdict must be misunderstood; let me understand the jury.

Erskine. The jury do understand their verdict.

Buller J. Sir, I will not be interrupted.

Erskine. I stand here as an advocate for a brother citizen, and I desire the word 'only' may be recorded.

Buller J. Sit down, sir; remember your duty, or I shall be obliged to proceed in another manner.

Erskine. Your Lordship may proceed in what manner you think fit; I know my duty as well as your Lordship knows yours. I shall not alter my conduct.[1]

Since the jury had refused to give an unqualified verdict, the situation was absolutely hopeless and there was nothing for it but to have the case argued before Mansfield in the court of King's Bench in November 1784. Mansfield upheld Buller's ruling that juries were allowed to decide on questions of fact only, indeed he could hardly have come to any other decision. However, Shipley had not been properly convicted by the jury and, therefore, his prosecutors were as far away as ever from succeeding in their case against him. He could be tried again but there was no guarantee that a second jury would be any more favourably disposed towards the prosecution than the first one had been. The case against Shipley was dropped. It is best known today not for the clash between Erskine and Buller but for Mansfield's classic dictum on press freedom, which sums up as much in its tone as in its vocabulary the latent hostility of many members of the eighteenth-century judiciary towards the alleged benefits of intellectual liberty.

To be free is to live under a government by law. The *liberty of the press* consists in printing without any previous licence, subject to the consequences of law. The *licentiousness* of the press is *Pandora*'s box, the source of every evil.[2]

[1] Lord Campbell, *Lives of the Lord Chancellors* (London, 1856–7), VIII, 276–7.
[2] Erskine, *Speeches*, I, 379.

Even those who were less alarmed at the political dangers inherent in a 'licentious' press, still had some reservations in the matter. Fifteen years earlier than Mansfield, Sir William Blackstone, one of the greatest English jurists of any age, had made much the same points in gentler language.

The Liberty of the Press is indeed essential to the nature of a free State; but this consists in laying no *previous* restraints upon publications, and not in freedom from censure for criminal matter when published.[1]

Neither Mansfield nor Kenyon, his successor, showed any inclination to compromise with the demand for reform as expressed in the verdicts of certain juries. As Holt pointed out in 1812, Kenyon was no less resolute in his way than Mansfield had been. 'With a just contempt of that popular but dangerous praise, of keeping pace with the liberality of the times, he inflexibly applied the law of the land to all the encroachments of public writers, and would not admit the imposing name of the liberty of the press to sanctify its licentiousness and protect its abuses.'[2] Yet there was little that men like Mansfield or Kenyon could do to prevent juries from taking the law into their own hands. When the fear of revolution grew more intense there were to be occasions when jurors could be more successfully browbeaten than they had been by Buller and his colleagues, but before that, in 1791, Charles James Fox introduced his bill in the House of Commons to give juries the right to decide on what was libellous. This bill reached the Lords and was then thrown out. Undaunted by a first failure, Fox introduced another bill in the following year, with the support of almost all those who were campaigning either for the extension or even the preservation of press freedom. There was continued opposition from Lord Kenyon and the law lords but despite this the bill survived its passage through both Houses to become Fox's Libel Act of 1792. In more ways than one it was well-timed. To a growing number of people, the existing law seemed to be unfair and, in the last resort, unworkable but the new statute was well-timed for reasons other than that. In 1789 with the revolution in France, the fear of revolution in England began to grow. Jacobins were seen to be at work everywhere, preparing for the overthrow of government, monarchy, and constitution. 1792 was not only the year of the Libel Act, it was also the year of the prosecution of Thomas Paine for publishing his *Rights of Man*.

[1] William Blackstone, *Commentaries on the Laws of England* (London, 1769), IV, xi, 151.
[2] F. L. Holt, *The Law of Libel* (London, 1812), p. 117.

7

Guardians of Public Morality:
(1) The Proclamation Society

THE PROCLAMATION AND THE PROCLAMATION SOCIETY

On 29 May 1787 the young William Wilberforce wrote a confidential letter to William Hey, assuring him that, 'in a very few days you will hear of a Proclamation being issued for the discouragement of vice.'[1] Wilberforce was much interested in continuing the work of the Society for the Reformation of Manners by founding another society which, this time, would be specifically concerned with the suppression of obscene or profane literature. He felt that such a society would more easily recommend itself to men of influence if its foundation coincided with a royal proclamation against vice and immorality. The Archbishop of Canterbury gave his support to the project and the King was easily persuaded of the need to issue such a proclamation: it appeared on 1 June as 'A Proclamation for the Encouragement of Piety and Virtue, and for preventing and punishing of Vice, Profaneness, and Immorality.' Apart from Sabbath breaking, drunkenness, and the usual preoccupations of such pronouncements, this proclamation of 1787 contained a precise reference to the need to suppress 'all loose and licentious Prints, Books, and Publications, dispersing Poison to the Minds of the Young and Unwary, and to punish the Publishers and Vendors thereof.' The dangers of literacy were at last recognised in this sphere as well.

Even before the proclamation was issued, Wilberforce had gone some way towards founding the society which was to celebrate it, the Proclamation Society. As he told William Hey, the King and the Archbishop were both sympathetic to the cause and the Duke of Montagu was prepared to be the first president. (Wilberforce believed that it would be better if his own name were not associated with the venture for the time being.) Once the proclamation was issued, bishops were instructed to return to their dioceses to ensure the carrying out of its provisions, and it was in their dioceses that Wilberforce proposed to visit them and solicit their support for his new society. He

[1] R. I. and S. Wilberforce, *The Life of William Wilberforce* (London, 1838), I, 132.

had no doubt of the righteousness of his mission, remarking in his journal, 'God has set before me as my object the reformation of manners'.[1] The great humanitarianism of Wilberforce is not entirely absent from his work for the Proclamation Society: drunkenness, after all, was a matter of life and death for a large number of people in the eighteenth century, and there was little sympathy for the misfortunes of the gamblers or the promiscuous. To condemn Wilberforce as a censorious prude for his work in this respect is no more just than to condemn him as an economic saboteur for his long and resolute fight against the slave trade.

Wilberforce took action because he did not expect that the government would, and indeed because he felt that the government could not deal with certain offences against morality.

In our free state it is peculiarly needful to obtain these ends by the agency of some voluntary association; for thus only can those moral principles be guarded, which of old were under the immediate protection of the government. It thus becomes to us, like the ancient censorship, the guardian of the religion and morals of the people. The Attorney-General and Secretary of State, who alone in our country can be thought at all to fill this post, are too much cramped by their political relations to discharge its duties with effect; yet some such official check on vice is absolutely needed. It is not here as with personal injury, which will always be suppressed by private prosecution; for though the mischief done by blasphemous and indecent publications and other incentives to licentiousness be greater than most private wrongs, yet it is so fractional, and divided amongst so many thousands, that individuals can scarcely be expected to take up the cause of virtue.[2]

Throughout the summer of 1787, Wilberforce gathered around him a body of men, of the greatest eminence in society, who were prepared to lend their support to the Proclamation Society. When the Society's prospectus was at last issued, it contained among the names of members those of the Archbishops of Canterbury and York, seventeen bishops, six dukes, and eleven other peers. Clearly the morality of the nation was no longer a matter of concern to the 'middle rank' alone. Among the most active of these supporters was Beilby Porteus, the Bishop of Chester, who was later to become the Society's president, in succession to the Duke of Montagu and Lord Bathurst. In 1779, preaching before the House of Lords on 'the Reformation of Manners,' Porteus had issued a stern warning about the 'grand corrupters' of youthful innocence, 'licentious NOVELS, licentious HISTORIES, and licentious systems of PHILOSOPHY,'[3] so

[1] *ibid.*, I, 130.
[2] *ibid.*, I, 131–2.
[3] *Works of the Rt. Rev. Beilby Porteus* (London, 1823), II, 259.

that it is not surprising to find that during his presidency of the Society, according to one narrator, 'many persons were prosecuted and punished for disseminating licentious books; and amongst other acts of beneficial interference, a check was in *some* measure given to that most pernicious custom of publicly exhibiting indecent prints'.[1] Certainly the founding of the Proclamation Society was followed by a wave of prosecutions for publishing obscene libels, some of the cases taking place in the court of King's Bench. In 1788 John Morgan was sent to prison for a year and pilloried for publishing *The Battles of Venus: A Descriptive Dissertation on the Various Modes of Enjoyment*, which was alleged to be 'Translated from the Posthumous Works of Voltaire,' and to have been printed at the Hague in 1760.[2] It was actually printed in London, later than 1760, and had nothing to do with Voltaire. A second case in 1788, against Lewis McDonald is worth mentioning because the book in question was that old favourite *The School of Venus*, and the translation was exactly the same as the one which had been in trouble in 1745.[3] In 1780 two more cases were brought in King's Bench, both against James Hodges, who was convicted in the first for publishing the ubiquitous *Memoirs of a Woman of Pleasure* and in the second for *A Dialogue between a Married Lady and a Maid*.[4]

Naturally, the supporters of the Proclamation Society and similar organisations had to face the objection that they were attempting to undermine the liberty of the press in a new way: but in this, as in questions of political freedom, arguments for liberty might always be countered by condemnations of authors and publishers for their licentiousness. Hannah More, for example, who was a supporter of the Proclamation Society and of the later Society for the Suppression of Vice, remarked in her essay *On the Religion of the Fashionable World*, 'While we glory in having freed ourselves from the trammels of human authority, are we not turning our liberty into licentiousness, and wantonly struggling to throw off the *divine* authority too?'[5] To Hannah More and to those who thought as she did 'we are no more at liberty to indulge opinions in opposition to the express word of God than we are at liberty to infringe practically on his command-ments'.[6] Like most of her sympathisers, she is deeply concerned with the moral effect of literature on women, children, and the working class. She fears 'immorality' rather than any sophisticated intellectual subversion of religious beliefs, though, to her evangelical piety,

[1] *ibid.*, I, 101.   [2] P.R.O., K.B. 28/347/4.   [3] P.R.O., K.B. 28/347/5.
[4] P.R.O., K.B. 28/353/5 and 6.
[5] *The Works of Hannah More* (London, 1801), VI, 114.
[6] *ibid.*, VI, 115.

Catholicism seemed as grave a peril as infidelity. What worries her most of all is not that men of intellectual eminence may fall prey to the snares of Gibbon or Hume but rather that her less gifted readers may be morally undone by 'the hot-bed of a circulating library'.[1] (A phrase which lends a nice ambivalence to the term 'hot-bed.') As in politics, so in morals, mass literacy was not an unmitigated blessing. If ministers of the Crown feared the collapse of established order as the result of political subversion on the part of the enemy below, moralists of Hannah More's persuasion envisaged a more general moral collapse through the corruption of the unsophisticated reader or listener. With dismay she recounts the spread of novel-reading among the lower orders.

May the Author be indulged in a short digression while she remarks, though rather out of its place, that the corruption occasioned by these books has spread so wide, and descended so low, as to have become one of the most universal, as well as most pernicious, sources of corruption among us. Not only among milliners, mantua-makers, and other trades where numbers work together, the labour of one girl is frequently sacrificed that she may be spared to read those mischievous books to others; but she has been assured by clergymen who have witnessed the fact, that they are procured and greedily read in the wards of our hospitals! an awful hint, that those who teach the poor to read, should not only take care to furnish them with principles which will lead them to abhor corrupt books, but that they should also furnish them with such books as shall strengthen and confirm their principles.[2]

The reading aloud of fiction in the family had been a common practice when the novels of Richardson and Fielding were published but the reading aloud of 'corrupt books' was now so widespread that even illiteracy was no longer an adequate protection for the chastity of an innocent mind.

In the hands of a critic like Hannah More such terms as 'novel' or 'circulating library' are so regularly employed as terms of abuse that we may justifiably wonder whether 'licentious books' meant anything like the same to these reformers as that phrase would do to a twentieth-century reader. So much of the criticism seems to apply to literature which was merely unedifying rather than obscene that we might be forgiven for supposing that these moralists were just being over-scrupulous about the sentimental fiction or the 'Gothic' novel which flourished so spectacularly during the last forty years of the eighteenth century. Certainly the prosecutions of 1788 and 1790 showed that favourites like *The School of Venus* and *Fanny Hill* or *Memoirs of a Woman of Pleasure* were still in circulation but, with the

[1] *ibid.*, VII, 205.   [2] *ibid.*, VII, 221–2.

exception of the *Essay on Woman*, there had not been a prosecution involving a newly-written piece of pornography since 1750. Was the pornography trade merely living on the profits of its past, Augustan glories?

In the years immediately preceding the foundation of the Proclamation Society there had appeared the first specimens of a new genre of periodical literature which was to unite the sexual scandals of high and low society, some rather feebly obscene verses and fiction (heavily strung with *doubles entendres*), curious correspondence which was no doubt contributed by the editors themselves on many occasions, and accounts of criminal prosecutions for sexual offences.[1] Some of the items may have slight historical interest but it would be stretching description too far to classify most of these publications as 'imaginative literature'. Yet the fact that so much of this material should now have begun to appear in periodical form suggests that editors and publishers envisaged a more permanent basis to the trade. The commercial advantages of periodical publication are obvious enough when one considers the nature of the subject-matter: serialised fiction of a more or less erotic kind could be manipulated with sufficient cunning to ensure that the casual reader was likely to become a continuing subscriber. This type of magazine, though coming to rely more and more on serialised fiction instead of social scandal, remained a feature of the pornography trade until the end of the Victorian period.[2] Disregarding the nature of its subject-matter, the basic format and appeal were not markedly different from those of its more respectable nineteenth-century contemporaries.

The earliest of these periodicals was *The Rambler's Magazine*, which had little enough in common with its namesake, edited by Samuel Johnson from 1750 to 1752. Indeed, the full title of this second *Rambler*, whose title-page was imitated from that of the staid

---

[1] Not only pornographic magazines are overwhelmed by 'curious correspondence'. In the later nineteenth century a largely bogus correspondence on the subject of flagellation continued intermittently in the *Family Herald* for eighteen years. Letters on the same topic, relating almost entirely to the whipping of girls, were received in such numbers by the editor of the *Englishwoman's Domestic Magazine* that in 1870 the magazine had to issue a special supplement to contain them all. Nor was this 'controversy' confined to Victorian periodicals. In 1965 an initial letter in the magazine *Penthouse*, on the same familiar topic, began an avalanche of correspondence which was still in progress eighteen months later and may still be continuing. Many of the letters in such exchanges, though carrying female signatures, are accounts of male fantasies. In the case of a magazine like *The Rambler* there is a high probability of editorial inspiration as well.

[2] *Paul Pry; Peter Spy*, and *The Ferret*, successively, purveyed scandal that was cheap both in tone and price. *The Exquisite; The Cremorne*, and *The Pearl* were their more expensive Victorian contemporaries.

Gentleman's Magazine, sufficiently indicates its aims and the nature of its contents: *The Rambler's Magazine; or, The Annals of Gallantry, Glee, Pleasure, and the Bon Ton: Calculated for the Entertainment of the Polite World; and to furnish the Man of Pleasure with a most delicious Banquet of Amorous, Bacchanalian, Whimsical, Humorous, Theatrical and Polite Entertainment.* The magazine first appeared in 1783 and circulated throughout the country, being sold at London, Oxford, Cambridge, York, Newcastle, Birmingham, and Bath. The first number was prefaced by the editor's address to his readers, an address which might have done much to stimulate the activities of Wilberforce and his associates.

We shall comprehend every Topic that engages the Bon Ton: every Place of public entertainment will furnish us with Subjects for our Design, as we propose giving the History of every Lady, whom the attracting charms of Gold can conquer, that resorts to any of the polite Assemblies; as well as the History of every married Lady, who for want of due attention being paid her at home by her Charo Sposa, forms some little amorous Alliance with a Party without Doors *pour s'amuser*, and to gratify herself for the Relief very frequently granted by Doctors Commons: and we shall illustrate the most striking passages of their Histories with elegant Copper-plates representing the various Situations in those critical Scenes.

Besides these Memoirs, our Readers will find such pleasant amorous Histories, as we think will be most conducive to their Entertainment, related in an easy, familiar Style, without the restraint of prudish Squeamishness. . . .

. . . To add to the Entertainment of our Readers, and to convey every Information of the amorous or humorous Kind, we shall attend Westminster-Hall, when any Trials for *Crim. Con.* are agitated before the sage and reverend Judges of the Court of King's Bench. The Evidence given by the Witnesses shall be carefully taken down in Short-hand and faithfully served up to the Public in the RAMBLER'S MAGAZINE.

Such also of the Trials at the Old Bailey as fall within our Plan, viz. Such as contain any Thing amorous, humorous, or gallant: whether for Rapes, privately Stealing &c. shall obtain a place in our Repository.[1]

The editor's gloating over the capital to be made out of the miseries of others is perhaps the most obscene thing in the magazine as a whole. The fiction and essays are almost always a pious fraud. *Memoirs of a Woman of Pleasure* and *Fanny Hill*, which ran as separate serials, have nothing more than their titles in common with

---

[1] *The Rambler's Magazine* I, (1783), 3–4. (*Crim. Con.* was the abbreviation for 'Criminal Conversation' between a man and a woman, or marital infidelity which entitled the injured partner of the marriage to bring an action for damages against the co-respondent. *The Crim. Con. Gazette* was published in twopenny numbers during 1830–1.

Cleland's novel. Nor does the *Essay on Woman* in any way resemble Wilkes's publication. Stories like *The Adventures of Kitty Pry* or *The History and Adventures of a Bedstead* are interspersed with tedious, pseudo-scholarly articles on 'The Laws of Flagellation,' 'Account of Grecian Courtesans,' and 'The Marriage Ceremonies of the Hotten-tots.' The total effect is, as a Massachusetts judge once remarked of *Forever Amber*, conducive to sleep but not to sleep with members of the opposite sex. Only the unremitting gullibility of its readers can have kept this *Rambler* alive for seven years. Although the real objection to such a publication is aesthetic rather than moral, the Proclamation Society might have taken notice of a letter which appeared in its pages in 1788, allegedly from Kitty Longfor't of Birch Rod Row, who describes how *The Rambler's Magazine* has been smuggled into her school.[1] Even though the letter was an editorial hoax, it might either reflect a true state of affairs or put ideas into the minds of the inhabitants of boarding schools. At all events, in August 1790 the magazine abruptly ceased publication. There is no direct evidence that this was the result of legal action or the threat of it by the Proclamation Society, though in the final number the editor promises that 'THE grievance complained of by the Duke of M—— shall not exist in future'.[2] (The Duke of Montagu was, of course, the first president of the Proclamation Society.) In March 1791 the *Rambler* was succeeded by *The Bon Ton Magazine; or Microscope of Fashion and Folly*, printed and published by William Locke and virtually identical in format to the earlier periodical. Though Locke was convicted of a libel on Clara Louisa Middleton in 1794, having described her adultery in the *Bon Ton* for June 1793, the magazine survived to die a more or less natural death in February 1796.[3] Its style was rather more euphemistic and its illustrations less explicit than those of the *Rambler* had been. During 1795 it ran concurrently with a brasher publication, *The Ranger's Magazine*, which complained that the *Rambler* had been 'too moral, and generally too timid,' and promised to 'pursue a contrary conduct'.[4] The *Ranger* with its detailed descriptions of available prostitutes, including prices and addresses, was unlikely to stay out of trouble for long: in June 1795, under what sounds like pressure from the Proclamation Society or its sympathisers the editor announced that he proposed to 'concur and unite' in 'the present general zeal for REFORMATION'.[5] He carried out this

[1] *ibid*. VI, (1788), 25.
[2] *ibid.*, VIII (1790), 282.
[3] P.R.O., K.B. 28/368/18.
[4] *The Ranger's Magazine: or, The Man of Fashion's Companion* I (1795), iii.
[5] *ibid.* I (1795), 286.

unlikely resolution in the only possible way, by ceasing publication forthwith.

Yet the reformers had more than these monthly periodicals to contend with. One annual publication which had earned their disapproval was *Harris's List of Covent-Garden Ladies*, which had been issued as an annual for a number of years.[1] Like the later feature in the *Ranger* it was a descriptive list of prostitutes complete with addresses and prices ranging from five shillings to five pounds. The physical descriptions of the women might have been regarded as a direct incitement to sexual immorality, though not every reader would feel impelled to hurry round to Miss Clicamp at 2, York Street, on finding her charms described as 'fortunate for the true lovers of fat, should fate throw them into the possession of such full grown beauties'.[2] Yet beneath the cynical bonhomie of the descriptions one detects all too often the plight of ageing whores and, at the other extreme, of children who would nowadays be below the age of consent. In 1794 the first prosecution for selling *Harris's List* was brought against James Roach who was convicted, sentenced to a year's imprisonment and ordered to find sureties of £200 for his good behaviour for three years afterwards.[3] A second case against James Aitken, who was indicted as 'John Aitken,' ended with him being fined £200 for selling the same edition of the book.[4] After this no more was heard of it.

Prosecutions of other books continued but whether because the Proclamation Society had lost some of its initial fervour or whether because the courts were still sometimes wary of condemning men for this type of offence in a private prosecution, the results of some of the cases must have seemed far from satisfactory. In 1798, for instance, when John Cole was prosecuted for publishing *Fanny Hill*, some mildly obscene 'riddles,' and 'The Delights of Venus,' (which had first appeared in about 1709 in *The Cabinet of Love* and had never been prosecuted before) he was convicted but merely required to find sureties to come up for sentence if and when summoned.[5] Worse still, so far as the reformers were concerned, two men were acquitted of obscene libel in the following year—in separate cases—for publishing a bawdy but popular poem of the time, 'The

[1] The earliest volume I have seen is for 1788 but this advertises 'The separate LISTS of many preceding Years.' Francis Place records a volume for 1786, also offering earlier 'lists'.

[2] *Harris's List of Covent-Garden Ladies: or, Man of Pleasure's Kalender* (London, 1788), p. 104.

[3] P.R.O., K.B. 28/370/5.

[4] P.R.O., K.B. 28/371/23.

[5] P.R.O., K.B. 28/387/2.

Plenipotentiary'.[1] This poem was attributed to an acquaintance of the Prince of Wales, Captain Morris, otherwise known as the author of *Songs, Drinking, Political, and Facetious* published some ten years earlier. However disconcerting these final verdicts might be to the Proclamation Society, there was no question of the campaign for moral reformation running out of energy at this stage. All that was needed was a more purposeful organisation of the reformers' enthusiasm, an organisation soon to be provided in the Society for the Suppression of Vice.

In its comparatively short career the Proclamation Society had naturally to concern itself with the surviving works of Augustan pornography and with a new species of more feebly written literature whose aim was to provide erotic stimulus and whose achievement must have been something far short of that. These were purely domestic problems but the reformers were becoming increasingly concerned over the deleterious moral effects of literature emanating from other European countries, particularly from France. In 1779, for example, Beilby Porteus had warned the House of Lords that such deplorable literature 'constituted a large and most pernicious branch of our commerce with a neighbouring kingdom'.[2] Of course, in another decade France was to be seen as the source of political corruption as well but the fear of French immorality was of earlier origin. To provide a moral scapegoat by associating various unpleasant sexual phenomena with other countries is natural enough: venereal disease to the English was the 'French pox' or 'French disease', which the French have reciprocated from time to time by labelling homosexuality or sadism as 'le vice anglais'. At the beginning of the nineteenth century the Society for the Suppression of Vice attributed the distribution of pornography to Italian migrants, while in Hannah More's view it was not only French writers—Rousseau particularly—but the Germans as well who were contributing to England's moral decline, Schiller being one of the culprits. Progressing from questions of morality to those of taste she adds a condemnation of 'the irruption of those swarms of publications now daily issuing from the banks of the Danube, which, like their ravaging predecessors of the darker ages, though with far other and more fatal arms, are overrunning civilised society'.[3]

The marked revival of moral censorship in England during the last two decades of the eighteenth century was the result of a number of coinciding developments but the moral welfare of newly-literate

[1] P.R.O., K.B. 28/391/12 and 13.
[2] *Works*, II, 259.
[3] *The Works of Hannah More*, VII, 41–42.

groups was the overwhelming impetus. In an age so conscious of education and the educative effect of all that was considered best in literature, it was inevitable that critics should have issued stern warnings of the likely result, in terms of moral conduct, of all that was worst in literature as well. This preoccupation with the power of erotic literature to corrupt its readers was much less evident in the earlier eighteenth century but, as the pre-Victorians and the Victorians themselves recognised, to believe in the educative power of literature is to believe in its ability to deprave and corrupt. In this they showed themselves more logical at least than those who would deny that books can corrupt while maintaining that 'good' books exert an influence for moral improvement. The moralists of the late eighteenth century were forced by the changing pattern of society to look around them and take stock: they found little comfort in what they saw. It is easy, though mistaken, to dismiss Hannah More as a foolish old maid with almost total inhibitions in matters of sex. It would be possible, though superficial, to debunk Wilberforce's motives and those of his associates in the Proclamation Society, just as one could do the same for him and his colleagues in the campaign against slavery. It is hard to accept that any supporters of censorship are not reactionary but these reformers, like those who introduced a new measure of censorship in the Race Relations Act of 1965, saw themselves as enlightened and even liberal. The only real fault, if it is a fault, which Wilberforce and Hannah More share, is that they voice their convictions in a manner which happens to displease the ears of the twentieth century. Neither of them could equal the taut denunciation by William Blake in his 'Auguries of Innocence', of a society threatened by the same impending moral catastrophe which they feared.

> The whore and gambler, by the state
> Licensed, build that nation's fate.
> The harlot's cry from street to street
> Shall weave Old England's winding-sheet.
> The winner's shout, the loser's curse,
> Dance before dead England's hearse.
> Every night and every morn
> Some to misery are born.
> Every morn and every night
> Some are born to sweet delight.
> Some are born to sweet delight,
> Some are born to endless night.

It was a view of the world which must have corresponded far more closely to the experience of many London prostitutes than did the synthetic gaiety of *Harris's List of Covent-Garden Ladies*.

SCEPTICISM AND TOLERANCE

However concerned the Proclamation Society may have been about the publication of heretical or blasphemous literature by 1787, the mid-eighteenth century was a period in which, perhaps by tolerance, perhaps by apathy, little action was taken against dangerous opinions of this kind. Yet the notoriety of Woolston's *Discourses Concerning the Miracles of Our Saviour* lingered, and however much his detractors might dismiss him as 'poor mad Woolston' the enemies of orthodox Christianity were prepared to use his books in their cause.[1] In 1746 Thomas Astley was fined a total of £100 for publishing the *Discourses* and even in France in 1770 one of the books condemned to the flames by the Parlement of Paris was *Discours sur les Miracles de Jésus-Christ*, diligently translated from Woolston's English text.[2] All the debating points for and against Trinitarian doctrine or biblical authority had been made long before the middle of the eighteenth century and there was little point in prolonging public controversy unless some new ground could be discovered to fight over. 'Who, born within the last forty years, has read one word of . . . that whole race who called themselves Freethinkers?' demanded Burke in 1790, 'Who now reads Bolingbroke? Who ever read him through? Ask the booksellers of London what is become of all these lights of the world.'[3] Four years later William Godwin, who could hardly be numbered as one of Burke's sympathisers, made much the same point when discussing deism in his *Enquiry Concerning Political Justice*. 'Yet fifty years after the agitation of these controversies their effects could scarcely be traced, and things appeared on all sides as if the controversies had never existed.'[4] There were practical results of the lull in theological disputes: Parliament showed its liberality towards religious minorities by removing certain restrictions on Catholics in 1778 and, in the following year, abolishing that requirement which obliged Nonconformist ministers to subscribe to almost all the Thirty-Nine Articles. There was a growing sympathy

---

[1] Even Leslie Stephen, a confessed agnostic by 1873, dismissed Woolston's outpourings as 'more significant of insanity than of intentional profanity', in his *English Thought in the Eighteenth Century* (1876). Yet, to a modern reader, though Woolston may seem scatterbrained or a crank, he is unlikely to appear insane on the strength of his writing, cf. *English Thought in the Eighteenth Century*, 3rd edn. (London, 1902), I, 89.

[2] James Anson Farrer, *Books Condemned to be Burnt* (London, 1904), p. 15.

[3] Edmund Burke, *Reflections on the Revolution in France* (London, 1790), p. 133.

[4] William Godwin, *Enquiry Concerning Political Justice*, 4th edn. (London 1842), I, 43.

even towards the Unitarians—so long as they were not renegade priests or bishops—a sympathy expressed by John Hey in 1796, some years before the Unitarians were officially granted freedom of worship.

We and the Socinians are said to differ, but about what? Not about morality or natural religion, or the divine authority of the Christian religion; we differ only about what we do not understand, and about what is to be done on the part of God; and, if we allowed each other to use expressions at will (and what greater matter could that be in what might almost be called unmeaning expressions?) we need never be upon our guard against each other.[1]

Not everyone would have gone quite as far as Hey in extending the hand of friendship to the Unitarians or to any other heretics, and of course the members of the Proclamation Society were on their guard against the spread of irreligion among the masses. The most general tolerance was for authors whom the masses were in no danger of reading or of hearing read, though even such writers as those came in for their share of hostile criticism. Looking back on the whole of the eighteenth century we might fairly conclude that the most powerful persuasives against Christian belief were to be found in the work of such men as Bolingbroke or, particularly, David Hume in the 'Essay on Miracles,' and Edward Gibbon in the fifteenth and sixteenth chapters of his *Decline and Fall of the Roman Empire*. Whatever one may feel about his philosophy, Hume was one of the great masters of English prose, and both he and Gibbon were among the truly formidable intellects of the eighteenth century, or, indeed, of any other period of English literature. Compared with them, most of their contemporaries or successors who led the onslaught on Christian belief seem ham-fisted in the extreme. The honest bludgeoning of Thomas Paine, for instance, in his *Age of Reason* appears crude and laborious when contrasted with the easy prose of Hume, where the argument is neat and clean as a razor in its attack.

A miracle is a violation of the laws of nature; and as a firm and unalterable experience has established these laws, the proof against a miracle, from the very nature of the fact, is as entire as any argument from experience can possibly be imagined.[2]

The skill, of course, is not merely in simplicity of expression but in the impression so easily conveyed to the unwary reader that there is nothing more to be said on the subject. Hume seems to be com-

[1] Quoted in Leslie Stephen, *History of English Thought in the Eighteenth Century*, 3rd edn. I, 424–5.

[2] *An Enquiry Concerning the Human Understanding*, ed. Selby-Bigge (Oxford, 1895), p. 114.

menting on an intellectual conflict that is already resolved, whereas Paine and his colleagues are preoccupied with issuing challenges and sounding the call to battle. Naturally, there were reasons why this second group and not more dangerous writers of the stamp of Hume should have been called to account. An author who raged against the obscenity or immorality of the Bible might be dealt with effectively enough by a court of law on the grounds that he had contravened the Blasphemy Act of 1698 but to attack the philosophy of Hume through the courts would have been an intimidating intellectual task for counsel and judges alike. It was considered best to leave other philosophers to question the full linguistic interpretation of such terms as 'miracle' or 'laws of nature' and to concentrate the forces of law against the honest indignation of men like Paine and Elihu Palmer. Much to the annoyance of these later writers, Hume had in any case taken the precaution of explaining that he only argued in the way he did to show that 'Our most holy religion is founded on *Faith*, not on reason; and it is a sure method of exposing it to put it to such trial as it is, by no means, fitted to endure'.[1] If this type of reservation saved Hume from censorship by courts of law, it earned him the reputation of a hypocrite among the anti-Christians of the next generation. As with Hume, so with Gibbon, the irony of *Decline and Fall* would have made it a difficult book to prosecute. Yet this technique too, 'Sapping a solemn creed with solemn sneer,' as Byron put it, offered Gibbon protection at the time yet later made him a target of abuse by certain deist martyrs.[2] Gibbon skirted blasphemy, as defined by the Act of 1698, with considerable skill. He criticised the inconsistencies of Mosaic narratives with regard to miraculous events, suggesting that if miracles had happened in biblical times, there was no reason why they should ever have stopped. But they had stopped—at least so far as most Protestants were concerned. The inference was that if eighteenth-century 'miracles' were nothing but delusions of the credulous, there was no cause to suppose that miracles had ever been anything else. As for the conversion of the Roman Empire to Christianity, Gibbon's explanation of that phenomenon is cynical in the extreme.

When the promise of eternal happiness was proposed to mankind on condition of adopting the faith, and of observing the precepts of the Gospel, it is no wonder that so advantageous an offer should have been accepted by great numbers of every religion, of every rank, and of every province in the Roman Empire.[3]

[1] *ibid.*, p. 130.
[2] Byron, *Childe Harold's Pilgrimage*, Canto III, stanza cvii, 5.
[3] *Decline and Fall of the Roman Empire* [Ch. XV], ed. Oliphant Smeaton (London, 1950), I, 452.

As well as escaping legal censorship Gibbon, though he was inevitably attacked for his views, attracted interest and even a slight sympathy from the most unlikely quarters. Hannah More remarked that at least he had concentrated his hostility to Christianity into specific chapters, which was less dangerous than laying it like a snare throughout the whole book. In 1826 Thomas Bowdler, fresh from his triumphant emasculation of Shakespeare's plays, produced his own edition of *Decline and Fall*, omitting the open attacks on Christianity but otherwise, yielding to no one in his admiration for Gibbon's work. To those who were by that time eager martyrs for the cause of Thomas Paine or Elihu Palmer, the duplicity of the great historian must have seemed clear beyond all doubt.

Of course, however great the intellectual power of men like Hume and Gibbon, their limited appeal to the reading public of the later eighteenth century made them easier to tolerate. They were unlikely to corrupt those literary and theological innocents who flocked to the circulating libraries and, in the name of Clara Reeve or Ann Radcliffe, transformed the English novel from a literary to a commercial success. A library with space on its shelves would have done much better to stock *The Mysteries of Udolpho* rather than the *Enquiry Concerning Human Understanding*, and even if *Decline and Fall* were available, how many of the innocents would have lasted out until the fifteenth and sixteenth chapters or appreciated the irony even if they had got that far? So men like Hume and Gibbon passed unmolested by any official censorship but it is small wonder that some of the most bitter attacks upon them should have come not from diehard clerics or embattled theologians but from those less-gifted deists and atheists, who regarded their two eminent predecessors as having been hypocrites when they should have been martyrs, and, indeed, as having been too clever by half.

Yet even in the mid-eighteenth century there were martyrs to be found, men of the new order with whom moral indignation weighed more heavily than any mere intellectual sophistry or logic-chopping. One man who suffered for his belief—or rather disbelief—in 1761 and whose memory was perpetuated by such deists as Richard Carlile in the early nineteenth century, was Peter Annett. When Annett published his views on the Pentateuch in the *Free Enquirer* between October and December 1761 he was much more harshly dealt with than Thomas Burnet or earlier critics of the Mosaic narratives. This can only have been because Annett represented the new type of sceptic whose objection to Christianity or the Bible was not to alleged illogicality or historical falsehood but rather to the fundamentally evil nature of Christian or biblical philosophy. On the threshold of practical democracy, where the most effective argument was the one which penetrated even to the least intelligent voter, it is not surprising that in matters of religion and politics alike the tone of argument should have become emotional (and even on occasion hysterical) rather than analytical, evangelical rather than intellectual. The new readers might have made nothing of Whiston's textual criticism of the Bible but in matters of morality one man's opinion was as good as another's. Of course the appeal to moral sense rather than to intellect was made by both sides and in 1759, for example, two years before Annett, a sermon preached by J. Witherspoon had advocated 'the trial of religious faith by its moral influence'.[1]

In Annett's case, almost any specimen of his style serves to show how indignation had replaced reason.

It is said that God tempted Abraham, by trying whether he would kill his only beloved son, at his command? a strange command from a good being! what good could this do to God, to Abraham, to his son, or to any one else? . . . It is objected that God only gave his command to try Abraham. But what an ignorant imputation upon God was this, as though he did not know the man's heart without so immoral a trial.[2]

In prosecuting Annett the authorities no doubt felt they were putting a stop to the career of a potential rabble-rouser, though there were 'rabble-rousers' on the other side of the question—John Wesley among them—who could certainly match Annett and his followers in their infectious indignation. Annett harps on the theme of the immorality of the Pentateuch and he concludes, 'We plead for no enormities, no immoralities, but to expose them to shew our detestation of them, and declare against impious, sanctified plots, dark insurrection, religious rebellion, and VILLAINY *consecrated with the name of* THE MOST HIGH.'[3] It is no surprise that Annett appeared to the court as an elderly down-and-out with 'some symptoms of wildness,' though one would not have expected him to recant—which he did—before the trial and obligingly plead guilty. The court, taking a realistic view of his poverty, fined him 6*s.* 8*d.* but also sentenced him to a month in Newgate, a year's hard labour, to appear twice in the pillory with a paper reading 'Blasphemy' on his head, and to find sureties for his good behaviour for the rest of his life.

The problem was not simply that the country had reached the

[1] J. Witherspoon, *The Trial of Religious Truth by its Moral Influence* (Glasgow, 1759).

[2] Peter Annett, *The Free Enquirer* [pub. Richard Carlile] (London, 1826), p. 27.

[3] *ibid.,* p. 96.

threshold of general literacy by the end of the eighteenth century and that, as a result, it faced what might be called the democratisation of literature. There were to be few men like Annett in the future who would recant in the face of prosecution. From now on, defendants in cases of seditious as well as blasphemous libel were not isolated dissenters who might be intimidated by the forces of law but eager martyrs for a variety of movements, in whose eventual triumph they had absolute confidence. Events in America and then in France had shown that reform or revolution was a practical possibility and that, if necessary, it could be accompanied by the rejection of religious belief. Extreme demands for press freedom were, under these circumstances, countered by extreme measures to control the press, introduced by ministers who were also convinced that revolution was a practical possibility. By 1792 it seemed that the stage was set for the last and greatest battle between the press and its censors: it was not a matter, for the press, of throwing off a few remaining restraints but rather of resisting the imposition of a political censorship which promised to be far more oppressive than anything the eighteenth century had known.

8

Political Censorship:
A Fight to The Finish 1792–1832

THE FLIGHT OF INTELLECT

In their general enthusiasm for democracy and a democratic culture, Thomas Paine and William Wordsworth sought equally to appeal to 'the essential passions of the heart' in 'a plainer and more emphatic language'[1] than most eighteenth-century authors had been accustomed to use: and there is a distinctly Wordsworthian tone to Paine's denunciation of Burke. 'He is not affected by the reality of distress touching his heart, but by the showy resemblance of it striking his imagination. He pities the plumage, but forgets the dying bird . . . he degenerates into a composition of art, and the genuine soul of nature forsakes him.'[2] For several years both men shared the same enthusiasm for the revolution in France and both were accepted, in their different ways, as the philosophers of democracy. It took some forthright criticism by Matthew Arnold to disabuse the nineteenth century of the idea that 'Wordsworth's poetry is precious because his philosophy is sound; that his "ethical system is as distinctive and capable of exposition as Bishop Butler's;" that his poetry is informed by ideas which "fall spontaneously into a scientific system of thought".'[3] Wordsworth and Paine, one for primarily aesthetic reasons and the other for political purposes accepted the unsophisticated values of 'democratic' literature. In Wordsworth's case this was artlessness for art's sake but to Paine it was the only effective style for preaching his political gospel to the masses. Both men were successful in their own way. Among the middle classes, Wordsworth's 'thought' was elevated to the status of a philosophy through the work of critics like Leslie Stephen, yet the ascendancy which the works and reputation of Paine achieved over the minds and sympathies of most influential members of the working classes is in many ways more remarkable. Both the *Rights of Man* and the *Age of Reason* were condemned by the courts but throughout the first quarter of the nineteenth century

---

[1] William Wordsworth, *Lyrical Ballads* (London, 1802), pp. vii–viii.

[2] Thomas Paine, *The Rights of Man* (London, 1791), p. 24.

[3] Matthew Arnold, *Essays in Criticism: Second Series* (London, 1888), p. 148.

there was no shortage of willing martyrs prepared to go—if not to the stake—to Newgate for six months or a year, in order that the philosophy of Thomas Paine should not go unread or unheard. Prosecutions of his works were undertaken on the grounds of blasphemy as well as sedition and Paine's admirers were quick to exploit this aspect of his writing in their pamphlet warfare.

Superstitition is on her death bed, her Doctors, the Priests, attend on her anxious for her recovery, Hark! 'The Age of Reason' is ringing her dying knell! the hag distorts herself—she cries for blood—for imprisonment—she is dead! The Sun of Reason shines.

> Virtue is truth
> Vice is a lie;
> Paine's Works shall live,
> The Bible shall die.[1]

Of course this level of argument was not one to appeal to everybody and so a number of the most able men of letters, concluding that the level of political and theological debate in England had sunk too low to be worth their attention, turned instead to the great intellectual leader among European nations, Germany. It was from Germany that Immanuel Kant's *Critique of Pure Reason* had come, though it had taken many years to appear in England. Later on, Karl Marx's *Das Kapital* was to suffer similar neglect. By comparison with German metaphysics, English discussions of politics and religion seemed to some observers like an aimless and drunken brawl. 'It is, after all,' said Thomas Carlyle, 'a blessing that, in these revolutionary times, there should be one country where abstract Thought can still take shelter; that while the din and frenzy of Catholic Emancipations, and Rotten Boroughs, and Revolts of Paris, deafen every French and English ear, the German can stand peaceful on his scientific watchtower; and, to the raging, struggling multitude here and elsewhere, solemnly, from hour to hour, with preparatory blast of cowhorn, emit his *Höret ihr Herren und lasset's Euch sagen*; in other words, tell the Universe, which so often forgets that fact, what o'clock it really is.'[2] So Coleridge could turn to Kant, and Strauss's *Leben Jesu* might become the great sensation among theological works of the nineteenth century, while the philosophy of Hegel absorbed men like T. H. Green, Benjamin Jowett, and Edward Caird. On the other hand, there were those who regarded such reverence paid to the aristocracy of German intellect as a betrayal of social democracy. In 1849 Charles Kingsley was to describe Strauss as 'a vile aristocrat, robbing the poor

[1] *Report of the Trial of Humphrey Boyle* (London, 1822), p. 26.
[2] *Sartor Resartus* (London, 1834), pp. 1–2.

man of his Saviour', and eight years later H. T. Buckle in his *History of Civilisation in England* remarked that the intellectual eminence of the few had been paid for in Germany by the ignorance and superstition of the many, and by 'indifference to material and physical interests'.[1] This is an absolute contrast, in Buckle's view, to the situation in America, where there is less learning but what there is has been more evenly shared among the population. At a more personal level and without specific relation to Germany, George Eliot's portrayal of Casaubon in *Middlemarch* (1871–2) is a warning against the excesses of what Carlyle venerates as 'abstract Thought'.

In England no aristocracy of intellect was to dictate the lines of political or theological debate; it was for the most part to be determined by the need to appeal to what the eighteenth century would have termed 'common capacities'. As Cobbett's *Political Register* announced triumphantly in 1816,

The *children* will also have an opportunity of reading, The wife can sometimes read, if the husband cannot. The women will understand the causes of their starvation and raggedness as well as the men, and will lend their aid in endeavouring to effect the proper remedy. Many a father will thus, I hope, be induced to spend his evenings at home in instructing his children in the history of their misery, and in warming them into acts of patriotism.[2]

Unhappily, in those troubled times it was no easy matter to find general agreement as to what constituted an act of patriotism. As the second Lord Ellenborough observed gloomily to the House of Lords, when putting the case for the other side, no good ever came 'from having statesmen at the loom and politicians at the spinning jenny'.[3]

THE FEARFUL EXAMPLE OF FRANCE

In November 1792 at the Crown and Anchor Tavern a meeting was held to form an association whose concern would be to preserve 'Liberty and Property' against 'Levellers and Republicans', and which proposed to attain this end by privately enforcing the laws against seditious literature. If the government would not take strong enough action through the courts to deal with the menace of such subversive books and pamphlets, then it remained for private citizens to group themselves together in this manner and begin prosecutions against the enemies of their country. To many people it must have seemed high time that some such action was taken, since in 1791 a

[1] *The Works of Charles Kingsley* (London, 1879), III, xxvii. H. T. Buckle, *History of Civilisation in England*, I, 219.
[2] 16 November 1816.
[3] *Parl. Deb.*, xli, 1591 (29 December 1819).

book had appeared which justified the revolution in France and would equally justify the overthrow of monarchy, constitution and Parliament in England. This book was, of course, Paine's *Rights of Man*, which had sold 200,000 copies in its first year and was now available in a cheap edition. Moreover, in 1792 a second part had been published, taking Paine's quarrel with Burke a stage further.

Nor was this a case of a single dangerous book circulating, nor of a single author who defied the law in matters of seditious libel. During the previous three years there had been an increasing number of attacks on the government and the royal family, many of which had resulted in prosecutions. One paper the *Morning Herald* got its publishers convicted three times for different seditious libels between March 1789 and March 1790, having suggested among other things that Pitt was using the madness of George III as an opportunity to establish himself as regent, and, indeed, dictator of the country.[1] In 1790-2 Sampson Perry was convicted for six libels (four of them seditious) in his paper the *Argus of the People*: sometimes he was content to attack the ministry, accusing Pitt and others of stock-jobbing, but as time went on he showed an alarming sympathy with the principles of the French revolution.[2] There was no lack of insults directed at the royal family: in 1792 the printer of the *Morning Post* and an associate were convicted of a libel on George III as patron of the arts.[3] John Walter, editor of *The Times* was convicted three times in 1789 of libels in his paper on various members of the royal family, including the Prince of Wales, Prince William, and the Dukes of York, Gloucester, and Cumberland.[4] He was sentenced to a total of two years' imprisonment and £250 in fines.

Throughout 1792 the battle between the government and a press, which all too often showed itself favourably inclined to the revolution in France, continued. It was in that summer that Jeremiah Samuel Jordan was prosecuted and pleaded guilty on a charge of seditious libel for having published the second part of the *Rights of Man* in February. That autumn, while some authors were openly supporting the revolution in France and others were gleefully promising the same thing in England, the association at the Crown and Anchor was formed with John Reeves as its leader. The association was founded as the result of a meeting on 20 November and there were soon attempts to form similar groups all over the country, in the hope that this would counteract the pernicious influence of French republicanism. The government and the loyalists now aimed to de-

[1] P.R.O., K.B. 28/349/33; 354/4; 357/26.
[2] P.R.O., K.B. 28/356/38; 357/23; 358/7; 363/2, 38 and 39.
[3] P.R.O., K.B. 28/361/22; 362/28.   [4] P.R.O., K.B. 28/350/35, 39 and 42.

stroy or at least weaken the opposition press by removing one of its principal supports. Thomas Paine was accordingly indicted for seditious libel in having published his *Rights of Man*.

Paine was not one of those men who in political trials at this time were induced through poverty or self-reliance to conduct their own defence: no less an advocate than Thomas Erskine was briefed for that task. Even before the day of the trial the principal actors in that drama found themselves caught up in it in various unexpected ways. Vigorous attempts were made in particular to persuade Erskine not to accept the brief for Paine's defence. At the end of November he was walking home alone, crossing Hampstead Heath in the evening darkness. Out of the gloom, like an apparition, appeared the figure of Lord Loughborough, who was to assume the office of Lord Chancellor in a few weeks. As the two men faced each other on the dark and deserted heath, Loughborough proclaimed with 'a deep hollowness in his voice', 'Erskine, you must not take Paine's brief.' Erskine, who was not apt to be impressed by melodramatic performances of this sort, replied abruptly, 'But I have been retained, and I will take it, by God.' There the meeting ended.[1] As it happened, Erskine's job was not made any easier when Paine slipped away to Paris before the trial began but there was still considerable sympathy for Paine's views, even in high places, and at the opening of the case the Attorney-General felt obliged to deny to the jury the truth of certain rumours, according to which he had appeared with great reluctance against Paine and the *Rights of Man*.

The *Rights of Man* began as an answer to Burke's *Reflections on the Revolution in France* (1790) but the scope of the argument soon spread to include England as well as France, and from there to a comparison between the absurdities of the English monarchy and the wisdom of the presidential system in the United States. Paine's thesis was simple and left little room for compromise.

All hereditary government is in its nature tyranny. An heritable crown or an heritable throne, or by what other fanciful name such things may be called, have no other significant explanation than that mankind are heritable property. To inherit a government, is to inherit a people, as if they were flocks and herds.[2]

According to Paine, the Glorious Revolution of 1689 had left the people with no right but the right of petitioning, thereby subjecting them to 'The fraud, hypocrisy and imposition of governments. . . . The farce of monarchy and aristocracy'.[3]

[1] Campbell, *Lives of the Lord Chancellors*, VIII, 295.
[2] *Rights of Man. Second Part* (London, 1792), p. 21.   [3] *ibid.*, p. 161.

The time is not very distant when England will laugh at itself for sending to Holland, Hanover, Zell, or Brunswick for men, at the expence of a million a year, who understood neither her laws, her language, nor her interest, and whose capacities would scarcely have fitted them for the office of a parish constable. If government could be trusted to such hands, it must be some easy and simple thing indeed, and materials fit for all the purposes may be found in every town and village in England.[1]

So much for the House of Hanover. Paine's was an uncomplicated view of English politics which saw obvious remedies for obvious problems: it is at once his strength and his weakness.

In the 1792 trial, which took place before Lord Kenyon on 18 December, the passages which I have quoted were included in the indictment, but worse was to come. When the prosecution had been brought Paine had decided to write a letter to the Attorney-General, containing what were described as 'the most impudent calumnies on his Majesty and his sons'. Erskine objected to the introduction of this letter in evidence, on the grounds that Paine was on trial for the *Rights of Man* and not for any letter he might have written to the Attorney-General. Lord Kenyon, however, overruled the objection and the odds against Paine's acquittal must have increased considerably. In any case, Erskine already had to contend with a special jury, who were not likely to be overwhelmed by any impassioned plea he might make for democracy and political freedom. Erskine suggested that in the first place the government had bribed one of the prosecution witnesses, a printer called Chapman, to buy up the entire edition of the *Rights of Man* on their behalf so that it could be quietly suppressed without the publicity of a trial. This seems an unlikely story, since there was more than one edition in existence and, in any case, the government must have known that if they had bought up this particular edition it would only have been a question of time before another appeared. At all events, Chapman denied the allegation. He claimed that the manuscript had been brought to him by Paine, who was drunk, at six o'clock one morning. Chapman printed the first part of the book and the second part as far as sheet H. On examining sheet I, he found that part of it seemed to have 'a dangerous tendency' and discontinued the printing. How he could have got so far without noticing the 'dangerous tendency' of the rest of the book remains unexplained.

Erskine's speech for the defence was powerful and long, three hours and forty minutes. He made no attempt to excuse Paine's remarks in the letter to the Attorney-General, since those remarks were not part of the indictment, and he challenged the prosecution's

[1] *ibid.*, p. 161.

134

method of citing passages from the *Rights of Man* out of their context. His main defence of the book, however, was that unless a man incites his readers to break the law—which, he insisted, Paine had not done —he cannot be guilty of seditious libel. Hostile criticism of existing political institutions is not in itself a seditious libel.

The Liberty of the Press consists in this, that any individual may teach his fellow-citizens doctrines in opposition to those under which they live; he may exercise his own faculties; he may provoke them to the exercise of theirs; he may persuade the whole people to agree with him in these doctrines; and he is not guilty; but if he shall teach it as a doctrine, that any individual may oppose the law of the land, may resist the legal authority, and may, by himself, or in conjunction with others, not merely disobey, but thwart and impede the settled order of society, he would be guilty of a libel upon the record. Shew me an expression like these in the book of Thomas Paine; shew me from any part of the evidence [which] the Attorney-General has brought forward, any thing to prove the evil mind of the Author.[1]

Despite all Erskine's powers of argument, a verdict of guilty was returned, though Paine was not there to hear it. The trial was none-theless followed by a great popular demonstration in favour of Erskine. The crowd unharnessed the horses from his carriage and themselves pulled him to his lodgings in Serjeant's Inn, among shouts of 'Erskine for ever,' 'Erskine and the Rights of Juries,' (recalling his conduct in the case of the Dean of St. Asaph) 'Erskine and the Rights of the Press', 'Erskine and the Liberties of the Press'. To have failed to sway a special jury in the circumstances of 1792 was no great discredit, and the special jury system remained an accepted part of the system of political censorship for another quarter of a century, by which time it seemed to operate in so scandalous a manner that it was a liability to the government rather than a support.

The crusade against the works of Thomas Paine continued and early in 1793 another publisher, Henry Delahay Symonds was sent to prison for a year and fined £100 for selling Paine's *Letter Addressed to the Addressers on the late Proclamation*.[2] Indeed, Symonds had been tried once before, on the same day, for seditious libel in publishing *The Jockey Club* and had been sentenced to a year's imprisonment and a fine of £100 for that as well. Yet the government and its supporters were not the only ones who were active at this time. If the formation of the association at the Crown and Anchor in November

---

[1] *The Trial at Large of Thomas Paine*, n.d., p. 15.
[2] A royal proclamation against seditious writings had been issued on 21 May 1792.

1792 had failed to stimulate believers in a free press into action, the outcome of Paine's trial in the following month soon remedied that. On 22 December the first meeting of the 'Friends to the Liberty of the Press' was convened by public advertisement at the Free-Mason's Tavern with a Member of Parliament, Gerard Noel Edwards, in the chair. Naturally enough, the meeting unanimously resolved that liberty of the press—'the free discussion of all matters of the Principles of Civil Government, and of all matters of public opinion'—was essential to the health of the government and constitution.[1] One of the supporters of this new association was Erskine himself and so it is not unexpected to find that the meeting reiterated his distinction between literature which incited men to break the law (and was therefore seditious and criminal) and literature which confined itself to commenting unfavourably upon existing political institutions, which was justifiable criticism and in no way criminal. At a second meeting of the Association in January 1793 Erskine himself took the chair and five hundred signatures were collected for a *Declaration of the Friends to the Freedom of the Press*. A third meeting in March with Richard Brinsley Sheridan in the chair resolved that ten thousand copies of the declaration should be printed and distributed. The *Declaration* was a reaffirmation of belief in a free Press and an attack on those bodies—in effect the Crown and Anchor association set up in the previous November—which employed paid informers to facilitate prosecutions of works whose political opinions it disliked.

The Friends to the Liberty of the Press, in their turn, provoked a great deal of acrimonious comment. In January 1793, in a sermon before the House of Lords, Samuel Horsley deplored the 'freedom of dispute, in which, for several years past, it hath been the folly in this country to indulge'.[2] Yet those who advocated a stricter political censorship were prepared to state their motives more specifically than this. As John Bowles put it in his *Short Answer to the Declaration of the Persons calling themselves the Friends of the Liberty of the Press*, 'As long as Anarchy shall reign in a neighbouring country, the project of introducing it into this will not be abandoned'.[3]

During the remaining years of the century the government spared no effort to curb the spread of seditious opinion and, indeed, by 1798 it seems a measure of their success that Charles James Fox could write, 'one can hardly conceive how any prudent tradesman can venture to publish any thing that can, in any way, be disagreeable to the mini-

---

[1] *Proceedings of the Friends to the Liberty of the Press* (1793), Sig. A^r.
[2] *Sermon Preached Before the Lords Spiritual and Temporal* (London, 1793), Sig. B^r.
[3] (London, 1793), p. 24.

sters'.[1] In 1793, after the successful prosecution of Paine, there was a spate of further prosecutions for seditious libel but the results were not altogether satisfactory from the government's point of view. Daniel Isaac Eaton was tried in June for publishing the *Rights of Man* but the jury would go no further than saying that he was guilty of publishing the book but without criminal intent. In the following month Eaton was tried again for another seditious libel, Paine's *Letter Addressed to the Addressers on the late Proclamation.*[2] Once again the jury refused to give an unqualified verdict but would only say 'guilty of publishing the pamphlet in question'. Although this was a special jury, the foreman's reply to Lord Kenyon's impatient cajoling was 'we cannot give any other verdict.'[3] (In 1794 Eaton was prosecuted yet again for publishing *Politics for the People: or Hog's Wash* and this time there was an unqualified verdict but it was one of not guilty.)

An even more frustrating case from the point of view of Lord Kenyon was the prosecution of Lambert and Perry, editor and printer of the *Morning Chronicle* for a seditious libel in their edition of 25 December 1792. They had reprinted the address to a society for political information set up at Derby, a society whose aim was the reform of Parliament so that those who paid taxes should also be entitled to vote. This address complained about the high level of taxation and the frequency of wars, adding, 'we are persuaded that the interests of the poor can never be promoted by the accession of territory, when bought at the expense of their labour and blood'.[4] Once again it was Erskine who appeared for the defence while Lord Kenyon summed up in a manner which was, to say the least, unsympathetic to the two defendants. His remarks were well-laced with warnings on the licentiousness of the press and the danger of importing revolution from France. At two o'clock in the afternoon the jury retired and Kenyon, believing that an early verdict was unlikely, went home. At seven in the evening the jury was taken in coaches to his house to deliver its verdict. 'Guilty of publishing but with no malicious intent.' Kenyon's reply was a flat rejection. 'I cannot record that verdict; it is no verdict at all.' The jury retired again and at nearly five o'clock in the morning returned a verdict of not guilty, in which Kenyon can have found little comfort.[5]

Yet it would be quite misleading to suggest that the government's campaign at the level of criminal prosecution was a complete failure. Not every publisher could afford to be defended by Erskine, so men

[1] H. T. Buckle, *History of Civilisation in England*, I, 449.
[2] *State Trials*, XXII, 753–822.   [3] *ibid.*, XXII, 822.
[4] *ibid.*, XXII, 956.   [5] *ibid.*, XXII, 1020.

like Henry Symonds, James Ridgway, and Daniel Holt were convicted and sent to prison or fined. In any case, the government did not always have to rely on the verdict of a jury to make its displeasure felt: a publisher could be penalised simply by having to face a prosecution, as one observer of the provincial scene noted in 1793.

The prosecutions that are commenced by government all over England against printers, publishers, &c., would astonish you; and most of these are for offences committed many months ago. The printer of the *Manchester Herald*, has had seven different indictments preferred against him for paragraphs in his paper; and six *different* indictments for selling or disposing of six different copies of Paine,—all previous to the *trial* of Paine. The man was opulent, supposed worth 20,000 l.; but these different actions will ruin him as they were intended to do.[1]

They might ruin him even if he were innocent, since the government could bring charges enough to bankrupt a man by the expenses of the case, though the jury acquitted him. So far as the *Manchester Herald* was concerned, the records of King's Bench include four indictments brought against Matthew Falkner and four against William Birch for seditious libels published in the paper between October and December of 1792.[2] The cases were not heard in Manchester but at Westminster, and the cost of contesting four or five such prosecutions at that distance would have been enough to bankrupt most publishers. The answer to this, as the radical press discovered, was to launch a public subscription to cover the cost of the defence and by this means some thousands of pounds were provided for defendants in the more celebrated cases. (After the three trials of William Hone in December 1817, nearly £2,500 was subscribed for him.)

Prosecutions were no longer instituted mainly in London, though provincial cases might at some stage be transferred to the court of King's Bench at Westminster. Manchester and Nottingham provided the cases of the *Manchester Herald* and Daniel Holt, while in 1793 Edinburgh saw one of the most notorious prosecutions of this kind brought against a young advocate, Thomas Muir. Muir was charged with sedition on the strength of having addressed meetings on parliamentary reform in language which, according to Lord Campbell fifty years later, 'in the years 1831 and 1832 would have been considered tame and conservative'.[3] Moreover, Muir was said to have distributed seditious literature, and a copy of the *Rights of Man* was found in his greatcoat pocket. The jurors in his case were selected by the presiding judge, and the jury was so packed that every member of it belonged to

[1] Buckle, *History of Civilisation in England*, I, 447.
[2] P.R.O., K.B. 28/365/7, 8, 9, 10.
[3] Campbell, *Lives of the Lord Chancellors*, VIII, 143.

an association hostile to parliamentary reform. A petition on Muir's behalf was organised during the case but the judge in his summing up scornfully insisted that 'no attention would be paid to such a rabble. What right have they to representation?'[1] Muir was found guilty and received the savage sentence of fourteen years' transportation. The House of Lords though urged to intervene on his behalf decided, on the advice of Lord Loughborough, not to do so.

In 1794 came the farce of the so-called 'Treason trials', when the government chose to prosecute twelve members of corresponding societies, including Horne Tooke, on charges relating to treasonable conspiracies to overthrow the constitution. The men were acquitted *en masse*, with Erskine once again appearing for the defence. Thwarted in its attempt to deal with men through the courts, the government began to legislate. As the crisis deepened, the Habeas Corpus Act was suspended and then in 1795 a new Act was passed by which all public meetings were forbidden unless publicly announced in the press five days before they were to take place: the purpose of the meeting had to be made clear in the announcement. Yet in its dealings with the press the ministry had other weapons which it could use without having to seek parliamentary sanction and without fear of disappointment through an obstinate jury. In the first place, a large number of newspapers were in the pay of the ministry—including those like *The Times* and the *Morning Herald* which, as we have seen, had been involved in prosecutions at the time. They were in the pay of the ministry in the sense that they received regular payments from the secret service accounts which, because they were secret, did not have to be disclosed to Parliament. Newspapers had, of course, always been subject to this political influence and the £5,000 a year which Pitt's administration distributed among them in the 1790s showed no increase on the sums paid out by Walpole's administration half a century earlier. Regular payments ranged from £100 a year to the *Public Ledger* to £300 a year for *The Times* and £600 a year for papers like the *Morning Herald* and the *World*. (The purchasing power of the pound was then about ten times as great as in the mid-twentieth century.) To attack the government and lose an allowance of £600 every year was a far greater financial disaster than to be convicted in a court of law and fined £100. On the other hand, the government had to consider the possibility that if, when a paper like the *Morning Herald* was in trouble with the courts, payment was stopped, the result might be a hostile journal completely beyond ministerial control.

Another weapon at the government's disposal and one which it frequently employed was the Attorney-General's power of filing an

[1] *ibid.*, VIII, 144.

ex-officio information against a publisher in cases of seditious libel. Once the Attorney-General had filed his *ex officio* information, the court would either demand bail of the defendant or, in default of bail, commit him to prison to await his trial. As the sums demanded in bail might be anything up to £1,000 many recalcitrant editors and publishers had no option but to spend six months or more in prison waiting to be tried. They might be acquitted but that was small compensation. Worse still, there was no time limit on the prosecution, so that a publisher might have the charge hanging over him as a threat, while being put to considerable expense at the same time. Not until 1819 was a law passed which required the Attorney-General to bring the case to trial within a year of filing the information. In 1796 John Smith spent seven months in prison waiting to be tried for selling a seditious libel, *A Summary of the Duties of Citizenship*. At his trial he complained that his health had deteriorated in Newgate and produced two doctors to substantiate this. Yet when he was found guilty, Lord Kenyon announced that the discipline of the prison at Clerkenwell was so salubrious as even to restore invalids to health, and he sent Smith there for two years.

Before the final decade of the eighteenth century was over it seemed possible that there would be no need for English revolutionaries to start their own uprising, since France would impose revolution on England by military force—this, at least, was the fear of many people. To others, such a solution to the political crisis was acceptable enough and they had no hesitation in saying so. As in the American revolutionary war, old-style patriotism was replaced for them by political ideals which knew no territorial limits. The war with France, which had begun in 1793, had gone badly and by 1798 a French invasion seemed quite likely. What if the French should come and find that England's will to resist had been undermined by republican propaganda? Indictments for seditious libel began to refer specifically to the crime of discouraging the King's subjects from 'resisting and opposing' the enemies of the Crown. The most important libel of this kind was published at the height of the invasion scare, by Gilbert Wakefield: it was *A Reply to some Parts of the Bishop of Llandaff's Address*. This was dangerous stuff indeed. The author attacked the corruption of the present ministry and the imposition of a military despotism on the country, referring, no doubt, not only to war-time measures in England but to the insurrection in Ireland during the previous year. Under these circumstances he would support any benevolent government rather than the one at present in control of Great Britain. If the French should invade, monarchists might resist them, but for his part he would offer them no opposition.

The government had already shown itself extremely sensitive to any comment on the war which might seem to show sympathy for Frenchmen and question its own moral position. In 1798, for example, James Stamp had been prosecuted for publishing a letter in the *Courier*, in which he had the temerity to suggest that French prisoners-of-war were being kept in insanitary conditions at Liverpool. The *Reply to the Bishop of Llandaff* was a far more serious matter than that. Prosecutions were brought against Wakefield and any other bookseller who dared to stock the publication. As a matter of fact, the first to be tried and sentenced was Jeremiah Samuel Jordan, who had published Paine's *Rights of Man* in 1792 and suffered for that as well. Soon afterwards Wakefield himself was sentenced to two years' imprisonment, while James Cuthell, who had never read the publication and had no idea that it might be considered seditious, was fined £50 when it was proved that one of his assistants had sold copies of it. There was to be no lasting peace with France for another seventeen years and during that time the government would have plenty of reasons for trying to suppress criticism of its conduct of the war.

In Ireland, no less than in the rest of the country, the press had become an object of ministerial concern before the massacres of 1798. In February 1797 Arthur O'Connor and the two proprietors of the *Northern Star* were imprisoned for seditious libel: three months later the premises of the newspaper were raided by English soldiers, who broke up the type and seized the presses. Lord Edward Fitzgerald and a group of Irish patriots established a successor to the *Northern Star*, which was to be called the *Press*. What Lord Edward and his friends did not know was that one of the shareholders, Leonard McNally, was a government agent whose brief was to keep a close watch on the development of the paper and report on it to his employers. Not surprisingly, within three months Peter Finnerty, the editor, had been charged and convicted of seditious libel. In 1793 Ireland had had its own Libel Act, similar to the Act of 1792 in England, but in those unhappy years when the hopes of many Irishmen must have been pinned on France rather than on England, freedom of the press was never likely to be much more than an admirable theory.

At Westminster the time had come for stricter control of the press by more legislation. The stamp duty on newspapers, which had begun at a penny a sheet in 1712, had been raised to a penny halfpenny in 1776 and then to twopence in 1789—at which time it had also been made illegal to hire out newspapers—and then in 1797 the stamp duty had almost been doubled, being raised from twopence to threepence halfpenny a sheet. The effect on newspaper prices of these succesive increases was predictable enough. The price of *The Times*, for instance, which had begun life in 1785 as the *Daily Universal Register*, rose from twopence halfpenny to sixpence in the first twenty years of its existence. Yet this increase in stamp duty was not enough on its own to curb the licentiousness of the press: even if it was now illegal to hire out newspapers at a penny a time, newspaper reading rooms were springing up—one had opened in Glasgow as early as 1794—where those of the rabble who could read might absorb the poison of democracy and sedition and might also read it aloud to, or otherwise infect, those who still remained illiterate.

To deal with this dangerous situation an Act was passed in 1799 'for the more effectual Suppression of Societies established for Seditious and Treasonable Practices'. Under the provisions of this law it became illegal to run a circulating library or a reading-room unless an annual licence was granted by two magistrates: the owner of an unlicensed library or reading room was liable to a fine of £100 a day. All places used for lecturing or debating, whether indoors or outdoors, had to be similarly licensed. Nor was this all. If the press was to be properly controlled, the means of production as well as those of distribution would have to be adequately supervised. All printers, letter founders, and printing press manufacturers were therefore to give notice of their trade to the Clerk of the Peace, with the exception of the royal printers and the presses of the two Universities. Strict accounts were to be kept of the sale of presses and type, while printers were to keep a copy of every book or pamphlet printed by them with the name and address of the person for whom they had printed it written upon that copy. Most important of all, the name and address of the printer was to appear on every publication issued by him: failure to do this entailed a fine of £20 for every *copy* of a book issued, so that an edition of five hundred copies with the name and address of the printer missing made him liable, in theory, to a fine of £10,000! In 1811 the government took a more realistic view of this penalty and the law was altered so that the maximum fine that could be imposed was £500. Not since the seventeenth century had the press been subject to such restrictions as this, even though in the reign of Queen Anne there had been the threat of a law which would require that publications should carry the author's name and address, there had never been a serious likelihood of legislation on the matter.

Unlike many attempts to control the press, the law of 1799 seems to have been effective, at least to the extent that printers registered themselves at the time. In another thirty years or so many of its provisions were disregarded but if it worked during political crisis and national danger, this was primarily what its supporters wanted. In its preamble, the Act refers to 'a traitorous Conspiracy . . . long . . .

carried on, in conjunction with the Persons from Time to Time exercising the Powers of Government in *France*, to overturn the Laws, Constitution, and Government, and every existing Establishment, Civil and Ecclesiastical, both in *Great Britain* and *Ireland*.' As time went on the bogy of subversion and revolution directed from France seemed little more than a shibboleth. If there was to be a revolution in the earlier nineteenth century, it would be English both in inspiration and character, coming not from abroad but below. In this sense, a later complaint in the Act seems more to the point when it refers to the criminality of those who have dispersed 'Papers of an irreligious, treasonable, and seditious Nature . . . among the lower Classes of the Community, either *gratis*, or at very low Prices'.

At the beginning of the nineteenth century the press, in theory at least, seemed less free than it had been at any time since the deposition of the Stuarts, nor did there appear to be any willingness on the part of the press or its enemies to seek a compromise. The legislation of 1799 might be taken as bearing powerful witness to Joseph Priestley's remark in the same year that there was 'no longer any hope of a peaceable and gradual reform'.

COMMUNISTS, ARISTOCRATS, AND THE CONDUCT OF WAR: 1800–1815[1]

The disillusionment of many would-be revolutionaries in England with the way in which the French revolution had developed—or, perhaps, degenerated—into the Empire of Napoleon, was by no means successful in uniting the country against the threat of a French invasion in the early years of the nineteenth century. Authors and publishers were still being fined and imprisoned for anti-war propaganda: Jonathan Panther was fined £100 and gaoled for three months in 1804 for such publications, while in 1805 despite the spirit of Trafalgar, Thomas Rickman was convicted for publishing Paine's letter *To the People of England*, on the invasion of England, a French invasion of course. By a choice irony, Paine was thrown into prison in France by the agents of that very revolution which he had done so much to defend: yet, as he would have been the first to recognise, the shortcomings of the revolutionaries hardly made the 'farce of monarchy and aristocracy' any easier to tolerate. In England the enthusiasm for revolutionary France was often replaced by a simple lack of inclination to resist a French invasion. 'What must I say if the French come?'

[1] The term 'communism' was not used in English politics until the 1840s but in its general application it describes certain views on communal ownership in the earlier nineteenth century.

demanded Thomas Spence in 1801, 'If they feelingly ask me what I am fighting for?' For this and for other sentiments he was fined £20 and sent to prison for a year. Between 1792 and 1795 he had been three times indicted and committed to prison for political libels but never before convicted. Spence was a communist, as opposed to Communist, who believed in the abolition of private property and the creation of an egalitarian society: the eccentric purity of his political vision would no doubt have got him into just as much trouble in France as in England. His political beliefs, as expressed in *The Restorer of Society to its Natural State* brought him before Lord Kenyon and a special jury in Westminster Hall. Despite its use of the word 'Citizen' as a form of address, Spence's views on society seem to relate much more to the dreams of a new and unattainable ideal like the Susquehanna dreams of Coleridge and Southey rather than to the reformation of a society as complex as those of England or France. It seems appropriate that in 1816 his disciples should have petitioned Parliament to do away with machinery. Eccentric purity took another form when the account of his trial was issued as a phonetic transcript— *Dh'e 'Imp'ort'ant Tri'al ov T'om'is Sp'ens*—in 1803.

At this time there was no censorship of war news and, indeed, one of Wellington's complaints during the peninsular campaign was that English newspapers were useful sources of military intelligence to the French, but presumably it was felt that by the time the enemy obtained information through the English newspapers it was no longer of much military value. So far as the press was concerned, news of the war travelled slowly. The Battle of Waterloo, not far distant geographically from London, had been over for four days when *The Times* published its official account, while *The Times* account of the Battle of Trafalgar appeared more than two weeks after the battle had been fought. It was not until the Crimean War that there was any real pressure by the army—or any real justification—for a press censorship of war news.

Government censorship at this time had not only to contend with those who offered moral support to the enemy or revealed military information: there were others as hostile to France as the government was and whose main objection was that the government was not prosecuting the war with sufficient skill or energy. In 1807 charges were brought against the *Morning Post* by the short-lived Whig administration for alleging that British soldiers were being transported in ships so rotten as to be in danger of sinking. Fortunately for the *Morning Post* there was a change of government and the charges were dropped. Less fortunate was Daniel Lovell who published a letter in the *Statesman* in 1812 claiming that money intended for the upkeep of prisoners of war was being retained for five or six months by the Commissioners of the Transport Board so that they could use it for stock-jobbing. He was fined £500 and sent to prison for eighteen months.

A favourite target of the libellers was the British Commander-in-Chief, the Duke of York, during the years 1808–10. In the Duke's case, the difficulty was that the truth of some of the 'libels' was evident to most impartial observers and would have been evident to a great many more, given the publicity of a trial. Not until the Libel Act of 1843 was it possible to put forward as a defence in a libel case that the libel was in fact true, but there was nothing to stop the country drawing its own conclusions. By 1810 when John Harriott Hart and Henry White were charged with having libelled the Duke of York by questioning his competence and condemning him as 'a prodigal spendthrift, licentious Debauchee, and double Adulterer', the Attorney-General was only too glad of an excuse to drop the case.[1] (White was also prosecuted the next year for an attack on the conduct of the war by 'our imbecile cabinet').[2] The most celebrated series of prosecutions involving the Duke of York was in 1808–9 and concerned *Major Hogan's Appeal*. Major Denis Hogan was a disgruntled army officer who had been denied promotion, and so he had put his case, unsuccessfully, to the Duke of York, as Commander-in-Chief. Later, according to Hogan, it was suggested to him that £600 discreetly distributed in bribes would ensure his promotion. Indignant at this, he prepared a pamphlet for publication, in which he proposed to reveal the corruption he had discovered in high military places: this pamphlet was duly advertised in the press. But before it could be put on sale, a well-dressed lady in a barouche called at the newspaper office for Hogan's address. When Hogan returned to his lodgings, he discovered £500 waiting for him with an anonymous letter which promised him that if he remained silent he would earn the gratitude of the royal family. Furious at this, he determined to return the money and, meanwhile, the whole story was made public by John and Leigh Hunt in their liberal or radical weekly, the *Examiner*, which they had started that year. The government brought a prosecution against them and against several other defendants who had published *Major Hogan's Appeal*. However, before the cases could be tried, a Member of Parliament, Colonel Wardle, produced an ex-mistress of the Duke of York before the bar of the House of Commons. This woman confessed that she had used her liaison (and the public knowledge of it) to extort money from gullible army officers who sought promotion. Under these circumstances the prosecutions had to be dropped and

[1] P.R.O., K.B. 28/433/34.   [2] P.R.O., K.B. 28/436/31.

the Duke of York was obliged to resign as Commander-in-Chief, only to be reappointed in May 1811.

The other great scandal of the war years, which involved the political freedom of the press, was the question of military flogging. In 1810 William Cobbett, who with three other men had been charged with seditious libel, was sentenced to two years' imprisonment for an article in his *Weekly Political Register* of 1 July 1809 criticising the manner in which a mutiny of the local militia at Ely had been put down by German mercenaries under General Auckland and the leaders of the mutiny sentenced to 500 lashes. A means of discipline, as Cobbett remarked, 'so conducive to the producing in them a disposition to defend the Country at the risk of their lives'. The complete libel for which Cobbett and the others were sentenced will be found in the second part of this book.

Two years later there was a pair of prosecutions, both for the publication of John Scott's article 'One Thousand Lashes'. This had first appeared in John Drakard's *Stamford News* and was then reprinted by John and Leigh Hunt in their *Examiner*. The Hunts were tried in London and Drakard in Lincoln a few weeks later. The article referred to the news of the sentence of a thousand lashes imposed upon a private, William Clifford, at Canterbury. The punishment ended, as a result of the victim's total insensibility, after 750 lashes had been inflicted. Another soldier, Corporal Curtis, was reprieved after 250 lashes on condition that he volunteered for service overseas. A number of other men had 2,600 lashes shared between them for 'disrespectful behaviour to their officers'. John Scott, in his article, compared the treatment of English soldiers, in this respect, unfavourably with that of their French counterparts. 'In short Buonaparte's soldiers cannot form any notion of the most heartrending of all exhibitions on this side hell—an English military flogging'. Despite the efforts of the Attorney-General (Sir Vicary Gibbs), and the hostility of Lord Ellenborough's summing up, the London jury acquitted the Hunts, deciding that this attack on military flogging was not seditious. The unexpected sequel to this was that when the case against Drakard was heard at Lincoln only a few weeks later he was found guilty and sentenced to eighteen months' imprisonment.

In the early years of the nineteenth century individuals showed themselves far more litigious in matters of personal defamation than they had ever been before. As if to fall in with the general trend, political criticism tended more and more to involve the denigration of an individual, whether the King, the Prince, or a humble Inspector of Taxes. In the last ten years or so of the eighteenth century there had been a number of libels on members of the royal family but in the opening years of the nineteenth there was a wider selection of targets. In 1804 Cobbett was convicted of libelling Lord Hardwicke, the Lord-Lieutenant of Ireland; three years later Colonel Draper was convicted of a libel on the Rt. Hon. John Sullivan, Under-Secretary of State for the Colonial Department, and in the following year, John Harriott Hart and Henry White were condemned for libelling the administration of public justice in England in general and Lord Chief Justice Ellenborough in particular. Such was the type of prosecution now being brought. At Cobbett's trial, Ellenborough had laid down the limits of press criticism of individuals in authority, using terms which if strictly interpreted would have left little room for criticism at all.

It has been observed, that it is the right of the British subject to exhibit the folly or imbecility of the members of the government. But, gentlemen, we must confine ourselves within limits. If, in so doing, individual feelings are violated, there the line of interdiction begins, and the offence becomes the subject of penal visitation.[1]

If ministers or others in public life had only to prove that their feelings had been 'violated', in order to obtain convictions for libel, the outlook for the press was bleak in the extreme. The logical answer to Ellenborough came sixteen years later from Jeremy Bentham.

'If individual feelings are violated'—i.e. in plain English, if, on the part of any one of the persons so situated, any uneasiness is in this way produced,—as often as any written discourse, productive of this effect, is published, every person, instrumental in the publication, is to be punished for it. Now, if there be any sort of proof by which, more than by any other a man's having experienced uneasiness, from the cause in question, is effectually demonstrated and put out of doubt, it is surely the fact of his having imposed upon himself the expense, and trouble, and odium, of prosecuting for it. Admit but this, the consequence is as satisfactory as it is simple. It is—that, in every case of libel, 'on the members of the government,' the

---

[1] F. L. Holt, *The Law of Libel* (London, 1812), p. 119.

When Lambert and Perry were prosecuted in 1792 for a seditious libel in the *Morning Chronicle*, Lord Kenyon made much the same point as Ellenborough. His words may explain why the jury (knowing that Kenyon had already decided the question of law on the libellous nature of the paper) used their only remaining power and acquitted the defendants on the question of fact. Kenyon said: 'I think this paper was published with a wicked, malicious intent, to vilify the government, and to make the people discontented with the constitution under which they live,—That is the matter charged in the Information; that it was done with a view to vilify the constitution, the laws, and the government of this country, and to infuse into the minds of His Majesty's subjects a belief that they were oppressed and on this ground, I consider it as a gross and seditious libel'. (Erskine, *Speeches*, II, 450–1.)

very act of prosecution is conclusive evidence of the guiltiness of the party prosecuted, and a verdict of guilty ought to follow, of course.[1]

Before long, Castlereagh, Sir Robert Peel and others had joined the list of victims of these libellous publications but no man was so frequently or mercilessly 'victimised' as the future George IV, both as Prince of Wales and as Prince Regent. Even before the end of the eighteenth century there was a growing need to check the outspoken comments on the future King. In 1797 and 1798 Mary Vint and Allan Macleod were convicted of a libel on the Prince which appeared in the *Gazetteer*, libelling him by commenting on his moral conduct.

The system of his conduct has been combined after excursions into the luxuriant regions of wild and reinless passion, he has infinitely extended the capacity of vice, and been himself the ingenious projector of her thousand engines to corrupt or emaciate or unnerve the mind.

Yet many people were prepared to forgive the Prince his amorous escapades and extravagant style of comfort, so long as they could believe in the political goodness of his heart. When he became King, it was thought, the liberal cause would prosper and the plight of the Catholics in Ireland might be heeded. As a matter of fact, when he became Regent in 1811, he reinstated the Duke of York as Commander-in-Chief and, to the dismay of liberals and radicals, retained the existing Tory administration, which two pro-Whig peers, Grey and Grenville, now refused to work with. As for the Irish, their cause was forgotten.

On 17 March 1812 the annual St. Patrick's Day dinner of the Benevolent Society of St. Patrick was held in London at the Freemason's Tavern in Great Queen Street, birthplace of the Association of Friends to the Liberty of the Press. When the King's health was proposed, according to *The Times*, 'This toast was drunk with three times three and was received with enthusiasm. It was followed by the air of *God Save the King*, which was sung in a very superior style and with full chorus.'[2] But when the toast of the Prince Regent was proposed, there were sounds of disapproval at the mention of his name, mingled with shouts of 'Change the subject!' Sheridan, who was present, protested in vain at the 'silent and surly manner in which the health of the Prince Regent had been drunk', but those who had been either silent or surly remained unmoved by this reproach. At the same time, when the insult to the Prince became known, the *Morning Post* reproved those responsible for it for their 'ungenerous, unmanly

---

[1] Jeremy Bentham, *The King against Edmunds and Others* (London, 1820), pp. 10–11.
[2] 18 March 1812.

conduct', and by way of affirming its own loyalty it addressed the Prince (in French, Italian, Spanish, and English), employing terms of flattery which were not so much extravagant as ludicrous. 'You are the *Glory of the People*—You are the *Protector of the Arts*—You are the *Maecenas of the Age*. Wherever you appear, *you conquer all hearts*, wipe away tears, excite *desire and love*, and win *beauty* towards you— You breathe *eloquence*—You inspire the Graces—You are an *Adonis in loveliness*.'[1] Leigh Hunt later said of the *Examiner* that it began by being of no party but reform soon gave it one. In this paper, on 22 March 1812, he examined the hysterical and sycophantic outburst of the *Morning Post*.

What person, unacquainted with the true state of the case would imagine in reading these astounding eulogies, that this 'Glory of the people', was the subject of millions of shrugs and reproaches! that this 'Protector of the Arts' had named a wretched foreigner his historical painter, in disparage- ment or in ignorance of the merits of his own countrymen!—that this 'Maecenas of the age' patronised not a single deserving writer!—that this 'Breather of eloquence' could not say a few decent extempore words, if we are to judge, at least, from what he said to his regiment on its embarkation for Portugal!—that this 'Conqueror of hearts' was the disappointer of hopes!—that this 'Exciter of desire' (bravo! Messieurs of the *Post*)—this '*Adonis* in loveliness,' was a corpulent man of fifty!—in short, this *delightful, blissful, wise, pleasureable, honourable, virtuous, true*, and *immortal* Prince, was a violator of his word, a libertine over head and ears in disgrace, a despiser of domestic ties, the companion of gamblers and demireps, a man who has just closed half a century without one single claim on the gratitude of his country, or the respect of posterity!

These are hard truths; but are they *not* truths? And have we not suffered enough—are we not now suffering bitterly—from the disgusting flatteries of which the above is a repetition? . . . Flattery in any shape is unworthy a man and a gentleman; but political flattery is almost a request to be made slaves. If we would have the great to be what they ought, we must find some means or other to speak of them as they are.

All too often Leigh Hunt has been dismissed as the author of a num- ber of facile, whimsical essays; a poet whose *Story of Rimini* is known as a verbal source of inspiration for Keats rather than for any excel- lence of its own; the man who in his later years was depicted by Dickens in the character of Harold Skimpole in *Bleak House*,'brilliant, vivacious, sentimental, but thoroughly selfish'. It is only fair that the verve and courage of the radical journalist should be set in the balance against all these.

At first there was an attempt to bribe John and Leigh Hunt with

[1] Leigh Hunt, *Autobiography* (London, 1850), II, 126.

the offer that if they would in future refrain from all comment on the Prince, they would neither be fined nor imprisoned on this occasion, if it should be necessary to bring them to trial. The offer was rejected and the trial began in the court of King's Bench on 9 December 1812 with Lord Ellenborough presiding. It was claimed by the *Examiner* that no less than five of the jurors were employees of the ministry but, whether this was true or not, John and Leigh Hunt were found guilty. Mr. Justice Grosse, sitting with Lord Ellenborough, pronounced sentence of two years' imprisonment and a fine of £500 on each of them, although according to Leigh Hunt it was Ellenborough who betrayed more signs of guilt than anyone else in court.

He knew that we were acquainted with his visits to Carlton-house and Brighton (sympathies not eminently decent in a judge), and with the good things which he had obtained for his kinsmen; and we could not help preferring our feelings at the moment to those which induced him to keep his eyes fixed on his papers, which he did almost the whole time of our being in court, never turning them once to the place on which we stood.[1]

Ellenborough's impartiality had not always been beyond question and there had been considerable disquiet in 1806 when, as Chief Justice of the King's Bench, he was appointed to a seat in the cabinet: if justice were to be seen to be done, it might be unfortunate for a man who was accused of libelling the government to have his case judged by a cabinet minister. As it happened, the Whigs were out of office by 1807—and Ellenborough was out of the cabinet—but then, as Sir Vicary Gibbs, the new Tory Attorney-General, remarked after an acquittal, 'We shall never get a verdict for the Crown while the Chief Justice is in opposition'. So far as seditious libels were concerned, however, Sir Vicary need not have worried: no one in the Tory party could have been more severe upon them than Lord Ellenborough.

The case of the Hunts was only one of many in which there were verdicts for the Crown. The belief that Ellenborough was present less as a judge than as a representative of the Prince's interests was shared by a number of people and found expression in Tom Moore's *Two-penny Post-Bag* (1813), in which the Prince says of the trial:

> *A compliment too to his Lordship the Judge*
> *For his speech to the Jury—and zounds! who would grudge*
> *Turtle soup, though it came to five guineas a bowl*
> *To reward such a loyal and complaisant soul?*
> *We were all in high gig—Roman Punch and Tokay*

[1] *Autobiography*, II, 134.

Travelled round, till our heads travell'd just the same way,
And we cared not for Juries or Libels—no—damme! nor
Ev'n for the threats of last Sunday's Examiner![1]

Nevertheless, the prosecution had succeeded. The two brothers went to prison on 3 February 1813, and were kept there until almost the last moment on 3 February 1815. Looking back on the whole sad episode in his *Autobiography* in 1850, Leigh Hunt remarked, 'I am no republican, nor ever was, though I have lived during a period of history when kings themselves tried hard to make honest men republicans by their apparent unteachableness'.[2]

By the time that John and Leigh Hunt emerged from their separate prisons, Europe was facing the final months of the Napoleonic wars and the prospect of a lasting peace to follow. Whether it would be a peace that implied more than the cessation of international hostilities seemed doubtful. Reform had replaced revolution as the political ideal of radicals in England but reform might have to be attained through a certain amount of violence and bloodshed, For the government to reduce the press to obedience would not in itself have been enough to thwart the aims of the reformers but it might have postponed the realisation of those aims for a considerable time—so, at least, the government seemed to think. The opening years of the nineteenth century had seen the most determined efforts by men like Sir Vicary Gibbs to bring the press to heel. In 1808 a law was passed giving the Attorney-General the power to arrest and hold to bail any publisher against whom he chose to file an *ex officio* information. Nor was this a power to be reserved for use in some great national emergency. Since 1760 two or three such informations, on an average, had been filed each year, but between 1807 and 1810 there were forty-two cases, twenty of them on a single day. True, this had been in a time of war, when any government might have been sensitive to the requirements of internal as well as external security, but the omens for the peace which followed in 1815 were hardly more encouraging. In the year of ultimate victory, the ministry raised the stamp duty on newspapers from threepence halfpenny to fourpence a sheet, so that, for example, the price of *The Times* was now sixpence halfpenny and most of that represented taxation. As a matter of fact, the government was only narrowly deterred from raising the duty to fourpence halfpenny in 1815. As the *Morning Chronicle* wrote on 3 June 1815, 'We fear that this tax is not for revenue. The press is in every way to be undermined'. That might well be true but in the next

---

[1] Thomas Moore, *Poetical Works* (London, n.d.), p. 445.
[2] *Autobiography*, II, 79.

five years the authorities were to show that there were more disagreeable ways of dealing with seditious literature than merely by
raising the stamp duty a halfpenny or so.

SEDITION'S HOST: 1815–22

In 1798 the *Anti-Jacobin* had apostrophised the opposition press in
the following lines.

> *Couriers* and *Stars*, Sedition's Evening Host,
> Thou *Morning Chronicle*, and *Morning Post*,
> Whether ye make the Rights of Man your theme,
> Your Country libel, and your God blaspheme,
> Or dirt on private worth and virtue throw. . . .[1]

Yet after 1815 the anti-government campaign was carried on by
publishers and periodicals, some of whom made the opposition press
of twenty years earlier seem almost moderate by comparison. Many
of the new publications advocated reform rather than revolution
but even these advocated their more limited policy with the greatest
vigour and tenacity. Few of the earlier books and pamphlets had
shown such hatred of government and will to violence, for instance,
as was now expressed in a pamphlet like *The Old Black Cock and his
Dunghill Advisers in Jeopardy*, which ended with a print of cabinet
ministers, judges, and priests hanged from lamp-posts under the sign
'Justice Triumphant'. The economic depression following the war,
when the capacity of industry surpassed the demands made upon it;
the rising price of food, as a result of the Act of 1815—known as
'Robinson's Act'—by which the importation of foreign corn was forbidden until the price of English corn had reached £4 a quarter; the
apparent opposition of Liverpool's administration to any degree of
parliamentary reform, all these were factors in the deteriorating situation. For the underfed, unenfranchised, and unemployed, the press
remained, in the words of *The Political House that Jack Built*, the thing

> that, in spite of new Acts,
> And attempts to restrain it,
> by Soldiers or Tax,
> Will *poison* the vermin
> That plunder the Wealth,
> That lay in the House
> That Jack built.[2]

And in case there should be any doubt as to the identity of the 'ver-

[1] *The Anti-Jacobin; or, Weekly Examiner*, 9 July 1798.
[2] *The Political House that Jack Built*, 23rd edn. (London, 1819), Sig. B2r.

min' they are depicted in a print as soldiers, priests, tax-inspectors, flunkeys, and lawyers. The title-page of the pamphlet has an engraving of 'The Pen and the Sword', showing a pair of scales in which a quill pen, on one side, weighs more than an *ex officio* information, bills of indemnity, and bank restrictions, on the other. But now an officer is adding his sword to this second pile.

Of course, although the press was subject to normal restrictions during the first eighteen months of peace, there were no political prosecutions in either 1815 or 1816. Yet even during these years anti-government feeling and growing support for radical reform seemed a sufficient danger for the Prince Regent to promise in the speech from the throne, in January 1817, that his government would 'omit no precaution for preserving the public peace, and for counteracting the designs of the disaffected'. Many of those in the crowds who watched him drive to Parliament to deliver this speech had openly hissed him, and something—either a stone or a bullet—had shattered the window of the state coach. In the previous month there was a riot in Spa Fields, as a result of which two men were convicted and one hanged, though rumours suggested that a government agent named Castles had acted as *agent provocateur* in the matter. Later in 1817 four men were acquitted on charges of high treason after the cross-examination of Castles who, it was revealed, had been a forger before he turned government spy.

In the political unrest of 1817 the government suspended the Habeas Corpus Act, passed a Seditious Meeting Act to give magistrates greater control over public meetings and lectures, and launched another campaign to silence the radical press. In March that year the Home Secretary, Lord Sidmouth, sent a circular letter to the Lords Lieutenant of England and Wales in which he announced, on the authority of the law officers of the Crown, that a man who sold books and pamphlets without a hawker's licence might be arrested on the orders of a magistrate and committed to prison. Naturally, this would only happen if the man's stock included books which the magistrate regarded as political libels. This ruling of Lord Sidmouth's—or rather of the law officers—was a bombshell. It seemed to follow that magistrates must become the censors of political literature in many cases. The Whig opposition, certain newspapers like *The Times*, and even a number of magistrates themselves, challenged or at least questioned the legality of this power. No court had ever ruled that magistrates possessed such jurisdiction over the book trade, no law had ever been passed which empowered them to act in such a manner. Indeed, Fox's Libel Act of 1792 had specifically given the authority to find a publication libellous to the jury. The Home Office's reply to this was that any magistrate possessed these powers over literature by virtue of his office. He must examine the publication complained of, he must 'exercise his own judgment and must decide for himself whether the matter so proved to have been published is blasphemous or seditious, and if he shall be of opinion that it is of that nature and of dangerous tendency, he will be clearly justified in committing the offender in default of his giving bail to answer the charge'.[1]

During some months of confusion over the power of magistrates, fears for the freedom of the press grew stronger. A few magistrates questioned their alleged powers, others decided to make the most of them. Naturally, a magistrate might commit a man to prison or allow him bail while waiting for a charge of seditious libel to be heard by a higher court, as he might in a number of other criminal cases. But Sidmouth's circular letter had inspired some magistrates to exceed their authority in no uncertain way. One bookseller, Peter Parkinson, was awarded £100 damages against a Staffordshire magistrate who had tried and condemned him for selling an allegedly seditious and unstamped newspaper, the *Black Dwarf*. Such proceedings should only have been undertaken by the Attorney-General or the solicitor of the Stamp Office. At the same time news was coming in from other parts of the country where booksellers had been arrested and imprisoned on the orders of magistrates, in a manner whose legality was in many cases not above question.

The controversy over the circular letter faded into comparative obscurity when the efforts of magistrates to impose a local political allegiance on the press were eclipsed by the series of prosecutions which the government itself instituted during 1817. Among the first of these was the prosecution of T. J. Wooler for seditious libels in his *Black Dwarf* on 12 February and 2 April 1817. Both articles were regarded as extremely inflammatory, suggesting as they did that reform was more likely to come about through violent action than by exercising the subject's right of petitioning Parliament. Many magistrates had tried to impose a local ban on the *Black Dwarf*, thus advertising it more widely than Wooler could have done, but neither of these two cases against Wooler himself was successful.

The way in which the geographical distribution of anti-government feeling was changing is shown by the place of origin of many of the major offences in 1817: Hampshire, Leicester, Cheshire, Macclesfield, Manchester, and Staffordshire now added to the flow of seditious libels. Eighteen prosecutions were brought in the court of King's Bench that year, the government setting a national example for local justices to follow. Four of these cases were in respect of Wooler's

[1] P.R.O., H.O. 42/165.

Black Dwarf; one was a prosecution of Richard Carlile for selling W. T. Sherwin's *Political Register*, the remaining thirteen dealt with William Hone's parodies, three of them being cases against Hone himself. William Hone, a man of strict evangelical upbringing, was later to become a preacher at the Weigh Bridge Chapel and it is something of an irony that the parodies should have been charged as both profane and seditious. Early in 1817 he had published three satires whose aim was political but whose form burlesqued certain parts of the Anglican liturgy. These parodies were written with great verve and panache, and disrespect to the government rather than the liturgy is clear throughout them: they were *John Wilkes's Catechism of a Ministerial Member; The Political Litany*, and the *Sinecurist's Creed*. James Williams, a Southampton bookseller, was the defendant in the first two trials for publishing the *Political Litany* and the *Sinecurist's Creed*. He was fined £100 and sent to prison for eight months for the first offence and then sentenced to a further four months' imprisonment on the second charge. In Staffordshire, Peter Parkinson was convicted on a charge of publishing the *Political Litany* but the issue was principally decided by the trials of William Hone himself. On Hone's fate depended those of other booksellers awaiting trial on almost identical charges for publishing the three parodies. The most significant name among these other defendants was that of Richard Carlile who, like Hone, had been in prison for four months waiting for the case to come on.

Hone's three trials were on three successive days, 18, 19, 20 December 1817. He was prosecuted by the Attorney-General, Sir Samuel Shepherd, and conducted his own defence. The Attorney-General had brought an *ex officio* information against him, so that this was Hone's first chance to defend himself, and the case was heard by a special jury. The first trial, relating to *John Wilkes's Catechism*, was before Mr. Justice Abbott. Hone's trials were remarkable in that he stood before the court not as a lonely political revolutionary but as the representative of an organised political opposition, which had identified itself beyond doubt in the life of the nation since 1815. More to the point, many members of that opposition were now in court to give Hone a sympathetic hearing. Though it could hardly claim to have much representation in Parliament, it was not a group devoid of all power and influence, as it showed by raising well over £2,000 for Hone through public subscription.

The three trials of William Hone were not remarkable so much for the administration of justice as for being a kind of gladiatorial contest between the uncompromising conservatism of Castlereagh and the unyielding demands of the radical reformers, who, with some justification, regarded the judiciary as no less reactionary than the government itself. Each side had chosen its champion and in the role of emperors at the arena sat the members of the special jury.

On the first day, the Attorney-General got up and began to read out the alleged libel, *John Wilkes's Catechism*, with due solemnity.

Question. What is you name?
Answer. Lick Spittle.
Q. Who gave you this name?
A. My Sureties to the Ministry, in my Political Change, wherein I was made a Member of the Majority, the Child of Corruption, and a Locust to devour the good Things of this Kingdom. . . .
Q. Rehearse the Articles of thy Belief.
A. I believe in GEORGE, the Regent Almighty, Maker of New Streets and Knights of the Bath;

And in the present Ministry, his only choice, who were conceived of Toryism, brought forth of WILLIAM PITT, suffered loss of Place under CHARLES JAMES FOX, were execrated, dead, and buried. In a few months they rose again from their minority; they re-ascended to the Treasury Benches, and sit at the right hand of a little man in a large wig; from whence they *laugh* at the Petitions of the People, who pray for Reform, and that the sweat of their brow may procure them Bread.[1]

To the consternation of Mr. Justice Abbott and the Attorney-General, the recital of this seditious and impious libel produced much amusement among the spectators, and when Sir Samuel Shepherd came to the line, 'I, the Minister, am the Lord thy Liege, who brought thee out of want and beggary into the House of Commons,' there were roars of laughter, quickly rebuked by Abbott.

Hone was reasonably lucky in having Abbott as his judge, a non-political lawyer who had never been a law officer of the Crown nor, for that matter, sat in Parliament. While the court was packed with Hone's supporters and Hone himself proved an extremely difficult defendant, Abbott did his best to see that justice was done. Hone's defence began with a rambling account of the manner of his arrest, recalling indignantly that he had been dragged to court on Ellenborough's orders 'when he was retiring for the purposes of nature' and treated with inhumanity and even brutality by Ellenborough at the preliminary proceedings. Abbott interrupted him pointing out that this was no defence against the charge on which he was being tried, and ordering him to answer that charge. This Hone proceeded to do at considerable length. He quoted an exhaustive list of earlier parodies of the liturgy for purposes of political satire, none of which had ever been prosecuted. He quoted from the Harleian

---

[1] *The First Trial of William Hone* (London, 1818), p. 7.

Miscellany, from Henry Fielding's journal the *Champion*, from the *Oracle*, which had produced political parodies of this sort at the behest of ministers of the Crown. He produced evidence to show that the present ministry had paid men to write just the sort of parodies for which they were now prosecuting him. He began to read one of these but Abbott hastily interposed to stop him. Hone protested, 'It is a Ministerial parody.' 'I know nothing of Ministerial or Anti-Ministerial parodies,' said Abbott wearily, 'you have stated enough of that publication for your purpose.' Although Hone objected to the way in which Abbott continually interrupted him, Abbott did this simply to point out again and again that what Hone was doing, citing other parodies which had not been prosecuted, was, in law, no defence against the charge which he faced. The fact that, in the twentieth century, a more obscene book has not been prosecuted is no defence, in theory, for the publisher of a less obscene book. Undeflected by Abbott's warnings, Hone pursued the argument further. If publishers and authors of such parodies were to be punished, might he look forward to the prosecution of Canning (who was to become Foreign Secretary in 1822 and Prime Minister in 1827) for his contributions to the *Anti-Jacobin*? There was cheering in the court at this suggestion and the conclusion of Hone's speech was greeted with further en-thusiasm by the spectators. When the Attorney-General addressed the jury, his speech was, in part, inaudible as a result of 'marks of disapprobation' from Hone's sympathisers. Abbott's summing up could hardly have been favourable towards Hone but he quite fairly pointed out to the jury that whatever he might think of the publication concerned his duty was 'to assist and not to direct them'. The jurors were out for a quarter of an hour before returning a verdict of not guilty, which caused an uproar of excitement in the court. It was a verdict from which the government could draw little comfort. The fact that the jury—and a special jury at that—had acquitted Hone, meant that the cases against Carlile and others who had published *John Wilkes's Catechism* had failed as well. Worse still, whatever Mr. Justice Abbott might declare the law to be, jurors were evidently impressed by the argument that other parodies had not been punished, because they were ministerial propaganda, so it would be unjust to punish those which attacked the ministry. And, finally, it had become clearer over a number of years that even a special jury was not going to condemn a man automatically because he published an attack on the government. The Whigs themselves were opposed to many of the government's measures for dealing with the press and there would be plenty of Whigs among the lists of special jurors.

There were two more cases against Hone to be heard, and after the *débâcle* of the first day, Mr. Justice Abbott was replaced by the far more formidable figure of Lord Ellenborough, who despite age and ill-health was determined to see that proper respect was paid to the process of law. The trial this time was for the *Political Litany* and once more the court was packed with Hone's supporters so that the atmosphere suggested the hustings rather than the Guildhall.[1] The offending passages were read out by the Attorney-General, and there were roars of laughter as he came to 'Son of George, we beseech thee to hear us. O House of Lords, that takest away so many thousands of pounds in pensions, have mercy upon us.' Ellenborough's anger grew as the trial progressed. Hone was by no means the most co-operative of defendants—and he hated Ellenborough: he flatly contradicted Ellenborough (usually incorrectly) on points of law and bickered with him constantly, while 'Long-continued acclamations here interrupted the proceedings of the Court.' By this time Ellenborough seemed to be in danger of losing control of the situation, especially since the officers of the court themselves appeared unable to deal with the disturbances. He accused the Sheriffs of not keeping order, while the Under-Sheriff claimed that he had gone down into the court but had been unable to find anyone creating a disturbance. 'Open your eyes, and see;' urged Ellenborough in exasperation, 'and stretch out your hands and seize. You must have observed somebody. Mark where the noise comes from, and note the man.' So the trial proceeded, the Sheriff having announced that he would arrest the first man he saw laughing.

Hone's defence followed the same pattern as on the previous day. He cited numerous examples of political parodies which had not been prosecuted, though this did not prevent Ellenborough in his summing up from describing Hone's work as 'a most impious and profane libel'. This time things were not quite so straightforward. The jurors were out for an hour and three quarters, but the verdict which they returned was again one of not guilty. This second trial illustrated more clearly than the first the increasing difficulties of conducting a political prosecution of this kind, when the defendant's sympathisers in court outnumbered his accusers. It was all very well for Ellenborough to instruct the officers of the court to 'mark where the noise comes from,' or to 'stretch out your hands and seize,' but the noise must have been coming from so many different places that it would have been an intimidating prospect for the Under-Sheriff to begin laying hands on the culprits.

On the third day, 20 December, Ellenborough again presided when Hone was tried for publishing the *Sinecurist's Creed*: it might have been sensible at this stage for the government to save face by

[1] *The Second Trial of William Hone* (London, 1818), *passim*.

dropping this final charge but it decided to fight on to the end. There were fewer disturbances this time, since the Sheriffs were reinforced by a strong body of peace officers, but two acquittals had not diminished Hone's intransigence. Among his other pleas of justification, he reminded the court that though he had been accused of parodying the creed, even Lord Ellenborough's own father, who had been Bishop of Carlisle, had entertained such misgivings about the contents of the creed that he wished clergymen to be absolved from the obligation of reciting it. Ellenborough said only, 'For common decency, forbear', but forbearance was not Hone's most striking characteristic. The jury acquitted him this time after being out for twenty minutes.

Hone's three trials broke the government's attack on the press in 1817 and in this lies their great significance. When Hone was acquitted, through his own unaided efforts and in the face of everything the Attorney-General and Lord Ellenborough could do, charges against other publishers who had issued the three parodies in question had to be dropped. In all, the government had brought eighteen prosecutions in the court of King's Bench during 1817 and had got convictions in only four of them. Of the fourteen acquittals, nine were the direct or indirect result of Hone's advocacy on those three days in December 1817.

There was one particularly good omen in the outcome of this trial: Hone had been acquitted by special juries. This was not new but it happened at a time when the whole special jury system was being attacked, particularly by Wooler and other partisans of a free press. During 1817, partly as the result of prosecutions brought against Wooler's *Black Dwarf*, there had been an investigation into the working of the special jury system and a number of disquieting facts were unearthed. These showed how carefully the names of jurors on such special lists might be chosen by the authorities. So few were the trusted and qualified special jurors in the City of London, for instance, that during the previous year 274 of them had been summoned to try 100 cases. Forty of these jurors were summoned more than twenty times and fifty of them over ten times during that period. A few had made a regular income of a guinea a week as what one is tempted to call 'professional jurors'. Of course, not all those summoned would actually be required at the trial but it was still a very small number to choose from. There were at least grounds for suspicion that a publisher charged with seditious libel might face a packed jury. It was probably fortunate for Hone that the scandal of the special jury system blew up in 1817 and the lists of special jurors were accordingly revised, so that they included more potential jurors who were not necessarily unswerving in their support of the political *status quo*.

After the failure of its campaign against the press in 1817 the government showed little inclination to start another series of prosecutions for the time being. Richard Carlile wrote in 1818 that the government was evidently sick with the prosecutions of 1817, and in 1818 'in London, the Press was free'. The political works of Thomas Paine circulated openly and without interference, which to Carlile was a sign of the times. Yet the triumph of Hone and the experience of Carlile were metropolitan: in the provinces the situation was more favourable to the government. In Warwick, for example, there was at one time a list of only fifty-four men from whom the panel of forty-eight special jurors for a case was chosen. It was in Warwickshire that the government brought its only major case in 1818 by prosecuting Joseph Russell, a Birmingham printer who had published Hone's *Political Litany*. Despite the fact that Hone had been acquitted on a similar charge in London three months earlier, Russell was found guilty and sent to prison for six months after a delayed trial.

Though 1818 may have been uneventful so far as political prosecutions were concerned, little was forgiven on either side. Publishers like Hone and Carlile remembered their months of imprisonment awaiting trial during the previous year, and Carlile described his accusers as 'anxious to glut your vengeance with punishment before trial'. In 1817 he had spent eighteen weeks in prison and, in the end, had not been tried. Early in 1818 the general election had resulted in an increased Whig representation in the House of Commons but the radical reformers were not prepared to wait patiently while the complexion of the House of Commons changed gradually over the years. Pamphlets and parodies became more savage, showing little sympathy or compassion for personal misfortune. In his *Man in the Moon*, for instance, Hone burlesqued the speech of the Prince Regent to Parliament, showing his contempt for the Prince's arrogance and a lack of sympathy with the mad King.

> *MY L-rds and G—tl——n,*
>   I grieve to say,
>   That poor old Dad,
>   Is just as—bad,
> As when I met you here
>   the other day.
> 'Tis pity that these cursed State Affairs
> Should take you from your pheasants and your hares
>   Just now:
>   But lo!
> CONSPIRACY and TREASON are abroad!
> Those imps of darkness, gender'd in the wombs

Of spinning-jennies, winding-wheels, and looms,
　　In Lunashire—
　　Oh, Lord!
My L—ds and G—tl——n, we've much to fear!

Reform, Reform, the swinish rabble cry—
Meaning, of course, rebellion, blood, and riot—
Audacious rascals! you, my Lords, and I,
Know 'tis their duty to be starved in quiet:
But they have grumbling habits, incompatible
With the respose of *our* august community—
They see that good things are with *us* come-at-ible,
And therefore slyly watch their opportunity
　　To get a share;
　　Yes, they declare
That we are not God's favourites alone—
That *they* have rights to food, and clothes, and air,
As well as you, the Brilliants of a throne!
Oh! indications foul of revolution—
The villains would destroy the Constitution![1]

The event which precipitated the final political struggle between the government and the press in 1819 was the massacre of 'Peterloo' on 16 August that year, when the Manchester authorities became apprehensive about a meeting in St. Peter's Fields, organised by the advocates of reform, and ordered the use of troops to disperse it. Men, women, and children were involved in the ensuing *melée* and it was afterwards claimed that eleven of them had been killed and 600 more or less severely injured. Whether or not these figures were exaggerated, the mood of the radical press became one of boiling anger. Violence of this sort clearly justified the use of violence in return. Within a few days, Sir Francis Burdett, Member of Parliament for Westminster, wrote his *Address to the Electors of Westminster*, in which he bitterly described 'the practical blessings of our glorious borough-monger's domination'.

What! kill men unarmed, unresisting, and, gracious God! women, too, disfigured, maimed, cut down, and trampled on by dragoons. Is this England? This a Christian land—a land of freedom?[2]

For publishing this address, Sir Francis was charged with seditious libel, tried and convicted at Leicester in March 1820, and sentenced to three months' imprisonment as well as a fine of £1,000.

A further aggravation of the political unrest during the summer of

---

[1] *The Man in the Moon*, 12th edn. (London, 1820).
[2] *The Trial of Sir Francis Burdett* (London, 1820), p. 6.

1819 had been the speech of the Prince Regent to Parliament at the end of the parliamentary session. As one pamphleteer put it,

The speech which he is reported to have delivered is one of the completest specimens of villainous impudence that was ever foisted upon the patience of the English people. 'Get ye down, ye race of ill-bred ignorant slaves,' is the language which it breathes in every line. It is a deliberate insult to the country at large, and the unfeeling wretch who looking with indifference on the miseries of the people could possess the heart to deliver it deserves to be cashiered for his misconduct.[1]

These sentiments too were prosecuted and condemned as a seditious libel. The temperature of the political debate had risen high before the Peterloo incident in August but when the blood of reformers was actually shed, widespread violence seemed not only likely but inevitable and even desirable. 'The blood so profusely and barbarously shed at Manchester on the never to be forgotten 16th of August incessantly cries aloud for vengeance', proclaimed the members of the Birmingham Union Society, in another condemned pamphlet, while other defendants had sold the *Republican* for 10 September, which urged the Manchester radicals to meet again, choosing this time a place that may be better fortified and in which they can arm themselves against any attempt to frustrate the purposes of their meeting.[2]

The outlook for a peaceful settlement, let alone the freedom of the press, was not encouraging. Government and radicals were each being driven to more and more extreme measures, while dislike of George III and loathing of the Prince Regent offered a dismal prospect for both this reign and the next. This was the time referred to so sombrely by Mrs. Gaskell in her *Life of Charlotte Brontë* (1857), the time 'when watchers or wakeners in the night heard the distant word of command, and the measured tramp of thousands of sad desperate men receiving a surreptitious military training, in preparation for some great day which they saw in their visions, when right should struggle with might and come off victorious: when the people of England represented by the workers of Yorkshire, Lancashire, and Nottinghamshire, should make their voice heard in a terrible slogan, since their true and pitiful complaints could find no hearing in Parliament'.[3] The government and the Prince Regent vigorously maintained that all the unrest was the work of a few unscrupulous agitators exploiting the existence of certain purely local hardships, 'and who

[1] P.R.O., K.B. 28/472/107.
[2] P.R.O., K.B. 28/472/76 and 25.
[3] *Life of Charlotte Brontë* (London, 1857), I, 114.

under the pretence of reform have really no other object but the subversion of our happy constitution'. In such a situation as this the ministry felt quite justified in launching another campaign to silence the radical press. The Attorney-General brought no less than thirty-three prosecutions against publishers in 1819 by way of *ex officio* informations and though only twelve of these resulted in convictions the others imposed a considerable financial burden and even financial ruin upon the defendants. At the same time, local magistrates did their best to apprehend and punish by fines, imprisonment, and flogging, those hawkers who sold radical publications like Cobbett's *Political Register*, Wooler's *Black Dwarf*, or Richard Carlile's *Republican* without a licence.

But to punish the publishers or vendors of such literature was, as Samuel Johnson had put it, like sleeping with one's doors open because by the law a thief might be hanged. Might it not still be possible to lock and bolt the doors of the constitution against seditious publications? Even if the old system of pre-censorship which had expired in 1695 could no longer be revived—though there was pressure on the government even in 1819 to try reviving it—there might be other ways of checking sedition at its very source. In December 1819 the government made clear how this was to be done. Three months earlier Lord Sidmouth, as Home Secretary, had claimed that magistrates had dealt so firmly with seditious literature that 'the worst description of poison has been considerably checked in many parts of the kingdom'.[1] But this was not enough. Despite Whig opposition, the Blasphemous and Seditious Libels Act was passed, giving magistrates greater powers to search for seditious or blasphemous literature and making transportation the punishment for a second offence under this Act. More directly effective was a second piece of legislation, the Newspaper Stamp Duties Act. Duties were now imposed on those periodical publications like the *Republican*, the *Black Dwarf* and Cobbett's *Weekly Register*, which had previously escaped because they were not, strictly speaking, newspapers. But by the new law any periodical publication of less than two sheets or costing less than sixpence or appearing more frequently than once every twenty-six days would have to pay duty. From now on 'Twopenny trash' would be 'Sixpenny trash'. The government made no secret of its motives in imposing this form of tax and the second Lord Ellenborough, who attributed the increased 'virulence and malignity' of the press to Hone's acquittals in 1817, explained the new law to the House of Lords.

It was not against the respectable press that this bill was directed, but

[1] P.R.O., H.O. 41/5/45.

against a pauper press, which, administering to the prejudices and the passions of a mob, was converted to the basest purposes, which was an utter stranger to truth, and only sent forth a continual stream of falsehood and malignity, its virulence and its mischief heightening as it proceeded.[1]

If there was to be any lasting political settlement it was essential, in Ellenborough's view, that such publications and their influence should be more strictly controlled.

The mischief arising from them in the deception and delusion practised upon the lowest classes, by means of the grossest and most malignant falsehoods, was such, that it threatened the most material injury to the best interests of the country, unless some means were devised of stemming its torrent.[2]

The Whig opposition wanted the Bill to be a temporary measure but they were heavily out-voted. In order to ensure that the new law was workable there was a provision by which all publishers and printers of periodical literature referred to by the Act were obliged to provide recognizances from which any fine imposed by a court might be deducted. In London the sum of such recognizances was to be £300 from the publisher himself and other similar sums from his sureties: in Edinburgh and Dublin the sums were also £300, and in the provinces £200. There was to be no question of a radical publisher issuing his newspaper first and then preparing to take the consequences: arrangements for his punishment had been made even before he had an opportunity to commit any offence.

Anyone who supposed that the imposition of duties and taxes would destroy the radical press was due for a disappointment but some radical newspapers disappeared and others carried on only under extreme difficulties. What had once sold for twopence was bound to cost sixpence by the simple addition of fourpence duty and, indeed, Cobbett found that it was now impossible to sell his *Political Register* for less. But while the periodical press might be shackled, the pamphleteers with their occasional lampoons or parodies were, in this respect, unmolested. In any case, it was not likely, whatever the financial difficulties, that in the mood of 1819–20 the voice of radical opinion would have been silenced. Indeed, the uproar and the prosecutions for seditious libel which the Peterloo affair had inspired were hardly over before the next controversy began. The Prince Regent had succeeded his father as George IV at the beginning of 1820 and by mid-August was having his wife, Queen Caroline, tried for adultery by the House of Lords. The radical press, on the principle that anyone

[1] *Parl. Deb.*, xli, 1591 (29 December 1819).   [2] *Parl. Deb.*, loc. cit.

who was an enemy of the new King must be a friend of theirs, rallied to the cause of the persecuted Queen. The crowds cheered her and smashed the windows of Castlereagh, the Foreign Secretary. Although she had been barred from the Coronation ceremony, a public subscription for a gift to mark her accession was opened under the trusteeship of the Duke of Leinster, the Earl of Oxford and others. In the appeal for funds which was published, her supporters promised that they would show 'her Majesty's nefarious persecutors that it is not in the power of an infamous government, a corrupt judicature or bribed majorities, of execrable perjurors, suborners of evidence or malignant conspirators to shut the hands of the people of England after they have opened their hearts'. This was prosecuted as a seditious libel but the jury in this case seems to have been sufficiently disenchanted with both the King and his ministers to acquit the publisher, Dennis O'Bryen. On the other hand, John Hunt who in the month before the Queen's trial published an article announcing that such a disgraceful proceeding would only have been possible in a Parliament filled with 'venal Borough Mongers, grasping placemen, greedy adventurers, and aspiring title-hunters, or the representatives of such worthies—a body, in short, containing a far greater proportion of public criminals than public guardians', was prosecuted and convicted for these sentiments.[1] He was sent to prison for one year and bound over for three more in the sum of £1,000 for this number of the *Examiner*.

The most unlikely writers and publishers now found a good word to say for this member of the royal family during the months of adversity. Jane Carlile, the wife of Richard Carlile who had assumed control of her husband's business when he was sent to prison for blasphemous libel in 1819, was now prosecuted for a reference to 'A King, vicious, malignant, implacable, despised, rejected and hated. A Queen virtuous, benignant, affable, honoured, caressed and loved.'[2] So Queen Caroline joined Thomas Paine in the pantheon of the radicals and republicans. On the other hand those who let their sympathies for George IV go so far as to attack the Queen as an adulteress were in trouble as well. Thomas Flindell, for instance, was imprisoned at Exeter for publishing a description of her as such a woman 'as would, if found on our pavement, be committed to Bridewell and whipped'.[3] Another case of this kind was brought against two men, Street and Mudford, for a libel on the Queen in the *Courier* of 14 December 1820, accusing her of having chosen 'to insult the King, abuse the Houses of Parliament, traduce the Nobility, deride

[1] P.R.O., K.B. 28/476/36.
[2] P.R.O., K.B. 28/476/13. [The libel was published in the *Republican*.]
[3] P.R.O., K.B. 28/476/67.

the Laws, and sneer at the religion, to court the addresses of prostitutes and the acclamations of pickpockets! to head public processions and defile the altars of God with factious and tumultuous thanksgivings that adultery is unpunished'.[1]

Queen Caroline may have been a pathetic figure but hardly, so far as adultery was concerned, a slandered innocent. She and George IV, for such time as they were together, had made each other equally miserable but the real point about the trial of 1820 was that the King himself was in no strong moral position to make charges of promiscuity or adultery against anyone. Before the end of the year the proceedings against the Queen were over yet the intense dislike of George IV, on the part of many people, endured and soon a new round of prosecutions began, in the early months of 1821, in respect of a ballad which appeared in the *Pasquin, or General Satirist* and elsewhere. Radicals like Thomas Dolby and Edward King now found themselves charged with criminal libel for issuing it. It seems to have spread rapidly in a number of slightly differing versions but it sums up as well as any other lampoon the cumulative contempt felt for the King by his enemies. There were also uncomplimentary references in it to Lord Liverpool, then Prime Minister, Lord Eldon, who as Lord Chancellor was known as 'Old Bags', Castlereagh, nicknamed 'Derry Down', and 'Doctor' Sidmouth, the Home Secretary.

> If you walk up Pall Mall
> You may pass by the gate
> Where an old hog of sixty
> Still wallows in state
> With his brown wig
> And his bladder chops white.
>
> Half drunk with white brandy,
> O'er heated with lust,
> This 'faithful defender'
> Of all that is just,
> In a proud pandemonium
> With well-guarded doors
> Is humbugged by Statesmen
> And fondled by whores
> For his brown wig
> And his bladder chops white.
>
> Derry Down and his Doctor
> And Liverpool sat
> With Old Bags and Duke Arthur
> In Council to chat

[1] P.R.O., K.B. 28/477/61.

> Of the brown wig
> And the bladder chops white.
>
> And three greater knaves
> And two greater fools
> Were never selected
> As infamous tools
> To a selfish old sinner
> Who cares not a jot,
> So he is reveng'd,
> If we all go to pot,
> For his brown wig
> And his bladder chops white.

Even after the controversy surrounding the Queen's trial was over, the attacks on George IV continued intermittently throughout the rest of the reign. In 1823, for example, Harvey and Chapman, printer and publisher of the *Sunday Times*, were found guilty of a libel on the King, though with some misgivings on the part of the jury, for suggesting that he had inherited his father's insanity and was being kept under lock and key in the Pavilion at Brighton. The heavy, over-emphatic irony described the King's devotion to his Queen and his intense distress at the 'excruciating sufferings of his agricultural subjects'. The defence claimed that this flattery was genuine and that no irony was intended but, the court decided, such unstinted praise of George IV could only be ironical. Also in 1824 John Hunt was fined £100 for publishing Byron's *Vision of Judgment* in the *Liberal* two years earlier. This was a libel on the dead George III and was condemned as seditious, the prosecution taking particular exception to the eighth stanza and the first half of the ninth.

> In the first year of freedom's second dawn
>   Died George the Third: although no tyrant, one
> Who shielded tyrants, till each sense withdrawn
>   Left him nor mental nor external sun;
> A better farmer ne'er brushed dew from lawn,
>   A worse king never left a realm undone!
> He died—but left his subjects still behind,
> One half as mad—and t' other no less blind.
>
> He died!—his death made no great stir on earth;
>   His burial made some pomp; there was profusion
> Of velvet, gilding, brass, and no great dearth
>   Of aught but tears—save those shed by collusion.

Not until the accession of the more good-natured and liberal William IV—'Silly Billy'—in 1830 was the prestige of the monarchy to recover from the impact of George IV both as King and Regent. Well might *The Times* remark on his death in 1830 that there could hardly be a wet eye in the whole kingdom.

During the unrest which followed Peterloo and continued throughout the summer of the Queen's trial in 1820, there were those who felt that a private association of prominent men ought to back up the government's attempts to control the press: this could be done by employing informers and bringing private prosecutions. If any odium were incurred it would be by such an association and not by the government. In December 1820 the Constitutional Association was formed under the aegis of the Duke of Wellington, 'the Waterloo Man', as William Hone called him, who regarded the demands for reform as something he could 'crush with his sword'. This Association was dedicated to prosecuting seditious libels, particularly those which the government might have overlooked. On the other hand, as Henry Brougham explained in the *Edinburgh Review* for June 1822 it was not without its channels of communication to the government and, no doubt, ministers of the Crown found it a useful weapon from time to time. They might draw the attention of the Association to a particular libel and encourage the members to prosecute without ever involving the government in the case. During 1821 Brougham and others questioned in Parliament the legality of such an Association, particularly since it had the support of a number of wealthy men and might, therefore, bring cases against publishers who could hardly afford to defend themselves. Indeed, if a case should reach the House of Lords, it could well be decided there by peers who were themselves members or supporters of the Association. It was bound to appear to many people as the most flagrant instance of a private body exercising a power over the press for which it was accountable to no one. One victim of the Association's activities was William Benbow, who was in trouble later on as a publisher of pornography. In 1821 the Association brought a charge against him which was political rather than moral, accusing him of a libel on George IV in two prints, the first known as *The Brightest Star in the State . . . or, . . . A Peep out of a Royal Window*, and the second called *The Royal Cock and Chickens, or the Father of his People*. According to Benbow, his accusers never dared to bring him to trial but the costs of the case were, nonetheless, so great that his bookseller's shop in the Strand was ruined and he had to begin all over again at other premises in Castle Street, near Leicester Square.

To begin with, the Constitutional Association received considerable support, some of it from that former admirer of the French Revolution, William Wordsworth, who wrote in December 1820, 'The objects of this association must be deemed of prime importance by every reflecting mind. If its regulations be found judicious. . . . I shall be happy to do all in my power to carry them into effect.'[1] It is only fair to add that when Wordsworth realised how much the Association was to be concerned with the prosecution of allegedly subversive literature, he became critical of it, on the sensible grounds that the only way to combat bad literature effectively was not to prosecute it but to publish what was good in reply.

Apart from attacks made upon it in Parliament, the reputation of the Constitutional Association was never much to be envied. Jurors showed themselves uneasy at the prospect of condemning a man or a woman for a political crime when the charge had been brought not by the government but by a private body. If the government was, apparently, prepared to let certain political literature circulate, why should the Constitutional Association try to prevent it? Worse still, it was rumoured that the Association was making money as a common informer. Throughout 1821 and 1822 it became increasingly discredited, and was defunct within two years of its inception. The sort of results which it achieved are well illustrated in its prosecution of Mary Anne Carlile, the sister of Richard Carlile, for publishing a *New Year's Address to the Reformers of Great Britain*, which attacked the British Constitution on the grounds that nothing was constituted except 'corruption in the system of government', and warned its readers that something more than good-natured petitioning would be needed to bring about reform of the parliamentary system. The interesting point is that another bookseller, David Ridgway in Manchester, had already been found guilty of publishing this same pamphlet and had been sent to prison. To that extent the omens for the Constitutional Association in its prosecution of Mary Anne Carlile were good. But Henry Cooper, Miss Carlile's counsel, carried out a withering cross-examination of James Rignall, the agent whom the Secretary of the Association had sent out to buy any pamphlets which he judged to be libellous. It now transpired that Rignall was a dismissed Customs officer. 'Good God!' exclaimed Cooper, 'to what a condition are we reduced, when, under the auspices of this blessed Association, discarded tide-waiters, and broken gaugers, are made judges of what is libellous, and leagued with an attorney, are to determine what may, and what may not, without the terror of a prosecution, issue from a free press'.[2] Despite the violent language

[1] Letter from Wordsworth to Lord Lonsdale, 18 December 1820 (Lonsdale MSS.).

[2] *Bridge-Street Banditti versus the Press. The Trial of Mary Anne Carlile* (London, 1821), p. 18.

which the 'libel' in question used, Cooper had made his point. After five hours the jury had still failed to agree and the case against Miss Carlile was dropped, despite an angry outburst from a representative of the Constitutional Association at the back of the court.

After the case against Miss Carlile in July 1821 hostility towards the Constitutional Association increased. Before the end of the year a criminal charge had been brought against it—or rather against certain of its officers, including the Secretary, Charles Murray—alleging that it had usurped the King's prerogative by bringing prosecutions for libel, and that it had extorted money from the defendants in such cases.[1] As it happened, the charge was dismissed but the enemies of the Association appear to have gained their end by blackening its reputation still further. Within another year its activities were over.

In the underworld of literature, those booksellers who specialised in publications which might easily have been condemned as seditious or blasphemous, decided that desperate times called for desperate measures. Some of the precautions adopted by these men were no less remarkable in their way than those of the unlicensed printers during the sixteenth or seventeenth centuries. There was, for example, a device by means of which a customer might buy a book without ever seeing the face of the man who sold it to him. A description of such an apparatus survives in the papers of the Treasury Solicitor.

This apparatus consists of two apertures in the back partition, one for the receipt of money, the other for the transmission of the publication from behind, over which is a round dial with numbers on it, and a movable hand which may be turned so as to point to any number. These numbers correspond with others affixed to a list of books stuck up on one side of the shop, so that any person by perusing the list may learn to what numbers to affix the hand of the dial.[2]

Such shops, where no word was exchanged between the customer and the invisible bookseller, were hardly the places for browsers but devices of this kind were popular enough. An even more elaborate model was found when Samuel Waddington was arrested and tried on a charge of blasphemous libel in 1822. The contrivance was no doubt one of Richard Carlile's own.

This apparatus consisted of a trunk or spout, which passed from the apartment on the first floor into the shop, and by the side of this spout was a board on which were written the titles of several works to be purchased, with hooks driven into the board by the side of each book. Close to this board was a cord (like a bell rope) also communicating with the first floor with a ring attached to the end of it. The mode of sale was this: The person

[1] P.R.O., K.B. 28/479/15.   [2] *State Trials* (New Series), I, 1368.

who desired to purchase any of these works pulled the cord and fixed the ring to the hook at the side of the book he wanted; and there was also a speaking tube communicating with the floor above. The cord being thus fixed to the hook apprised the person above what was the book wanted, or a bag was let down through the spout, and the price of the work being deposited therein by the person wishing to become purchaser, the bag ascended, and the book was then let down through the spout, and the purchaser received it at the lower mouth in the shop.[1]

Of course, the protection offered by such ingenuity against either police raids or the persistent probing of a common informer was slight indeed: the second device certainly did Waddington little good, since he was apprehended and later sentenced to a year's imprisonment. In any case, for some booksellers there was no doubt as much attraction in the prospect of being caught and becoming martyrs for their beliefs as in baffling the informers and the police.

Remote from the day-to-day hazards of selling condemned books, the questions of press freedom were debated in more general terms. Voices like those of Coleridge and Bentham were raised in favour of liberty of expression, even if only because it was the lesser of two evils. In his periodical the *Friend*, which appeared in 1809–10, Coleridge first of all examined the assumption, on which so much political censorship was based, that inflammatory opinions will incite their readers to violence and revolution. He thought the assumption unwarranted, pointing out that one had to balance 'the incomparably greater mischief of the overt-acts, if we suppose them actually occasioned by the libel', against the 'very great improbability that such effects will be produced by such writings'.[2] How many of Thomas Paine's hundreds of thousands of readers had been incited to political acts of violence by reading him? 'It is proved, likewise, by experience, that the frequency of open political discussion, with all its blameable indiscretions, indisposes a nation to overt-acts of practical sedition or conspiracy.'[3] Nor was Coleridge representing an extreme or eccentric view in challenging the official belief that men were incited to violence by political literature. In 1791 the *Gentleman's Magazine*, reviewing the *Rights of Man*, had observed, 'It is well our Revolutionists speak so freely as they do. Their declamations have no effect on the general mind of the nation, and serve to put the wiser and better part on their guard.'[4]

Of course, it would have been a rash man who tried to maintain that under no circumstances could political argument provoke an individual to take political action. Coleridge finds it improbable that

[1] *ibid.*, I, 1368.   [2] *The Friend*, 4th edn., I, 119.   [3] *ibid.*, loc cit.
[4] *Gentleman's Magazine*, LXI, pt. 2 (1791), 740.

men are moved to violence by what they read, and the *Gentleman's Magazine* holds that there is no general effect on readers from books like the *Rights of Man*. The danger of individuals succumbing to the influence of seditious literature remained. Yet even so, as Jeremy Bentham put it in his essay *On the Liberty of the Press and Public Discussion* (published by William Hone in 1821), 'In all liberty, there is more or less of danger: and so there is in all power. The question is —in which there is more danger—in power limited by this check, or in power without this check to limit it.'[1] This question was, of course, a purely rhetorical one for a man like Bentham after the events of 1815–20. As for Lord Ellenborough's suggestion that anything which hurt the feelings of ministers of the Crown must be a political libel, Bentham made short work of that in his pamphlet *The King against Edmunds and Others* (1820). Some years earlier, when Daniel Isaac Eaton was tried for publishing Paine's *Age of Reason* in 1812, Shelley had written an open letter to Lord Ellenborough, attacking the whole idea of punishing men for the expression of their opinions or beliefs, on the rather romantic assumption that belief 'is an involuntary operation of the mind, and, like other passions, its intensity is purely proportionate to the degrees of excitement. Volition is essential to merit or demerit'.[2] Yet knowing the recipient of the letter, Shelley adds more prosaically, 'I have not addressed this letter to you with the hope of convincing you that you have acted wrong.'[3]

To the government as well as to the radicals and the advocates of press freedom, it was evident by this time that even the present level of political censorship could hardly be maintained for much longer. It was not simply a case of the strength of radical feeling defying all suppression but again, as so often in the past, the growth and the economic development of the press made current methods of censorship inadequate. In a few years, for instance, governments had to give up all idea of either buying up newspapers or paying them subsidies to ensure their loyalty, simply because the market value of an influential newspaper had increased to a point where the government could not afford the price of financial control.

The fate of press freedom had been linked for so long to that of political or parliamentary reform that it was hard to see that either question could be settled without the settlement of the other. For

[1] *On the Liberty of the Press and Public Discussion* (London, 1821), p. 13. The opposite view was expressed by John Reeves, who had no doubt of the power of libels. 'The pen militant might save the expense of many regiments'.
[2] *Shelley on Blasphemy* (London, 1883), p. 7.
[3] *ibid.*, p. 14.

both causes the ten years preceding the Reform Bill of 1832 was a period of advancement, not always uniform and not without certain ominous setbacks. Time and chance removed some of the most resolute opponents of the radicals and their press. Infirmity and intellectual decline soon overtook Castlereagh, the moving spirit of Lord Liverpool's administration, of whom Shelley had written in the *Masque of Anarchy*, 'I met murder on the way—He had a mask like Castlereagh.' Indeed, no radical journalist or political agitator could have contrived a much worse end than the one which Castlereagh inflicted on himself when, at the age of fifty-three, he slit his own throat with a penknife.

TOWARDS THE FREEDOM OF THE PRESS 1822–1832

As the influence of Canning replaced that of Castlereagh, the ministry which had been so implacably opposed to any measure of compromise with the reformers or the press now assumed a more liberal complexion. Administrations of greater or less moderation succeeded each other during these ten years and during the administration of the Duke of Wellington in 1828–30 the fulfilment of dreams of a free press and universal suffrage must have seemed to many people as far away as ever. Wellington's period of office showed that a major clash between government and press was still easily provoked. In 1829 the government brought cases against the printers and publishers of the *Morning Journal* and the *Standard*, charging them with seditious libel as well as with libelling the King and Wellington himself. There was little support for this action outside government circles and, as *The Times* put it, 'Why resort to the official prosecutor, who never yet in any age saved a feeble ministry from contempt, or added authority to a strong one?'[1] All that the ministry had achieved, in the view of *The Times*, was to confer the glories of martyrdom on the *Morning Journal*. Throughout the spring and summer of 1829 the *Morning Journal* had attacked the government on every possible issue. It had accused Peel, Wellington, and Parliament as a whole, of cynical indifference towards the plight of the silk weavers in Lancashire who were on the point of starvation. It alleged that the King disliked and distrusted Wellington but was nonetheless in his power. On the strength of the Catholic Emancipation Act, it described the ministry as being under the influence of 'pro-Popery ruffians.' To the *Morning Journal*, as to a great many observers, the danger to the Established Church now seemed to come from Catholicism rather than from Thomas Paine and the deists. Five separate cases were brought against Robert

[1] 25 December 1829.

Alexander, and others against the various printers of his *Morning Journal*. Three prison sentences were passed on Alexander himself and he was fined £300 for such sentiments as these in the *Morning Journal* of 17 July 1829, quoted in one of the indictments against him.

We leave so important a question to be answered by the silent response of the reader's own heart. But we can imagine a case and one not of mere visionary application when the devolvement of Royal Honours upon the next in Succession would place in the hands of the Prime Minister of such a Sovereign all the power and patronage of the Crown. If such a Minister were an honest one, no danger might be created, no abuse of power might be indulged in, no arbitrary measures sanctioned, no family interest erected into a monopoly of all the gifts of the King. But if it should happen, as it might happen, that the Minister of such a Sovereign were an ambitious soldier of vast wealth and great family connections, proud, overbearing, grasping, dishonest and unprincipled, a man having the army at his command, the navy at his nod, every situation under the Crown at his disposal, every sinecurist, every Commissioner of Taxes, every dignitary of the Customs and Excise at his mercy, what could not such a man do to overturn the very throne itself and prostrate to the earth the laws and liberties of England?

The preoccupation of the *Morning Journal* with the plight of the Lancashire silk weavers is one indication of a change in emphasis on the part of the extreme opposition press. Of course political reform remained one of the great objectives but there was a growing concern with the economic condition of the industrial classes as well as with their political deprivation. Whig as well as Tory ministries faced the problem of suppressing literature which encouraged strikers, industrial agitators or rick-burners. In 1829, as the result of the strike of carpet weavers at Kidderminster, Humphrey Price was sent to prison for a year for publishing two poems, 'A Kidderminster Weaver's Wife's Dream,' and 'The Complaint of a Kidderminster Weaver's Wife to her Infant,' which described the moral superiority of the strikers' cause and were held to be libels on the master manufacturers. There were some prose libels as well but the two poems, at least, are worth preserving and will be found in the second half of this book.

Two veteran journalists or publishers turned their attention to similar problems. In December 1830 Richard Carlile published his *Address to the Insurgent Labourers*, for which, and for the third number of the *Prompter*, he was at once prosecuted. In the *Address*, it was alleged, he had deliberately incited the agricultural workers to destroy farm property. There were certainly grounds for this accusation.

As yet there is no evidence before the public that you are incendiaries or

174

even political rebels. Much as every thoughtful man must lament the waste of property, much as the country must suffer by the burnings of farm produce now going on, were you proved to be incendiaries, we should defend you by saying that you have more just and moral cause for it than any king or faction that ever made war had for making war. . . . Yours is a state of warfare, and your ground of quarrel is the want of necessity of life in the midst of an abundance.

Just to show that he had not lost all interest in pure politics, Carlile included a few passing remarks on the monarchy in the *Prompter*. 'We want no mummeries and nonsense wherewith to please savages and fools in the present day.' At his trial the jury, after a first retirement, reported to the Recorder of London that there seemed no prospect of their reaching a verdict that day. The Recorder warned them that if they did not return a verdict, they would be locked up for the night without any refreshment or heating. (It was 10 January.) When the jury was sent back in this manner, there were sounds of protest from the spectators but at 1.45 a.m. the jurors had had enough and agreed on a verdict of guilty, which Carlile—with some justification—claimed had been obtained under duress. He was sent to prison for two years, fined £200 and bound over in the sum of £1,000. But there were official misgivings over the case. Carlile paid neither the fine nor the surety, and he was released from prison after eight months of his sentence had been served.

The second well-established journalist to clash with the government over much the same question was William Cobbett, who was prosecuted for remarking in *Rural War* of those agricultural labourers who had taken to rick-burning, 'it is unquestionable that their acts have produced good, and great good too.' He pointed out that by destroying produce these men were not depriving themselves or their families of food, since they could not afford to buy it in any case. Cobbett was tried in July 1831 and when he entered the court there was an outburst of applause, which he acknowledged by remarking, 'Gentlemen, if the truth prevails we shall beat them.' Like so many of his contemporaries he welcomed the opportunity of turning the court into a political arena. After a retirement of 15 hours the jury was still unable to reach a verdict, they were six for conviction and six for acquittal. The Whig government apparently thought the matter had gone far enough and the case against Cobbett was dropped.

Despite the way in which successive ministries, by bringing such prosecutions as those against Alexander, Carlile or Cobbett, reminded the press of the powers which authority might exercise if it chose, in many small ways the government's statutory powers over the press were being gradually eroded. In 1811 Lord Holland had tried in vain to check the Attorney-General's power of prosecuting political libels on *ex officio* informations but in 1819 a bill was passed which required the Attorney-General to bring the case to court within twelve months of the information. It could no longer be used as a weapon to intimidate dissident publishers or journalists by keeping a prosecution suspended over them. In 1825 the Attorney-General's right to have cases of criminal libel heard by a special jury was abolished and in the same year the law of 1819 was repealed which limited the size of a newspaper sheet to 32 inches by 22 inches, while the duty was reduced to 2d. on supplementary sheets containing only advertisements. (In 1836 the stamp duty on newspapers was reduced from the rate of 4d. a sheet, imposed in 1815, to 1d. a sheet, and in 1855 this so-called 'Tax on knowledge' was abolished altogether.) The Attorney-General's power to file *ex officio* informations remained but was rarely used. Lord Campbell recalled that when as Sir John Campbell he had been Attorney-General during the 1830s, he had filed only one such information in seven years. This was against Feargus O'Connor, the Chartist leader, for libels in the *Northern Star* 'inciting the people to insurrection and plunder.' His reason for exercising this right was that 'I wished to take upon myself the whole responsibility of the prosecution'.[1]

The decline in the number of prosecutions for what we should regard as political offences, especially between 1821 and 1834, is shown by two sets of statistics. The first of these was a return by order of the House of Commons of informations for political libels and seditious conduct during the years 1808–21. In these thirteen years no less than seventy prosecutions were instituted in cases of seditious libel but, despite the special jury system, convictions were obtained in no more than thirty-four of these cases. As we have already seen, the fifty-one prosecutions brought during the fateful years of 1817 and 1819 produced no more than sixteen convictions. During the next thirteen years, 1821–34, there were thirty-six prosecutions (many of them in 1821 and 1822) but twenty-seven of them ended with convictions. The number of convictions for blasphemous libel during the same period, seventy-two, seems remarkably high but there were special reasons for this which will be explained in the next chapter.

The growing freedom of the press was a portent of more general change in the climate of political opinion. The Reform Bill of 1832 was by no means enough to satisfy all the demands of the radicals but it went considerably beyond what many of its critics thought likely. Even a proportion of those who remained dissatisfied could be

[1] *Lives of the Lord Chancellors*, 4th edn. (London, 1857), VII, 178n.

persuaded that the bill and the Whig administration which fostered it offered the best practical means to still further reforms in the political system. The firebrands of the radical press, who had suffered the penalties of political censorship under earlier administrations, now acquired an improbable respectability. William Hone retired to the life of evangelical piety; William Cobbett, with only three years of life left to him, became Member of Parliament for Oldham in 1832; and even the apparently incorrigible Richard Carlile remarked after the passing of the Reform Bill that he might now become 'what is commonly called a ministerial man'. On the government side as well, men began to profess a new belief in political tolerance. 'There is no man', said Sir Robert Peel in 1832, 'who has had official experience connected with the Press, who can fail to be sensible of the danger of any crusade rashly directed against it. There are considerations of delicacy and prudence always to be attended to; and if you were to produce a hundred libels of the most disgusting nature, and at the same time show me that the Attorney-General had not prosecuted one of them, I should certainly not, from those two premises alone, draw the conclusion that he must necessarily have neglected his duty'.[1]

The Reform Bill and the new style of monarchy robbed the literature of political protest of some of its foremost authors and publishers—just as it deprived those who were still totally dissatisfied with these first reforms of the support of an articulate middle-class. To many of the pre-1832 reformers it now seemed that they had got what they wanted, whether they had got what the industrial workers and the agricultural labourers wanted was another matter. In any case, too many of the unenfranchised classes were soon to be concerned with the prospect of slow starvation rather than whether or not they might elect Members of Parliament. With the passing of George IV, however, attacks on the monarchy declined, and after the accession of the more tolerant William IV and later the serious-minded young Victoria—whose quality of moral earnestness was a match for that of many of the radical reformers—even the imposition of a monarchy became easier to bear. Political criticism became, if not milder, less dangerous and the need for political censorship diminished. A careful eye had to be kept on the publications of Chartists or Irish nationalists but rarely to the extent of prosecuting their publishers.

Many early and eminent Victorians looked back, almost incredulously, at the speed with which freedom of speech and of the press had been established, as well as at the completeness of this revolution.

[1] *Parl. Deb.*, 3rd series, xii, 1162–3 (21 May 1832).

Lord Campbell described the change from a politician's and a lawyer's point of view.

In the year 1834, being a candidate to represent the city of Edinburgh in Parliament, I was reproached for not being sufficiently liberal in my opinions. I said truly, that, although Attorney-General to the Crown, I had uttered sentiments for which, forty years before, I should have been sent to Botany Bay.[1]

Many like H. T. Buckle in 1857 rejoiced over 'the rapid progress of democratic opinions', or, like Mrs. Gaskell in the same year, marvelled how 'rapid have been the changes for the better'. Others, like Leigh Hunt, observed the young Victoria's readiness 'to fall in with every great and liberal measure', and threw away their republican banners. Still others, with rather more political sophistication, like Disraeli, linked the new democracy and the free press by looking back at the weak and frightened governments of George IV as King and Regent, wondering how they could have imposed themselves on the country for so long, and remarking how impossible such an imposition would be 'To us, with our "Times" newspaper every morning on our breakfast table, bringing, on every subject which can interest the public mind, a degree of information and intelligence which must form a security against any prolonged public misconception'.[2] As the echoes of self-congratulation faded, other Victorian voices began to debate how free a free press could expect to be.

[1] *Lives of the Lord Chancellors*, VII, 273n.
[2] *Coningsby: or, The New Generation* (London, 1844), I, 154.
cf. H. T. Buckle, *History of Civilisation in England*, I, 457; Mrs. Gaskell, *The Life of Charlotte Brontë*, I, 114; Leigh Hunt, *Autobiography*, II, 78.

9

Guardians of Public Morality:
(2) The Society for the Suppression of Vice

GODLINESS AND CLEANLINESS

The French revolution illustrated the connection between good morals and the order and peace of society more than all the eloquence of the pulpit and the disquisitions of moral philosophers had done for many centuries. The upper ranks in society, the generality of men of rank and fortune, not always the most inquisitive on other subjects, were among the very first to take alarm at those irreligious and profligate doctrines by which the French democracy sought to shelter the profligacy of its conduct. . . . The levity and licentiousness of French manners had already made an alarming progress in the higher, and what were called, the fashionable circles, from whence they must pass on to the other orders.
                                        —*The Annual Register* (1798)

The causal connection between sexual immorality and political subversion, whether in print or in fact, was not always as evident to observers as it was to the author of this passage in the *Annual Register*. Yet irreligion—or, more specifically, anti-clericalism—had been a feature of the French revolution and such irreligion as existed in the English radical movement of the early nineteenth century was anti-clerical too. Certainly, it seemed that blasphemy was a tool of political revolution and that obscene literature by accustoming its readers to moral subversion would prepare them for political insurrection as well. The period when unorthodox religious beliefs— or the lack of any religious belief—could be dismissed with mild contempt was coming to an end. No longer were Anglican theologians like Samuel Horsley content to put down their intellectual opponents like Joseph Priestley, the Unitarian, with a piece of neat sarcasm. ('The conviction of the orthodox Trinitarian, that his philosophy is Plato's and his creed St. John's, will alleviate the mortification he might otherwise feel in differing from Dr. Priestley'.) Instead the cry was 'The Church in danger', and men rallied to the defence of that Church even if only because it was part of the established order. This particular attitude towards the Church of England, quite openly political, is well illustrated by the response of Lord Thurlow, whose reign as Lord Chancellor ended in 1793, when a group of Presbyterians met him to ask that certain laws, which disqualified them from holding civil offices, should be repealed. 'Gentlemen', said Thurlow, 'I'll be perfectly frank with you. Gentlemen, I am against you, and for the Established Church, by God. Not that I like the Established Church a bit better than any other church, but because it *is* established. And whenever you can get your damned religion established, I'll be for that too. Good morning to you'.[1]

As the contagion of revolutionary thought and sympathy spread during the final decade of the eighteenth century, the government itself still showed some inertia in the matter of prosecuting blasphemous publications, perhaps because it believed that to prosecute them was to publicise them or perhaps because it felt that private organisations like the Proclamation Society were well able to deal with the offenders. Certainly, the Proclamation Society showed itself willing to undertake the task in the case of Thomas Paine's *Age of Reason*. In 1797 a prosecution was brought against an impecunious bookseller, Thomas Williams, for issuing the book, and Erskine who had defended Paine in the *Rights of Man* trial appeared this time for the Proclamation Society. There were two other publishers of the book, neither of whom was prosecuted: Daniel Isaac Eaton was authorised by Paine to publish it but Eaton left the country at the time of the case against Williams; H. D. Symonds produced a pirated edition but sold this with answers to Paine's arguments and an extremely hostile account of Paine's life by Francis Oldys.

Although Paine's book attacked Christianity as a whole, Lord Kenyon, who presided at the trial of Williams, made much of the technical offence which it committed of denying the doctrine of the Trinity. Such a denial remained criminal by the Blasphemy Act of 1698 and was, in theory, enough to condemn the book. Of course, Paine was not an atheist but a deist, though this made no difference so far as the court was concerned. His creed was 'I believe in one God, and no more; and I hope for happiness beyond this life'.[2] In attacking the Bible and the doctrines of Christianity, Paine set up an alternative 'word of God' and 'revelation'. These were 'THE CREATION WE BEHOLD'.[3] Science was to Paine, as to Samuel Clarke almost a century earlier, the means of demonstrating the being and nature of God. Indeed, Paine's God is described with the vagueness and euphemism of quasi-religious jargon as 'The Almighty Lecturer'.[4] It

[1] Campbell, *Lives of the Lord Chancellors*, VII, 319.
[2] *Theological Works of Thomas Paine* (London, 1827), p. 3.
[3] *ibid.*, p. 22.
[4] *ibid.*, p. 29.

is perhaps unfair to charge Paine with having sired those popular religious cults of the nineteenth century whose connections with orthodox Christianity were either extremely tenuous or non-existent but he bears at least part of the responsibility. At all events, a deist work like the *Age of Reason*, written by an apologist for the French revolution could only be regarded as blasphemous and Williams went to prison for a year. It is to Erskine's credit that when he discovered the poverty of Williams and his family, he urged the Proclamation Society to exercise some charity towards them but this, apparently, the Society felt disinclined to do.

A case which was in many ways more interesting than that of the *Age of Reason* was one which never came to court. In March 1796 Matthew Gregory Lewis's novel *The Monk* had been published, the latest in a succession of 'Gothic' novels which went back at least as far as Horace Walpole's *Castle of Otranto* (1764) and, in the opinion of some people, to Thomas Leland's *Longsword, Earl of Salisbury* (1762), or even Smollett's *Ferdinand Count Fathom* (1753). Most of these novels, although fruitful for the psychoanalyst, contained little which their readers could regard as indecent, however sensational their style might be. By comparison, the tone of *The Monk* was sensuous, sensual, and often sadistic, so that the Marquis de Sade himself thought it the best of '*ces romans nouveaux*', describing it as '*supérieur, sous tous les rapports, aux bizarres élans de la brillante imagination de Radcliffe*'.[1] But there were those in England who were unlikely to share the enthusiasm of the Marquis for scenes of rape in burial vaults and other trappings of Lewis's fiction. T. J. Mathias, for instance, in the fourth dialogue of his *Pursuits of Literature* (1797) proclaimed,

> Another Cleland see in LEWIS rise.
> Why sleep the ministers of truth and law?
> Has the State no controul, no decent awe,
> While each with each in madd'ning orgies vie,
> Pandars to lust and licens'd blasphemy?[2]

In February 1797, Coleridge in the *Critical Review* had accused Lewis of trying to 'inflame the fleshly appetites' and, more significantly, of pouring contempt on the Bible.[3] In August the *Monthly Review* claimed that the vein of obscenity running through *The Monk* made the book totally unfit for general circulation. Yet it was the charge of blasphemy rather than that of obscenity from which Lewis

---

[1] *Oeuvres Complètes du Marquis de Sade* (Paris, 1966–7), X, 14–15.
[2] *The Pursuits of Literature* (London, 1797), pp. 44–45.
[3] *Critical Review*, XIX (1797), p. 198.

had most to fear. In the novel Donna Elvira does not allow her daughter Antonia, fifteen years old, to read the Bible except in an expurgated version drawn up by Donna Elvira herself.

That prudent mother, while she admired the beauties of the sacred writings, was convinced that, unrestricted, no reading more improper could be permitted a young woman. Many of the narratives can only tend to excite ideas the worst calculated for a female breast: every thing is called plainly and roundly by its name; and the annals of a brothel would scarcely furnish a greater choice of indecent expressions. Yet this is the book which young women are recommended to study, which is put into the hands of children, able to comprehend little more than those passages of which they had better remain ignorant, and which but too frequently inculcates the first rudiments of vice, and gives the first alarm to the still sleeping passions.[1]

For just such attacks on the Bible men were fined and imprisoned during the next fifty years and it would have been no mitigation in Lewis's case that he was a professing Christian. Under the provisions of the Blasphemy Act of 1698 such an attack was as criminal as denial of the Trinity. Critics like Mathias began to demand the prosecution of Lewis for blasphemous libel and obscene libel as well. The Attorney-General, Sir John Scott, later Lord Eldon, apparently initiated proceedings in the court of King's Bench but at this point Lewis took fright. In February 1798 an entirely new edition of his novel was issued with the title of *Ambrosio: or, The Monk* and with all the 'objectionable' passages cut out. The reward for this compliance was that no further proceedings were taken against the book or its author.

It is no coincidence that the Gothic novel as a genre should have developed and thrived so remarkably at a time when the standards of moral censorship were becoming much stricter. Given the Gothic trappings, the most ordinary stories became subtly suggestive and though, for instance, no one would have dreamt of prosecuting Ann Radcliffe or her publisher for obscene libel, even in her comparatively benign narratives the same overtones of morbid sexuality and sadism are present. Her novels are essentially studies of the characters and sufferings of persecuted heroines in elaborate and evocative settings. The other prisoners of the Gothic nightmare exist only in relation to the heroine, and for the greater part of the story the one indispensable relationship is that between the hypersensitive victim and her sinister, ruthless persecutor. What must have given the stories greater impact is that beneath the fancy dress the central character is always a middle-class English girl of the later eighteenth century, doomed to submit

---

[1] *The Monk* (New York, 1952), p. 258.

to a man whose 'polluted touch would freeze her heart in horror,' or confined by her captors in a bedroom whose door cannot be fastened on the inside. Then, as Mrs. Radcliffe never tires of reminding her readers, these heroines are of a very special type. They are distinguished by hypersensitivity in all emotional matters, by their delicacy of sensibility and physical beauty, by their sweetness of nature, their modesty and gentility, and by the ease with which beauty as well as grief will move them to tears. These heroines, not their more robust sisters, are the chosen victims of tyrants and libertines, the prisoners of Gothic castles and abbeys. They are the natural and inevitable partners of men like Montoni in the *Mysteries of Udolpho* (1794), or Schedoni in *The Italian: or, The Confessional of the Black Penitents* (1797). Of course, the rape which is threatened never takes place and, in this sense, Mrs. Radcliffe's novels are less obscene than *Clarissa* but the reader is treated to a volume or so of anticipation.

This is merely one aspect of the Gothic novel but it is a highly significant one and while in England the force of moral censorship confined the genre to suggestion and symbolism in this matter, the Marquis de Sade showed another heroine in *Justine* (1791) enduring more explicit horrors in the Gothic surroundings of the convent of Sainte-Marie des Bois or the castle where Roland holds her captive and which is described very much in the style that Ann Radcliffe used three years later to depict Udolpho.[1] More recent literature supports the view that in the Gothic novel eighteenth-century readers were approaching—albeit subconsciously—territory that would have been forbidden them, had it been more clearly mapped out. A century and a half after Udolpho came the castle of Roissy in 'Pauline Reage's' *Histoire d'O* (1954), a castle complete with cells, refectory, and dungeons.[2] Two years later, in Jean de Berg's novel *L'Image* the young victim reaches the climax of her sufferings in a chapter called 'La Chambre Gothique'. In 1967 in an anonymous novel *Harriet Marwood, Governess*, published in America, the victim is male but the climax of the story is again in the Gothic surroundings of a Breton

[1] 'Enfin nous vîmes un château perché sur la crête d'une montagne, au bord d'un précipice affreux, dans lequel il semblait prêt à s'abîmer: aucune route ne paraissait y tenir; celle que nous suivons, seulement pratiquée par des chèvres, remplie de cailloux de tous côtés, arrivait cependant à cet effrayant repaire, resemblant bien plutôt à un asile de voleurs qu'à l'habitation de gens vertueux.' *Oeuvres Complètes du Marquis du Sade*, III, 268.

[2] 'Elle était dans une pièce ronde et voûtée, très petite et très basse; les murs et la voûte étaient de pierre sans aucun revêtement, on voyait les joints de la maçonnerie. . . . La chaleur des radiateurs . . . ne suffisait pas cependant à venir à bout de l'odeur de vase et de terre qui est l'odeur des anciennes prisons, et dans les vieux châteaux, des donjons inhabités.' *Histoire d'O* (Paris, 1962), pp. 59–60.

castle dungeon, where 'for him . . . the lasting basis of their love was established in a single night'.[1] At a far lower level, the same morbid sexuality persists in a comic-book series like *Tales from the Crypt* with such tales as 'The High Cost of Dying', where in an 'old world' setting, necrophiliac doctors gloat over 'glamorised' corpses.[2] Without reading back too much from these later imitations into the Gothic fiction of the eighteenth and early nineteenth centuries it is not hard to see why so long as the genre maintained its reticence at the level of literal description the censors could hardly interfere with it, while at much deeper levels it exercised a powerful attraction for its many thousands of readers. Nor was the censorship always irksome, for as Ann Radcliffe realised and De Sade, to his cost, did not, there is a profound truth for the novelist in Voltaire's remark that the art of boring people is to tell them everything: 'Le secret d'ennuyer est le secret de tout dire'.

Yet by 1796 *The Monk* had made the underlying preoccupations of the Gothic novel much more explicit and the forces of censorship were brought into play. Like the Jacobean drama of two centuries earlier this species of fiction had gone beyond what was to be tolerated, in its search for new and more lurid excitement. When a so-called 'parody' of *The Monk* was published in 1798 as *The New Monk*, all the Gothic trappings were dispensed with and the readers were left with an unattractive picture of what such fiction might degenerate into, once the fancy dress was put away. The setting is Mrs. Rod's boarding school with a complement of girls, a crew of flagellators, and a flogging-room presided over by a male porter: sections of the book would fit without alteration into certain volumes of Victorian pornography. Feeble though *The New Monk* may be, it must have made the censors wonder whether they had not missed something in the Gothic novel proper and whether, perhaps, even the strictest moral censorship could stifle the less admirable human emotions at all levels of expression.

In the last few years of the eighteenth-century the government and bodies like the Proclamation Society were too much engaged with literature which openly flouted the law to spend their time in exploring the various levels of meaning in the Gothic novel. The sad truth was that for all its efforts—or perhaps lack of effort—the Proclamation Society seemed to be making little headway against the menace of obscene books and prints. The seventh report of the Society's committee, published in 1795, recorded only one successful prosecution of this kind and a second which was not yet concluded. These

[1] *Harriet Marwood, Governess* (New York, 1967), p. 165.
[2] *Tales from the Crypt* (New York, 1964), pp. 52–72.

may have been the two prosecutions against publishers of *Harris's List of Covent-Garden Ladies*, indeed there is no record of any other cases at the time. Four years later, in its report for 1799 the committee reported more prosecutions for obscene libel, revealing with horror that some of this 'moral poison' had even found its way into 'a female seminary of education' and reminding its supporters that 'The publication of obscene books and prints is an offence which attracted the Society's earliest attention; and to which, as to an object of the first importance, it has uniformly continued to direct its regard'. But unhappily for the Society, the courts did not yet seem to regard such offences with quite the same urgency: hence the discharge of John Cole after his convictions in 1798 and the acquittals of Thomas Skillern and James Fentum in the following year.[1] Skillern and Fentum had both published 'The Plenipotentiary' and when Skillern was charged he replied that 'the said indictment and the matters therein contained are not sufficient in law, and that he needs not nor is he bound by any law of the land in any manner to answer thereto'.[2] This was a plea which the court accepted and though the coarsest words in the poem had been represented by no more than their first and last letters there was little encouragement for the Proclamation Society in these acquittals. No wonder that at the turn of the century there was a growing feeling that the Society was lacking in vigour and that a new accession of energy was needed.

To make matters worse, this was a time when such organisations as the Proclamation Society should have been making a much greater impact, since the temper of the age was so sympathetic to them and this sympathy was to become yet more evident during the first quarter of the nineteenth century. Critics and censors alike strove for a new moral standard in literature. In vain might Byron assure his publisher, John Murray, that no girl would ever be seduced by reading *Don Juan: Blackwood's Magazine* knew better and with a severity which might seem more appropriate to Robert Montgomery or the *Evangelical Magazine*, *Blackwood's* dismissed it as 'a filthy and impious poem', in which 'every species of sensual gratification' was laid bare 'to the eye of man—and of *woman*'. Even as unlikely a figure as Sir Walter Scott was involved in a small literary scandal in 1801 when with the assistance of other editors he was preparing new editions of certain medieval romances. John Leyden, the editor who was working on *Sir Tristram*, discovered that one line of that poem contained the word *queynt*, the medieval version of *cunt*, which was also used by Chaucer in 'The Miller's Tale'. Leyden complained that

[1] P.R.O., K.B. 28/387/2, 3 and K.B. 28/391/12, 13.
[2] P.R.O., K.B. 28/391/12.

the text of *Sir Tristram* had become too 'free and easy' at this point and refused to have any more to do with it. The Duke of Roxboroughe suggested that such words should be retained, since the poems were in medieval English, but he refused to have the work dedicated to him. Scott himself completed the edition but when it was published the line containing the offending word had to be omitted in all but twelve copies, reserved for him and his friends.[1]

The great age of expurgation had begun and by 1805 when James Plumptre published his *Collection of Songs* suggestive lines like Shakespeare's 'Under the greenwood tree/Who loves to lie with me' were altered to the less objectionable 'Under the greenwood tree/ Who loves to work with me'. Seven years later Plumptre, having gone to work on the dramatists, produced *The English Drama Purified* but the most popular expurgation of this sort was undoubtedly Thomas Bowdler's *Family Shakespeare* (1818), to which he prefaced the following remarks.

It certainly is my wish, and it has been my study, to exclude from this publication whatever is unfit to be read aloud by a gentleman to a company of ladies. I can hardly imagine a more pleasing occupation for a winter's evening in the country, than for a father to read one of Shakespeare's plays to his family circle. My object is to enable him to do so without incurring the danger of falling unawares among words and expressions which are of such a nature as to raise a blush on the cheek of modesty, or render it necessary for the reader to pause, and examine the sequel, before he proceeds further in the entertainment of the evening.[2]

Before condemning Bowdler out of hand, it is worth remembering the remark, made nine years earlier, of no less a critic than Coleridge with reference to the far more genteel writing of Addison and Steele in the *Spectator* and *Tatler*. It might almost be the verbal inspiration for Bowdler's own comment. 'A man—I will not say of delicate mind and pure morals, but—of common good manners, who means to read an essay, which he has opened upon at hazard in these volumes to a mixed company, will find it necessary to take a previous survey of its contents'.[3] Such was the moral sensitivity of readers by 1818 that the remarks made by Bowdler seem hardly out of the ordinary. Nonetheless, he found certain plays of Shakespeare impossible to expurgate adequately if they were to remain comprehensible to their readers, these plays included *Othello*; *Measure for Measure*, and the second part of *Henry IV*. Here is his advice on *Othello*:

[1] Arthur Johnston, *Enchanted Ground: The Study of Medieval Romance in the Eighteenth Century* (London, 1964), p. 180.
[2] *The Family Shakespeare*, 4th edn. (London, 1825), I, xvii–xviii.
[3] *The Friend*, III, 326.

THIS tragedy is justly considered as one of the noblest efforts of dramatic genius that has appeared in any age or in any language; but the subject is unfortunately little suited to family reading. . . . I would advise the transferring it from the parlour to the cabinet.[1]

In 1830 appeared the first volumes of the *Family Classical Library*, edited on the same principles and promising in its prospectus, 'those Authors, whose works may with propriety be read *by the youth of both sexes*'.[2] It was perhaps surprising, in the light of this promise that for its nineteenth volume the *Library* chose the satires of Juvenal but any reader who expected to find these published intact was in for such sharp reminders as this one about the sixth satire. 'I do not suppose that any class of females who can read at all, will ever be permitted to read it'.[3] Before long even the Bible was being condemned for its obscenity, in terms far stronger than M. G. Lewis would have dared to use in *The Monk*. 'Its heroines are strumpets', proclaimed the atheist Charles Southwell in 1841, 'an account of whose debaucheries is fit only for the hell of human imagination; assassinating Jezebels, the tale of whose lewdness and infamy would put Fanny Hill or Harriet Wilson to the blush'.[4] Of course, the atheists of the nineteenth century could be as puritanical as any believer but not only atheists were disturbed about some of the contents of the Bible in this respect. Here is the view of a Christian, Richard Lalor Sheil, Vice-President of the Board of Trade.

The Bible contains tales of atrocity at which human nature shudders. Part of the holy writings consists of history, and of the narration of facts of a kind that cannot be mentioned in the presence of a virtuous woman, without exciting horror. Should a woman be permitted to read in her chamber, what she would tremble to hear at her domestic board? Should she con over and resolve, what she would rather die than utter?[5]

The Bible, like the plays of Shakespeare, was something which could inspire unease as well as cultural or spiritual reverence in the minds of many readers: this unease, as well as reverence, created the market for Lamb's *Tales from Shakespeare* and collections of Bible stories for children.

If the Bible and Shakespeare were morally suspect in this respect,

---

[1] *The Family Shakespeare*, X, 245 and 247.

[2] *Prospectus of the Family Classical Library* (London, 1830), p. 4.

[3] *The Family Classical Library: Juvenal and Persius* 2nd edn. (London, 1831), p. xii.

[4] *The Trial of Charles Southwell* (London, 1842), p. 4. The passage was originally published in the fourth number of the *Oracle of Reason* in November 1841.

[5] *ibid.*, p. 74.

there was little that could be said for the robust bawdry of seventeenth century poems like Charles Cotton's *Scarronides: or, Virgil Travestie.* The existence of such burlesque poems seemed to Francis Place, writing in 1836, clear evidence of the debased values of the seventeenth century reading public.

The grossness the nastiness and the obscenity with which the Burlesque Poems abound did not prevent the principal booksellers in London from publishing them openly and with their names on the title page. This with the sale of so many editions may be taken as unquestionable evidence of the taste of that portion of the people who could afford to purchase a volume containing nearly 400 pages.[1]

Francis Place was a careful observer of the changing standards of his time. As a young man he could, for instance, recall seeing *Harris's List of Covent-Garden Ladies* openly displayed by booksellers in Fleet Street between the Racing Calendar and the Book of Common Prayer, 'all three being bound in red and lettered with gold'.[2] Yet by 1819 the reformation had spread throughout the book trade and even the singing of bawdy street ballads had come to an end.

The causes of their being discontinued to be sung are various among others a more active Police. The Association against republicans and levellers also contributed to this end, John Reeves and his associates together with the magistrates extinguished them. The association printed a large number of what they called Loyal songs, and gave them to the ballad singers; if any one was found singing any but Loyal songs, he or she was carried before a magistrate who admonished and discharged him or her, they were then told they might have loyal songs for nothing, and that they would not be molested while singing them. . . . Another cause of their discontinuance was the proceedings of the Society for the Suppression of Vice.[3]

Clearly, by the beginning of the nineteenth century, when even the great books of the past might be objects of suspicion, there were going to be hard times ahead for the publishers of such *jeux d'esprit* as *Fanny Hill* or 'The Plenipotentiary'. All that appeared to be needed to translate literary taste into positive action was an organisation on the lines of the Proclamation Society which, with the vigour of a new enterprise, would attack the evil of obscene publications through a series of private prosecutions. In 1801, after several years in which the Proclamation Society seemed to have had only a moderate success in the cases which it had brought, there appeared a *Proposal for Establishing a Society for the Suppression of Vice and the*

[1] B.M., Add. MSS. 27, 825 f.21.
[2] B.M., Add. MSS. 27,825, f.131.
[3] B.M., Add. MSS. 27,825, ff. 144–45.

Encouragement of Religion and Virtue. This heralded almost a century of activity, by that organisation which was known, for short and rather to its own chagrin, as 'The Vice Society'.

EARLY CAMPAIGNS OF THE VICE SOCIETY: 1802-25

In the *Proposal* of 1801 it was suggested that the Vice Society should include among its aims the exposure of selling by false weights and measures; the prevention of cruelty to animals; and the punishment of those who seduced women, and very often children, into the trade of prostitution. Inevitably, there was also a promise to suppress the publication of 'Licentious and Obscene Books and Prints'. Taken as a whole, it seemed a Society which many humane people would be glad to support but, sadly, the false weights and measures, as well as the fate of animals and humans, were all too often forgotten in the frenzy to put pornographers behind bars. In 1817 George Prichard, the Secretary of the Society, was examined before the Police Committee of the House of Commons and the evidence which he gave then presents a good general picture of the Society's work during its earlier years. His opening remarks on the subject of obscene books and prints show a distinct tendency towards xenophobia and say little for the previous efforts of the Proclamation Soceity.

The Society first entered upon their investigation into the state of this trade shortly after its institution in 1802; at which period prosecutions for such offences being almost unknown, so little disguise and concealment were used by dealers of this class, that, with no great difficulty, important discoveries were soon made as to its nature and extent. It was early ascertained, from indubitable testimony, that several foreigners (having their head quarters in London) of apparent respectability, and considerable property, were united together in partnership for the principal, and almost exclusive, purpose of carrying on an extensive traffic in obscene books, prints, drawings, toys, &c. The agents, by whom the partners of this house disseminated their merchandise, were about thirty in number, chiefly consisting of Italians, under the assumed character of itinerant hawkers, by whom they established a systematic trade throughout great part of the United Kingdom.[1]

Among the areas visited annually by these men, who travelled singly or in pairs, were Brighton, Maidstone, York, Manchester, Norfolk, and Suffolk. Not all were Italians, despite the Vice Society's insinuation that no decent Englishman would stoop to such iniquity: in 1820, for example, William Moore was convicted at Maidstone Quarter Sessions on a charge of selling snuff boxes, representing men

[1] *Report of the Society for the Suppression of Vice* (London, 1825), p. 29.

189

and women partly naked in the act of 'carnal copulation'.[1] There was a series of prosecutions for similar offences in 1816, involving Anthony Holstein, Peter Paris, and Ireland Ward Pitts.[2] As Prichard pointed out to the Police Committee in the following year, the Napoleonic wars had by a happy chance cut off these pedlars from most of their sources of supply for obscene ornaments but with the resumption of normal trade with the Continent the scourge had returned. Of course, it would have taken more than a major European war to bring this commerce to an end and it is no surprise to find in 1812 that Thomas Wirgman was arrested for 'publishing' what is described as an obscene tooth-pick case, 'containing on the inside lid thereof one obscene, filthy, and indecent picture representing the naked persons of a man and woman in an indecent, filthy, and obscene situation, attitude and practice'.[3]

Even in its earliest months in 1802 the Vice Society had taken swift action against books and prints, so that the number of prosecutions for obscene publication rose sharply. One of the Italian hawkers, Baptista Bertazzi, enjoyed the doubtful honour of being dealt with by Lord Ellenborough himself for selling obscene prints.[4] James Aitken, who had been in trouble in 1795 for selling *Harris's List of Covent-Garden Ladies*, was now sent to prison for six months for publishing *The Amours of Peter Aretin*, a charge which involved the publication of obscene prints as well.[5] His wife Ann went to prison for six months for selling a print called 'The Convent Well Supplied', of which we know no more than that it depicted the sexual acrobatics of four men and two women.[6] At the same time Alexander Hogg was convicted of obscene libel for publishing *A New and Compleat Collection of the most Remarkable Trials for Adultery*.[7] This collection had been published by J. Gill in 1799 and the significance of the prosecution is that the Vice Society was striking at one of the best-selling forms of quasi-pornography. Of course, in its preface the book's aim was piously stated as that of shaming adulterers into a sense of their sin, and most of the contents of the two volumes consisted of short-hand transcripts of trials for 'Adultery, Fornication, Cruelty, and other Criminal Conversation', heard in Doctors' Commons or the court of King's Bench. A great deal of pornography or near-pornography was made up of just such accounts as these and

[1] P.R.O., K.B. 28/474/35.
[2] P.R.O., K.B. 28/456/33 and K.B. 28/458/32.
[3] P.R.O., K.B. 28/443/16.
[4] P.R.O., K.B. 28/404/56.
[5] P.R.O., K.B. 28/401/28.
[6] P.R.O., K.B. 28/404/57.
[7] P.R.O., K.B. 28/401/29.

it would have been difficult at the time to prosecute Alexander Hogg or anyone else merely for reporting what had gone on in court. At the same time, the Vice Society was clearly displeased by the way in which accounts of this sort, mingling scandals in high society with illicit sexual relationships, had such a ready and apparently insatiable market. Gill's edition of these trials happened to be embellished by illustrations of the culprits in their various acts of immorality and it was on these pictures, not on the court reports, that the Society saw its chance of basing a successful case. In this case it was judged that the pictures depicted 'carnal copulation' and were therefore obscene, though carnal copulation does not necessarily imply more than kissing or embracing. If the Vice Society hoped to put a stop to books of this genre it was to be disappointed and when, for instance, A. Moore published his *Annals of Gallantry; or, The Conjugal Monitor* in 1814–15, the illustrations by 'J. Cruickshank' were of a rather more burlesque kind and neither they nor the court reports evidently offered sufficient basis for a prosecution.

That other genre of eighteenth- and nineteenth-century pornography, the monthly magazine of serial stories, scandal, and bawdy, had been the subject of prosecutions for obscenity before the founding of the Vice Society and in 1801, perhaps as the last expiring blow of the Proclamation Society, Isaac Aldrich was prosecuted and imprisoned for a year for publishing his *New Rambler's Magazine*.[1] So many more-or-less pornographic periodicals had similar titles to this that the succession of them becomes rather confusing: this was the second of at least five such publications which appeared between 1783 and 1830. To a modern reader the most striking thing about Aldrich's *New Rambler* is not its obscenity but its feebleness, and it appears that his customers must have been exceptionally easy to please.

From 1802 onwards the Vice Society began to make a considerable impact both on the trade in pornography and upon the courts. Well might Holt in his *Law of Libel* (1812) remark that 'The punishment for obscene writings, prints, etc., has become more frequent in the present period'.[2] Yet not everyone was entirely happy about the legality of the Society's actions, and at Bertazzi's trial in 1801 the defence counsel had hinted at these misgivings. But Lord Chief Justice Ellenborough had no doubt on the matter at all.

Something has been said about the persons, who have formed themselves into this Society, having acted contrary to the law; it does not appear to me

[1] P.R.O., K.B. 28/397/19.
[2] F. L. Holt, *The Law of Libel* (London, 1812), p. 67.

they have done so, by any thing they have done in prosecution of the purposes of the Society; but looking at this prosecution only, so far from seeing any thing which trenches upon law, I conceive they have done very properly in taking an interest in the morals and happiness of Society, and in exerting themselves to prevent the contagion of these infamous publications. It appears to me they have deserved the thanks of all men, and I do not know one rule of law upon which they have at all trenched.[1]

When Prichard gave evidence before the Police Committee of the House of Commons many years later, he was able to quote other unsolicited support for the work of the Society, including the expressed belief of one magistrate who remarked in the course of a case of obscene libel that 'the mischief done to the community by such offences greatly exceeds that done by murder: for, in the latter case, the mischief has some bounds; but no bounds can be set to the pernicious consequences of a crime, which tends to the entire corruption of morals'.[2] With the sympathy of many judges and magistrates on its side, the Society had brought between thirty and forty prosecutions by 1817, 'in all of which', said Prichard, 'they have invariably succeeded'.[3] By that time, dealers in pornography had at least been driven underground, although there were still certain booksellers who did not regard themselves as pornographers but who might nonetheless attract the interest and attention of the Society.

Certainly there had been plenty of prosecutions of publishers or booksellers on charges of obscene libel during the eighteenth century but they had been sporadic and quite unlike the campaign against obscene literature which the Vice Society now seemed able to sustain both financially and morally. Moreover, there is a certain amount of truth in the belief that as censorship grew stricter the styles of pornography became more vicious. The pornographers found themselves herded into a cultural ghetto and, for example, subjects like lesbianism which Henry Fielding in *The Female Husband* (1746) or William King in *The Toast* (1732) had been able to depict without fear of prosecution were now dealt with according to the rules of that ghetto. A more rigid distinction between 'literature' and 'pornography' widened the already present gulf between sexual fantasy and reality. Elements of fantasy certainly exist in *Fanny Hill*, yet it has a certain amount in common with, say, the realism of *Moll Flanders* and a lot in common with the memoirs of an actual whore, as in *An Apology for the Conduct of Teresa Constantia Phillips* (1748–9)—better known in the trade as 'Con' Phillips.

By the early nineteenth century pornography was so rigorously

[1] *Report of the Society for the Suppression of Vice* (1825), p. 37.
[2] *ibid.*, p. 35.   [3] *ibid.*, p. 31.

excluded from the ordinary world as to be in danger of becoming what Havelock Ellis called the fairy tales of adult society. Of course, the heroes and heroines of such literature had always been shown accomplishing feats of sexual endurance hardly likely to be found outside the pages of fiction and there was—and is—a pornographers' myth about female orgasm, making it comparable to male ejaculation, which goes back at least as far as *L'Escole des Filles* in 1655. Pornographic fiction now showed greater psychological and physiological unreality: every orifice of the female body was available to the protagonist of such stories, and the more unorthodox or unnatural the act, the more gratified the heroine was—once her resistance had been overcome by persuasion or force. The leading actors now appeared more often whip in hand and pornography—but not only pornography—made the most of a market for flagellant literature: the difference in the pornographic type was that the victims frequently came to enjoy the procedure sooner or later. Even stranger physiological myths eventually grew up in the nineteenth century, insisting that girls were bewitched by the contact of birch and pudenda or that their buttocks could blush with embarrassment independently of their faces, since the heart is able to send the blood in either direction.[1]

To return to the Vice Society, its members and those who shared its views on literature and morality had two principal preoccupations with publications whose decency they might question. First and most important, they were preoccupied with a class of literature which could be described as criminally immoral in that it 'depraved and corrupted' its readers. (Obviously the ability of certain books to deprave and corrupt had long been an assumption of puritan criticism but by this time it was more generally held, and in 1868, in Regina *v.* Hicklin, the legal definition of obscenity was that it must be capable of depraving and corrupting its readers. This still remains the case today.) The second preoccupation was with a type of literature which might 'bring a blush to the cheek of modesty,' but except in cases of extreme coarseness of language this was not generally regarded as a matter for legal censorship. In this respect, authors, editors, and the circulating libraries were encouraged by the moral climate of the age to be their own censors: if they failed, it was reviewers or readers rather than the courts which took them to task. In many cases the nineteenth, like the twentieth, century put such books beyond the reach of the law, though it was not until 1954, in the case of Stanley Kauffman's novel *The Philanderer* that Mr. Justice Stable ruled, 'The charge is not that the tendency of the book is either to shock or to dis-

[1] *The Romance of Chastisement; or, Revelations of the School and Bedroom* (1870), pp. 62 and 82.

193

gust, that is not a criminal offence'.[1] Yet even Thomas Bowdler or the Vice Society would not have prosecuted a publisher of *Othello*, however crimson the blushes on the cheek of 'a young person'.

One pornographer whose activities and tribulations were very much a sign of the times was Edward Rich, prosecuted and sent to prison in 1806 and again in 1809. At the first trial he was accused of publishing two obscene books, *The Frisky Songster* which included 'Oyster Nan' as well as a number of ballads of the type which Francis Place refers to, and *The Voluptuarian Museum*.[2] This second book was characterised by a type of prurient gloating over 'luscious incitements' and 'light rebounding springiness of flesh' which was more intense in expression but less vigorous in action than most pornography of the eighteenth century. At his second trial he was prosecuted for publishing 'The Delights of Venus', which had appeared in the early eighteenth century, without interference, in *The Cabinet of Love* but which had been criminal since the trial of John Cole in 1798.[3] Yet if Rich was a victim of the growing disapproval of Augustan literature of this kind, he was also shrewd enough to be in tune with the less attractive demands and fashions of the contemporary market for pornography. At his second trial his books were described as being of a type whose effect on readers was to 'incite and encourage them to indecent practices and the commission of crimes against nature and particularly the crime of bestiality'.[4] It is no surprise to find that one of the books featuring most prominently in the case—and a sign of things to come—was *Manon la Fouetteuse: or, The Quintessence of Birch Discipline*. At his first trial Rich was sentenced to ten months' imprisonment and a fine of £100 but when he appeared a second time Lord Ellenborough, who presided, apparently decided that he was dealing with a true professional and so sent the bookseller to prison for two years and ordered him to be pilloried.

Shortly after the second trial of Rich a number of sentences—including death sentences—were passed for homosexual conduct and a well-organised homosexual brothel was discovered at the White Swan in Vere Street. Public curiosity and the tendency for pornographers to search out the less explored aspects of sexual conduct made it inevitable that this new subject should be exploited. It had, of course, occurred in eighteenth-century writing but now it became—for the time being—something of a preoccupation. Naturally, the

[1] Stanley Kauffmann, *The Philanderer* (London, 1957), p. 278.
[2] P.R.O., K.B. 28/418/54.
[3] P.R.O., K.B. 28/428/22. cf. K.B. 28/387/2.
[4] P.R.O., K.B. 28/428/22.

authorities regarded such literature as a cause of sexual depravity—as did the Vice Society—but in this particular instance it appears that art imitated life and not the other way round. In 1813 Robert Holloway was sent to prison for eighteen months for having gratified public curiosity over the Vere Street scandal in an obscene libel, *The Phoenix of Sodom; or, The Vere Street Coterie.*[1] In his evidence to the Police Committee of the House of Commons four years later, George Prichard revealed that articles 'representing a crime, which ought not to be named among Christians, which they termed *"the new fashion"* ' had been made and sold openly at Stapleton prison near Bristol.[2] The crime not to be named among Christians, as any number of earlier and contemporary indictments make clear, is sodomy: the only doubt, to judge from other literature of this time, is whether it was invariably 'the new fashion' in homosexual conduct only. Prosecutions shortly after this certainly refer to literature which describes illicit heterosexual conduct, as in the case against John Clarke in 1820.[3]

> Her body was a lott'ry fair
> To prick where'er it pleas'd you,

begins one of his verses and he promises satisfaction from his heroine 'Whatever whim besiege you'.

Organised opposition to the activities of the Vice Society only began when the Society took to bringing prosecutions for blasphemous libel and, even then, the victims of such prosecutions were ready to congratulate the Society on its work in dealing with pornographers. But occasionally a publisher or bookseller would get the better of the Society, even in a case of obscene libel. One of the few men to succeed in doing this was William Benbow, whom we have already met as the defendant in a case of political libel brought against him by the short-lived Constitutional Association. In 1822 Benbow had begun to publish yet another *Rambler's Magazine: or, Fashionable Emporium of Polite Literature,* still in the tradition of those rather feebly obscene periodicals which had appeared from time to time during the previous half-century. In the *Rambler* for April 1822 Benbow announced that he was about to publish a new translation of Louvet de Couvray's romance *Les Amours du Chevalier de Faublas,* which had a certain transvestite element and which, as Benbow remarked, existed in English only in an old and expurgated edition. But then in June came another announcement: Benbow had

[1] P.R.O., K.B. 28/445/10.
[2] *Report of the Society for the Suppression of Vice* (1825), p. 32.
[3] P.R.O., K.B. 28/473/57.

been prosecuted by the Vice Society for publishing *Faublas* and for certain material in the *Rambler*, including the frontispieces for January and February 1822. These two prints are hardly suggestive to modern eyes, let alone obscene: they represented Vulcan netting his wife Venus in bed with Mars, and a portrayal of Leda and the Swan. The passages objected to in the novel, *Faublas*, were not less decent than some to be found in the pages of Fielding or Smollett. Benbow's counsel, when the case came on at Quarter Sessions, made much of the fact that the two allegedly obscene prints were a great deal less obscene than many passages from classical literature: descriptions in prose or verse of those same events which the prints depicted were considered part of the education of a gentleman, even of a member of the Vice Society. He was probably wise to encourage the suspicions of a middle-class jury with regard to 'gentlemanly' education. The prosecution had made a great point of the fact that one of the passages objected to ended with six stars or asterisks, thus suggesting something unprintable: the Vice Society's next move, predicted Benbow's counsel acidly, 'would be to indict the firmament and stars for indecency'.[1] He made a point too of the fact that *Faublas* had been available for many years from the circulating libraries, though he said nothing about this earlier edition being an expurgated one. Finally, he hinted that the morals of certain members of the Vice Society might not bear too close scrutiny. The jury must have taken the point. Earlier that same year there had been an unfortunate case involving one of the Society's supporters, the Bishop of Clogher, who had been charged with homosexual offences and, when bailed, had absconded. Benbow had given this incident excellent publicity at the time in the *Rambler*.

It took only a little while for the jury to find Benbow not guilty of publishing an obscene libel, and he celebrated this in the September number of the *Rambler* by printing a letter from an improbable 'J. Smith' of 'London', who announced his resignation from the Society because of the hypocrisy and immorality of its members. Yet Benbow and his fellow victims could expect little sympathy, even from those who had been attacked by the Vice Society for other reasons. Richard Carlile who had been prosecuted by the Society and imprisoned for blasphemous libel, addressed its members on the subject of prosecutions brought for obscenity and remarked, 'Had you confined yourself to this, no honest or moral man would have complained or objected to your conduct as a society'.[2] It is an equally sad comment on human

[1] *Rambler's Magazine: or, Fashionable Emporium of Polite Literature* (London, 1822), p. 354.
[2] *The Republican*, II, 182 (25 February 1820).

nature that the pornographers shed few tears when the blasphemers were put behind bars, and many political libellers disliked the blasphemers and pornographers in equal proportions. In this respect, the Vice Society inspired a philosophy of *sauve qui peut* among its chosen victims. Yet it was the Society's new concern with blasphemy (which provoked it to bring fourteen prosecutions for blasphemous libel in the period 1817-25 as compared with twenty for obscenity) which first stimulated real opposition to its activities. Blasphemy, after all, had a certain intellectual respectability about it in terms of freedom of religious belief, making Members of Parliament and others willing to stand up and defend the rights of publishers or authors to disagree with the doctrines of the Church of England or even the doctrines of Christianity as a whole. But it was a very different matter in the emotional climate of the early nineteenth century to stand up and defend the rights of those same people to publish enticing presentations of crimes 'not named among Christians', nor, for that matter, among contemporary blasphemers either.

THE VICE SOCIETY AND THE SUPPRESSION OF BLASPHEMY

Even without the vigilance and dedication of the Vice Society the crime of blasphemous libel would hardly have gone unnoticed or unpunished during the first quarter of the century. There was, for instance, the prosecution of the elderly Daniel Isaac Eaton in 1812 before the Society's campaign began. Eaton had published what he called the 'Third Part' of Paine's *Age of Reason*, which was merely a collection of Paine's occasional essays on Christianity assembled by Eaton and added to the first two parts of the *Age of Reason*. Of course, these first two parts themselves remained criminal, as they had been when Williams was convicted in 1797, and in 1819 Carlile was sent to prison for publishing them. Paine himself had died in New York in 1809 so that publishers could now edit his work to suit themselves without fear of the author's displeasure. Prince Smith defended Eaton in 1812 and from this advocate's lips came the first of many protests about the leniency shown to more intellectually sophisticated writers like Hume and Gibbon, as compared with the severity with which the law treated Thomas Paine's forthrightness.

The endeavours of all questioners of the divine revelation, from Lord Herbert of Cherbury to Mr. Gibbon—the endeavours of Hume—were to insinuate Deism by all the arts of philosophy, rhetoric and declamation; and the question whether less danger was to be apprehended from such writers than from Paine was easily decided. It was a question between the vulgarity and abuse of the latter, and the artful sophistry of Gibbon

197

the specious philosophy of Hume, and the witty sarcasms of Voltaire.[1]

Lord Ellenborough invited the jury as 'Christian men to say whether the present was not an atrocious libel on the Christian religion'.[2] Eaton was found guilty forthwith, sent to prison for eighteen months and ordered to be pilloried. Eaton died in prison but his appearance in the pillory was not all that Ellenborough would have wished. According to a later account, 'the people, so far from shewing the least incivility towards him, expressed the greatest indignation at his having been put there'.[3]

Inevitably, Paine's views on Christianity were a great deal less restrained than those of Hume or Gibbon because he belonged to an age which chose to discuss theology in terms of moral indignation. He attacked the morality of the Bible on the grounds that it was either foolish,

Loving enemies, is another dogma of feigned morality . . . to love in proportion to the injury, if it could be done, would be to offer a premium for a crime.[4]

or repugnant.

Whenever we read the obscene stories, the voluptuous debaucheries, the cruel and torturous executions, the unrelenting vindictiveness, with which more than half the Bible is filled, it would be more consistent that we call it the work of a Demon, than the word of God. It is a history of wickedness, that has served to corrupt and brutalize mankind.[5]

Such attacks were not allowed to pass unchallenged by the law and yet, in certain respects, the law itself was becoming more lenient. When Thomas Williams was tried in 1797 for selling the *Age of Reason*, Lord Kenyon had reminded the court of the criminality of denying the doctrine of the Trinity. Now, in 1813, an Act was passed which made such a denial no longer criminal, and the words 'deny any one of the Persons in the Holy Trinity to be God', were removed from the provisions of the Blasphemy Act. This Act of 1813 was intended 'for the further relief of Protestant Dissenting Ministers and Schoolmasters', but more specifically it was intended to grant freedom of worship to Unitarians. How much freedom, in practice, it would give to the press was by no means certain. John Wright, a Unitarian,

[1] *State Trials*, XXXI, 955.

[2] *ibid.*, XXXI, 950.

[3] *Gentleman's Magazine*, LXXXV (1815), 452. (The same account includes a reference to the punishment of Shebbeare in 1759, who 'came upon the pillory in full dress, attended by his servant in livery, who held an umbrella over him.')

[4] *Theological Works of Thomas Paine* (*Age of Reason* Part II), p. 84.

[5] *Theological Works of Thomas Paine* (*Age of Reason* Part I), p. 13.

described the Trinity as 'ridiculous' in 1817 and an attempt to prosecute him for this was abandoned. On the other hand, Mr. Justice Best at the trial of Samuel Waddington in 1822 for publishing a blasphemous libel (Elihu Palmer's *Principles of Nature*) ruled that denial of the Trinity was still criminal in such cases, despite the Act of 1813. 'The legislature, in passing that Act, only thought of easing the consciences of Dissenters, and not of allowing them to weaken the faith of the members of the Church'.[1] His brother judges agreed with him that the Act of 1813 'while relieving from penalties those who deny the doctrine of the Trinity, made no change in the Common Law as to blasphemous libels'.[2]

At the time when the Vice Society launched this particular campaign it is probably fair to say that the government would have been prepared to turn a blind eye to a number of publications which could have been prosecuted to conviction as blasphemous, if only for the simple reason that so many people now felt the publicity of prosecution would do more for a book than merely allowing it to circulate in some obscurity. Once the attractions of martyrdom were removed it is likely that men on the other side of the question— Richard Carlile, for example—would have found the cause of Paine and Palmer less compelling. The Vice Society, on the other hand, could bid for nothing short of total suppression. Of course the Society thereby stimulated Carlile and his sympathisers, and laid itself open to precisely the same kind of objection as the government had done. Why prosecute men for publishing the works of Paine and Palmer, while taking no action against those who publish Hume, Gibbon, Bolingbroke, and the other sceptics of the eighteenth century? Naturally, the Society believed that those for whose spiritual welfare it felt particularly responsible were more likely to be affected by the blunt onslaught of Paine than by the cool logic of Hume—in which they were probably right. But there was another consideration: it was, after all, rather too late to begin censoring works which had been circulating freely for half a century or more. Had the books been pornographic it would, nonetheless, have been possible but juries would have been less sympathetic in the case of anything which might be written in a spirit of moral earnestness or 'philosophical inquiry'. Books like the *Age of Reason* had never really circulated freely in England and there was, therefore, a better chance of continuing to suppress them. Under such circumstances it is not surprising that those who were now prosecuted turned on Hume and Gibbon, almost as savagely as they turned on the Vice Society, with the

[1] *State Trials* (New Series), I, 1342.
[2] *ibid.*, I, 1339.

righteous anger of the less able who have seen the more able escaping their due punishment.

They let the great Deistical works repose upon the shelves of the book-sellers, while they direct all their arrows against poor Thomas Paine. They touch not Bolingbroke's heavy quartos, because Bolingbroke was a Tory, and a Lord; they touch not David Hume, because Hume was a silly admirer even of the persons of princes, and a great advocate for hereditary Govern-ment and legitimacy; they touch not Adam Smith, because Adam Smith was a Scotchman and a hypocrite. . . . They touch not Gibbon, because Gibbon was a sinecure placeman and an advocate for the American war. But Thomas Paine they fear, and they have feared him of old; he exposed their solid system of finance; he raised the fabric of American freedom; he laid bare the rotten borough system, and the still more rotten Church and State.[1]

The other thing which Thomas Paine did, but which this supporter of Richard Carlile's in 1819 forbore to mention, was to unite about as many readers against some of the causes he advocated as for them, by his general approach and style. For this reason alone, his pros-ecutors might have done better to leave him alone.

The two books which provoked the Vice Society on one side and Carlile and his supporters on the other to a frenzy of activity were both American in inspiration and, partly, in origin. Paine's *Age of Reason* was written in Paris after a long period in America, while Elihu Palmer's *Principles of Nature* had first appeared in America in 1801. There is a simplicity and optimism in Palmer's work which seems to go beyond anything in Paine. Like Paine, he attacks Christianity as a great moral evil and describes in terms of righteous anger the 'crimes of ecclesiastical despots'. He urges that religious dogma should be replaced by what he calls, rather hopefully, a belief in 'the great cause of human existence', and feelings of reverence for 'the mighty power by which the universe is sustained.'[2] 'Man's highest happiness', he adds, 'consists in perspicuously discovering his true connection with nature', and he saw the future in terms which make Victorian optimism or the hopes of Candide seem cautious and restrained by comparison.[3] The nineteenth century is to witness the great progressive movement towards the millennium, as indicated by the heading of the book's last chapter. 'Commencement of the Nineteenth Century; Christianity; Deism; Reason; Science; Virtue; Happiness'. Palmer's book was very much a product of the American

[1] *The Opening Speech and Reply of Mr. Fleming at the British Forum* (London, 1819), p. 16.
[2] *The Deist, or, Moral Philosopher* (London, 1819), I, 163 and 182.
[3] *ibid.*, I, 158.

—as opposed to the English—mind at the beginning of the nineteenth century, since few people in England could see the future determined by quite the rational and tranquil sequence of Palmer's prediction: many, if not most, of those who bought this banned book during the 1820s must have done so to demonstrate their support for a free press rather than their faith in Palmer's philosophy. By comparison, the *Age of Reason* was a more sophisticated book but in prosecuting it, the Vice Society built it into a rallying point for those who wished to show their continuing loyalty to freedom of expression, deism, the radical cause, or simply to the memory of the late Thomas Paine.

Hostilities began in 1819 when Carlile published the *Age of Reason*, despite the fate of its previous publishers, and the *Principles of Nature*. The Vice Society brought a prosecution against him but Carlile boasted that they would never get a conviction. He claimed that what they really wanted to do was to keep him in prison, as he had been kept in prison in 1817 for eighteen weeks when the government prosecuted him for publishing Hone's parodies, so that when he was acquitted he would already have served a sentence of several months. When he heard that the Attorney-General himself had taken over the prosecution which the Society had brought, he maintained bravely, 'Some persons have ventured to tell me, that the Attorney-General was sensible of the general opinion respecting the Society for the Suppression of Vice, and considered it dangerous to leave a prosecution of that nature in their hands'.[1] Defying his enemies even from prison, he issued the reprint of the *Principles of Nature* in his periodical the *Deist, or, Moral Philosopher* and in the dedication to the Vice Society he taunted his persecutors by reminding them that without their 'kind assistance' publication of the book could never have been so financially rewarding to him. Carlile had always enjoyed emphasising the effect of prosecutions on the sale of his publications and had actually dedicated his second edition of the *Political Litany* to Sir Samuel Shepherd, the Attorney-General, telling him that the enormous increase in its circulation was entirely due to the unsuccessful prosecutions brought against Carlile and Hone, and inviting him to have another try.

Carlile may have been something of an over-eager martyr but whatever one's views of this and of his publications, it is difficult not to admire his very great courage, his absolute determination to resist oppression or intimidation to the uttermost, and the splendid panache with which he set about his well-nigh victorious enemies. In the face of the coming trial, at which he had no financial alternative but to

[1] *ibid.*, I, iv.

defend himself, he concluded his dedication of the *Principles of Nature* with these words.

I flatter myself, (perhaps vainly) from the deep interest you have taken to circulate my publications amongst the more virtuous part of the community, that each of your Members will do me the honour to grace your libraries with this volume. I feel it incumbent on me to say, that its completion may be fairly attributed to your kind assistance, and have earnestly to entreat a continuation of that assistance to the completion of a Second Volume. I am, &c.

> Your grateful Protégé,
> THE PUBLISHER.[1]

The trial may have been a disaster for Carlile but at least he got his second volume.

The case itself was heard by Lord Chief Justice Abbott and a special jury: the court clearly had the utmost sympathy with the Attorney-General's legal argument that 'Christianity is, undoubtedly, a part of the common law of the land, and therefore a part of the constitution.'[2] Any attack on it was bound to be criminal. This was, of course, the law as laid down by Chief Justice Hale at the trial of John Taylor in 1676, and it was to be upheld in the case of Susannah Wright four years after the prosecution of Carlile. At his own trial, Carlile seemed less concerned to clear himself of the charges than to use the occasion for the dissemination of propaganda. He argued that if only the special jury heard the books read which were alleged to be blasphemous, they would acquit him at once. He read them long extracts from the *Age of Reason* and the whole of Palmer's *Principles of Nature*. If nothing else had secured his conviction, this would have done. He was found guilty and fined £1,000 with two years' imprisonment for publishing the *Age of Reason*, and then fined another £500 with a year's imprisonment for publishing the *Principles of Nature*. Despite all his bravado, the Vice Society was amply revenged, and if a sentence of such severity was not enough to deter others from following his example, then there was little hope of suppressing the two books by means of criminal proceedings.

What followed was a prolonged struggle not so much between the Vice Society and the press as between the Vice Society and the Carlile family and its friends. With Carlile in Dorchester prison, the running of his publishing and bookselling business passed to his wife Jane, whose first action was to issue a full account of her husband's trial complete with everything he had read out from the works of Paine

---

[1] *ibid.*, I, iv.
[2] *The Mock Trials of Richard Carlile* (London, 1822), p. 5.

and Palmer. To reprint these passages was in itself to publish a blasphemous libel, and so Jane Carlile too was put on trial before Lord Chief Justice Abbott and a special jury in 1820 but, though she was found guilty, the indictment was quashed on a technicality. Undaunted by this narrow escape, she went on to publish Carlile's magazine, the *Republican*, including in it some letters which Carlile himself had written from prison to the Reverend William Wait of Bristol. These letters attacked the government and amounted, according to the indictment, to an incitement to murder. Jane Carlile was tried again in January 1821, found guilty and sentenced to two years' imprisonment. But this was to be a fight to the bitter end, and control of the business now passed to Carlile's sister, Mary Anne Carlile. A case brought against her by the Constitutional Association in 1821 failed when the jury disagreed, but on the same day she was also tried on a charge of publishing a blasphemous libel, *An Appendix to the Theological Works of Thomas Paine*. In this second case there was no disagreement; she was found guilty, sent to prison for a year and fined £100. But in the sphere of religious debate, as in that of political discussion, the government and the Vice Society were no longer dealing with isolated individuals who might easily be intimidated, nor even with one remarkably persistent family. Carlile himself had issued an open and general challenge before his wife was convicted a second time. He wrote it from prison and it appeared in the *Republican* on 27 October 1820.

In consequence of the verdict of Guilty given against Mrs. Carlile for selling Sherwin's Life of Paine and No. 9, vol. 1 of the *Republican*, she is now liable to banishment [under the provisions of the Blasphemous and Seditious Libels Act 1819 a second conviction might incur the penalty of banishment] for serving in the shop, according to our glorious Constitution; the business will therefore be managed by Mary Anne Carlile, sister of R. Carlile, on behalf of the infant children, or rather on behalf of the whole family. In case the house, 55, Fleet Street, should again be exposed to the violence of the legal thieves, the business will be opened as near to the spot as possible immediately, of which due notice will be given. As this kind of business might be said to be renewed every week, or at least it depends on the periodical publications, we can begin anywhere with half-an-hour's preparation, and laugh at the Vice Society and all the influence they can use against it. If one web be destroyed, a few hours work will spin another, stronger and better than before.

So far as the Vice Society was concerned, this type of statement might be challenging but it was hardly encouraging, and it is small wonder that in the *Report* for 1825 there was a hint that lack of funds might make continued prosecutions of this kind impossible.

With the Carlile family in prison, there was no absence of supporters to keep the business going and to suffer as martyrs in their turn. From 1821 until 1824 the series of prosecutions continued. One of those brought to trial in 1822 was Humphrey Boyle, an assistant in Carlile's shop who had sold a pamphlet in which the Bible was alleged to be an obscene libel. When his trial came on, Boyle put up a spirited defence.

Shall I instance that disgusting scene described as occurring between Lot and his daughters? Shall I take you to the bed-chamber of Onan and Tamar, or to the road-side where Tamar is playing the harlot with her father-in-law, Judah? Can we, for a moment, reflect with serious minds upon the debaucheries of David and his sons, or think without shame of the beastly comparisons made by the Book of Ezekiel?[1]

The expected answer to every question in this peroration was 'no', and there was, therefore, some consternation in the courtroom when Boyle announced, 'Gentlemen, the first extract I shall read to you is the story of Lot and his daughters.'

At this intimation, several ladies who sat in a box close to the Bar, began to move out of Court; and on seeing this Mr. Adolphus [counsel for the prosecution] got up and moved that the ladies and boys be ordered out of Court while the Defendant was reading those portions of Scripture.[2]

Boyle solemnly read Genesis xix, 27–38; xxxviii, 9–10; Deuteronomy xxiii, 1; Ezekiel xxiii, 1–21, adding, 'If all this be not obscenity, then the Vice Society never found anything of the kind existing'.[3] It was a vigorous defence but, unhappily and predictably for Boyle, it made no difference to the outcome of his trial and he went to prison for eighteen months.

For two years longer the procession of martyrs for the cause of Thomas Paine's *Age of Reason* and Elihu Palmer's *Principles of Nature* wound its way through the courts *en route* for Newgate and the other prisons of London: Samuel Waddington, Susannah Wright, Charles and Joseph Trust, William Campion, William Tunbridge and others more evidently inspired by Carlile than by the books for which they suffered, disappeared temporarily from the scene of the conflict to serve their sentences. As they were condemned, they protested not only against the activities of the Vice Society but, as so often before, against the impunity which seemed to attend the works of 'hypocrites' like Hume and Gibbon. As Susannah Wright put it at her trial in

---

[1] *Report of the Trial of Humphrey Boyle* (1822) p. 15.
[2] *ibid.*, p. 15.
[3] *ibid.*, p. 17.

1822—she had been indicted a long time before but because she was pregnant the Vice Society had the trial postponed for a year, in case her condition should attract sympathy—the laws governing freedom of speech in matters of religion actually encouraged the contemptible duplicity of authors like Hume and Gibbon.

Although by 1824 sentences were getting more savage (three years each for Campion and Perry, who published the *Age of Reason* and the *Principles of Nature* respectively) the end of this particular struggle was almost in sight. After all, even the Vice Society must have realised that the material which they were prosecuting so assiduously was principally composed of personal indignation directed mainly at the Old Testament. The amount of space devoted to attacking the Christian religion as described in the New Testament—even in a book like the *Age of Reason*—was very limited indeed. Of course, neither Paine nor Carlile wished to take arguments against religion too far, since they were loyal to the idea of deism, to a belief in a supreme being, and a belief in life after death. The Vice Society might also have considered that, whatever else it led to, there was little future for deism itself as a religion—not because of its truth or falsity but rather because of its vagueness of belief and lack of formal organisation. The last great popular religion, Methodism, had indeed survived but largely because John Wesley and his associates had set up a system of class meetings, which acted rather like Communist cells in carrying on the work of the movement in the areas which the Wesleyans had visited. Another drawback to deism, as interpreted by men like Richard Carlile, was that it was too dependent on rather narrow and negative issues like anti-clericalism, which were as much political as theological and which were therefore likely to prove unproductive if the political situation in the country improved.

There had naturally been a considerable feeling of sympathy for Carlile, even among those who did not share his views on Christianity. When he was prosecuted in 1819, for instance, the Reverend Robert Aspland, editor of the *Monthly Repository*, attacked the proceedings on the grounds that 'Christianity wants not the assistance of Crown lawyers'.[1] W. J. Fox, a Unitarian minister, preached a sermon on the occasion of Carlile's conviction, 'The Duties of Christians towards Deists,' in which he took up the refrain that the authorities had made no attempt to prosecute the real villains like Gibbon, whose 'insidious artifice' was more likely to corrupt his readers than Paine's forthrightness. In Carlile's case, he observed, what was being punished was not deism but honesty.

The Vice Society itself was coming in for its fair share of hostility,

[1] *The Monthly Repository Extraordinary* (London, 1819), p. 10.

even from those not directly involved by its proceedings and in March 1823, when the case against Mary Anne Carlile was referred to, Joseph Hume launched an attack on the Society in the House of Commons, while William Wilberforce and others hurried to its defence. When Hume asked how blasphemy was to be defined for legal purposes, Wilberforce repeated a reply he had made to someone else who had asked him that same question. 'If you desire to go as near as you safely can to blasphemy, I only hope that you will find that you have overstepped the mark, and incurred the punishment which you have tempted.'[1] Such advice did nothing to mollify the supporters of Carlile, who were now more convinced than ever that, in the words of Robert Aspland, 'Laws against blasphemy have, in truth, been framed by Christian governors and legislators in the spirit, not of Christ, but of his enemies and persecutors'.[2]

By the time Carlile came out of prison he had stirred up controversy enough to win the support of a significant number of people for his right to publish, even if not for the views that he wished to publish. He rebuilt his business and founded the Joint Stock Book Company, which offered the investor interest at the rate of 5% and the option of concealing his identity. Another expedient of Carlile's was that of calling himself 'the Reverend Richard Carlile,' which made it legal for him to address certain meetings on a Sunday, or at least diverted the attention of the law. Yet he caused some consternation among deists by announcing in 1832 his conversion to Christianity, 'after Fourteen Years of Obstinate Infidelity'. Though he was later to be in trouble for publishing a seditious libel, his *Address to the Insurgent Labourers* (1831), he was issuing the *Theological Works of Thomas Paine* in 1827 without any apparent interference. As Lord Chief Justice Abbott had put it at Carlile's trial in 1819, the question which would now decide the fate of a book in a case of blasphemy was whether it was 'a work of candid and impartial inquiry into the truth of the evidence of that which it is so important to us all not to be mistaken in, or is it a work of calumny and scoffing?'[3]

Not all opinions on matters of religious belief were tolerated even by 1827. In October that year an apostate clergyman of the Church of England, Robert Taylor, was sent to prison for a year as the result of a blasphemous address which he had delivered to the Christian Evidence Society (an organisation dedicated to exposing what it believed to be the fictitious nature of the Bible), but the fact that he

[1] *Life of William Wilberforce*, V, 173.
[2] Robert Aspland, *An Inquiry into the Nature of the Sin of Blasphemy* (London, 1817), p. 22.
[3] *State Trials* (New Series), IV, 1425.

was an apostate may have had much to do with this. With the collapse, or rather termination, of the Vice Society's campaign against blasphemy and its return to the old hunting ground of obscene books and prints, publishers like Carlile were in little danger of appearing in the courts for what they had issued. Yet blasphemous libel remained—and remains—an offence, and there were to be some remarkable examples of it during the reign of Victoria.

BLASPHEMY AND LITERATURE

Few of the publications with which we have just been concerned would now be regarded as works of great literary distinction, or works of imaginative literature at all, yet in the early nineteenth century a number of such books, almost for the first time in the literary history of England brought trouble to their authors and publishers because of laws and attitudes relating to blasphemy. Critics, even those of considerable sophistication, were less hardened than jurists and reacted with all the astonishment of the young Wordsworth first hearing 'The voice of Woman utter blasphemy'.[1] Faced with the certain hostility of the critics and possible legal action as well, publishers were naturally very cautious about issuing any book likely to be regarded as blasphemous. The medievalist Joseph Ritson, who shared Shelley's vegetarianism and hatred of Christianity, had edited the romance of *King Alisaunder* for publication by Nicol in 1802 but even in the case of a scholarly work of limited circulation Nichol was dismayed by the blasphemous tone of the editor's remarks and nine pages of the book had to be altered before it was issued.[2] In 1811 Shelley himself was sent down from Oxford for circulating *The Necessity of Atheism* and in 1813 he had *Queen Mab*, written when he was eighteen, privately printed, though he later tried to suppress it. The printer of this private edition removed his name from it, in case of trouble, but at this stage *Queen Mab* did not attract the attention of the authorities or the Vice Society. On the other hand, after Shelley's first wife, Harriet Westbrook, had committed suicide in 1816 by drowning herself in the Serpentine, Lord Eldon, as Lord Chancellor, denied Shelley the custody of the children of the marriage, in 1817, on the grounds that Shelley was an atheist and a believer in free love. *Queen Mab* was offered as evidence of this. Then in 1821 a publisher called William Clarke pirated *Queen Mab* and reissued it while Shelley was in Italy. There was no legal means of preventing this, since Lord Eldon had ruled in the case of Southey's *Wat Tyler*, which

[1] *The Prelude* (1805), Bk. VII, l. 417.
[2] Arthur Johnston, *Enchanted Ground*, p. 135.

had been pirated in 1817, that libellous works—whether seditious or blasphemous—did not enjoy the protection of copyright. But in Clarke's case retribution followed swiftly through the action of the Vice Society. *Queen Mab* and Shelley had soon become the subjects of disapproving notices. *The Investigator*, reviewing this new edition of the poem, was horrified to find that it had gone beyond mere deism to the ultimate revolt of atheism. 'Compared with this Don Juan is a moral poem and Cain a homily. . . . Our blood curdled in our veins as we waded through nine cantos of blasphemy and impiety, such as we never thought that anyone, on the outside of bedlam, could have uttered.'[1] In less melodramatic terms, the *Gentleman's Magazine* reflected on Shelley's death in 1822, 'Percy Bysshe Shelley is a fitter subject for a penitentiary dying speech, than a lauding elegy; for the muse of the rope, rather than that of the cypress; the muse that advises us "Warning to take by others' harm and we shall do full well." '[2] And Winthrop Mackworth Praed, still a schoolboy, wrote in the *Etonian* in 1821, 'when I consider his powers of mind, I am proud that he was an Etonian: when I remember their perversion, I wish he had never been one'.

In 1822 the Vice Society prosecuted William Clarke for his edition of *Queen Mab*: there was no question of prosecuting Shelley since he was not responsible for this publication of the poem and, in any case, was drowned in the wreck of the *Ariel* in July 1822. The poem was first prosecuted on the evidence of such passages as the following, quoted in the 1822 indictment.

> I was an infant when my mother went
> To see an atheist burned. She took me there:
> The dark-robed priests were met around the pile;
> The multitude was gazing silently;
> And as the culprit passed with dauntless mien,
> Tempered disdain in his unaltering eye,
> Mixed with a quiet smile, shone calmly forth;
> The thirsty fire crept round his manly limbs;
> His resolute eyes were scorched to blindness soon;
> His death-pang rent my heart! the insensate mob
> Uttered a cry of triumph, and I wept.
> 'Weep not, child!' cried my mother, 'for that man
> Has said, There is no God.'[3]

Other passages in the indictment might have been objected to on rather broader moral grounds than those of blasphemy.

[1] *The Investigator* V (1822), 361.
[2] *The Gentleman's Magazine*, pt. 2 (1822), 623.
[3] P.R.O., K.B. 28/478/53.

Chastity is a monkish and evangelical superstition, a greater foe to natural temperance even than unintellectual sensuality; it strikes at the root of all domestic happiness, and consigns more than half of the human race to misery, that some few may monopolize according to law. A system could not well have been devised more studiously hostile to human happiness than marriage.

I conceive that from the abolition of marriage, the fit and natural arrangement of sexual connection would result.[1]

Of course, the blasphemous nature of *Queen Mab* had been established when a copy was produced for Lord Eldon's inspection in 1817, so that it was not surprising when Clarke was found guilty and sent to prison for four months, which naturally stimulated public interest in the poem. Richard Carlile managed to get hold of 180 copies of the privately printed edition of 1813, after Shelley's death, and also produced his own expurgated edition, which encountered no trouble from the Vice Society or the courts. But the story of *Queen Mab* was not yet over and twenty years later the most respectable Victorian publishers were being prosecuted and convicted for reprinting it as part of Shelley's *Poetical Works*. By comparison with much of Shelley's other work this youthful poem seems laboured and it is a sad reflection on the popularity which censorship confers upon a mediocre work, at the expense of more accomplished literature, that H. Buxton Forman could write in 1888, 'To this day, I believe, there are ten who know Shelley as the author of *Queen Mab* for one who knows that he wrote *Prometheus Unbound*'.[2] It would not be hard to parallel this in the twentieth century by, say, a comparison between *Lady Chatterley's Lover* and *Sons and Lovers* among the novels of D. H. Lawrence.

Shelley was by no means the only man of letters, or of learning, to feel that he had been unjustly treated by Lord Eldon, though no one else described Eldon with the bitterness reserved for him in Shelley's *Masque of Anarchy* (1819), where the Lord Chancellor comes second in the procession, immediately after Castlereagh.

> Next came Fraud, and he had on,
> Like Eldon, an ermined gown;
> His big tears, for he wept well,
> Turned to mill-stones as they fell.
>
> And the little children, who
> Round his feet played to and fro,

[1] *ibid.*

[2] H. Buxton Forman, *The Vicissitudes of Queen Mab* (Shelley Society's Papers, Part I) (London, 1888), p. 22.

Thinking every tear a gem,
Had their brains knocked out by them.[1]

Byron's encounter with Eldon was no more satisfactory than Shelley's. In 1822 he had published his poem *Cain: a Mystery*, which received a hostile series of reviews on the grounds of its allegedly blasphemous nature. The *Edinburgh Review* spoke for many critics in its denunciation of Byron's new poem.

Of 'Cain, a Mystery', we are constrained to say, that, although it abounds in beautiful passages, and shows more *power* perhaps than any of the author's dramatical compositions, we regret very much that it should ever have been published. It will give great scandal and offence to pious persons in general—and may be the means of suggesting the most painful doubts and distressing perplexities, to hundreds of minds that might never otherwise have been exposed to such dangerous disturbance. . . . The fact is, that here *the whole argument*—and a very elaborate and specious argument it is—is directed against the goodness or the power of the Deity, and against the reasonableness of religion in general; and there is no answer so much as attempted to the offensive doctrines that are so strenuously inculcated.[2]

This was a general opinion, which Wordsworth put more concisely and smugly in 1827. 'Lord Byron has spoken severely of my compositions. However faulty they may be, I do not think I ever could have prevailed upon myself to print such lines as he has done.'

Byron's poem was never prosecuted but it was pirated by William Benbow. In February 1822 John Murray brought an action against Benbow, seeking an injuction to prevent him from selling this unauthorised edition. The injunction was granted but later dissolved by Lord Eldon on the grounds that *Cain*, like *Queen Mab*, was a blasphemous poem and, therefore, not entitled to the protection of copyright. Byron was unsuccessful in attempting to prevent the young William Dugdale from pirating *Don Juan*, copyright being refused because of the poem's anti-government bias. When Lord Eldon was asked to prevent the sale of a pirated edition of a scientific work, Lawrence's *Lectures on Physiology, Zoology, and the Natural History of Man*, the piratical publisher alleged that the book denied the immortality of the soul and was not entitled to legal protection. Lord Eldon agreed. Under these circumstances, it is hardly remarkable that when Onwhyn pirated John Joseph Stockdale's publication, *The Memoirs of Harriette Wilson*, in 1826, such scandal and scurrility should have been judged undeserving of the law's protection.

---

[1] *The Masque of Anarchy* (London, 1832), p. 3. In this first edition of the poem Eldon's name was represented by an initial letter only.
[2] *The Edinburgh Review*, XXXVI (1822), p. 437.

The religious controversies of the first quarter of the nineteenth century had, inevitably, generated more heat of moral indignation than light of logical or metaphysical discussion. Yet before the accession of Victoria or William IV new Acts of Parliament had established a further degree of religious liberty by 'emancipating' both Catholics and Nonconformists. If the Church was still in danger, the danger was not represented by the writings of men like Paine and Palmer. Once the publicity of the Vice Society's prosecutions was over, interest in Palmer's work died almost completely and Paine remained interesting for what he was rather than for what he wrote. Much of the residual influence of Paine's 'theology' could have been absorbed without too much difficulty into the 'Broad Church' philosophy of certain later Victorians. Indeed, it is hard to believe that some of those who continued to promote Paine's writings on religion really had much in common with his views beyond a dislike of Christianity. By the mid-nineteenth century 'the Church in danger' meant to many people not the Church in danger from deism or atheism but the Church in danger from the new attraction of Roman Catholicism, or from the Anglo-Catholicism of the Oxford Movement. Even by the time that Victoria came to the throne, the counter-reformation was under way. Those pious evangelicals who, through the Vice Society and in other ways, had fought the good fight against Daniel Isaac Eaton or the Carlile family were now faced with opponents of a rather different style and calibre, men like John Henry Newman, Edward Pusey, and Henry Edward Manning. The Church of Rome was re-established and the Church of England seemed to wake from a century of defensive apathy. The vogue was now not for warnings against deism or infidelity but for the *Awful Disclosures of Maria Monk*, first published in 1833, *The Confessional Unmasked*, and, later still, Walter Walsh's *Secret History of the Oxford Movement*.

Blasphemous libel remained a crime, though logic and the evidence of the natural sciences entered more and more into the discussion of religious belief. The attitude of the law remained substantially that of Mr. Justice Best at the trial of Mary Anne Carlile in 1821. 'Is this a temperate discussion, or the writing of a person who attempts not to argue, but to vilify and degrade, to excite prejudices in our mind and not to convince our judgment?'[1] The first quarter of the century had certainly been a time when propagandists on both sides of the question had done their best, in outbursts of self-righteousness, to 'excite prejudices' in the minds of their readers. It is a nice irony that the book which stood at the centre of so much vindictiveness and hysterical denunciation should have been called the *Age of Reason*.

[1] *State Trials* (New Series), I, 1047.

THE MIDDLE YEARS OF THE VICE SOCIETY

When its campaign against blasphemy was over, the Vice Society still faced the Herculean task of trying to control, and if possible suppress, the trade in pornography. As Francis Place pointed out, the Society and its sympathisers had successfully put an end to the singing of obscene street ballads but only to the extent of driving them from the streets into the pubs and into the pages of such publications as *Duncombe's Drolleries*, published and sold by John and Edward Duncombe during the 1820s and later. The Coal Hole, in the Strand; the Cave of Harmony, and the Cyder Cellars, in Maiden Lane, were among the most celebrated of the 'chanting cribs' in early Victorian London, where the entertainment was organised at first on an amateur and then on a professional basis. From these beginnings developed the music halls of the later nineteenth century. The permitted level of obscenity varied from one 'crib' to another, from 'out-and-outers', where no ladies—unless of easy virtue—were admitted, to others of the more decorous kind described by Thackeray in the first chapter of *The Newcomes*. Not all establishments were as innocuous as the 'Cave of Harmony' in Thackeray's novel and those of a different type, including the Grapes in Suffolk Street, Southwark Bridge Road, were advertised in such publications as the *Swell's Night Guide*, which says of the Grapes,

This is a chaunting crib, and on very gigantic dimensions, conducted with much spirit and order. Good chaunting, spicy mots, and tolerable lush may be had here. Admission thrums.[1]

For the uninitiated middle-class, the *Guide* adds that 'mots' are whores, 'lush' is drink, and 'thrums' is threepence.

Yet the Vice Society, if it could not prevent the singing of obscene songs in such establishments, could at least prosecute those who put them into print, as it prosecuted the Duncombes in 1829. Indeed by this time the Society had to deal with a new and, in many respects, more professional generation of pornographers; men who were, in most cases, in their late twenties or early thirties when the series of prosecutions in 1829–30 was launched against them. Apart from the Duncombes, there was George Cannon, John Benjamin Brookes, and a young man who was to plague the authorities for the next four decades, William Dugdale. All these were prosecuted at the time, as they were to be on a considerable number of occasions before the passing of the Obscene Publications Act in 1857, when the govern-

---

[1] *The Swell's Night Guide: or, A Peep through the Great Metropolis under the Dominion of Nox* (1846), p. 38.

ment took upon itself at least some of the duties of the Vice Society. Apart from *Duncombe's Drolleries* and *Fanny Hill* (the latter had also been cited in the prosecutions of 1820[1]) the cases of 1829–30 involved two books which, to judge from the frequency of their appearance, were among the most popular pornographic novels of their time, the *Memoirs of a Man of Pleasure* and the English translation of the French eighteenth-century novel *Histoire de Dom B . . ., portier des Chartreux.*[2]

In 1857, when the Obscene Publications Bill was being debated, Lord Campbell claimed that the Vice Society, since its foundation fifty-five years earlier, had brought 159 cases against pornographers and had been successful in no less than 154 of them. There was, of course, considerable support for the Society's activities, since it was now an accepted dogma that pornography's chief attribute was an almost magical power to deprave and corrupt its readers. Few men would have repudiated this basic assumption as coolly as Lord Macaulay was to do, when reviewing Leigh Hunt's edition of Restoration dramatists in the *Edinburgh Review* for January 1841.

We find it difficult to believe that, in a world so full of temptation as this, any gentleman whose life would have been virtuous if he had not read Aristophanes and Juvenal will be made vicious by reading them.

To make matters worse, Zachary Macaulay, the historian's father, had been one of the founder members of the Vice Society.

---

[1] P.R.O., K.B. 28/473/57.

[2] Among other titles worth noting in this batch of prosecutions are the *New London Rambler's Magazine* (P.R.O., K.B. 28/509/21) and De Sade's *Juliette* (P.R.O., K.B. 28/515/13). At least three of the five *Rambler's Magazines* published between 1783 and 1829 were prosecuted as obscene and two of these cases, against Isaac Aldrich in 1801 and John Duncombe in 1829, ended with convictions: William Benbow was, of course, acquitted in 1822. The prosecution of George Cannon in 1830 for publishing *Juliette*, in French, marks the entry of De Sade into the history of English censorship. This is one of the earliest English references to De Sade and, probably, the earliest of all to *Juliette*. It certainly suggests that his work was better known and more generally available in England during the early nineteenth century than has been supposed. 'Pisanus Fraxi', for example, records only a German edition of *Justine und Juliette* (1874) abridged to 155 pages, and a 'new edition', of *Justine et Juliette* published in Brussels in 1875. (*Index Librorum Prohibitorum*, pp. xxxii, and 466.)

Victoria:
(1) 'If All Mankind Minus One . . .'
J. S. Mill (1859)

'TOWARDS THE PERFECT DAY'

To those Victorian liberals who, in the years after 1850, surveyed the history of English censorship and took stock of the contemporary situation, it was clear that though the campaign for a free press might never end in absolute victory, most of the major battles had been won. Since the troubled years immediately succeeding the Napoleonic wars, prosecutions for seditious and blasphemous libel had grown rarer and less certain of success, even if convictions for obscene libel might more easily be obtained. By the latter half of the century, the dispute was no longer between those who regarded liberty of the press as the only safeguard against tyranny or corrupt government and those who regarded it as subversive of responsible government: it was a dispute between believers in an absolute or utopian freedom of expression and those who saw press freedom as a political compromise. In the view of this last group, men should not be free, for instance, to incite one another to acts of violence and murder, or to endanger the peace of their country by publishing its official secrets to a potential enemy. The more extreme view was that since even tyrannicide may sometimes be morally preferable to political stability, to urge assassination or revolution may also be the nobler course of action. So if one senses dissatisfaction on the part of a writer like John Stuart Mill in his essay *On Liberty* (1859), this is because Mill puts the case for absolute freedom of expression, if not of action.

If all mankind minus one, were of one opinion, and only one person were of the contrary opinion, mankind would be no more justified in silencing that one person, than he, if he had the power, would be justified in silencing mankind.[1]

Only from a position as uncompromising as this could Mill in 1859 have described the law in its control of the press as being 'as servile to this day as it was in the time of the Tudors'.[2] Even Mill has to qualify

[1] J. S Mill, *On Liberty* (London, 1859), p. 33.   [2] *ibid.*, p. 31.

this by adding that, of course, there is 'little danger' of the law being
put into force 'except during some temporary panic'.[1] Mill's major
and reasonable fear for the liberty of the Victorian press was that as
censorship by government intervention declined, a censorship imposed by 'public opinion' would take its place. Lord Macaulay had
already given it as his view that this was just what had been happening
in England for the past century and a half. Indeed, the Vice Society or
the Constitutional Association might reasonably claim to represent
certain sectors of public opinion. Ironically, from Mill's point of view,
when this new power of censorship appeared it operated mainly in a
sphere with which he was not much concerned. It was 'public opinion',
as represented by Mudie's and W. H. Smith's libraries or bookstalls,
which imposed a ban on books alleged to be not blasphemous and
seditious but obscene or indelicate. As a spokesman for W. H. Smith
told George Moore in 1883, explaining the firm's refusal to stock his
novel *A Modern Lover*, 'Two ladies from the country wrote to me
objecting to the scene in which the girl sat to the artist. After that I
naturally refused to circulate the book unless a customer said he
wanted particularly to read Mr. Moore's novel'.[2] In economic terms,
at least, 'two ladies from the country' and their sympathisers might
prove to be as ruinous as Lord Ellenborough or the Vice Society.
Although these developments lay some years in the future, it is interesting to see that while Mill in the essay *On Liberty* makes a
number of references to events of 1857 and 1858 involving freedom
of expression, he makes no mention of Lord Campbell's Obscene
Publications Act of 1857.

The Victorian preoccupation with press freedom is illustrated
from a more optimistic standpoint than Mill's by the appearance of
such books as James Routledge's *Chapters in the History of Popular
Progress, Chiefly in Relation to the Freedom of the Press and Trial by
Jury 1660–1820* (1876) or James Anson Farrer's *Books Condemned to
be Burnt* (1892). Though it was inevitable, and to some extent justifiable, that such books should be the occasion for self-congratulation
by Victorian liberals, a passage from Farrer's preface indicates how
unmistakably Victorian in taste that occasion was to be.

I trust that no one will be either attracted or alarmed by any anticipations
suggested by the title of my book. Although primarily a book for the
library, it is also one of which no drawing-room table need be the least afraid.
If I have found anything in my condemned authors which they would have

[1] *ibid.*, p. 31.
[2] Quoted in Norman St. John Stevas, *Obscenity and the Law* (London, 1956),
p. 76. This appears to be another version of the story told by Moore of Mudie's
library in *Literature at Nurse* (London, 1885), p. 3.

done better to have left unsaid, I have, in referring to their fortunes, felt under no compulsion to reproduce their indiscretions. But, in all of them put together, I doubt whether there is as much to offend a scrupulous taste as in many a latter-day novel, the claim of which to the distinction of burning is often as indisputable as the certainty of its regrettable immunity from that fiery but fitting fate.[1]

The taste for partisan histories of this kind derives from that period in the middle of the nineteenth century when under the aegis of veterans like Mill or of Herbert Spencer in his *Social Statics* (1851) the libertarians had put their case—with rather more sophistication than some of their recent predecessors—against the restraint of individual freedom by governments. Not all the most eminent minds of the day thought alike. Thomas Carlyle, writing to his brother 'in hot *haste*', accused Mill of having written 'as if it were a sin to control, or coerce into better methods, human swine in any way;—as if the greater and the more universal the "liberty" of human creatures of the *Swine* genus, the more fatal all-destructive and intolerable were not the "slavery" the few human creatures of the *Man* genus are thereby thrown into, and kept groaning powerless under.'[2] Carlyle must have had many sympathisers but it was a sufficiently unfashionable view to be confined to thoughts and private correspondence for the most part.

Each advocate of the freedom of the press or of public discussion imposed his own interpretation on that freedom, and not all supporters of a free press were as ready as Mill to condemn restraint by 'public opinion' or 'good taste'. J. A. Froude in 'A Plea for the Free Discussion of Theological Difficulties', in *Fraser's Magazine* in 1863, made a point of stating his difference with Mill on this issue.

Mr. Mill demands for every man a right to say out his convictions in plain language, whatever they may be; and so far as he means that there should be no Act of Parliament to prevent him, he is perfectly just in what he says. But when Mr. Mill goes from Parliament to public opinion, when he lays down as a general principle that the free play of thought is unwholesomely interfered with by society, he would take away the sole protection which we possess from the inroads of any kind of folly.[3]

And then Froude illustrates his point with what one might think was the classic Victorian reservation about freedom of expression.

If a man persists in talking of what he does not understand, he is put down;

[1] James Anson Farrer, *Books Condemned to be Burnt* (London, 1892), p. viii.
[2] *New Letters of Thomas Carlyle*, ed. Alexander Carlyle (London, 1904), II, 196.
[3] *Fraser's Magazine*, LXVIII (1863), 280.

if he sports loose views on morals at a decent dinner party, the better sort of people fight shy of him, and he is not invited again.[1]

Froude was, after all, Carlyle's disciple and, later, the great man's literary executor but, to be fair to him, he would have no resort to coercion by Act of Parliament and thus grants the Press a freedom not only unthinkable to most of his contemporaries but far in advance of anything the twentieth century has permitted. As to public opinion, Froude himself knew what its disapproval might mean, since he had been condemned by one section of it. In 1849 his novel *The Nemesis of Faith*, the story of an Anglican's loss of faith, had been publicly burnt in the hall of Exeter College, Oxford, of which Froude was then a Fellow. The burning of the book by Sewell, the Senior Tutor, was followed, in Froude's words, by 'A peremptory demand . . . from the Rector and the College authorities for the resignation of my fellowship'.[2] And whatever his faith in public opinion, Froude concludes his argument in complete agreement with Mill on the main issue by demanding 'free discussion through a free press which is the best instrument for the discovery of truth, and the most effectual means for preserving it'.[3]

Mill, Spencer, Froude and their contemporaries lived to see their belief in liberty considerably modified by the later fashions of nineteenth-century thought, and six years after Mill's death T. H. Green delivering his *Lectures on the Principles of Political Obligation* at Oxford in 1879–80, condemned on moral grounds any purely negative liberty based on mere absence of restraint and substituted a positive power of 'doing or enjoying something worth doing or enjoying'. In 1873 Sir James Stephen's *Liberty, Equality, Fraternity* was reprinted from the *Pall Mall Gazette* and in this Stephen pointed out that Mill's absolute liberty, unrestrained by 'public opinion', was incompatible with democracy. As a biologist, T. H. Huxley writing in the *Nineteenth Century* for February 1890 could only equate absolute liberty or 'individualism' with the law of the jungle.

Probably none of the political delusions which have sprung from the 'natural rights' doctrine has been more mischievous than the assertion that all men have a natural right to freedom, and that those who willingly submit to any restriction of this freedom, beyond the point determined by the deductions of *a priori* philosophers, deserve the title of slave.[4]

[1] *ibid.*, LXVIII, 280.
[2] Waldo Hilary Dunn, *James Anthony Froude: A Biography 1818–1856* (Oxford, 1961), p. 147.
[3] *Fraser's Magazine*, LXVIII (1863), p. 291.
[4] *Nineteenth Century*, XXVII (1890), p. 182.

Nonetheless, Huxley would have been incensed had the authorities curtailed his own liberty to the extent of prosecuting him for blasphemy after his attacks on 'superstition' and 'bibliolaters' during the *Origin of Species* controversy.

Naturally there were few later Victorians who would admit that they wanted to restrict the political or religious freedom of the press which had been established on the high plateau of mid-nineteenth century libertarian sentiment. From this plateau philosophers like Mill scanned the horizon of the future and historians like Macaulay or Buckle looked back on the course of national development with considerable satisfaction. It was, in the end, the historians rather than the philosophers who justified the existence of a free press. Quarter of a century before Macaulay, Henry Hallam's *Constitutional History of England* had first described the system of literary censorship in the seventeenth century as part of the royal prerogative against which his heroes had fought. He makes some partial excuse for the fact that Parliament, no less than the Crown, was ready to maintain the apparatus of censorship but his condemnation of that apparatus is as forthright as Macaulay's. He quotes with satisfaction such incidents as Archbishop Whitgift's blundering condemnation of the works of the Hebrew scholar Hugh Broughton because of their views on the descent of Christ into hell—views so reasonable that the Archbishop was later obliged to adopt them himself.

Certainly it was the historians rather than the philosophers who would have convinced the waverers that past experience showed the inexpediency of attempting to muzzle the Press, but it would be unfair to give the impression that the historians were concerned merely with expediency. A later historian than Hallam or Macaulay, William Stubbs, published his *Constitutional History of England* in 1874–8, at a time when some political philosophers were having more than second thoughts on the question of liberty. Stubbs is an interesting case of the historian whose view of literature and its dissemination reflects a contemporary passion for intellectual liberty with such optimism as to overlook the phenomenon of Tudor and Stuart censorship. Stubbs ended his history with the close of the Middle Ages and chose the printing press as 'an apt emblem or embodiment of the change' between the medieval and the modern. Yet in presenting this emblem as something almost unaffected by the censorship of ideas, Stubbs fixes his gaze not on the immediate historical future of the sixteenth century but on a more remote, ideal prospect.

The real change is that by which every man comes to be a reader and a thinker; the Bible comes to every family, and each man is priest in his own household. The light is not so brilliant but it is everywhere, and it shines more and more unto the perfect day.[1]

Not a word to indicate the horrors of two centuries, during which imprisonment, torture, disfigurement, and execution were the rewards of many authors and publishers, nothing to suggest the more subtle methods of political and financial coercion by which the press had been threatened in the eighteenth and even at the beginning of the nineteenth century. Perhaps it is wrong to expect that such things should have their place in this passage since, despite the limits of his *History*, Stubbs seems to be no longer thinking of the Tudors and the Stuarts. It is hard to escape the conclusion that the light which is everywhere falls by courtesy of Bentley, Moxon, and the family magazines, and that for Stubbs, as for so many of his contemporaries, the perfect day towards which it shone was Victorian England.

THE POLITICAL FREEDOM OF THE VICTORIAN PRESS

Before much of Victoria's reign had passed, the relevant question which political journalists or publishers had to ask was not how much they could say without fear of being prosecuted for seditious libel but what they would have to say in order to be prosecuted. A newspaper like the *Daily Telegraph*, founded in 1855, had nothing to fear as the result of referring, in a discussion on House of Lords reform to 'the chartered lords of misrule ogling in the ancient face of bigotry', or attacking the Royal family for 'seeking pensions *in forma pauperis* for their daughters whom it should be their pride and pleasure to support'.[2] However much certain political leaders might cherish secret dreams of controlling the press, it was evident by 1832 that any attempt at general censorship would be hopeless. By the middle of the century the press had outgrown the censorship of 1815 or 1820, in economic terms alone, just as the press of the eighteenth century outgrew the licensing system. *The Times*, which had had a circulation of less than 7,000 copies when the government began its series of press prosecutions in 1817, had achieved a circulation of 70,000 copies by 1861. In 1815 the price of *The Times* had reached 7*d.*, most of which represented the cost of stamp duty on newspapers. There was growing opposition to this measure of control and during the 1830s men like Henry Hetherington, editor of the *Poor Man's Guardian*, openly defied the law by issuing their publications unstamped and going to prison when the authorities caught up with

[1] William Stubbs, *Constitutional History of England*, Library edn. (Oxford, 1880), III, 664–5.

[2] Lord Burnham, *Peterborough Court* (London, 1955), pp. 14 and 15.

them. Stamp duty was finally abolished in 1855 and the tax on paper
in 1861. As a result, the price of a paper like *The Times* fell to 3*d.* and,
since the paper no longer had to be printed on separate sheets, each
stamped at the Stamp Office, printing on continuous rolls or 'webs'
was introduced at once. The process had long been known but the
existing law made it an impossible one to use. A web machine could
now be bought for £600 and would produce 7,000 copies an hour,
making mass circulation figures a possibility.[1] When the tax on paper
was abolished in 1861, the *Daily Telegraph* had already reached a
figure of 150,000 copies and *Reynold's Weekly* one of 350,000.

Yet far from choosing to attack the press, successive governments
of Victoria's reign gave it further protection against certain types of
prosecution. The Quarter Sessions Act of 1842 deprived magistrates
of the right to try cases of blasphemous, seditious, or defamatory
libel, thereby ensuring that no longer was a mere Justice of the Peace
to enjoy the power of exercising a local political censorship. Further
protection was given to newspapers in their reporting of debates,
trials, or meetings. As early as 1840 the Parliamentary Papers Act
had laid down that if a libel was published by order of Parliament, it
was a complete defence for the publisher to say that he had published
it by virtue of this order.[2] Still more comprehensive was the Newspaper Libel Act of 1888, which indemnified newspapers against libel
actions in respect of their reporting of parliamentary or judicial
proceedings as well as *bona fide* public meetings. Again, it further
restricted the power of would-be prosecutors by enacting that no case
could be brought without the order of a judge in chambers. The only
reservations in this Act were that a newspaper should remain liable to
prosecution if it reprinted any blasphemy or obscenity in its report.
When Henry Vizetelly was prosecuted in 1888 for publishing English
translations of *La Terre* and other novels of Zola, the Solicitor-
General warned reporters that a newspaper whose report included
any of the passages objected to would be liable to a prosecution for
obscene libel.

If the press accepted political power, it accepted a substantial
measure of responsibility as well and, under such circumstances, it
was easier for the government to decide that the best thing to do with
any lunatic extremist was to consign him to oblivion by not according
him the publicity of a trial. When copies of a newspaper sold by the

[1] *Peterborough Court*, p. 3.
[2] This Act was the outcome of the Stockdale *v.* Hansard case of 1839, in which
Hansard had been successfully sued for publishing parliamentary proceedings
containing statements libellous outside the boundaries of parliamentary privilege.
The Act of 1840 reversed the decision of the court.

hundred thousand, it was increasingly difficult for one man to make anything like the impact that Hone or Carlile had done with their primitive equipment half a century earlier. A paper like the *Daily Telegraph* might sell as many copies in a week as the *Rights of Man* had sold in ten years. Attacks on the monarchy or on the monarch herself, which would have merited prosecution under George III or George IV now passed almost unnoticed. Charles Bradlaugh, for instance, who provoked plenty of controversy in other ways, denounced members of the Royal Family with almost complete impunity in his *Impeachment of the House of Brunswick*. 'I loathe these small German breast-bestarred wanderers, whose only merit is their loving hatred of one another. In their own land they vegetate and wither unnoticed; here we pay them highly to marry and perpetuate a pauper prince-race. If they do nothing they are "good". If they do ill, loyalty gilds the vice till it looks like virtue.'[1] As it happened, Bradlaugh's book received no worse treatment than being ground under the foot of Lord Randolph Churchill in a rhetorical gesture during a Commons' debate in 1880.

Just as it was felt best to ignore those squibs which commented cynically on the relationship between the widowed Victoria and her servant John Brown, naming her as 'Mrs. John Brown,' so there were other circumstances in which it was judged best to treat attacks upon her as a nuisance rather than a danger. In 1851, for example, the clerk to the Leamington magistrates wrote to Hyde Clarke, warning him that certain handbills he was issuing were 'treasonous', and that if he persisted in distributing them some action would have to be taken against him. Hyde Clarke, whose sanity may well be doubted, claimed to be the rightful heir to the Crown, as fifteenth in succession from Edward III. In his printed propaganda he was waging a campaign of vilification against Victoria. The direct cause of this was the Sugar Act of 1846, which he regarded as lending support to the system of slavery in America and for which he held the Queen responsible. He referred to her as 'Mrs. Albert Guelph' and his favourite recommendation for dealing with her was as follows.

TO THE TOWER
Mrs. Manning was hung for one murder only.[2]
The Roman Catholic Bible says 'God makes no distinction of persons.'

[1] *The Impeachment of the House of Brunswick*, 8th edn. (London, 1881), p. 99. Bradlaugh proposed that Victoria should reign for the rest of her life and then the monarchy should be abolished. He dedicated the eighth edition of his book 'to Lord R. H. S. Churchill and Sir H. D. Wolff, as some acknowledgement of their effectual advertisement of the sixth and seventh editions'.

[2] Marie Manning and her husband were hanged in 1849 for the murder of Patrick O'Connor.

221

For well over another year Hyde Clarke continued this one-sided contest, annoying a number of people and provoking a letter in the *Leamington Courier* which suggested that it might be as well to restrain him but that there should be no question of a prosecution. The clerk to the magistrates wrote to Palmerston at the Home Office a week later, enclosing a copy of this letter and indicating the advisability of avoiding a prosecution.[1] There, it seems, the matter ended. As the Queen's reign passed, she became less the subject of political attacks than of irreverent speculation. According to Swinburne's little fantasy *La Soeur de la Reine*, she had had an illegitimate daughter by Lord Russell, while a pornographic novel of about 1860, *The Festival of Love; or, Revels at the Fount of Venus* was one of a number 'Dedicated, by permission, to Her Most Gracious Majesty, The Queen.' Some attacks on individuals associated with the Queen were so scurrilous—if true—that action had to be taken, as when in 1842-3 the publishers of such periodicals as the *Age*; the *Satirist or the Censor of the Times*, and later the *Weekly Despatch*, were prosecuted and convicted for imputing homosexuality to the Duke of Brunswick.[2] Typical of such attacks was the epigram, published in the *Age* on 6 February 1842, 'on hearing from Mrs. Denniston that the Duke of Brunswick abused the writers of the "Age" '.

> To do so he prudence or courage must lack
> Yet it sometimes *is* the case
> That men will do behind your back,
> What they will not do to your face.

Naturally there were still occasions when a man's opinion of monarch, ministers, or, for that matter, a private citizen, might get him into trouble. Yet a jurist like Sir James Stephen—not always of the most liberal opinions in such matters—reflected the general feeling in his maxim that 'Every person who takes a public part in public affairs submits his conduct therein to criticism'.[3] The law was no more intended to protect a politician or a civil servant from criticism than it was to protect an author or a painter from the judgments of his critics.

To many people it seemed that the press might do more harm by the information it published than by its opinions and, for example, Victoria herself seems to have been less put out by personal attacks

---

[1] P.R.O., O.S. 4239.

[2] P.R.O., K.B. 28/565/16 and K.B. 28/567/24.

[3] Sir James Fitzjames Stephen, *A Digest of the Criminal Law* (London, 1877), p. 189.

upon her than by the 'leakage' to *The Times* of her private conversations with Lord Granville in 1859, when she invited him to form an administration following the fall of Lord Derby's government. Earlier in the same decade, even more urgent matters of security had to be considered during the Crimean War. There was some consternation immediately before the war when the British ultimatum to Russia appeared in *The Times* almost before it had had time to reach St. Petersburg. The war itself showed the potential threat to national or military security of a press which could publish what it liked, or at least such information as it could get hold of from its correspondents. This had never really been a problem before but in November 1854 Lord Raglan wrote from the Crimea to the Secretary of State for War, complaining bitterly of a dispatch from *The Times* war correspondent, William Russell, which had been published on 23 October. Raglan pointed out that this dispatch contained 'details connected with the Army', and he added, 'The knowledge of them must be invaluable to the Russians'. Raglan goes on to cite some of the details now available to the Russians, including British losses from cholera, the effects of Russian artillery fire on British positions, the disposition of British artillery and gunpowder, as well as references to troop movements. Russell's reaction was to lay the responsibility for any 'censoring' that had to be done on the editor of the paper himself, since it was very hard for a correspondent in the field to know what might be useful information to the enemy and what might not. The faster news travelled, the more dangerous its publication became and, though the matter was less serious in 1854 than Lord Raglan claimed, by 1914 a complete system of military censorship was ready. Worse than the disclosure of military information to the enemy, in many ways, was the publication of news likely to undermine morale at home. There had been stories of mismanagement in the Napoleonic wars, though perhaps not of anything quite so grotesque as consignments of boots arriving in the Crimea—all for the left foot, or of supplies which by some accident were delivered to the Russian army instead of the British, or, more sinister still, of shady dealings over the supply of preserved meat to the army, which led *Punch* to remark that 'One man's preserved meat is another man's poison'. A curb of some sort seemed desirable in the interests of security as well as morale, and, as Justin McCarthy pointed out, the fact that the French appeared to have managed their part of the war better than the British was a tribute to the greater freedom of the British press.

Once the war was over, the sense of urgency in this matter diminished and for the rest of the century the only increase in security was provided by the Official Secrets Act of 1889, an Act which seemed at the time to be 'so drafted as to be difficult to understand'.[1] It was directed not so much against the press as against espionage in times of peace and provided a penalty of a year's imprisonment (or life imprisonment in the case of anyone in a position of trust) for disclosing official secrets to a foreign power. The significance of the Official Secrets Act, so far as the press was concerned, was not apparent for another quarter of a century, when it was used as the ultimate threat in the event of failure by the press to agree to a voluntary censorship in matters of national security.

The nineteenth century had come to accept the view which Erskine had urged without success at the trial of Paine's *Rights of Man* in 1792, that no political opinions, however forcibly expressed should be regarded as criminal unless they advocated violence, murder, or some breach of the law. After 1832 there were still authors and editors who felt that the causes which they supported could only succeed through violence, or at least through preparations for violence. Henry Hetherington, for example, published advice to working class radicals in his *Poor Man's Guardian* of 25 May 1833 on how to protect themselves against physical assault by their opponents. He urged each man to carry with him to political meetings some bread, cheese, and a large knife with long blade and stout handle, 'for it is a pity he should run the risk of being starved'. This was tantamount to advocating violence and it is no surprise to find that Hetherington was charged with seditious libel and convicted. Seven years later when the Chartist leader Feargus O'Connor was charged with seditious libel published at Leeds in the *Northern Star* of 13 July 1839, the indictment made clear that the offence was not merely one of insulting the Crown, or the constitution but rather of inciting resistance and obstruction to 'the Laws and Government of this Realm', and calling on his readers—and hearers, since this was a printed report of a speech O'Connor had made—'to overturn and change the Laws and institutions of the Realm and to make insurrections, riots, routs, and tumultuous and illegal assemblies, and to arm themselves for the purpose of more effectually obstructing and resisting the Laws and Government of the Realm'.[2] O'Connor had accused the government of attempting to 'put down the cause of the people by physical force', and dismissing the argument that the people should oppose physical force by moral force alone, he promised a 'warm reception' for any further use of physical force by the authorities. O'Connor's speech had industrial as well as political implications: he urged, 'let the whole

[1] Sir James Stephen, *A Digest of the Criminal Law*, 5th edn., ed. Sir H. Stephen and H. L. Stephen (London, 1894), p. 49.
[2] P.R.O., K.B. 28/551/9.

country strike on a given day and never return to their callings till they had worked out their political and social salvation'. In calling for the strike alone, O'Connor would have been guilty of a criminal libel by the law of the time but in advocating violence he put himself beyond the bounds of toleration even in Victoria's England. He was sent to prison for eighteen months.

Other Chartists were tried and convicted for what they had written or said; indeed, in the same year as O'Connor, John Collins and William Lovett were gaoled for distributing pamphlets which condemned the conduct of the London Metropolitan Police, who had been brought in to break up a Chartist meeting in the Bull Ring at Birmingham. Yet a cause which was to have a much longer and closer association with violence was that of Irish Nationalism. There were few prosecutions for seditious libel in connection with this, if only because, despite their great literary tradition, Irishmen discovered that dynamite was more effective than dialectic in the battle for national freedom. Two Irishmen who overstepped the bounds of Victorian political tolerance were John Mitchel and Charles Gavin Duffy who had published articles in the *United Irishman* and the *Nation* on the technique of vitriol throwing, or sympathising with the Irish insurrection of 1848. By a stroke of fortune for them, both prosecutions failed. Duffy made his way to Australia, became Prime Minister of Victoria, and received a knighthood. Mitchel, after being convicted as a rebel, escaped to the United States, where, by some quirk of personality, he became an advocate for the retention of negro slavery.

When men were convicted for their political views during the earlier period of Victoria's reign it was because they advocated violence as the only solution to a particular problem, whether it was a problem represented by Chartism or Irish Nationalism. Towards the end of the Queen's reign, however, there was a new kind of political literature which was beyond the bounds of political toleration. It was a literature associated with the new 'Anarchists', 'Nihilists' and other groups. Unlike the Irish Nationalists, or even the Chartists, their aims were very general and the whole world was their territory. If they applauded the assassination of English officials in Ireland, it was because they approved of the assassination of 'tyrants' everywhere. To the Victorians the physical danger threatened by such groups seemed very real, and the more sinister because those who were dedicated to violence and subversion seemed often to be foreigners. Even the pornographers made the most of this, hoping perhaps to add a certain *frisson* to such works as the *Amatory Experiences of a Surgeon* (1881), or the *Power of Mesmerism* (1880) by describing them on their title-pages as 'Printed for the Nihilists: Moscow'. The bombs which Orsini threw in Paris in 1858, killing ten people and wounding more than 150 had their origin in England; popular melodramas showed plotters scheming to blow up various places and people, and when, in 1867, the Fenians killed and wounded a number of victims in an attempt to blow open Clerkenwell prison, it seemed no more than a fulfilment of the worst fears. Whatever John Stuart Mill might say, there were limits to the political opinions which could be tolerated in practice: indeed, it was not Mill but Erskine who had provided a formula for political freedom of the press in this respect.

One of the most remarkable of these extremist publications to be prosecuted was the German-language journal *Freiheit*, which involved three men in legal proceedings for advocating and supporting assassination through its pages. Since 1861 it had been illegal by statute to advocate an act of murder, whether the intended victim was a British subject or not. In 1881 Johann Most was successfully prosecuted for approving the murder of a foreign sovereign—the Czar of Russia— in the *Freiheit*. He praised 'the most energetic of all tyrant haters, the Russian Nihilists', deplored the fact that 'here and there even Socialists . . . abominate regicide', and concluded 'what one might in any case complain of that is only the rarity of so-called tyrannicide. If only a single crowned wretch were disposed of every month, in a short time it should afford no one gratification henceforward still to play the monarch'.[1]

In the following year cases were brought against William Mertens and Frederick Schwelm for articles in the *Freiheit* on 13 May and 27 May 1882. The article for which Mertens was tried and convicted applauded the recent assassination of Lord Cavendish, who was Chief Secretary to the Lord Lieutenant of Ireland, and Thomas Burke, the Permanent Under-Secretary. The two men were stabbed to death in Phoenix Park, Dublin, though the murder was at once denounced by Parnell and the Irish Nationalists. Perhaps it was this which now led the *Freiheit* to advocate the murder of Parnell also. The *Freiheit* of 27 May, commenting on the prosecution of earlier numbers proclaimed, 'The international gang of monarchs has made a great mistake imagining to close the mouths of the London Social revolutionists by prosecuting the *Freiheit*'.[2] Certainly there were similar publications which succeeded the *Freiheit* and, for instance, there was a case ten years later involving David Nicholl's paper, the *Commonweal*. The paper had attacked the trials and sentences of the so-called 'Walsall

[1] *Law Reports*, 7 Q.B.D., 1881, pp. 244–59. Alexander II was assassinated on 13 March 1881.
[2] P.R.O., D.P.P. 4/14.

Anarchists' in 1892. The police raided the *Commonweal*'s offices and Nicholl himself was tried and sent to prison for eighteen months. Those who wondered whether a free press could ever be as free as Mill and others advocated in the mid-nineteenth century now received their answer. Some of the rulers of Victorian England might have been prepared to concede that it is a man's moral duty to advocate assassination if his country and its inhabitants are at the mercy of an intolerable tyranny: yet this state of affairs remained hypothetical, since they could not regard themselves—and chose not to regard the established rulers of other countries, in this context—as tyrants.

BLASPHEMY AND HONEST DOUBT

In the first ten years or so of the Queen's reign it seemed as if the Victorians might after all, return to the theological battles of the earlier nineteenth century, with very little change of either positions or tactics. This involvement with past controversies is well-described by the hero of Charles Kingsley's *Alton Locke* (1850), who refers to the prison chaplain as a man 'like most of his class, "attacking extinct Satans", fighting manfully against Voltaire, Volney, and Tom Paine; while I was fighting for Strauss, Hennell, and Emerson. . . . He had never read Strauss—hardly even heard of him; and, till clergymen make up their minds to do that, and to answer Strauss also, they will, as he did, leave the heretic artisan just where they found him.'[1] Certainly the trials for blasphemous libel during the 1840s seemed to cover a lot of old ground. When Hetherington was tried and convicted before Lord Denman and a special jury in December 1840, it was for publishing Haslam's *Letter to the Clergy of all Denominations*, which contained such comparatively well-worn sentiments about the Bible as 'I for one, however, renounce the book; I renounce it as a vile compound of filth, blasphemy, and nonsense, as a fraud and a cheat, *and as an insult to God*'.[2] Nor were the sentiments of the Attorney-General any less predictable: Hetherington, he said, had published the book, 'careless of the effect it might have on the morals of the unthinking working classes'.[3] Hetherington was sent to prison for four months but this, the first conviction for blasphemy for some years, provoked substantial sympathy for Hetherington from newspapers like the *Sun*, the *Morning Chronicle*, and the *Weekly Despatch*. The *Sun* attacked the bringing of such a prosecution and, more specifically, the part played in it by the Attorney-General, Sir John Campbell.

[1] *The Works of Charles Kingsley* (London, 1879), III, 322.
[2] *A Full Report of the Trial of Henry Hetherington* (London, 1840), p. 3.
[3] *ibid.*, p. 22.

In the following year, a Royal Commission considered the question of bringing such prosecutions for blasphemous libel, and concluded, 'There is no instance, we believe, of the prosecution of a writer or speaker who has applied himself seriously to examine into the truth of the most important of all subjects, and who, arriving at his own convictions of scepticism or unbelief, has gravely and decorously submitted his opinions to others, without any wanton and malevolent design to do mischief'.[1] It would be hard to devise a more question-begging statement than this one and, for the time being, the series of prosecutions continued with Charles Southwell being sent to prison in 1842 for a year, and fined £100 for yet another attack on the morality of the Bible. Southwell was the editor of the *Oracle of Reason*, which like so many publications proclaiming 'reason' on their title-pages, showed little evidence of it elsewhere. It was Southwell who attacked the 'obscenity' of the Bible and denounced its heroines as worse strumpets than Fanny Hill or Harriette Wilson. Like a number of his colleagues, Southwell also makes an appeal to anti-semitic feeling by dubbing the Bible 'The Jew Book'. His moral self-righteousness and good nose for impure literature might have been the envy of many an evangelical clergyman. In his defence he quoted Cardinal Wiseman's criticism of Protestant over-reliance on biblical authority, as well as Richard Lalor Sheil's attack on the indecency of certain episodes in the Bible. The two Catholics made improbable allies for the unfortunate atheist and his quotations from them did him no good.

With Southwell in prison, editorship of the *Oracle of Reason* passed to George Jacob Holyoake. In the strength of his moral convictions, on which he based his atheism, and a certain cultural puritanism, Holyoake was a true Victorian. 'The marriage service of the Church,' he later protested, 'contains things no bride could hear without a blush, if she understood them.'[2] Eight months after taking over the *Oracle of Reason*, Holyoake himself was tried for blasphemy at Gloucester assizes before Mr. Justice Erskine. When lecturing at Cheltenham in May, Holyoake had said in reply to a question, 'I am of no religion at all—I do not believe in such a thing as a God. The people of this country are too poor to have any religion. I would serve the Deity as the government does the subaltern—place him on half-pay.'[3] It seems a mild enough jibe but Holyoake was found guilty without delay and sent to prison for six months.

[1] Quoted in Hypatia Bradlaugh Bonner, *Penalties upon Opinion* (London, 1934), p. 70.
[2] G. J. Holyoake, *The Origin and Nature of Secularism* (London, 1896), p. 121.
[3] G. J. Holyoake, *The Last Trial for Atheism in England* (London, 1850), p. 25.

Of course, anti-clericalism and attacks on the alleged immorality of the Bible had long been the stuff of trials for blasphemy but there was another series of prosecutions at this time, which dealt not only with the same topics but with the same book which had caused so much trouble in the reign of George IV. In 1840–1 four different cases were brought against those who attempted to issue unexpurgated editions of Shelley's *Queen Mab*. The most significant of these was a case brought against Edward Moxon, one of the most eminent and respectable bookmen of the Victorian era, the publisher of Wordsworth, Tennyson, Browning, and Hood, among others. Moxon had already published Shelley's *Poetical Works* with a selection from *Queen Mab* included, and, finally, he decided to issue a complete edition of the *Works*. The prosecution brought against him in 1841 was something of a test case. There are conflicting accounts of how the case came about—it may have been begun by Hetherington or by Linton, one of Moxon's acquaintances—yet in either event it was not motivated by disapproval of *Queen Mab* but by a desire to see if there was one law for the 'low booksellers of the Strand' and another for the aristocratic booksellers of Dover Street. Moxon's counsel, Talfourd, claimed that the passages objected to in *Queen Mab* were no more impious than some of those put into the mouths of the fallen angels by Milton in *Paradise Lost* nor less decent than others in the novels of Fielding and Richardson. Moxon was nevertheless found guilty, though he was merely bound over in his own recognizances, for which Linton and others sportingly offered to supply the money. At this trial, Lord Denman rather pointedly suggested that if the doctrines in a particular book were irreligious, the answer lay not in an appeal to courts of law but in 'confuting the sentiments themselves.' When two more prosecutions were brought in respect of *Queen Mab*, later in the same year, both defendants were acquitted and from then on the poem circulated without interference.

The common law judges had agreed in 1842 that a decent denial of the truth of the Christian religion was not criminal and this was repeated twenty-five years later in Starkie's *Slander and Libel* with the observation, 'A wilful intention to pervert, insult, and mislead others by means of contumelious abuse applied to sacred subjects, or by wilful misrepresentations and artful sophistry, calculated to mislead the ignorant and unwary, is the test of guilt'.[1] Though as late as the end of the nineteenth century a more conservative lawyer like Sir James Stephen might continue to argue that any denial of the truth of Christianity in general or the existence of God amounted to blasphemy, there was little support for such a view. In practice, most trial

[1] Quoted in Stephen, *Digest of the Criminal Law*, 5th edn., p. 97.

judges were careful to point out that it was not criminal merely to deny the truth of Christianity or to advocate atheism, so long as this was done honestly and decently.

The fact that the amount of unbelief in the Victorian age was greater but the number of prosecutions for blasphemy smaller than in any earlier period has much to do with the quality of that unbelief. It was not a scepticism voiced in the polished sarcasm of Gibbon or the exultant gibes of Thomas Paine but, for the most part, a reluctant and scrupulously honest unbelief. Indeed, the scruples of some Victorians could get them into ridiculous situations and one thinks, for instance, of the naturalist P. R. Gosse who believed in the literal truth of the first two books of Genesis and was then confronted by the work of Sir Charles Lyell in geology and Darwin in biology. Gosse sought refuge in the only conceivable explanation which would reconcile his allegiances to Genesis and science. The world had indeed been created six thousand years ago as described in Genesis but it was created with the appearance of a world which had already existed for millions of years—hence the fossils. As Edmund Gosse recalled, his father's theory was interpreted by an unsympathetic press as meaning 'that God hid the fossils in the rocks in order to tempt geologists into infidelity'.[1] It is—or was—fashionable to write of the hypocrisy of the Victorians, and yet in following the intellectual pilgrimages from faith to doubt or doubt to faith of, say, George Eliot, Newman, Clough, Tennyson, J. A. Froude, and many of their contemporaries, the modern reader finds an integrity and scrupulousness hard to match in any other period, often reflecting Gerard Manley Hopkins's description of 'That night, that year/Of now done darkness I wretch lay wrestling with (my God!) my God.' As George Gissing pointed out in the *Private Papers of Henry Ryecroft* (1903), if there was a national vice in this respect it was not hypocrisy but self-righteousness.

The honesty, the seriousness, the sobriety of the critics of Christianity perfectly matched the idea which the interpreters of the law had put forward of 'decent' dissent. Many of these critics never reached the point of atheism nor, for that matter, of orthodox belief but remained in that ill-defined intellectual limbo for which T. H. Huxley coined the name of 'agnosticism'. Tennyson himself spoke for them in lines of self-conscious resonance.

> There is more faith in honest doubt,
> Believe me, than in half the creeds.

The new reservations about Christianity were based on arguments

---

[1] Edmund Gosse, *Father and Son* (London, 1907), p. 120.

which no court of law could either refute or proscribe. If the evidence of man's origins in Sir Charles Lyell's *Principles of Geology* (1844) or Charles Darwin's *Origin of Species* (1859) was going to demolish the authority of the Old Testament, it would do so in a way which no law of blasphemous libel could prevent. Strauss's *Leben Jesu* (1835); Charles Hennell's *Inquiry Concerning the Origin of Christianity* (1838), and Ernest Renan's *Vie de Jésus* (1863) had examined the four gospels critically and, in many people's minds thrown doubts on certain aspects of their historical authenticity but all this had been done as dispassionately as though the text in question had been, say, the *Annals* of Tacitus, not in terms of hysterical propaganda or insult. The only possible reaction, as Lord Denman suggested and Charles Kingsley insisted, was not to censor such publications or their imitators but to answer their arguments. Indeed, new intellectual forces might operate in more ways than one, and if the conclusions of Lyell and Darwin led P. R. Gosse into a hopeless attempt to reconcile his religious beliefs with his scientific integrity, they also led John Stuart Mill towards a belief in 'creation by intelligence' in his *Three Essays on Religion*.

It is hardly surprising that by 1888 Mrs. Humphrey Ward in *Robert Elsmere* could describe her hero's loss of faith without causing a fraction of the indignation which followed J. A. Froude's *Nemesis of Faith* almost forty years earlier. Perhaps by that time the fact that Christianity had survived half a century of the new science and the new criticism made its defenders more tolerant. Yet as early as 1866 the National Secular Society had been founded and with this new organisation to support him Charles Bradlaugh had begun to champion the secularist cause in his *National Reformer*. Once again, Bradlaugh illustrates the truth that, Catholic or agnostic, evangelical or atheist, the parties to the dispute were all Victorians under the skin. Bradlaugh, once described by the *Northern Echo* as 'a Puritan who has lost his way', was the epitome of upper middle-class respectability in many ways: a political liberal, a philanthropist, a martyr for conscience's sake, a sober and upright man, he happened also to be a republican, an atheist, and an advocate of birth control. One of the ironies of Bradlaugh's character is that, in so many respects a revolutionary, he should have been an associate of the Reverend Stuart Headlam's work through the Guild of St. Matthew, only to part company with him when Headlam, accepting the need for nationalisation of the land, became a Socialist.

Bradlaugh's *National Reformer*, though it never provoked a prosecution for blasphemous libel, laboured under two significant difficulties. W. H. Smith refused to stock it, which put it in quite good company but obviously reduced its circulation, and the government, though unwilling to bring a prosecution for blasphemy, made indirect attempts to suppress it. Under the Act of 1819 for suppressing seditious and blasphemous libels the government was still entitled to demand sureties from a publisher against his issuing such libels, a law which applied to any periodical selling at less than sixpence. The *National Reformer* sold at twopence and Bradlaugh, as its owner, should have paid over to the Inland Revenue sureties of £400 required of him. This he did not do, and so became liable for penalties of £50 a day so long as the paper continued to appear and £20 for every copy issued. On 3 May 1868 Bradlaugh announced the opening of the *National Reformer* Defence Fund to resist this attempt by the Commissioners of the Inland Revenue to suppress the paper. He declared that he was publishing it in defiance of the government and of the Act of 1819, which he alleged was merely a law for the suppression of 'cheap Democratic and Freethought literature'. The Commissioners of the Inland Revenue issued a writ for the recovery of the money now due as the penalty for continuing to publish the paper without giving recognizances. At £50 a day and £20 a copy, Bradlaugh announced that by this time he must owe them a well-nigh incalculable sum. The *National Reformer* for 24 May was headed with the proclamation 'Prosecuted by Her Majesty's Government'. The government had taken action, as it was legally entitled to do, but at this point it began to have second thoughts. The Act of 1819 was, after all, an instrument of censorship which public opinion in 1868 would have found intolerable if the matter had really come to a head. Certainly any prosecution of a newspaper on the grounds of an Act passed in the troubled times of half a century earlier was going to reflect badly on the government. Bradlaugh and John Stuart Mill presented petitions to the House of Commons for the repeal of the law in question. However, the legal process had been set in motion and Bradlaugh was duly summoned before the Court of Exchequer in June 1868. Only ten jurors were present and when the Attorney-General was asked if he wanted more to be summoned so that the case could proceed, he declined. By December there was a general election and a Liberal government was formed, yet in February 1869 the case was begun again and adjourned. That summer the Act of 1819 was repealed and the case against the *National Reformer* was dropped. No doubt there were those who would gladly have suppressed the paper by indirect means but they misjudged both the character of Bradlaugh and the mood of mid-Victorian politics. Despite the ban on it by W. H. Smith, the *National Reformer* survived and even flourished.

However respectable Bradlaugh and his paper might appear to be, so long as there was some limit to the manner in which Christianity might be denied it was probable that someone sooner or later would overstep that limit. In 1881, under the aegis of the Freethought Publishing Company, G. W. Foote and William Ramsay—both prominent members of the National Secular Society—launched a new weekly paper, the *Freethinker*. Those who wondered what would constitute blasphemous libel in the last quarter of the nineteenth century were about to find out. Neither Bradlaugh nor his new associate Annie Besant was responsible for what appeared in the *Freethinker*, though they shared the same offices. Indeed, Mrs. Besant accused the paper of lowering the tone of Freethought advocacy and thereby playing into the hands of its enemies. The cause of all the trouble was that the *Freethinker*, which was far more bitterly anti-Christian than any other publication of the time, had begun to publish a series of so-called 'Comic Bible Sketches', presumably in the hope that a sufficiently violent campaign would destroy the basis of religious belief by making it a matter for automatic ridicule. As a matter of fact, it did much to discredit the Freethought movement among influential sympathisers, particularly by alienating Bradlaugh in this matter from Foote and his colleagues. Both the manner of attacking the Bible and the appeal to anti-semitism would have been unattractive to Bradlaugh. There is a description of one of the 'Comic Bible Sketches' in Mrs. Humphrey Ward's novel *Robert Elsmere*, published five years after the case ended. Robert Elsmere, walking through the working-class area of London to which he has chosen to devote himself, sees a placard advertising the *Freethinker* outside a rather shabby little shop which specialises in such literature. 'Read "Faith and Fools". Enormous Success. Our "Comic Life of Christ" now nearly completed. Quite the best thing of its kind going. Woodcut this week—Transfiguration.'[1] The paper itself, when Robert buys and opens it, is described as containing 'a caricature of the Crucifixion, the scroll emanating from Mary Magdalene's mouth, in particular, containing obscenities which cannot be quoted here'.[2] This sort of thing appeared for about six months without provoking any action on the part of the authorities and, indeed, it may be that the government had decided to let well alone. Yet in the summer of 1882 a Member of Parliament, Sir Henry Tyler, obtained a *fiat* from the Director of Public Prosecutions to prosecute the publishers of the *Freethinker* for blasphemy. Bradlaugh, as well as Foote and Ramsay, was prosecuted at first but he argued successfully that he should be tried separately and when this happened, in April 1883, before Lord

[1] *Robert Elsmere* (London, 1888), III, 167.
[2] *ibid.*, III, 167.

Coleridge, he proved to the satisfaction of the jury that he was not responsible for the *Freethinker* and was duly acquitted. Lord Coleridge laid much emphasis on the existence of a malicious and mischievous intention being necessary to constitute an act of blasphemy. Mere denial of Christianity was not enough. Bradlaugh's trial was followed by the trial of Foote and Ramsay with Coleridge again presiding and interpreting the law of blasphemy in the sense most favourable to the defendants. Nonetheless, these two men had published the material objected to, which Bradlaugh had not, and to that extent at least the case against them was stronger. The jury disagreed and the prosecution was dropped. But in the meantime another prosecution had been brought against the two men for a 'Comic Bible Sketch' in the rather inappropriately-styled 'Christmas Number' of the *Freethinker* for 1882. This second case was, in fact, the first to be tried and the defendants were perhaps less fortunate in having Mr. Justice North as their judge. He insisted that even to deny the existence of God was technically blasphemous and, as both he and Coleridge pointed out, it was no defence for the two accused to produce other anti-Christian literature which had not been prosecuted, such things were not relevant to the case. The first jury disagreed but a second jury found the two men guilty. Foote was sentenced to a year's imprisonment and Ramsay to nine months.

Though there was no other case of this kind in the later nineteenth century, it is worth considering the difficulties of the 'Comic Bible Sketches' prosecutions. These were cases which the government itself was evidently reluctant to undertake, though it was content to let Sir Henry Tyler represent the powers of censorship. The publications themselves were, by all accounts, extremely offensive and could hardly come within the bounds of a 'decent' denial of the Christian religion, yet it was difficult to obtain a verdict against the defendants. Four separate juries produced one conviction and that was after Mr. Justice North's rather illiberal interpretation of the law. If this was the best that attempts at censorship through courts of law could achieve it was evidently high time that Christianity renounced the protection of these courts altogether, unless the law against blasphemy could be made a great deal stricter in practice. This last possibility was one which still had its attractions for some people. In March 1883 an announcement appeared in the press from the newly-formed Society for the Suppression of Blasphemous Literature.

We propose to get up cases, as our funds will allow, against Professor Huxley, Dr. Tyndall, Herbert Spencer, Swinburne, the author of 'Supernatural Religion,' the publishers of Mill's works, the publishers of Strauss's works, Leslie Stephen, John Morley, the editor of the *Jewish World*, Dr.

Martineau, and others, who by their writings have sown widespread un-belief, and in some cases rank Atheism, in cultivated families.[1]

It is quite a change to find that 'cultivated families' rather than the 'unthinking working classes' had become the chief cause for concern. Yet it is hard to take the announcement seriously, not because there was any lack of people who would have been pleased to see T. H. Huxley, Leslie Stephen, and, certainly Swinburne, behind bars but rather because of the hopelessness of persuading a judge and jury to put them there. Perhaps the announcement was an improbable *jeu d'esprit* on the part of the National Secular Society. Even in the twentieth century prosecutions for blasphemous libel were not to be unknown, in extreme cases, but for all practical purposes it had now been left to editors, publishers, librarians, booksellers, and—above all—authors to exercise their own censorship where matters of religious opinion were concerned. Often this personal 'censorship' was motivated by prudent self-interest which had nothing to do with fear of prosecution. It took no court of law in 1879, for instance, to induce A. J. Balfour, with an eye to his political future to alter his *Defence of Philosophic Scepticism* to *A Defence of Philosophic Doubt*.

Before leaving the question of the censorship of religious opinion in Victoria's England, it is worth recalling that one body of men was subject to restraints which did not apply to writers in general: the clergy of the Church of England. The power of the Anglican Church to punish its priests for what they had written or published was not accompanied by any power to prevent such publications and, of course, the heretics included those who were too sympathetic towards Roman Catholic doctrine as well as those who seemed to be moving towards unbelief. There were many evangelical clergyman who urged the suppression of 'Catholic' interpretations of Anglican doctrine, though not all of them were like the Reverend C. P. Golightly, so obsessed with 'the task of annihilating Newmanism . . . that he trembled to walk the streets at night, lest he might fall into a Tractarian ambush'.[2] As heretics of both extremes were to discover, the Universities as well as the Church itself had the power to deal with dissident clergy among their members. In 1841 Newman's *Tract XC*, in which he asserted the Catholic nature of the Thirty-Nine Articles, was condemned by the Heads of Houses at Oxford. Two years later Pusey was suspended from preaching for two years by the Vice-Chancellor after a sermon in which he seemed to approve the Roman doctrine of transubstantiation. These were University and Church

[1] Hypatia Bradlaugh Bonner, *Charles Bradlaugh* (London, 1898), II, 332.
[2] Geoffrey Faber, *Oxford Apostles: A Character Study of the Oxford Movement* (London, 1954), p. 416.

matters but in Newman's case an understanding was reached that no further action would be taken against him provided that no more *Tracts for the Times* were issued. It is not surprising that Newman should have accepted the condition, since, as he later wrote, 'From the end of 1841, I was on my death-bed, as regards my membership with the Anglican Church,' and four years later he was received into the Church of Rome.[1] Yet there were others who could neither accept what Rome had to offer nor, on the other hand, reject Christian belief: they were obliged to make the best of the Church they had got and in doing so sometimes make trouble for themselves.

In 1860 there appeared *Essays and Reviews*, which contained seven essays by seven of the ablest men in the Anglican Church: Benjamin Jowett, Mark Pattison, Frederick Temple, Baden Powell, C. W. Goodwin, H. B. Wilson, and Rowland Williams. Temple became Headmaster of Rugby and Archbishop of Canterbury; Pattison was to be Rector of Lincoln College, Oxford; Jowett became Master of Balliol ten years later and was Professor of Greek at the time; Baden Powell was also at Oxford, as Savilian Professor of Geometry; Goodwin was a Fellow of Christ's College, Cambridge; Wilson had taught at Oxford for a quarter of a century, while Williams was Vice-Principal and Professor of Hebrew at St. David's College, Lampeter. By any standards, the heretics made an impressive array but this did not prevent the book from being condemned as a whole. Two of the essays, all of which sought somehow or other to reconcile religious belief and contemporary thought, provoked particular censure, and the contributors to the book were dubbed *Septem contra Christum*. Critics saw in Williams's essay on 'Bunsen's Biblical Researches' a demand that the divine nature of biblical revelation should be ignored and that the Bible should be treated with the same objectivity as any other historical document: the heresy of Strauss in the mouth of an Anglican. Wilson's essay, 'Séances historiques de Genève: The National Church,' also expressed reservations about some of the contents of the Bible and went on to suggest that if the Church of England would abandon its insistence on subscription to the Thirty-Nine Articles, it would attract those who at present stood outside it and might thus become a truly national Church. It seemed the ultimate expression of the Broad Church ideal. Both Williams and Wilson were charged with heresy in the ecclesiastical courts and though they were convicted by the Court of Arches in 1862 this decision was reversed when they appealed to the Privy Council. The efforts of their enemies, it seemed, had come to nothing. In the mean-

[1] John Henry Newman, *History of My Religious Opinions* (London, 1865), p. 147.

time, Pusey—who had himself been in trouble in 1843 for his 'pro-Catholic' sermon—was one of those who brought a case against Jowett in the Vice-Chancellor's court at Oxford. (Jowett's contribution to *Essays and Reviews* was an essay 'On the Interpretation of Scripture,' which amounted to another plea for treating the Bible as an historical document rather than a divine revelation whose authenticity was beyond question.) In the end this case against Jowett was dropped. If it seems inappropriate to find a rebel like Pusey attacking a rebel like Jowett—even though their two rebellions were of opposite persuasions—it is worth recalling that Wilson, who was now regarded as perhaps the greatest heretic of *Essays and Reviews*—had been one of the leaders of the attack on Newman's very different kind of heresy as expressed in *Tract XC*.

Wilson and Williams were not the only two against whom action was taken in the ecclesiastical courts at this time. In 1862 J. W. Colenso, the Anglican Bishop of Natal, had published yet another attack on the Pentateuch in his *Pentateuch and the Book of Joshua Critically Examined*. For this heresy he was deposed and excommunicated but then something happened which no one could really have anticipated. Colenso, deciding that, for a colonial bishop, possession is ten points of the law, refused to move and continued as Bishop of Natal. In 1866 the temporal courts declined to interfere, although another bishop was consecrated, and so the Diocese of Natal enjoyed two rival bishops for some years to come.

Whatever penalties had been imposed on Colenso, Wilson, or Williams by the ecclesiastical courts, those courts would have had no power to suppress the books or essays which had caused all the trouble, so their powers of direct censorship were very limited. Yet indirectly they might have done much to dissuade clergymen from expressing dangerous opinions. In general, once the trials for blasphemy in the 1840s were over, any further convictions for blasphemous libel in the temporal courts were, if not freaks, at least a matter of luck. It is not entirely unrealistic to say that, for instance, in 1883 Ramsay and Foote were unlucky in their judge. So far as the imaginative literature of the Victorian period is concerned, a publisher like F. S. Ellis might insist on Swinburne withdrawing two allegedly blasphemous sonnets from *Songs Before Sunrise* (1871) before he would issue the book but there can have been few other periods of history which would have taken as one of their great poetic achievements the kind of self-torturing doubt which animates Tennyson's *In Memoriam*. Most authors were perfectly safe from censorship in this respect. No one would have tried to prosecute Samuel Butler for his jibes at Christianity in the *Fair Haven* (1873) or for his representation of it as 'Sunchildism' in *Erewhon Revisited* (1901). In mid-century, a poet like A. H. Clough could write in a style and tone which would probably have seemed blasphemous to most eighteenth-century believers because of the doubts which were generated and not blasphemous enough to Thomas Paine because the poet was prepared to do no more than doubt.

> Through the great sinful streets of Naples as I past,
>> With fiercer heat than flamed above my head
> My heart was hot within me; till at last
>> My brain was lightened when my tongue had said—
>> Christ is not risen!

>> Christ is not risen, no—
>> He lies and moulders low;
>> Christ is not risen.

So Clough begins *Easter Day* but no Victorian doubter was allowed to have his brain 'lightened' by so simple an incantation as that, and so in the second part of the poem Clough restores the balance, leaving both scales suspended and immobile.

> Though He be dead, He is not dead
>> In the true creed
>> He is yet risen indeed;
> Christ is yet risen.

Censors habitually envisage men as being incited to various undesirable forms of action by literature which must, therefore, be suppressed. Clough and those who shared his uncertainties escaped censorship because according to the law their doubt was 'honest' or 'decent'. But quite apart from this, the effect of their writing is less to incite mental activity in respect of questions of religious belief than ultimately to induce a state of paralysis.

II

Victoria:
(2) 'Smacks and Laughter Echoed
Through the Grove . . .'
The Pearl (September 1879)

A BLUSH ON THE CHEEK OF MODESTY

It is all too easy to exaggerate or to misinterpret the Victorian concern over allegedly indecent literature, to deduce from a few unrepresentative reviews that it would have been quite possible for George Eliot, Mrs. Gaskell, George Moore, Thomas Hardy or their publishers to have been prosecuted for issuing obscene libels. As a matter of fact it was unusual for a book by a major novelist to be banned by a circulating library and even that ban was by no means permanent. On the other hand, after the Obscene Publications Act of 1857 there was a major effort to deal with the 'poison' of pornography, which succeeded in driving the more sophisticated part of the trade to refuges in Paris and Brussels. Literature which was, arguably, of some real literary merit was not much interfered with by the law until the last twenty years or so of the nineteenth century. Indeed, when Lord Campbell introduced his bill in 1857, he made it clear that he had no intention of preventing the circulation of 'literature' as opposed to pornography, even though he might disapprove of the moral standards of some of that literature. Producing a copy of *La Dame Aux Camélias*, he announced that much as he disapproved of it, it was not against such publications that the new law was aimed.

The official censorship of pornography by law is easy enough to trace and describe in the Victorian period but, naturally, the most important form of moral censorship was one with which the law was not directly concerned. It was a censorship exercised ultimately by booksellers and libraries, penultimately by publishers or editors, and in the first place by authors themselves. And when all this was done there still remained the individual censorship of the buyer or the borrower. The purpose of Victorian censorship is related closely to that scene pictured by Bowdler in the introduction to his edition of Shakespeare, the scene in which a father is reading aloud to his family. This is the audience to whom a majority of Victorian writers and

239

publishers were compelled to think of themselves as catering. 'At our social table, we shall suppose the ladies and children always present', said Thackeray, laying down his editorial policy in the first number of the *Cornhill* in November 1859. Under these circumstances it was not surprising that so many publications made a direct, domestic appeal in their titles, whether in the *Family Library*; *Household Words*, or the *Englishwoman's Domestic Magazine*. Given this family audience, as envisaged by Bowdler, if Dickens had decided to describe Nancy's profession in *Oliver Twist* as Defoe had described Moll Flanders's, a father's embarrassment in reading aloud to his children would hardly have been less in 1938 than in 1838. This reading aloud of books in the family had been common in the mid-eighteenth century among the middle classes and since then, as Hannah More pointed out, had spread lower down the social scale. It was no longer, therefore, a matter of mere squeamishness about 'free' expressions. The Victorians and their immediate predecessors regarded literature as an educative agent, at a time when the education of the lower orders seemed to be the panacea for moral and social ills: in this sense, literature was to serve the intellectual and moral needs of the community rather than to amuse a few sophisticated individuals. Like the Puritans of the seventeenth century, many Victorian moralists felt it was not enough that a book should be free from impurity, books should contribute to the moral improvement of their readers, hence the criticism aimed at novelists like Scott that though they were devoid of the 'immorality' of Byron they were also devoid of moral instruction.

'We must now at least educate our new masters', said Robert Lowe, future Liberal Chancellor and Home Secretary, after the passing of the 1867 Reform Bill, and three years later Forster's Education Act went some way towards doing this. Yet a most important ingredient in the Victorian attitude towards literary censorship was the belief that the desire for education on the part of the masses would be satisfied, whatever the government did. The Sunday School system and its adjuncts had ensured that a large proportion of those masses was already literate if not educated: it was now a question of whether they should be well or badly educated by the literature made available to them. When, for instance, *The Times* sent a correspondent to investigate the literature available on railway station bookstalls in 1851 he was not merely appalled to find most of them piled high with 'unmitigated rubbish' and mildly erotic pulp fiction; what shocked him most of all was the missed opportunity to provide really worthwhile nourishment for the 'hungry minds'.[1] For this reason the article ends with high praise for W. H. Smith, the 'Schoolmaster' who had ac-

[1] *The Times*, 9 August 1851.

quired a monopoly of bookstalls on the North Western Railway that year, and for Longmans who were bringing out a 'Traveller's Library' of worthwhile literature. There was no room for frivolity—let alone indecency—when the education of the 'new masters' was at stake. Some critics even regarded imaginative literature in general as dangerous and misleading. 'Literature is a seducer,' the *Westminster Review* had warned in 1825, 'we had almost said a harlot. She may do to trifle with; but woe be to the state whose statesmen write verses, and whose lawyers read more in Tom Moore than in Bracton'.[1]

A belief that men can be improved intellectually or morally by what they read entails the corollary that a certain type of literature may cause intellectual or moral deterioration. In 1868 the so-called 'Hicklin Judgment' laid down that pornography or obscenity was to be recognised by its power to deprave and corrupt its readers. Whether or not a particular person is corrupted by reading a particular book is ultimately beyond proof or disproof, just as whether a particular man is deterred from committing a particular murder by the knowledge that he may be hanged cannot be finally determined: in neither case are the people in question under 'laboratory conditions' at the appropriate time. All that can be said with certainty is that some critics would sincerely agree with William Burnaby that it is impossible that 'any ill man can talk a good one into a new Frame or Composition', while others like Lord Campbell or James Douglas, the literary watchdog of the *Sunday Express* during the 1920s, regard pornography as no less dangerous than prussic acid in the hands of the unwary. Those who oppose the 'deprave and corrupt' theory may well point to the lack of any reliable evidence to support it, yet they are faced with the proposition that if a 'bad' book cannot debase its readers nor can a 'good' book improve them. In this respect, the attitude of a critic towards pornography is only a part of his attitude towards the much larger question of whether literature is capable of shaping personality and conduct, and what the duties of an author are with regard to the moral and aesthetic intentions of his work. Since the questions which pornography raises are part of the most fundamental question of literary criticism, they are unlikely ever to receive a definitive answer. Nor are we likely to find an answer to the psychological problem of whether a man is promiscuous or practices a sexual perversion because of the pornography he has read or whether he reads such pornography because his natural inclinations are towards promiscuity or perversion. There can be no single answer, since no literature—pornographic or not—works in the same way for all its readers. Some people certainly find erotic qualities in quite 'respectable' art which are

[1] *The Westminster Review*, IV (July 1825), p. 166.

absent for others. What, in any case, has to happen to a reader before he can be regarded as depraved and corrupted?

Though the questions raised by pornography may be unanswerable, it is nonetheless interesting to know what certain people thought the answers were. To many Victorians it seemed that the effects of reading pornography, while morally undesirable, were in the end physiological. In 1857, the year in which Lord Campbell, introducing his Obscene Publications Bill, described obscene literature as 'a poison more deadly than prussic acid, strychnine or arsenic', Dr. William Acton published *Functions and Disorders of the Reproductive Organs*, in which he described how boys who were excited to 'self-indulgence' by erotic literature became destined for an early grave. Acton's work is often quoted in discussions of Victorian sexual morality and yet, one suspects, Acton's fame rests largely on the industry and righteousness with which lesser men popularised—and frequently travestied—his beliefs. Among other things, the lesser men firmly established what might be called the physiological theory of pornography, or indeed of imaginative literature as a whole. Ruddock's *Lady's Manual of Homoeopathic Treatment* (1876) lists among the causes of early sexual maturity in girls, spiced food, bad ventilation, late hours, dancing, and 'novel-reading'.[1] Towards the end of the century, the theory was further developed and, for instance, John Thompson in *Man and his Sexual Relations* (1889) insists that if his regimen for sexual continence (cold baths, wet compresses, chest expander, and dumb bells) is to succeed, then most literature, like tobacco, alcohol, spice, and feather beds, is to be avoided.

Read no fashionable papers, novels, or magazines that are full of love-tales. Nearly all the novels that deluge our bookstalls are seasoned with exciting references to the exercise of amativeness. Many allusions in these publications are decidedly objectionable, though frequently very delicately covered over with a thin gauze of fashionable refinement. On this account, however, they are all the more objectionable; they may be thoughtlessly recommended to a young person, in whose mind they may awaken lewd thoughts and licentious reveries.

Read books that will furnish the mind with useful knowledge, such as Combe's 'Constitution of Man', and 'Moral Philosophy'; Fowler's 'Human Science'; Cowen's 'Science of a New Life'; Weaver's 'Mental Science'; and, though I may not be able to accurately measure myself, I can honestly say that in all such cases as are now under consideration, there is no better work than my own on 'Body, Brain, Mind, and their inter-relationships'.[2]

[1] E. H. Ruddock *The Lady's Manual of Homoeopathic Treatment*, 6th edn. (London, 1876), p. 25.
[2] John Thompson, *Man and his Sexual Relations* (Scarborough, n.d.), pp. 159–60.

The same horror of fiction is echoed in Sylvanus Stall's *What a Young Boy Ought to Know*, which was first published in the United States in 1897, then in England, and with other books in the same series enjoyed a wide circulation until the end of the First World War.

As I told you in an earlier Talk that you could not injure the body without impairing the mind, so neither can you starve, defile, or injure the mind without injuring the body as well. Read histories and biographies. Read about the sciences and arts. Read of travels and explorations. Read about morals and religion, but do not read stories and trash. The world is too full of good books, and there are too many things in the realm of the actual and the real, concerning which you cannot afford to be ignorant, to permit of the reading of worthless books.[1]

Similar advice was offered by Stall in *What a Young Husband Ought to Know*. He, like his colleagues in England feared the physical effects of indiscriminate reading—masturbation among adolescents and too frequent sexual intercourse among their elders. As regards the former practice, Dr. Adam Clark issued what must be a classic Victorian warning to the young, and, incidentally, redefined the physiological relationship between the reading of inflammatory literature and inevitable death and damnation. Pornography might work more slowly than prussic acid but none the less effectively. Their solitary indulgence provoked by it, Clark warns adolescents, is 'several degrees worse than common whoredom, and has in its train more awful consequences . . . the muscles become flaccid and feeble, the tone and natural actions of the nerves are relaxed and impeded; the understanding confused; the memory oblivious; the judgment perverted, and the will undermined and wholly without energy to resist; the eyes appear languishing and without expression, and the countenance vacant; appetite ceases, for the stomach is incapable of performing its proper office; nutrition fails; terrors, fears, and tremors are generated; and thus the wretched victim drags out a miserable existence, till, superannuated even before he has time to arrive at man's estate, and with a mind often debilitated even to a state of idiotism, his worthless body tumbles into the grave, and his guilty soul (guilty of self-murder), is hurried into the awful presence of its judge.'[2] Some of the 'victims' are said to have been driven to suicide— no doubt after reading accounts of this kind.

By the standards of his time, Lord Campbell was hardly guilty of exaggeration when he compared obscene literature with arsenic and

[1] *What a Young Boy Ought to Know* (Philadelphia, 1909), p. 152. Of course, Stall also advises, 'Never read, handle, or listen to the reading of a book or paper which you might not ask your Mamma or Papa to read aloud with you'. p. 130.

[2] John Thompson, *Man and his Sexual Relations*, p. 77.

the more orthodox poisons. Of course, it is foolish to suggest that the standards of taste or morality remained unaltered during the whole of Victoria's reign. (To measure that reign in later terms, it was equal to the gap which separates the publication of Browning's *Asolando* from the publication of Ian Fleming's *Casino Royale*.) But belief in the power of pornography to deprave and corrupt remains the official motive of censorship in the twentieth century as in the nineteenth and there was little modification of the attitude by the Victorians. What was poisonous to Lord Campbell in 1857 was poisonous to Dr. Adam Clark thirty years later and, for that matter, to James Douglas thirty years later still. Yet the later Victorians had to consider the existence of obscenity in types of serious literature which had not hitherto been suspect. As each decade passed, the standards of morality expected in literature became stricter and a greater number of writers found themselves in rebellion against such standards. Even by absolute standards, what was tolerable in 1840 was not necessarily tolerable in 1870: this represented moral improvement. Yet in 1840 and for some time afterwards novelists and poets had generally lived up to the moral expectations of their readers and critics but as the attitude of the critics became more repressive, the writers themselves rebelled—or at least felt that it was no longer cause for a bad conscience if they should disagree profoundly with their critics in this respect. Swinburne, Rossetti, George Moore and others seemed almost to revel in their notoriety, and by the end of the nineteenth century there was a serious breach between such writers and the upholders of conventional literary morality.

Stricter standards in law and morality not only caused rifts of this kind but widened the gap between literature and pornography to almost unbridgeable dimensions. This gulf had been growing throughout most of the eighteenth century and now, as the respectable writers of Victorian England became more and more restrained in their choice of subject matter, so the pornographers grew more outrageous, their publications showing a degree of perversity, as well as perversion, unknown in the eigthteenth century in England and rivalled in Europe as a whole only by the works of the Marquis de Sade.[1] If the gulf was

---

[1] The influence of De Sade on English writers of the nineteenth century may have been more direct than has been supposed. The first known translation of *Justine, Opus Sadicum: a Philosophical Romance* dates from 1889. Yet the French original of the novel was known to Swinburne and others long before this. Moreover, we know from the account of the trial of George Cannon in 1830 (P.R.O., K.B. 28/515/13) that *Juliette* was already circulating in French by this time, if not in English. *The Inutility of Virtue*, which dates from about the same time, discusses and illustrates some of the aberrations of De Sade's novels in very similar terms. There are further parallels between the 'cut up' as described in *The Romance of*

bridged at all, those who managed it were rebels from the side of 'literature', like Swinburne or, allegedly, Oscar Wilde, who slipped across to perpetrate a nimble piece of flagellant or homosexual fantasy and then returned to temporary respectability. There were some publishers, like John Camden Hotten, who managed to carry on business on both sides of the gulf and some, like Henry Vizetelly, who were consigned to perdition with the pornographers for publishing what would now be regarded as classics of French nineteenth-century literature. Yet the traffic between the two sides was small indeed, and for those who wished to make the journey to respectability the figures of W. H. Smith and Charles Mudie loomed like perpetual sentinels before the bookstalls and circulating libraries.

So far as the Victorian reader was concerned, there were two paths to destruction, the first being the more obvious one of deriving erotic stimulus from books and thus plunging into promiscuity and an early grave. The second and less obvious path lay through the continued reading of literature which was so shocking—though not necessarily erotic—that it brought a blush to the cheek of a young person. The danger was that as the young person became inured to certain words and phrases the blush would appear less and less promptly, until finally all sense of shame was lost and the young person became capable of acts and thoughts which would once have been quite impossible. It is rare for this second type of literature to suffer the consequences of legal censorship—as Mr. Justice Stable was later to point out, in *The Philanderer* case of 1954, it is not a criminal offence to shock one's readers—yet to most Victorians such publications were sufficiently offensive and potentially dangerous to warrant a censorship outside the law.

It would, of course, be wrong to ignore the division which the Victorians themselves made between books for the drawing room and books for the library, just as there was one standard of decorum when the ladies were present and another for the smoking room.[1] The reader whose knowledge of Latin and Greek would carry him through Apuleius, Martial, Aristophanes, and Petronius, would certainly find material in the library which would not have been tolerated in translation in the drawing room. Even a play like Sophocles' *Oedipus Tyrannos* was hardly suitable for family reading, so that it is not surprising to find it very circumspectly translated by men like E. H.

[1] An extreme example of this distinction is the *Edinburgh Review*'s verdict on various translations of the *Arabian Nights*. 'Galland for the nursery, Lane for the library, Payne for the study, and Burton for the sewers.' CLXIV (1886), 184.

Chastisement (1866), p. 62, and similar incidents in *Justine* and *La Nouvelle Justine*. (*Oeuvres Complètes du Marquis de Sade*, III, 196 and VI, 386.)

Plumptre, the Dean of Wells, while Campbell and Abbott judiciously pruned the original text for use in schools. Nonetheless, the Victorian preoccupation with morality as a whole was an infinitely greater influence than mere concern about indecency. The worship of 'Great Books' was a worship based largely on their moral value and even if the theme of *Oedipus Tyrannos* involved incest, it was still a Great Book. Charlotte M. Yonge, a pious but popular novelist of High Anglicanism, pointed out in 1899 that lapses from decency or decorum 'do not do anything like the amount of harm equal to the benefit of the great book itself to the mind and character'.[1] After all, it was the moral and the educative value of great literature which made it worth expurgating. The greatness of the literature remained beyond question even if precautions had to be taken with it before it was made available to a general readership: in the case of a poet like Juvenal—whose greatness was not generally self-evident—a number of liberties could be taken with the text itself. When, for instance, the *Family Classical Library* offered the first satire of Juvenal in translation, it was faced with those lines in which Juvenal describes how every upstart in Rome has a triumphal statue raised to him and deserves to have it urinated upon, 'Cuius ad effigiem non tantum meiere fas est.' The translator on this occasion approached his task gingerly and evasively.

> Where, midst triumphal statues raised on high,
> One's spleen must ever and anon descry
> That some barbarian mongrel, some unknown
> Egyptian, Arabarch, dared plant his own!
> Whose titled effigies one's choice compel
> For purpose that we care not here to tell.[2]

The editors of the *Index Expurgatorius of Martial* (1868) accused Bohn's Library of deliberately mistranslating lines from classical authors, in the interests of propriety. Horace's advice,

---

[1] Quoted in Kathleen Tillotson, 'Charlotte Yonge as a Critic of Literature', in *A Chaplet for Charlotte M. Yonge*, ed. Georgiana Battiscombe and Marghanita Laski (London, 1965), p. 60. Charlotte Brontë expresses something of the same faith in great literature, in a letter of advice. 'If you like poetry, let it be first-rate; Milton, Shakespeare, Thomson, Goldsmith, Pope (if you will, though I don't admire him), Scott, Byron, Campbell, Wordsworth, and Southey. Now don't be startled at the names of Shakespeare and Byron. Both these were great men, and their works were like themselves. You will know how to choose the good and avoid the evil; the finest passages are always the purest, the bad are invariably revolting; you will never wish to read them over twice.' Mrs. Gaskell, *Life of Charlotte Brontë*, I, 140.

[2] *Family Classical Library: Juvenal and Persius*, p. 12.

Quod ut superbo provoces ab inguine,
Ore adlaborandum est tibi

had appeared as 'But for you to raise an appetite in a stomach that is nice, it is necessary that you exert every art of language.' As earlier commentators had recognised, 'inguine' is not 'stomach' but 'genitals,' and 'ore' is not 'language' but 'tongue.' Indeed, comparisons were made between these lines and those in Suetonius which describe the vices of Tiberius.[1] None of these circumlocutions, however, had quite the charm of the descriptions used by a female correspondent of the *St. James's Gazette* when writing on 'The Ex-Khedive's Harem', and substituting for 'eunuch' such phrases as 'a species of giant', and 'a great big fat personage'.[2]

The Victorians mistranslated and expurgated so that Great Books might live and—more than that—so that there might be a flow of culture from the library to the drawing room and the schoolroom. Only by such a traffic in ideas, such a current of serious literature, were new readers to be saved from frivolity—'the moral imbecility of an inward giggle'. Better that schoolboys should read of the sexual catastrophe which overtook Oedipus than that their reading should be frittered away in the perusal of rubbish, even of disinfected rubbish. Yet once that concession had been made, there still remained a need to censor books in the interests of morals and manners. As Coleridge put it,

We have only to suppose society innocent, and then nine-tenths of this sort of wit would be like a stone that falls in snow, making no sound because exciting no resistance; the remainder rests on its being an offence against the good manners of human nature itself.[3]

Manners and morals were increasingly in the custody of authors, publishers, editors, booksellers, and librarians: most of these custodians needed no prompting by the law to remind them of their trust. Before turning to the underworld of Victorian literature it is worth examining the operation of literary censorship without the law, a restriction voluntarily accepted and playing an infinitely greater part in determining the nature of Victorian literature than any law of obscene libel could have done.

THE GOOD MANNERS OF HUMAN NATURE

One of the most penetrating studies in the corruption of the 'young

[1] *Index Expurgatorius of Martial* (London, 1868), p. vi.
[2] J. W. Robertson Scott, *The Story of the Pall Mall Gazette* (London, 1950), p. 255.
[3] Coleridge, *Literary Remains* (London, 1836–9), I, 141–2.

person's' innocence appeared in Henry James's novel *The Awkward Age* in 1899: with casual irony James exploits the horror of Mrs. Brookenham at the thought that certain books of Michett's, 'abject, horrid, unredeemed vileness from beginning to end,' might fall into the hands of her children, apparently unaware that the moral example of her own social set is very much worse as an influence than any book could be.[1] In the preface which he later wrote for this novel, James compares the attitude in England and France towards the problem of the 'female young' in this respect. In France they are excluded from all discussion which might prove dangerous, thus avoiding any need to 'sacrifice' the discussion.

Such sacrifices strike [the French] as gratuitous and barbarous, as cruel above all to the social intelligence; also as perfectly preventable by wise arrangement. Nothing comes home more, on the other hand, to the observer of English manners than the very moderate degree in which wise arrangement, in the French sense of a scientific economy, has ever been invoked.[2]

There were those who had good reason to feel more strongly than James about this matter, including George Moore who wrote indignantly in 1885, 'We must write as our poems, our histories, our biographies are written, and give up once and for ever asking that most silly of all silly questions, "Can my daughter of eighteen read this book?"'[3] Moore's remedy is simple and direct, 'Let us renounce the effort to reconcile those two irreconcilable things—art and young girls'.[4] Yet though Moore suffered from the censorship of the circulating libraries during the 1880s and 1890s, he was able to see the true relation of literature and censorship, as he described it in discussing fiction of the 1850s with Edmund Gosse many years later.

A prose epic implies the existence of a man of genius, and genius, I suppose, cannot be censored. It will find a way out, so it is said, though all the doors and windows are barred—up the chimney, through the keyhole.[5]

Few of the early Victorian novelists, those writing in the 1850s included, found the moral conventions of their time irksome, though Thackeray might protest in his preface to *Pendennis* (1850), 'Since the

[1] *The Awkward Age* (London, 1899), p. 61.

[2] *The Awkward Age* (London, 1909), p. x. [The preface was written for this collected edition of the novels.]

[3] George Moore, *Literature at Nurse: or, Circulating Morals* (London, 1885), p. 21.

[4] *ibid.*, p. 21.

[5] George Moore, *Avowals* (London, 1936), p. 85.

author of *Tom Jones* was buried no writer of fiction among us has been permitted to depict to his utmost power a MAN'.[1] Thackeray, like Fielding, can take the reader into his confidence and explain the difficulties of telling such a story but Thackeray is excusing what he has done rather than arguing that he should have been permitted to go a great deal further in his description of a 'MAN.' It was not for another thirty years or so that English novelists took up his complaint in earnest that 'Society will not tolerate the Natural in our Art.' Thackeray's great contemporary, Dickens, rarely gives the impression that he is being prevented from writing in a manner or about subjects which he would have chosen but for the temper of the age. Sometimes, however, there is room for 'improvement' even in the most cautious novelist, and Dickens had felt obliged to expurgate the 1841 introduction to *Oliver Twist*, in which he had specified that Nancy was a prostitute. Other writers were satisfied with the merest indication of some incident in a story so that, for instance, the only physical evidence provided at the scene of Hetty Sorrel's seduction in *Adam Bede* is the discarded handkerchief which Arthur Donnithorne retrieves at the end of Chapter XLVIII. Even so, the indelicacy of George Eliot's novel still displeased a minority of her critics.[2]

Among the later Victorians too the strong sense of moral obligation is still far more in evidence than a bitter impatience with the prudery of literary conventions. It is quite in keeping with this that, for instance, Walter Pater should have suppressed the 'Conclusion' of his *Renaissance* (1873) for fifteen years after the first edition, on the grounds that it could mislead some of the young men into whose hands it might fall. It was finally reprinted only after some 'slight changes.' The sensitivity of even the most sophisticated Victorian men of letters in this respect is well illustrated by an anecdote of Henry James's in *The Middle Years*, recalling a luncheon party of

[1] *The Works of William Makepeace Thackeray* (London, 1894), III, xi. Thackeray adds, 'Society will not tolerate the Natural in our Art. Many ladies have remonstrated with me and subscribers left me, because in the course of the story, I described a young man resisting and affected by temptation. My object was to say, that he had the passions to feel, and the manliness and generosity to overcome them. You will not hear—it is best to know it—what moves in the real world, what passes in society, in the clubs, colleges, mess-rooms,—what is the life and talk of your sons. A little more frankness than is customary has been attempted in this story; with no bad desire on the writer's part, it is hoped, and with no ill consequence to any reader. If truth is not always pleasant; at any rate truth is best, from whatever chair—from those whence graver writers or thinkers argue, or from that at which the story-teller sits as he concludes his labour, and bids his kind reader farewell.' III, xi–xii.

[2] *The Saturday Review* of 26 February 1859, feared that *Adam Bede* and novels of a similar type would create 'a literature of pregnancy'.

Tennyson's at Aldworth. One of the guests, Sabine Greville, happened to mention one of her relatives, Mademoiselle Laure de Sade, which, as James describes it, sent Tennyson off into a tirade against 'the scandalous, the long-ignored, the at last all but unnameable author' of the same surname. For some while the great man held forth on the viciousness of the Marquis and all his works, to the mild bewilderment of his guests, none of whom except for Henry James had the faintest idea of what he was talking about.[1]

On the whole the Victorians managed to adapt their style to the moral conventions of their literature. Thomas Hughes, for example, could hardly have expected ready acceptance of *Tom Brown's Schooldays* (1857) if he had included an overt and graphic warning against public school homosexuality but the warning is conveyed in other terms with the introduction of 'one of the miserable little pretty white-handed curly-headed boys, petted and pampered by some of the big fellows, who wrote their verses for them, taught them to drink and use bad language, and did all they could to spoil them for everything in this world and the next.' Hughes later added a note saying that an old Rugboean had written to him pointing out that such relationships were not always as bad as that. 'But', said Hughes, 'I can't strike out the passage; many boys will know why it is left in.'[2] Had he been able to use what language he chose the warning itself might well have been more succinct, less laboured and, therefore, less impressive. Certainly nothing could be more significant in tone than, 'many boys will know why. . . .' If they did not know, they would assuredly begin to think.

One of the most remarkable displays of euphemistic cavorting appears—of all places—in Carlyle's *History of Frederick the Great*, which occupied him from 1851 until 1865. He describes Frederick's *Congé de l'Armée des Cercles et des Tonneliers*, a piece of mildly bawdy verse composed to celebrate the flight of the French after the battle of Rossbach, which elaborates with no great subtlety the theme that the rear view of the French army is the only gratifying one. Carlyle quotes lines of the poem, with appropriate asterisks, hinting heavily at what the asterisks conceal and describing how Frederick 'sings the charms of the rearward part of certain men. . . . He rises to the heights of Anti-Biblical profanity, quoting Moses on the Hill of Vision; sinks to the bottomless of human or ultra-human depravity, quoting King Nicodemes's experiences on Caesar (happily known only to the learned); and in brief, recognises that there is, on occasion, considerable beauty in that quarter of the human figure,

[1] Henry James, *The Middle Years* (London, 1917), pp. 99–100.
[2] *Tom Brown's Schooldays*, 2nd edn. (London, 1857), p. 257.

when it turns on you opportunely.'[1] So long as the conventions of Victorian literature gave him the chance for this kind of display, Carlyle can have had little to complain about. It would be interesting to know how many uninstructed readers hurried away to find out about Caesar and Nicodemes, which they would hardly have done if Carlyle had merely reprinted the original, unexpurgated French poem without comment.

A difficulty which publishers, and occasionally authors, had to face was that an outraged printer would simply refuse to set the type for a book of which he disapproved. In Chapter XXIX of *Vanity Fair*, Thackeray remarks lightly, 'The curses to which the General gave a low utterance, as soon as Rebecca and her conqueror had quitted him, were so deep, that I am sure no compositor in Messrs. Bradbury and Evans's establishment would venture to print them were they written down.' To some later Victorians, the matter was by no means a joke. John Addington Symonds received a stern reprimand from the compositor who was setting the type for the second volume of *Studies of the Greek Poets* (1875), and in the same year the English printers of the *Kama Sutra*, translated by Sir Richard Burton and F. F. Arbuthnot, refused to complete production of the book. Of course, the standards of propriety set by most of the later Victorian publishers and editors matched anything which the most scrupulous printer might require, though these standards provoked a mood of rebellion among certain writers, whether of the 'Fleshly school' of Rossetti, Swinburne and others, or of the novel of 'realism' and 'naturalism' championed by George Moore and Thomas Hardy. Even in the earlier years of Victoria's reign the censorship of authors by publishers and editors had produced some disagreements, as when, in 1851, John Chapman finally rejected Eliza Lynn's novel *Realities* because she refused to revise certain passages which, according to Chapman, 'excited the sensual nature and were therefore injurious'.[2] Chapman went on to explain, 'as I am a publisher of works notable for their intellectual freedom it behoves me to be exceedingly careful of the *moral* tendency of all I issue'.[3] In the end, the book failed to find a publisher and appeared at the author's expense. The censorship of a novel by one publisher—or, indeed, by all publishers—did not prevent its publication so long as the author could find a printer willing to produce the book, and such printers

---

[1] *History of Friedrich II of Prussia, called Frederick the Great* (London, 1858–1865), V, 210.

[2] Quoted in Kathleen Tillotson, *Novels of the Eighteen-Forties* (London, 1962), p. 62.

[3] *ibid.*, p. 62.

certainly existed. As in so many other aspects of Victorian censorship, it was likely to be economic considerations which finally ensured a book's suppression.

The case of Eliza Lynn is unusual in the history of early Victorian publishing in that the author refused to co-operate with the publisher's suggestions. Eight years later, though *Adam Bede* sold well and was acclaimed by most reviewers, there were hostile critics of George Eliot's fiction and, perhaps as a consequence of this, John Blackwood wrote to her before the publication of *The Mill on the Floss* in 1860 asking her to alter her description of Mrs. Moss in that novel as 'a patient, loosely-hung, child-producing woman'. Blackwood seemed to feel that such a description might offend some readers, though he was not offended by it himself, and George Eliot obligingly emended it to 'a patient, prolific, loving-hearted woman', thereby, presumably, giving offence to no one.[1]

Even later Victorian authors did not necessarily get to a point of conflict with their publishers in this matter, since most of them knew perfectly well what the reputation of a given publisher was and they accepted the situation. For instance, when Dante Gabriel Rossetti wrote to Alexander Gilchrist in 1861 about which of Blake's poems should be included in Gilchrist's study of Blake, to be published by Macmillan, he wrote, 'And *Long John Brown* and *Little Mary Bell*,—Merciful Powers!—if indeed McMillan had a branch in Holywell Street!—or our editor's name were Swinburne!!'[2] Holywell Street was, of course, notorious in Victorian London as being the centre of the pornography trade, and it seemed to Rossetti that Macmillan was the epitome of Victorian prudery. Three years later, however, he submitted a collection of Swinburne's poems to the same publisher, only to have them rejected with a hint that the collection would be acceptable if expurgated—which would certainly not have been acceptable to Swinburne. As Rossetti explained to Swinburne, 'I mentioned the St. Dorothy as an unobjectionable poem, but Mac had some funky reminiscences of the allusions to Venus, so really it seemed a bad look out'.[3]

Swinburne himself drew together many of the threads in the tangled web of extra-legal censorship. He was faced with demands for expurgation from Macmillan and from F. S. Ellis, who published *Songs before Sunrise* in 1871. Still more significant was the incident in

[1] Geoffrey and Kathleen Tillotson, *Mid-Victorian Studies* (London, 1965), p. 68.
[2] *Letters of Dante Gabriel Rossetti*, ed. Oswald Doughty and J. R. Wahl (Oxford, 1965), II, 419.
[3] *ibid.*, II, 521.

1866, when Moxon published Swinburne's first series of *Poems and Ballads*, including the treatment of lesbianism in 'Anactoria'. It was rumoured that *The Times* was about to publish a review of the book which would include a demand that the publisher be prosecuted. The reviewer was to be Eneas Sweetland Dallas, and Moxon took fright. Without consulting Swinburne, they withdrew the book, while those copies still on the market fetched five guineas each. There the matter might have ended, at least for the time being, but for the intervention of John Camden Hotten, the English publisher—or rather pirate— of Mark Twain, James Russell Lowell, and Bret Harte, as well as a range of mainly flagellant pornography. Hotten now brought out *Poems and Ballads* unexpurgated and both he and Swinburne survived unscathed by the law, though roughly handled by the reviewers and certain sections of 'public opinion', including Mudie's Library which withdrew Swinburne's poems from its shelves. In August 1866 Swinburne wrote to Charles Augustus Howell, 'I got an anonymous note today threatening to "cut off my stones" within six weeks if my poems are not withdrawn, and then brand me as a ——. I don't see the connection of ideas—but you shall see the note.'[1] It might seem a happy coincidence for Hotten that Swinburne had a certain gift for producing flagellant pornography and was therefore able to assist the other side of the publishing business by collaborating on *The Romance of the Rod*, but Hotten suffered from that weakness so prevalent among the publishers of pornography; whatever his literary ethics, his commercial morals were a great deal worse. Swinburne had reason to consider himself cheated by Hotten and when the publisher died in 1873 at the age of forty-one, Swinburne's reaction was not sympathetic. 'When I heard he had died of a surfeit of pork chops, I observed that this was a serious argument against my friend Sir Richard Burton's view of cannibalism as a wholesome and natural method of diet.'

Naturally, editors of magazines could exercise the same degree of censorship as publishers, though sometimes a magazine would accept material which a publisher had refused. So, for instance, the sonnets which Ellis had made Swinburne remove from *Songs Before Sunrise* in 1871 appeared in the *Examiner* two years later. In general, though, it was the magazine editors with their reliance upon a family readership who were more sensitive to the dangers of printing material which might be considered unsuitable. Nine years after defending his own outspokenness in the preface to *Pendennis*, Thackeray became editor of the *Cornhill* and rejected a story, *Mrs. General Talboys*, by no less

[1] *Letters of Algernon Charles Swinburne*, ed. C. Y. Lang (New Haven, 1959–62), I, 173–4.

an author than Trollope because of the moral tolerance shown by the central character towards divorce or marital separation, and illegitimacy. Later still, authors like Thomas Hardy faced extreme difficulty in persuading editors to serialise their fiction. Leslie Stephen, as editor of the *Cornhill*, had already been uneasy over such novels as *Far from the Madding Crowd* but no editor would print *Tess of the d'Urbervilles* unexpurgated. It went the rounds of *Murray's* and *Macmillan's*, finally appearing with suitable alterations in the *Graphic*. Needless to say, if editors were unwilling to accept *Tess* they were far more hostile to *Jude the Obscure* which followed it. Yet both Hardy and Trollope, to deal with the two authors in question, would survive despite magazine censorship, since there was less difficulty in producing fiction in book form. *Mrs. General Talboys* appeared in the second series of Trollope's *Tales of All Countries*, while both *Tess* and *Jude* were published without difficulty, despite much hostile criticism of the later novel. (Questions of decency or delicacy were not the only considerations in banning literature from periodicals. In 1860 the *Cornhill* ended serialisation of Ruskin's *Unto this Last* after three instalments because it was 'too deeply tainted with socialistic hurry'.[1] Serialisation then began in *Fraser's* but was discontinued there after only four instalments.) The sums of money paid for serial rights were sometimes very large indeed and the author who took a moral stand on behalf of his work did so at considerable cost. George Eliot, for instance, was offered £10,000 by the *Cornhill* for *Romola*, though she accepted £7,000 for a shorter version of the story.

The most significant conflict which seemed to be developing between the forces of literature and the forces of censorship—though not on the whole the forces of censorship by law—concerned the freedom of the novelist to depict life as he saw it, rather than life as it was considered proper for the young person to see it. As Henry James put it, 'our English system is a good thing for virgins and boys and a bad thing for the novel itself, when the novel is regarded as something more than a simple *jeu d'esprit* and considered as a composition that treats of life at large and helps us to *know*.'[2] James chose his words well: the one thing that the most earnest and narrow-minded of Victorians could not bear was the idea that the novel—or any other form of literature—should be a mere *jeu d'esprit*. Yet it was equally difficult to accept that the novel should be free to reflect life realistically or naturalistically without somehow organising its material into a species of moral fable. The move towards realism encountered opposition of various kinds and by 1859 George Meredith

[1] J. W. Robertson Scott, *The Story of the Pall Mall Gazette*, p. 75.
[2] *The Parisian*, 26 February 1880.

was saying triumphantly of his *Ordeal of Richard Feverel*, 'I have offended Mudie and the British nation,' though the truth of the matter seems to have been that he offended more readers by his incomprehensibility than by any indecency or indelicacy in that book. In the case of novelists like Hardy or George Moore, or English versions of Zola's novels the conflict was sharper, and the circulating libraries (and in Zola's case the law) pronounced their obscenity far more readily than they would have done in the case of such *jeux d'esprit* as the novels of 'Ouida'. Critics might condemn Ouida's novels as containing nothing but 'fine names and all the phraseology of fashionable vice', but they were nonetheless popular and profitable to those who circulated them.[1] Moore, comparing his own 'banned' fiction with some of that which Mudie continued to stock, described Ouida's *Moths* (1880) as a story which tells 'how a dissolute adventuress sells to her lover the pure white body and soul of her daughter, and how in the end Vera, disgraced and degraded by her ignoble husband, goes off to live with the tenor with whom she fell in love at the beginning of the story.'[2] As a matter of fact Mudie was reported to be considering the withdrawal of *Moths* from his libraries but, as Ouida wrote confidently and correctly to Chatto, her publisher, Mudie could no more afford to withdraw a novel of hers than one of Disraeli's. As time went on, the censorship of Mudie's Library became less strict and in the catalogue for 1904 both *A Modern Lover* and *Jude the Obscure* were listed. Yet even in 1904 Mudie's Select Library remained extremely cautious in its choice of French literature. At the head of the catalogue of works in French it is announced that books marked with an asterisk are 'suitable for family reading'. Not more than about five per cent of the books are asterisked and, of course, one looks in vain for Rousseau's *Confessions*; Daudet's *Sappho*; Dumas's *La Dame aux Camélias*; Zola's *La Terre* and their like.

The extent and nature of the power exercised by Charles Mudie and W. H. Smith over the Victorian book trade is worth considering, since they bore such great responsibility for shaping the literary tastes of the reading public in the later nineteenth century. Books had been expensive to buy even in the eighteenth century, hence the popularity of circulating libraries then, and this continued to be the case throughout the greater part of the nineteenth century. A publisher could normally count on the commercial success of a new novel only if it appealed to the circulating libraries and, more specifically, to Smith and Mudie. There were a few cheap editions but the usual form of publication was a three-volume novel selling at a guinea and

[1] *Pall Mall Gazette*, 21 September 1867.
[2] *Literature at Nurse: or, Circulating Morals*, p. 17.

255

a half, aimed for purchase by libraries rather than by individuals. When, for instance, Blackwood published *The Mill on the Floss* in 1860, despite the success of *Adam Bede* a year earlier, he bought the rights of 4,000 copies of a three-volume edition as compared with only 1,000 copies each of the 12s. and 6s. editions. As for the author, she received £2,000 for the larger edition, as against £210 for the other two together. Mudie had set up as a bookseller in 1840 and had started his library two years later. From London, the library spread to Birmingham and Manchester, its subscribers numbering more than 25,000. If Mudie liked a book, he bought it in large quantities: 2,400 copies of Macaulay's *History of England*; 2,000 copies of George Eliot's *Felix Holt*, and 2,000 copies of Livingstone's *Travels*, but no copies of a book for the library or for sale if it was felt to be indecorous. Mudie himself died in 1890 but the institution which he had founded survived until almost the outbreak of the Second World War.

The parents of W. H. Smith were strict Methodists and his father was a newsagent. Smith inherited both an interest in the retail book trade and a Nonconformist conscience. During the earlier years of Victoria's reign the bookstalls of the London railway stations had become notorious as the places where undesirable and, allegedly, pornographic literature could be bought: for this reason they were often frequented by those who had not the least interest in travelling anywhere by train. Such was the state of affairs on which *The Times* reported in its article 'The Literature of the Rail', on 9 August 1851.

Are we turning this rushing and roaming over the land to real advantage? Is the most made of the finest opportunity yet offered to this generation for guiding awakened thought and instructing the eager and susceptible mind? The question forcibly occurred to us the other day in a first-class carriage, in which two young ladies and a boy, for the space of three mortal hours, were amusing themselves and alarming us by a devotion to a trashy French novel, most cruelly and sacrilegiously misplaced. A volume of *Eugene Sue* was in the hands of each. The cover of the books was light green, and we remembered to have seen a huge heap of such covers as we hastily passed the bookstall at the station on our way to the carriage. Could it be possible that the conductors of our railways, all-powerful and responsible as they are, had either set up themselves, or permitted others to establish on their ground, storehouses of positively injurious aliment for the hungry minds that sought refreshment on their feverish way? Did they sell poison in their literary refreshment rooms, and stuff whose deleterious effects 20 doctors would not be sufficient to eradicate?

The answer to these questions was 'yes', but in that same year the twenty-six year old W. H. Smith had acquired a monopoly of the bookstalls on the North Western Railway and two years later added control of the bookstalls on the Midland Railway to his empire. Volumes of rubbish and near-pornography were replaced by works of moral and intellectual improvement, which in the hands of Smith became a source of considerable profit. Yet not everyone was satisfied that the bookstalls were now safe enough and in 1853, for example, Smith received a reproachful letter pointing out that three copies of Byron's *Don Juan* had been seen on his bookstall at Waterloo Station, and that he was also rather lax in his attitude towards the writings of Dumas the younger. (This was probably a reference to *La Dame Aux Camélias*, which had caused some controversy in 1850 when *Traviata*, based on the novel, had been produced in London.) Smith himself went into politics and became First Lord of the Admiralty, in which capacity he remains best known as the model for Sir Joseph Porter, K.B.E., the 'ruler of the Queen's navee' in *H.M.S. Pinafore*. To his bookstalls he added a circulating library—closely associated with Mudie's both in financial interests and moral standards—and a bookselling business. He died the year after Mudie but subsequently both firms united at least in their determined rejection of such pernicious literature as George Moore's novel *Esther Waters* in 1894. This was an exercise of that power so pungently described by George Moore himself nine years before.

Instead of being allowed to fight, with and amid, the thoughts and aspirations of men, literature is now rocked to an ignoble rest in the motherly arms of the librarian. That of which he approves is fed with gold; that from which he turns the breast dies like a vagrant's child; while in and out of his voluminous skirts run a motley and monstrous progeny, a callow, a whining, a puking brood of bastard bantlings, a race of Aztecs that disgrace the intelligence of the English nation. Into this nursery none can enter except in baby clothes; and the task of discriminating between a divided skirt and a pair of trousers is performed by the librarian. Deftly his fingers lift skirt and under-skirt, and if the examination prove satisfactory the sometimes decently attired dolls are packed in tin-cornered boxes, and scattered through every drawing-room in the kingdom, to be in rocking-chairs fingered and fondled by the 'young person' until she longs for some newer fashion in literary frills and furbelows.[1]

The effect of the moral zeal exhibited by Smith, Mudie, and their kind was twofold. In the first place it contributed towards the great alienation of many writers from contemporary standards of morality or 'respectability'—though this would have happened even if Mudie and Smith had never gone into business at all. In the case of George Eliot and John Blackwood, one feels that author and publisher shared a moral view which enabled alterations to be made to a book without

[1] *Literature at Nurse: or, Circulating Morals*, pp. 18–19.

bitterness or controversy: the same moral identity was shared by the novelist and the majority of critics or book buyers. Yet in 1891, the year of W. H. Smith's death, Oscar Wilde delivered what seemed to be the final rejection of the values which Smith and Mudie represented, in his preface to *The Picture of Dorian Gray*. '*There is no such thing as a moral or an immoral book. Books are well written, or badly written. That is all.*'[1] And in the very next sentence Wilde, who was in so many ways the antithesis of writers like Moore and Hardy, addresses the opponents of realism. '*The nineteenth century dislike of Realism is the rage of Caliban seeing his own face in a glass.*'[2] It seemed that on the enchanted island of the Aesthetes there could be no other role for Smith, Mudie and their kind but that of the monster.

The second consequence of moral and commercial censorship was to drive rejected authors to find other means of getting their work into circulation. It was the price of novels which made so many readers dependent upon the circulating libraries and the only answer, as George Moore showed with *A Mummer's Wife* in 1884, was to bring out a book in a cheaper edition, gambling on the hope that it would sell in sufficient numbers to make the loss of the 'three-volume' market a matter of no great importance. The gamble proved worthwhile and Moore's publisher, Henry Vizetelly published new novels as 6*s.* and even less, while he issued others for no more than 1*s.* each, in many cases, or 6*d.* for a novella.

Vizetelly was one of the natural enemies of those who believed themselves to be the private guardians of public morality and when, in March 1886, the National Vigilance Association was founded with the purity of literature as one of its aims, it soon turned its attention to his activities. The Association was in many respects a revival of the Society for the Suppression of Vice which had got into financial difficulties during the 1870s and ceased to function. By 1888 the National Vigilance Association had brought an unsuccessful prosecution against a publisher of the *Decameron* and a successful one against Henry Vizetelly for publishing English translations of the novels of Zola, a case which will be more fully discussed in the next section of this chapter. The Association was criticised in *Truth* for not taking action against certain attacks which had been published on the celibacy of priests and the practice of the confessional, attacks which might well have been condemned as indecent. However, it is no surprise that the vigilantes overlooked these attacks, since they were the work of Kensit, himself a leader of the N.V.A. In 1890 the Association brought a successful case against the exhibitors of Jules

[1] Oscar Wilde, *The Picture of Dorian Gray* (London, n.d., i.e. 1891), p. vi.
[2] *ibid.*, p. vi.

Garnier's illustrations of the works of Rabelais and continued its fight against the pernicious influence of French culture well into the twentieth century, ending with a triumphal destruction order for Balzac's *Contes Drolatiques* in 1909. Of course, many of the prosecutions brought by the Association involved no more than 'photographs' of one sort or another and in many ways its most significant achievements were private ones. The Annual Report for 1890 describes one of these.

During the year we have had several cases in which we prosecuted under Lord Campbell's Act. In the cases of *Cox* and *Wilcox*, heard at the end of 1889, counsel for the defendants consented to an order for the destruction of about 120 photographs. The defendants were committed for trial, but that effete survival of a respectable antiquity, the grand jury, threw out the bill.

Shortly after this, a man wrote a letter to our office stating that he had sent a large parcel of immoral publications to a railway station in the north of London, and desiring us to obtain possession of the books and to destroy them, expressing at the same time his contrition and intention of amendment. The books were obtained and destroyed.[1]

Not all possessors of 'immoral publications' needed the fear of God put into them by the example of court proceedings before they called on the Association for help. There is a particularly enthusiastic paragraph in the Report for 1896, referring to the widow of the translator of the *Kama Sutra*.[2]

An incident of [*sic*] which any society might congratulate itself was the fact that it was this Association that was selected by the late Lady Burton during her life to destroy a large number of the books of her late husband, which, in her opinion, could not judiciously be read by an indiscriminate public, and in this connection it was our privilege to burn, on one occasion, books to the value of £1,000.[3]

Such zeal was not without its effect on the book trade in general. John C. Nimmo, for instance, took fright after the attempted suppression of the *Decameron* and the successful suppression of Zola. The *Memoirs* of Count Carlo Gozzi, which John Addington Symonds had translated for him were briskly emasculated, if not eviscerated, before

---

[1] *National Vigilance Association. Fifth Annual Report* (1890), pp. 21–22.
[2] Sir Richard Burton is a good example of a Victorian scholar who, by publishing in the right form and for the right audience, was able to issue material which, under other circumstances, a court of law might have judged obscene. His work was even well-received by many reviewers. Yet the young Burton's *First Footsteps in East Africa* (1856), was censored by its publisher who tore out the appendix—written in Latin—which dealt with the sexual customs of certain tribes.
[3] *National Vigilance Association, Eleventh Annual Report* (1896), p. 25.

they appeared and the publication of Symonds's *Giovanni Boccaccio* was delayed for eight years until Nimmo felt that all was safe once more.

The standards of the National Vigilance Association were not markedly different from those of Mudie or Smith in moral terms, except that Smith and Mudie were looking for books to exclude from their lists while the N.V.A. was looking for books to include in its own, for a rather different purpose. The inevitable effect was to push certain writers and publishers towards the twilight zone between literature and pornography. Naturally the gulf between literature and pornography remained and certainly Moore, Hardy, Symonds, and many others would have been very upset to be classified with the denizens of Holywell Street. What had happened was that the territory along the side of the gulf belonging to literature had been reclassified by the arbiters of literary fashion. Along this precipice now roamed the 'Aesthetes' and the poets of the 'Fleshly school', novelists of realism or naturalism and publishers of 'translations from the French', or of serious-minded literature on birth-control. From time to time one of these suspects leapt the gap and gained the opposing cliff, which was hardly to be wondered at.

IN THE TWILIGHT

Thackeray, it seemed to Walter Bagehot, was as near to the edge of the precipice as a decent or self-respecting author might safely venture, 'perpetually treading as close as he dare to the borderline that separates the world which may be described in books from the world which it is prohibited to describe'.[1] Of course Thackeray is skilful, more so than most other authors who incur risks of this kind. 'He never violates a single conventional rule; but at the same time the shadow of the immorality that is not seen, is scarcely ever wanting to his delineation of the society that is seen'.[2] As time went on, it had become more difficult to tread as close to the borderline as Bagehot felt Thackeray had done, simply because it was no longer so easy to be sure just where that borderline was: it ran, presumably, somewhere through the twilight zone.

In Victorian London pornography had been driven into a ghetto which could be located on the map as running just to the north of the Strand, along Holywell Street, and through Wych Street and parts of Fleet Street. Later the trade moved north and west to Leicester Square, Charing Cross Road, and thence to Soho. The rules

[1] Walter Bagehot, *Literary Studies* (London, 1879), II, 210.
[2] *ibid.*, II, 210.

of the trade were almost as strict in their way as the rules of Mudie's or Smith's, and the would-be buyer of pornography had no trouble in finding somewhere to make his purchases. Meantime, there were publishers in Piccadilly, like John Camden Hotten, or in Henrietta Street, like Henry Vizetelly whose status so far as the law was concerned might seem ambiguous. Vizetelly published respectable literature, as he thought, and went to prison; Hotten published pornography as a sideline and died in 1873 still a free man. In Bond Street itself, by a more curious anomaly still, Sotheby's auctioned such works as *Peregrine Penis, New Frisky Songster* without risking either liberty or reputation. Between the areas of legality and illegality there was this third area, whose designation was more doubtful and whose existence was principally the result of the Obscene Publications Act of 1857.

The Obscene Publications Bill was introduced in the House of Lords by Lord Campbell, who from his vantage point on the judicial bench had for some time viewed the trade in pornography as it appeared in the cases tried before him. He was disturbed by both its nature and extent. In the spring of 1857 two cases had particularly impressed on him the need for action to suppress the sale and distribution of this 'poison'. The first was the trial of William Dugdale on 11 May for selling obscene prints and the second the trial of William Strange which followed on the same day. Strange was tried for selling *Paul Pry* and *Women of London*: like Dugdale, Strange was found guilty but in this second case Lord Campbell went to the lengths of examining the literature complained of and declared it to be 'most infamous'; he thought it 'high time that an example should be made'.[1] So Strange went to prison for three months and Dugdale —who was an old hand at this sort of thing—for a year.

Both these cases had been the results of investigations and ruses on the part of the Vice Society, still zealous as ever more than half a century after its foundation. Indeed, Lord Campbell gave it full credit for its achievements in the fight against obscene literature: one

---

[1] *The Times*, 11 May 1857. From the account of the trial, *Women of London* seems to have been a periodical publication, like the more celebrated *Paul Pry*. Michael Sadleir records a book, *Women of London*, whose author later produced *The Women of Paris: A Romance*. This was one of the 'Anonyma' series of racy but not pornographic novels of the 1860s, later published in a uniform edition. The series took its name from *Anonyma, or Fair but Frail. A Romance of West End Life* published by George Vickers in 1864. It included a number of biographies of the famous and infamous, including Cora Pearl; 'Skittles', and Lola Montez. This was a type of literature which serious-minded Victorians might deplore but would not, as a rule, attempt to suppress through the courts. (Michael Sadleir, *XIX Century Fiction* (London, 1951), II, 8–12.)

hundred and fifty-four convictions and, in the last twenty-three years, no less than thirty-seven of the fifty-seven shops selling pornography had been put out of business. Lord Campbell proposed that in order to make this offence easier to deal with—for, after all, there were still twenty shops at which such literature could be bought—the police should be able to obtain warrants from magistrates to search for publications of this kind. The new law was also to empower magistrates to grant a destruction order in respect of material brought before them, if they judged it to be indecent. This process of seeking a destruction order was not, strictly speaking, a criminal proceeding: in itself it did not put the owner of the goods in danger of a fine or prison. What was to happen in practice was that a body like the National Vigilance Association would first bring a case, seeking a destruction order, and if they were successful in that they would then go on to prosecute the man in question for having published an obscene libel. This was not invariably successful, since though a magistrate might condemn a book as obscene a grand jury might equally find that the defendant had no case to answer.

Those who opposed Lord Campbell's Bill did so on the grounds that it might, logically, be made to apply just as much to the works of the Restoration dramatists as to the sort of literature which Strange had been sent to prison for publishing, just as much to a painting like Correggio's *Jupiter and Antiope* as to one of Dugdale's pornographic prints. (Indeed, the National Vigilance Association subsequently brought a prosecution against a man who had sold photographs of certain French paintings.) Lord Campbell's answer to this shows, as clearly as anything could, the Victorian reverence for Great Books. He had no intention, he said, of trying to censor such books or pictures and the new law would be aimed only at 'works written for the single purpose of corrupting the morals of youth, and of a nature calculated to shock the common feelings of decency in any well regulated mind'.[1] Whether or not a man chose to read the Restoration dramatists was a matter for his own taste and judgment, not for the law. The difficulty was, of course, in establishing a common agreement as to what constituted a well-regulated mind or what were 'the common feelings of decency', or whether the fact that some people were undoubtedly very shocked by the novels of Zola or Thomas Hardy was reason enough for bringing a prosecution. Yet no twentieth-century legislator could have been more positive than Lord Campbell that his proposals were in no way meant to interfere with literature and the arts. And so he produced a copy of *La Dame Aux Camélias* and announced that, much as he disapproved of the

[1] *Parliamentary Debates*, CXLVI, 329 (25 June 1857).

book, he had no wish to see such publications banned by the new law.

Whatever Lord Campbell might say, no one was likely to feel free to publish a book like *Sodom: or, The Quintessence of Debauchery* by virtue of its historical interest or value as a commentary on heroic drama. The very preamble of the 1857 Act indicated that it was intended to make censorship more strict. 'Whereas it is expedient to give additional Powers for the Suppression of the Trade in Obscene Books, Prints, Drawings, and other Obscene Articles . . .' Campbell himself seemed quite well pleased with the immediate results of the Act and there is little doubt that the pornographers operated cautiously for a while but eleven years later the *Saturday Review* reported that the situation was as bad as ever and that 'the dunghill is in full heat, seething and steaming with all its old pestilence'. Six shops in Holywell Street and three more in Wych Street were quite openly displaying their infamous wares. This renaissance of obscenity was in part the result of renewed activity by the indefatigable William Dugdale, now out of prison again and publishing as never before. Whatever Lord Campbell's Act had done, it had certainly not suppressed this sort of trade but then no new law would have been needed to deal with Dugdale and his tribe, no new resolve on the part of the authorities was necessary. The stricter censorship imposed by the law did not push the pornographers into the sphere of illegality, they were there already, but it did bring within danger of prosecution some of the inhabitants of the twilight zone. Many of these were publishers who did not regard their books as pornographic but were often men of intense moral earnestness who would have found support among a large number of law-abiding contemporaries, men who detested Dugdale and all his works as heartily as Campbell had done. Campbell himself might even have had misgivings about his new law, had he known that one of its first major casualties was to be a publication of the Protestant Electoral Union.

The aim of the Protestant Electoral Union was to 'restore and maintain the Protestant Constitution of the Empire as established by the Revolution of 1688', so that the Union was not best pleased by memories of Catholic Emancipation in 1828 or by the restoration of the Catholic ecclesiastical hierarchy in England. A further irritation was the annual grant made by the government to the Catholic college of Maynooth in Ireland. From 1845 until 1869, when the grant was abolished at the disestablishment of the Irish Church, motions were introduced in the Commons every year demanding an end to this subsidy, which went towards the training of future priests. There was a great deal of anti-Catholic literature in the nineteenth century which claimed that female penitents were exposed to indecent questions—and worse—by priests during confession. Such literature had circulated ever since the Reformation but in Victorian England it was much more the work of evangelical Christians than of non-Christians. One such publication was the Protestant Electoral Union's *The Confessional Unmasked*, a compilation from the works of Roman Catholic theologians, though it might be argued that some of the passages were quoted misleadingly out of context. This book had been available since 1836 in various editions and, the Protestant Electoral Union claimed, contained material used at Maynooth. The Protestant Electoral Union itself had bought the existing stock of an edition of *The Confessional Unmasked* and the stereo plates from which it had been printed. The previous proprietor was none other than William Strange, very possibly the same William Strange who had been sent down for three months by Lord Campbell in 1857 for selling obscene literature. Of course, the new owners were simply trying to demonstrate the obscenity which, they alleged, the practice of confession involved but in carrying out this demonstration they had to publish material which was *ipso facto* obscene. The book, as it was now published, contained descriptions of sexual predicaments and eccentricities which could hardly have failed to bring it to the attention of the law. In 1867 copies of the book were seized from a Wolverhampton bookseller, H. Scott, and their destruction ordered by a magistrate. Scott appealed against this but the order was confirmed by Sir Alexander Cockburn in the Court of Queen's Bench in Regina *v.* Hicklin (1868). It was in this case that the literary and medical view of pornography was enshrined in law, in the so-called 'Hicklin Judgment', whose terms remain basically unaltered at the present day.

The test of obscenity is whether the tendency of the matter charged as obscenity is to deprave and corrupt those whose minds are open to such immoral influences and into whose hands a publication of this sort might fall.[1]

But since, in their own eyes, the criminals in this case were still clad in the armour of righteousness, the battle did not end there. They published an expurgated edition, apparently not expurgated enough, since when George Mackay used it in a series of lectures at Lymington he was sent to prison for fifteen months. Then Steele, the Secretary of the Protestant Electoral Union, published an account of Mackay's trial, including some of the material objected to, and in 1871 he too was successfully prosecuted.

Lord Campbell would have shown more sympathy towards the

[1] *Law Reports*, 3 Q.B.D., 1867–8, p. 371.

prosecution in a later case when Charles Bradlaugh and Annie Besant were indicted in 1877 for publishing the *Fruits of Philosophy*. As usual, Bradlaugh was involved in a moral crusade which so happened to challenge the standards of most of his contemporaries. *The Fruits of Philosophy: An Essay on the Population Problem* by Charles Knowlton, an American, had first been published in England in 1834 by James Watson and later by George Jacob Holyoake. The objection to the book was that it advocated birth control rather than self-restraint as the solution to over-population and poverty. Charles Watts had taken over Holyoake's business and continued to sell the book until 1876, when a prosecution was brought against him for publishing an obscene libel and the work was suppressed. At this point Bradlaugh, believing less in the wisdom of the book's contents than in its right to circulate, and Annie Besant deliberately challenged the law by producing another edition, issued by their Freethought Publishing Company. In their preface to this new edition they admitted that part of Knowlton's book 'seems to us full of philosophical mistakes, and as we are neither of us doctors, we are not prepared to endorse his medical views; but since progress can only be made through discussion, we claim the right to publish all opinions so that the public may have the material for forming a sound judgment'.[1]

At the beginning of the trial the Lord Chief Justice remarked that 'the question was not merely whether the book was obscene in the coarser sense of the term, but whether its tendency was to vitiate public morality'.[2] The Solicitor-General, Sir Hardinge Giffard, was convinced that it was one of those books 'tending to create morbid feelings and lead to unlawful practices'.[3] Which amounted to saying that if people believed there were ways of preventing conception they would be less inclined to control their sexual emotions or to refrain from sexual intercourse. The fact that the publication was 'sold in the streets at 6*d*. a copy' seemed to Sir Hardinge to be proof of its power to corrupt the morals of the British public. The defence offered by Bradlaugh and Mrs. Besant was that the book which they had published was no more obscene than *Tristram Shandy* or the novels of Fielding, but the trouble with this argument was that they were often using 'obscene' as a synonym of 'coarse', which neither their accuser nor their judge was doing. According to Mrs. Besant, illustrations of the reproductive organs in books used by the special schools of art in South Kensington were 'immeasureably more obscene' than those in the *Fruits of Philosophy*. Even when she turned from what she defined as 'obscene' and began to talk about the book's power to stimulate, she still seems to have misjudged the attack

[1] *The Times*, 19 June 1877.   [2] *ibid.*   [3] *ibid.*

which was being made upon her and her book. 'Medical or physiological books had no tendency to arouse sexual feelings, which were rather aroused by glowing descriptions and amorous passages such as were to be found in Fielding or Congreve'.[1]

Bradlaugh cited the work of Acton and suggested that if the *Fruits of Philosophy* was obscene so was *Functions and Disorders of the Reproductive Organs*. But it was, of course, no defence simply to cite other books which might be more obscene than the one in question: neither the works of Acton nor the novels of Fielding and Sterne were on trial but the *Fruits of Philosophy* was. When Dr. Drysdale gave evidence for the defence, the Lord Chief Justice asked him, referring to the book, 'Is there anything in it calculated to excite sensual or libidinous feelings?' 'Certainly not', said Drysdale, 'indeed, on me it had the contrary effect'.[2] There was laughter in court but even Drysdale had not answered the prosecution's most significant argument, that the book corrupted its readers not by arousing their passions but by removing the fear of pregnancy (and, therefore, reducing their self-restraint) when their passions were roused by other means. Another witness for the defence was Bohn, the publisher, who claimed that there was little difference between the book on trial and other books on physiology. Yet Bohn had to admit that times were changing and that when Bell and Co. took over his own business they were obliged to withdraw from circulation such works as the *Memoirs of the Count de Grammont* and editions of Rabelais.

There seemed to be no question of acquitting Bradlaugh and Mrs. Besant and thereby indicating that the book was not obscene but here, as in the case of *The Confessional Unmasked*, the moral zeal and sincerity of the defendants was beyond dispute. They exemplified the best Victorian qualities unluckily harnessed to one of the most unacceptable causes. The jury was out for an hour and a half, after which the foreman announced, 'We find that the book is calculated to deprave public morals, but we entirely exonerate the defendants from any corrupt motives in publishing it'. The Lord Chief Justice ordered them to return a verdict of guilty but sentence was postponed for a week. Though Bradlaugh and Mrs. Besant were each sentenced to six months' imprisonment, and fined £200, they were released on bail after promising not to circulate further copies of the book. When the trial ended *The Times*, though condemning the book, referred to its publishers as 'this well-intentioned pair'. It must have been something of a relief to many people when the conviction was quashed, on appeal, because the indictment was bad. Other distributors of such literature attracted less attention and no consoling comments from

[1] *ibid.,*   [2] *The Times*, 21 June 1877.

266

The Times. In the following two years, for instance, Edward Truelove suffered both imprisonment and confiscation of his stock because of his persistence in selling Robert Dale Owen's *Moral Physiology* and J. H. Palmer's *Individual, Family, and National Poverty.* More than 1,400 copies of these were seized from his premises and destroyed in 1880.

In other cases there were no extenuating circumstances whatever, no reservations about the good intentions of the accused. When Henry Vizetelly appeared at the Central Criminal Court in October 1888 on charges of obscene libel (for publishing translations of Zola's *La Terre*; *Pot Bouille,* and *Nana*) the Recorder had remarked, 'There is a great distinction between this case and "The Queen *v.* Hicklin". There the object of the publication was no doubt extremely good.'[1] It is uncertain whether Vizetelly could ever have believed that his translations of nineteenth century French literature would bring him into conflict with the law. He had published translations of *Mademoiselle de Maupin,* Daudet's *Sappho,* novels of Maupassant and Paul Bourget, and the greater part of Zola's fiction. Henry James wrote favourably of Zola in 1880 but publications like the *Methodist Times* turned on Zola and James as well.

We have never been able to believe in the moral intention of Zola, and it has always been a marvel to us that such a critic as Mr. James should seriously contend for them. Zolaism is a disease. It is a study of the putrid. Even France has shown signs that she has had enough of it. No one can read Zola without moral contamination.[2]

Vizetelly published a wide range of fiction, travel books, and translations. He published George Moore's attack on the censorship of the circulating libraries, *Literature at Nurse; or, Circulating Morals*: he issued Moore's novels at six shillings, and later at three and sixpence to break the monopoly of Mudie and Smith. He published the Mermaid Series of sixteenth and seventeenth century English dramatists, in unexpurgated editions, and employed such men as Havelock Ellis, Swinburne, J. A. Symonds, and Edmund Gosse to edit the volumes. Smith and Mudie had no reason to sympathise with his activities but Vizetelly might reasonably have assumed that he was one of those against whom the 1857 Act was not intended to operate. He ran a special series of translations, selling for as little as a shilling and described by him as 'Translations of the best examples of recent French fiction of an unobjectionable character'. In its

[1] *The Times,* 1 November 1888.
[2] *Pernicious Literature* (1888), p. 24. This booklet, issued by the National Vigilance Association, quoted the remarks of the *Methodist Times.*

267

review of this series, the *Sheffield Independent* remarked, 'They are books that may be safely left lying about where the ladies of the family can pick them up and read them. The interest they create is happily not of the vicious sort at all.' The corollary of this was that Vizetelly sold his translations of Flaubert and Zola at a higher price and called them 'Realistic Novels' so that his readers might know what to expect. His interest in European fiction extended to Russia as well as France and editions of Dostoyevsky and Tolstoy mingled with those of Flaubert and the Goncourt brothers. At the very least Vizetelly could claim that he priced and advertised his novels carefully and honestly but he reckoned without the moral zeal of the National Vigilance Association which brought the case against him in respect of Zola's novels in 1888. He was prosecuted by the Solicitor-General, who was assisted by a future Prime Minister, H. H. Asquith, and Asquith later recalled how the French Press at the time had referred to 'la pudeur effarouchée de l'avocat Asquith', and how he had spent 'the best part of a fortnight in the Long Vacation, with scissors and a pot of paste at hand, in a diligent quest for the most objectionable passages in M. Zola's voluminous works'.[1] When the passages objected to were about to be read out, the jury indicated that the obscenity of the writing was such that they would prefer to have none of it read aloud. Clearly the case was hopeless. Vizetelly changed his plea to guilty, undertook to withdraw the books from circulation and was fined £100. There was a chorus of approval from the Press. 'In future', said *The Times*, 'anyone who publishes translations of ZOLA'S novels and works of similar character will do so at his peril, and must not expect to escape so easily as Mr. VIZETELLY.'[2] *The Times* also made the point that the fine of £100 was small compared with the financial loss of having to withdraw the novels in question from circulation.

Vizetelly had tried to anticipate the trial by sending to the Treasury Solicitor *Extracts Principally from English Classics: Showing that the Legal Suppression of M. Zola's Novels would Logically Involve the Bowdlerizing of some of the Greatest Works in English Literature*. The extracts ranged from Shakespeare to Rossetti, from Fielding to Swinburne, supported by acknowledgements of the greatness of Zola's Rougon-Macquart series of novels from critics like Henry James and Andrew Lang. 'I ask for my own and other publishers' guidance', wrote Vizetelly, 'whether, if Zola's novels are to be interdicted, "Tom Jones" and "Roderick Random", "Moll Flanders" and "The Country Wife", "The Maid's Tragedy" and "The Relapse",

[1] *Memories and Reflections* (London, 1928), I, 89.
[2] *The Times*, 1 November 1888.

in all of which the grossest passages are met with, will still be allowed to circulate without risk of legal proceedings'.[1]

Six months later Vizetelly was in trouble again for novels other than those in the first trial, indeed they were books published long before that first trial but which he had allowed to continue to circulate. Of the eight novels in question, five were by Zola (*How Jolly Life Is; Fat and Thin; The Rush for the Spoil; His Excellency Eugène Rougon,* and *Abbé Mouret's Transgression*); two were by Maupassant (*A Woman's Life,* and *A Ladies' Man*), and the eighth was Paul Bourget's novel *A Love Crime.* The National Vigilance Association had again taken action and in May 1889 Vizetelly appeared at the Central Criminal Court, pleading guilty to further charges of publishing obscene libels. The Solicitor-General described him as a man who specialised in the publication of French literature and unexpurgated editions, as though that were crime enough in itself, but the truth was that Vizetelly now had little heart for the fight. He was seventy years old, his health was poor, and he was in considerable financial difficulties. The Recorder remarked that there was little point in fining him, since he had not the money to pay, and sent him to prison for three months.

If the Act of 1857 had not, according to Lord Campbell himself, been aimed against such publications as *La Dame Aux Camélias,* it was certainly interpreted thirty years later as being aimed against the novels of Zola and Maupassant. Even publishers who might regard themselves as being the disseminators of serious literature were dragged willy-nilly into the twilight zone by the operation of the law. The fact that the *Decameron* had escaped destruction in 1886 was a matter of extreme irritation to a number of people and in 1900 a bookseller who had sold copies of the *Heptameron of Queen Margaret of Navarre* was tried for obscene libel at the Central Criminal Court. Fortunately, when the jury heard that she had also sold the *Encyclopaedia Britannica* and the *Edinburgh Review,* she was acquitted.[2] In 1909 came the destruction of Balzac's *Contes Drolati-*

---

[1] *Extracts Principally from English Classics* (London, 1888), p. 2.

[2] R. V. Thomson (1900), 64 J.P. 456. A point which the jury was asked to consider was whether the fact that the book was sold for 1s. 11d. would 'clearly tend to the corruption of morals'. A further point of interest occurs in the remarks of the Common Serjeant in this case. 'In the Middle Ages things were discussed which if put forward now for the reading of the general public would never be tolerated. In towns buried from the corrupt times of the Roman Empire, now disinterred or in the course of being disinterred, there are discovered pictures of the most lewd and filthy character. Nobody would think of destroying those pictures, but to sell photographs of them in the streets of London would be an indictable offence.'

ques and in the course of a civil action in 1915 Mr. Justice Younger suggested that a prosecution should be considered in respect of Elinor Glyn's novel *Three Weeks*, which had been published eight years earlier.[1] The rigour with which the law was enforced against such literature of the past as the *Contes Drolatiques*, and later the *Satyricon* of Petronius, made it unlikely that the authorities would look favourably on any new literary *genre* which required unusual tolerance on their part. When, for instance, Havelock Ellis published *Sexual Inversion*, which he had written in collaboration with J. A. Symonds, the book was treated by most of those concerned as if it had been a piece of homosexual pornography. George Bedborough, who had sold it, was prosecuted in 1898 and not only pleaded guilty but led the police to the real publisher, de Villiers, who was operating under the disguise of the 'University Press' at Watford, but de Villiers committed suicide before he could be charged. 'He took with him . . . a lot of information which might have been useful to us', said Chief-Inspector Edward Drew disconsolately.[2] *Sexual Inversion* had, of course, been published first of all in Germany but the English police dismissed it as 'grossly obscene', though purporting to be 'of a classical or medical character'.

So long as the law was interpreted with such illiberality, a publisher might feel that if he had to go to prison, he would at least do something worth going to prison for. It certainly appeared that the trade in books not regarded as obscene in the literary world generally had already put some publishers and booksellers beyond the pale of the English law. As early as the 1850s certain little pocket volumes had appeared—the so-called *Works of Aristotle* or Ovid's *Art of Love*—undated and with nothing more to identify the publisher than 'Published for the Booksellers' on the title-page. If such comparatively innocuous works had to be disowned because they might get their publishers into trouble, then life was clearly going to be hard for publishers like Hotten with a sideline in pornography but a principal interest in respectable literature. Hotten did his best to justify his more shady products by pedantic-sounding titles. He claimed, for instance, that after the death of H. T. Buckle a collection of booklets had been found in the historian's study and Hotten, recognising his duty to the promotion of scholarship, published these in 1872 under the collective title of 'The Library Illustrative of Social Progress'. As a matter of fact, what this imposing description concealed was such unedifying trifles as *Lady Bumtickler's Revels* and *Madame*

[1] Glyn *v.* Western Feature Film Company Ltd.
[2] *Joint Select Committee Report on Lotteries and Indecent Advertisements* (1908), p. 41.

Birchini's Dance, the former piece being remarkable even in the world of pornography for being written in the form of an opera. One of Hotten's best-sellers, and one which he sold openly, was *A History of the Rod* by 'the Reverend William Cooper'. Like much of his other literature, this is a curious rather than an erotic book, though occasionally the author's detached, pseudo-academic manner breaks down in such enthusiastic phrases as 'dressed in a *négligé* costume that heightened the charms of her person'. In fact, 'the Reverend William Cooper' was James Glass Bertram, a marine economist and author of *The Harvest of the Sea. A Contribution to the Natural and Economic History of the British Food Fishes*, who also adopted the *nom de plume* of 'Margaret Anson' for another book of Hotten's, *The Merry Order of St. Bridget*. Hotten carefully avoided prosecution and disposed of his stock very slowly. He printed up to 500 copies of private editions but at his death in 1873 no more than fifty copies of any one title had been sold and the remaining stock was hastily disposed of to Bouton of New York, where the market was less restricted.

With the disappearance of Vizetelly from the literary scene in 1889, a new and rather bizarre champion of 'questionable' literature appeared in the person of Leonard Smithers, a Sheffield solicitor who moved to London and during the 1890s became the publisher of Oscar Wilde, Aubrey Beardsley, Ernest Dowson, Arthur Symonds, and of the *Savoy*, which Beardsley edited after leaving the *Yellow Book*. Of course, Smithers's claim that he would issue anything which other publishers were afraid of, referred, for instance, to the works of Wilde, after Wilde's imprisonment or to Beardsley's *Venus and Tannhauser* rather than to mere pornography. Indeed Smithers, who was a bookseller as well as a publisher, ended his partnership with H. S. Nichols because of the latter's enthusiasm for the lower reaches of pornographic literature. If Smithers had a speciality, in erotic literature as in any other type, it was the handsomely-produced book intended for a necessarily rather limited market. These publications included editions of such works as Sir Richard Burton's translation of *The Arabian Nights* (privately printed at first) or Dowson's translation of Balzac's *La Fille Aux Yeux d'Or*. As a bookseller, first in the Charing Cross Road and then in Bond Street, Smithers acquired the reputation of being a dealer in pornography and, indeed, of publishing such books as *Teleny: or, The Reverse of the Medal*, a novel of emotional and physical homosexual relationships. On the evidence of Hirsch, who ran the Librairie Parisienne in Coventry Street and who saw the novel in manuscript, it was the work of several pens probably including Wilde's. 'It was evident to me that several writers of unequal literary merit had collaborated in this anonymous but profoundly interesting work.' That is certainly the impression which the novel gives to a modern reader.

Smithers evaded prosecution, and in this respect was more fortunate than either a reputable publisher like Vizetelly or other less reputable publishers of the 1890s, and when at last he went out of business it was bankruptcy rather than the law of obscene libel which put a stop to his activities. Smithers had shown just how far a careful man might go without ultimately incurring the penalties of the law: he was as near as he could have been to the darker verge of the twilight realm of Victorian literature.[1]

THE UNDERWORLD OF VICTORIAN LITERATURE

In *London Labour and the London Poor* (1851) Henry Mayhew discusses the street trade in 'pornography' during the mid-nineteenth century and his is the view which most of his contemporaries must have had of the underworld of literature. He describes how these traders 'live chiefly by professing to dispose of "sealed packets" of obscene drawings and cards for gentlemen; but this is generally a trick adopted to extort money from old debauchees, young libertines, and people of degraded or diseased tastes; for the packets, on being opened, seldom contain anything, but an odd number of some defunct periodical'.[2] This was what Mayhew described as 'the Sham Indecent Street-Trade', though there was also a genuine trade of this kind,

---

[1] So long as the tree of Freudian knowledge remained untouched, some Victorian writers were free of inhibitions and an 'emotional censorship' which is almost universal in the twentieth century. William Johnson *alias* William Cory, for instance, was a master at Eton whose poems in *Ionica* (1858) addressed to his young 'playmates' might well have caused suspicion and unease fifty or a hundred years later. There may be nothing sinister in his belief, expressed in 'A Study of Boyhood' that his 'lady-nature dwells in hearts of men', or in the descriptions in 'Mercurialia'.

> Sweet eyes that aim a level shaft
> At pleasure flying from afar,
> Sweet lips just parted for a draught
> Of Hebe's nectar . . .

but few twentieth-century schoolmasters would care to publish views of this kind.

Novels like Mrs. Wetherell's *Queechy* (1854) provoked some disquiet because of the loving intensity with which they dwelt upon relationships between 'interesting' little girls and men old enough to be their fathers but who became their husbands instead. Mrs. Wetherell wrote without the benefit of Freudian views on childhood sexuality, or she would not have written at all on this subject. Yet her Fleda and Nabokov's Lolita, though distinct in their moral reactions, inhabit a similar state of emotional development.

[2] *London Labour and the London Poor* (London, 1864), I, 229.

closely associated with sources of supply in Holywell Street. The sham of the façade concealed a greater reality.

As in so many other periods, one of the most significant characteristics of pornography in the Victorian age is its dependence on the literature and moral values which it burlesques. The two following passages illustrate one aspect of this phenomenon.

My dear Middleton, I can produce more effect by one caning than twenty floggings. Observe, you flog upon a part the most quiescent; but you cane upon all parts, from the head to the heels. Now when once the first sting of the birch is over, then a dull sensation comes over the part, and the pain after that is nothing; whereas a good sound caning leaves sores and bruises in every part, and on all the parts which are required for muscular action.[1]

Those women who give most satisfaction to the amateurs of discipline, are called governesses, because they have by experience, acquired a tact and a *modus operandi*, which the generality do not possess. It is not the merely keeping a rod, and being willing to flog, that would cause a woman to be visited by worshippers of the birch: she must have served her time to some other woman who understood her business, and be thoroughly accomplished in the art.[2]

In both cases there is a tone of cool appraisal, almost of connoisseurship, yet the second comes from William Dugdale's edition of *Venus School Mistress*, which he published after the prison sentence to which he was condemned by Lord Campbell in 1857, while the first is taken from a book whose respectability must surely have been beyond question, Captain Marryat's novel *Midshipman Easy* published in 1836. What distinguishes these two passages is not their tone but the motive which inspires them. The means of attempting to enforce discipline and moral order is turned by the pornographer into the means of promiscuous pleasure and the destruction of moral order. Elsewhere in Victorian pornography, cherished moral beliefs and social institutions suffer a similar fate. The figures of the family and the schoolroom become the denizens of the literary brothel: cousins pair off without the least inhibition; uncles exercise a sexual tyranny over nieces and nephews; fathers seduce their daughters and corrupt their sons; sons unite with mothers; brothers and sisters form homosexual or heterosexual liaisons. 'We are thus a "happy family", bound by the strong ties of double incestuous lust,' says the narrator of *The Romance of Lust* at the end of his four-volume marathon.[3]

---

[1] *Midshipman Easy* (London, 1862), p. 21 (Ch. V).
[2] See Pisanus Fraxi alias H. S. Ashbee, *Index Librorum Prohibitorum* (London, 1877), p. 401.
[3] *The Romance of Lust: or, Early Experiences* (London, 1873), IV, 129.

The key to Victorian pornography is surely not, as many people believe, its flagellant content—which exists as much in other literature as in pornography—but rather this incestuous burlesque. The 'happy family' was an ideal of moralists and pornographers alike. Linked as parody must be to its model, much pornographic writing in the later nineteenth century shows as strong an aversion to orthodox sexual activity as the most scrupulous novelist could do. Sadism, sodomy, fellatio, cunnilingus, lesbianism, coprophilia, all serve to displace procreative processes which, in the end, might lead to the constitution or the reconstitution of family life. The purpose of pornography, like a great deal of satire, is not to create moral values but to ridicule or destroy them. In the nineteenth century a number of books, like *The Inutility of Virtue*, reflected the opinions of De Sade in their mockery not only of sexual orthodoxy but of all current morality. If so much Victorian pornography now seems tediously repetitive this is, in great measure, because it is aimed at targets which are no longer as morally vulnerable as they were in the nineteenth century. What is pornographic varies from age to age and from society to society, so that *Fanny Hill* or *The School of Venus*, which may have been morally subversive in the mid-eighteenth century, do not necessarily seem so in the twentieth. The twentieth-century reader, though disapproving of incest, is less likely than his Victorian predecessor to be either stimulated or outraged by jibes against the 'happy family', but much more likely to be affected by later and perhaps more ingeniously perverse writing whose effect is to ridicule faith in racial tolerance and the equality or emancipation of women. 'Votes for women' in reality prepares the way for *Histoire d'O* in fantasy.

It is no valid criticism of pornography to complain that it merely presents a dream world or that it constitutes what Havelock Ellis called the fairy tales of the adult world which help to make many of its readers' lives more tolerable. In this sense, the fantasies of most human minds are no less important than their experience of reality. In Victorian pornography, particularly, no one need look very far to see, in merely physical terms, the impossibility of much of the activity described. No less unreal are the settings of many of these novels. Edward Sellon, for example, opens his novel *The New Epicurean*, which Dugdale published in 1865, with a description of the house and gardens in which the ensuing orgies take place, 'a suburban villa, situate in extensive grounds, embosomed in lofty trees, and surrounded with high walls'. This baroque dream, with its ornamental gardens, erotic statuary, paintings by Watteau, and Louis Quinze furniture is described by Sellon as the 'happy valley', and he was certainly well-read enough to have intended a reference to the happy valley of *Rasselas* from which Johnson's hero makes his pilgrimage to the 'real' world of the eighteenth century, only to retreat again, despondent and disillusioned. The happy valley has an important part to play in the pornography of the Victorians and such books as 'Colonel Spanker's' *Experimental Lecture* (1879) do their best to provide it even in a Metropolitan setting with a large, secluded house in Park Lane concealing a spacious conservatory, filled with palms and exotic flowers, which is the scene of the action. Burlesques of the 'real' world must often operate through such fantasies and to condemn pornography for doing so is to show the naïvete of the churchman who complained of *Gulliver's Travels* that it was a wicked book and that, for his part, he did not believe a word of it.

The pornography in which these characteristics are most prominent is, naturally, of a comparatively sophisticated kind and circulated among a smaller readership than the products of 'Paul Pry' or 'Peter Spy', yet its influence remained considerable though its editions were very limited. None of Hotten's private publications, for instance, appeared in editions of more than 500 copies, some were as small as 250. Those periodical publications which in the last quarter of the century marked—according to one's view of the matter—the heights or depths of the pornographers' achievements, were produced in smaller numbers. The *Cremorne* of 1882 (dated 1851) and the *Boudoir* of 1883 circulated in an edition of 300 copies, while the more celebrated *Pearl* of 1879–80 was apparently limited to 150 copies. The publishers sold these at prices which were exorbitant even by the standards of pornography. The *Boudoir* sold for half a guinea an issue and the *Cremorne* for a guinea. A set of the *Pearl* for 1879–80 cost twenty-five pounds! Even the Christmas Numbers and the Christmas Annual of the *Pearl*—wretchedly produced little volumes of some sixty pages—were sold at three guineas. A book of only seventy-seven pages like *Letters from Laura and Evelina*, which was devoted to hermaphroditism, as its companion *Sins of the Cities of the Plain* was to homosexuality, sold in 1883 at six guineas. At the other end of the social scale, publications like *Paul Pry* and, later, *Peter Spy* and the *Ferret*, with their love of scandal and earthy humour, were hawked about the streets at a penny and were printed in editions of several thousand copies. Like their more sophisticated contemporaries they emanated usually from the shops and presses of Holywell Street and contained something of the same material, adapted to a more easily satisfied market.

Periodical literature like the *Pearl* followed the pattern laid down by earlier magazines, including Dugdale's *Exquisite* of the 1840s, by including a number of serial stories, some occasional features and verse, but the *Pearl* contained no illustrations except in its special numbers. The policy of the *Pearl* was to run three serials concurrently on the usual assumption that one of these could be devoted to sex in High Society, one to sex 'in the family', and one to flagellation. So it began with *Sub-Umbra, or Sport Amongst the She-Noodles* (the adolescent hero's adventures with his female cousins); *Miss Coote's Confession* (flagellation at home and at school); *Lady Pokingham, or They All Do It* (homosexual and unorthodox heterosexual activity among the upper classes). The serials were interspersed with literary parodies of the style of Samuel Johnson and of such favourite poems of the family circle as Charles Wolfe's 'Burial of Sir John Moore' or Thomas Moore's 'Meeting of the Waters', and 'The Harp that Once through Tara's Halls'. These were accompanied by limericks, some of which were of an anti-erotic obscenity calculated to turn all but the strongest stomach, while others might normally have appeared elsewhere but in the later nineteenth century could hope for no other outlet than this.

At the Parish Church, South Hackney, by the Rev. C. A. White, John Henry Bottomfeldt, of Hamburgh, to Sarah Jane Greens, of South Hackney. (Vide 'Daily Telegraph', January 3, 1875)

> How lovely everything now seems
> When joined in one by Hymen's belt,
> For now John Henry has his Greens
> And Sarah Jane her Bottom-feldt.[1]

Few items were as innocent as this or as good-natured and many of the *jeux d'esprit* were directed against the enemies of pornography, whom the editor of the *Pearl* described variously as 'moral and hypocritical swine' or 'piggywiggies'. Bogus advertisements were published, ridiculing such figures as Spurgeon, the great Baptist preacher, while the magazine was described on its title-page as being published for the Society of Vice.[2] The shafts of such publications as this were directed against morality rather than against religious doctrine and so it is no suprise to find Annie Besant and her views being ridiculed in an extremely unpleasant poem, 'The Fruits of Philosophy', in the *Pearl* for March 1880.

[1] *The Pearl* (September 1879), I, 117.
[2] Rev. J. Spurgeon will Address the Young Women's Christian Association on the subject of
CIRCUMCISION
With practical examples of the advantage of removing the hood or foreskin from the Penis.
Admission to women only. No collection. (*Pearl*, November 1880, III, 197.)

I   'Aretine's Postures'

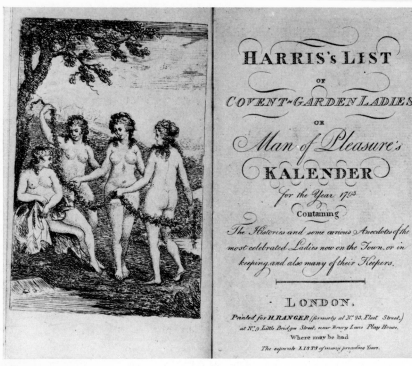

II *Harris's List of Covent-Garden Ladies* (1793)

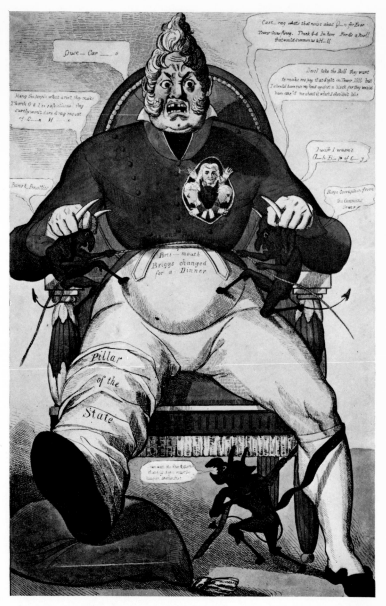

III *The Brightest Star in the State or A Peep out of a Royal Window* (1820)

IV *Mars, Venus and Vulcan*, from the *Rambler's Magazine* (1822)

V *Leda*, from the *Rambler's Magazine* (1822)

VI   *The Guard of Honor*, from the *New London Rambler's Magazine*
(1829)

VII   *Mrs. Nesbit, as Cornet FitzHerbert,* from the *Exquisite* (1842)

VIII   *La Correction Conjugale*, from the *Exquisite* (1844)

IX *A Father's Love*, from the *Freethinker* (1883)

THE

FERRET.

An Inquisitive, Quizzical, Satirical, and Theatrical Censor of the Age.

No. 2.]   SATURDAY, JANUARY 29, 1870.   [One Penny.

BENEFIT BA

CONDUCTED BY   PETER SPY.

CHAM

A MUSIC HALL CANTEEN.

X   Public display – 1870: *The Ferret*

The
original
French skin
boots 12½ gns.

Elliott
Knightsbridge
Bond Street and Now
KINGS ROAD
CHELSEA

(Reproduced by courtesy of Elliott of Knightsbridge)

XI   Public display – 1967: New Elliott at 120 Kings Road

XII   Pictures from an exhibition: Jules Garnier

XIII   Pictures from an exhibition: Ernest Normand

(Reproduced by courtesy of the Robert Fraser Gallery, London W.1)

XIV   Pictures from an exhibition: Jim Dine and Eduardo Paolozzi

MANUAL

OF

Classical Erotology

(De figuris Veneris)

BY

FRED. CHAS. FORBERG

LATIN TEXT AND LITERAL ENGLISH VERSION.

FIRST VOLUME

MANCHESTER
One Hundred Copies
PRIVATELY PRINTED FOR VISCOUNT
JULIAN SMITHSON M. A., AND FRIENDS

1884

JACQUES DESROIX

La

Chambre
Jaune

ROMAN

PARIS
CHARLES CARRINGTON, *Libraire-Éditeur*
13, FAUBOURG MONTMARTRE

1902

XV   Genuine and bogus title-pages published by Charles Carrington

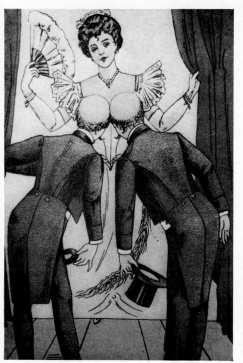

XVI   Chief Inspector Drew's obscene pictures (1908)

At times a certain literary talent is evident in such publications and there are strong reasons to suppose that one of the *Pearl's* poems, 'Frank Fane—A Ballad' may have been wholly or partly the work of Swinburne, though he may well not have authorised its appearance here. In other respects, the irreverence of the *Pearl*'s parodies is reflected in many other publications, where poems like Longfellow's 'Excelsior' and other parlour favourites are reduced to terms of the most ludicrous obscenity. Even that most cherished form of family entertainment, the Christmas pantomime, was not spared and in 1879 it was burlesqued with a certain amount of skill in *Harlequin: Prince Cherrytop*, whose authors showed a good ear for the ponderous humour of the traditional pantomime, as in the dialogue between the Lord and Lady in Waiting.

> *Lord.* Good morning, Lady Clara, you, I see,
> Are waiting for the King as well as me.
> *Lady.* As well as I is grammar, Sir, I ween,
> Beside, I wait not for the King, but Queen.
> *Lord.* I stand corrected, 'Tis the only way
> That I can stand, excuse the jest, this day.

Other more exalted individuals and institutions were treated with the same irreverence and a particularly obscene book might be announced as dedicated 'with permission' to the Queen, while such items as *Cythera's Hymnal: or, Flakes from the Foreskin* (1870) were given descriptions like 'Oxford: Printed at the University Press, For the Society for promoting Useful Knowledge'. It is not in the least extraordinary that by 1880 the pornographers were invoking political anarchy by proclaiming books to be the work of the Nihilists in Moscow. The claim had some truth philosophically if not geographically.

The relationship of moral anarchy to the conventional values of the time was closer than a mere parody of verbal or literary forms to its model. Greater insistence on the value of family life was accompanied by books like *Letters from a Friend in Paris* (1874) which offered incest on a scale and with intricacy hardly matched elsewhere outside the pages of De Sade. In *Teleny: or, The Reverse of the Medal* (1893)—as though homosexuality itself were not rejection enough—both Camille Des Grieux and his mother are seduced by Teleny. In 'wicked uncle' novels like *The Yellow Room: or, Alice Darvell's Subjection* (1891), the code of the nursery is incongruously adapted to the fantasies of the brothel. In *The Autobiography of a Flea*, parent and clergy join the more distant uncle in debauching the heroines. In such works as Hotten's *Madame Birchini's Dance* or

277

Fashionable Lectures, the psychological truths of Victorian pornography are uncomfortably evident when the whores are made to dress up as the mothers of their clients.

The morality of the school, as well as the morality of the family, became by the same irony the subject-matter of pornography. Teachers seduced their pupils of either sex, pupils seduced one another, flagellation was introduced under the pretext of discipline and blossomed into an aphrodisiac. It was no good for the chivalrous William Acton to claim that when men supposed women capable of experiencing physical pleasure with their husbands or lovers, they were slandering British womanhood: the pornographers knew better and at the least touch or suggestion their heroines might become Maenads capable of acts of sexual depravity hardly to be matched by their male counterparts. They were the very opposite of those heroines so dear not only to Acton but, more significantly, to Smith and Mudie.

Some men, whose names became quite well known, devoted their lives to the pornography trade, whether as authors, publishers, or retailers. The identity of the authors of much Victorian pornography is uncertain but occasionally there emerges a man like Edward Sellon (1818–66), who had been a Captain in the Indian Army, driven the Cambridge Mail until the development of rail travel had put an end to it, and opened some fencing rooms in London. During the 1860s he wrote a number of novels for Dugdale, including *The New Epicurean*; *Phoebe Kissagen*; *The Adventures of a Schoolboy*; *The New Lady's Tickler*, and *The Ups and Downs of Life*, which was said to be his autobiography. Some of the novels contained his own illustrations. But Sellon was by no means a stable personality. In April 1866, after writing a farewell letter to a friend and a poem to one of his casual mistresses—his own marriage was a disaster for both parties—Sellon shot himself at Webb's Hotel in Piccadilly. There is a humour even in his pornographic writing but too often, one suspects, it is unintentional.

The colour came and went in the cheeks of her beauteous companion, who faintly sighed out, 'Ah, Marie, what are you doing? Oh, joy; oh blissful sensation! Ah, is it possible—oh—oh—ur—r—r—r,' she could no longer articulate.[1]

'Mon Dieu,' ejaculated the dark beauty, who I now began to think was a Frenchwoman.[2]

Neither Sellon nor his publisher, Dugdale, can really have hoped for

[1] *The New Epicurean* (A new edition) (London, 1875), p. 30.
[2] *ibid.*, p. 25.

literary immortality but it might have been some consolation to them to know that *The New Lady's Tickler* was still being read by the British army in Flanders during the First World War.[1]

Early Victorian publishers of pornography may not have had to encounter the hazards of Lord Campbell's Obscene Publications Act of 1857 but they nonetheless faced a redoubtable opponent in the Society for the Suppression of Vice, which continued to flourish as a guardian of literary morals. Among these publishers, George Cannon who died in 1854 seems to have avoided further difficulties with the law after the prosecution of 1830 (for publishing De Sade's *Juliette* and other books) until being gaoled in 1853. When prosecuted, some publishers of this kind claimed that they had only taken to the trade because they were starving and had not enough money to support their families. As a matter of fact, men like Cannon did reasonably well out of pornography and a few, like William Dugdale, very well. At the other extreme were those like Jack Mitford, the publisher of the *New London Rambler's Magazine* (1827–9), who died in 1831 after following the road from riches to rags, or more specifically from Mitford Castle to St. Giles's Workhouse.[2] Yet most men had more to fear from prison than from financial ruin. Edward Duncombe, who with his brother John had a hand in publishing Mitford's *New Rambler*, was tried and sentenced for publishing obscene literature in 1829; 1833; 1835; 1838; 1853; and 1856. It was, one might suppose, more of a vocation than a trade but, nevertheless, a financially rewarding one. The Duncombe brothers were responsible for such collections of bawdy verse as *Duncombe's Drolleries* and *Labern's Original Comic Song Book*, as well as for stories like 'Kitty Pry's' *Mysteries of Venus* and 'Terence O'Tooleywag's' *Adventures of an Irish Smock*. They also reprinted older books and when Edward Duncombe was sent to prison in 1851 it was for publishing the irrepressible *Fanny Hill*. By then the sentence imposed was two years, as compared with six or eight months which had been the custom in the 1830s.

---

[1] C. M. Bowra, *Memories 1898–1939*, p. 87.

[2] 'He received a classical education, was originally in the navy, and fought under Hood and Nelson. Besides "The Scourge", he edited "The Bon Ton" magazine, and "Quizzical Gazette", and was the author of a sea song once popular, "The King is a true British Sailor". He was an irreclaimable drunkard, thought only of the necessities of the hour, and slept in the fields when his finances would not admit of payment of a twopenny lodging in St. Giles's. His largest work was "Johnny Newcome in the Navy", for which the publisher gave him the generous remuneration of a shilling a day till he finished it. He died in St. Giles's workhouse in 1831.' Graham Everitt, *English Caricaturists and Graphic Humourists of the Nineteenth Century* (London, 1893), p. 129n.

During the earlier years of Victoria's reign there were a number of men like Cannon who had a chance encounter with the law but managed to keep out of the courts for much of their lives. This was true, for instance, of Edward Dyer who was convicted in 1828 of publishing *The Story of Dom B . . .* and in 1853 of publishing *Fanny Hill* but who seems to have kept out of trouble in the meantime. Even Renton Nicholson, editor of the *Town*, and his associates were unlucky enough to be prosecuted for obscene libel in respect of six issues of that periodical in 1838 but the jury found them not guilty. Renton Nicholson's paper was a scandal sheet and regaled its readers with stories that were bawdy rather than erotic. While editing and writing the *Town* he also edited a High Church paper called the *Crown* and, according to his own account, derived much amusement from launching attacks in the *Crown* on the immorality of the *Town* and then replying to them. Later he forsook literature to become 'Baron Nicholson' and to hold his mock-trials in various taverns, before transforming this into the 'Judge and Jury Show' with *tableaux vivants* provided by girls in flesh-coloured tights.

When William Dugdale appeared in court it was no mere accident or misfortune. By the time that Lord Campbell's Obscene Publications Act became law in 1857 Dugdale had served at least nine prison sentences for publishing obscene books and prints, which is hardly remarkable when one considers the scale on which he worked. Using the *aliases* of H. Smith, Turner, Young, and Brown, he issued a wide range of pornographic fiction from his premises in Holywell Street, Wych Street, and Drury Lane, the novels usually selling at three guineas or just double the price of a three-volume novel of the more orthodox kind. Of course, Dugdale's novels were not in three volumes and were much cheaper to produce, which was perhaps just as well for him since they were seized by the police in large quantities, more than 800 volumes in 1851 and 3,000 in 1856. The arrest and prosecution of Dugdale in 1851 was typical of many such cases. The Vice Society, acting as informant, complained to the Metropolitan Police that Dugdale was selling obscene books and prints at 16 and 37 Holywell Street and on 2 September 1851 a party led by Inspector Lewis of the Thames police (who had the powers of search of a Customs officer) and Sergeant Chadwick of the Metropolitan Police (F division), accompanied by strong-arm men from the Vice Society, set out to raid these premises. As soon as they appeared in Holywell Street, Dugdale's lookout gave him the 'office'—warned him that men from the police office were coming—and rushed inside. By the time the authorities reached 37 Holywell Street, which was Dugdale's headquarters, the shop was so securely bolted and barred that it was nearly impossible to break in. For ten minutes the search-party cooled its heels while a hostile crowd, composed mainly of other inhabitants of the area, gathered. Then Dugdale appeared saying, 'Now, Chadwick, you may come in', but there was some further disturbance in which the stalwarts of the Vice Society seem to have been set upon by the employees of Holywell Street. The ten minutes grace was enough for Dugdale to burn certain prints, of which the police found the charred remains, but the raiders took possession of some 'French lithographic prints', lithographic stones and other items. In all, they seized 882 books, 870 prints, 110 catalogues, 9 lbs. of letterpress, as well as stones and copperplates. At Bow Street, two days later, Dugdale protested that some of the books seized were advertised in the most reputable newspapers, others were sold at public auctions, and an edition of the *Memoirs of Harriette Wilson* had been found not to be an obscene libel some years earlier. He said nothing, however, of certain other and less discreet little books like *The Amorous History and Adventures of Raymond de B——, and Father Andouillard*, which dealt in types of behaviour that might well have put Harriette Wilson to the blush. Dugdale was committed for trial to the Middlesex Sessions later that month, where he was sent to prison for two years. Yet on this occasion Dugdale had a small triumph when he appealed to the court of Queen's Bench against his conviction for obtaining and procuring obscene prints with the intention of selling them, and of possessing them with the intention of selling them. The conviction for obtaining the prints stood but the court agreed with Dugdale that it was no crime merely to possess them. Nonetheless, he still went to prison for two years. A few years later Dugdale brought a successful action against an agent of the Vice Society who broke into his premises and removed certain books but by 1857, when he and William Strange were tried before Lord Campbell, he seems to have lost much of his resilience. His appeal to Campbell for clemency was hardly coherent and he reached 'the highest pitch of excitement', opening a penknife and attempting to use it either on himself or, possibly, on a Vice Society witness who was standing near him in court. He was restrained and sent to prison for a year but when he was at liberty again he began to publish on a scale which would have done credit to many a legitimate firm. His productions included the novels of Sellon and the first publication of a manuscript, which he believed to be genuine, of *Don Leon*, a poem allegedly by Byron which includes a detailed account of the sexual aberrations that caused the failure of the Byron marriage. Neither the style nor contemporary references in the poem support the view that this is the work of Byron. Dugdale's new enthusiasm for his trade ultimately attracted the attention of the Vice Society and the police again, and he died in prison at the age of sixty-eight in 1868.

It is true, as C. R. Dawes suggests in his unpublished *Study of Erotic Literature in England*, written in 1943, that there seems to have been a decline in the production of pornography during the 1840s, and there were certainly few criminal prosecutions in either this decade or the 1860s. The most productive periods, perhaps because they coincide with campaigns against pornography, appear to have been the 1830s, the 1850s, and the last thirty years or so of the century. Certain references in cases of 1851 suggest that the drive against pornography at that time may have been connected with an attempt to improve the image of London for the benefit of visitors to the Great Exhibition. In the later years of the nineteenth century the gulf between rich and poor among the pornographers seems to have been much greater: those who appeared in court were usually not much more than street traders who had been selling photographs of one kind or another. Next to the street traders were the small retailers, whose methods of doing business, as described by an agent of the Vice Society at the trial of Alfred Carlile in 1845, were the same then as now.

I went to the shop two or three times before the day when the sale took place, and bought several innocent publications. On the day in question, the prisoner showed me a French print in the window, which I had asked to see. I asked him if he had anything more curious, and he at length invited me to go into the back shop. He then shewed me several indecent prints. I asked him the price, and selected two which I produce. These form the subject of the present indictment.[1]

The small dealers were obviously very vulnerable to tactics of this sort, whether their adversaries were agents of the Vice Society or the police. When Inspector James Brennan of the Metropolitan police was given the job of 'cleaning up' the Holywell Street area in 1870, plain clothes officers found the Vice Society's methods worked admirably. Five shops were dealt with in this manner and in every case the officers were invited into the 'back room.' Only one of the booksellers, William Saunders, who had been to prison already, began to have suspicions. He tried to escape the trap by offering to post the material and then by demanding a letter of introduction before he would hand it over, but all in vain. Also in January 1870 the Vice Society and the police turned their attention to the street traders, who, according to Henry Mayhew, had always felt a certain injustice inherent in the greater protection enjoyed by the booksellers of Fleet

[1] *Cox's Criminal Law Cases* (London, 1846), I, 229.

Street, Wych Street, and Holywell Street, from whose shops the traders themselves were supplied. But in 1870 the police were getting at these booksellers through the hawkers. In January 1870, for instance, the police began to round up newsboys—most of them in their late teens or early twenties—who had been selling the first two numbers of the *Ferret*, particularly because of complaints about the print 'A Music Hall Canteen,' which appeared on the cover of the second number for 29 January. When they appeared at the Mansion House police court it was said that the newsboys had brought the *Ferret* at twenty-six copies for a shilling and had made profits of more than four shillings a day. The newsboys protested that they had bought the *Ferret* from a bookseller in Russell Court, Charles Grieves, *alias* Young, a man whom Dugdale had employed for many years as the printer of his more sophisticated productions. The newsboys were dismissed with fines of 2*s*. 6*d*. or four days' imprisonment, while the police investigated the matter more fully.[1] 960 copies of the paper were found on the premises of the printer and no less than 2000 copies at the shop of Grieves himself, together with copies of such earlier publications as *Peter Spy* and *Every Woman's Book*. *Every Woman's Book; or, What is Love?* contained advice on birth control. It had first been published by Richard Carlile in 1825 in the *Republican* and was afterwards reprinted separately. Grieves appeared at the Middlesex Sessions in February 1870 and was sentenced to a year's imprisonment with hard labour.[2]

Certainly, a bookseller who wished to remain out of prison was well-advised to avoid displaying anything which might cause offence and, possibly, contravene the Metropolitan Police Act of 1839 or the Town Police Clauses Act of 1847. He would also have to be very sure that any customer who penetrated to the back room of the shop was a genuine amateur of the books and pictures he was selling. Sooner or later he might make a mistake but this was much less likely if he was selling very highly priced books to a small clientele. Hence the comparative good fortune of men like Charles Hirsch of the Librairie Parisienne—who numbered Oscar Wilde among his customers—Edward Avery, an associate of Swinburne, and, in his later years, Leonard Smithers. As a matter of fact, after twenty-five years of immunity, Avery had the bad luck in 1900 to sell an expensively produced book to a plain clothes officer and when his shop in Greek Street was raided the full extent of his trade was discovered. The police did not dispute the lavishness of his publications, which were rarely printed abroad, but Avery went to prison for four months after pleading guilty. He may have felt it was a small price to pay for

[1] *The Times*, 29 January 1870.   [2] *The Times*, 17 February 1870.

quarter of a century of profitable trading. There were a number of measures which the big dealers like Avery could take to protect themselves. It was, for instance, an easy matter for the publisher of a book to ante-date it on the title-page and to attribute it to a non-existent publisher or to one long since dead. *The Autobiography of a Flea* is clearly a product of the later nineteenth century yet it bears the date 1789, whereas 1889 would be more accurate. Many books were attributed to 'George Peacock' or 'William Holland' as publishers and given dates between 1777 and 1788. Hotten claimed that Peacock had been the original publisher of most of the items in the so-called 'Library Illustrative of Social Progress.' Another device was to claim that the book had been published abroad, in Paris or Moscow, or even in the case of Burton's translation of the *Kama Sutra*, at Benares. Sometimes the place of publication was a proclaimed fiction, indicating that the publisher had no intention of making it easier for the police to catch him, and so books were published at 'Mons Veneris' or, in the case of *Teleny*, at 'Cosmopoli'. Publishers of English pornography and curiosa abroad took similar precautions. Charles Carrington announced *The Memoirs of Dolly Morton* (Paris, 1899), by 'Hughes Rebell,' *alias* Georges Joseph Grassal, as being published in Philadelphia for the 'Society of Private Bibliophiles,' and *Flossie, A Venus of Fifteen* (Paris, 1897), as 'Printed for the Erotica Biblion Society of London and New York.' One of Carrington's most ambitious productions was a Latin text with English translation of Friedrich Karl Forberg's *Manual of Classical Erotology* (*De Figuris Veneris*), a book which Carrington issued in 1899 and which has obvious claims to be a work of scholarship. Yet even this was prudently described as 'Privately Printed for Viscount Julian Smithson M.A., and friends, Manchester, 1884.' Indirectly, Carrington did the state of learning some service by publishing, for instance, editions of Aristophanes and defensively claiming that they were the work of the Athenian Society.

'Unfortunately,' said the Vice Society's Report for 1868, 'a long experience has shown that, though the vigorous enforcement of the law is for the time attended with the best effects, offences of this class have always a tendency to revive'.[1] The Society might feel like a latter-day Canute facing the flood-tide of Victorian pornography but its moral dedication was unswerving. In the thirty-four years from 1834 to 1868 the Society was responsible for the seizure or destruction of no less than 129,681 obscene prints; 16,220 books and pamphlets; five tons of letterpress in sheets; 16,005 sheets of obscene songs,

[1] *Society for the Suppression of Vice. Occasional Report and Appeal* (London, 1868), p. 7.

catalogues, and handbills; 5,503 cards, snuff boxes etc.; 844 engraved steel and copper plates; 428 lithographic stones; 95 woodblocks; 11 printing presses, and 28 cwt. of type. This was at least some reward for a century or so of moral vigilance. Of course the Society looked for assistance and substantial results in consequence of Lord Campbell's Obscene Publications Act of 1857 but there were other forces at work to thwart Lord Campbell's good intentions. 'The powers of the Act were immediately put in force, and with so much effect that the trade seemed effectually checked, until it was resuscitated, and a new phase developed in the history of vice, by the perversion to these degrading purposes of the discoveries of photography and the stereoscope; and the improvements in the postal service introduced facilities for secret trading that were previously unknown.'[1] Certainly the techniques of photography were sufficiently developed by the mid-nineteenth century for the purpose of pornography and—in a more orthodox sphere—Delacroix had announced the superiority of photography to sketching while photographers like J. Watson were experimenting with 'dorsal nudes' by the process known as wet collodion. As to the postal trade, the Post Office Protection Act of 1884 made it possible for the recipient of obscene material to lodge an official complaint but the postal authorities were not empowered to open letters without a warrant from the Home Secretary. An adjunct to this Act of 1884 was the Indecent Advertisements Act of 1889, since those traders who hoped to supply their customers by post would have to contact them generally by means of advertisements, which quite often appeared in sporting papers like the *Winning Post*. But long before either of these two Acts became law pornographers were making use of improved postal services to speed their goods—mainly photographic and, indeed, stereoscopic—on their way. Among the first of these was a mysterious 'Jacques & Co.' who operated from Southampton Buildings in Holborn and whose method of promoting its stereoscopic gems was to circularise such likely customers as members of the Army, the Navy, and the two Universities. Jacques and Co. were never brought to justice but their successor, Deplangue, who moved the business to Camden Town, was twice caught and, on the second occasion, sent to prison for two years at the Central Criminal Court in April 1866. As life became increasingly hazardous for both the shopkeepers and the postal traders, there were obvious advantages in withdrawing to the Continent and continuing operations from Paris or Brussels. There was little that the Vice Society could do to track down an advertiser and bring him to court if he had a French or a Belgian address—or for that matter a Dutch one.

[1] *ibid.*, p. 5.

By 1870 the Vice Society was, in any case, in acute financial difficulty and it announced early that year that it had not been able to pay the costs of its last twenty-eight prosecutions. It maintained a precarious existence for much of the following decade before insolvency overtook it. In 1886, however, the National Vigilance Association followed this redoubtable predecessor. The law was further reinforced by such Metropolitan Police officers as Inspector James Brennan, who on 25 February 1870 was presented with £5 from the Police Reward Fund by the Bow Street magistrate, in recognition of his efforts to suppress the trade in obscene photographs. The time had clearly come for pornographers to consider the advisability of withdrawal to neutral territory.

Such a withdrawal was, as a rule, only possible for the more accomplished dealers, so that the run-of-the-mill booksellers and street-traders were obliged to stay behind and take their chance. The more sophisticated customers had always had direct connections with the Continent. Monckton Milnes, later Lord Houghton, was indebted to his Paris supplier, Fred Hankey—son of a British general and cousin of the Governor of the Bank of England—as well as to some adroit smuggling via the diplomatic bag and the Foreign Office, for the very fine collection of obscene books, pictures, and *objets d'art*, which he assembled at Fryston. The Customs Consolidation Act of 1853 prohibited the importing of obscene books and pictures but even such items as came under Customs scrutiny on their way to Fryston were well-concealed. Milnes showed a laudable literary taste in preferring the more polished literature of French pornography to its cruder English counterpart and the fact that so many of the books were in French made it unlikely that the Customs would recognise them as worth detaining. When there were pictures which might have given away the nature of the book, Milnes instructed that the pages should be gummed together, where necessary, to hide the illustrations from prying eyes. One of the most proficient smugglers who conveyed Hankey's discoveries to Milnes was Harris, the manager of the Covent Garden Opera, who was so curiously shaped as to be able to conceal quarto volumes in the curve of his back and was also responsible for piloting some very curious statuary past the Customs.

Naturally, a man like Monckton Milnes, a Member of Parliament, later a peer, involved in political and social issues, editor and biographer of Keats, friend of Swinburne and Nathaniel Hawthorne, was unlikely to show the representative tastes of those who paid for smuggled goods. There was another and less ingenious level of smuggling which the Vice Society and its sympathisers soon dis-

286

covered, a level at which dealers made rather amateur efforts to get past the Customs carrying suitcases evidently fitted with false bottoms or panels. A German dealer caught at Hull in November 1866, using this method, was fined the considerable sum of £100 in the following month. This was clearly not the method to appeal to a really professional supplier. Much easier and much safer was the system of posting goods from France or Belgium to individual customers. By the very nature of their work, the Customs authorities could hardly hope to examine every suspicious parcel, and even when they discovered a book or pictures, the sender would be beyond their jurisdiction. So it happened that after the prosecutions of the late 1860s and the early 1870s, in which men like Inspector Brennan had played so effective a part, the emigration of English pornography began. *The Romance of Chastisement* and a number of manuscripts written for Hotten were sold to Hartcupp of Brussels on Hotten's death in 1873 and published there the next year. These included *The Charm, The Night School, The Beautiful Jewess*, and *The Butcher's Daughter*. Hartcupp produced another batch of flagellant pornography, the work of St. George H. Stock, in 1875 and a year later the English Ambassador in Brussels was instructed to register a protest with the Belgian government. This resulted in the Belgian police raiding Hartcupp's premises at 128, Boulevard Central, and destroying part of his stock. But it was to take more than one—or more—police raids to prevent the publication of this expatriate literature. At about this time, for instance, there appeared in Brussels *Curiosities of Flagellation*, in Paris *The Woman of Pleasure's Pocket Companion*, and in Leipzig *The Harem Storyteller*. French publishers like Jules Gay, in flight from their own government, had taken the publication of pornography as far south as Geneva, Bordighera, and San Remo. There is no reason to doubt the claim of English pornography which was announced as being published in Naples. Yet it was Holland and Belgium which proved most lenient in their attitude towards pornography, and it was to Brussels that publishers like Jules Gay and Auguste Poulet-Malassis had fled, from Paris, earlier in the 1860s.[1] Even English publishers who had reached the comparative safety of France often preferred to have their work done for them by printers in Belgium or Holland.

Relationships, in this respect, became very close between England and the Continent during the last thirty years or so of the nineteenth century. Yet publication abroad had its disadvantages and the

---

[1] They continued their operations from the Belgian capital, while bribing the guard of the Brussels–Paris night express to deliver their publications to a contact in Paris.

number and nature of misprints in so many otherwise quite well-produced books make clear that they were too often the work of printers to whom English was not a first language. In a number of books, including the *Pearl* which was supposed to originate in London, the printer is inclined to put the inverted commas, at the beginning of a piece of dialogue, at the base of the first letter instead of above it. This is, of course, a German practice. In other books it is the French form of inverted commas, as in *Dolly Morton*, «underground station», which appears from time to time.[1] But these eccentricities are excusable by comparison with the number of more general errors, which at times make nonsense of a text. Carrington was one among the few publishers of his kind to go to the trouble of printing and proof-reading to a reasonably high standard.

Carrington was perhaps the best-known and most proficient publisher of English pornography abroad. According to Vernon Symonds, Carrington was an errand boy, vanboy, and lavatory attendant before selling books from a barrow in Farringdon market. Despite the illnesses of his later life, he was one of the most successful of expatriate publishers. When he died, blind and syphilitic, in a lunatic asylum, 'His mistress provided a magnificent funeral and his tortured body was consigned to earth by the Catholic Church'.[2] His real name was Paul Ferdinando and for many years he attracted the attention of the police on both sides of the English Channel. Despite two expulsion orders by the French authorities, he and his shop in Montmartre survived and he remained in business until shortly before his death in 1922. Carrington, who was of Portuguese extraction, had left England for France before the end of the nineteenth century and those who worked for him in London or elsewhere were merely distributors. These were the only men to suffer the consequences of law. His list of publications is impressive, and apart from those already referred to it included *My Secret Life* and French translations of English pornography. For some time there had been almost simultaneous publication in French and English of certain items, like *Colonel Spanker's Experimental Lecture* (1879) which appeared as *Conférence Experimentale par Le Colonel Cinglant* (1880).[3] One of Carrington's contributions to this cultural exchange was *La Chambre Jaune* (1902) by 'Jacques Desroix,' an adaptation of *The Yellow Room* (1891), though toned down a little perhaps for fear of offending the French authorities. Another precaution which

---

[1] *The Memoirs of Dolly Morton* (Philadelphia, 1904), p. 34.

[2] Quoted in Alec Craig, *The Banned Books of England* (London, 1962), p. 71.

[3] Despite their amusement at 'Le Vice Anglais' the French seem to have been ready customers for the flagellant pornography of the Victorians.

Carrington took on a number of occasions was to produce two versions of the same book, one which could be supplied to genuine customers and the other which omitted the more obscene passages and could be openly displayed.

Among others who left England at this time was Henry Hayler, a photographer whose work might be euphemistically described as 'family groups', and H. S. Nichols, the partner of Leonard Smithers. Both men were about to be prosecuted and, indeed, Nichols was on bail at the time he absconded. Nichols opened a shop in Paris at 27, Place de la Madeleine, at about the same time that another expatriate, H. Ashford, went into business at 31 Passage de Harve. Nichols eventually made his way to America and though Ashford died in 1902 his postal trade was carried on by his widow.

The French police were not always as obliging to their English colleagues as they might have been, principally because they were not much concerned with postal or other traffic in books from France to England: it was for the English Customs or postal authorities to deal with that. There was hardly more than a token co-operation in serving expulsion orders on Carrington in 1901 and 1907, and the Sûreté took a similar attitude when it was proved that Dolly Ashford was sending obscene photographs to England or Nichols was selling copies of the *Pearl*, presumably second-hand survivors of the edition of 1879–80 or perhaps cheap reprints for the new trade. In at least one case, involving a bookseller called Keary in 1907, the French police refused to take any action at all. Keary had published the *Illustrated Artistic Encyclopaedia*, which contained pictures of naked women considered by the English police to be obscene. As Chief Inspector Drew explained in the following year, a picture of a naked woman might in any case be considered indecent by the police but that would not necessarily mean a prosecution of the publisher. On the other hand, obscene pictures did entail a prosecution. An obscene, as opposed to an indecent, picture was one in which 'the hair is clearly shown on the private parts'.[1] But the Chef de Sûreté wrote to the Assistant Commissioner at Scotland Yard explaining that pubic hair was not considered to be obscene by the French and, therefore, no action could be taken against Keary.

Once the more sophisticated trade had been driven out of England and the pattern of publishing forbidden books abroad was established, the way was clear for the Obelisk Press of Jack Kahane, the Olympia and Ophelia Presses of M. Maurice Girodias and their many contemporaries. Naturally, the trade in pious frauds and cheaply-

[1] *Joint Select Committee Report on Lotteries and Indecent Advertisements* (1908), p. 40.

produced, feebly written obscenity continued in England, much of it at the level of literary achievement represented elsewhere by the mass-produced romantic novelette: in many cases the two types of literature may fulfil the same purpose for opposite sexes. The one thing which Victorian pornography illustrates and which twentieth-century pornography confirms is that this particular genre is not nearly so interesting in itself as the reactions which it inspires. H. S. Ashbee, perhaps the most diligent and patient seeker after curious and forbidden books that English bibliography or criticism has ever known, wrote wisely of his friend James Campbell, *alias* James Campbell Reddie, in 1885, 'James Campbell viewed erotic literature from a philosophic point of view—as illustrating more clearly than any other human nature and its attendant foibles'.[1] It seems hardly too much to suggest that if we knew nothing of Victorian society except through its pornography, we might guess a great deal of the rest.

[1] *Catena Librorum Tacendorum* (London, 1885), p. xlviii.

The Twentieth Century:
'Plus ça Change . . .'

Nothing is more misleading than the appearance of finality accompanying the reaction of one generation against its immediate predecessor and, in this respect, no rejection can have seemed more absolute than that of the Victorians by their descendants in the first half of the twentieth century. Now that Victorian literature has become one of the most overcrowded areas of academic research, now that the physical possessions of the Victorians—their paintings, furniture, and bric à brac—are in such urgent demand, now that so many 'modern' social and religious controversies seem in a curious way to parallel the arguments of believers, sceptics, liberals, and 'realists' of the nineteenth century, the debunking of the Victorians begins to look like an amusing but unimportant interruption in the consolidation of their beliefs and achievements. The fame of General Gordon has been relayed to millions who have never heard of Lytton Strachey, whose acerbity already exudes the fateful charm of quaintness over a distance of nearly fifty years.

In practice, history and human nature are never quite as uncomplicated as that and one might easily point out any number of facets of contemporary life which would make the Victorians as eager to disown us as the most rabid anti-Victorian of the 1920s would have been to disown them. Censorship, particularly the censorship of literature which discusses frankly the relations of the sexes might seem a case in point. Yet the principles on which Victorian censorship was based were older than the Victorians, deeply rooted in the evangelical morality and liberal philosophy of the later eighteenth century, and there was no good reason why the influence of such principles should fade away just because the Victorian era was over. What has occurred in the last hundred years or so is less a change of principles than one of taste and, in this sense, the most remarkable feature of literary censorship is not how much its standards have altered but how little, in essence, they have changed. To take the most obvious example, one might expect that between the Obscene Publications Act of 1857 and the Obscene Publications Act of 1959 something like a revolution had taken place. The principal innovation in the 1959 Act was to make statutory provision for the acquittal of works whose publication would be in the interests of literature, science, or learning. Yet this had been implied by Lord Campbell in 1857, although the courts later chose to ignore this implication. Both Acts were designed to suppress pornography and to allow works of literature free circulation. So Lord Campbell gave his blessing to *La Dame aux Camélias* and his successors to *Lady Chatterley's Lover*, a novel which for all its alleged indecency blends the plot of a Victorian novelette with a truly Victorian moral earnestness of treatment. Both the 1857 and the 1959 Acts accept the hypothesis that literature may deprave and corrupt its readers, though the later Act with a Victorian regard for Great Books specifies literary merit as an extenuating circumstance. 'Podsnappery,' the prudish concern of the Victorians for the susceptibility of the 'Young Person,' is not exclusively Victorian. Many enlightened critics regard the banning of 'Horror Comics' in 1955 as an act of progress and few enemies of literary censorship are on record, for instance, as advocating the circulation of the works of the Marquis de Sade among adolescents. Indeed, though it is easy enough to laugh at those who ask, 'Would you like your child to read this book?' the question itself seems immortal, it is only the answers which change. In July 1968 in *Inter-Racial Books for Children*, the librarian of a New York high school demanded the withdrawal of Hugh Lofting's 'Dr. Dolittle' stories from libraries on the grounds that Lofting was 'a white racist' whose African characters were made to appear quaint and ridiculous. On 2 August 1968 *The Times*, in an account of the *Books for Children* supplement published by the Advisory Centre for Education, announced that, 'Sinbad the Sailor, Andrew Lang's Fairy Books, some of Grimms' fairy tales, Jane Eyre, and Hoffman's Struwwelpeter are named today as examples of books which are likely to be "positively harmful" for most young children of between five and seven.' The supplement in question also concedes that there may be some truth in assertions that 'Cinderella encourages boot-fetishism, that Alice in Wonderland and Tom up the chimney in the Water Babies are about the birth process, and that the Three Blind Mice is a straightforward essay on castration.' The taboos of Freudian hypothesis are evidently as ingenious as anything devised by the Victorians.

It must have brought some consolation to the shades of Charles Mudie and W. H. Smith that booksellers of the twentieth century continued to operate their own form of censorship. When *Lady Chatterley's Lover* was openly published in 1960, Smith's refused to stock it and B. H. Blackwell would supply it only 'on demand'.[1]

[1] In 1966 Smith's banned nine books on legal advice.

Among periodical literature recently banned by Smith's is the science fiction magazine *New Worlds* and the July 1968 number of *Playboy*, the latter ban caused by a number of shots from films included in the magazine, none of which seemed more remarkable than the stills displayed by a good many cinemas. Among enterprises which began later than Smith's and ended earlier was Boot's circulating library, which on one occasion refused a book of Wyndham Lewis's called *False Bottoms* because the title was vulgar, and so the title became *The Revenge for Love*.[1]

In politics as in morals, twentieth-century censorship has inherited both the general beliefs of the Victorians and those beliefs which the Victorians themselves had inherited from the later eighteenth century. The twentieth century believes, as Thomas Erskine believed, that freedom of expression does not entitle a writer to advocate violence. In the case of seditious literature no less than in the case of literature which is obscene the assumption is that men are moved to action by what they read. Coleridge's view that men were not brought to revolution by reading the *Rights of Man*—nor presumably would they be brought to racial hatred by reading *Mein Kampf*, in this view—is unacceptable to legislature and judicature alike. So the Race Relations Act of 1965 accepts the hypothesis that readers can be inspired to hatred and violence at the behest of a writer: to publish such 'inspiration' would be criminal anyway and the only remarkable thing about the new law is that it should emphasise the criminality of doing this in respect of racial groups. Perhaps the successors of the twentieth century may regard this nervous preoccupation with matters of race as no less curious than the Victorian sensitivity towards sex. In both cases the matters are not so much taboo as subjects for endless discussion.[2]

A prosecution which involved a certain amount of race hatred but much more than that alone was brought against Guy Aldred, the English distributor of the *Indian Sociologist* in 1909. It is a case which clearly illustrates the limits of toleration in political discussion. In that year an Indian Nationalist, Madan Lal Dhingra, who was also a student at the University of London, chose to play his part in the 'liberation' of India by going one night to the Imperial Institute and shooting dead Sir W. Curzon Wyllie, who was a member of the Indian Civil Service, and Dr. Cowas Lalcaca. He was convicted of

---

[1] In 1898 T. Mullett Ellis's novel *God is Love*, though well-reviewed, was banned by Smith's because its title was objectionable.

[2] Censorship rarely works in the way anticipated. The 1965 Act, intended to protect racial minorities against the intolerance of the majority, is now used to fine and gaol members of the minorities.

293

these crimes and sentenced to death, though he and his nationalist colleagues clearly regarded such acts as deeds of selfless patriotism. *The Indian Sociologist*, a journal published in Paris by an Indian who claimed to have taught at Oxford, Krishnarva, declared Dhingra to be a martyr for the cause and announced the foundation of several scholarships to commemorate his assassination of 'a Governmental flunkey.' The English printer of the *Indian Sociologist* had already been sent to prison for four months in July 1909 and in September it was Guy Aldred, describing himself as an 'Anarchist Communist', who was convicted of seditious libel for producing copies of it at the Bakunin Press in Shepherd's Bush (Bakunin was the name of a Russian anarchist.) Aldred was sentenced to a year's imprisonment by Mr. Justice Coleridge, who had reminded the jury in his summing up that all incitement to 'rebellion, insurrections, outrages, assassination,' must be illegal.

As well as directly preventing incitement to violence, political censorship in the twentieth century—no less than in the nineteenth or eighteenth—must indirectly maintain political stability by outlawing certain forms of comment on the monarchy, the legislature and the judicature. Attacks on the Royal Family have generally been ignored unless they seemed to threaten more than the personal reputation of the individual attacked. The law ignores comments on the personal shortcomings of a monarch but could not ignore the kind of attack made on George V by the *Liberator* in November 1910. This paper was republican and was published in Paris by an American, Edward Holden James, and distributed in England by Edward Mylius. In an article entitled 'Sanctified Bigamy,' in November 1910, the *Liberator* alleged that before his marriage to the daughter of the Duke of Teck in 1893, George, who was not even heir apparent at the time, had married the daughter of a British Admiral, Sir Michael Culme-Seymour in Malta in 1890. When his elder brother died and he became heir to the throne, he was said to have deserted his wife and bigamously married the future Queen. There was no real evidence to support this story but rumours of it had appeared earlier in such papers as the *Brisbane Telegraph*. The *Liberator*, which sought to discredit the monarchy rather than to reinstate the King's first 'wife', followed up its article with a further squib in December 1910. 'The *Daily News* of London informs us that the King plans to visit India with his wife. Would the newspaper kindly tell us which wife?'

Since James was safely in Paris there was nothing the English courts could do about him but when Mylius was tried in February 1911 the special jury had not the least hesitation in finding him guilty of a libel on the King (who sent an official denial of the story to the court) and Mylius went to prison for a year, still protesting the truth of the account given in the *Liberator* of the King's 'first marriage.' This was not only a case of an insult offered to the monarch: if the story in the *Liberator* was accepted, then the children of George V who succeeded to the throne would have had no right to do so—there were alleged to be children of the first 'marriage'—and Edward VIII, George VI, and Elizabeth II would have been usurpers. For that reason alone the jibes of the *Liberator* could not merely be ignored.

Courts of law have proved themselves, on the whole, to be more sensitive than Parliament in the twentieth century to comments which might undermine their authority. Such comments may be contempt of court either because in the most straightforward sense, they bring the court into contempt or because in some other way they make it harder for justice to be done. The freedom of the press in commenting on the actions of the courts was summed up in 1900 by Lord Russell of Killowen in terms which apply to the nineteenth and twentieth centuries alike.

Any act done or writing published calculated to bring a Court or a Judge of the Court into contempt or to lower his authority, is a contempt of court . . . subject to one and an important qualification. Judges and Courts are alike open to criticism, and if reasonable argument or expostulation is offered against any judicial act as contrary to the law or the Public Good, no court could or would treat that as contempt of court.

The limits of 'reasonable argument or expostulation' are unfortunately not defined until someone has crossed them as, for instance, the editor of the *New Statesman* did on 28 January 1928 in his comments on Mr. Justice Avory's conduct of the trial of Marie Stopes on an action brought against her by the editor of the *Morning Post*. 'We cannot help,' said the *New Statesman*, 'regarding the verdict given this week in a libel action brought by the Editor of the *Morning Post* against Dr. Marie Stopes as a substantial miscarriage of justice . . . prejudice against her aims ought not to be allowed to influence a court of justice in the manner in which they appeared to influence Mr. Justice Avory in his summing up. . . . The serious part of this case, however, is that an individual owning to such views as those of Dr. Stopes cannot apparently hope for a fair hearing in a court presided over by Mr. Justice Avory—and there are so many Avorys.' It can hardly have been a great surprise to Clifford Sharp, the editor of the *New Statesman*, when he was summoned before the court to apologise and pay the costs of his appearance there.

More serious is the contempt of court which may prejudice potential jurors against an accused person before the trial begins. In

November 1967 Times Newspapers Ltd. were fined £5,000 for publishing an article in the *Sunday Times* of 29 October which included a photograph of a defendant in a pending trial. The caption referred to the defendant as a man who 'took to politics after unedifying career as brothel-keeper, procurer, property racketeer.' At his trial the defendant in this case submitted that the action of the *Sunday Times* in publishing such material made it impossible for him to be tried by an impartial jury. He was overruled by the Recorder. Under these circumstances absolute freedom of the press would be incompatible with the impartial administration of justice and, indeed, in 1965 the working party of 'Justice' and the International Press Institute under the chairmanship of Lord Shawcross recommended only two changes in the law relating to contempt of court. They suggested that all proceedings for contempt of court should require the sanction of the Attorney-General and that newspapers should be allowed to comment 'responsibly' on a case between trial and appeal.

If there is a distinction to be made between what may broadly be called political censorship in the nineteenth century and political censorship in the twentieth it is surely that in the twentieth century the censor is much less concerned with the danger of civil war or revolution and much more concerned with the perils of conquest or destruction by external enemies. The Official Secrets Act instead of being a quaint and rather puzzling piece of legislation has been reinforced by further Official Secrets Acts of 1911 and 1920 to become perhaps the most irksome form of censorship in which political material may be involved. As early as 1898 Rudyard Kipling had been obliged to censor his book *A Fleet in Being: Notes of two Trips with the Channel Squadron* because, it was alleged, the book betrayed naval secrets and then with the outbreak of war in 1914 the need for a stricter censorship in such matters was obvious enough. J. L. Strahan-Davidson wrote to the *Morning Post* on 28 April 1915 recalling how during the Franco-Prussian war, Moltke had told a Prussian officer in 1870 to come to England and 'study each morning every line coming from France in the correspondence columns of the British newspapers.' By spending his time in doing this, according to Moltke, the officer concerned would do more for his country than by any act of gallantry on the field of battle. So in the First World War the War Office set up a censorship of cables, while the Defence of the Realm Act made it criminal to publish unauthorised military information or to undermine public confidence in the nation's war effort. Already a press bureau had been set up, to operate henceforward in peace as well as war, to which editors might submit copy for censorship and thus be relieved of any fear of prosecution. In a number of cases, however, editors who had done this saw other newspapers publish the 'censored' material without submitting it to the press bureau and no penalty was incurred. From this period of preoccupation with military security grew the system of censorship through the issue of 'D notices.' These notices, issued by the Ministry of Defence amount to a request to a newspaper not to publish the information to which they refer. They do not have the effect of prohibiting publication but are an indication that a newspaper which ignores the request and publishes the information may be subject to prosecution under the Official Secrets Act.

The two most common objections to the Official Secrets Act and the D notice system are that they may be applied to information which is not really a matter of security, and that they may be used to inhibit the discussion of material which is political as well as military. In the first case, for example, it is doubtful whether such information as the staff holiday rota at Broadmoor really merits or requires the protection of a D notice. Much more serious is the use of a threat of prosecution under the Official Secrets Act to prohibit the publication of information relevant to political discussion. After the trial and before the execution of Sir Roger Casement in 1916 copies of his so-called 'Black Diaries', which had been made by Scotland Yard, were circulated to certain people with the object of proving that he was a homosexual and thus destroying any lingering sympathy for the man or his cause. When a copy of these diaries came into the hands of Mr. Peter Singleton-Gates in 1925 he wrote and was about to publish a full account of the contents of the diaries and the manner in which they had been used. Just before the book appeared he was summoned to the Home Office, where the Home Secretary and a legal adviser interviewed him. To put it simply, he seems to have been ordered to withdraw the book and threatened with proceedings under the Official Secrets Act if he did not comply. The diaries remained unpublished for another thirty-four years. If this was an unwarranted interference with political discussion, the issues are less clear in the case of two Oxford undergraduates who were sent to prison for publishing an article in *Isis* which attempted to demonstrate what they regarded as the danger and the futility of British military policy towards the Soviet Union. In doing this they revealed information which was acquired, apparently, during National Service and so violated undertakings given in respect of the Official Secrets Act.

It is a tribute either to the maturity or perhaps to the docility of the British press to realise how rarely in peace or, particularly, in war it has found itself in direct conflict with the law or with governmental power. During the Second World War the government was empowered under Regulation 2D of the Defence (General) Regulations to suppress any newspaper which it deemed guilty of 'systematic publication of matter calculated to foment opposition to the prosecution of the war to a successful issue'. In July 1940 the *Daily Worker* which, in the roseate glow of the Molotov-Ribbentrop pact of 1939, had been condemning the war against Germany and the manner of fighting it, was warned by the government of the dangers of such an editorial policy. (J. B. S. Haldane was chairman of the editorial board and Sean O'Casey was one of its members.) But the *Worker* took little notice of the warning. By January 1941 it was supporting the 'People's Convention' in its demands for a 'People's Government' and a 'People's Peace'. On 1 January the *Worker* had announced 'The legend of the anti-Fascist war is dying' and followed this on 20 January with a cartoon called 'Their Gallant Allies', ridiculing the allies of the British government, including the Free French and the Polish leader Sikorski, who holds a banner reading 'War on U.S.S.R. Peace with Italy.' Reporting on the Communist Congress in London, also in its issue of 20 January the *Worker* announced, 'They proclaimed their solidarity with the rest of the world's workers, whether in Berlin, Turin, Paris, or Shanghai. All were equal victims of the capitalist system.' The next day the Home Office announced the suppression of the *Worker* and of the *Week*, a cyclostyled Communist magazine, while the offices of the paper were raided by Scotland Yard Special Branch. The next day in the House of Commons the Home Secretary, Herbert Morrison, explained that the action had been taken, 'because it is and has been for a long period the settled and continuous policy of these papers to try to create in their readers a state of mind in which they will refrain from co-operating in the national war effort and may become ready to hinder that effort'. On the other hand, Aneurin Bevan, while expressing his 'detestation' of the *Worker*'s propaganda, tabled a motion regretting the suppression. The ban remained until after the Soviet Union had been involved in the war, at which time it was judged safe to allow the *Worker* to circulate again. Yet the effectiveness of the ban on the *Worker* was, to say the least, doubtful. Two months later there were complaints in the House of Commons that it was still circulating in pamphlet form and Douglas Hyde in his autobiography *I Believed* describes the clandestine manner in which the banned paper was produced and the dedication of its supporters who would cycle through the blitz with batches of the day's issue for delivery to factories and to sympathetic trades union organisations. That aspect of the *Worker*'s conduct is certainly in the best tradition of Cobbett or Hone.

No other paper in the twentieth century has come close to suppression in quite the same way, with the possible exception of the *Daily Mirror*, which in the end showed more regard for self-preservation than the Cobbett-Hone tradition allows. In 1942 the *Mirror* published one of Donald Zec's cartoons with a caption contributed by 'Cassandra'. The cartoon showed a torpedoed sailor on a raft above the caption, 'The price of petrol has been increased by one penny (Official).' Despite the *Mirror*'s protest that this was merely a warning against the wastage of petrol, the government chose to see it as a comment on the profits of the petrol companies. The owner and editor of the *Mirror* were called to the Home Office and warned by Morrison that if the paper repeated this indiscretion it would be closed under the 2D regulation.

At this level of political writing the twentieth century has a more obvious censorship than the second half of the nineteenth not because the philosophy of political censorship has changed since the Victorian period but by virtue of a growing sense of insecurity in international affairs. Political censorship in England is designed to keep the peace of the realm, a peace of the kind which is approved by the established order and which, in turn, preserves that established order against all but 'constitutional' change. This truism applies as much to the nineteenth century as to the twentieth, and as much to the sixteenth century as to the nineteenth. The general test to be applied in considering whether a publication ought to be censored or not is whether, as Mr. Justice Coleridge put it in 1909, it may result in 'rebellions, insurrections, outrages, assassinations'. The difference between the Victorians and ourselves in this respect is that they were principally concerned with the fearful consequences of incitement to all these things, whereas we have become more conscious of them as the consequences of nothing more dramatic than publishing information. As a result, we are not able to accept the absolute freedom of expression advocated by Mill and his sympathisers but, for all practical purposes, nor were the Victorians either.

Mill, in insisting on the right of men to express themselves freely in matters of religious belief—or disbelief—must have realised that of all areas of discussion this was the one nearest to the state of perfect liberty. Despite the case of the *Freethinker*'s 'Comic Bible Sketches' in 1883, there was little more that could be done by the end of the nineteenth century to confer greater freedom of debate, since so few restraints remained. The situation might be imitated by the twentieth century but there remained little scope for alteration. It is a symptom of something approaching absolute tolerance that it was never even thought necessary to repeal the Blasphemy Act of 1698, since it was impossible to imagine that an attempt would ever be made to enforce its provisions. To the twentieth century as to the nineteenth it is evident that the survival of Christianity must depend, among other things, on its ability to do without 'the assistance of crown lawyers'. If people cannot be made good by Act of Parliament, they certainly cannot be made devout. In religion as well as in politics what the censor fears is physical violence and the determining question in such cases of blasphemy as the present century has witnessed seems to have been the likelihood of violence resulting from the offensiveness of the blasphemy expressed. In 1917 the House of Lords upheld the opinion of the majority of Victorian jurists that the propagation of anti-Christian doctrines was not criminal, 'apart from scurrility and profanity'. No publications of the stature of even the *New Statesman* or the *Daily Worker* have suffered for their views on religion either the rebuke or suppression which those two papers did for other comments. Indeed, the last case of blasphemy, of the slightest literary significance, was the prosecution of William Gott in 1921–2. Gott was a bizarre figure with a number of previous convictions for blasphemous libel, offences against the Defence of the Realm Act, and sending obscene books through the post. He was fifty-five years old and described euphemistically as not well educated—or less euphemistically by his own counsel as 'ignorant'. In November 1921 Gott, surrounded by a large crowd, was selling various publications of his own in Stratford Broadway. The papers, which sold at twopence each, included the *Liberator; God and Gott,* and the *Rib Tickler: or Questions for Parsons.* Gott's style was abusive rather than argumentative and, for instance, his description of Christ entering Jerusalem 'like a circus clown on the back of two donkeys', would have earned him no converts and offended secularists of the Bradlaugh type as well as Christians. There was no physical violence on this occasion but when the crowd became restive and there were cries of 'Disguisting! Disgusting!' and 'You ought to be ashamed of yourself', the police moved in and arrested Gott. When he was tried at the Central Criminal Court in December before Mr. Justice Avory, the first jury failed to agree but a second jury found him guilty. He was described rather quaintly by a police witness as 'a Socialist and Atheist of the worst type'. The jury had, however, recommended clemency, which Mr. Justice Avory interpreted as nine months' hard labour. At this point there was an intervention on Gott's behalf when a voice from the court called to the judge, 'Love thy enemy and forgive him seventy times seven.' 'You have been guilty of gross contempt of court in making that exclamation,' said Mr. Justice Avory to the 'voice', 'and I fine you £5 for it.'[1]

Gott appealed against his conviction in January 1922 but the Lord Chief Justice upheld it on the grounds that there had been no mistrial and that the remarks which Gott had published were such that it did not require 'a strongly religious person' to be outraged by them.[2] This was the fourth time that Gott's *Rib Ticklers* had brought him to prison and, indeed, half the trials for blasphemous libel in the twentieth century had been trials of Gott. Whether he reformed his ways or died after this, or whether it no longer seemed worthwhile prosecuting him is uncertain, but in 1922 he disappeared from the scene of events.

In 1930 the Blasphemy Laws (Amendment) Bill was introduced in the House of Commons, a bill whose effect would have been to remove blasphemy or blasphemous libel from the calendar of crime. There was considerable sympathy for this measure and a certain amount of practical support. The bill passed its second reading before the Home Secretary indicated that while, in general, he approved of such a bill he would be obliged to suggest certain amendments which would provide for prosecutions against men of the scurrility of Gott. As Home Secretary he saw it to be his duty to prevent 'breaches of the peace by unbridled attacks upon religious feeling'.[3] Those who were the most enthusiastic supporters of the bill rejected any such compromise, viewing it as surrender, while many of their sympathisers appeared happy to accept the limitations which the Home Secretary proposed. At all events, the bill was dropped. Yet what had already been demonstrated in the courts was now confirmed by Parliament: for the future it was going to take a man of extreme persistence, and even ingenuity, to get himself prosecuted for blasphemous libel.

It would be wrong to suggest that English courts in the earlier twentieth century misinterpreted Lord Campbell's Act of 1857, though there is good reason to think that they may have disregarded Campbell's personal intentions. The difficulty was, in part, that this legislation preceded the more controversial developments in realistic or naturalistic fiction, which in the years immediately following the Act appeared in terms of *Adam Bede* or *The Ordeal of Richard Feverel*. Certain reviewers might find such novels objectionable but fiction of

---

[1] *The Times*, 10 December 1921.

[2] *The Times*, 17 January 1922.

[3] The attackers might need the law's protection quite as much as those whose beliefs they challenged. In 1902, for instance, John Kensit, Secretary of the Protestant Truth Association was fatally wounded when addressing an anti-Catholic meeting in Birkenhead.

this type could never come within the scope of the new law. Had not Campbell held up a copy of *La Dame aux Camélias* and promised that the Act would not interfere with such works because they could be regarded as serious literature? But thirty years later would he have held up *A Modern Lover* or Vizetelly's translations of Zola or, later still, *Jude the Obscure*, and said the same? The fact that he would almost certainly not have granted them such immunity is no reflection on the integrity of his intentions but rather a sign of the change in literary style and taste. Because of their subject-matter and the manner in which they dealt with it such books as these would have seemed to Campbell, as to the later Victorians, incapable of literary merit.

Yet while the English law and the majority of English critics seemed to think in terms of the law of 1857, there were those among the most eminent of English and Irish writers who claimed larger and larger areas of human experience as legitimate material for discussion. The organisation of the pornography trade in the twentieth century has differed little from its organisation in the nineteenth and the basic dichotomy has remained between the small retailers of crude, cheaply-produced publications, who operate in London and the producers of more sophisticated material who operate in Paris (and more recently the United States), and elsewhere beyond the reach of the English law. Because the law was almost static in its view of obscenity, while the views of writers themselves had changed considerably, many writers were to become dependent on the more sophisticated pornographers for the distribution of their work. The fact that there was rarely in the earlier twentieth century a prosecution involving a work of serious pretensions is largely the result of prudence on the part of English publishers: knowing that they could expect little sympathy from the courts, they were ready to suppress a book in the face of threats or hostile comments on the part of reviewers. Sometimes, as in the case of Methuen who had published Lawrence's *The Rainbow* in 1915, a publisher did not choose to take the hint: Robert Lynd, supported by James Douglas and Clement Shorter condemned *The Rainbow* as 'reminiscent of Diderot's *La Religieuse*' in its worst pages. A destruction order was granted for the book and Methuen were fined. Lawrence's troubles were, of course, by no means over. *Women in Love* was attacked as obscene in 1921, though there was no real danger of a prosecution, and it is not hard to see why the decision was taken in 1928 that *Lady Chatterley's Lover* should not be published in England but by Orioli in Florence, and that copies should be sent from there to subscribers in England. At first it was hoped to do this through booksellers but in the end the distribution in England had to be undertaken by Richard Aldington and Enid Hilton. Naturally it was impossible to obtain international copyright for such a book and Lawrence lost financially, though he gained in notoriety, through the appearance of pirated editions.

There were other hazards, quite apart from the threat of legal action, attendant upon the publication of allegedly obscene books in England. In the case of James Joyce's *Ulysses*, which was published in Paris by Shakespere and Company in 1922, plans existed to produce the book in England as well. It had been recommended by T. S. Eliot to the Hogarth Press but no printer could be found who was willing to undertake the production of the book. From 1922 until 1936 *Ulysses*, like many of its shabbier contemporaries, was obliged to run the gauntlet of the Customs, who in 1923 seized all but one copy of a complete edition of the novel. In 1936 it was published without interference in London, following the decision of a United States District Court in New York in 1933 that a complete edition of *Ulysses* imported by Random House was not obscene. (Even in the United States *Lady Chatterley's Lover* was not allowed to circulate at this time, though it was once again America which gave a lead when Grove Press was acquitted after publishing Lawrence's novel in 1959, the year before the trial in England.)

The free circulation of *Ulysses* in England was officially decided upon at a meeting between the Director of Public Prosecutions and the Attorney-General, Sir Donald Somervell, K.C., in November 1936. According to the official minutes of the meeting, now in the custody of the Public Record Office at Mepol. 3/930, the Attorney-General decided that no action should be taken against the English publishers of *Ulysses*, the Bodley Head, on the grounds that the definition of obscenity laid down by the Hicklin judgment of 1868 was inadequate.

In his view the question of intention has to be taken into account as in criminal law generally: the context has also to be considered. No one today would, he thought, be found to hold that such books as those of Havelock Ellis on sexual matters were obscene, nor any medical book dealing with sexual aberrations. Standards in these matters were constantly changing— as conventions and taste changed.

If he were challenged in the House of Commons his answer would be on the line that it was a well established principle of law that the intention of a writer had to be taken into account as well as the general setting or context of the book. On applying these tests to 'Ulysses' he was of opinion that the book was not obscene and having regard, in addition, to its established position now in literature he had decided to take no action.

The Postal and Customs authorities were informed of the decision but it is, perhaps, as well for the Attorney-General's peace of mind that he had not read those samples of the 'new criticism' demonstrating the irrelevance of the author's intention in any critique of a work of literature, and that he had not heard the opinion of Lord Justice Salmon in the *Last Exit* appeal.[1] 'However pure and noble the intent may have been if in fact the book taken as a whole tended to corrupt and deprave a significant proportion of those likely to read it, it was obscene within the meaning of the word in the Act.'[2]

During the late 1920s and early 1930s the moral censorship of literature was, if not stricter, at least more obtrusive than it had been for some considerable time. To many people this appeared to be the work of Sir William Joynson-Hicks, who was appointed Home Secretary in 1924 and who had no illusions about either pornography or controversial literature of alleged literary merit.

To discriminate in favour of a book which in the opinion of many will debauch the young, because in the minds of some it is a work of art, seems to me quite indefensible. I was told by a correspondent to some periodical who was pleading the case for a book that I had 'banned', that I had not the intelligence to appreciate its merits. The merits of the book may be as great as its admirers claim—and I confess I found it to contain much that, from a purely literary standpoint, excited admiration—but surely its merits were not strictly material to the issue; it was the demerits of the book which I was asked by the publishers to consider—not whether it possessed something of greatness, but whether it would tend to corrupt and deprave the public mind. On that point I could find only one answer, and my view was subsequently confirmed by the courts.[3]

Joynson-Hicks, popularly known as 'Jix', had been created Viscount

[1] See, for example, 'The Intentional Fallacy' in W. K. Wimsatt, Jr., and Monroe C. Beardsley, *Verbal Ikon* (Kentucky, 1954), pp. 3–18.

[2] *The Times*, 1 August 1968.

[3] Viscount Brentford, *Do We Need a Censor?* (London, 1929), pp. 18–19. Joynson-Hicks who, in addition to other attacks, was lampooned in *The Sink of Solitude* and *The Policeman of the Lord*, defended his conduct in more general terms as well.

'Those who object to all forms of censorship cannot, I imagine, realise the extent of the traffic which goes on in filthy literature, and still more filthy photographs. In the course of my administration at the Home Office I had to place an embargo on pictures coming into this country of such a character that, whatever artistic merit they might possess, I am quite sure that not one hundred people in the country would be prepared to support or even excuse them. I know, from my examination of the letters passing to certain shops on the continent, the nature of the traffic, the kind of person who indulges in it, and the harm that is done in consequence: is the Executive to allow this evil to go unchecked? I am very glad indeed to say that, during my term of office, a much happier liason [sic] took place between the French Police and ourselves, and considerable efforts are being made, both in France and in Germany, to stem the output of these vicious publications.' *Do We Need a Censor?*, pp. 12–13.

Brentford and retired from the Home Office by the time that he wrote these words. He does not mention the name of the book in question but the circumstances hinted at suggest that it was Radclyffe Hall's *The Well of Loneliness* which Jonathan Cape was about to publish in 1928 but withdrew after seeking Home Office advice as to the likelihood of a prosecution. The book was subsequently published in Paris but copies intercepted by the Customs were declared obscene by magistrates' courts and destroyed. At Bow Street on 9 November 1928 Norman Birkett, appearing for the publishers, announced that he had a number of distinguished witnesses who would give evidence that the novel was a work of literature and not obscene. The magistrate refused to hear them, remarking, 'How can the opinion of a number of people be evidence?'

Despite protests from many of the most eminent men of letters of the time, this adherence to the letter rather than to the spirit of the 1857 law persisted. During the next few years destruction orders were granted for contemporary works like Norah James's *The Sleeveless Errand* and Edward Charles's *The Sexual Impulse* and, more significantly, for English translations of much older literature including the *Greek Anthology*; the *Satyricon* of Petronius, and two translations from Pierre Louys, *Aphrodite* and *Les Chansons de Bilitis*. Among other books of historical interest issued by the Fortune Press and banned at this time were Brantôme's *Vies des Dames Galantes* and two translations by the Reverend Montague Summers, whose reputation as a demonologist and connoisseur of the curious was considerable, *De Daemonialitate* by the seventeenth-century author Ludovico Maria Sinistrari and *Histoire de Magdelaine Bavent* (1652). It is a further indication of the more liberal attitude of courts in the United States that when a prosecution was brought against the publisher of *The Well of Loneliness* in 1929 he was acquitted on appeal, counsel for the defence being Morris Ernst, who was to do battle on behalf of *Ulysses* four years later. In England, *The Well of Loneliness* remained unpublished until 1949 and other books like 'Sheila Cousins's' *To Beg I am Ashamed*, the autobiography of a London prostitute, were withdrawn by English publishers in the face of hostile reviews.

As the gulf widened between so many serious writers and their critics—both literary and legal—a new type of expatriate publisher appeared, a type of which perhaps Jack Kahane, a Mancunian, is the best example. Charles Carrington had been dead for nine years by the time that Kahane established the Obelisk Press in Paris in 1931. Yet the Obelisk Press and, later, the Olympia and Ophelia Presses of Kahane's son, Maurice Girodias, were concerned with a wider trade both in terms of clientele and authors than Carrington had been. The Obelisk Press published many books which had substantial claims as literature, alongside ephemera whose authors assumed various pseudonyms. (Kahane himself became 'Cecil Barr' as the author of novels like *Suzy Falls Off* and *Daffodil*.) Among books which had been condemned by the English courts, the Obelisk Press issued Wallace Smith's *Bessie Cotter*; James Hanley's *Boy*, and Norah James's *The Sleeveless Errand*. Among books which would never have been published in England in the first place, the Obelisk Press was responsible for Frank Harris's *My Life and Loves* and Henry Miller's *Tropic of Cancer*. And apart from these it published such books as Cyril Connolly's *The Rock Pool* which was withdrawn by its English publishers.

If a book was issued as though it had been published abroad, the author might be freed from certain consequences of English law but he might equally be exposed to all the hazards of piracy. Count Geoffrey Potocki de Montalk, a poet and right-wing propagandist, claims a great deal of one's sympathy for what he suffered at the hands of the English courts and, subsequently, the pirates. Count Potocki de Montalk, who lived in London and argued his claims to the throne of Poland, had prepared a little book of five poems, two of which were adapted from Rabelais and Verlaine. The title of the collection was *Here Lies John Penis*. The first attempt to have these poems printed was not successful, since on the casual advice of a policeman the author took them to a firm who happened also to be the printers of the *Methodist Recorder*. Undaunted by this, he approached a second printer who agreed to undertake the printing but subsequently took the poems to the police. In 1932, Count Potocki de Montalk was tried and convicted of 'publishing' these poems to the printer. The Recorder then asked him what punishment he thought he deserved. To his eternal credit—and true to his royalist sympathies —Count Potocki de Montalk suggested several years in Buckingham Palace, upon which the Recorder sent him to prison for six months. While he was in prison, the poems were published without his permission. From this 'Paris edition' which was, in fact, printed in north London, he received nothing but six complimentary copies. As for the poems themselves, despite the use of words to which exception might have been taken in 1932, their tone is gentle, humorous, and without malice. It is hard not to feel that anyone who believed he was being corrupted by them must already be in urgent need of psychiatric attention. Count Potocki de Montalk remains an active translator of European poetry, and *Here Lies John Penis* is soon to appear in its first authorised edition, in America.

The Olympia Press and the Ophelia Press, founded by Maurice Girodias in 1953, presented much the same appearance as the Obelisk Press, except that it was on the whole the Ophelia Press which specialised in mere pornography, while the Olympia Press issued many works of literary or historical importance.[1] These two presses dominated the world of expatriate publishing after the Second World War, though the Obelisk Press survived as well, and the new presses often took over books which were established favourites, such as *The Adventures of Father Silas* (another translation of *Histoire de Dom B . . .*) or *The Young and the Evil*, which had first been published by the Obelisk Press in 1933 and whose authors were Charles Henri Ford and Parker Tyler. Some of the publications of the Olympia Press—the works of Samuel Beckett, for instance—circulated freely in England and might as well have been published for the first time in London as in Paris, yet many of the 'classics' like De Sade or Guillaume Apollinaire would have been prosecuted on sight in England and there would have been scant judicial sympathy for less prepossessing volumes represented in the Olympia list by *White Thighs* or *The Sexual Life of Robinson Crusoe*. In the 1960s it is to America rather than to England that such enterprises as the Olympia Press have made their way and, in certain respects, the word 'expatriate' is hardly applicable. As a glance at, say, a list of Grove Press publications would show, there is a freedom to publish in the United States which seems greater than any the English-speaking world has known before. Translations of *Les Cent Vingt Journées de Sodome*; *Histoire d'O*, and Apollinaire's *Les Onze Mille Verges* are published and circulate with little interference, as do reprints of 'Victoriana' like *The Autobiography of a Flea*; the *Pearl*, and *The Lustful Turk*. Some Olympia Press books have been published in the United Kingdom but these are, in many cases, pious frauds. The Publisher's Foreword to these English editions proclaims that the series 'is to become the image of the newly-won liberties: the right for everyone to think, to write and to read freely—for pleasure alone'. The foreword does not add that the series has been expurgated for the English market, nor indeed would a reader know this unless he had read the

[1] A comparison of some titles shows the difference between the two presses.

Olympia Press: Jean Genet, *Our Lady of the Flowers*, and *The Thief's Journal*; Samuel Beckett, *Molloy. Malone Dies. The Unnamable*; Raymond Queneau, *Zazie dans le Métro*; Lawrence Durrell, *The Black Book*; Pauline Réage, *The Story of O*; William Burroughs, *The Naked Lunch*.

Ophelia Press: Count Palmirio Vicarion, *Lust*; Angela Pearson, *Whips Incorporated*; Marcus van Heller, *Terror* and *Nightmare*; Miles Underwood, *Under the Birch*; Hilary Newton, *Without Shame*, and Peter Lewys (i.e. Pierre Louys), *The She-Devils*.

original Paris editions. The English editions of the Olympia Press are quite as much an image of Thomas Bowdler and his kind, in this respect, as they are of 'newly won liberties'. In the 'Fifth Volume' of Frank Harris's *Life and Loves*, 'an irreverent treatment by Alexander Trocchi', there is a case in point. In the Paris edition, pages 173 to 179 containing descriptions of cunnilingus, lesbianism, flagellation, and sodomy, are reduced to a page and a half in the English edition. The only line which survives expurgation in the last three pages or so of this description is, 'I laughed. And then I had an inspiration.' As a token of newly-won liberties it seems, to say the least, inadequate.[1]

The censorship which expatriate literature incurs is, of course, incurred more often by the purchaser than the publisher, since it is the Customs and Excise which attempts to control its entry into the United Kingdom. Obscene books and horror comics are listed among prohibited imports and Customs officers are armed with a 'Stop List' of books to be seized on sight. This is a cyclostyled list and could hardly include all or even most of the books objected to. The list issued during the 1950s concentrated much more on books written only to satisfy the demand for pornography and much less on the banned works of established authors. This may well have been because no Customs officer at that time needed to be told that *Lady Chatterley's Lover* or *The Tropic of Cancer* should be seized. At the end of the 'Stop List' was a general instruction that all books emanating from the Olympia or Ophelia Presses should be carefully examined.[2] In doubtful cases a legal opinion would be sought, after which the book would either be confiscated or returned to its owner: this form of censorship applied to all books in all languages, though a book in anything but a common European language would hardly be detected in the first place. An importer whose book is confiscated may appeal against the decision to destroy it but such appeals are rare. A first 'offender' is generally warned and no further action taken but a traveller who is 'professional' enough to have hidden a book with considerable ingenuity is likely to be shown less leniency.

The Obscene Publications Act of 1959 was prompted by a series of prosecutions for obscene libel brought against well-known and reputable publishers in 1954, a series which resulted in two convic-

[1] *My Life and Loves: Fifth Volume* (Paris, 1959), pp. 173–9; (London, 1966), pp. 181–2.

[2] One of the books most hunted by Customs officers during the 1950s was *I'll Spit on Your Graves*, a translation of *J'Irai Cracher Sur Vos Tombes*, which Boris Vian wrote and published in 1947 under the pseudonym of 'Vernon Sullivan'. It was prosecuted and banned in France. There has been no complete French edition since then. A pious fraud appeared in 1967.

tions and three acquittals.[1] The Act allowed expert evidence to be
called in defence of the book and, in turn, by the prosecution to rebut
that defence. A later amendment gave the publisher the right to a
trial by jury, rather than making him submit to the decision of a
magistrate as to whether or not the book should be condemned. The
first case before a jury was misleading; it was the trial of Penguin
Books in 1960 for publishing *Lady Chatterley's Lover*. Despite the
greater hostility in the tone of counsel for the prosecution than has
been customary since, the Crown presented a weak case. No witnesses
were called to rebut the expert evidence given for the defence and
many of the defence witnesses were not cross-examined. The jury,
who were rumoured to be nine to three for acquittal after reading the
book and before hearing evidence, never had to consider one of the
most important provisions of the 1959 Act. They found the book was
not obscene and so were absolved from deciding whether despite its
obscenity, publication would be in the interests of literature, science,
or learning. In the case of *Last Exit to Brooklyn* by Hubert Selby, Jr.,
for which Calder and Boyars were prosecuted in 1967 the proceedings
were very different. The prosecution called a number of witnesses to
rebut the expert evidence given for the defence and the jury found
that the novel was obscene. Counsel on both sides, as well as the
judge, made it clear to the jurors that they might be disgusted by the
book, it might make them feel physically sick, but that was not
enough to condemn it: it must deprave and corrupt by inciting its
readers to act as the characters in the novel acted. Even if the book
was obscene by those standards, the jurors must still consider whether
its publication might not be in the public interest as being of benefit
to literature, science, or learning. It seems a strong defence, particularly since *Last Exit to Brooklyn* presents the most unenviable
characters and situations. Yet the jury found it to be obscene and
found that it was not in the interests of art or learning that it should
be published. All forms of censorship, even liberalising ones, have
their shortcomings, but in the case of the 1959 Act the shortcomings
have not really been evident until the *Last Exit* trial. It is, perhaps,
being too optimistic to suppose that a jury would, as Judge Rogers
put it, find that 'the effect of reading the book was to horrify, shock,
disgust, and nauseate', and still retain sufficient detachment to consider whether it might not, after all, be uncorrupting. The difficulty
is that this asks of jurors a type of objectivity not universal even
among literary critics and very rare among ordinary readers. As to

[1] Convicted: Werner Laurie for *Julia*; Hutchinson for *September in Quinze*.
Acquitted: Secker and Warburg for *The Philanderer*; Arthur Barker for *The
Man in Control*; Heinemann for *The Image and the Search*.

deciding whether the publication of an obscene book might be in the interests of learning, this is an even less realistic question to put to a jury. The jurors are not likely by their unaided efforts to be in a position to decide what is in the interests of learning or art. The common-sense attitude seems to be that it would be difficult to think of any book whose publication would not somehow be in their interests but the jury, having heard two conflicting sets of opinions, can hardly do more than make an arbitrary decision. Above all, it seems quite unreasonable to suppose that a jury which honestly believes a book to be obscene—and therefore capable of depraving and corrupting the innocent—will sanction the circulation of that book because it will promote the study of literature. Few jurors are concerned with literature as an art or an academic discipline but most of them are concerned with morality. After the trial of Calder and Boyars the *People* began an investigation into 'The Dirty Book Trade'. In an article published on 3 December 1967 it described the bookshops of Soho, including a number of addresses of shops which its readers would be able to note and avoid. It also published a photograph of a young girl at a counter holding a magazine open at a picture of two naked women. The bookshops of Soho are not thronged with young girls but with very much older men; young girls would find their contents either incomprehensible or tedious—perhaps on occasion revolting. But such photographs as this one have their relevance to parental fantasies. Counsel for the prosecution in the *Last Exit* trial did not ask jurors if they would like their daughters to read this book: he did not need to.

As it happens, *Last Exit* escaped in the end. On 31 July 1968 the Court of Appeal quashed the conviction of the publishers on the grounds that the trial judge had failed to put to the jury the defence case on the alleged obscenity of the book, and, particularly, that he had not given sufficient direction on the question of whether, even if the book was obscene, publication might not still be for the public good. Yet, as the Court of Appeal repeated, the decision must be the jury's. 'The jury must set the standards of what is acceptable, of what is for the public good, in the age in which we live.' On the question of what is meant by the terms 'deprave' and 'corrupt' the Court of Appeal was more circumspect. 'No one has ever tried to define in law the meaning of the words "deprave and corrupt". It would be a good thing, I agree, if the legal meaning were explained.' Perhaps in the case against the English publisher of *My Secret Life*, to be tried at Leeds Assizes, someone may produce a plausible explanation of these terms.

The Act of 1959 has been modified in various ways. In 1964, as the result of the prosecution of Mayflower Books for publishing *Fanny Hill*, in which the case was decided by a magistrate without the defendants having the chance to go before a jury, the law was changed so that in a criminal prosecution for obscenity a publisher might claim the right to trial by jury. The other significant amendment at that time made it an offence for a publisher to possess even the typescript of an obscene book, if it could be reasonably inferred that his intention was publication of it. Yet there remained one process, at least, which did not involve a jury. In 1966 when Sir Cyril Black began proceedings privately against the publishers of *Last Exit*, he applied successfully to the Marlborough Street magistrate for a destruction order in respect of the book. This, naturally, involved no trial by jury, though criminal proceedings against the publishers were taken subsequently by the Crown. The Criminal Justice Act of 1967, however, has since provided that no destruction order may be sought by a private citizen without leave from the Director of Public Prosecutions. It has always seemed to publishers that their chances of acquittal are better before a jury than before a magistrate, and though the *Last Exit* case does nothing to confirm this view, it seems that in future almost every decision will be made by a jury.

Two organisations were founded in 1967 to provide financial aid to publishers prosecuted under the Obscene Publications Act and the Race Relations Act of 1965 respectively. The Free Art Legal Fund was inspired by the prosecution of Calder and Boyars but it also proposed 'to provide for the defence of any future cases brought against those who, in the opinion of the Trustees, are genuinely concerned with the Arts in this country'. This condition is, presumably, intended to discourage hopeful pornographers from applying for assistance. In July 1967 the Free Speech Defence Committee was set up to collect funds for the defence of 'five British patriots', who were charged under the Race Relations Act with publishing material designed to incite racial hatred in the Racial Preservation Society's *Southern News*. Four of the five defendants were acquitted at Lewes Assizes in March 1968 and charges against a fifth were dropped.

It is easy to point to absurdities in the hypothesis that readers may be depraved or corrupted by what they read, the hypothesis upon which the English law rests. Anyone with a taste for such absurdities will find it catered for in books like Morris Ernst's and Alan Schwartz's *Censorship: The Search for the Obscene* (New York, 1964), which shows how few people, according to the investigations of Dr. Kinsey and others, have ever experienced sexual stimulus as a usual reaction to reading erotic literature or literature in general, and how the literature which does stimulate has a way of being the most un-expected kind, as the findings of Morris Ernst and others, summarised by Leo M. Alpert, indicate.

Over ten years ago the Bureau of Social Hygiene of New York City sent questionnaires to ten thousand college and normal school women gradu-ates. Twelve hundred answers were received; and of those seventy-two persons who replied that the source of their sex information came from books, mentioning specific volumes, not one specified a 'dirty' book as the source. Instead, the books listed were: the Bible, the Dictionary, the Ency-clopaedia, novels from Dickens to Henry James, Shakespeare, circulars for venereal diseases, medical books, and Motley's *Rise of the Dutch Republic*. In answer to the question of what things were most stimulating sexually, of the 409 replies, 9 said 'Music', 18 said 'Pictures', 29 said 'Dancing', 40 said 'Drama', 95 said 'Books', and 218 noted very simply 'Man'.[1]

Information of this sort does not invalidate the belief that readers may be affected for the worse by what they read but it does argue the futility of a moral censorship of literature. Censorship is a social phenomenon, while literature is an individual experience, and in the light of this it is futile to speculate as to whether a given book—pornographic or not—has a cathartic or stimulating effect. What is cathartic to one reader may be stimulating to another. The hypo-thesis that some readers may be 'depraved' by a book is open to fewer objections than the assumption that no one can ever be affected for the worse—or, logically, for the better—by literature. The case against censoring a book is not that the hypothesis of the censors is wrong but that most readers do not need the protection of censorship and those who do will find their stimulus elsewhere. In terms of literature, *The Scourge of the Swastika* may become a refuge for those who are denied access to *Les Cent Vingt Journées de Sodome*: in terms of life, when Swinburne read De Sade he found the technique of the Mar-quis inept compared with that of Eton.

Of course, terms like 'deprave' and 'corrupt' have an inherent imprecision and emotive effect which makes their use in discussion hardly possible. For most purposes, certainly for the purposes of the law, they are taken to mean that a reader is encouraged by a book to imitate the behaviour described, stimulated to orthodox or unortho-dox sexual acts. This leads to the further question of whether, on occasion, such 'depravity' might not be a good thing. If it involved certain perversions, it might still be condemned almost universally but not so universally in other cases. The permissive, if naïve, attitude is illustrated by D. H. Lawrence in his attack on Sir William Joynson-Hicks.

[1] *Harvard Law Review*, LII (1938), 73.

The late British Home Secretary, who prides himself on being a very sincere Puritan, grey, grey in every fibre, said with indignant sorrow in one of his outbursts on improper books: '—and these two young people, who had been perfectly pure up till that time, after reading this book went and had sexual intercourse together!!!' *One up to them*! is all we can answer.[1]

Yet if Joynson-Hicks was a late disciple of nineteenth century puritanism, Lawrence himself was one of the prophets of twentieth century puritanism: it is not the least surprising that Professor Vivian de Sola Pinto, at the trial of Penguin Books in 1960, should have described *Lady Chatterley's Lover* as 'a moral tract as well as a novel'. The new puritanism of the twentieth century insists that sex must be free of taboo, inhibitions, unhealthy feelings of guilt, sexual experience is to be rid of what Georges Bataille described as the sense of transgression. This puritanism of mental hygiene is as comic and, in certain respects, as sinister in its way as the puritanism of the Victorians. It is such philosophies as this which pornography exists to undermine and Lawrence, within a few lines of the passage quoted above, recognises the common enemy.

But even I would censor genuine pornography, rigorously. It would not be very difficult. In the first place, genuine pornography is almost always underworld, it doesn't come into the open . . . you can recognize it by the insult it offers, invariably, to sex, and to the human spirit.

Pornography is the attempt to insult sex, to do dirt on it. This is unpardonable. Take the very lowest instance, the picture post-card sold underhand, by the underworld, in most cities. What I have seen of them have been of an ugliness to make you cry. The insult to the human body, the insult to a vital human relationship! Ugly and cheap they make the human nudity, ugly and degraded they make the sexual act, trivial and cheap and nasty.[2]

Sir William Joynson-Hicks himself could not have made a more powerful case, though in his own experience Lawrence is obliged to admit 'how strong is the will in ordinary, vulgar people, to do dirt on sex'.[3]

The more sophisticated pornographers, like so many satirists, seem to echo Cardinal Newman's belief in the involvement of the human race in some 'terrible aboriginal calamity', though they see the calamity in terms other than Newman's. The good intentions and the moral capabilities of the human race are, to the pornographer, a matter for scepticism and cynicism, as they are to the satirist. Since the pornographer's effect is to subvert the prevailing moral values of

[1] D. H. Lawrence, *Pornography and Obscenity* (London, 1929), p. 12.
[2] *ibid.*, pp. 12–13.
[3] *ibid.*, p. 14.

society, what is 'pornographic' will vary from time to time and from place to place. Thus *Fanny Hill* may have been pornographic in London in the mid-eighteenth century but not in America in the mid-twentieth. (For that matter, even in the twentieth century the works of Andrey Sinyavsky and Yuli Daniel, which are taken for legitimate political satire in the West, are 'a mixture of bad taste, vulgarity and pornography' in the Soviet Union.)[1] Wilkes's *Essay on Woman* was morally subversive so long as the philosophy of Pope's *Essay on Man* had currency but now it appears as little more than a bawdy parody at a mainly verbal level. There was not a great deal of sadistic or flagellant literature in England until the humanitarianism of the nineteenth century abolished the judicial flogging of women and curtailed it in the case of men. As the Victorians preached the ideal of family life, incest and homosexuality assumed greater importance in later nineteenth-century pornography. As women achieved emancipation in life, they became enslaved in literature; a novel like *Histoire d'O* is a complete example of this. In the nineteenth century when women were idealised rather than emancipated, the pornographers replied to this idealisation by showing the 'heroines' of their novels in grotesque lesbian situations. Harriet Beecher Stowe might fight the evils of slavery through *Uncle Tom's Cabin* but a pornographic novel like *The Memoirs of Dolly Morton* urged the pleasures of owning a troupe of coloured girls who were obliged to submit to their master's sexual fantasies. Not, of course, that this would make him more affectionate or considerate towards them, since the prevailing philosophy of the book is 'a nigger is no better than a hog'.[2] As the ideal of racial integration gained ground, the pornographers switched their emphasis to the danger threatened by Negroes and Africans. Zane Merritte's *Voodoo* (Paris, 1958), for instance, is not much more than a saga of 'gringoes' in the hands of black rapists and sadists. 'Marcus van

[1] *On Trial: The Case of Sinyavsky and Daniel*, ed. Leopold Labedz and Max Hayward (London, 1967), p. 253. The words were used by the State Prosecutor at the trial in February 1966. This vindictive prosecution, violating truth and Soviet law, reflects a belief that the relation between the ideals on Communist society and the works of these two authors is parallel to the relation between pornography and ideals in the west. This moral subversion was said, in 'expert evidence', to exist in Sinyavsky's writing, since, 'The typical ideas expressed in these works range from Freudianism through anti-Semitism and sex to "God-seeking".' *On Trial*, p. 248. Blasphemy against Lenin and the Soviet system was also alleged against Sinyavsky and Daniel, while the attack on them by Dmitri Eremin in his article, 'The Turncoats', in *Izvestia*, 13 January 1966 has significant echoes of Lawrence's denunciation of pornography, which I have already quoted. 'They spit poison at the whole of progressive mankind, at its ideals, at its holy struggle for social progress, for democracy, for peace.' *On Trial*, p. 94.

[2] *The Memoirs of Dolly Morton*, p. 175.

Heller', with rather more sophistication, tells the story of a West Indian Jack-the-Ripper in *Nightmare* (1960) and of a gang of Algerian thugs and rapists in *Terror* (1959). In another novel of the same vintage, 'Ataullah Mardaan's' *Kama Houri* it is a Pakistani who is the white heroine's tormentor. Even in *J'Irai Cracher sur Vos Tombes*, which is theoretically on the side of the oppressed American Negro, the sexual encounters of black and white are calculated to rouse prejudices rather than promote tolerance. At a lower level of pornography which is cheaply produced but expensively sold, the menace of this particular species of black power almost reaches the proportions of a sexual Armageddon between the races. There seems to be comparatively little anti-Jewish pornography, discounting the Nazi propaganda of men like Julius Streicher, perhaps because anti-semitic feeling had for so long had an outlet in more general literature.

Pornography reflects the *alter ego* of an individual as much as of a society. In the eighteenth century, the age of enlightenment in France, the birth of 'liberté, égalité, fraternité,' De Sade responded to the new democracy by constructing a world of tyranny in his novels, a world in which the most barbaric cruelties inflicted on the poor became the amusement of the rich. Yet despite the massacre of so many of the characters of his fiction, De Sade remained in fact a sincere advocate for the abolition of capital punishment. It is a bizarre thought that if he had kept his writings to himself, the term 'Sadism' might now mean something like 'Opposition to judicial execution'.

In literary terms, pornography is destructive of moral aspirations, as satire may be, and yet, depending on one's view of the human race and its predicament, pornography may be as necessary as satire. The fiction of De Sade or the satire of Swift can only aim to mock human nature as it is, not to transform it into anything better. It is a recognition of something more than the darker side of human nature that while the propagandist of the new order prophesies that the heavens shall declare the glory of man, he hears at his shoulder a derisive chuckle.

Because the discussion or description of sexual activity is somewhat easier now than it was before the Obscene Publications Act of 1959, there is a popular supposition that censorship, if not extinct, must be in a rapid decline. The fact that no English publisher has yet risked reprinting an eighteenth-century favourite like *The School of Venus* or an American novel like *Candy*, unexpurgated, suggests that this same supposition is not shared by the book trade. More to the point, it is open to the Crown to take action against literature under the law of seditious libel, to say nothing of the Official Secrets Act; the Race Relations Act, and even such an unlikely piece of legislation as the Prices and Incomes Act of 1966, which includes a promise of fines of up to £500 for those who incite workers to strike in contravention of the terms of that Act. If literary censorship is less strict in certain respects than it used to be, this may be just as much a reflection of the diminished status of literature as a token of liberal attitudes in government. In the sixteenth century, despite the harshness of censorship laws, the printers of the 'Martin Marprelate' tracts or the activities of a Jesuit press like Parsons's seemed a significant threat to the stability of the state, regardless of what we might regard as the amateurishness of some of their products. Yet though it might be a comparatively easy matter to set up a press for the dissemination of one's views, the condition of national literacy—or rather illiteracy—remained a barrier to anything like universal communication. But for all that, during the whole period of pre-censorship by licensing it is doubtful whether any political or religious argument was silenced by want of a printing press. Seditious literature during the seventeenth and even the earlier eighteenth century was dangerous enough to be answered by the most barbaric penalties. In the case of John Matthews, the young printer who was hanged in 1719 for supporting the claims of the Pretender, it was still possible for one humble individual to seem a threat to the constitution and the government. Though the penalties were not as harsh, the menace of subversion seemed no less powerful at the close of the eighteenth century and in the early years of the nineteenth. The anti-government presses of men like William Hone or Richard Carlile achieved influence beyond anything that Parsons or Matthews had known. William Cobbett could compete with the national press, indeed for many people he was the national press. Yet with the development of more elaborate methods of printing in the nineteenth century, the sort of pamphlets and periodicals which many radicals had issued were no longer professional enough to hold their own: the format of such literature alone would suggest the eccentricity or mere nuisance-value of its publisher. By the middle of the century the *Daily Telegraph* sold more copies in a week than most radical tracts had sold in ten years. To have stated their case with comparable effect at this time, Hone or Cobbett or Carlile would have needed a web offset press costing £600 and capable of producing 7,000 copies an hour. Even then they might have had to rely on Smith and Mudie for the distribution of their work. Their impact would have been reduced to that of a paper like Bradlaugh's *National Reformer*.

The progress of printing, to say nothing of more recent means of communication, appeared to dictate that audiences would grow while sources of opinion decreased in number. A twentieth-century William

Hone would achieve little with a portable printing press—however seditious his publications—and to judge by the fate of certain individuals who have tried to launch new national newspapers, he would probably gain nothing by investing in more sophisticated equipment. He might accomplish something with his own radio programme—but while there is a monopoly of radio, he would have to be acceptable to those who exercise that monopoly.[1] To make any appreciable impact on the nation he would need his own television station but, since that too would be illegal, he would once again have to be acceptable to those who control one of the existing channels. Ultimately, his fate would not be in the hands of the government nor of the courts but rather of the programme planners and—in Hone's case, no doubt—of their legal advisers. To censor Hone or his type it would no longer be necessary to prosecute him but merely to ignore him, and the actions of those who silenced him would be even less available to public inspection or comment than the behaviour of Parliament or the court of King's Bench. In this situation the twentieth century may have as its censors men who are tolerant, urbane, and independent, or self-conscious, timid, and conformist: the system provides for either possibility. But of whatever type they are, the censors will remain with us, perpetuating the condition described by Lord Radcliffe in his Rede Lecture of 1961.

A man may glitter with new and valuable ideas or burn with wise thoughts or passionate feelings, but if he is to communicate them to any circle wider than that of his own immediate friends he has got to render them acceptable to the real licensers of thought today, the editors, the publishers, the producers, the controllers of radio and television.[2]

Dissenting voices may be heard but their dissent must itself be approved by the 'controllers of radio and television', so that when, for instance, the B.B.C. devised a programme in which it could be criticised by the public, it was stipulated that only 'responsible' criticism would be broadcast. On other occasions individual criticisms may be presented to viewers, though often to be turned aside by bland humour or a quick retort.

Yet Hone in the twentieth century would still have a hope of making his view known, by an act of violence sufficiently 'newsworthy' to attract the attention of the mass media. In this respect, dynamite and demonstrations have helped to bring a range of issues

---

[1] The last man to be put to death in England for his views, though they were expressed under unusual circumstances, was not a publisher but a broadcaster, William Joyce, alias 'Lord Haw-Haw' in 1946.

[2] Lord Radcliffe, *Censors* (Cambridge, 1961), p. 2.

from Welsh separatism to American foreign policy into the foreground of that area now fashionably known as 'public debate', into which the majority of the public will never enter. The single and perhaps permanent division of classes in the society of the future may well be between speakers and listeners, actors and spectators: it would prove a far more effective barrier than any mere economic distinction between rich and poor has ever been. At present, the political demonstrator is well advised to accept the approved cause or attitude of a protest group towards which the attention of 'public debate' is drawn, accommodating the nuances of his personal beliefs to general slogans. His only hope of fulfilment beyond this may be through an act of violence.

I return to the point made at the end of my first chapter. The relevant question at any stage of human history is not 'Does censorship exist?' but rather, 'Under what sort of censorship do we now live?' The technology of the later twentieth century offers the means of silencing men—without the danger of making them martyrs—by the most effective method of all, by ignoring them. It is a bloodless and almost silent censorship but, nonetheless, it might have been the envy of the Tudors and the Stuarts.

Select Bibliography

I make no attempt in this bibliography to list all works previously referred to in footnotes. My principal concern is to indicate those books, articles, and manuscript sources to which the text is more indebted than an occasional footnote would suggest.

GENERAL BIBLIOGRAPHY

1. *Manuscript sources*
   British Museum Add MSS. 16,919.
   British Museum Add MSS. 27,825.
   Corporation of London Records Office. Sessions Books 1683–93.
   Dawes, C. R. *A Study of Erotic Literature in England*, 1943. (British Museum at Cup. 364 d. 15.)
   Public Record Office Series King's Bench 28.
   — Home Office 42.
   — Home Office 45.
   — Director of Public Prosecutions 4.
2. *Reports*
   Cobbett's *State Trials* 33 vols. London, 1809–26.
   The English Reports 1900–32.
   Hansard's *Parliamentary Debates* 1803, etc.
   Journals of the House of Commons.
   Journals of the House of Lords.
   State Trials (New Series), ed. Sir J. Macdonnell, 8 vols. 1888–98.
3. *Books and Periodicals*
   The Annual Register 1758–1826.
   Bowman, W. D., *The Story of 'The Times'*, London, 1931.
   Buckle, H. T., *A History of Civilisation in England*, 2 vols. London, 1857–61
   Campbell, John, Lord, *Lives of the Lord Chancellors*, 10 vols. London, 1856–7.
   Cobbett's *Parliamentary History*, 36 vols. London, 1806–20.
   Craig, Alec, *The Banned Books of England*, London, 1962.
   Edinburgh Review 1803–74.
   Farrer, James Anson, *Books Condemned to be Burnt*, London, 1904.
   Fraxi, Pisanus, [H. S. Ashbee], *Index Librorum Prohibitorum*, London, 1877.

— *Centuria Librorum Absconditorum*, London, 1879.

— *Catena Librorum Tacendorum*, London, 1885.

Gentleman's Magazine; or, Monthly Intelligencer, 1731–1833.

Haight, Anne Lyon, *Banned Books*, London, 1955.

Holdsworth, W., *History of the English Law*, 13 vols. London, 1903–52.

Holt, F. L., *The Law of Libel*, London, 1812.

Hyde, H. Montgomery, *A History of Pornography*, London, 1964.

Jackson, Holbrook, *The Fear of Books*, London, 1932.

James, Louis, *Fiction for the Working Man 1830–1850*, London, 1963.

Macaulay, T. B., *History of England*, 5 vols. London, 1849–61.

Nokes, G. D., *History of the Crime of Blasphemy*, London, 1928.

Odgers, W. Blake, *A Digest of the Law of Libel and Slander*, London, 1911.

Reade, Rolf S., [Alfred Rose], *Registrum Librorum Eroticorum*, 1936.

Routledge, James, *Chapters in the History of Popular Progress, Chiefly in Relation to the Freedom of the Press and Trial by Jury*, London, 1876.

St. John Stevas, Norman, *Obscenity and the Law*, London, 1956.

CHAPTER BIBLIOGRAPHIES
CHAPTER 1

Cleland, John, *Fanny Hill: Memoirs of a Woman of Pleasure*, London, 1964.

Huxley, T. H., *Hume* (English Men of Letters Series), London, 1878.

Montgomery, Robert, *Poetical Works*, London, 1836.

Rolph, C. H. [C. R. Hewitt] (ed.), *The Trial of Lady Chatterley*, London, 1961.

CHAPTER 2

Arber, Edward, (ed.). *A Transcript of the Registers of the Company of Stationers of London: 1554–1640*, 5 vols. London, 1875–94.

—, *The Term Catalogues: 1668–1709; with a Number for Easter Term 1711*, 3 vols. London, 1903.

Atkyns, Richard, *The Original and Growth of Printing*, London, 1664.

Blount, Charles, *A Just Vindication of Learning, or an Humble Address to Parliament on behalf of the Liberty of the Press*, London, 1679.

—, *Reasons Humbly Offered for the Liberty of Unlicensed Printing; to* which is subjoined the *Just and True Character of Edmund Bohun, the Licenser of the Press*, London, 1693.

Bohun, Edmund, *The Diary and Autobiography of Edmund Bohun*, Beccles, 1853.

Clyde, W. M., *The Struggle for the Freedom of the Press from Caxton to Cromwell*, London, 1934.

Foxon, David, 'Libertine Literature in England: 1660–1745', *Book Collector*, XII, 1963.

L'Estrange, Roger, *Considerations and Proposals in Order to the Regulation of the Press*, London, 1663.

—, *A Seasonable Memorial upon the Liberties of the Press and Pulpit*, London, 1680.

Luttrell, Narcissus, *A Brief Historical Relation of State Affairs from September 1678 to April 1714*, 6 vols. Oxford, 1857.

Pepys, Samuel, *The Diary of Samuel Pepys*, ed. H. B. Wheatley, 10 vols. London, 1952.

Williams, J. B., *A History of English Journalism*, London, 1908.

CHAPTER 3

[Addison, Joseph,] *Thoughts of a Tory Author Concerning the Press*, London, 1712.

Copies Taken from the Records of the Court of King's Bench, London, 1763.

The Craftsman's Doctrine and Practice of the Liberty of the Press, London, 1732.

[Defoe, Daniel,] *An Essay on the Regulation of the Press*, London, 1704.

An Essay for the Press, London, 1712.

Hanson, Laurence, *Government and the Press 1695–1763*, London, 1936.

Lecky, W. E. H., *A History of England in the Eighteenth Century*, 8 vols. London, 1883.

Oldmixon, John, *Memoirs of the Press, Historical and Political: 1710–1740*, London, 1742.

Quintana, Ricardo, *Swift: An Introduction*, London, 1962.

State Law: or, The Doctrine of Libels Discussed and Examined, 1729.

Swift, Jonathan, *The History of the Last Four Years of the Queen*, London, 1758.

[Tindal, Matthew,] *Reasons Against Restraining the Press*, London, 1704.

Trevelyan, G. M., *England Under Queen Anne: Ramilles and the Union with Scotland*, London, 1932.

—, *England Under Queen Anne: The Peace and the Protestant Succession*, London, 1934.

Williams, Basil, *The Whig Supremacy 1714–1760*, Oxford, 1962.

CHAPTER 4

Barrow, Isaac, *The Works of the Learned Isaac Barrow, D.D.*, London, 1687

Clarke, Samuel, *A Discourse Concerning the Being and Attributes of God*, London, 1749.

Collins, Anthony, *A Philosophical Enquiry Concerning Human Liberty*, London, 1890.

Cudworth, Ralph, *The True Intellectual System of the Universe*, 3 vols. London, 1845.

Stephen, Leslie, *A History of English Thought in the Eighteenth Century*, 2 vols. London, 1902.

Tillotson, John, *The Works of the Most Reverend Dr. John Tillotson*, London, 1720.

Willey, Basil, *The Eighteenth Century Background*, London, 1953.

CHAPTER 5

Addison, Joseph, *The Spectator*, ed. G. A. Aitken, 8 vols. London, 1898.

An Account of the Societies for the Reformation of Manners, London, 1699.

Collier, Jeremy, *A Short View of the Immorality and Profaneness of the English Stage*, London, 1698.

Richardson, Samuel, *The Correspondence of Samuel Richardson*, ed. A. L. Barbauld, 6 vols. London, 1804.

— *Selected Letters of Samuel Richardson*, ed. John Carroll, Oxford, 1964.

Steele, Richard, *The Guardian*, 2 vols. London, 1756.

— *The Tatler*, ed. G. A. Aitken, 4 vols. London, 1898.

Straus, Ralph, *The Unspeakable Curll*, London, 1927.

Watt, Ian, *The Rise of the Novel*, London, 1957.

Wood, Anthony à, *Athenae Oxoniensis*, 2 vols. London, 1721.

CHAPTER 6

Aeropagitica: An Essay on the Liberty of the Press [Dedicated to Charles James Fox, whose campaign to alter the law of libel was successful in 1792]. London, 1791.

[Bingley, William], *A Sketch of English Liberty!* 1768.
Biographical, Literary, and Political Anecdotes, 3 vols. London, 1797.
Considerations on Proceedings by Information and Attachment, London, 1768.
A Digest of the Law Concerning Libels, London, 1765.
Erskine, Thomas, *The Speeches of the Hon. Thomas Erskine*, 4 vols. London, 1810.
A Summary of the Law of Libel, London, 1771.

CHAPTER 7

The Bon Ton Magazine; or, Microscope of Fashion and Folly, 1791–6.
More, Hannah, *The Works of Hannah More*, 8 vols. London, 1801.
Porteus, Beilby, *The Works of the Rt. Rev. Beilby Porteus*, 6 vols. London, 1823.
The Rambler's Magazine: or, The Annals of Gallantry, Glee, Pleasure and the Bon Ton, 1783–90.
The Ranger's Magazine: or, The Man of Fashion's Companion, 1795.
Tompkins, J. M. S., *The Popular Novel in England 1770–1800*, London, 1932.
Wilberforce, R. I., and S., *The Life of William Wilberforce*, 5 vols. London, 1838.

CHAPTER 8

The Anti-Jacobin Review; or, Weekly Examiner, 1797–8.
Aspinall, A., *Politics and the Press c. 1780–1850*, London, 1949.
Bentham, Jeremy, *The King Against Edmunds and Others*, London, 1820.
— *On the Liberty of the Press and Public Discussion*, London, 1821.
Bowles, John, *A Short Answer to the Declaration of the Friends of the Liberty of the Press*, London, 1793.
Cobbett's *Political Register*, 1802–35.
Eaton, D. I., *The Proceedings on the Trial of Daniel Isaac Eaton* [For publishing the second part of the *Rights of Man*], 1793.
Hone, William, *The Three Trials of William Hone*, London, 1818.
Hunt, James Leigh, *Autobiography*, London, 1850.
Proceedings of the Friends to the Liberty of the Press, London, 1793.
Stout, G. D., *The Political History of Leigh Hunt's Examiner*, St. Louis, 1949.
Wickwar, W. H., *The Struggle for the Freedom of the Press: 1819–1832*, London, 1925.

CHAPTER 9

Bowdler, Thomas (ed.), *The Family Shakespeare*, 10 vols. London, 1825.

Coleridge, S. T., *The Friend*, ed. H. N. Coleridge, 4 vols. London, 1844.

Johnston, Arthur, *Enchanted Ground: The Study of Medieval Romance in the Eighteenth Century*, London, 1964.

Parreaux, André, *The Publication of The Monk*, Paris, 1960.

A Proposal for Establishing a Society for the Suppression of Vice, 1801.

Praz, Mario, *The Romantic Agony*, London, 1933.

Quinlan, M. J., *Victorian Prelude*, New York, 1941.

The Rambler's Magazine: or, Fashionable Emporium of Polite Literature, 1822.

The New London Rambler's Magazine: or, Annals of Gallantry, Glee, Pleasure, and Bon Ton, 1829.

Varma, Devendra P., *Gothic Flame*, London, 1957.

CHAPTER 10

Arnstein, Walter L., *The Bradlaugh Case: A Study in Late Victorian Opinion and Politics*, Oxford, 1965.

Burnham, Edward Frederick Lawson, Lord, *Peterborough Court*, London, 1955.

Bonner, Hypatia Bradlaugh, *Charles Bradlaugh*, 2 vols. London, 1894.

— *Penalties upon Opinion*, London, 1934.

Cockshut, A. O. J. (ed.), *Religious Controversies of the Nineteenth Century*, London, 1966.

— *The Unbelievers: English Agnostic Thought 1840–1890*, London, 1964.

Cook, E. T., *Delane of The Times*, London, 1915.

Dasant, A. I., *John Thaddeus Delane*, 2 vols. London, 1908.

Dunn, Waldo Hilary, *James Anthony Froude: A Biography 1818–1856*, Oxford, 1961.

Hallam, Henry, *The Constitutional History of England*, 2 vols. London, 1846.

Ideas and Beliefs of the Victorians, London, 1949.

Stephen, J., *A Digest of the Criminal Law*, London, 1877.

Stubbs, William, *The Constitutional History of England*, 3 vols. Oxford, 1880.

Willey, Basil, *More Nineteenth Century Studies: A Group of Honest Doubters*, London, 1956.

CHAPTER 11

Auchincloss, Louis, 'The Two Ages of Thackeray', in *Reflections of a Jacobite*, London, 1961.

Bagehot, Walter, *Literary Studies*, 2 vols. London, 1879.

Brodie, Fawn M., *The Devil Drives: A Life of Sir Richard Burton*, London, 1967.

Buckley, J. H., *The Victorian Temper*, London, 1952.

Chew, S. C., *Swinburne*, Boston, 1929.

Ffrench, Yvonne, *Ouida: A Study in Ostentation*, London, 1938.

Fryer, Peter, *The Birth Controllers*, London, 1965.

Grosskurth, Phyllis, *John Addington Symonds*, London, 1964.

National Vigilance Association. Annual Reports, 1887–1926.

Nesbitt, G. L., *Benthamite Reviewing*, New York, 1934.

Pope-Hennessey, James, *Monckton Milnes: The Flight of Youth*, London, 1951.

Report of the Joint Select Committee on Lotteries and Indecent Advertisements, 1908.

Rossetti, Dante Gabriel, *Letters of Dante Gabriel Rossetti 1835–1870*, ed. O. Doughty and J. R. Wahl, 2 vols. Oxford, 1965.

Saturday Review, 1855–96.

Scott, J. W. Robertson, *The Story of the Pall Mall Gazette*, London, 1950.

Smithers, Jack, *The Early Life and Vicissitudes of Jack Smithers*, London, 1939.

Society for the Suppression of Vice. Occasional Report and Appeal, London, 1868.

Swinburne, Algernon Charles, *Letters of Algernon Charles Swinburne*, ed. C. Y. Lang, New Haven, 1959–62.

Thackeray, W. M., *The Works of William Makepeace Thackeray*, 26 vols. London, 1894.

Tillotson, Geoffrey and Kathleen, *Mid-Victorian Studies*, London, 1966.

Tillotson, Kathleen, *Novels of the Eighteen-Forties*, Oxford, 1954.

Wilde, Oscar, *The Letters of Oscar Wilde*, ed. R. Hart-Davies, London, 1962.

CHAPTER 12

Aldington, Richard, *Portrait of a Genius But . . .*, London, 1963.

Alpert, L. M., 'Judicial Censorship of Obscene Literature', *Harvard Law Review*, LII (1938), 40–76.

Brentford, William Joynson-Hicks, Viscount, *Do We Need a Censor?* London, 1929.

Brome, Vincent, *Frank Harris*, London, 1962.

Chandos, John (ed.), *To Deprave and Corrupt* . . ., London, 1962.

Dawson, Thomas, *The Law of the Press*, London, 1927.

Edelman, Maurice, *The 'Mirror': A Political History*, London, 1966.

Ellis, Havelock, *More Essays of Love and Virtue*, London, 1931.

Ernst, Morris L., and Schwartz, Alan U., *Censorship: The Search for the Obscene*, New York, 1964.

Girodias, Maurice (ed.), *The Olympia Reader*, New York, 1965.

Joyce, James, *Ulysses* (Appendices A and B, relating to the American publication of the novel), London, 1952.

Justice and International Press Institute, *The Law and the Press*, London, 1965.

Kahane, Jack, *Memoirs of a Booklegger*, London, 1939.

Kauffmann, Stanley, *The Philanderer* (The summing up by Mr. Justice Stable at the trial of Secker and Warburg in 1954 is reprinted here), London, 1957.

Lawrence, D. H., *Pornography and Obscenity*, London, 1929.

— *À Propos of Lady Chatterley's Lover*, London, 1930.

Orioli, G., *Adventures of a Bookseller*, Florence, 1937.

Radcliffe, Cyril John, Viscount, *Censors*, Cambridge, 1961.

Wertham, F., *The Seduction of the Innocent*, London, 1955.

Appendix

The following appendix consists of a collection of documents intended to illustrate various aspects of the history of literary censorship. These documents are, primarily, extracts from legislation, official reports, and books which were censored or, at least, prosecuted. A number of others, like John Morley's review of Swinburne's *Poems and Ballads* or George Moore's *Literature at Nurse*, are reprinted here as echoes of controversies provoked by unofficial censorship.

The extract from George Moore's *Literature at Nurse* appears by permission of Mr. J. C. Medley and Mr. R. G. Medley.

I am grateful to Count Potocki de Montalk for allowing me to reprint his five poems from *Here Lies John Penis*. The first authorised edition of the poems is to be published by the Frijon Press, 2 Lennox Street, Toronto 4, Ontario. It will include the French text and exact translation of Verlaine, as well as additional material by Richard Aldington, L. V. Kelly and Count Potocki de Montalk himself, who is contributing a substantial foreword.

For information relating to the case of the *R.P.S. Southern News* I am indebted to Mr. C. Wheddon and Mr. Alan Hancock.

DOCUMENTS

Appendix

REFUSAL OF THE HOUSE OF COMMONS TO RENEW
THE LICENSING ACT 1695

17 April 1695

The Commons cannot agree to the Clause marked A;

1st, Because it revives, and re-enacts, a Law which in no-wise answered the End for which it was made; the Title and Preamble of that Act being to prevent printing seditious and treasonable Books, Pamphlets, and Papers: But there is no Penalty appointed for Offenders therein; they being left to be punished at Common Law, as they may be without that Act; whereas there are great and grievous Penalties imposed by that Act for Matters wherein neither Church nor State is in any ways concerned.

2. Because that Act gives a Property in Books to such Persons, as such Books are, or shall be, granted to by Letters Patents, whether the Crown had, or shall have, any Right to grant the same, or not, at the time of such Grant.

3. Because that Act prohibits printing any thing before Entry thereof in the Register of the Company of Stationers, except Proclamations, Acts of Parliament, and such Books as shall be appointed under the Sign Manual, or under the Hand of a principal Secretary of State; whereby both Houses of Parliament are disabled to order any thing to be printed; and the said Company are empowered to hinder the printing all innocent and useful Books; and have an Opportunity to enter a Title to themselves, and their Friends, for what belongs to, and is the Labour and Right of, others.

4. Because that Act prohibits any Books to be imported, without special Licence, into any Port in *England*, except *London*; by which means the whole foreign Trade of Books is restrained to *London*,

unless the Lord Archbishop of *Canterbury*, or the Lord Bishop of *London*, shall, in Interruption of their more important Affairs in governing the Church, bestow their Time *gratis* in looking over Catalogues of Books, and granting Licenses; whereas, the Commons think, the other Ports of the Kingdom have as good Right as *London* to trade in Books, as well as other Merchandizes.

5. Because that Act leaves it in the Power either of the Company of Stationers, or of the Archbishop of *Canterbury*, and Bishop of *London*, to hinder any Books from being imported, even into the the port of *London*; for if one or more of the Company of Stationers will not come to the Custom-house, or that those Reverend Bishops shall not appoint any learned Man to go thither, and be present at the opening and viewing Books imported, the Custom-house Officer is obliged to detain them.

6. Because that Act appoints no Time wherein the Archbishop, or Bishop of *London* shall appoint a learned Man, or that one or more of the Company of Stationers shall go to the Custom-house to view imported Books; so that they, or either of them, may delay it till the Importer may be undone, by having so great a Part of his Stock lie Dead; or the Books, if wet, may rot and perish.

7. Because that Act prohibits any Custom-house Officer, under the Penalty of losing his Office, to open any Pacquet wherein are Books, until some or one of the Company of Stationers, and such learned Man, as shall be so appointed, are present: Which is impracticable; since he cannot know there are Books, until he has opened the Pacquet.

8. Because that Act confirms all Patents of Books granted, and to be granted; whereby the sole Printing of all, or most of the Classick Authors are, and have been for many Years past, together with a great Number of the best Books, and of most general Use, monopolized by the Company of Stationers; and prohibits the importing any such Books from beyond Sea; whereby the Scholars in this Kingdom are forced not only to buy them at the extravagant Price they demand, but must be content with their ill and incorrect Editions; and cannot have the more correct Copies, which are published abroad, nor the useful Notes of Foreigners, or other learned Men, upon them.

9. Because that Act prohibits any thing to be printed till licensed; and yet does not direct what shall be taken by the Licenser for such License; by colour whereof great Oppression may be, and has been, practised.

10. Because that Act restrains Men bred up in the Trade of Printing, and Founding of Letters, from exercising their Trade, even in an innocent and inoffensive Way, though they are Freemen of the Company of Stationers, either as Masters or Journeymen; the Number of

Workmen, in each of those Trades, being limited by that Act.

11. Because that Act compels Master Printers to take Journeymen into their Service, though they have no Work or Employment for them.

12. Because that Act restrains all Men, who are not licensed by the Bishop, from selling innocent and inoffensive Books, though never so useful, in any Part of *England*, except Freemen of the Company of Stationers, who may sell without such License; so that neither Church nor State is taken care of thereby; but the People compelled to buy their Freedom of Trade in all Parts of *England* from the Company of Stationers in *London*.

13. Because that Act prohibits any one not only to print Books, whereof another has entered a Claim of Property in the Register of the Company of Stationers, but to bind, stitch, or put them to Sale; and that under a great pecuniary Penalty; though it is impossible for a Bookbinder, Stitcher, or Seller, to know whether the Book brought to him were printed by the Proprietor or another.

14. Because that Act prohibits Smiths to make any Ironwork for any Printing Press, without giving Notice to . . . Company of *Stationers*, under the Penalty of 5 *l.*; whereas he may not know to what Use the Iron bespoke of him, and forged by him, may be put.

15. Because that Act prohibits printing and importing not only heretical, seditious, and schismatical Books, but all offensive Books; and doth not determine what shall be adjudged offensive Books: So that, without Doubt, if the late King *James* had continued in the Throne till this time, Books against Popery would not [sic] have been deemed offensive Books.

16. Because that Act subjects all Mens Houses, as well Peers as Commoners, to be searched at any time, either by Day or Night, by a Warrant under the Sign Manual, or under the Hand of one of the Secretaries of State, directed to any Messenger, if such Messenger shall, upon probable Reason, suspect, that there are any unlicensed Books there; and the Houses of all Persons free of the Company of Stationers are subject to the like Search, on a Warrant from the Master and Wardens of the said Company, or any one of them.

17. Because the Penalties for Offences against that Act are excessive; it being in the Power of the Judges, or Justices of the Peace, to inflict what Punishment they please, not extending to Life or Member.

Lastly, there is a Proviso in that Act for *John Streater*, That he may print what he pleases, as if the Act had never been made; when the Commons see no Cause to distinguish him from the rest of the Subjects of *England*.

Ordered, That a Message be sent to the Lords, to desire a Con-

ference upon the Subject-matter of the Amendments made by them to
the said Bill.

(Journals of the House of Commons, XI, 305–6)

AN ACT FOR THE MORE EFFECTUAL
SUPPRESSING OF BLASPHEMY AND
PROFANENESS (1698)

9 Will. III c. 35

Whereas many Persons have of late Years openly avowed and published many blasphemous and impious Opinions contrary to the
Doctrines and Principles of the Christian Religion greatly tending
to the Dishonour of Almighty God and may prove destructive to the
Peace and Welfare of this Kingdom Wherefore for the more effectual
suppressing of the said detestable Crimes Be it enacted by the Kings
most Excellent Majesty by and with the Advice and Consent of the
Lords Spiritual and Temporal and the Commons in this present
Parliament assembled and by the Authority of the same That if any
Person or Persons having been educated in or at any Time having
made Profession of the Christian Religion within this Realm shal by
writing printing teaching or advised speaking deny any one of the
Persons in the Holy Trinity to be God or shal assert or maintain that
there are more Gods than One or shal deny the Christian Religion
to be true or the Holy Scriptures of the Old and New Testament to
be of Divine Authority and shal upon Indictment or Information in
any of His Majesties Courts at Westminster or at the Assizes be thereof
lawfully convicted by the Oath of Two or more credible Witnesses
such Person or Persons for the First Offence shall be adjudged incapable and disabled in Law to all Intents and Purposes whatsoever
to have or enjoy any Office or Offices Imployment or Imploym$^{ts.}$
Ecclesiastical Civil or Military or any Part in them or any Profit or
Advantage appertaining to any of them And if any Person or Persons
so convicted as aforesaid shal at the Time of his or their Conviction
enjoy or possess any Office Place or Imployment such Office Place or
Imployment shal be voyd and is hereby declared void And if such
Person or Persons shall be a second Time lawfully convicted as aforesaid of all or any the aforesaid Crime or Crimes that then he or they
shall from thenceforth be disabled to sue prosecute plead or use
any Action or Information in any Court of Law or Equity or to be
Guardian of any Child or Executor or Administrator of any Person
or capable of any Legacie or Deed of Gift or to bear any Office
Civil or Military or Benefice Ecclesiastical for ever within this Realm

and shall also suffer Imprisonment for the Space of three Years without Bail or Mainprize from the Time of such Conviction.

PROVIDED always and be it enacted by the Authority aforesaid That no Person shall be prosecuted by virtue of this Act for any Words spoken unless the Information of such Words shal be given upon Oath before One or more Justice or Justices of the Peace within Four Days after such Words spoken and the Prosecution of such Offence be within Three Months after such Information.

PROVIDED also and be it enacted by the Authority aforesaid That any Person or Persons convicted of all or any of the aforesaid Crime or Crimes in manner aforesaid shal for the First Offence (upon his or her or their Acknowledgement and Renunciation of such Offence or erronious Opinions in the same Court where such Person or Persons was or were convicted as aforesaid within the Space of Four Months after his her or their Conviction) be discharged from all Penalties and Disabilities incurred by such Conviction Any Thing in this Act contained to the contrary thereof in any wise notwithstanding.

JOHN TUTCHIN AND THE OBSERVATOR
1702–1704

[The following passages are those quoted in the indictment at Tutchin's trial.]

Observator No. 11 Saturday, the 30th of May, 1702

At the same time we consider the French king's success in his bribery and corruption, we ought to lament the sad state of our own country which affords so many instances of treachery. If we may judge by our national miscarriages, perhaps no nation in Europe has felt the influences of French gold more than England: and worthy it is our greatest lamentation, that our dear country should be thus weakened by men of mercenary principles; when countries inferior to us in strength and riches, are secured from attempts of this nature only by the fidelity of their people. What is the reason that French gold has not affected Holland as well as England; but that their ministry is such as is entirely in the interest of their country, and altogether incorruptible? They prefer men that are knowing in their posts and are active in business: when, in England, we find out offices for men, not men for offices. And a title of honour gives a man a title to a great employment he is altogether ignorant of. By this, and by preferring of men by interest and favour, has the excise, the customs, and other branches of the revenue intolerably sunk: and by this means has the navy of England, our chief support, been hitherto perfectly bewitched. And can Lewis spend his money better, than in getting men into offices in England, who are either false, or ignorant in the business, or are his friends?

No. 23. Saturday, the 11th of July, 1702.

And this is a prerogative of singular advantage to the people of England; in that their representatives are the judges of the maladministration of their governors; that they can call them in question for the same, and can appoint such to wear the crown who are fittest for government: which they have often done, and indeed which is the privilege of all free people, who are authorised by the laws of God and nature, to chuse their own governors.

No. 19. Saturday, the 12th of June, 1703.

Take one time with another, the mismanagements of the navy have been a greater tax on the merchants, than the duties raised by parliament: we never had a better navy, but the wisdom of the managers thereof is like a bottomless pit, past finding out.

No. 20. Wednesday, the 16th of June, 1703.

What avails it a man of learning and parts, to qualify himself for the service of his country on the ocean? If he has knowledge enough to advise Neptune himself, if he has no interest, he shall have no preferment. How much does it look to our nation's disadvantage, to have men in eminent stations in the navy, who have not so much as an idea, a notion, a thought of naval affairs? To have men to superintend the building of our floating castles, who know not the nature of any part of the management? To have men employed in the victualling, who qualify themselves for that post by learning to write their names, which is indeed a post for a philosopher bred to the sea?

No. 27. Saturday, the 10th of July, 1703.

Countryman. Truly, Master Observator. I have no very good news for you; Mr. Daniel de Foe has pleaded guilty to the indictment against him, for writing and publishing, The Shortest Way with Dissenters; and he is to be sentenced to stand three times in the pillory, to pay a fine of 200 marks, and to find security for his good behaviour for seven years.

Observator. The Court could do no otherwise than convict him, upon his pleading guilty; *habemus confitentem reum* is very often the voice of courts of judicature, it is the ease of judges and juries; if Daniel de Foe was in expectation of Coleman's black box, he has found a pillory instead of it. I do not trouble my head about the custom of giving the pillory to authors, which is the punishment of bakers. You talked just now of turning author, have a care of your

334

candle; you see which is the Shortest Way with Authors; you must all enter yourselves into the regiment of Colonel Foe; the law of England directs that no man shall be fined *ultra tenementum*; and I make no question, but the justice of the court has fined Mr. Foe answerable to his estate: his security for his good behaviour for seven years, without doubt, was rationally considered, as to the legality thereof. For my part, I am only acquainted with old laws of England, the ancient birthrights and immunities of Englishmen: this I take to be the foundation of new laws.

No. 17. Saturday, the 20th of May, 1704.

Countryman. Master Observator, there is another plot against you.

Observator. Prithee, man, there is a plot against the queen, and the whole nation; is it any wonder then, that there are plots against me? The high-fliers are now plotting against every honest man in England. I will tell you more of it, the next time we meet.

Countryman. I fancy some sort of people plot against you because you endeavour to countermine their plots against the queen and nation.

Observator. You are right enough; but that shall not hinder me from detecting their designs, and from opening the people's eyes: but prithee, what plot is this?

Countryman. Why, Sir, it is a plot preparatory to your trial; and if they cannot effect this plot, I suppose you will never be tried. They insinuate into the citizens of London, that you have lately written very scandalously, maliciously and treasonably, and I do not know how many other lies, against them, the said citizens; and by this means they are minded to set your jurors against you.

Observator. This is likely enough; they will leave no stone un-turned, to suppress the truth. I understand, I should have been prosecuted by bill the last sessions, but that the high-fliers did not like the jury; nay, they say they do not like the two sheriffs, because they will not pack juries to find innocent men guilty.

DEPRAVE AND CORRUPT—SOME
PORNOGRAPHERS' VIEWS: 1683–1882

(1) *The Whore's Rhetorick* (1683)

After the disjunction, be very industrious to drive away that re-pentance, or melancholy rather, which naturally succeeds fruition. . . . It will not be amiss during this intervall, to divert him with an aery Song, or some jocular, and facetious Novel, that may remove all marks of sadness, and prepare him for a second assault. (p. 44)

Besides the Male Picture prescribed for your use, you must be stockt with others of a different nature to operate on your visitants more effectually than the similitude of your *Ganymede* could affect your self. . . . These obscene Images do produce marvellous effects towards the propagation of Love, they insinuate at every pore of the Eye an extravagant desire to gratifie the sensitive appetite, they spur Men on by an irresistible impulse towards the venereal Bed; from whence he ought at no time be suffered to come off a winner. (pp. 168 and 170)

(2) *A New Atlantis for the Year One Thousand Seven Hundred and Fifty Eight* (1758)

Having soon reached her teens, and by the means of her chamber-maid got a translation of Ovid's Art of Love, Rochester's Works, and the Memoirs of a Woman of Pleasure, all her doubts about her inward feelings vanished; she was convinced what use she was designed for, and made acquainted with the canal thro' which it was to be admitted; which, with her new-disciplined fingers, she used frequently to explore: whose capacity and wants increasing daily, one of the middle-sized dildo tribe was procured for her private amusement; through it her French maid, well skilled in such practices, would in the moment of rapture, dart a warm injection; nay, some-times artfully gird it to her loins, and act the man with her young mistress, who grown too sensible of the inefficacy of all such weak misrepresentations, was determined to enjoy the essence ere long. (pp. 52–53)

(3) *Harris's List of Covent-Garden Ladies* (1789)
    Miss W——d, No. 55, *Wells Street, Oxford Road*

Although she has not been nine months upon the *pavé de Londres* (having received a complete boarding school education, where she not only learnt to dance and speak French, but also was initiated into all the mysteries of the cyprian school, having read *les Bijoux* Indiscrets; the *Woman of Pleasure*; *Rochester's Poems*); she is *au fait de tout*. Add to this, she has often viewed with rapture all *Aretin's* postures, and longed for the practice, as well as the theory. No wonder then that she should be inclined to give delight in every possible attitude, and has no kind of objection to yield, with becoming modesty, to take a *coup à Levretta*. (p. 38)

(4) *The Cremorne. A Magazine of Wit, Facetiae, Parody, Graphic Tales of Love, etc.* No. 2 (1851, i.e. 1882).
[From the speech of the Devil in *St. Anthony Settled at Last*.]
    'Now if he was reading some book a bit naughty,

336

That would make his balls itch and his prick to feel rorty,
A good English classic, say 'praps "Fanny Hill",
Or something of that sort, I'd let him sit still'. (p. 49)

From THE FIFTEEN PLAGUES OF A MAIDEN-HEAD, LONDON, 1707

The Sixth Plague

Pox take the thing Folks call a Maiden-head,
For soon as e'er I'm sleeping in my Bed,
I dream I'm mingling with some Man my Thighs
Till something more than ord'nary does rise;
But when I wake and find my Dream's in vain,
I turn to Sleep only to Dream again,
For Dreams as yet are only kind to me,
And at the present quench my Lechery.

The Fifteenth Plague

Alas! I care not, Sir, what Force you'd use,
So I my Maiden-head could quickly lose:
Oft do I wish one skill'd in *Cupid*'s Arts,
Would quickly dive into my secret Parts;
For as I am, at Home all sorts of weather,
I skit,—as Heaven and Earth would come together,
Twirling a Wheel, I sit at home, hum drum,
And spit away my Nature on my Thumb;
Whilst those that Marry'd are, invited be
To Labours, Christnings, where the Jollitry
Of Women lies in telling, as some say,
When 'twas they did at Hoity-Toity play;
Whose Husband's Yard is longest, whilst another
Can't in the least her great Misfortune smother,
So tells, her Husband's Bauble is so short,
That when he Hunts, he never shews her Sport.
Now I, because I have my Maiden-head,
Mayn't know the Pastimes of the Nuptial Bed;
But mayn't I quickly do as Marry'd People may,
I'll either kill myself, or shortly run away.

From THE WORKS OF LUCIAN, LONDON, 1711. VOL. I.

When I came home, I very fortunately found the Maid by herself
in the Kitchen, and complemented her upon her Handiness in her
Function. To which she briskly made answer, that she was as dextrous

in Bed, as in the Kitchen. This unexpected Answer surpris'd me very much; and going up to her, to play with her, but she stepping back a little, Have a care, says she, how you come too near me, unless you have a mind to be burnt; for if I touch you but with my Finger, I shall set you all in a flame, so that neither Doctor nor Deity can cure you. I laugh'd at her Pertness and Reply; and calling her every now and then the charming Cook-maid: You little think, says she, very briskly again, what a charming Cook I am; for I can dish you up all manner of Ways, if I please; nay, and cut you as small as Herbs for the Pot. I am not unsensible, says I, what you can do; for already I find myself I know not how, but as hot withal as if I were upon a Stove. At this she burst out a laughing, saying withal, that she was a famous Witch; and if she had but set a Spell upon me, she cou'd pault me with Stones, and I shou'd never be able to endeavour an Escape from her Persecution, but kindly submit to the fascinating Torment. I was but too sensible, I told her, of the Influence she had over me, and that it was no longer in my Power to be absent from her. After some Difficulties, I brought her to Terms, and she assur'd me, as soon as ever her Mistress was in Bed, she wou'd come to me. When her Master was come home, and Supper concluded, we toasted a few Healths together; and I, pretending to be somewhat drowsie, withdrew: I was no sooner got into my Chamber, but I was surpris'd to see it all strow'd over with Roses, some loose, and others in Bundles; nay, and my Man's Bed remov'd out of the Room. When she had dispatch'd her Mistress, she came to me, and we fell to work upon an Entertainment she had prepar'd for us: Healths and Kisses went plentifully about, and in a little time we adjusted the Preliminaries of Love. We shall soon see, says she to me, whether you are the Man you brag you are; for as my name is *Palæstra*, so was I never worsted in *Cupid's* Field. I accepted the Challenge, and she undress'd, telling me, Now the Stage is clear, prove your Manhood; and if I find you a capable vigorous young Man, I'll teach you some Curiosities in these Matters; Come strip, and to it. While you exert your Courage I'll be Umpire, and will give you Directions what to do; be sure to obey my Orders. Sound the Charge (says I then), and take care that our Engagement be warm and fierce, and show equally Conduct and Gallantry. At this, she being stark naked, Come, Sir, strip, strip, and take heed to the Word of Command. Anoint your Body with those Perfumes, and Make ready. Advance my Thighs. Ground me on the Bed. Draw your Baggonet of Generation. Put it in the Muzzle of the Piece. Mount the Breach. Maintain your Ground, Push your Baggonet. Again. Again. Again. Briskly, my lad. Courage. Advance. Make good your Footing. Attack again; but preserve your Fire.

Now, now, now: Give fire! Oh, ye Gods! cry'd she, all in Rapture, how I expire in Extasie and Delight. The Fantasticalness of her Expressions made me less moved with the tumultuous Bliss, and without any Concern, when the Parly was sounded, My charming Lady, (says I to *Palæstra*) you see now how dextrous I am at my Arms, tho' you hudled over your Words of Command with so much Precipitation. At this Repremand she gave me a gentle Spat on the Cheek; You are a Rogue, Sirrah, says she; but a dear one: Take care that you never receive greater Dammage in these Engagements than what you have done from me, then you will be always eager to renew the Combat. After having compos'd herself again a little, Now, says she, I must try your Skill in another sort of Exercise, which is call'd the Kneeling Posture; with that she threw herself upon the Bed on her Knees; Now to Arms, cries she, begin your Attack in *Fossè*, in the Center, between those two Bastions; Briskly, my Lad, Push on; gain Ground upon 'em; what repuls'd! Go on again; seize the Enemy. The Counterscarp is unmann'd; lay hold of the Opportunity. If you find your self fainting, redouble your Efforts; thrust your Sword up to the Hilts, and continue it there till fresh Orders. Ah! ah! ah! ah! my Dear, cries she, now I find you are quite spent. But I cou'd not forbear Laughing, ready to split my Sides. Now, said I, to her, 'tis time that I command a little. Get up and rectifie your Disorders, and wipe my Weapon with your softer Hand; and then return it, and lull me to sleep. Thus we dallied away the Night, and I was so transported with the Huzzy, that I never reflected upon what occasion'd my Journey.

(The Ass. pp. 117–20)

From John Henry Meibomius, *A Treatise of the use of Flogging in Venereal Affairs*, London, printed for E. Curll, 1718.
[The following passages are those quoted in the indictment of Curll in 1725.]
(1) Your Father has prov'd by many Examples, how much FLOG-GING prevails in *Venereal Affairs*, which I have no occasion to respect or offend the Ears by a second Reading, although I knew a Person at *Venice*, who could not be sollicited to a *Love-Encounter*, any way but by the Blows of his Mistress's Fist (p. 16).
(2) But what you could not so readily believe upon my Affirmation was, that there are Persons who are stimulated to *Venery by Strokes of Rods, and worked up into a Flame of Lust by Blows*; and that the *Part*, which distinguishes us to be *Men*, should be Raised by the Charm of invigorating Lashes. But I will convince you, my Friend *Cassius*, that it is so, and when I have proved by the Testimony of no vulgar Authors that

there are many Experiments of the Truth of it, I shall add some Reasons and Arguments why others have conceived it, and I think it possible and practicable. I shall not now make many Words of the stinging the Parts with young Nettles for *Monytius Taventius*, in his 2d. book *of the Organs of Generations*, asserts, That if Sterility is suspected from the Shortness of the *Penis*, that the Defect may be amended, and the Part extended by the Use of that Discipline. Besides your admired Petronius prescribes the same Method to excite a languid Inaptness to Pleasure. *Eucolpio*, in the Words of the Author, says, 'That Part of my Body, in which I was formerly a very *Achilles*, was quite languid and dead, it retired, cold as it was, colder than Winter into my Belly; and cover'd with a thousand Wrinkles, and all look'd more like a Bag of Leather in the Water than a Man'. When *Enothea*, the Priestess of *Priapus* had promised him, that she would make it as stiff as a Horn, *she mixes up the Juice of Water-Cresses with Southern-wood, and besprinkles his Thighs; then she takes a Rod of young Nettles, and gently stings all the Parts from the Navel.*

But I am to give you an Account of a rougher and stronger *Flagellation*; and the first I shall cite upon this Head, is *Johannes Picus*, Count of *Mirandola*, who flourished about a Century and a half ago. He in his 3d. Book *against the Astrologers*, Chap. 27 relates this of an Acquaintance of his, 'There is now alive, says he, a man of a prodigious, and almost unheard of kind of Lechery: For he is never inflamed to Pleasure, but when he is whipt; and yet he is so intent on the Act, and longs for the Strokes with such an Earnestness, that he blames the Flogger that uses him gently, and is never thoroughly Master of his Wishes unless the Blood starts, and the Whip rages smartly o'er the wicked Limbs of the Monster. The Creature begs this Favour of the Woman whom he is to enjoy, brings her a Rod himself, soak'd and harden'd in Vinegar a Day before for the same Purpose, and intreats the Blessing of a whipping from the Harlot on his Knees; and the more smartly he is whipt, he rages the more eagerly, and goes the same pace both to Pleasure and Pain. (pp. 5–8) (3) 'It is certain upon the Oath of credible Persons, that not many Years since, there lived a Man not of a Salaciousness, resembling that of Cocks, but of a more wonderful, and almost incredible sort of Lechery; who the more Stripes he received, was the more violently hurried to Coition. The Case was prodigious, since it was a Question which he desired most, the Blows, or the Act itself, unless the Pleasure of the last was measured by the Number of the former: Besides, it was his manner to heighten the Smartness of the Rod with Vinegar the Day before it was to be used, and then to request the Discipline with violent Entreaties. But if the *Flogger*, seemed to work slowly, he flew into a Passion, and abused him. He was never contented unless the Blood sprung out, and followed the Lash; a rare Instance of a Man who went with an equal pace to Pleasure and Pain, and who, in the midst of Torture, either satisfied or excited a pleasing Titulation, and a furious itch of Lust'. We may add another too of the same Nature to these, from *Otho Brunselsius*, a famous Physician, who in his *Physical Dictionary*, under the Word *Coition*, says, 'That at *Munich*, the Seat of the Duke of *Bavaria*, there lived a Man who never could enjoy his Wife, if he was not soundly flogged to it before he made his Attempts'. I subjoin a new and late Instance, which happen'd in this City of *Lubeck*, where I now reside: A Citizen of *Lubeck*, a Cheesemonger by Trade, living in the *Millers*-Street, was cited before the Magistrates, among other Crimes, for Adultery; and the Fact being proved, he was banished. A Courtesan with whom this Fellow had often an Affair, confessed before the Deputies of the Senate, that he never could have a forcible Erection, and perform the Duty of a Man, 'till she had whipped him on the Back with Rods; and that when the Business was over, that he could not be brought to a Repetition, unless excited by a second Flogging. The Adulterer at first denied the Charge; but being seriously pressed about the Subject, he confessed the Fact (pp. 9–11).

(4)   When will the clasping *Theletusa* rise
          To my embrace with waving *Loins* and *Thighs*?

                                                                                        (p. 24)

(5)   Such luscious Songs as pierce the secret Chine,
          Tickle the Loins, and work the lustful Spine.

                                                                                        (p. 26)

(6)   When Music, and when Wine to Lust conspire,
          Provoke the Blood, and set the Loins on fire.

                                                                                        (p. 26)

(7) And in *Apuleius*, B.VIII. the *Industry of the Sides* is a Potency in Lust. 'They brought, says he, a lusty Countryman well furnished with an Industry of Sides, and a Length of Label.'

                                                                                        (p. 32)

(8)   Unruly Tumors, panting for Delight,
          Erect the Nerve, and stimulate the Fight,
          Nor cease to glow, till *Venus* often try'd
          In mirthful Pleasure *first my languid Side*.

                                                                                        (p. 33)

(9)   I have beheld the wearied Lover go
          From the fair Dame ridiculously slow,

His *Sides* all *faint*, exhausted all below.

(p. 34)

(10)   Languid and cold, he moves to work with pain,
And dribbles at the lovely Sport in vain;
When at the best, 'tis like a Stubble fir'd,
Flashes in haste, and is in haste expir'd.

(p. 52)

[Nos. 5, 6, 8, 9, 10, are translations of the following passages:
Cum carmina lumbum

(5)   Intrant, & tremulo scalpuntur ubi intima versu.

(*Persius, Satires, I, 20–1*)

(6)   Nota Bonae secreta Deae, cum tibia lumbos
Incitat, & cornu pariter vinoq; feruntur.

(*Juvenal, Satires, VI, 314–15*)

(8)   Et inquietus inguina arrigat tumor,
Neque incitare cesset, usque dum mihi
Venus jocosa molle ruperit latus.

(*Tibullus, Priapea, II, 43–5*)

(9)   Vidi ego cum foribus lassus prodiret amator,
Invalidium referens, emeritumque latus.

(*Ovid, Elegies, III, xi, 13–14*)

(10)   Frigidus in Venerem fertur frustraque laborem,
Jucundum trahit, & si quando ad praelia ventum,
Ut quando in stipulis vanus sine viribus ignis
Incassum furit, &c.

(*Virgil, Georgics, III, 97–100*)

Curll's edition of Meibomius gives both Latin and English versions of these quotations. His text of the lines from Virgil differs considerably from that normally accepted.

Frigidus in Venerem senior frustraque laborem,
Ingratum trahit, et si quando ad proelia ventum est,
Ut quondam in stipulis magnus sine viribus ignis
Incassum furit.

Nonetheless, when Conington published his translation of Virgil in 1882 these lines were omitted and there are no notes on them in his edition of the text published in 1858.]

FROM EX ORE TUO TE JUDICO, VOX POPULI VOX DEI (1719)

[When Matthews was tried and convicted of high treason, two passages from this pamphlet were quoted in the indictment. A third passage was introduced in the trial by Matthews's counsel, apparently a disastrous decision since it was a much more damning excerpt and was eagerly taken up by the Attorney-General. In the original pamphlet this passage follows immediately the first one quoted in the indictment, after the words 'to make us happy'. These are printed together here, since they form the opening of the pamphlet and the second passage in the indictment, which concludes the pamphlet, is printed as a second excerpt.]

(1) [The pamphlet begins by dismissing the allegation that the Pretender was not the legitimate son of James II.]

To all true lovers of liberty, Vox Populi, Vox Dei.

From the solemnity of the Chevalier's birth, the moral impossibility of putting an imposter on the nation after the manner pretended, and the disappointment in the attempt of proving him so, I think it's demonstration, if hereditary right be any recommendation, he hath that to plead in his favour; and all assertors of limited monarchy must allow, that ought to be preferred, if the person having it is endowed with other qualities fit to govern. And the great opinion all courts have of this prince's virtues, shews he only wants to be known by us to be admired, and that we only want the enjoyment of him to make us happy. I hope some patriot will rouse up the people to shake off this arbitrary government, and animate them with the saying of the noble Roman, who defended the Capitol,

Livy: quousque tandem, &c.

How long will you be ignorant of your strength? Count your numbers: sure you ought to fight with more resolution for liberty than your oppressors do for dominion.—Count your numbers.

(2) I will conclude with these remarks. First, That every assertor of hereditary right must be a Jacobite. 2dly, That every Whig who makes 'Vox Populi' his rule of government must be so. And, 3dly, Every assertor of limited monarchy must be so, the Chevalier being endowed with all princely virtues; so that all rights concur in him.

From JEAN BARRIN, VENUS IN THE CLOISTER, LONDON, 1724

[The following passages are those quoted in the indictment of Edmund Curll in 1725 which are taken from Curll's edition.]

(1) He spoke not one word, but leaning his head in a melancholy posture he looked upon her with eyes full of languishing, which spoke for him. After which, taking her by the hand through the grate, he said unto her with a very moving air,

'We must then change our method and love otherwise than we did before. Can you do this Virginia? For my part I can retrench nothing of my love. The rules which you prescribe me cannot be received by a true lover.'

At last he exaggerated with so much fire the excess of his passion that he entirely disconcerted her, and drew from her a promise to grant him a few days that one only thing that could make him perfectly happy. He then made her come nearer to the grate, and having made her get upon a stool of a convenient height, he conjured her to let him satisfy at least his sight, since all other liberties were forbidden. She obeyed him after some resistance, and gave him time to handle those places consecrated to chastity and continence. She on her side would also satisfy her eyes with the like curiosity and the father, who was not insensible, found easily the means to gratify her and she obtained of him what she desired with less difficulty than what he obtained from her. This was the fatal moment to them both and what our spies desired, who contemplated with a most extraordinary satisfaction the most beautiful parts of the naked body of their companion, which the father discovered to their view and handled with all the transports of a furious lover. One while, they admired one part, then another, according as the officious father turned and changed the situation of his paramour, so that while he considered her before he exposed her posteriors to their view, for her petticoats on both sides were taken up as high as her girdle.

(2) It would be malicious and ungrateful to censure the diversions of nuns and friars, for I should say to such people, Is it not true that continency is a gift of God, which He bestows gratis on whom He pleases, and of which He does not grant the bounty to any but to those whom He will vouchsafe to honour? This being supposed, He will not make those give any account of that gift who have not received it.

(3) The good father, looking very attentively upon the person who spoke to him and who was very beautiful and well made, forgot the place he was in and imagining himself to be in free conversation, so much was he transported, asked him if the young woman was handsome, what age she might be of, and how often he had to do with her. The other having answered him that he found her an accomplished beauty, that she was no more than eighteen, and that he had kissed her three times, *Ah, qual gusto, Signor*, cried he out aloud, which is to say, 'Ah, Lord, what pleasure!'

(4) As soon as Vespers were over, Dosithea, as though she had not been all this while addressing herself to Heaven, went immediately and prostrated herself in her oratory. She prayed, wept, and sighed but all to no purpose. She found herself more oppressed than ever, and in order to insult anew and with greater violence that opinionated nature, takes her discipline in hand, and pulling up her coats and smock to her very navel, and tying them about her with a girdle, she

344

had no mercy on her poor thighs and that which had caused all her sufferings, which then lay entirely bare and uncovered. This rage having lasted some time, her strength failed her by this cruel act, she had scarce so much left as to set her clothes at liberty, which exposed her more than half naked. She rested her head upon her mattress, and making reflection upon the state of poor mortals, which she called miserable and wretched, being born with such movements which they condemned, though it was impossible to repress them, she fell into a very great weariness, but it was an amorous one which the fury of her passion had caused and made this young thing taste such a pleasure which ravished her to the very skies. At this moment, nature, inciting all its forces, broke through all the obstacles which opposed its sallies, and that virginity which till then had been in prison, delivered it without any aid or succour, with the utmost impetuosity, leaving its keeper extended on the floor as a certain sign of her being discomfited.

Agnes. Ah, Lord, I wish I had been present.

Angelica. Alas, my dear, what pleasure would that have been to thee! Thou wouldst have seen that innocent half naked, her mouth smiling with those amorous, gentle contractions of which she knew not the cause. Thou wouldst have seen her in an ecstasy, her eyes half dying, and without any strength or vigour fall beneath the laws of undisguised nature, and lose in defiance to all her care that treasure, the keeping of which had cost her so much pain and trouble.

Agnes. Very well, and it is in this that I should have placed my pleasure, to have considered her thus naked and curiously to have observed all the transports that love would have caused in the moment she was vanquished.

(5) After this manner do they kiss who truly love each other, by amorously darting out their tongue between the lips of the beloved object. For my part, I find nothing in the world more sweet and delicious when one does it as one should do, and I never put it in practice but I am ravished with ecstasy and so feel all over my body an extraordinary titillation and a certain *je ne sais quoy*, which I am not able otherwise to express than only by telling thee that it is a pleasure which pours itself out with a sort of sweet impetuosity over all my secret parts, which penetrates the most profound recess of my soul, and which I have right to call the sovereign pleasure.

(6) Thou must know then that Frederick, taking the benefit of our enclosures being open, got very early into the convent disguised like a workman and, watching his opportunity, conveyed himself into Eugenia's cell after her, breaking her noviceship, where he found her stark naked, the weather being very hot. She knew him, and turning

about with a smile asked him what he wanted. He answered only, 'My dear, my life, my soul', and could say no more after these words. She put on her smock and came up to him. He immediately put his hand you may guess where. She, all surprised, asked if he was not ashamed to treat her after this manner. All this signified nothing, he answered her closely in his arms and in a languishing voice cried, 'Kiss me, my soul', which she had no sooner done but he threw her upon the mattress and ran over her breasts and other more secret parts with a thousand kisses, and then proceeded unto pleasures more particular which made her, if she was not so before, a perfect woman.

Agnes. And how came you to know all this?

Angelica. I'll tell thee. I thought I saw one of the workmen enter her cell and tipping softly along the dormitory, made up to her door, which having a large chink between the boards, so I saw what I tell you. The first thing I beheld was Eugenia all naked with Frederick sitting by her, holding in his hand . . . which extremely surprised me, imagining to myself that she could never enjoy that excess of pleasure I afterwards found she did. Said I to myself, 'Lord, what pain must poor Eugenia undergo? How is it possible he should not tear her to pieces?' These were my thoughts but I suppose he treated her very gently on account of her youth, for she was but bare fifteen. While I was thus busied in my thoughts, I heard Frederick say, 'Eugenia, my dear, turn upon your back', which after she had done, he got up and put his —— into her ——. For my part I was quite frightened when I heard her cry out as if she were in excessive pain. This gave me, as thou may'st well imagine, a great deal of uneasiness, for I did not dare to come in for fear of surprising of them, which might have had, perhaps, very ill consequences. However, a moment after I saw her move her legs and embrace her lover with both her arms, after such an extraordinary manner, and sufficiently expressed the utmost satisfaction. Frederick was no less pleased with this encounter. 'Ha', said he, 'what pleasure dost thou give me!' In short, after endeavouring to exceed each other in the amorous combat, they softly sighed and then for some small space reposed in an ecstasy.

(7) Don Grassio immediately without any ceremony embraced me after such an amorous manner, and gave me just grounds to believe that I should soon be the most happy creature living. My modesty combating with my passion made me receive his first caresses with some reluctance and inward shame, but a little after I returned them in so sensible a manner as he did not expect. Upon which, throwing off his coat, he gently laid me upon it on the floor and kissed me a thousand times, nor were his hands without employ. I received all this like a true child of Venus, and we repeated it more than once but with

a pleasure still more exquisite. He bestowed on me such kisses as would raise jealousy in the gods. Ah, how full of tenderness are these embraces, how agreeable and delicious his touches. 'Let me', said he in a trembling tone, 'Let me put my mouth between thy bubbies, and let this hand cover this mountain sacred to love and Venus, and with this other repose upon they lovely thighs.'

(8) I saw Pierrot musing, as it were in a brown study, and then staring of a sudden sent out a loud sigh and flew immediately into his little house, where he lies and keeps his books. I followed, moved by a certain curiosity to see the sense of this sudden flight, when bounding to the door which he had only put to and forgot to fasten, I saw him throw himself upon the bed and handle his plaything with a very deep sigh or two. 'Alas, poor boy,' said I to myself, 'he is without a woman. So am I without my Don Grassio.' I perceived that since he had no other conveniency that he was resolved to make use of what nature had given him. 'What,' thought I, 'shall I stand this, and see that thrown away which may be better elsewhere bestowed? No, no, if he has some occasion, I'll go and content him after a more agreeable manner.'

Agnes. And you say he is young and handsome?

Angelica. To a wonder. He is no more than one and twenty, of a middling stature, his hair of light brown and the finest in the world, his eyes very amorous and languishing, his face unexceptionable, his lips softer than the softest velvet, and his legs admirably turned: but then he kissed, Agnes—oh, I cannot express what!

Agnes. No more of your raptures, but continue your narration.

Angelica. Well, to go on regularly, after I had seen what I told you at the door, all trembling as I was, I resolved to know. But love exceeded my fear and made me enter boldly without waiting his coming to let me in.

Agnes. Indeed, I think you were very forward to one you have so little knowledge of.

Angelica. You are mistaken, I have been acquainted with Pierrot these two years. There have passed indeed some little liberties between us but he never came to the grand point. The poor boy, in the condition he was in, was more surprised than I, as not doubting but I had been an eye-witness of all the postures and gestures with which love had inspired him. I could not help smiling to see how unmoveable he sate, not being capable to move a finger. I came up to the bed-side, smiling, and he taking my hand with his left, for his right hand was not quite disengaged, 'Ah, Angelica,' said he, 'My love, my heart, what do we do!' And then drawing me to him, threw me on the bed and kissed my breasts, with eyes so soft and languishing that I no ways doubted of the consequences. Upon which I leaped up and went to secure the door and stop up all the holes. Then coming back with somewhat the air of a prude, said to Pierrot, 'I took this precaution to say something in particular to thee'. Upon which, interrogating me, he was going to put his hand . . . 'Ha! Pierrot!' said I, 'What wouldst thou do? Take away thy hand there!' But was, Agnes, all was in vain. The poor boy! And my conscience, I believe, was the first time, by the awkwardness of his manner, fell suddenly into a kind of fainting, which when I perceived I was frightened. But presently my fears were over, when I saw by an involuntary discharge of his summation, before he reached the counterscarp, his vigour lost.

Agnes. Possible disappointment indeed. Poor Pierrot!

Angelica. Say rather poor Angelica. However this did not last long. The champion rallied his forces and pushed so furiously in the attack that he gained the fort entirely with the effusion of much blood.

FROM THOMAS WOOLSTON, A DISCOURSE ON THE MIRACLES OF OUR SAVIOUR (1727)

[The following passages are those quoted in the indictment of Woolston, on which he was tried and convicted in 1729. The same passages were quoted when Astley was tried and convicted in 1746.]
(1) I. I will show, that the Miracles of Healing all manner of Bodily Diseases, which *Jesus* was justly famed for, are none of the proper Miracles of the *Messiah*, neither are they so much as a good Proof of his Divine Authority to found a Religion.

II. That the litteral History of many of the Miracles of Jesus, as recorded by the Evangelists, does imply Absurditys, Improbabilities and Incredibilitys consequently, they, either in whole or in part, were neither wrought, as they are commonly believed now a days, but are only related as Prophetical and Parabolical Narratives of what would be mysteriously and more wonderfully done by him. (pp. 3–4.)

(2) St. *Augustin* not only says, that *if we examine into Jesus's Miracles by humane Reason, we shall find he did nothing great, considering his Almighty Power, and considering his Goodness, what he did was but little*, but he tells us also, that *such Works as Jesus did, might be imputed to, and effected by magic Art.* (pp. 10–11.)

(3) Moreover History affords us Instances of Men, such as of *Apollonius Tyanaeus*, *Vespesian*, and of the *Irish Stroker*, *Greatrex*, who have miraculously cured Diseases to the Admiration of Mankind, as well as our Jesus; but if any of them, or any other greater Worker of Miracles, than they were, should withal assume to himself the Title of a Prophet, and Author of a new Religion, I humbly conceive, we ought not to give heed to him. (p. 11.)

(4) The Fathers, upon whose Authority I write, will tell such Orators, that *Jesus*, if his Miracles are to be understood in the litteral sence, did not only as foolish Things, as any Impostor could do, but very injurious ones to Mankind. I shall not here instance in the seemingly foolish and injurious things which Jesus did for Miracles, intending under the next Head to speak to some of them. But they are such, if litterally true, as our Divines do believe, as make us take him for a *Conjuror*, a *Sorcerer* and a *Wizard* rather, than the *Messiah* and Prophet of the most High God. (pp. 14–15).

(5) And so I come to speak to a

2. Second Miracle of Jesus, and that is, that of his *casting the Devils out of the Madman or Madmen, and permitting them to enter into the Herd of Swine, which thereupon ran down a Precipice and were all choaked in the Sea.*

To exorcise or cast Devils out of the Possess'd, without considering the Nature of such a Possession, or the Nature and Power of the Devil, we'll allow to be not only a kind and beneficient Act, but a great Miracle. But then, be the Miracle as great as can be imagin'd, it is no more, than what false Teachers, *Workers of Iniquity*, and even some Artists amongst the *Jews* have done before, consequently such a Work of *Exorcism* in our Saviour could be no Proof of his Divine Authority. And if there was no more to be said against this Miracle; this is enough to set it aside, and to spoil the Argument of *Jesus*'s Divine Power from it. But there are many Circumstances in the Story litterally consider'd, that would induce us to call the Truth of the Whole into Question. How came these Madmen to have their dwelling amongst the Tombs of a Burying Ground? where was the Humanity of the People, that did not take Care of them in Pitty to them, as well for the Safety of others? Or if no Chains, as the Text says, which is hardly credible, could hold them, it was possible surely as well as lawfull to dispatch them, rather than their Neighbours and Passengers should be in Danger from them. Believe then this Part of the Story who can? (pp. 31–2.)

(6) But then it's unlikely (without better Reason than at present we are apprised of) that our Saviour would permit the Devils to enter into a Herd of them to their Destruction. Where was the Goodness and Justice of his so doing? Let our *Divines* account for it, if they can. It is commonly said of our Saviour, and I believe it, that his Life was entirely Innocent, that his Miracles were all useful and beneficial to Mankind, and that he did no Wrong to any one. But how can this be rightly said of him, if this Story be litterally true? The Proprietors of the Swine were great Losers and Sufferers; and we don't read that *Jesus* made them amends, or that they deriv'd such Usage from him.

The Proprietors of the Swine, it seems, upon this Damage done them by *Jesus*, desire him to depart out of their Coasts, to prevent farther Mischief, which was gentler Resentment, than we can imagine any others would have made of the like Injury. I know not what our Divines think of this Part of the Story, nor wherefore Jesus escaped so well; but if any *Exorcist* in this our Age and Nation had pretended to expel the Devil out of one possess'd, and permitted him to enter into a Flock of Sheep, the People would have said, that he had bewitch'd both; and our Laws and Judges too of the last Age, would have made him to swing for it. (pp. 33–4.)

(7) If this Miraculous Story had been recorded of *Mahomet* and not of *Jesus*; our *Divines*, I dare say, would have work'd it up to a Confutation of *Mahometanism*. *Mahomet* should have been, with them, nothing less than a Wizard, an Enchanter, a dealer with familiar Spirits, a sworn slave to the Devil; and his *Mussulmen* would have been hard put to it to write a good Defence of him.

When our Saviour was brought before *Pilate* to be arraign'd, try'd, and condemn'd, *Pilate* put this Question to the *Jews*, saying *what evil hath Jesus done*? If both or either of the Stories above had been litterally true of *Jesus*, there had been no need of false Witnesses against him. The Merchants of the Temple were at hand, who could have sworn 'that he was the Author of an Uproar, and Riot, the like was never seen on their Market-day; that they were great Sufferers and Losers in their Trades; and, whether he or his Party had stolen any of their Goods or not, yet some were embezzled and others damag'd; and all through the outragious Violence of this unruly Fellow against Law and Authority,' If such Evidence as this was not enough to convict him of a Capital Crime; then the *Swine-Herds* of the *Gadarenes* might have deposed, how they 'believed him to be a *Wizard* and had lost two thousand Swine through his Fascinations. That he bid the Divils to go into our Cattle is not to be deny'd. And if he cured one or two of our Countrymen of a violent Possession; yet in as much as he did us this Injury in our Swine, we justly suspect him of Diabolical Practices upon both.'

Upon such Evidence as this, *Pilate* asks the Opinion of Jews, saying, *what think you*? If they all had condemn'd him to be guilty of Death, it is no wonder, since there is not a *Jury* in *England* would have acquitted any one arraign'd and Accused in the like Case.

It is well for our litteral *Doctors*, that such Accusations were not brought against *Jesus*; or their Heads would have been sadly puzzled to vindicate his Innocence, and to prove the Injustice and Undeservedness of his Death and Sufferings. (pp. 37–9.)

(8) And so I pass to a

3. Third Miracle of Jesus, and that is *his Transfiguration on the Mount*. And this is the darkest and blindest Story of the whole Gospel, which a Man can make neither Head nor Foot of; and I question whether the Conceptions of any two thinking *Doctors* do agree about it. (p. 39.)

(9) St. *Augustin* himself owns, that the whole of it might be perform'd by Magic Art; And we know, in these our Days that some Jugglers are strange Artists at the imitation of a Voice, and to make it as if it came from a far of, when it is uttered close by us; and can cast themselves too into different forms and shapes, without a Miracle, to the Surprise and Admiration of spectators. (p. 40.)

(10) Our Divines, I suppose would not have him thought such a *Posture-Master* for the whole World. (p. 41.)

(11) In short, for all the imaginary greatness of the Miracle (which there is a way to reduce and lessen) of Jesus's feeding his thousands with a few Loaves, there must be some Fascination or Enchantment (condemn'd by the Laws of the *Jews* as well as of other Nations) in the Matter; or the People, if they had stay'd one Day, would not two, much less three *to faint*, but would, especially the Women and Children have been for returning, the first Night, home. (pp. 51–2.)

(12) I will also take into Consideration the Miracle of *Jesus*'s curing *the Blind Man, for whom Eye-Salve was made of Clay and Spittle*; which Eye-Salve, whether it was balsamick or not, do's equally affect the Credit of the Miracle. If it was naturally medicinal, there's an End of the Miracle; and if it was not at all medicinal, it was foolishly and impertinently apply'd, and can be no otherwise accounted for, than by considering it, with the Fathers, as a figurative Act in Jesus.

I will also take into Consideration the several Stories of *Jesus*'s raising of the dead; and, without questioning his actual bringing of the Dead to Life again, will prove from the Circumstances of those Storys, that they are parabolical, and are not litterally to be apply'd to the Proof of Jesus's Divine Authority and Messiahship; or, for Instance, *Jesus*, when he raised *Jarius*'s Daughter from the dead, would never have turned the People out of the House, who should have been his best and properest Witnesses.

I will also Consider the Miracle of Jesus's *Cursing the Fig-Tree*, for its not bearing Fruit out of Season; which, upon the bare mention of it, appears to be a foolish, absurd, and ridiculous Act, if not figurative.

I will also consider the Journey of the Wisemen out of the East, with their (litterally) senseless and ridiculous Presents of *Frankincence* and *Myrrhe* to a new-born Babe. If with their *Gold*, which could be but little, they had brought their Dozens of Sugar, Soap, and Candles, which would have been of use to the Child and his poor Mother in the Straw, they had acted like wise as well as good Men. But what, I pray, was the Meaning and Reason of a Star, like a *Will a Whisp*, for their Guide to the Place, where the Holy Infant lay. Could not God by Divine Impulse, in a Vision or in a Dream, as he ordered their Return Home, have sent them on this important Errand; but that a Star must be taken or made out of Course to this Purpose? I wonder what Communication passed between these Wise Men and the Star, or how they came to know one anothers Use and Intention. But the Fathers shall speak hereafter farther to the senselessness of this Story litterally; and make out the Mystery and true meaning of it. (pp. 53–5.)

(13) I will also, by the Leave of our *Divines*, take again into Consideration the miraculous Conception of the Virgin *Mary*, and the Resurrection of *Jesus* from the Dead. I do believe, if it may so please our *Divines*, that *Jesus* was born of a pure Virgin, and that he arose from the Dead; but speaking too briefly, in the *Moderator*, to these two Miracles, they took Offence. I will therefore give them a Review, and speak Home to them; particularly to Christ's Resurrection, the Evangelical Story of which litterally, is such a Complication of Absurditys, Incoherences, and Contradictions, that unless the Fathers can help us to a better Understanding of the *Evangelist* than we have at present, we must of Necessity give up the Belief of it. (pp. 55–6.)

(14) In the mean Time, our Divines may go on in their own Way, if they think fit, and admire *Jesus* of old, and celebrate his Power and Praises for healing of bodily Diseases, and doing other notable Feats according to the Letter of the Evangelical Story; but I am for the spiritual *Jesus* and *Messiah*, who cures the worse Distempers of the Soul, and do's other mysterious and most miraculous Works, of which those recorded in the Evangelists are but Figure and Parable. This is the Primitive and concurrent Opinion about the true Messiah, which the Fathers universally adher'd to. Whether our *Jesus*, at this Day, be such a spiritual *Messiah* to his Church, or whether she do's not stand in need of such a one, is the Question that our Divines are to see to. But I will add here, what I believe, and shall have another Opportunity to prove, that God on purpose suffer'd or empower'd *false* as well as *true* Prophets; *bad* as well as *good* Men, such as *Apollonius*, *Vespesian*, and many others to cure Diseases, and to do other mighty Works, equal to what are litterally reported of *Jesus*, not only to defeat us of all Distinction between true and false Miracles, which are the Object of our bodily Senses, but to raise and keep up our Thoughts to the constant Contemplation of *Jesus*'s spiritual,

mysterious, and most miraculous Works, which are the Object of our Understandings, and loudly bespeak the Power, Wisdom and Goodness of God, and which are to be the absolute Demonstration of *Jesus*'s Divine Authority and Messiahship to the Conversion of *Jews* and *Infidels*.

I have no more to do at present, but, like a *Moderator*, to conclude with a short Address and Exhortation, to *Infidels* and *Apostates*, the two contending Partys in the present Controversy. And

First, to *Apostates*, I mean the Writers against the *Grounds* and *Scheme*. Whether you, *Grave Sirs*, who account your selves Orthodox *Divines*, tho' there is little but Contradiction and Inconsistency amongst you, do like the Name of *Apostates* which is given you, I much Question: But it is the properest, I could think of, for your Desertion of Primitive Doctrine about Prophecy and Miracles. I could, not improperly, have given you a worse *Title*, but I was willing to Compliment you, rather than Reproach you with this.

But setting aside the Title of *Apostates*, whether it be, in your Opinion, opprobious [sic] or not; you may plainly perceive, that I am, *Sirs*, on your side, as to the Truth of Christianity, and if you'll accept of my Assistance, for the Proof of *Jesus*'s Messiahship from Prophecy, upon the Terms of the Allegorical Scheme proposed in my *Moderator*, you shall find me your hearty Abettor. Upon the Allegorical Scheme I don't doubt, but we shall soundly drub and maul *Infidels*, and beat them out of the Field of Battle. If you, being wedded to the litteral Scheme, will not accept of my Assistance, you may go on in your own Way, and see the Event of the Controversy, which in the End will turn to your Dishonour.

You, *Sirs*, can't but be sensible, how those two great Generals, Mr. *Grounds*, and Mr. *Scheme*, with their potent Armies of Reasons, and Authorities against your litteral Prophecies, have greivously [sic] distress'd and gall'd you; and, if you don't make an honourable Retreat in Time, and seek to *Allegorists* for help, will gain a compleat Victory, and Triumph over you.

Instead of the help of *Allegorists*, you, I find, under the Disappointment of your litteral Scheme, chuse rather to have Recourse to *Jesus*'s Miracles: But what little Dependence there is upon his Miracles, in your Sense, I have in *Part* proved in this Discourse; and this I have done (give me leave repeatedly to declare it) not for the Service of your unbelieving Adversaries, but to reduce you to the good old Way of interpreting Oracles, which, upon the Testimony of the Fathers, will, one Day, be the Conversion of the *Jews* and *Gentiles*.

Whether you, *Sirs*, will be pleas'd with this short Discourse on

Christ's Miracles, I much Question. But before you put your selves into a Rage against it, I beg of you to read St. *Theophilus* of *Antioch*, *Origen*, St. *Hilary*, St. *Augustin*, St. *Ambrose*, St. *Jerome*, St. *Chrysostom*, St. *John* of *Jerusalem*, St. *Theophylact*, and other occasional ancient Pieces on one Part or other of the *Evangelists*; and you'll find, how they countenance such a Discourse as this on Miracles, and will abundantly assist me in the Prosecution of it.

I expect, *Sirs*, that some of you will be ready to rave against me for this Discourse; but this is my Comfort, that if your Passion should arise to another Prosecution of me, you can't possibly separate any of mine from the Opinions of the Fathers to ground a Prosecution on: And what Dishonour in the End will redown [sic] to Protestant and pretendedly learned *Divines* of the Church of *England* to persecute again the Fathers for primitive Doctrine, I desire you to think on.

But as I suppose you'll have more Wit, *Sirs*, than to prosecute me again for this Discourse; so I hope you'll have more Ingenuity than odiously (after your wonted manner) to represent me to the Populace, for Profaneness, Blasphemy and Infidelity. If you dislike the whole or any Part of this Discourse, appear like Men and Scholars, from the *Press* against it. Use me as roughly in Print as you think fit, I'll not take it ill.

Veniam petimus, dabimusq; vicissim.

I desire nothing more than to be furiously attack'd from the *Press*, which, if I am not much mistaken, would give me a long'd for opportunity to expose your Ignorance to more Advantage.

Be not longer mistaken, *Good Sirs*. The History of *Jesus*'s Life, as recorded in the *Evangelists* is an emblematical Representation of his Spiritual Life in the Soul of Man; and his Miracles are Figures of his mysterious Operations. The four Gospels are in no Part a litteral Story, but a System of mystical Phylosophy or Theology.

If you are resolv'd not to come into this Opinion, I beg of you again, before you break forth into a Passion, to try to vindicate the litteral Story of the three Miracles spoken to in this Discourse, *viz.* those of Jesus's *driving the Buyers and Sellers out of the Temple; Of his exorcising the Devil out of the Madman; and of his Transfiguration on the Mount*; which if you are able to defend against the Fathers and my Objections, I'll give up the Cause to you, and own my self (what I am farr enough from being) an impious Infidel and Blasphemer, and deserving of the worst Punishment. In the mean time I make bold again to assert, that the litteral Story of Christ' Life and Miracles is an absurd and incredible Romance, full of Contradictions and Inconsistencys. (pp. 59–64.)

From THE SCHOOL OF VENUS, *or*; THE LADIES' DELIGHT REDUCED INTO RULES OF PRACTICE, LONDON, 1744.

[The following extract is one of those condemned in the prosecution of 1745.]

Katy. I am so far from repenting that were it to do again, it should be my first work. What a comfort is it to love and be beloved, I am sure I am much mended in my health since I had the use of a man.

Fanny. You are more airy a great deal than before, and they that live to see it will one day find you as cunning and deep a whore as any in the nation.

Katy. Truly, cousin, I was a little shame-faced at first, but I grow every day bolder and bolder, my fucking-friend assuring me he will so well instruct me that I shall be fit for the embraces of a king.

Fanny. He is a man of his word, you need not doubt what he promises. What advantages have you now over other wenches in receiving so much pleasure, which enlivens thee and makes thee more acceptable in company!

Katy. I tell you what, since Mr. Roger has fucked me, and I know what is what, I find all my mother's stories to be but bugbears and good for nothing but to fright children. For my part, I believe we were created for fucking, and when we begin to fuck we begin to live, and all young people's actions and words ought to tend thereto. What strangely hypocritical ignorants are they who would hinder it, and how malicious are those old people who would hinder it in us young people because they cannot do it themselves! Heretofore, what was I good for but to hold down my head and sew? Now nothing comes amiss to me. I can hold an argument on any subject, and that which makes me laugh is this: if my mother chide, I answer her smartly, so that she says I am very much mended, and she begins to have great hopes of me.

Fanny. And all this while she is in darkness as to your concerns.

Katy. Sure enough, and so she shall continue as I have ordered matters.

Fanny. Well, and how goes the world with you now?

Katy. Very well, only Mr. Roger comes not so often to see me as I could wish.

Fanny. Why, you are well acquainted with him then?

Katy. Sure enough, for we understand one another perfectly.

Fanny. But did not what he did unto you at first seem a little strange?

Katy. I'll tell you the truth. You remember you told me much of the pleasure and tickling of fucking? I am now able to add a great deal

355

more of my own experience, and can discourse as well of it as any one.

Fanny. Tell me then, I believe you have had brave sport, I am confident Mr. Roger must be a good fuckster.

Katy. The first time he fucked me I was upon the bed, in the same posture you left me, making as if I had been at work. When he came into the chamber, he saluted me and asked me how I did. I made him a civil answer and desired him to sit down, which he soon did close by me, staring me full in the face, and all quivering and shaking asked me if my mother was at home, and told me he met you at the bottom of the stairs and that you had spoken to him about me, desiring to know if it were with my consent. I returning no answer, but smiled, he grew bolder and immediately kissed me, which I permitted without struggling, tho' it made me blush as red as fire for the resolution I had taken to let him do what he would do unto me. He took notice of it and said, 'What do you blush for, child? Come, kiss me again.' In doing of which he was longer than usual and thrusted his tongue into my mouth. 'Tis a folly to lie, that way of kissing pleased me, that if I had not before received your instructions to do it I should have granted him whatever he demanded.

Fanny. Very well.

Katy. I received his tongue under mine, which he wriggled about, then he stroked my neck, sliding his hand under my handerchief he handled my breasts, thrusting his hands as low as he could.

Fanny. A very fair beginning.

Katy. The end will be as good. Seeing he could not reach low enough, he pulled out his hands again and, whilst he was kissing and embracing me, by little and little he pulled up my coats 'till he felt my bare thighs.

Fanny. We call this getting of ground.

Katy. Look here. I believe very few wenches have handsomer thighs than I, for they are white, smooth, and plump.

Fanny. I know it, for I have often seen and handled them before now, when we lay together.

Katy. Feeling them, he was overjoy'd, protesting he never felt the like. In doing this his hat, which he had laid on his knees, fell off and I casting my eyes downwards perceived something swelling in his breeches, as if it had a mind to get out.

Fanny. Say you so, madam?

Katy. That immediately put me in mind of that stiff thing, which you say men piss with and which pleaseth us women so much. I am sure when he first came into the chamber 'twas not so big.

Fanny. No, his did not stand then.

356

Katy. When I saw it I began to think there was something to be done in good earnest, so I got up and shut the door, least the maid should surprise us, who was below stairs. I had much ado to get away for he would not let me stir 'till I told him it was only to fasten the door. I went and set the maid to work in the out-house, fearing she might come up and disturb us if she heard any noise. Having made all sure, I returned and he, taking me about the neck and kissing me, would not let me sit as before upon the bed but pulled me between his legs and thrusting his hand into the slit of my coat behind handled my buttocks, which he found plump, round, and hard. With his other hand he takes my right hand and, looking me in the face, put it into his breeches.

Fanny. You are very tedious in telling your story.

Katy. I tell you every particular. He put his prick into my hand and desired me to hold it. I did as he bid me, which pleased him so well that every touch made him almost expire, he guiding my hand as he pleased, sometimes on his prick, then on his cods and hair that grew about it, and then he bid me grasp his prick again.

Fanny. This relation makes me mad for fucking.

Katy. This done, says he, 'I would have you see what you have in your hand,' and so made me take it out of his breeches. I wondered to see such a damned great tarse, for it is quite another thing when it stands. He, perceiving me a little amazed, said, 'Do not be frightened, girl, for you have about you a very convenient place to receive it,' and upon a sudden pulls up my smock round about my arse, feeling my belly and thighs. Then he rubbed his prick against my thighs, belly, and buttocks, and lastly against the lips of my cunt.

Fanny. This is what I expected all this while.

Katy. Then he took me by it, rubbing both the lips of it together, and now and then plucked me gently by the hairs which grew about. Then opening the lips of my cunt he thrust me backwards, lifted my arse a little higher, put down his breeches, put by his shirt and draws me nearer to him.

Fanny. Now begins the game.

Katy. I soon perceived he had a mind to stick it in. First with his two fingers he opened the lips of my cunt and thrust at me two or three times pretty smartly, yet could not get it far in, tho' he stroked my cunt soundly. I desired him to hold a little for it pained me. Having breathed, he made me open my legs wider and with another hard thrust his prick went a little farther in. This, I told him, pained me extremely. He told me that he would not hurt me much more and that when his prick was in my cunt I should have nothing but pleasure for the pain I should endure, and that he endured a share of the pain for

357

my sake, which made me patiently suffer two or three thrusts more, by which means he got in his prick an inch or two farther. Endeavouring still to get more ground, he tortured me so as I cried out. This made him try another posture. He takes and throws me backwards on the bed, but being too heavy he took my two thighs and put them upon his shoulders, he standing on his feet by the bedside. This way he gave me some ease, yet was the pain so great to have my cunt stretched so by his great tarse. Then once more I desired him to get off, which he did. For my part, my pain was so great that I thought my guts were dropping out of the bottom of my belly.

Fanny. What a deal of pleasure did you enjoy! For my part, had I such a prick I should not complain.

Katy. Stay a little, I do not complain for all this. Presently he came and kissed me and handled my cunt afresh, thrusting his finger in to see what progress he had made. Being still troubled with a standing prick and not knowing what to do with himself, he walked up and down the chamber 'till I was fit for another bout.

Fanny. Poor fellow, I pity him: he suffered a great deal of pain.

Katy. Mournfully pulling out his prick before me, he takes down a little pot of pomatum which stood on the mantle-tree of the chimney. 'Oh,' says he, 'this is for our turn,' and taking some of it he rubbed his prick all over with it to make it go in the more glib.

Fanny. He had better have spit upon his hand and rubbed his prick therewith.

Katy. At last he thought of that and did nothing else. Then he placed me on a chair and by the help of the pomatum got in a little further, but seeing he could do no great good that way, he made me rise and laid me with all four on the bed, and having rubbed his tarse once more with pomatum he charged me briskly in the rear.

Fanny. What a bustle is here to get one poor maidenhead! My friend and I made not half this stir. We had soon done and I never flinched for it.

Katy. I tell you the truth verbatim. My coats being over my shoulders, holding out my arse I gave him a fair mark enough. This new posture so quickened his fancy that he, no longer regarding my crying out, kept thrusting on with might and main, 'till at last he perfected the breach and took entire possession of all.

Fanny. Very well, I am glad you escaped a thousand little accidents which attend young lovers, but let us come to the sequel.

Katy. It now began not to be so painful. My cunt fitted his prick so well that no glove could come straighter on a man's hand. To conclude, he was so sovereign at his victory, calling me his love, his dear, and his soul, and this while I found his tarse rub up and down in my body so that it tickled all the faculties of my cunt.

Fanny. Very good.

Katy. He asked me if I were pleased. I answered 'yes.' 'So am I,' said he, hugging me close unto him, and thrusting his hands under my buttocks he lifted my cunt towards him, sometimes handling the lips thereof, sometimes my breasts.

Fanny. This was to encourage and excite him.

Katy. The more he rubbed, the more it tickled me, that at last my hands on which I leaned failed me and I fell flat on my face.

Fanny. I suppose you caught no harm by the fall?

Katy. None, but he and I dying with pleasure fell in a trance, he only having time to say, 'There have you lost your maidenhead, my fool.'

Fanny. How was it with you? I hope you spent as well as he?

Katy. What a question you ask me! The devil can't hold it in when it is a-coming. I was so ravished with the pleasure that I was half besides myself. There is not that sweetmeat or rarity whatsoever that is so pleasing to the palate as spending is to a cunt. It tickleth us all over and leaves us half dead.

Fanny. Truly, I believe you did not believe it half the pleasure you have found it.

Katy. Truly, no. 'Tis impossible 'till one have tried it. So soon as he withdrew, I found myself a little wet about my cunt, which I wiped dry with my smock, and then I perceived his prick was not so stiff as before but held down its head lower and lower.

Fanny. There is no question to be made of it.

Katy. This bout refreshed me infinitely and I was very well satisfied. Then he, caressing and kissing me, told me what a great deal of pleasure I had given him. I answered he had pleased me in like manner. That, he said, rejoiced him more than anything. We then strove to convince one another who had the most pleasure. At last we concluded that we had each of us our share, but he still said he was the better pleased of the two because I was so well satisfied, which compliment I returned him.

Fanny. There is a great deal of truth in what you say, for when one loves another truly they are better satisfied with the pleasure they give each other than with that they themselves enjoy, which appears by a woman who if she really love a man she will permit him to fuck her, tho' she herself have no inclination thereunto, and of her own accord will pull up her smock and say, 'Get up, dear soul, and take thy fill of me. Put me in what posture you please, and do what you will with me.' And on the contrary, when the woman hath a mind to be fucked, tho' the man be not in humour, yet his complaisance will be as great towards her.

Katy. I am glad I know this, I will mind Mr. Roger of it as I see occasion.

Fanny. Therein you will do very well.

Katy. After a little pause he got up his breeches and sat down by me, told me he should be bound unto you so long as he lived, how he met you at the stairs' foot, where with your good news you rejoiced the very soul of him, for without such tidings the agony he was in for the love of me would certainly have killed him, that the love which he had so long had for me encouraged him to be doing but he wanted boldness and rhetorick to tell me his mind, that he wanted words to express my deserts, which he found since he enjoyed me to be beyond his imagination. And therefore he resolved to make a friendship with me as lasting as his life, with a hundred protestations of services he would do me, entreating me still to love him and be true unto him, promising the like on his part, and that he would have no friendship for any woman else, and that he would every day come and fuck me twice. For these compliments I made him a low curtsey and gave him thanks with all my heart. He then plucked out of his pockets some pistachios, which he gave me to eat, telling me it was the best restorative in the world after fucking. Whilst he lay on the bed, I went down to look after the maid, and began to sing to take off all suspicion. I stayed a while, devising how to employ her again. I told her I was mightily plagued with Mr. Roger and knew not how to be rid of him, yet found her out such work as assured me I should not be molested in our sport by her.

Fanny. In truth, you are grown a forward wench.

Katy. When I was got upstairs again, I shut the door and went to him, whom I found lying on the bed holding his standing prick in his hand. So soon as I came, he embraced and kissed me, making me lay my powerful hand on his prick, which did not yet perfectly stand, but in the twinkling of an eye it grew as stiff as a stake by virtue of my stroking.

Fanny. This we call rallying, or preparing to fuck again.

Katy. I now began to be more familiar with it than before and took a great deal of satisfaction with holding it in my hand, measuring the length and breadth of it, wondering at the virtue it had to please us so strangely. Immediately, he pushed me backwards on the bed, throwing up my coats above my navel. I suffered him to do what he pleased. He seized me by the cunt, holding me by the hairs thereof, then turned me on my belly to take a prospect of my buttocks, turning me from side to side, slapping my arse, playing with me, biting, tickling, and reading love lectures to me all this while, to which I gave good attention, being very desirous to be instructed in these mysteries.

360

At last he unbuttoned his breeches, putting his prick between my buttocks and thighs, which he rubbed up and down and all to show me how to act my part when we fucked in earnest.

Fanny. I am sure your person and beauty pleased him extremely.

Katy. That is not my discourse now, but he put me in a hundred postures, incunting at every one, showing me how I must manage myself to get in the prick farthest. In this I was an apt scholar and think I shall not in haste forget my lesson. At last we had both of us a mind to ease ourselves. Therefore he lay flat on the bed with his tarse upright, pulled me upon him, and I myself stuck it into my cunt, wagging my arse and saying, 'I fuck thee, my dear.' He bid me mind my business and follow my fucking, holding his tongue all this while in my mouth and calling, 'My life, my soul, my dear fucking rogue,' and holding his hands on my buttocks. At last the sweet pleasure approaching made us ply one another with might and main, 'till at last it came, to the incredible satisfaction of each party.

Fanny. This was the second bout.

Katy. Then I plainly perceived all that you told me of that precious liquor was true, and knew there was nothing better than fucking to pass away the time. I asked him who was the inventor of this sport, which he was not learned enough to resolve me, but told me the practique part was better than the theorique. So, kissing me again, he once more thrust his prick into my cunt and fucked me dog-fashion, backward.

Fanny. Oh, brave! This was the third time he fucked you.

Katy. He told me that way pleased him best because in that posture he got my maidenhead, and besides his prick this way went further in my body than any other. After a little repose he swived me again, wheelbarrow fashion as you showed me before, with my legs on his shoulders.

Fanny. This was four times, a sufficient number for one day!

Katy. This was the parting fuck. At that time in swiving me he told me he demonstrated the greatness of his affection unto me.

Fanny. I should desire no better evidence. But how long did this pastime last?

Katy. 'Twas near night before we parted.

Fanny. If you were at it less than three hours, sure his arse was on fire.

Katy. I know not exactly how long it was but this I am sure, the time seemed not long to me, and if his arse was on fire I found an extinguisher which did his business. And this, cousin, is the plain truth of what hath befallen me since last I saw you. Now, tell me, what is your opinion of it all?

Fanny. Truly, you are arrived to such a perfection in the art of fucking that you need no farther instructions.

Katy. What say you cousin?

Fanny. Why, I say you have all the terms of art as well as myself, and can now without blushing call prick, stones, bollocks, cunt, tarse, and the like names.

Katy. Why, I learned all this with more ease than you can imagine, for when Mr. Roger and I are alone together, he makes me often name these words, which amongst lovers is very pleasing.

Fanny. Incunting is when one sheathes his prick in a cunt and only thrusts it in without fucking.

Katy. But, he tells me, in company modesty must be used and these words forborne.

Fanny. In truth, when my friend and I meet, we use not half such ceremonies as does Mr. Roger and you. Tell me, therefore, what is the difference between occupying or fucking and sheathing or incunting?

Katy. Occupying is to stick a prick into a cunt and wriggle your arse 'till you spend, and truly that word expresseth it fuller than any other. Fucking is when a prick is thrust into a cunt and you spend without wriggling your arse. Swiving is both putting a prick into a cunt and stirring the arse but not spending. To incunt or insheath is the same thing and downright sticking a prick into a cunt, and bears no other denomination but prick in a cunt.

Fanny. There are other words which sound better and are often used before company, instead of 'swiving' and 'fucking', which is too gross and downright bawdery, fit only to be used among dissolute persons. To avoid scandal, men modestly say, 'I kissed her, made much of her, received a favour from her,' or the like. Now let us proceed to the first explanation which you mentioned, and 'tis as good as ever I heard in my life. I could not have thought of the like myself.

Katy. You compliment me, cousin, but I do not well know what you mean, they express fucking by so many different words.

Fanny. This is not unknown to me. For example, the word 'occupying' is proper when a man takes all the pains and labour. Incunting is called insheathing from a similitude of thrusting a knife into a sheath. But men amongst themselves never use half these ceremonies, but talk as bawdy as we women do in our gossipings or private meetings. If on one side we tell our gossips or those that we trust in our amours, 'I fuck'd with him and pleased him well,' or 'He fucked me and pleased me well,' on the other side, when they are among their companions, they say of us, 'Such a one has a plaguy wide cunt.' Another tells of a straight cunt and the pleasure he received.

'Tis ordinary for two or three young fellows, when they get together, to give in their verdicts upon all the wenches that pass by saying among one another, 'I warrant you that jade will fuck well. She looks as tho' she lacked it. She hath a whorish countenance.'

(*The School of Venus.* pp. 47–68)

FROM THE FREE ENQUIRER (1761)

[Peter Annett was tried and condemned for blasphemous libel in 1763 on the evidence of passages from the *Free Enquirer* Nos. 3–9. The passages which follow here are all those which the indictment quotes from Nos. 3–5 of the periodical.]

The Free Enquirer, No. 3. Saturday, 31 October 1761.

(1) By the description and character *Moses* gives us of God, the character of *Moses* himself may be known.

After God had made man, he placed him in a garden, upon the fruit whereof he was to live: but he was forbad to eat the fruit of one tree in particular, which was called the tree of knowledge of good and evil: on pain of dying the same day.

There was in the same garden a serpent, who knew the properties of that tree, (by experience, no doubt, for how could he otherwise know them) and that the fruit thereof was not mortal; for so he told Mrs. *Adam*: and added, that God knew otherwise than what he told her husband. Said he, I assure you, ye shall not die; that day ye eat thereof, your eyes shall be opened, and ye shall be as the Gods are, knowing good and evil. And so it happened; not as God spoke, but as the serpent spoke! The woman and her good man did eat, but did not die thereupon. The eyes of them both were opened, they saw they were naked, which they knew not before, and God himself confessed *behold the man is become like one of us* (Gods) *to know good and evil. And now lest he put forth his hand and take also of the tree of life, and eat and live for ever* he drove him out of the garden, and set cherubs for sentinels, with flaming swords to guard the tree of life. From whence it appears, that this God was a jealous God towards man, and lest he, having the knowledge of a God, should live, like one, if he eat of the tree of life—*therefore lest man should put forth his hand, and take of the tree of life and eat and live forever. Therefore the Lord God sent him forth from the garden of Eden.* The God of *Moses*, who had before made the world in six days, and by a council of Gods made man; though he had surveyed every day's work as it went on, and pronounced it all very good, day by day, and blessed the whole. Yet after man had acquired the knowledge of good and evil, and saw with his own eyes; his God (according to *Moses*) was so enraged, that he cursed the serpent, the woman, the man, and all the earth; and put enmity into the man and into the serpent, and perpetuated the same envious nature between the mankind and the serpent kind, which should induce them to bruise and spitefully to injure each other.—All this was occasioned because the parents of mankind resolved to know good from evil; and to see for themselves. Thus tyrannical, thus wrathful, and thus revengeful, does *Moses* represent the all-beneficent God to be.

Moses allows of more gods than one; for though *Israel* was to worship only their own God, and have nothing to do with other Gods, they were not to revile them; for that would argue infidelity; and all priests love idolaters better than infidels: for a stupid idolater may be brought from one superstition to another; but an infidel despises them all. *Moses*, as was before observed, allows of more gods than one. *Elohim* signifies gods in the plural number. Whenever, therefore, *Elohim* is mentioned you are to understand a synod or council of gods. Thus, *God said, let US make man.* Here was a council called upon this grand affair, for to speak to himself would have been preposterous. *And the Lord God said, behold the man is become like one of US to know good and evil.* Whom did God council with, and take to his assistance, when he said, *let US make man, after our image, in our likeness*: or to whom did he compare himself, when he said, *the man is become like one of US*? Not to angels, they were his creatures, and had no more knowledge than what he gave them. It must be to his associate gods or the expressions are absurd.

Before *Adam* was turned out of the garden of *Eden*, God used to take a walk in it in the cool of the day, and converse with him as a man: for all *Moses*'s gods were in the form of man, though perhaps not male or female. *Let us make man in our image after our likeness.*

The doctrine of God's being in the form of man, seems to be maintained in the New Testament, *Phil.* ii. 6. The writer speaking of Christ Jesus saith, *he was in the form of God;* and *Heb.* i. 3. that the son was *the express image of his person*. But I hope this is to be ascribed to the ignorance of translators, blunders of copyers, or insertions of interpolators.

(2) But further; that the God of *Moses*, of *Abraham, Isaac*, and *Israel*, appears to be a finite personal God, in form of man, is further evident in *Gen.* xvii. 1. When *Abraham* was ninety-nine years old, the Lord appeared to him, and said, *I am the Almighty God*. Was he not then the Almighty God? or did he lie unto his servant *Abraham*? or does the historian lie, who tells us, *Abraham fell on his face, and God talked with him*?

As this God's person was finite, so was his sight, as I observed before; for *Gen.* xi. when men conspired to build a tower, whose top might reach to heaven, *the Lord came down to see the city and the tower which the children of men builded*. But if he could have seen it from above, he need not have come down to see it; and lest they should get to heaven that way, he confounded their speech, for he saw nothing could restrain them from doing what they intended.

(3) Was it the will of *Moses*'s God to keep mankind in ignorance, lest man should know more than God, and rebel? or did keeping them ignorant make them wicked? for we find *Gen.* vi. *it repented the Lord that he had made man, and it grieved him at his heart*. May it not hence be inferred, that he knew not how his workmanship would turn out; and that he was disappointed in his expectations? For he that knows what will be the event of his own act beforehand, can never repent after it is done, because he would regulate his proceedings so as to prevent any cause of grief for doing it; and repentance on account of disappointment can only be the effect of mistaken conduct and ill founded expectation.

The God of *Moses* was also subject to be tired, and to want rest and refreshment: for after he had been working six days, in making the world, he rested a whole day and was refreshed. *Ex.* xxxi. 17. therefore he blessed the seventh day and considered poor labouring men, ordaining it a day of rest for them too, that they might be refreshed by rest as he had been. This indeed betokened a feeling pity in this case, but what pity had he on the whole world, when he saved only *Noah* and his family out of it, and did not attempt to mend it, but resolved to drown it? Could he not repair his own work? would it not have been far better to do so, then to have destroyed it? But he had not then a *Moses* to mollify his anger, as when he would have destroyed all *Israel* upon their affronting him with a golden calf; and again, when the spies disheartened the people from attempting to conquer the land which the Lord promised to give them. In *Noah*'s time, to make men better, God is said to have destroyed them, and to have sowed the earth again with the same seed; which, as soon as it grew again, produced the same fruit! and after he found that all the evils in the world arose from his cursing it, he at last, when he smelt the grateful savour of *Noah*'s sacrifice, resolved to curse it no more; as he found all things, as well as man, being cursed, evil was natural to them; *the imagination of his heart being evil from his youth*. If the curses had been washed away by the flood, there might have been some hopes that man and the earth might possibly become better; but we see they were not; for the serpent goes upon his belly still, woman still finds pain in bringing forth children, and poor men still eat their bread by the sweat of their brow: the earth brings forth thorns and thistles still, and so things are like to go on till they altogether make one common and general bonfire.

(4) All these citations from the writings of *Moses*, which are a necessary introduction to his life, are corroborating evidences, that *Moses* taught the people, who were under his discipline, contemptible and false notions of the deity: therefore they discover to us that all his pretentions to familiarity with God, and of receiving his laws from Heaven, were calculated to govern an ignorant multitude, and to keep them in a state of subjection, under the rod of authority; but could not have a natural tendency to make them a wise and good people.

The Free Enquirer, No. 4. Saturday, 7 November 1761.

(1) When he was grown up, the princess adopted him for her son, called him *Moses*, which signifies one drawn out, or taken up, i.e. a foundling: and gave him a princely education, in all the learning in *Egypt*, then a very polite nation. Thus the tenderness of the princess ignorantly nourished a viper, destined to gnaw the vitals of *Egypt*. *Moses* was brought up in the best way of acquiring the utmost knowledge that *Egypt* could give, or he receive; which enabled him to be a profound politician, a great naturalist, and a skilful *magician*: which latter art was in great esteem at that time in *Egypt*, and some think he was admitted into the order of their priests, and consequently into the secrets of priestcraft; by which advantage he was qualified for what he afterward undertook. His education fed his ambition, which, with revenge, appear to have been the reigning passions of this *meekest* of men!

(2) It was by the side of a desert, through which he afterwards led the *Hebrews* to a new settlement, that he kept the flock of Jethro his father-in-law. No doubt, in the many years he had lived there, he had well surveyed all the parts about it, made himself thoroughly acquainted with the conveniency of *Mount Sion*, and the nature of the *Red Sea*. Here it was that he contrived the plot; here the plan was laid, which he afterwards successfully effected, of raising his name to the highest dignity, of being the deliverer, and prince of his people, their law-giver, and their deputy God. Here then we leave him, contemplating how to bring his purpose to pass, which he revealed to his father *Jethro*, the old priest of *Midian*, and had his encouragement and advice in the affair. There is no doubt to be made, but he kept a correspondence with his brother *Aaron*, and sister *Miriam*, in *Egypt*, by whom he might now receive information that he might be sure to find his nation ready for a revolt, if he could but open the way.

The Free Enquirer, No. 5. Saturday, 14 November 1761.

(1) The story goes that after the death of the King, who, as *Moses*

feared, would put him to death, for the murder he had committed in *Egypt*, *Moses* led the flock of *Jethro*, his father-in-law, the Priest of *Midian*, on the back side of the desert, by mount *Horeb*; here the Lord appeared to him to send him into *Egypt*. The waiting so long for an opportunity, makes it seem as if the Lord was fearful of sending him before; and that a miraculous power is not to be depended on, when the miracle-worker's life is in danger: for it is worthy of remark, that all those whom fame reports to have been great miracle-workers, when their persons have been in danger, never depended for safety on their miraculous power, though they pretended to be possessed of power supernatural.

Hard by *Mount Horeb*, the angel of the Lord (it is said) appeared unto *Moses* in, or as, a flame of fire *out of the midst of a bush*, or in a bush; *and he looked, and behold the bush burned with fire, and the bush was not consumed.* By the way, the bush did not burn; for if it had, it would have been consumed. *Moses* looked upon it some time, and seeing the bush remained as at first, went near to observe it more perfectly. As he went on, we read, that *God called to him out of the midst of the bush*, or, a voice seemed to come from the bush; where observe, that which was before thought to be an *angel*, is exalted to a *God*; and if the voice, or the history that relates it, said true, it was THE GOD OF ISRAEL. The voice called MOSES! MOSES! He answered, *Here am I*; he might have said, *I am coming.* Not so hasty—The voice called to stop his coming. *Draw not nigh hither*; stand still and pause. Sacred things are not to be pried into and too closely examined with carnal eyes, or common sense; that would reveal, and consequently unsanctify the plot.

(2) After the King of *Egypt*, whom *Moses* feared, was dead; Moses declares himself to be invested with a commission from God to deliver the *Israelites* from their bondage. The Lord is not said to have come down to see and hear their cry before, and to have taken notice of it: for *Moses* had no dependence that miracles would have broke his halter.

After *Moses* had received his commission from his God, he asked him (it is said) in what name he should deliver his message? and God said, I AM THAT I AM, which seems to mean no more than I AM WHAT I AM. Tell them I AM hath sent me to you, which commentators will have to signify existence, and therefore this was the very God; but it appears to signify no more than, *I am what I told you before*; for he afterwards relinquishes this name *I AM*, for the former, as what they would better understand. *Tell them, the Lord God of your fathers, of Abraham, Isaac, and Jacob hath sent me to you. This is my name for ever, and my memorial unto all generations.*

And at the latter part of this commission, to shew how worthy it is to be a commission from God, he says, *And I will give the people favour in the sight of the Egyptians; and it shall come to pass, that when ye go, ye shall not go empty; but every woman shall borrow of her neighbour, and that of her that sojourneth in her house, jewels of silver, and jewels of gold, and raiments; and ye shall put them upon your sons, and upon your daughters; and ye shall spoil the Egyptians.* A very pretty contrivance for God truly, whereby it is tolerably evident that *it was* the God of *Moses* that commanded it! That his people might have wherewith to subsist in their journeyings, they were to impose on the credulity of their good-natured neighbours and lodgers, break their faith with them, and rob them deceitfully under the name of borrowing! Are these things worthy the commission of the God of truth? if they are, they are miracles indeed!

Moses seeming to fear that God was about to send him on an unsuccessful attempt, and to tell the people a story they would not believe; therefore some proof was necessary to claim attention. This God then told him how to perform three cunning tricks, as proofs of his mission: *viz.* to turn a stick into a serpent, and the serpent into a stick again; to make his hand seem leprous in an instant, and in an instant well again; also to pour water on the ground, and so poured to look like blood. But it may be supposed his father-in-law, the priest of *Midian*, was capable of teaching him such feats as these; and as priests in those times were conjurors and fortune-tellers, *Moses* sure was not so dull as to serve him forty years after being previously qualified in all the learning of *Egypt*, and remain ignorant of the current practices of his profession.

Moses made several excuses, as being unwilling to go: nothing like pretended modesty makes an ambitious man seem worthy of the honour his soul thirsts to obtain. Here the historian shews his art in his representation of *Moses*. But these excuses at last made the Lord angry, and he ordered him to join his brother *Aaron* with him to be his speaker. An artful association! that *Aaron* might be an assistant in miracle working, and carrying on the plot. *Moses* was to be a God, and *Aaron* his prophet. So with *Moses*'s head-piece, and *Aaron*'s tongue, the deep design is attempted in a regular and well digested manner; that neither the King nor the Court might perceive the drift of it before it was effected.

Moses, after asking leave of his father-in-law, (so said, perhaps, that the father might not appear to be concerned) he essayed to go into *Egypt* with his wife and sons, setting them upon asses. And he was further commissioned to *say unto Pharaoh, Israel is my son, even my first-born. And I say unto thee let my son go, that he may serve me:*

and if thou refuse to let him go, behold I will slay thy son, even thy first-born. This appears to be an after-thought, that the Lord and *Moses* may be excused for destroying all the first-born in *Egypt*. Or as the next words are, *And it came to pass, by the way in the inn, that the Lord met him, and sought to kill him.* It looks as tho' the Lord met *Pharaoh*'s first-born son in the inn, and would have killed him, which would not have been fair, before *Moses* had delivered his message to *Pharaoh*; and the Lord had known whether *Pharaoh* would let *Israel* go or not. It does not appear wherefore the Lord came to the inn. Had he been toiling? or was he on a journey, and put in there to refresh himself? Is not this a horrid diminution of the majesty of God? does it not plainly appear, that the God of *Moses* was in the form of man, as well as the God of *Muggleton*? This God likewise behaved strangely in the inn; he was going to kill somebody, though it is difficult to understand who.

(3) *Egypt* being a very superstitious nation; the only method was to pretend a commission from the God of the *Hebrews*, to prevail on the King to give them a respite two or three days to worship their God; and to be able to confirm this commission by prodigies, *Moses* and *Aaron* had a few tricks to begin with ready at hand, and they were dexterous in performing them whenever they pleased. For *Egypt* being full of religion, was full of revelations and miracles; so that the proof of a revelation was the working of a miracle, and by such works was any new Godship confirmed, and made the object of veneration and worship. But when two Gods set their wits against each other, he was to be preferred, who proved to be most powerful in miracle-working.

(4) *Moses*, we read, went and made his complaints to the Lord, and told him, that, by the message he had sent him with, he had done his people more harm than good. But his God renewed his promise of giving them a plentiful country to comfort him, and repeated his charge. This is only the dressing up the relation to make it appear something singular and wonderful. They had not yet shewn their skill to *Pharaoh* in a miraculous manner, because he had not yet called for a miracle to prove their mission. But the next time they appeared before the King, they shewed their dexterity in turning *Aaron*'s conjuring wand into a serpent. The King's conjurors being called for, shewed the King that they could do the same; only the history says, that *Aaron*'s rod swallowed up their rods: that might be, it remained longer a serpent after all theirs had done wriggling; for the *Hebrews* generally expressed themselves in figures, which are not to be literally taken. But this explanation is to account some way for the expression, supposing there was something like truth in the

history. We do not read that the trick of making his hand leprous was shewn the King, perhaps it was too mean a miracle to be done before him and his magicians. And as the King saw nothing extraordinary in *Moses*'s miracles, he refused to let *Israel* go.

(5) *Pharaoh* is to be diverted with tricks and sleight of hand, until a fit opportunity to execute the plot appears. And God is made to play with *Pharaoh*, to divert himself, as it were, with tormenting him before he kills him; as a cat does with a mouse. He orders him to let his people go, threatens if he does not, and brings plagues upon him according to his threatenings, yet every time professes to harden his heart that he might not let them go, until he had plagued him as long as he pleased! nay until he had done all the wonderful things he could do, to shew himself worthy of such a people! and at last, that the people might be worthy of such a God; every woman was to borrow of her neighbour and of her lodger jewels of silver and of gold, and raiments, to make off with them, and choose those who confided in their honesty. What is it the *profession* of religion cannot sanctify? What better cloak to cover any scheme, and what more powerful pretence than that of supernatural revelation, which bears down and subverts the laws of moral good and evil, by stopping the mouth of contradiction.

JOHN WILKES, THE NORTH BRITON, No. XLV,[x] Saturday, 23 April 1763 Genus ORATIONIS *atrox, & vehemens*, cui opponitur *lenitatis & Mansuetudinis*. CICERO.

"*The King's Speech* has always been considered by the legislature, and by the public at large as the *speech of the Ministers.*[y] It has

---

[x] The passages included within the inverted commas are the *only* passages to which any objection is made in the INFORMATION filed in the *King's-Bench* by the *Attorney-General* against the publisher Mr. George Kearsly.

[y] Anno 14 G.II. 1740. Duke of Argyle.
The King's Speech is always, in this House, considered as the Speech of the Ministers.
—LORDS Debates, vol. 7, p. 413.
    Lord Carteret.
When we take his Majesty's Speech into consideration, though we have heard it from his own mouth, yet we do not consider it as his Majesty's Speech, but as the speech of his Ministers. p. 425.
    Anno 7 G.II. 1733. Mr Shippen.
*I believe it has always been granted, that the speeches from the Throne are the compositions of ministers of state; upon that supposition we have always thought ourselves at liberty to examine every proposition contained in them; even without doors people are pretty free in their marks upon them: I believe no Gentleman here is ignorant of the reception the speech from the throne, at the close of the last session, met with from the nation in general.—*COMMONS Debates vol. 8, p. 5.
    Anno 13 G. II. 1739. Mr. Pulteney, now Earl of Bath.

regularly, at the beginning of every session of parliament, been referred by both houses to the consideration of a committee, and has been generally canvassed with the utmost freedom, when the minister of the crown has been obnoxious to the nation. The ministers of this free country, conscious of the undoubted privileges of so spirited a people, and with the terrors of parliament before their eyes, have ever been cautious, no less with regard to the matter, than to the expression of *speeches*, which they have advised the sovereign to make from the throne, at the *opening* of each session. They well knew that an* honest house of parliament, true to their trust, could not fail to detect the fallacious arts, or to remonstrate against the daring acts of violence committed by any minister. The speech at the *close* of the session has ever been considered as the most *secure* method of promulgating the favourite court-creed among the vulgar; because the parliament, which is the constitutional guardian of the liberties of the people, has in this case no opportunity of remonstrating, or of impeaching any wicked servant of the crown."

"This week has given the public the most abandoned instance of ministerial effrontery ever attempted to be imposed on mankind. The *minister's speech* of last Tuesday is not to be paralleled in the annals of this country. I am in doubt whether the imposition is greater on the sovereign or on the nation. Every friend of his country must lament that a prince of so many great and amiable qualities, whom England truly reveres, can be brought to give the sanction of his sacred name to the most odious measures, and to the most unjustifiable, public declarations, from a throne ever renowned for truth, honour, and unsullied virtue." I am sure all foreigners, especially the king of Prussia, will hold the minister in contempt and abhorrence. He has made our sovereign declare, *My expectations have been fully answered by the happy effects which the several allies of my crown have derived from this salutary measure* of the definitive treaty. *The powers at war with my good brother, the king of Prussia, have been induced to agree to such terms of accommodation as that*

---

* The House of Commons in 1715 exhibited *Articles of impeachment of high treason, and other high crimes and misdemeanours against* Robert *Earl of* OXFORD, *and Earl* MORTIMER. Article 15 *is for having corrupted the sacred fountain of truth, and put falshoods into the mouth of Majesty, in several speeches made to parliament.* See the Journal of the House of Commons, Vol. XVIII, Page 224.

His Majesty mentions heats and animosities. Sir, I do not know who drew up this speech; but whoever he was, he should have spared that expression: I wish he had drawn a veil over the heats and animosities that must be owned ONCE *subsisted upon this head;* for I AM SURE NONE NOW SUBSIST. Vol. II, p. 96.

great prince has approved; and the success which has attended my
negotiation, has necessarily and immediately diffused the blessings of
peace through every part of Europe. The infamous fallacy of this
whole sentence is apparent to all mankind: for it is known, that the
king of Prussia did not barely *approve*, but absolutely *dictated*, as
conqueror, every article of the terms of peace. No advantage of any
kind has accrued to that magnanimous prince from *our negotiation*,
but he was basely deserted by the *Scottish* prime minister of *England*.
He was known by every court in Europe to be scarcely on better
terms of friendship *here*, than at *Vienna*; and he was betrayed by us
in the *treaty of peace*. What a strain of insolence, therefore, is it in
a minister to lay claim to what he is conscious all his efforts tended to
prevent, and meanly to arrogate to himself a share in the fame and
glory of one of the greatest princes the world has ever seen. The King
of *Prussia*, however, has gloriously kept *all* his former *conquests*, and
stipulated security for his allies, even for the *elector of Hanover*. I
know in what light this great prince is considered in Europe, and in
what manner he has been treated here; among other reasons perhaps,
for some contemptuous expressions he may have used of the *Scot*:
expressions which are every day echoed by the whole body of *Englishmen* through the southern part of this island.

The *Preliminary Articles of Peace* were such as have drawn the
contempt of mankind on our wretched negotiators. All our most
valuable conquests were agreed to be restored, and the *East-India
company* would have been infallibly ruined by a single article of this
fallacious and baneful negotiation. No hireling of the minister has
been hardy enough to dispute this; yet the minister himself has made
our sovereign declare, *the satisfaction which he felt at the approaching
re-establishment of peace upon conditions so honourable to his crown,
and so beneficial to his people.* As to the *entire approbation* of parliament, which is so vainly boasted of, the world knows how that was
obtained. The large debt on the *Civil List*, already above half a year
in arrear, shews pretty clear the transactions of the winter. It is,
however, remarkable, that the minister's speech dwells on the *entire
approbation* given by parliament to the *Preliminary Articles*, which I
will venture to say, he must by this time be ashamed of; for he has
been brought to confess the total want of that knowledge, accuracy
and precision, by which such immense advantages, both of trade and
territory, were sacrificed to our inveterate enemies. These gross
blunders are, indeed, in some measure set right by the *Definitive
Treaty*; yet the most important articles, relative to *cessions, commerce*,
and the FISHERY, remain as they were, with respect to the *French*.
The proud and feeble *Spaniard* too does not RENOUNCE, but

only DESISTS *from all pretensions, which he may have formed, to the right of Fishing* . . . where? Only *about the island of* NEW-FOUNDLAND . . . till a favourable opportunity arises of *insisting* on it, *there, as well as elsewhere.*

"The minister cannot forbear, even in the *King's Speech*, insulting us with a dull repetition of the word *oeconomy*. I did not expect so soon to hear that word again, after it had been so lately exploded, and more than once by a most numerous audience, *hissed* off the stage of our *English* theatres. It is held in derision by the *voice of the people*, and every tongue loudly proclaims the universal contempt, in which these empty professions are held by *this* nation. Let the public be informed of a single instance of *oeconomy*, except indeed in the household." Is a regiment, which was completed as to its complement of officers on the *Tuesday*, and broke on the *Thursday*, a proof of *oeconomy*? Is the pay of the *Scottish Master Elliot* to be voted by an *English* Parliament, under the head of *oeconomy*? Is this, among a thousand others, one of the convincing proofs of a *firm resolution to form government on a plan of strict oeconomy*? Is it not notorious, that in the reduction of the army, not the least attention has been paid to it? Many unnecessary expences have been incurred, only to increase the power of the crown, that is, to create more lucrative jobs for the creatures of the minister? The *staff* indeed is broke, but the discerning part of mankind immediately comprehended the mean subterfuge, and resented the indignity put upon so brave an officer as marshal *Ligonier*. That step was taken to give the whole power of the army to the crown, that is, to the minister. Lord *Ligonier* is now no longer at the head of the army; but lord Bute in effect is; I mean that every preferment given by the crown will be found still to be obtained by *his* enormous influence, and to be bestowed only on the creatures of the *Scottish* faction. The nation is still in the same deplorable state, while *he* governs, and can make the tools of *his* power pursue the same odious measures. Such a retreat, as he intends, can only mean the personal indemnity, which, I hope, guilt will never find from an injured nation. The negotiations of the late inglorious *peace* and the *excise*, will haunt him wherever he goes, and the terrors of the just resentment which he must be sure to meet from a brave and insulted people, and which must finally crush him, will be for ever before his eyes.

"In vain will such a minister or the foul dregs of his power, the tools of corruption and despotism, preach up in *the speech that spirit of concord and that obedience to the laws, which is essential to good order*. They have sent the *spirit of discord* through the land, and I will prophesy, that it will never be extinguished, but by the extinction of their power. Is the *spirit of concord* to go hand in hand with the PEACE and EXCISE, through this nation? Is it to be expected between an insolent EXCISEMAN, and *a peer, gentleman, freeholder*, or *farmer*, whose private houses are now made liable to be entered and searched at pleasure? *Gloucestershire, Herefordshire*, and in general all the *cyder* countries, are not surely the *several counties* which are alluded to in the *speech*. The *spirit of concord* hath not gone forth among them, but the *spirit of liberty* has, and a noble opposition has been given to the wicked instruments of oppression. A nation as sensible as the *English*, will see that a *spirit of concord* when they are oppressed, means a tame submission to injury, and that a *spirit of liberty* ought then to arise, and I am sure ever will, in proportion to the weight of the grievance they feel. *Every* legal *attempt of a contrary tendency* to the *spirit of concord* will be deemed a justifiable resistance, warranted by the *spirit of the English constitution.*"

"A despotic minister will always endeavour to dazzle his prince with high-flown ideas of the *prerogative* and *honour* of the *crown*, which the minister will make a parade of *firmly maintaining*. I wish as much as any man in the kingdom to see *the honour of the crown maintained* in a manner truly becoming *Royalty*. I lament to see it sunk even to prostitution. What a shame was it to see the security of this country in point of military force, complimented away, contrary to the opinion of Royalty itself, and sacrificed to the prejudices and to the ignorance of a set of people, the most unfit, from every consideration, to be consulted on a matter relative to the security of the house of *Hanover*." I wish to see the honour of the *crown* religiously asserted with regard to our allies, and the dignity of it scrupulously maintained with regard to foreign princes. Is it possible such an indignity can have happened, such a sacrifice of *the honour of the crown of England*, as that a minister should already have kissed his majesty's hand on being appointed to the most insolent and ungrateful court in the world, without a previous assurance of that reciprocal nomination which the meanest court in Europe would insist upon, before she proceeded to an act otherwise so derogatory to her honour? But *Electoral Policy* has ever been obsequious to the court of *Vienna*, and forgets the insolence with which *Count Colloredo* left England. Upon a principle of *dignity* and *oeconomy*, lord *Stormont*, a *Scottish* peer of the loyal house of *Murray*, kissed his majesty's hand, I think, on Wednesday in the *Easter* week; but this ignominious act has not yet disgraced the nation in the *London Gazette*. The ministry are not ashamed of doing the thing in private; they are only afraid of the publication. Was it a tender regard for the honour of the late king, or of his present majesty, that invited to court *lord George Sackville, in these first days of peace,* to share in the general satisfaction, which all good courtiers received in the indignity offered to Lord *Ligonier,* and on the advancement of —? Was this to shew *princely* gratitude to the eminent services of the accomplished general of the house of *Brunswic,* who has had so great a share in rescuing *Europe* from the yoke of *France;* and whose nephew we hope soon to see made happy in the possession of the most amiable princess in the world? Or is it meant to assert the honour of the *crown* only against the united wishes of a loyal and affectionate people, founded in a happy experience of the talents, ability, integrity, and virtue of those, who have had the glory of redeeming their country from bondage and ruin, in order to support, by every art of corruption and intimidation, a weak, disjointed, incapable set of — I will call them anything but *ministers*—by whom the *Favourite* still meditates to rule this kingdom with a rod of iron.

The *Stuart* line has ever been intoxicated with the slavish doctrines of the *absolute, independent, unlimited* power of the crown. Some of that line were so weakly advised, as to endeavour to reduce them into practice: but the *English* nation was too spirited to suffer the least encroachment on the antient liberties of this kingdom. 'The *King of England* is only the first magistrate[1] of this country; but is invested by law with the whole executive power. He is, however, responsible to his people for the due execution of the royal functions, in the choice of ministers, &c. equal with the meanest of his subjects in his particular duty.' The personal character of our present amiable sovereign makes us easy and happy that so great a power is lodged in such hands; but the *favourite* has given too just cause for him to escape the general odium. The *prerogative* of the crown is to exert the constitutional powers entrusted to it in a way not of blind favour and partiality, but of wisdom and judgment. This is the spirit of our constitution. The people too have their *prerogative,* and I hope the fine words of D R Y D E N will be engraven on our hearts.

Freedom *is the English Subject's* Prerogative.

JOHN WILKES AND THOMAS POTTER, AN ESSAY ON WOMAN, 1763

Awake, my Fanny, leave all meaner things;
This morn shall prove what rapture swiving brings!

[1] In the first speech of JAMES I to his *English parliament,* March 22, 1603, are the following words, *That I am a* SERVANT *is most true . . . I will never be ashamed to confess it My principal honour, to be the* GREAT SERVANT *of the commonwealth.* Journal of the House of Commons, Vol. I, Page 145.

Let us (since life can little more supply
Than just a few good fucks, and then we die)
Expatiate free o'er that loved scene of man,
A might maze, for mighty pricks to scan;
A wild, where *Paphian Thorns* promiscuous shoot,
Where flowers the Monthly Rose, but yields no Fruit.
Together let us beat this ample field,
Try what the open, what the covert yield;
The latent tracts, the pleasing depths explore,
And my prick clapp'd where thousands were before.
Observe how Nature works, and if it rise
Too quick and rapid, check it ere it flies;
Spend when we must, but keep it all we can:
Thus godlike will be deem'd the ways of man.

I.   Say, first a woman's latent charms below,
What can we reason but from what we know?
A face, a neck, a breast, are all appear
From which to reason, or to which refer.
In every part we heavenly beauty own.
But we can trace it only in what's shewn.
He who the hoop's immensity can pierce,
Dart thro' the whalebone fold's vast universe,
Observe how circle into circle runs,
What courts the eye, and what all vision shuns,
All the wild modes of dress our females wear,
May guess what makes them thus transform'd appear.
But of their cunts the bearings and the ties,
The nice connexions, strong dependencies,
The latitude and longitude of each
Hast thou gone through, or can thy Pego reach?
Was that great Ocean, that unbounded Sea,
Where pricks like whales may sport, fathom'd by Thee?

II.   Presumptuous Prick! The reason would'st thou find
Why form'd so weak, so little, and so blind?
First if thou canst, the harder reason guess
Why form'd no weaker, meaner, and no less.
Ask of thy mother's cunt why she was made
Of lesser bore than cow or hackney'd jade?
Or ask thy raw-boned Scottish Father's Tarse
Why larger he than Stallion, or Jackass?
Of Pego's possible, if 'tis confess'd

376

That wisdom infinite must form some best,
Where all must rise, or not coherent be,
And all that rise must rise in due degree;
Then, in the scale of various Pricks, 'tis plain,
God-like erect, BUTE stands the foremost man,
And all the question (wrangle e'er so long)
Is only this, If Heaven placed him wrong.
Respecting him, whatever wrong we call,
May, must be right, as relative to all.
When frogs would couple, labour'd on with pain,
A thousand wriggles scarce their purpose gain:
In Man a dozen can this end produce,
And drench the female with spermatic juice.
Yet not our pleasure seems God's end alone,
Oft when we spend we propagate unknown;
Unwilling we may reach some other goal,
And sylphs and gnomes may fuck in woman's hole.
When the proud Stallion knows whence every vein
Now throbs with lust, and now is shrunk again;
The lusty Bull, why now he breaks the clod,
Now wears a garland, fair Europa's God:
Then shall Man's Pride and Pego comprehend
His actions and erections, use and end,
Why at Celaenae Martyrdom, and why
At Lampsacus adored chief Deity.
Then say not Man's imperfect, Heaven in fault,
Say rather, Man's as perfect as he ought;
His Pego measured to the female Case,
Betwixt a woman's thighs his proper place;
And if to fuck in a proportion'd sphere,
What matter how it is, or when, or where?
Fly fuck'd by fly may be completely so,
As Hussey's Duchess, or yon well-bull'd cow.

III.   Heaven from all creatures hides the Book of Fate
All but the page prescribed, the present state,
From boys what girls, from girls what women know
Or what could suffer being here below?
Thy lust the Virgin dooms to bleed today:
Had she thy reason would she skip and play?
Pleased to the last, she likes the luscious food,
And grasps the prick just raised to shed her blood.
Oh! Blindness to the Future, kindly given,

That each may enjoy what fucks are mark'd by Heaven.
Who sees with equal Eye, as God of all,
The Man just mounting, and the Virgin's fall;
Prick, cunt, and bollocks in convulsions hurl'd,
And now a Hymen burst and now a world.
Hope, humbly, then, clean girls; nor vainly soar;
But fuck the cunt at hand, and God adore.
What future fucks he gives not thee to know,
But gives that Cunt to be thy blessing now.

By the KING

A PROCLAMATION

For the Encouragement of Piety and Virtue, and for preventing and punishing of Vice, Profaneness, and Immorality.
GEORGE R.

WHEREAS We cannot but observe, with inexpressible Concern, the rapid Progress of Impiety and Licentiousness, and that Deluge of Profaneness, Immorality, and every Kind of Vice, which, to the Scandal of our Holy Religion, and to the evil Example of our loving Subjects, hath broken in upon this Nation: We therefore esteeming it Our indispensible Duty to exert the Authority committed to Us, for the Suppression of these spreading Evils, fearing lest they should provoke God's Wrath and Indignation against Us, and humbly acknowledging that We cannot expect the Blessing and Goodness of Almighty God (by whom Kings reign, and on which We entirely rely) to make our Reign happy and prosperous to Ourself and Our People without a Religious Observance of God's Holy Laws: to the Intent that Religion, Piety, and Good Manners, may (according to Our most hearty Desire) flourish and increase under Our Administration and Government, have thought fit, by the Advice of Our Privy Council, to issue this Our Royal Proclamation, and do hereby declare Our Royal Purpose and Resolution to discountenance and punish all Manner of Vice, Profaneness, and Immorality, in all Persons of whatsoever Degree or Quality, within this Our Realm, and particularly in such as are employed near Our Royal Person; and that for the Encouragement of Religion and Morality, We will, upon all Occasions, distinguish Persons of Piety and Virtue, by Marks of Our Royal Favour: And We do expect and require, That all Persons of Honour, or in Place of Authority, will give good Example by their own Piety and Virtue, and to their utmost contribute to the discountenancing Persons of dissolute and debauched Lives, that they, being reduced by that Means to Shame and Contempt for their loose

378

and evil Actions and Behaviour, may be thereby also enforced the sooner to reform their ill Habits and Practices, and that the visible Displeasure of good Men towards them, may (as far as it is possible) supply what the Laws (probably) cannot altogether prevent. And We do hereby strictly enjoin and prohibit all Our loving Subjects, of what Degree or Quality soever, from playing, on the Lord's Day, at Dice, Cards, or any other Game whatsoever, either in Public or Private Houses, or other Place or Places whatsoever: And We do hereby require and command them, and every of them decently and reverently to attend the Worship of God on the Lord's Day, on Pain of Our highest Displeasure, and of being proceeded against with the utmost Rigour that may be, by Law. And, for the more effectual reforming all such Persons, who, by reason of their dissolute Lives and Conversation, are a Scandal to Our Kingdom, Our further Pleasure is, and We do hereby strictly charge and command all Our Judges, Mayors, Sheriffs, Justices of the Peace, and all other Our Officers and Ministers, both Ecclesiastical and Civil, and all other Our Subjects, to be very vigilant and strict in the Discovery and the effectual Prosecution and Punishment of all Persons who shall be guilty of excessive Drinking, Blasphemy, profane Swearing and Cursing, Lewdness, Profanation of the Lord's Day, or other dissolute, immoral, or disorderly Practices; and that they take care also effectually to suppress all publick Gaming Houses and other loose and disorderly Houses, and also all unlicensed Publick Shews, Interludes, and Places of Entertainment, using the utmost Caution in licensing the same: Also to suppress all loose and licentious Prints, Books, and Publications, dispersing Poison to the Minds of the Young and Unwary, and to punish the Publishers and Vendors thereof; and to put in Execution the Statute made in the Twenty-Ninth Year of the Reign of the late King *Charles* the Second, intitled, *An Act for the better Observation of the Lord's Day, commonly called* Sunday; and also an Act of Parliament made in the Ninth Year of the Reign of the late King *William* the Third, intitled, *An Act for the more effectual suppressing of Blasphemy and Profaneness*; and also an Act passed in the Twenty-First Year of Our Reign, intitled, *An Act for preventing certain abuses and Profanations on the Lord's Day, called Sunday*; and all other Laws now in Force for the punishing and suppressing any of the Vices aforesaid; and also to suppress and prevent all Gaming whatsoever, in Publick or Private Houses, on the Lord's Day; and likewise that they take effectual Care to prevent all Persons keeping Taverns, Chocolate Houses, Coffee Houses, or other Publick Houses whatsoever, from selling Wine, Chocolate, Coffee, Ale, Beer, or other Liquors, or receiving or permitting Guests to be

379

or remain in such their Houses in the Time of Divine Service on the Lord's Day, as they will answer it to Almighty God, and upon Pain of Our highest Displeasure. And for the more effectual Proceeding herein, We do hereby direct and command all Our Judges of Assize and Justices of the Peace, to give strict Charge at their respective Assizes and Sessions, for the due Prosecution and Punishment of all Persons that, contrary to their Duty, shall be remiss or negligent in putting the said Laws in Execution; and that they do, in their respective Assizes and Quarter Sessions of the Peace, cause this Our Royal Proclamation to be publicly read in open Court before the Charge is given. And We do hereby further charge and command every Minister, in his respective Parish Church or Chapel to read or cause to be read this Our Proclamation at least Four Times in every Year, immediately after Divine Service, and to incite and stir up their respective Auditors to the Practice of Piety and Virtue, and the avoiding of all Immorality and Profaneness. And to the End that all Vice and Debauchery may be prevented, and Religion and Virtue practised by all Officers, Private Soldiers, Mariners, and others who are employed in Our Service by Sea and Land, We do hereby strictly Charge and Command all Commanders and Officers whatsoever, that they do take Care to avoid all Profaneness, Debauchery, and other Immoralities, and that by their own good and virtuous Lives and Conversation, they do set good Examples to all such as are under their Care and Authority; and likewise to take Care of and inspect the Behaviour of all such as are under them, and punish all those who shall be guilty of any of the Offences aforesaid, as they will be answerable for the ill Consequences of their Neglect herein.

Given at Our Court at *St. James's*, the First Day of *June*, One thousand seven hundred and eighty-seven, in the Twenty-seventh Year of Our Reign.

GOD SAVE THE KING.

PROSPECTUS OF THE SOCIETY FOR ENFORCING THE KING'S PROCLAMATION (1787)

WE, the undersigned, truly sensible of His Majesty's tender and watchful concern for the happiness of his people, manifested in his late royal Proclamation, and being convinced of the necessity, in the present juncture, of our attending to His Majesty's call on all his faithful subjects to check the rapid progress of impiety and licentiousness, to promote a spirit of decency and good order, and enforce a stricter execution of the laws against vice and immorality, do agree to form ourselves into a Society, for the purpose of carrying His Majesty's gracious recommendation into effect.

2. With this view we will be ourselves, and will countenance and encourage others in being, vigilant in the effectual prosecution and punishment of such criminal and disorderly practices as are within the reach of the law.

3. We will endeavour to afford the Magistracy such assistance in the discharge of their duty as the nature of the case may require.

Duke of Montagu, President

Duke of Buccleugh	Archbishop of Canterbury
Marlborough	York
Northumberland	Bishop of Hereford
Grafton	Chichester
Chandos	St. Asaph
*Marquis of Buckingham	*Salisbury
Lord Ailesbury	Peterborough
Hopetoun	Ely
Dartmouth	Rochester
Guilford	Chester
North	Oxford
Radnor	Lincoln
Effingham	Bangor
Brudenell	Lichfield
Harcourt	Gloucester
*Muncaster	Norwich
	Llandaff
	St. David's
	Bristol
*Sir Lloyd Kenyon	*Mr. Morton Pitt
*William Dolben	*Samuel Thornton
Henry Hoghton	*Wilberforce
James Long	*Edwards Freeman
*Charles Middleton	Richard Milnes
*Mr. Mainwaring	*Rev. Dr. Glasse
*Brook Watson	

Note. The names to which asterisks are annexed are those of members of the Committee.

From HARRIS'S LIST OF COVENT-GARDEN LADIES: *or*, MAN OF PLEASURE'S KALENDER, FOR THE YEAR 1788

Containing The Histories and some curious Anecdotes of the most celebrated Ladies now on the Town, or in keeping, and also many of their Keepers.

London: Printed for H. Ranger. Where may be had, The separate
LISTS of many preceding Years. [Price 2*s*. 6*d*.]
[Prices of women range from 5*s*. to £5, but usually £1—£2.]
(1) Introduction.
By thus extending our researches we shall be able to suit every
constitution and every pocket, every whim and fancy that the most
extravagant sensualist can desire. Here may they learn to shun the
dreadful quicksands of pain and mortification, and land safe on the
terra firma of delight and love. (p. 14.)

(2) Miss W-lk-ns-n, [Wilkinson] No. 10, *Bull-and-Mouth Street.*

> Forbidding me to follow she invites me,
> This is the mould of which I made the sex,
> I gave them but one tongue to say us nay,
> And two kind eyes to grant.

Here we present our readers with as pretty a man's woman as ever
the bountiful hand of nature formed; a pair of black eyes that dart
resistless fire, that speak a language frozen hearts might thaw, and
stand as the sweet index to the soul; a pair of sweet pouting lips that
demand the burning kiss, and never receives it without paying with
interest; a complexion that would charm the eye of an anchorite; a
skin smooth as monument alabaster, and white as Alpian snow; and
hair that so beautifully contrasts the skin, that nought but nature can
equal. Descend a little lower and behold the semi-snow-balls.
'Studded with rose buds, and streaked with celestial blue,' that want
not the support of stays; whose truly elastic state never suffers the
pressure, however severe, to remain, but boldly recovers its tempting
smoothness. Next take a view of nature *centrally*; no *folding lapel*,
no *gaping orifice*, no *horrid gulph* is here, but the *loving lips* tenderly
kiss each other, and shelter from the cold a small but easily stretched
passage, whose *depth* none but the *blind boy* has liberty to *fathom*;
between the tempting *lips* the *coral headed tip* stands centinal, sheltered
by a *raven coloured-bush*, and for one half guinea conduct the *well
erected friend* safe into *port*. She is a native of Oxfordshire, and has
been a visitor on the town about one year, is generally to be met with
at home at every hour excepting ten at night, at which time she visits a
favourite gentleman of the Temple. (pp. 29–30.)

(3) Miss Sophia M-rt-n, [Martin] No. 11, *Stephen Street, Rathbone
Place.*

Oh! the transporting joy!

Impetuous flood of long-expected rapture, she is a charming black
beauty; her vivid eyes speak the liveliness of her disposition, and the
joy she conceives in the hour of bliss. As yet she hath not approached

the verge of satiety; she is not so hackneyed in the ways of man as to be merely passive, she enjoys the pleasure, and though she is very fond of a *noun substantive* that can *stand* by itself, yet she loves to make it *fall*, and indeed the stoutest man cannot *stand* long before her; many a *fine weapon* she has made a *mere hanger* and the most stubborn steel hath melted in her *sheath*; yet no one complains, but rather rejoices at the debility she produces, and wishes for repetition which she enjoys with a *gou* peculiar to herself, and is possessed of every *amorous* means to produce it, as she is of every luscious one to destroy it.—To be met with at any of the genteel houses about St. James's. (pp. 31–2.)

(4) Mrs. H-w-rd, [Howard] No. 14, *Moor's-place, Lambeth.*
     Her brows are arch'd and rather full and thin
     To shade the dazzling light that dwells therein.
Although Mrs. H-w-rd cannot be more than twenty-six, she has been a true sportswoman, at the cyprian games, for at least twelve years, and has within these late ones contracted such an habit of intimacy with the gin bottle, that unless a person is particularly partial to it, it is almost intolerable, to approach her. At Brighton, this last season, she was the favourite girl at Mrs. John—n's, and had she not, through a foolish fondness, gave the preference to her dear Mr. Sh-m, [Shism] it is in general believed Mr. W—, [Wood] the capital Brewer, would have taken her under his own protection; she is rather too short, and too fat, fine dark hair; and eyes and eye-brows that answer very well to her motto; the *grove* below is *well thatched*, and ample enough in size to *take in* any guest, but still she has learnt the knack of *contracting* it, and a small made gentleman may feel the tender friction. When she elopes from her dear fellow, she is to be met with at Mrs. J-ns-n's, [Johnson's] in German street, and does not turn away any money offered her. (p. 72).

(5) Miss C——p, [Clicamp] No. 2, *York Street, Middlesex Hospital.*
     Give me a nymph with all her charms,
     A full grown nymph to fill my arms;
     And leave to them that cannot feel,
     The insipid things they call genteel.
. . . fraught with every melting charm that can be found in the field of Venus, fortunate for the true lovers of fat, should fate throw them into the possession of such full grown beauties. (p. 104).

Harris's List of Covent-Garden Ladies . . . For the Year 1793
     [The following passages are two of those quoted in the indictments

of James Roach and James Aitken in 1794, when both men were tried and convicted on charges of publishing an obscene libel.]

(1)   Miss Ke-t, [Kent] No. 9, *Warren Street, Tottenham Court Road.*
Whenever she is offering incence at the shrine of Venus, her whole frame is agitated with pleasure, her eyes languish, her breasts heave, and her limbs quiver; while involuntary sighs and murmurs burst forth from her tender bosom, provoking the transports of the happy priest who administers with her. (pp. 11–12).

(2)   Miss S--wyn, [Selwyn] *Chelsea.*
It is questionable, as a certain author says, whether the enjoyment of a woman be not more luscious when dressed than in *puris naturalibus*; and it is demonstrable that one thus enjoys her in a twofold manner, for it is an axiom in sensuality that the sight contributes very much to its gratification; by preferring her dressed, it must not however be understood to mean her when encumbered with all the articles that complete the court or ball dress: of stiff stays, she should by all means, be divested; white seems the most voluptuous dress; her hair elegantly dressed and highly perfumed; the head-dress adorned with large feathers, but an indispensable article in the dress of a young woman, is a very large nosegay of natural flowers, or artificial ones well scented, and which she should wear on the left side of her bosom, as high as the ear, this mode of wearing them being reckoned exceeding lascivious, and indeed there is no appendage in the whole catalogue of female dress which raises lust so powerfully as those enormous bouquets which our woman of fashion wear, their luxurious perfume not only provoke [sic] desires but aggravate [sic] very much venereal enjoyments. (pp. 88–9).

FOX'S LIBEL ACT (1792)
32 GEO. III, C. 60
Whereas doubts have arisen whether on the trial of an indictment or information for the making or publishing any libel, where an issue or issues are joined between the King and the defendant or defendants, on the plea of not guilty pleaded, it be competent to the jury impanelled to try the same to give their verdict upon the whole matter in issue; be it therefore declared and enacted . . . that, on every such trial, the jury sworn to try the issue may give a general verdict of guilty or not guilty upon the whole matter put in issue upon such indictment or information; and shall not be required or directed, by the court or judge before whom such indictment or information shall be tried, to find the defendant or defendants guilty, merely on the proof of the publication by such defendant or defendants of the

paper charged to be a libel, and of the sense ascribed to the same in such indictment or information.

II. Provided always, that, on every such trial the court or judge before whom such indictment or information shall be tried, shall, according to their or his discretion, give their or his opinion and directions to the jury on the matter in issue between the King and the defendant or defendants, in like manner as in other criminal cases.

III. Provided also, that nothing herein contained shall extend, or be construed to extend, to prevent the jury from finding a special verdict, in their discretion, as in other criminal cases.

IV. Provided also, that in case the jury shall find the defendant or defendants guilty, it shall and may be lawful for the said defendant or defendants to move in arrest of judgement, on such ground and in such manner as by law he or they might have done before the passing of this Act; any thing herein contained to the contrary notwithstanding.

FOUR CRIMINAL LIBELS: 1792–1833

[The names of the defendants are given before the title of the publication. Each case ended with a conviction.]

(1) Libel on George III. William Williams and Richard Tattersall. *The Morning Post and Daily Advertiser*, 17 March 1792.

The Academy was founded on his [Sir Joshua Reynolds's] merit. Now mark the sequel. With royal reluctance he was called to the chair, with royal reluctance he received the honour of knighthood, with royal and utter neglect he was treated, and once with royal effrontery cheated. The Empress of Russia has the cheat in her possession and is ready to shew and to prove it but indeed it proves itself at sight. Beautiful, excellent, and unrivalled as his pictures were, yet they passed in annual review without royal favor or praise or smile. What the first Charles would have seen at a single glance and flown to cover with reward and honour, the malignant eye of a sordid Hanoverian turned from with disgust and resentment, reasonless disgust and unfounded resentment. Charles, the elegant, the liberal, the magnificent Charles. But why do I name them together? Hyperion to a satyr. Apollo and Marsias. Burgundy and hogwash.

(2) Seditious Libel. Jane Carlile. *The Republican*, Vol. III, no. 8. 16 June 1820.

I will now come to the point with you, and tell you more than you seem to ask, lest you should say that I evade the question. In the first place I hold the destruction of tyrants by putting them to death suddenly and violently, or if you should think I am not sufficiently explicit, by assassinating them, to be an act just, moral, virtuous and legal, agreeable to the law of nature which should be the foundation of all other law. A tyrant is the common destroyer of his species and any member of that community in which he dwells and plays the tyrant that shall receive any injury from him may, in my opinion, meritoriously put him to death. The moralist or a man with the most humane mind will stand aloof and ask himself the following question, which would have been the greatest outrage on the laws, morals, and welfare of this society, that this man who is an avowed and admitted tyrant should fall by the hand of one whom he has injured, or that he should have lived to have made unhappy, miserable and in continual fear for their lives and properties every member of this society that should not feel disposed to flatter and applaud his wicked measures! Give me an answer to this last question in the same frank and candid manner in which I am answering your question and I will give you my opinion of your morality and virtue. With respect to the plot and measures in which those men whom you call Cato-street Conspirators were seduced and involved by our ministers and their agents. They have my decided disapprobation but as I consider that a majority of the present ministers are tyrants and enemies to the interests and welfare of the people of this country, so also am I bold to confess that if any man who has suffered unjustly under their administration should be so far indifferent about his own life as to slay any one or more of them, I would tune my lyre to sing his praises. I consider it to be a want of virtue and true courage that makes a man seek companions to perform such an act. It is a proof that he calls upon others to do that which he has not resolution to do single-handed, and in seeking men that will co-operate with him he is sure to fall in with the most vicious of mankind and mar all the good he might have done as an individual. I condemn an association for such purposes. [This was part of a letter written by Richard Carlile, from Dorchester prison to the Rev. William Wait of Bristol.]

(3) Thomas Dolby. *A Political Dictionary* 1820.

Common law, judge law, the terrae incognitae of lawyers, any thing the Judge pleases. For example, the fining of Mr. Davison three times in the midst of his defence or Mr. Clement for publishing Thistlewood's Trial. Mem. Chief Justice Pemberton used to boast he had made more law (common law) in his time than the King and both Houses of Parliament. Some of the present judges appear inclined to follow his example.

King's Speech. A few insipid ungrammatical sentences recited by Hum to his Parliament and for which Hum receives a million a year, usually announcing just and necessary wars, the improvement of the revenue, the flourishing state of commerce and agriculture, a seditious and blasphemous people—all of which is seldom perceived by any body but Hum and his Ministers. Mem. as the royal speech grows every year more short and inane it may be presumed that in time it will go entirely out of fashion and Parliament be assembled and prorogued without such an unmeaning formality. The people would not regret the loss of Hum's speech, provided the million a year remained in their pockets.

(4) Henry Hetherington and Thomas Stevens. *The Poor Man's Guardian.* 25 May 1833.

The axe of the law like the sword of Damocles is suspended by a single hair above our heads. Let us then counteract the assassin by a vigilance equal to his own.—Remember, by violating the law we should only add to its rigour, by obeying the law we shall destroy it hereafter.—Let us then obey the law, let us obey it for our own sakes but let us obey it only for the sacred purpose of overthrowing it . . . You see, my friends, we cannot be too cautious against the blood-thirsty men, having missed your lives in their murderous assault upon you at Cold Bath Fields, they now resort to the agency of spies for your blood. What they fail to accomplish by undisguised ferocity they now seek by emissaries and hired perfidy! What a horrible crew! but follow our advice, brother Reformers and you will defeat all their machinations—As to their open day assaults upon your persons we deem it unnecessary to offer any advice on this head. The fate of Cully and Brooke must have taught you ere this how the truncheon of the hired assassin can be most safely repelled, but as regards the more dangerous because the more covert attack of the vile emissary, your obvious safeguard will be the openness and strict legality of your proceedings, seek no object that is illegal, and seek no legal object by illegal means, or should events induce you to do either, be previously assured that in whatever steps you take you will have the support of the great bulk of your countrymen . . . But now, Mr. Editor, I have a little bit of a secret to tell you, a word to the wise is enough and no mistake. The sports of the great, unboiled, would at once be put an end to if these hired bludgeoners were fully convinced that for the future the working man always goes to public meetings with bread and cheese in his pocket, a hard crust of bread and a very small piece of cheese and also a knife, that's of course, for surely you would not have the poor man break his teeth against the hard crust or nibble at the cheese like a mere mouse? No, the working man must have a knife—It need not be made with a joint, that would be an unnecessary expence, a strong straight knife carried in a sort of large scissors-sheath, will serve admirably for cutting bread and cheese, and also for any other incidental purposes. The cheese knife may be made very sharp at the point in order that you may pick out anything detrimental in your victuals etc. but the back of your knife should increase in size up to the haft, where it should be very thick indeed, almost as thick as the back of a sword, but that's nothing to the purpose. I only mean that every working man should at every public meeting have in his pockets some bread and cheese, and also whatever may be, for it is a pity he should run the risk of being starved.

From THOMAS PAINE, THE RIGHTS OF MAN, LONDON, 1792

[The following passages are those quoted in the indictment at Paine's trial for seditious libel in December 1792.]

(1) All hereditary government is in its nature tyranny. An heritable crown, or an heritable throne, or by what other fanciful name such things may be called, have no other significant explanation, than that mankind are heritable property. To inherit a government, is to inherit the people, as if they were flocks and herds. (p. 21).

(2) The convention met at Philadelphia, in May 1787, of which General Washington was elected President. He was not at that time connected with any of the State Governments, or with Congress. He delivered up his commission when the war ended, and since then had lived a private citizen.

The Convention went deeply into all the subjects; and having, after a variety of debate and investigation, agreed among themselves upon the several parts of a federal constitution, the next question was, the manner of giving it authority and practice.

For this purpose, they did not, like a cabal of courtiers, send for a Dutch Stadtholder, or a German Elector; but they referred the whole matter to the sense and interest of the country. (p. 47).

(3) The History of the Edwards and the Henries, and up to the commencement of the Stuarts, exhibits as many instances of tyranny, as could be acted within the limits to which the nation had restricted it. The Stuarts endeavoured to pass those limits, and their fate is well known. In all those instances, we see nothing of a constitution, but only of restrictions on assumed power.

After this, another William, descended from the same stock, and claiming from the same origin, gained possession; and of the two evils, *James* and *William*, the nation preferred what it thought the least, since, from circumstances, it must take one. The act, called the Bill of Rights, comes here into view. What is it, but a bargain, which the parts of the government made with each other to divide powers, profits, and privileges? You shall have so much, and I will have the rest; and with respect to the nation, it said, for *your share*, YOU *shall have the right of petitioning*.

This being the case, the Bill of Rights is more properly a Bill of Wrongs, and of insult. As to what is called the Convention Parliament, it was a thing that made itself, and then made the authority by which it acted. A few persons got together and called themselves by that name. Several of them had never been elected, and none of them for that purpose.

From the time of William, a species of government arose, issuing out of this coalition Bill of Rights; and more so, since the corruption introduced at the Hanover succession, by the agency of Walpole; that can be described by no other name than a despotic legislation. Though the parts may embarrass each other, the whole has no bounds; and the only right it acknowledges out of itself, is the right of petitioning. Where then is the Constitution either that gives or restrains that power?

It is not because a part of the Government is elective, that makes it less a despotism, if the persons so elected, possess afterwards, as a Parliament, unlimited powers. Election, in this case, becomes separated from representation, and the candidates are candidates for despotism. (pp. 52–3).

(4) The attention of the Government of England (for I rather chuse to call it by this name, than the English Government) appears, since its political connexion with Germany, to have been so completely engrossed and absorbed by foreign affairs, and the means of raising taxes, that it seems to exist for no other purposes. Domestic concerns are neglected; and with respect to regular law, there is scarcely such a thing. (p. 56.)

(5) With respect to the two Houses, of which the English Parliament is composed, they appear to be effectually influenced into one, and, as a legislature, to have no temper of its own. The minister, whoever he at any time may be, touches it as with an opium wand, and it sleeps obedience.

But if we look at the distinct abilities of the two Houses, the difference will appear so great, as to shew the inconsistency of placing power where there can be no certainty of the judgement to use it. Wretched as the state of representation is in England, it is manhood compared with what is called the House of Lords; and so little is this nick-named House regarded, that the people scarcely enquire at any time what it is doing. It appears also to be the most under influence, and the furthest removed from the general interest of the nation. (p. 63).

(6) Having thus glanced at some of the defects of the two Houses of

Parliament, I proceed to what is called the Crown, upon which I shall be very concise:

It signifies a nominal office of a million sterling a year, the business of which consists in receiving the money. Whether the person be wise or foolish, sane or insane, a native or a foreigner, matters not. Every ministry acts upon the same idea that Mr. Burke writes, namely, that the people must be hood-winked, and held in superstitious ignorance by some bugbear or other; and what is called the Crown answers this purpose, and therefore it answers all the purposes to be expected from it. This is more than can be said of the other two branches. The hazard to which this office is exposed in all countries, is not from any thing that can happen to the Man, but from what may happen to the Nation—the danger of its coming to its senses. (pp. 107–8).

(7) I happened to be in England at the celebration of the centenary of the Revolution of 1688. The characters of William and Mary have always appeared to me detestable; the one seeking to destroy his uncle, and the other her father, to get possession of power themselves; yet, as the nation was disposed to think something of that event, I felt hurt at seeing it ascribe the whole reputation of it to a man who had undertaken it as a job, and who, besides what he otherwise got, charged 600,000 l. for the expence of the little fleet that brought him from Holland. George the First acted the same close-fisted part as William had done, and bought the Duchy of Bremen with the money he got from England, 250,000 l. over and above his pay as King; and having thus purchased it at the expence of England, added it to his Hanoverian dominions for his own private profit. In fact, every nation that does not govern itself, is governed as a job. England has been the prey of jobs ever since the revolution. (pp. 116–17).

(8) The fraud, hypocrisy and imposition of governments, are now beginning to be too well understood to promise them any long career. The farce of monarchy and aristocracy, in all countries, is following that of Chivalry, and Mr. Burke is dressing for the funeral. Let it then pass quietly to the tomb of all other follies, and the mourners be comforted.

The time is not very distant when England will laugh at itself for sending to Holland, Hanover, Zell, or Brunswick, for men, at the expence of a million a year, who understood neither her laws, her language, nor her interest, and whose capacities would scarcely have fitted them for the office of a parish constable. If Government could be trusted to such hands, it must be some easy and simple thing indeed, and materials fit for all the purposes may be found in every town and village in England. (p. 161.)

390

From PROCEEDINGS OF THE FRIENDS TO THE LIBERTY OF THE PRESS ON DECEMBER 22, 1792; AND JANUARY 19 AND MARCH 9, 1793. PRINTED BY ORDER OF THE COMMITTEE, 1793

Free-Mason's Tavern, December 22, 1792

Gerard Noel Edwards, Esq., M.P. in the Chair

Resolved Unanimously,

1. That the Liberty of the Press is a right inseparable from the principles of a free government, and essential to the security of the British constitution.

2. That this Liberty consists in the free discussion and examination of the Principles of civil Government, and of all matters of public opinion.

3. That no writing ought to be considered as a public Libel, and made the subject of criminal prosecution, unless such writing shall appear to be published with a design to excite the People to resist the Civil Magistrate, or obstruct the execution of the existing laws.

4. That such publications may become proper objects of prosecution, and that the Executive Government is entrusted with powers amply sufficient for that purpose.

5. That we have therefore seen with uneasiness and alarm the formation of certain Societies, which under the pretence of supporting the Executive Magistrate, and defending the Government against sedition, have held out general terrors against the circulation of Writings, which, without describing them, they term Seditious; and entered into Subscriptions for the maintenance of Prosecutions against them; a proceeding doubtful as to its legality, unconstitutional in its principle, oppressive in its operation, and destructive of the Liberty of the Press.

6. That such associations have appeared to us the more exceptionable from an attentive observation of their proceedings. Whilst mutually binding and engaging themselves to enforce the execution of the Laws against seditious Libels, they have themselves produced and circulated publications, containing doctrines long since exploded, and which, if admitted, would prove the Revolution to be an act of rebellion, and the title of the reigning Family to the throne of these kingdoms to be founded in usurpation and injustice.

THE PLENIPOTENTIARY (C. 1792)

[This ballad, which was the subject of a number of prosecutions for obscene libel between 1798 and 1820, exists in slightly differing versions. It is said to be the work of a friend of the Prince of Wales, Captain Morris, but its singing was by no means confined to the rowdier celebrations of the Carlton House set. It seems to have been sung for five or six years before appearing in print, which would account for the variant forms. It was sung to *The Terrible Law* or *Shawnbuee*.]

The Dey of Algiers, when afraid of his ears,
A messenger sent to our court, sir,
As he knew in our state the women had weight,
He chose one well hung for the sport, sir.
He searched the Divan till he found out a man
Whose b—— were heavy and hairy,
And he lately came o'er from the Barbary shore
As the great Plenipotentiary.

When to England he came, with his p—— in a flame,
He showed it his Hostess on landing;
Who spread its renown through all parts of the town,
As a pintle past all understanding.
So much there was said of its snout and its head,
That they called it the great Janissary;
Not a lady could sleep till she got a sly peep
At the great Plenipotentiary.

As he rode in his coach, how the whores did approach,
And stared, as if stretched on a tenter;
He drew every eye of the dames that passed by,
Like the sun to its wonderful centre.
As he passed thro' the town not a window was down
And the maids hurried out to the area,
The children cried, 'Look, there's the man with the cock,
That's the great Plenipotentiary.'

When he came to the Court, oh, what giggle and sport,
Such squinting and squeezing to view him,
What envy and spleen in the women were seen,
All happy and pleased to get near him.
They vowed from their hearts, if men of such parts
Were found on the coast of Barbary,
'Tis a shame not to bring a whole guard for the King,
Like the great Plenipotentiary.

The dames of intrigue formed their c—— in a league,
To take him in turns like good folk, sir;

392

The young misses' plan was to catch as catch can,
And all were resolved on a stroke, sir.
The cards to invite flew by thousands each night,
With bribes to the old secretary,
And the famous Eclipse was not let for more leaps
Than the great Plenipotentiary.

When his name was announced how the women all bounced,
And their blood hurried up to their faces;
He made them all itch from the navel to breech,
And their bubbies burst out all their laces;
There was such damned work to be f—— by the Turk,
That nothing their passion could vary;
All the nations fell sick for the Barbary p——
Of the great Plenipotentiary.

A Duchess whose Duke made her ready to puke,
With fumbling and f—— all night, sir,
Being first for the prize, was so pleased with its size,
That she begged for to stroke its big snout, sir.
'My stars!' cried her Grace, 'its head's like a mace,
'Tis as high as the Corsican Fairy;
I'll make up, please the pigs, for dry bobs and frigs,
With the great Plenipotentiary.'

And now to be bor'd by this Ottoman Lord
Came a Virgin far gone in the wane, sir,
She resolved for to try, tho' her c—— was so dry,
That she knew it must split like a cane, sir.
True it was as she spoke, it gave way at each stroke,
But oh, what a woeful quandary!
With one terrible thrust her old piss-bladder burst
On the great Plenipotentiary.

The next to be tried was an Alderman's Bride,
With a c—— that would swallow a turtle,
She had horned the dull brows of her worshipful spouse,
Till they pointed like Venus's myrtle.
Thro' thick and thro' thin, bowel deep he dashed in,
Till her c—— frothed like cream in a dairy,
And expressed by loud farts she was strained in all parts
By the great Plenipotentiary.

The next to be kissed, on the Plenipo's list,
Was a delicate Maiden of Honour,
She screamed at the sight of his p——, in a fright,
Tho' she'd had the whole palace upon her.
'O Lord', she said, 'what a p—— for a maid!
Do, pray, come look at it Cary!
But I *will* have one drive, if I'm ripped up alive,
By the great Plenipotentiary'.

Two sisters next came, Peg and Molly by name,
Two ladies of very high breeding,
Resolved one should try while the other stood by
And watched the amusing proceeding.
Peg swore by the gods that the Mussulman's cods
Were as big as both buttocks of Mary;
Molly cried with a grunt, 'He has ruined my c——
With his great Plenipotentiary'.

The next for a shag came the new Yankee flag;
Tho' lanky and scraggy in figure,
She was fond of the quid, for she had been well rid
From Washington down to a nigger.
'Oh my! such a size! I guess it's first prize,
It's a wonder, quite next Ni-a-gary;
W-a-l-l, now I'm in luck, stranger, let's f——
Bully for the great Plenipotentiary'.

All heads were bewitched and longed to be stitched,
Even babies would languish and linger,
And the boarding-school Miss, as she sat down to piss,
Drew a Turk on the floor with her finger.
For fancied delight, they all clubbed for a shite,
To frig in the school necessary,
And the Teachers from France f—— à la distance
With the great Plenipotentiary.

Each sluice-c—— bawd, who'd been s——d abroad
Till her premises gaped like a grave, sir,
Found luck was so thick, she could feel the Turk's p——,
Tho' all others were lost in her cave, sir.
The nymphs of the stage did his ramrod engage,
Made him free of their gay seminary;

394

And the Italian Signors opened all their back doors
To the great Plenipotentiary.

Then of love's sweet reward, measured out by the yard,
The Turk was most blest of mankind, sir,
For his powerful dart went right home to the heart,
Whether stuck in before or behind, sir.
But no pencil can draw this great-pintled Bashaw
Then let each c—— loving contemporary,
As cocks of the game, let's drink to the name
Of the great Plenipotentiary.

[Later versions of the ballad included an additional stanza.
With joy and delight they gaz'd at the sight
For it rose like a May pole to view, sir,
With his c—s large and hard at the root of his y—d
To behold it made their c—ts spew, sir.
Miss Prue on her back discover'd her crack
Which was small yet was plumb and was hairy,
Then his wonderful p—— touch'd her home to the quick,
The new Plenipotentiary.]

From CHEAP REPOSITORY TRACTS (1795)

[These Tracts were issued by evangelicals to further the reformation of manners among the lower orders of society and to combat the immoral influence of such other literature as might fall into innocent hands. *The Story of Sinful Sally* is one of the most engaging of these Tracts.]

The Story of Sinful Sally
Told by herself
Shewing

How from being SALLY of the GREEN, she was first led to become SINFUL SALLY, and afterwards DRUNKEN SAL, and how at last she came to a most melancholy, and almost hopeless End! being therein a Warning to all young Women both in Town and Country

COME, each maiden, lend an ear,
    Country lass and London belle!
Come and drop a mournful tear
    O'er the tale that I shall tell.

I that ask your tender pity,
    Ruin'd now and all forlorn,

Once, like you, was young and pretty,
  And as cheerful as the morn.

In yon distant cottage sitting
  Far away from London town,
Once you might have seen me knitting
  In my simple kersey gown.

Where the little lambkins leap,
  Where the meadows look so gay,
Where the drooping willows weep,
  Simple Sally used to stray.

Then I tasted many a blessing,
  Then I had an honest fame;
Father, Mother, me caressing,
  Smil'd, and thought me free from blame.

Then amid my friends so dear,
  Life it speeded fast away:
O, it moves a tender tear,
  To bethink me of the day!

From the villages surrounding,
  Ere I well had reached eighteen,
Came the modest youths abounding,
  All to Sally of the Green.

Courting days were thus beginning,
  And I soon had proved a wife:
Oh! if I had kept from sinning,
  Now how blest had been my life!

Come, each maiden, lend an ear,
  Country lass and London belle!
Come ye now and deign to hear,
  How poor Sinful Sally fell.

Where the hill begins inclining,
  Half a furlong from the road,
O'er the village white and shining,
  Stands Sir William's great abode.

Near his meadow I was tripping,
  Vainly wishing to be seen,
When Sir William met me skipping,
  And he spoke me on the green.

Bid me quit my cloak of scarlet,
  Blam'd my simple kersey gown:
Ey'd me then so like a varlet,
  Such as live in London town.

With his presents I was loaded,
  And bedeck'd in ribbons gay;
Thus my ruin was foreboded,
  O how crafty was his way!

Vanished now from cottage lowly,
  My poor parents' hearts I break;
Enter on a state unholy,
  Turn a mistress to a rake.

Now no more by morning light
  Up to God my voice I raise;
Now no shadows of the night
  Call my thoughts to prayer and praise.

Hark! a well-known sound I hear!
  'Tis the Church's Sunday bell;
No; I dread to venture near;
  No; I'm now the child of Hell.

Now I lay my Bible by,
  Choose that impious book so new,
Love the bold blaspheming lie,
  And that filthy novel too.

Next to London town I pass,
  (Sinful Sally is my name)
There to gain a front of brass,
  And to glory in my shame.

Powder'd well, and puff'd and painted,
  Rivals all I there outshine;

397

With skin so white, and heart so tainted,
   Rolling in my chariot fine.

In the park I glitter daily,
   Then I dress me for the play,
Then to masquerade so gaily,
   See me, see me tear away.

When I meet some meaner lass,
   Then I toss with proud disdain;
Laugh and giggle as I pass,
   Seeming not to know a pain.

Still at every hour of leisure
   Something whispers me within,
O! I hate this life of pleasure,
   For it is a life of sin.

Thus amidst my peals of laughter
   Horror seizes oft my frame:
Pleasure now—Damnation after,
   And a never-dying flame.

'Save me, save me, Lord,' I cry,
   'Save my soul from Satan's chain!'
Now I see salvation nigh,
   Now I turn to sin again.

Is it then some true repentance
   That I feel for evil done?
No; 'tis the horror of my sentence,
   'Tis the pangs of hell begun.

By a thousand ills o'ertaken
   See me now quite sinking down;
Till so lost and so forsaken,
   Sal is cast upon the town.

At the dusk of evening grey
   Forth I step from secret cell;
Roaming like a beast of prey,
   Or some hateful imp of hell.

Ah! how many youths so blooming
  By my wanton looks I've won;
Then by vices all consuming
  Left them ruined and undone!

Thus the cruel spider stretches
  Wide his web for every fly;
Then each victim that he catches
  Strait he poisons till he die.

Now no more my conscience troubled,
  Deep I plunge in every sin;
True; my sorrows are redoubled,
  But I drown them all in gin.

See me next with front so daring,
  Band of ruffian rogues among;
Fighting, cheating, drinking, swearing,
  And the vilest of the throng.

Mark that youngest of the thieves,
  Taught by Sal he ventures further;
What he filches Sal receives,
  'Tis for Sal he does the murder.

See me then attend my victim,
  To the fatal gallows tree;
Pleas'd to think how I have nick'd him,
  Made him swing while I am free.

Jack I laughing see depart,
  While with Dick I drink and sing:
Soon again I'll fill the cart,
  Make this present lover swing.

But while thus with guilt surprising,
  Sal pursues her bold career,
See God's dreadful wrath arising,
  And the day of vengeance near!

Fierce disease my body seizes,
  Racking pain afflicts my bones:

Dread of Death my spirit freezes,
    Deep and doleful are my groans.

Here with face so shrunk and spotted
    On the clay cold ground I lie;
See how all my flesh is rotted,
    Stop, O stranger, see me die!

Conscience, as my breath's departing,
    Plunges too his arrows deep,
With redoubled fury starting
    Like some giant from his sleep.

In this pit of ruin lying,
    Once again before I die,
Fainting, trembling, weeping, sighing,
    Lord, to thee I'll lift my eye.

Thou can'st save the vilest harlot,
    Grace, I've heard, is free and full;
'Sins that once were red as scarlet,'
    Though canst make as 'white as wool'.

Saviour, whom I pierc'd so often,
    Deeper still my guilt imprint!
Let thy mighty Spirit soften
    This my harden'd heart of flint.

Vain, alas! is all my groaning,
    For I fear the die is cast;
True, thy blood is all-atoning,
    But my day of grace is past.

Saviour! hear me, or I perish!
    None who *lives* is quite undone;
Still a ray of hope I'll cherish,
    'Till eternity's begun.

FROM THE ANTI-JACOBIN REVIEW: OR, WEEKLY EXAMINER,
4 DECEMBER 1797

[Those who agreed with John Reeves that 'The pen militant might save the expense of many regiments', attempted to neutralise the influence of Paine and other authors of 'seditious' literature by loyalist propaganda, much of which appeared in the pages of the *Anti-Jacobin*. By 1797 the 'terror' in France and the threat of a French invasion inspired the loyalist writers to some of their best satire. 'La Sainte Guillotine' was introduced to readers of the *Anti-Jacobin* with the words, 'We have been favoured with the following specimen of Jacobin Poetry, which we give to the world without any comment or imitation. We are informed (we know not how truly) that it will be sung at the Meeting of the Friends of Freedom; an account of which is anticipated in our present Paper.']

La Sainte Guillotine
A New Song
Attempted from the French
Tune, 'O'er the vine-cover'd hills and gay regions of France.'

From the blood bedew'd valleys and mountains of France,
See the Genius of Gallic INVASION advance!
Old Ocean shall waft her, unruffled by storm,
While our shores are all lin'd with the *Friends of Reform*.[1]
Confiscation and Murder attend in her train,
With meek-eyed Sedition, the daughter of PAINE;[2]
While her sportive *Poissardes* with light footsteps are seen
To dance in a ring round the gay *Guillotine*.[3]

To London, 'the rich, the defenceless',[4] she comes—
Hark! my boys, to the sound of the Jacobin drums!
See Corruption, Prescription, and Privilege fly,
Pierced through by the glance of her blood-darting eye.
While patriots, from prison and prejudice freed,
In soft accents shall lisp the Republican Creed,
And with tri-colour'd fillets, and cravats of green,
Shall crowd round the altar of *Saint Guillotine*.

See the level of Freedom sweeps over the land—
The vile Aristocracy's doom is at hand!
Not a seat shall be left in a House *that we know*,

[1] See the Proclamation of the Directory.
[2] The '*too long calumniated* author of the Rights of Man'.
—See a Sir Something Burdet's speech at the Shakespeare, as referred to in the *Courier* of Nov. 30.
[3] The Guillotine at Arras was, as is well known to every Jacobin, painted '*Couleur de Rose*'.
[4] See *Weekly Examiner*, No. 11. Extract from the *Courier*.

But for *Earl Buonaparte* and *Baron Moreau*.—
But the rights of the Commons shall still be respected,
Buonaparte himself shall approve the elected;
And the Speaker shall march with majestical mien,
And make his three bows to the grave *Guillotine*.

Two heads, says the proverb, are better than one,
But the Jacobin choice is for Five Heads or none.
By Directories only can Liberty thrive;
Then down with the ONE, Boys! and up with the FIVE!
How our bishops and judges will stare with amazement,
When their heads are thrust out at the *National Casement*![1]
When the *National Razor*[1] has shaved them quite clean,
What a handsome oblation to *Saint Guillotine*!

PROSECUTIONS FOR OBSCENE LIBEL: 1801–53

[The following passages were those cited by the Crown when a number of well-known publishers were prosecuted for issuing certain 'favourite' banned books, and one or two less popular works. The first name in each heading is that of the publisher: the prison sentences ranged from six months to two years.]

(1) Isaac Aldrich. *The New Rambler's Magazine*, January 1801.

(i) Thus Love on one side has been known to produce Love, and as in the course of excitation in making electrical experiments the jars will now and then discharge themselves accidentally or involuntarily, as well as by the safer and more natural application of the smooth round knob blunthead of the discharging rod, so in courtship or in amorous dalliance between the sexes, involuntary coliquations will now and then happen, and at best courtship and dalliance is no other than charging the battery on the one side and heating or preparing the genial oven of nature on the other for the connection and maturation of the genial juice.

(ii) Sir, I cannot refrain from acquainting you with the inexpressible felicity I enjoy owing to the lucky rencontre with your New Rambler's Magazine for March last. You must know then that above a fortnight ago, while my cousin and her husband were at tea with my spouse and me, my husband produced your said magazine, when the principal article that attracted our attention was 'the Plan whereby the licentious part of the human species may indulge their natural propensities without disturbing the peace of regular families'. It is impossible to describe how we were all electrified when we read

[1] *La petite Fenêtre*, and *la Razoire Nationale*, fondling expressions applied to the Guillotine by the Jacobins in France, and their pupils here.

about small societies of married people, where the men were all common to each woman and the women all common to each man, and at the same time so easily kept from the knowledge of the world. A conversation on the subject ensued, when each of us appeared tremblingly alive to the theme and frankly owned that however for the sake of outward decency we might restrain our wandering desires, yet we could not help being very unhappy and languid under the chains of eternal bondage to one subject only, though ever so amiable. Well, what should we do but agree to make a trial, and accordingly we immediately changed partners, and if you can conceive anything of the highest scenes of voluptuousness, you may have some idea of the poignant pleasures of that memorable evening. But that is not all. We have added another amiable couple to our delectable society, and have laid down rules to regulate ourselves by, viz. That we are to have no private or clandestine meetings or intrigues, and to meet but once a week at such of our houses as are most convenient. By these regulations we neither cloy ourselves nor hinder business, and yet our spirits are constantly kept in high glee in expectation of the next meeting. Lord, Sir, if you could but conceive the transports three high mettled couples are capable of bestowing on each other! Nay, the men have sworn eternal friendship and reciprocal services in the way of trade, and we are in fact in the highest state of fraternal felicity. Both men and women of us now follow our business more steadily and soberly than formerly, and keep close at home and are so guarded in public that the most probing eye cannot discover any cause for scandal. We only wish to add one couple more to our happy society, if we can find them discreet and sober and in all respects to our mind, for you know we must not have anything to do with blackguards or such who have no character to lose, for our security entirely consists in the mutual interests we have in keeping each other's secrets, and defending the characters of one another. I could add a great deal more to prove that it is the most just, fair, and happy scheme of lewdness that ever was invented, and liable to no bad consequences following. Future occasions will give rise to further amplifications, so I now conclude, Yours, Margery G——

London, March 19, 1800

P.S. I forgot to tell you that at our meetings we give up all claims of private or exclusive property in each other and determine by lot who shall be partners for the evening, to which we most rigorously submit to prevent every plea for dissention or strife.

(iii) Isaac no sooner had entered her apartment and she had perused the letter than she began to view the bearer very attentively.

Isaac appeared more amiable and desirable in her Ladyship's eyes than ever. Her passion began to operate in its full force. 'Come nearer,' said she, 'Isaac, you are not afraid of a woman or you would not have lived so long with your mistress. You have a well-turned leg and thigh, and those breeches display the manly contour of your limbs amazingly.' Saying this, she stroked his Nankeen breeches in such a manner that poor Isaac lost two of his front bu——ns, which were forced off despite of his teeth. Such an exhibition now presented itself that Lady W——y could no longer subdue her rage for gratification and as he had made no efforts to seize the opportunity that presented itself she resolved it should not be lost. She with dexterity threw him upon his back upon the sopha and like another St. George subdued the dragon.

(iv) A Riddle

For length and strength I am admir'd
For work that's warm I am requir'd:
And very often I am plac'd
By open legs to be embrac'd.
Then soon again I'm put to use,
As I to nourishment conduce.
When women take me into hand
I'm guided just as they command,
For I've no eyes, as I may say,
(Tho' I've a head) to see my way.
Sometimes one part looks deeply red
Yet soon again the colour's fled.
Then guess me rightly, if you can,
And you shall be a charming man.

(v) A noble knight delights in hardy deeds of arms.
Perhaps some ladies love sweet musick's charms.
Rich men hoard riches, whereso'er they be.
Infants love dandling on their mother's knee.
Coy maids love something. Nothing I'll express.
Keep the first letter of each line and guess.

(2) Edward Rich. *The Voluptuarian Museum* 1806.
    (i) I could now at my pleasure explore these luscious incitements, which love to retire from the public gaze. I could feel as well as view that light rebounding springiness of Flesh, so pleasing to the touch in the breasts, in buttocks, in thighs or belly.

(ii) Never was Europa half so well unvirgined, though the puissant might of a bull obliged her longing gap.

(iii) Her rear beauties were not inferior to her front. O heavens, what a bum!!! Which Jews might kiss and Infidels adore.

(iv) She hired two young girls in the bloom of youth and in the highest perfection of loveliness, whom she obliged to lay naked in the same bed with her when she received the embraces of her paramours, whom she directed to indulge themselves in every sense of feeling with her sweet companions, now moulding their swelling bubbies, now roving over the smooth expanse of their ivory bellies, or grasping the plumpness of their snowy thighs, but more especially playing with their moss grown cells, till the engine of her adoration was in the finest condition imaginable, when she would make them conduct it where she expected it and by dint of such powerful helps was made happy by a performance she could never have so well otherwise obtained.

(v) Enthusiasts are generally lively in their passions and when her white thighs were expanded, her polished belly displayed, both of which might rival the objects of my former amours, she seemed possessed of an absolute furor of sensuality. She scarce waited for the insertion of my canonical staff ere she darted towards me, with one motion throwing her arms around my shoulders, her legs about my back and began heaving, wriggling, twisting and pressing, as if the very devil was in her.—'O, the precious doctrine! O, the balm of life,' cries she, 'Do not let me lose a drop of my dear teacher's instructions! Give me a long sermon! And every thrust more potent than the proceeding, Ah, repeat that sentence again, it went to my very heart. I could keep you forever in my pulpit.'

(3) John Duncombe. *Duncombe's Drolleries* 1829.

Oyster Nan

As Oyster Nan stood by her tub,
To shew her wicked inclination
She gave her noble parts a scrub
And sighed for copulation.

A vintner of no little fame,
Who excellent white and red could sell ye,
Observing of this dirty dame
As she was scrubbing of her belly,

'Come in, come in you dirty slut,
This is a rare convenient minute.
I'll lay the itching of your cunt,
Humph! I say the devil's in it.'

With that flap cap'd Nanny smiled,
And fain would blush but could not,
Saying, 'How soon we are beguiled
To do the thing we should not.'

From the door they went behind the bar
And as by common fame reported
'Twas there upon a leather chair
This loving couple kiss'd and courted.

But being called by company,
As he was taking pains to please her,
'I am coming, Sir,' said he,
'And so am I, my dear,' said she, 'Sir.'

Her molehill belly swelled about
Into a mountain quickly after,
And when the little brat crept out
It caused a mighty laughter.

But now she's learnt the pleasing game,
Although much shame and pains it cost her,
She daily ventures at the same
And opens still her rare fat oysters.

(4) John Duncombe. *The New London Rambler's Magazine* 1829
(from 'The Guard of Honour').

Now a little dog may do more good in a *certain* way than a bad
man—he can tickle with his tail, he can lick with his tongue, and
create a vibration which will end in preserving his mistress from evil
ways. A lovely girl that lays down to sleep seldom has a recollection
that her seat of honour lays in front and is exposed to every base
invader but her little lap dog has, by instinct, found out that there is
a treasure she possesses which cannot be dispensed with only on
honourable terms. He will bark and bray, arouse the sleeper and frequently drive away the ravisher. In this case, the story which alludes
to the plate is plain and simple; it was a favourite dog, and proved the

guardian of its young mistress. She was indulging in one of those voluptuous slumbers, girls of seventeen do generally give way to, when a person who had been a little favoured made his *entrée* softly and sweetly to the lady's bedside, but he saw the dog all alive and ready to grasp at whoever touched the —— of his mistress. No one dared to do so, and the guard of honour was left in its proper station at the *fountain of beauty*, on its mossy bed.

[The *New Rambler* was advertised as being published by J. Mitford at 19, Little Queen Street, but this was where John Duncombe operated from. He may have taken on Mitford's name as an *alias*.]

(5) George Cannon. D. A. F. De Sade, *Juliette ou les Prospérités du Vice* 1830.

La fille de dix-huit ans se mit à genoux devant elle; Clairwil lui appuya le con sur le visage, en frottant de toutes ses forces les lèvres de son vagin et son clitoris sur le nez, la bouche et les yeux de cette fille à qui elle recommanda de le lécher. Une fille postée à droite, l'autre à gauche, étrillaient vigoureusement mon amie qui, tenant une poignée de verges de chaque main, se vengeait sur les deux culs des coups qu'elle recevait; à cheval sur le crâne de celle qui léchait le con, je lui présentais le mien à sucer; ici la putain déchargea, mais avec des cris, des convulsions et des blasphèmes qui caractérisaient l'un des délires les plus lubriques et les plus luxurieux que j'eusse encore observés de mes jours; la jolie figure contre laquelle s'était escrimée la tribade était inondée de foutre.

—Allons, sacredieu! faisons autre chose, s'écria-t-elle, sans se donner le temps de respirer, jamais je ne me repose quand mon sperme est en train de couler; travaillez-moi, putains! secouez-moi, fouettez-moi, branlez-moi de la plus forte manière!

La fille de dix-huit ans se couche sur l'ottomane, je m'assieds sur son visage, Clairwil se campe sur le mien, j'étais sucée, je le rendais; elevée au-dessus de moi, la plus jeune des filles faisait baiser ses fesses à Clairwil, qu'une autre fille enculait avec un godemiché; la plus mince des quatre filles, inclinée, branlait, avec ses doigts, le clitoris de Clairwil, presque établi sur ma bouche, et présentait, pendant ce temps-là, son con aux mêmes pollutions exercées par la main de mon amie. De cette manière, notre libertine branlait un cul avec sa langue, était gamahuchée, on l'enculait, et on lui branlait le clitoris.

[In the indictment these lines from *Juliette* and from other publications in French were specially translated into English by the Crown, for the benefit of the jurors. It is a nice irony that the first translation of De Sade into English should have appeared not to satisfy the demands of the pornographers but at the behest of the Treasury Solicitor.]

(6) Edward Duncombe. *Memoirs of a Man of Pleasure* 1835.

Full of this thought, he began to be very familiar with Maria's petticoats, at which she seemed at first offended, but as her inclinations were individually the same as Charles's, after a little struggle she permitted him to survey the throne of mighty love in all its budding bloom. It formed a tempting protruberance divided in the middle like a downy peach, its edges tinged with deep vermillion, which gave a lustre to the radiant whiteness of the neighbouring mount. No shaggy shrubs had yet disfigured the sacred vale but all was smooth as polished ivory. Charles silently gazed for some time with wonder and amazement and then in a transport pressed the mysterious spot with his wanton hands and allowed his little fingers to search its inmost recesses.

(7) William Dugdale. *The Amorous History and Adventures of Raymond de B——, and Father Andouillard,* 1851.

I then saw again, not without much astonishment, the Trustee flat upon his belly with a young girl under him, whose neck he was devouring with kisses, and who was also extended almost at full length upon a table, which appeared to have been put there for the express purpose. She was stripped to her shoulders, and his weapon engulphed, as it were, in her backside; his stones pressed on her plump buttocks, and he was peeping every minute through the hole in the screen, to watch the beautiful Julia, who was flogging a girl about 12 years old with all her strength, and the widow, who had just whipped a boy about the same age, who was reading before her with his pantaloons down to his heels, keeping him between her thighs and pressing with one of her hands, which was round his body, his naked arse upon her private parts, and holding a most tremendous rod in the other.

(8) George Cannon. *The Adventures of Sir Henry Loveall,* 1853.

(i) A violet bank was near; I bore her to it, overcome by all she felt, by all she heard, my boldest proceedings met with sufferance. Gods! I arrived at the summit of my designs. In a few moments I was engulphed in a sea of super-inexpressible delight. I had penetrated the rosy folds of my Louisa! Her murmurs died away! The joys, the titillating joys took their place! Her melting embrace mixed with mine! We came together! She could have died for me, the dear possessor of her maidenhead, and perhaps at that very instant, I for her.

(ii) I lay undermost, and drew her on me, smiling in her angelic face. She returned it and, straddling, sheaths my champion in her wanton scabbard. Ah! how luxurious her fleshy thighs! her fine formed buttocks as they prominated. She was tickled to the very soul, her very actions showed it, the novelty incomparably delighted her. She would try it again and was so much pleased with this method of playing on the Flute of Cupid, she for that evening would have no other music but what struck upon the same plan. I indulged her till my instrument was as mute as a blind man's broken fiddle, or to speak more justly, like that at least began to make most horrible discord.

(iii) She sank upon my bosom and I bore her to the only bed in the hut—that but a crazy one I promise you—she suffered me to lay her on it, while I bared her beauties to the sight. As she lay looking with the most languishing sensibility, I separated her charming thighs, imprinted on them my warm kisses, and entered the moss-grown retreat. As she felt me she deeply sighed and, 'Is it, oh, is it,' cried she, 'the last? For heaven knows how long I must experience, oh, raptures so enchanting! Oh bliss so sweet—yet, oh, so quickly past! Must I,' said Louisa, 'wait for months again to feel thee? Ah, Loveall! To the hilt! Spare me not! there!—transport!—transport!' Then the warm tide came rushing on again. She clos'd upon me—and in one delicious thrilling was almost overpaid for future consequences.

[Although the prosecution of Cannon was not until 1853, the novel in question dates from the early years of the nineteenth century, as the figurative and rhetorical style suggests.]

From COBBETT'S WEEKLY POLITICAL REGISTER, SATURDAY 1 JULY, 1809.

[The following passage is the one for which Cobbett was tried and convicted in June 1810.]

The mutiny amongst the Local Militia which broke out at Ely was fortunately suppressed on Wednesday by the arrival of four squadrons of the German Legion Cavalry from Bury under the command of General Auckland. Five of the ringleaders were tried by a court martial and sentenced to receive 500 lashes each, part of which punishment they received on Wednesday and a part was remitted. A stoppage for their knapsacks was the ground of complaint that excited this mutinous spirit, which occasioned the men to surround their officers and demand what they deemed their arrears. The first division of the German Legion halted yesterday at Newmarket on their return to Bury.

—*Courier* (Ministerial) *Newspaper*   Saturday 24th of June 1809.
Summary of Politics, Local Militia and German Legion.

See the motto English Reader! See the motto and then do pray
recollect all that has been said about the way in which Buonaparte
raises his soldiers—well done, Lord Castlereagh! This is just what it
was thought your plan would produce. Well said, Mr. Huskisson!
It really was not without reason that you dwelt with so much earnestness upon the great utility of the foreign troops whom Mr. Wardle
appeared to think of no utility at all, poor Gentleman! he little
imagined how a great genius might find useful employment for such
troops. He little imagined that they might be made the means of
compelling Englishmen to submit to that sort of discipline which is
so conducive to the producing in them a disposition to defend the
Country at the risk of their lives. Let Mr. Wardle look at my motto
and then say whether the German soldiers are of no use. Five
hundred lashes each! Aye, that is right! Flog them. Flog them. Flog
them! They deserve it and a great deal more. They deserve a flogging
at every meal time. 'Lash them daily, Lash them duly.' What, shall
the rascals dare to mutiny and that too when the German Legion is
so near at hand! Lash them. Lash them. Lash them! They deserve
it. O yes, they merit a double-tailed cat.—Base dogs! What, mutiny
for the sake of the price of a knapsack! Lash them! Flog them! Base
rascals! Mutiny for the price of a goat's skin and then upon the
appearance of the German soldiers they take a flogging as quietly as
so many trunks of trees! I do not know what sort of a place Ely is but
I really should like to know how the inhabitants looked one another
in the face while this scene was exhibiting in their town. I should
like to have been able to see their faces and to hear their observations
to each other at the time. This occurrence at home will, one would
hope, teach the loyal a little caution in speaking of the means which
Napoleon employs (or rather which they say he employs) in order to
get together and to discipline his conscripts. There is scarcely any one
of these loyal persons who has not at various times cited the hand-
cuffings and other means of force said to be used in drawing out the
young men of France. There is scarcely one of the loyal who has not
cited these means as a proof, a complete proof, that the people of
France hate Napoleon and his Government, assist with reluctance in
his wars and would fain see another revolution. I hope, I say, that the
loyal will hereafter be more cautious in drawing such conclusions
now that they see that our 'Gallant defenders' not only require
physical restraint in certain cases but even a little blood drawn from
their backs and that too with the aid and assistance of German

troops. Yes, I hope the loyal will be a little more upon their guard in drawing conclusions against Napoleon's popularity. At any rate, every time they do in future burst out in execrations against the French for suffering themselves to be 'chained together and forced at the point of the bayonet to do military duty' I shall just republish the passage which I have taken for a motto to the present sheet. I have heard of some other pretty little things of the sort but I rather choose to take my instance (and a very complete one it is) from a public print notoriously under the sway of the ministry.

From T. J. WOOLER, THE BLACK DWARF, 12 FEBRUARY and 2 APRIL, 1817.

[The two passages which follow are those in respect of which the two prosecutions were brought against Wooler.]
(1) 12 February 1817.

The people of this country have heard a great deal about the *right* of petition; and notwithstanding a thousand proofs of its inefficacy, they seem as fond of it as ever. But some tub must be thrown out to the whale. There must be found some way or other to dissipate the well grounded discontent that so universally prevails; and like a breakwater, the *right of petitioning* is thrust forward to stop the current of popular dissatisfaction. All this is very well. But what purpose will it answer. Like all other delusions, it will be found out at last, and then good bye to petitioning. In the literal acceptation of the term, nothing is, or can be so ridiculous. The RIGHT of *petitioning*. Bravo! John Bull! Bravo. You have the *right* of petitioning, have you? And your ancestors obtained it for you, did they? And Hampden bled for the right of petitioning, did he? And Sydney was beheaded, and Russell, for the *right of petitioning*. And your ancestors sent Charles to the block, and drove James to the —— for the right of petitioning, did they? And you possess the *right*, Johnny? Do you? And are charged 60 millions a year for it, are you. Well you may call it one of your DEAREST RIGHTS, for you have paid dear enough for it, in all conscience. But you are a good sort of a fellow; and being no great judge of the value of diamonds, it is the same to you, whether you have *glass*, or french paste. It must *glisten* a little, to please your imagination, and you are as pleased as the poor Indian who gives his gold or his treasure for a bauble. But the savage is the better off, of the two; for though he gets but a *bauble*, it is *something* at least; but you, John, have got *nothing* for your liberty, but have had your *pocket picked* into the bargain.

You have the right of *petitioning*, you say. Yes, you have indeed. And you petition away with a vengeance. You see those whom you petition have a voracious appetite for such kind of food. They swallow them as fast as the serpent of Moses swallowed all the other serpents. Only you have fed them a little too fast, and having to pick out of so many, they are now become a little nice. They want *respectful* petitions. They would have the politest epithets bestowed upon them; and if you will flatter their vanity, and rely upon their wisdom, faith you may use your *right* of *petitioning* as frequently as you please. You will assist trade by it. Lawyers will find parchment dearer, and the tailors will get it cheaper to make measures with.

But in reality, master Bull, you estimate all this boasted right *a little* too highly. Are you not aware that you only have it in common with the *free burgesses* of the Mogul; and the independent slaves of the Dey of Algiers? Do you not see that the right of petition, in the sense you enjoy it, is only what you cannot be deprived of—no, not even if you were lashed to your work daily by a herd of slave-drivers. Do you not perceive that the MAN must be destroyed, before the *power of complaining*, can be taken from him? And what is your *right of petitioning* more than the *power of complaining*, and that LIMITED too by those who tell you, that you have an *undoubted right to grumble*. When you present such petitions, as your masters deem fit to be received, what do you get by it. A clerk who ought to be sent to school to learn to read; is set to mutter over your petition. Then it is moved, as there is nothing *disrespectful* stated, that it do lie *on* the table. If the table will hold it, well and good, it MAY lie there; if not, it will lie *under* the table, until the sweeper comes and clears the floor, for the reception of more petitions. And what good do you get by all this? Literally none. You tell your *omnipotent* representatives what they very well knew before hand, that you are very much distressed, and very sorry for it. They say they are very sorry too; and that your petition ought to lie on the table for consideration; and that a *proper* time ought to be taken for such consideration. But then they, poor souls! are so busied for your good, throughout the session, that the proper time never comes, and your grievances are never redressed. It is sometimes hinted that they are only temporary, and will cure themselves; and there is no doubt of that; only be patient for *half a century*, and if the grievances do not die away, why YOU WILL; and that is the same thing. Now you see, that while you possess the *right of petitioning*, and they possess the right of *neglecting your petitions*, it is just the same thing as if you had no right at all.

This is the BEST side of the question. This is the view of the case when your petitions are deemed to be *fit* to be received. For you see that your *right* of petitioning, is confined to a peculiar mode of expression. If your pockets are picked, you must not pray the House of Commons to hang a minister—you must civilly ask them to be so kind as not to let him do it again. If your valuable constitution is injured, or totally destroyed, you must only ask for its renovation in the most mild and gentlemanly terms. The House must not be *insulted*! Oh! no! the house must not be insulted. Although every body knows that the House of Commons, collectively taken, speaks neither the voice of the people, nor attends to the wishes of the people; although every body knows that a majority of that house, are—what it would not be prudent to say; although the experience of ages has proved it the ready servant of the existing minister; and that therefore it is neither *rationally nor constitutionally* the representative of the public; yet all this is to be veiled in silence. We may petition the house for reform, if in the same breath we will admit that it wants no reform; we may entreat it to restore us the blessings of our constitution, and give us back our rights, if we will confess that our rights have not been infringed upon, and that the blessings of the constitution have never been impaired. Such is now the state of the RIGHT of petition. We must suppress the remonstrance of truth, and the firm tone of justice, and then our complaints may be heard—and despised.

The terms imply this—the right of petition is only the privilege of slaves. Free men would blush to hear it boasted of, in its modern acceptation.

But were our ancestors fools then, and slaves? No, neither. They were men, but not scholars. They approached their monarchs with petitions, it is true; but then they carried arms in their hands to support them. They did not *mean* to petition, when they employed a term which custom had familiarly applied to addresses to the throne. The first complaint was a petition, in its modern signification, the second, was the determination to enforce it. Would *petitioning* have ever obtained the constitution? How then can petitioning be expected to preserve it. Was John *petitioned* to sign Magna Charta:— Was Charles *petitioned* to lay down his head upon the block:—was James *petitioned* to abdicate his throne? Or was William *petitioned* to accept the Bill of Rights? No! no! the *right of petitioning* with our ancestors meant the right of laying their grievances before the *highest authority*, and demanding, or ENFORCING an attention to their wrongs. With them, then, you see that the right of petitioning, meant the power of obtaining redress. With you, it means nothing—but that you may assemble, in your parishes, *when you can get leave* of the rector and churchwardens; in your towns, if *the mayor chooses* to call a meeting; in a tavern, if you choose to be taunted with the rebuke, that you are not ALL *the inhabitants* of the town; in the fields, if you wish to be *called a mob*, and to be surrounded with soldiers;

and when you have met, you may state your opinions, and make speeches, and call yourselves freemen, and say you are taxed by those whom you never elected; and yet that you are all free men, all free-born Englishmen, every one of you; and that you will claim your rights, you will! that you will. You may then buy as many skins of parchment as you please, you may indeed; and write your petition out fair, and get all your neighbours to sign it; and then you can take it to a member of parliament, and ask him to present it; which many of them will do for you. But then some will tell you that you are a parcel of fools, or rogues, that they know better than you, and that they will take care to prevent the possibility of your obtaining your wishes. Now, is not this a blessed right, Master Bull? And ought you not to be very grateful for it, and very proud of it?

But this is all tolerably fair yet. The House of Commons is atten-tion itself, compared to another quarter, to which you are also *privi-leged* to carry your petitions. I beg your pardon; no, you are only privileged to SEND them there. Now, your ancestors, Master Bull, never thought much about petitioning the House of Commons. That is a modern invention. They did not understand any thing about petitioning their *immediate servants*. They sent such men there as would do their duty properly; and when *the people were aggrieved,* they set their servants to *petition the crown,* and to give it a broad hint about the necessity of redressing the matters complained of. But when one got as careless of the interests of the people as the other, it became necessary that the people should go to the Crown with *their own* complaints. But mark, what a dextrous plea was invented to save the Crown any trouble in this matter. The Crown had never *been accustomed* to receive petitions *from the* people, and *therefore* would not receive them, except from one or two *favored bodies,* who it was expected would give the Crown no great trouble that way.

Thus, you see, that your right of petitioning the crown, is merged in the *right* of sending a deputation to the office of the Secretary of State for the home department, and as the crown NEVER returns ANY ANSWER to those that are sent there, you may believe, *if you will,* that the King ever takes the trouble to read them; or that his ministers ever pay any attention to them. I say, you MAY believe this. I do not mean to tell you they do not. But it is the same to you, whether they do, or whether they do not; for you have never been the better for either the trouble of the one, or the attention of the other.

(2) 2 April 1817.
We start from the contrast of what we were with what we are, with as much astonishment, as if we could not have anticipated the change.

But those who will not attend to their own affairs, must take from experience the lesson that others will invariably deceive them, or betray them. Our ministers have done both. The nation has to reproach them with the most infamous duplicity, the most dreadful treachery. They promised us that they would fight *our battles*, and they have *fought their own*. They talked of patriotism, when they meant *plunder*; and told us we were fighting the battles of *regular government* abroad, when they have been reduced to the necessity, even in the boasted success of our arms, to destroy that constitution themselves, which they pretended they called upon us to *pay*, and *combat* to *defend*. The constitution which France could not assail, nor ever wished to injure, has perished at Stephen's; perished ignobly, and *without a struggle*, among the *representatives of the people*, the *guardians of the public purse*. Have our ministers any further object to achieve? or will they be satisfied with the annihilation of our most important laws? Will they be satisfied with our toil as slaves, or must we *bleed* to appease their hatred of the cause of freedom and reform? If we must, we have only to request of them, in the language of Ajax, to destroy us in the open light of heaven, breathing our appeal to the God of Freedom, against the agents of slavery and degradation.

We embarked in the *last war* to conquer France, and we have conquered *ourselves*: our ministers have scarcely breathed from the contest against freedom abroad, and they are already in full armed mail against liberty at home. They would destroy the very name;—but it is immortal. It starts fresh from the scythe of persecution. The blood of one martyred patriot is the dew that waters the soil from whence shall spring a thousand, and ten thousand heroes. The ministers might as well attempt to veil the sun by Act of Parliament, as to destroy public sentiment by legislative restrictions. These are attempts that destroy themselves, and that provoke the crisis which might have been avoided. The delusions practiced by the ministers are now seen through, and despised, or hated. It was not to subdue France, but to subjugate England to *their* yoke, that they have *taxed*, and *lied*, and urged us on to fight those who were not our enemies. We have been impoverishing our strength against the French, that we might be at last an easy prey to our junto of rough riders and political jockies. They have pushed us on to dangers, while they gained something by every step we took; and now, when a nation of paupers *supplicate for food*, they are threatened with imprisonment, and even death. Every man that falls a victim to this state of things, is *virtually murdered*: and although the laws of man may not be able to reach, or punish the murderers, heaven's all-seeing eye will mark them, and demand a signal retribution from the guilty head.

What phantom have we been pursuing throughout the lamentable history of the present reign? What infatuation has led *freemen*, and Englishmen, on to the committal of such dreadful outrages against the cause of freedom? What fiend could have instigated a wish in Britain to become the despotic masters of America; to plant there the tree of tyranny, which we fondly flattered ourselves we had destroyed at home? The nation never completely recovered from the effects of that wanton crusade against the principles of freedom. We had wandered from the leading star of happiness, and have never been able to recover our way; until at last we fell into the labyrinth of guilt and folly, which led us to oppose the least advances to happiness in any quarter of the globe, and proclaim ourselves the *general* champions of *'legitimate despotism'*, throughout the wondering world. Folly led to folly, and crime brought on crime. All the evils that were attendant upon the French revolution, are fairly attributable to the mean jealousy of the English ministers, and the astonishing infatuation of the English people. Our *apparent success*, has been purchased at the expence of all we have. We are like the German Baron, who laid out all his property in the purchase of arms to defend it; like us, at last, he found he had *nothing to defend*. And yet our ministers dare talk of the GLORY we have acquired. Sad specimen indeed of *glory*, and dearly purchased is the empty boast! Is it, then, *glorious* to have restored the most oppressive systems of political degradation, and the most infamous control of religious opinions? Is it *glorious* to England, that Lord *Castlereagh*, and his ferocious friends on the Continent, should have restored the Pope? Is it *glorious* for England, that the wretched Ferdinand should remount the throne of Spain, under the protection of Lord Castlereagh, over the mangled bodies of those mistaken men who fought for his title, who bled for his defence, and who escaped a thousand deaths from his enemies, to perish like felons by *his orders*? Is this *glory* worthy of England to achieve, or Englishmen to *boast of*? No! no! leave the authors of *such glorious deeds* to groan and sweat under their load of honours. Let those who have usurped the name of Englishmen, and identified themselves with these *praiseworthy consequences*, take all the *glory* to themselves; and since we are not likely to appreciate the full value of such services, they had better hasten to the regions which their influence has so much blessed. Perhaps Ferdinand will treat them as he has treated his *best friends*, and spare them the account to which their own country must call them, if they provoke the crisis to which their cupidity and folly seems to wish to hasten us.

All hopes, however, of awakening any commiseration for the people in the bosoms of the present ministry are absurd. They are the decided authors of our calamities, and they will not believe that a nation so deeply injured as England has been, can ever pardon them the guilt of their misconduct. They feel they do not deserve the forgiveness of the country; and would now *coerce us into silence*, because they *tremble at our complaints*. Nothing operates so forcibly upon the nerves of the murderer as the fancied spectre of his victim: the wounds he has inflicted are ever bleeding in his eyes; the cold mangled form impedes his every step; and he cannot *cease to apprehend*, although the lifeless corse is incapable of vengeance. Every eye that is bent on his scowling forehead seems to question him of his guilt, and every accent in his ears sounds like the denunciation of his crime. It is thus with the ministers and the *constitution*. It lies mangled beneath their feet. Their rashness has aimed at it a mortal blow; and they look fearfully round to see if any are interested in its fate. Every eye that dares to look at them, seems to them the eye of an avenger. They know how dear the victim of their fury was to every Englishman, and they would fain hope that not an English spirit survived to mourn its fate, or to rise in vengeance upon their misdeeds. They would call themselves the *government*, and make *their will* the *general law*; but they dare not. They must strike yet again at our vital interests before they can accomplish this. They must make us fools as well as paupers, before we can consent to breathe entirely at their mercy.

WILLIAM HONE, THE LATE JOHN WILKES'S CATECHISM OF A MINISTERIAL MEMBER (1817).

A CATECHISM,
That is to say,

An Instruction, to be learned of every Person before he be brought to be confirmed a Placeman or Pensioner by the Minister.

:::::::::::

Question. What is your name?
Answer. Lick Spittle.
Q. Who gave you this Name?
A. My Sureties to the Ministry, in my Political Change, wherein I was made a Member of the Majority, the Child of Corruption, and a Locust to devour the good Things of this Kingdom.
Q. What did your Sureties then for you?
A. They did promise and vow three things in my Name. First, that I should renounce the Reformists and all their Works, the pomps and vanity of Popular Favour, and all the sinful lusts of Independence. Secondly, that I should believe all the Articles of the Court Faith.

417

And thirdly, that I should keep the Minister's sole Will and Commandments, and walk in the same, all the days of my life.

Q. Dost thou not think that thou art bound to believe and to do as they have promised for thee?

A. Yes, verily, and for my own sake, so I will; and I heartily thank our heaven-born Ministry, that they have called me to this state of elevation, through my own flattery, cringing, and bribery; and I shall pray to their successors to give me their assistance, that I may continue the same unto my life's end.

Q. Rehearse the Articles of thy Belief?

A. I believe in GEORGE, the Regent Almighty, Maker of New Streets and Knights of the Bath; And in the present Ministry, his only choice, who were conceived of Toryism, brought forth of WILLIAM PITT, suffered loss of Place under CHARLES JAMES FOX, were execrated, dead, and buried. In a few months they rose again from their minority; they re-ascended to the Treasury Benches, and sit at the right hand of a little man in a large wig; from whence they *laugh* at the Petitions of the People, who pray for Reform, and that the sweat of their brow may procure them Bread.

I believe that King James the Second was a legitimate Sovereign, and that King William the Third was not; that the Pretender was of the right line, and that George the Third's Grandfather was not; that the dynasty of Bourbon is immortal; and that the glass in the eye of Lord James Murray, was not Betty Martin. I believe in the immaculate purity of the Committee of Finance, in the independence of the Committee of Secresy, and that the Pitt system is everlasting. Amen.

Q. What dost thou chiefly learn in these Articles of thy Belief?

A. First, I learn to forswear all conscience, which was never meant to trouble me, nor the rest of the tribe of Courtiers. Secondly to swear black is white, or white black, according to the good pleasure of the Ministers. Thirdly, to put on the helmet of impudence, the only armour against the shafts of patriotism.

Q. You said that your Sureties did promise for you, that you should keep the Minister's Commandments: tell me how many there be?

A. Ten.

Q. Which be they?

A. The same to which the Minister for the time being always obliges all his creatures to swear, I the Minister am the Lord thy liege, who brought thee out of Want and Beggary, into the House of Commons.

I. Thou shalt have no other Patron but me.

II. Thou shalt not support any measure but mine, nor shalt thou frame clauses of any bill in its progress to the House above, or in the Committee beneath, or when the Mace is under the table, except it be mine. Thou shalt not bow to Lord COCHRANE, nor shake hands with him, nor any other of my real opponents; for I thy Lord am a jealous Minister, and forbid familiarity of the Majority, with the Friends of the People, unto the third and fourth cousins of them that divide against me; and give Places, and thousands and tens of thousands, to them that divide with me, and keep my commandments.

III. Thou shalt not take the Pension of thy Lord the Minister in vain; for I the Minister will force him to accept the Chilterns, that taketh my Pension in vain.

IV. Remember that thou attend the Minister's Levee day; on other days thou shalt speak for him in the House, and fetch and carry, and do all that he commandeth thee to do; but the Levee day is for the glorification of the Minister thy Lord: In it thou shalt do no work in the House, but shall wait upon him, thou, and thy daughter, and thy wife, and the Members that are within his influence; for on other days the Minister is inaccessible, but delighteth in the Levee day; wherefore the Minister appointed the Levee day, and chatteth thereon familiarly, and is amused with it.

V. Honor the Regent and the helmets of the Life Guards, that thy stay may be long in the Place, which thy Lord the Minister giveth thee.

VI. Thou shalt not call starving to death, murder.

VII. Thou shalt not call Royal gallivanting adultery.

VIII. Thou shalt not say, that to rob the Public is to steal.

IX. Thou shalt bear false witness against the People.

X. Thou shalt not covet the people's applause, thou shalt not covet the People's praise, nor their good name, nor their esteem, nor their reverence, nor any reward that is theirs.

Q. What dost thou chiefly learn by these Commandments?

A. I learn two things—my duty towards the Minister, and my duty towards myself.

Q. What is thy duty towards the Minister?

A. My duty towards the Minister is, to trust him as much as I can; to fear him; to honor him with all my words, with all my bows, with all my scrapes, and all my cringes; to flatter him; to give him thanks to give up my whole Soul to him; to idolize his name, and obey his word; and serve him blindly all the days of his political life.

Q. What is thy duty towards thyself?

A. My duty towards myself is to love nobody but myself and to do unto most men what I would not they should do unto me; to sacrifice to my own interest even my father and mother; to pay little reverence to the King, but to compensate that omission by my servility to all that are put in authority under him; to lick the dust under the feet of my superiors, and to shake a rod of iron over the backs of my inferiors; to spare the people by neither word or deed; to observe neither truth nor justice in my dealings with them; to bear them malice and hatred in my heart; and where their wives or properties are concerned, to keep my body neither in temperance, soberness, nor chastity, but to give my hands to picking and stealing, and my tongue to evil speaking and lying, and slander of their efforts to defend their liberties and recover their rights; never failing to envy their privileges, and to learn to get the Pensions of myself and my colleagues out of the People's labour, and to do my duty in that department of public plunder unto which it shall please the Minister to call me.

Q. My good Courtier, know this, that thou art not able of thyself to preserve the Minister's favour, nor to walk in his Commandments, nor to serve him, without his special protection; which thou must at all times learn to obtain by diligent application. Let me hear therefore, if thou canst rehearse the Minister's Memorial.

A. Our Lord who art in the Treasury, whatsoever be thy name, thy power be prolonged, thy will be done throughout the empire, as it is in each session. Give us our usual sops, and forgive us our occasional absences on divisions; as we promise not to forgive them that divide against thee. Turn us not out of our Places; but keep us in the House of Commons, the land of Pensions and Plenty; and deliver us from the People. Amen.

Q. What desirest thou of the Minister in this memorial?

A. I desire the Minister, our Patron, who is the disposer of the Nation's overstrained Taxation, to give his protection unto me and to all Pensioners and Placemen, that we may vote for him, serve him, and obey him, as far as we find it convenient; and I beseech the Minister that he will give us all things that be needful, both for our reputation and appearance in the House and out of it; that he will be favourable to us, and forgive us our negligences; that it will please him to save and defend us, in all dangers of life and limb, from the people our natural enemies; and that he will help us in fleecing and grinding them; and this I trust he will do out of care for himself, and our support of him through our corruption and influence; and therefore I say Amen. So be it.

Q. How many tests hath the Minister ordained?

A. Two only, as generally necessary to elevation: (that is to say) Passive Obedience and Bribery.

Q. What meanest thou by this word Test?

A. I mean an outward visible sign of an inward intellectual meanness, ordained by the Minister himself as a pledge to assure him thereof.

Q. How many Parts are there in this Test?

A. Two; the outward visible sign, and the inward intellectual meanness.

Q. What is the outward visible sign or Form of passive obedience?

A. Dangling at the Minister's heels, whereby the person is degraded beneath the baseness of a slave, in the character of a Pensioner, Placeman, Expectant, Parasite, Toadeater, or Lord of the bedchamber.

Q. What is the inward and intellectual meanness?

A. A death unto freedom, a subjection unto perpetual Thraldom: for being by nature born free, and the children of Independence, we are hereby made children of slavery.

Q. What is required of persons submitting to the Test of Passive Obedience?

A. Apostacy, whereby they forsake liberty; and faith, whereby they steadfastly believe the promises of the Minister, made to them upon submitting to that Test.

Q. Why was the Test of Bribery ordained?

A. For the continual support of the Minister's influence, and the feeding of us, his needy creatures and sycophants.

Q. What is the outward part or sign in the Test of Bribery?

A. Bank notes, which the Minister hath commanded to be offered by his dependents.

Q. Why then are beggars submitted to this Test, when by reason of their poverty they are not able to go through the necessary forms?

A. Because they promise them by their Sureties; which promise, when they come to lucrative offices, they themselves are bound to perform.

Q. What is the inward part or thing signified?

A. The industry and wealth of the people, which are verily and indeed taken and had by Pensioners and Sinecurists, in their Corruption.

Q. What are the benefits whereof you are partakers thereby?

A. The weakening and impoverishing the People, through the loss of their Liberty and Property, while our wealth becomes enormous, and our pride intolerable.

Q. What is required of them who submit to the Test of Bribery and Corruption?

A. To Examine themselves, whether they repent them truly of any signs of former honour and patriotism, stedfastly purposing henceforward to be faithful towards the Minister; to draw on and off like his glove; to crouch to him like a Spaniel; to purvey for him like a

Jackall; to be as supple to him as Alderman Sir WILLIAM TUR-
TLE; to have the most lively faith in the funds, especially the Sinking
Fund; to believe the words of Lord Castlereagh alone; to have
remembrance of nothing but what is in the Courier; to hate MAT-
THEW WOOD, the present Lord Mayor, and his second Mayoralty,
with all our heart, with all our mind, with all our soul, and with all
our strength; to admire Sir JOHN SILVESTER, the Recorder,
and Mr. JOHN LANGLEY;[1] and to be in charity with those only
who have something to give.

Here endeth the Catechism.

FROM MINUTES OF EVIDENCE GIVEN TO THE POLICE COMMITTEE OF
THE HOUSE OF COMMONS BY THE SECRETARY OF THE SOCIETY FOR
THE SUPPRESSION OF VICE (GEORGE PRICHARD), 1817.

Jovis, 15° Die Maii, 1817,
The Hon. Henry Grey Bennett in the Chair
George Prichard, Esq. called in and examined.

1. *Q.* In your former examination before the Committee, you stated,
that one of the objects of the Society was the prosecution of dealers
in obscene books, prints, &c. What was the state in which the Society
found this trade when they first directed their attention to it?

A. The Society first entered upon their investigation into the state
of this trade shortly after its institution in the year 1802; at which
period prosecutions for such offences being almost unknown, so little
disguise and concealment were used by dealers of this class, that, with
no great difficulty, important discoveries were soon made as to its
nature and extent. It was early ascertained, from indubitable testimony, that several foreigners (having their head quarters in London)
of apparent respectability, and considerable property, were united
together in partnership for the principal, and almost exclusive, purpose of carrying on an extensive traffic in obscene books, prints,
drawings, toys, &c. The agents, by whom the partners of this house
disseminated their merchandize, were about thirty in number, chiefly
consisting of Italians, under the assumed character of itinerant
hawkers, by whom they established a systematic trade throughout
great part of the United Kingdom. The names of the artists were,
also, ascertained by whom the prints were designed and engraved.
These itinerants, after being provided with a considerable stock, were
accustomed to disperse themselves in parties of two, and sometimes

---

[1] Otherwise Jack Ketch.

would travel singly in different directions throughout the country; and when their stocks were exhausted, their confederates in London were accustomed to convey fresh supplies by the waggons. These itinerants, at stated intervals, would rendezvous at towns previously agreed upon, and concert their future plans of proceeding. The places which they principally visited were, Brighton, Maidstone, York, Manchester, and the counties of Norfolk and Suffolk. The same species of trade, and by similar means, was also carried on by others; and it was ascertained from the testimony of a frame-maker, as well as from other credible sources of information, that the principals and agents generally concerned therein, amounted in number to at least six hundred. From their own and other incidental information, it was discovered that the principal vent for their commodities were schools, and chiefly those for females, into which they would contrive to introduce these articles by means of servants. Women were also employed as agents in this trade, who would gain admission into schools for females under the pretext of purchasing cast-off clothes from servants. It also appeared, that opulent tradesmen, of fair reputations, were concerned in the same trade, who obtained large importations from the continent, in return for the works of native artists. Many of the keepers of ballad-stalls were also implicated in these transactions, and several booksellers were known to be in the habit of supplying country orders of the same kind. The foregoing description is as concise an outline as can well be given of the state of this trade at the time when the Society first entered upon the investigation of it; and its early records furnish ample and circumstantial particulars in proof of the general facts I have stated.

2. *Q.* What steps did the Society take in consequence of these discoveries?

A. Having obtained undoubted evidence of the practices I have before detailed, they immediately sent cautionary letters to almost all the schools for female education in and about the metropolis, and to the Head-masters of the different public schools. They afterwards prosecuted two itinerant dealers to conviction, and have continued, up to the present time, to watch the trade with a vigilant eye, until, by successive prosecutions, they have reduced it to a state of comparative insignificance.

3. *Q.* How many prosecutions have the Society carried on against these offenders?

A. Between thirty and forty, in all of which they have invariably succeeded; the Society being particularly careful not to enter upon any prosecution, in which there may seem to be the most distant probability of failure.

4. *Q.* Have the various prosecutions of the Society apparently tended to the diminution of these offences?

A. So much so as to render it now a matter of great difficulty to succeed in making purchases, which heretofore could be effected with comparative ease. A very common answer now returned to applications made for such articles is, that it is very difficult to procure them in consequence of the prosecutions of the Society for the Suppression of Vice; the very name of which proves of considerable efficacy in spreading dismay among the trade, and driving many, who before derived an entire subsistence from it, into other occupations.

5. *Q.* How many prosecutions have the Society instituted during the last twelve months?

A. In consequence of the renewed intercourse with the continent, incidental to the restoration of peace, there has been a great influx into the country of the most obscene articles of every description, as may be inferred from the exhibition of indecent snuff boxes in the shop windows of tobacconists. These circumstances having tended to a revival of this trade, the Society have had occasion, within the last twelve months, to resort to five prosecutions, which have greatly tended to the removal of that indecent display, by which the public eye has of late been so much offended.

6. *Q.* Was not this description of goods introduced into the kingdom from the continent also during the war?

A. To a very small extent comparatively, though the advantages of obstructed intercourse in this respect were in some degree counteracted by the great quantities manufactured at the prisons for prisoners of war.

In proof of the extent of this evil, I beg leave to give in the following letter, received from the late Mr. Birtill, of Bristol, under date, Bristol, 6th December 1808.
'Sir,

'The Bristol Society for the Suppression of Vice being about to dissolve, and the agents before employed having moved very heavily, I took my horse and rode to Stapleton prison, to inquire into the facts contained in your letter: inclosed are some of the drawings which I purchased, in what they call their market, without the least privacy on their part or mine; they wished to obtrude on me a variety of devices, in bone and wood, of the most obscene kind, particularly those representing a crime, which ought not to be named among Christians, which they termed "*the new fashion.*" I purchased a few, but they are too bulky for a letter; yet I will forward them if desired. Straw platt was tendered me by at least thirty of the prisoners, who carry it about with them.

'This market is held before the door of the turnkey every day, between the hours of ten and twelve; and the space being small, I think it impossible for him not to be privy to the description of articles sold.

'I have waited on the Mayor, who, in conjunction with a respectable Magistrate for the county (Thomas Daniel, Esq.), has sent an official letter to the Duke of Portland, who is Lord High Steward of this City, enclosing proofs of this abominable practice, and requesting his interference with the proper officers, and that a total stop be put to it. Perhaps your very useful Society might, with the enclosed, still further this object; or, if we are applying to the wrong persons, advise us of the most efficient mode of acting.

'The prison is a pleasant walk of three miles, and is the promenade for the youth of both sexes of this city in fine weather, as well as the resort of strangers; so that the mischief is incalculable.

'Please to make my best acknowledgements for the humane attention of your Committee, while I feel sorry and ashamed that our citizens should have suffered an evil of such magnitude to lie at their doors unremoved for so long a time.

'Any future communications might be addressed either to the Mayor, or to the Rev. T. T. Biddulph, J. Fort, or to,

Sir,

Your very obliged servant,

'JOHN BIRTILL.'

Addressed,
'*George Prichard, Esq.*
31, *Essex Street, Strand.*'

In consequence of the foregoing letter, the Society made representations to the Transport Board, and the then Duke of Portland, who caused instructions to be dispatched to the Agents for Prisoners of War at Bristol, and the result was the entire suppression of the evil. Similar communications were afterwards made to the Agents for Prisoners of War at Norman Cross, Dartmoor, Chatham, Yarmouth, Foxton, and Edinburgh.

7. *Q.* What appears to be the present state of this trade?

A. From collateral evidence, the Society has reason to think that it is now reduced to a very low ebb, particularly in consequence of a very recent prosecution by the Society; but which it is intended to discontinue, in consequence of the parties having delivered up a considerable magazine of obscene books, upwards of 1200 obscene prints and drawings, and all the copper-plates in their possession, from which many of the prints were struck off. From indirect information received by the Society, and which there is every reasonable ground for believing, this was the great and almost only remaining source of supply to the inferior dealers throughout the kingdom.

8. *Q.* How is it, that when such offences seemed so much to abound, these prosecutions were so rare previous to the institution of this Society?

A. The offences were but little known by those who, from their province or situation in life, might naturally be supposed to be inimical to such practices; for dealers and customers, being alike conscious of guilt, used every precaution against detection, and carried on the trade in concealment. When these offences were first brought to light by the Society, Magistrates have expressed their astonishment at the extent of the evil, of the great prevalence of which they before had no conception.

9. *Q.* It seems strange that the Society should come to the knowledge of offences so little known to the police: how is this to be accounted for?

A. Because it is one of those offences for the detection of which there are no rewards, and Magistrates can only be supposed to have knowledge of such crimes as become the subjects of information before them. How duly Magistrates have been impressed with the enormity of this offence when brought before them by the Society, may be inferred from the following recorded observation of a Magistrate by whom one of these delinquents was tried; viz. 'That the mischief done to the community by such offences greatly exceeds that done by murder: for, in the latter case, the mischief has some bounds; but no bounds can be set to the pernicious consequences of a crime, which tends to the entire corruption of morals.'

10. *Q.* Are we to understand from your last answer, that the Society would recommend that the system of rewards should be extended to the detection of this species of offence?

A. By no means; as it would tend to the introduction of great abuses by attracting the common informer. On the other hand, individuals are deterred from coming forward on the occasion, by personal timidity and the expenses attendant on prosecution. These difficulties become obviated by means of the Society, through whom the moral feelings of the country can, with irresistible power, be brought to bear upon this as well as all other offences that are open and scandalous violations of the laws, passed for the preservation of public morals and decency.

11. *Q.* But can the Society itself act without employing a number of agents, whose practices are open to the same objections that attach to the common informer?

A. The Society seldom employs more than one agent, whose office is not *to find out* offenders; but to ascertain the correctness of such information as is received from respectable individuals, and to qualify himself for giving evidence on the occasion. In using the means necessary for detection, he is strictly prohibited from using falsehood, or of alluring to sale by the offer of a price. The public is the usual source of that information on which the Society acts, as I could prove by the production of those letters which usually give rise to their proceedings; but which cannot be brought forward without a breach of that confidence reposed in them by their correspondents, with respect to whom it is their custom to preserve strict secrecy. The idea which has gone abroad, that the Society send among the public numbers of secret spies and informers, is utterly without foundation, and has originated in the misrepresentations of many of the public journals, the editors of which (from not understanding the true character of the Society, or the real nature of their proceedings) have too hastily admitted into their columns the misrepresentations of those evil-disposed persons, who are ever attempting to render the Society unpopular by disseminating the most unfounded calumnies. The Committee endeavour, by all the means in their power, to make the well-disposed members of society understand, that the Institution is to be considered as an instrument in their hands for putting in force the existing laws against the more open and daring violations of public decency. With this view the Committee avail themselves of every opportunity of inviting all persons, duly impressed with the importance of such considerations, to communicate to the Society what they may discover within the sphere of their observation. With private vice and folly, and such as extends not to the public the influence of its bad example, the Society have nothing to do, and never interfere; and being entirely dependent on public opinion for their existence and support, they must of necessity be particularly careful of maintaining it by the general propriety of their measures, as the loss of the public esteem would inevitably be productive of their downfall.

12. *Q.* By what description of persons are the proceedings of your Society generally controlled?

A. By individuals of the most respectable classes in society, both clergy and laity, as its printed Reports show.

13. *Q.* In what courts do you usually institute your prosecutions?

A. Sometimes at the Quarter Sessions, but mostly in the Court of King's Bench. Although suits in the latter court are much more expensive, yet they gain more publicity, and denunciations against offenders from a court of the highest jurisdiction in the kingdom, tend to infuse a greater degree of dread among persons prone to such offences.

14. *Q.* Have the Courts, before whom these prosecutions have been brought, generally approved of them; or has not the legality of the Society's associating for such purposes been brought into question?

A. The Court of King's Bench has been pleased on such occasions to declare its high approval of such prosecutions; and the Lord Chief Justice, in the trial of a man named Bertazzi, in adverting to some observations of counsel for the defence, insinuating that it was illegal for persons to associate for the objects pursued by the Society, and particularly for the prosecution of offenders, was pleased to say—'Something has been said about the persons, who have formed themselves into this Society, having acted contrary to the law; it does not appear to me they have done so, by any thing they have done in prosecution of the purposes of the Society; but looking at this prosecution only, so far from seeing any thing which trenches upon law, I conceive they have done very properly in taking an interest in the morals and happiness of society, and in exerting themselves to prevent the contagion of these infamous publications. It appears to me they have deserved the thanks of all men, and I do not know of one rule of law upon which they have at all trenched.' And on the occasion of another prosecution, for the same offence, the same high authority was pleased to observe—'Whether these prosecutions will have the effect of suppressing this infamous practice I do not know; if they have not, I cannot tell what must be done to put an end to it.'

15. *Q.* Has it not been objected, that such things derive a publicity from prosecutions, the ill-effects of which more than counterbalance their supposed advantages?

A. Such certainly has been one of the objections urged against the Society's prosecutions; but that it has no foundation in fact, will appear from the following rule, always adopted in Court with respect to these proceedings, viz. that the indictments are never read openly in Court; but are, with the libel, handed up to the Bench and the Jury, so that not even the name of the libel escapes. That this is the case will appear from the observations of the Attorney General upon one of the Society's prosecutions, viz. 'I cannot but congratulate the Society upon the very satisfactory result of their last prosecution, by which they have established, by the highest authority, that gentlemen of the first rank may not only, with perfect propriety, lend their assistance to the bringing offences to light, and offenders to punishment; but that, in so doing, they will be protected from any thing that might be injurious to their characters, or distressing to their feelings; and have also given a practical proof that prosecutions, which, from the manner in which they sometimes have been conducted, have been more injurious to the interests of morality than the practices which they sought to suppress, may be brought under consideration before the most crowded audiences, in a manner not to offend the most chaste ear of female virtue, or in the smallest degree to promote the progress of vice. I hope I shall be excused for adding these observations upon an occurrence, which has given me much satisfaction.'

16. *Q*. What is the legal description of the offence under consideration? and do you think the law as it at present stands adequate to its reformation?

A. It comes under the description of a libel, the printing and publishing of which is indictable at common law, as tending to a breach of the peace. According to the law of libel (as at present understood by Magistrates) it certainly is by no means adequate to the suppression of such offences; for if an itinerant dealer is detected in the very act of selling obscene prints at a school, he cannot be apprehended without a warrant, which cannot be obtained until after a bill of indictment is presented and found against him by a grand jury, in order to which (a thing almost impossible) his name must be previously obtained. These difficulties enable itinerant dealers sometimes to escape with impunity, and to carry on their nefarious practices at other places. I do not see how this evil can be effectually put a stop to, unless constables and all other persons are enabled to seize such offenders without a warrant[1] (as in cases of treason and felony), and to carry them before a justice of the peace, to be held to bail, or committed for want of sureties to take their trial at the ensuing Quarter Sessions or Assizes.

17. *Q*. Does the circumstance of these publications being introduced into seminaries for female education rest upon undoubted evidence?

A. The fact has been verified, by the evidence brought forward on such trials, and has been adverted to by the Court of King's Bench in pronouncing its judgement in the following terms in the King v.——: 'We cannot hear without horror and disgust the arts you have practised to render the wholesome seminaries of female education the scenes of pollution and vice. At the same time, what has passed upon this occasion, must strike all persons with horror and disgust; it has opened a scene which it will be well for those who have the tuition and care of youth, males as well as females, seriously to reflect upon, and in future to guard against with the most attentive caution.'

---

[1] This difficulty has since been happily obviated by a circular, declaratory of the law, from a late Minister of the Home Department; by which magistrates were instructed, that, for all acts committed by individuals, tending to a breach of the peace, they had a power of immediate commitment in default of bail.

18. *Q.* Have you reason to suppose that the evil with respect to schools is now effectually remedied?

A. Though it is probably much diminished, yet that it still continues to exist in a degree, appears from a report of what passed at Union Hall no longer ago than the month of September last, and which was as follows: viz. Union Hall—Infamous Case—'James Price was brought up by an inspector of hawkers' licenses, charged with hawking goods from house to house not having a license. The inspector stated, that being at Richmond, on Wednesday last, he observed the defendant going about from house to house selling twine and snuff-boxes; he went up to him, and asked him for his license; the defendant produced one, which was out of date, and acknowledged he had no other. The defendant now pleaded great poverty, and said he was ignorant his license had expired, and the magistrate was about to discharge him; when, upon further investigation, it was discovered that many of the snuff-boxes had indecent and obscene engravings, and pictures upon them, some of them very highly finished; and, on being closely interrogated by the worthy magistrate, in consequence of some information conveyed to him, the defendant was obliged to confess that he was in the habit of exposing these boxes to sale at Ladies' Boarding Schools, and of disposing of many of them to the young pupils. The magistrate animadverted in severe terms on the conduct of the defendant, and regretted that his power of punishing him extended no further than fining him ten pounds, which he did; and the defendant not being prepared to pay that sum, the magistrate committed him to the house of correction for three months, or until the fine was paid.'

I do not think that any degree of vigilance, that can be exercised by the heads of schools can effectually guard against this evil, unless the law is rendered more effectual against such offenders, as suggested in my answer to a former question.[1]

19. *Q.* How do the Society dispose of the obscene articles which come into their possession?

A. They are always destroyed in the presence of two members of the Committee, except a few specimens, which are preserved as evidence of the convictions, which have from time to time been obtained by the Society. These specimens are kept in a tin box secured by three different locks; one of the keys of which is kept by the treasurer, one by a member of the Committee, and one by the secretary; so that the box can at no time be opened, but with the concurrence of these three persons.

---

[1] See former Note; from which it appears, that this difficulty is now removed.

From J-B. LOUVET DE COUVRAY, THE AMOURS OF THE CHEVALIER DE FAUBLAS, 4 VOLS., LONDON: (WILLIAM BENBOW), 1822.

[The following passages are those quoted in the indictment of Benbow on charges of obscene libel. At his trial the jury decided that the book was not obscene.]

(1) A profound silence reigned for some moments. Are you asleep already, my sweet child, said the Marchioness in a gentle tone.—Oh! no, I am not asleep. She threw herself into my arms, and pressed me against her bosom. Oh, heaven! cried she, with an astonishment very naturally assumed, if it was assumed, it is a man! and then, quickly repulsed me: what! is it possible?—Madam, replied I, trembling, I told you so; You told me so, sir, but was it to be believed? Well, you must not remain in my house—or at least another bed must be prepared for you.—Madam, it is not me, it is the Marquis—But, sir, speak then in a lower tone—you must not remain in my house, you must go away.—Well, madam, I'm going. She then took hold of me by the arm. You are going away! where, and what to do? To awake my maids; to hazard your life in jumping out of the window! to discover, in all probability, to my servants, that I have had a man in bed with me!—Pardon me, madam, be not angry; I am going to recline in the arm chair. Yes, undoubtedly you must—but what a fine resource, (still holding me by the arm) fatigued as you must be! to remain in the cold, and to injure your health! you deserve that I should treat you with this rigour—well, rest there, but promise that you will be prudent. Provided, madam, that you will pardon me.—No, I do not pardon you! but I have still more regard for you, than you have for me. See how cold your hand is already! And out of pity she put it on her ivory bosom. Guided by nature, and by love, this happy hand descended a little; I knew not the stimulus which caused my blood to boil. No woman, said the Marchioness in a milder tone, ever experienced the embarrassment in which you place me. Ah! pardon me then, my dear mamma! Your dear mamma, indeed! you have a great regard for your dear mamma, little libertine that you are! Her arms which had at first repulsed me, gently drew me towards her: presently we were so close to each other, that our lips came in contact, and I was emboldened to print a burning kiss upon hers. Faublas, said she in a voice scarcely audible, is this what you promised me? Her hand strayed; a raging flame circulated in all my veins—Ah! madam! pardon me, I die—Ah! my dear Faublas—my friend!—I continued motionless. The Marchioness felt for my embarrassment, which could not displease her—She kindly aided my inexperience, and I received, with as much astonishment as pleasure, a charming lesson, which I repeated more than once.

We employed several hours in this agreeable exercise; I began to fall asleep on the bosom of my fair mistress, when I heard the noise of a door which opened gently; somebody entered and advanced on tip-toe; I was without arms, in a house with which I was unacquainted, and I could not help experiencing a sensation of alarm. The Marchioness guessed who it was, told me in a whisper to take her place, and give her mine, and I immediately obeyed her.

Scarcely had I changed places, when some one opened the curtains on the side which I had just quitted. Who comes to wake me thus, said the Marchioness? The person hesitated a few moments, but presently explained himself, without replying to her. And what a strange whim is this, sir? continued she, the time too that you choose sir, is also very improper; without consideration for me, and without respect for the innocence of this young person, who perhaps is not asleep, or who may awake! you are very unreasonable, I beg you will retire. The Marquis insisted, and endeavoured to appease his wife by some very comic excuses. No, sir, said she, I will not, it shall not be, I assure you, you shall not, therefore I beg you will retire; she jumped out of bed, took him by the arm and put him out of the door.

My beautiful mistress returned to me laughing, was not that well done; said she, you see what I have refused on your account. I felt that I owed her a remuneration, which I offered her with ardour, and she accepted with gratitude: so complaisant is a woman of twenty-five when she loves! and so fertile are the resources which nature gives to a novice of sixteen! (Vol. I, pp. 21–3).

(2) I found her in her boudoir, negligently reclining upon an ottoman; an elegant dishabille, instead of concealing, showed her charms to advantage. She rose as soon as she saw me. How charming you look in this dress, Mademoiselle du Portail! how well this gown becomes you! and as soon as the door was shut: Oh! how happy I am to see you, my dear Faublas, how your punctuality flatters me! my heart told me you would find the means of coming in spite of your two fathers. I only replied by the most tender embraces; and compelling her to take the position from which she rose to receive me, *I proved to her that her lessons were not forgotten*; when we heard a noise in the adjoining room. Dreading to be surprised in a situation by no means equivocal, I rose precipitately, and thanks to my convenient garments, I had only to change my posture, for my disorder to be repaired. The Marchioness, without appearing embarrassed, merely put that in order which was most necessary; this was only the affair of a moment. (Vol. I, pp. 31–2.)

(3) I ran home. Jasmin told me my father was gone out, and that a pretty girl had been waiting for me above an hour. A pretty girl,

Jasmin? I flew to my apartment. Ah! Justine, is it thee! Jasmin was right when he told me it was a pretty girl: I embraced her.—Keep that for my mistress, said she, pretending to be sullen. For thy mistress, Justine? Thou art as good as her.—Who told you so?—I think so; it rests with thee to make me certain of it. I embraced her again, and she suffered me to do so, still repeating,—Keep that for my mistress. My God! how well you look in your own dress added she; and will you ever quit it again, to disguise yourself as a woman? —To-night, for the last time, Justine: after that I shall always be a man,—at thy service, sweet girl.—At my service?—Oh, no; at the service of Madame—At hers and thine at the same time, Justine. Hey dey, so you must have two at a time!—I feel, my dear, that is not too much. I embraced Justine, and my hands strayed upon her snowy hills, which she scarcely defended.—How impudent he is, said Justine. What has become of the modesty of Mademoiselle du Portail?—Ah, Justine, thou knowest not how one night has changed me!—That night also made an alteration in my mistress; the next day she was pale and fatigued. My God! when I saw her, I was not at a loss in guessing that Mademoiselle du Portail was a very nice young man.

I was going to embrace her again. For this time, she prevented it by recoiling a few paces: my bed was behind her; she fell on her back; and by an accident which might, perhaps, be expected, I lost my equilibrium at the same moment.

Some minutes after, Justine, who was in no haste to repair her disorder, asked, with a smile, what I thought of the little piece of waggery she had played the Marquis. (Vol. I, pp. 94–5).

(4) A door, which I had not observed, opened all at once. The Marchioness entered. To fly into her arms—to give her twenty kisses—to carry her to the alcove—to place her on the springing couch—and to plunge with her into a delightful extacy, was the affair of a moment. The Marchioness recovered her senses at the same time with myself. I asked her how she did. What say you? replied she, with an astonished air.—I repeated: My dear little mamma, how do you do?—She burst into a fit of laughter: I thought I had misunderstood you; the *how do you do* is excellent; but if I was unwell, it would have been a very queer time to ask me such a question. Do you think that this exercise would agree with a sick person? (Vol. I, pp. 96–7.)

(5) When I see thee, my dear friend, I think no more of what I have suffered for thee. How well you look in your male attire! How handsome! how charming you are! but what a pity, added she, rising with an air of gaiety, that they must be laid aside. Come on, make way for Mademoiselle du Portail. At these words she undid, with a single

433

stroke of her hand, all the buttons of my waistcoat. I revenged myself on her neck-handkerchief, which I had already considerably deranged, and which I now took entirely away. She continued the attack, and I was pleased with her vengeance; we took off all without replacing anything. I showed to the half-naked Marchioness the alcove, and once more she let me conduct her there. (Vol. I, p. 100.)

(6) She threw herself upon the sofa. Her husband cried out, and then embraced her, saying, If you knew how I loved you!—If you loved me, monsieur, you would have had more consideration for me, more respect for yourself, more tenderness for a child who is, perhaps, more to be pitied than blamed. What are you doing, monsieur? Leave me. If you love me, you will not go to inform an unhappy father of the errors of his child; you will not go and relate this adventure to M. de Rosambert, who will laugh at it, make a jest of you, and spread a report that I have received in my house a girl of intrigue! But, monsieur, have done; what you would do is nothing to the purpose.—Madam, I love you.—It is not sufficient to say so; it must be proved.—But for these three or four days, my love, you would not let me prove it.—It is not such proofs as these that I demand of you, monsieur. But monsieur; have done then, I say.—Come on, madam, my love.—Indeed, monsieur, that is very ridiculous!—We are alone.—It would be better if there were other persons here; that would be decent. Have done then, I say; have we not always time to do those things! Leave me alone.— What! married people! at your age? in a boudoir! on a sofa! like lovers! and when I have something else to request of you.—Well, my angel, I'll say nothing to Rosambert, nothing to M. du Portail.—You can promise well.—I'll give you my word.—Well then! Stop a moment; give me the pocket-book; leave it with me.—With all my heart; there it is. (There was a short silence.) Indeed, monsieur, said the Marchioness, in a voice almost extinct, you desired it; but it is very ridiculous.

I heard them stammer, sigh, and die away both together. One may imagine what I suffered under the sofa during this strange scene. I could have strangled the actors with my own hands; and in the excess of my spite I was tempted to discover myself, to reproach the Marchioness with this new species of infidelity, and repay the Marquis for the bitter mortification he made me undergo, without knowing it. (Vol. I, pp. 122–3.)

(7) While speaking, she had drawn my sword, and was fencing before me: Be on your guard, chevalier, said she.—I know not if the Viscomte is redoubtable, but I know well it is not in that; it is not thus that I ought to combat with the Marchioness. Dare she accept another kind of encounter?—(She flew to my arms.)—Ah, Faublas!

said she, laughing; ah! if there were no greater murderers!—It is not, mamma, among men that they seek for heroes.

I then placed the Marchioness in a situation which rendered her unable to combat with me, and she took it kindly. (Vol. I, p. 132.)

(8) My sleep was not of long duration. I could not resist the accustomed impression of this kiss, which burnt my lips, and made my heart beat. For this time, I was not deceived by a vain dream; it was no longer a fugitive shadow which embraced me; even in my bed, and presently in my arms, I found a living body in voluptuous contact with my own. But gently—blunderer as I am, I was going to tell the simple fact in simple language, and the fair reader is already blushing; let us, then, endeavour to clothe this affair in decent phraseology.

I felt myself taken hold of in a very delicate manner, and gently drawn towards it by a charming little hand, which I kissed. Do not be displeased with me, for, with all your scruples, you would have done as I did. A thousand seductive attractions would not have been offered you in vain; like me, you would have wandered with delight over so many charms with a caressing and curious hand, enchanted at the result of your researches; like me, you would have said in a whisper, lest your servant in the next room should hear you: Charming spirit! how beautiful thy form! how soft thy skin!

I repeated this very flattering compliment several times; I wished more than once to prove that it was sincere. Vains désirs un convalescent, s'il peut dans une heureuse nuit! souvent recommencer les mêmes discours, répéte mal aisement les mêmes actions. Le doux combat venait de s'engager, il n'était pas de simple politesse; je me rapelle trop bien que mon adversaire s'y complaisait. Hélas! Faublas s'y trouva trop peu préparé; Faublas y fut presqu' aussitôt vaincu. Encore si le revenant, moins taciturne, avait bien voulu causer familièrement avec moi; mais il s'obstinait à ne pas repondre un mot. C'était un sûr moyen de me rendormir, moi que, comme tout d'autres, aime assez à parler quand je n'ai rien à faire.

When I woke again, the sun was rising, and I was alone in my chamber. I recommenced my search, already so often made without effect. My two doors and four windows were fast, and the walls seemed incapable of containing a secret door, nor was there any opening in the floor, or sliding compartment in the ceiling. How, then, could this *female* spirit penetrate into my room? The doctor had neither wife nor daughter, and the house was only inhabited by men. From whence then came this *tempting* spirit, whose *sex* I had proved? Did Lisette journey from the other world into this, to be revenged of her poor Lucas?

A farmer's wife in my arms! No! I would rather believe myself

435

the Titan of the timid Aurora, or the modern Endymion of some haughty goddess, who had clothed herself in a human form. Oh! my Sophia! It seems to have been predestined that thy husband should not remain faithful to thee, even for three weeks; but at least the incense which belongs to thee, has only burnt at the shrine of a divinity.

I was anxious to lay this adventure before Count Rosambert, from whom it was very astonishing that I received no direct intelligence. I wrote him a letter of three large pages, the two first were occupied about Sophia, and I crowded into the third, the inconceivable history of my beautiful ghost.

I waited the night following, but it did not come until the eighth night. Impelled by an eager desire of knowing the nocturnal beauty who visited me, I demanded her appellation, for whether nymph or goddess, a name she must have. How long she had loved me, for without infatuation, I flattered myself that I had pleased her; in what place she had met me, for she treated me at least like an acquaintance. These questions, and several others less embarrassing, obtained me no answer. At last, of all the known means to make a woman speak, I employed the most decisive, but the malicious female demon, with an unshaken presence of mind, exhausted my resources without suffering a single exclamation to escape her.

I was mortified the more, as this impolite silence became, in consequence of circumstances, a species of ingratitude; I endeavoured to conduct myself in such a manner as to obtain some thanks. All my efforts, however, were useless, for I found with regret that the females of the other world, although very sensible to *certain* terrestrial joys, possess not, on the most interesting occasions, the tender prattle, and the affectionate converse of our earthly dames.

An enemy to the accusing day, my discreet spirit waited not the rising Aurora. When I heard her prepare for her departure, I endeavoured to retain her; but she placed the fore finger of her right hand on my mouth, her left hand upon my heart, and on my forehead two kisses; then, slipping from me with a sigh, quickly escaped I know not where. I merely thought I could distinguish a cracking as if the wall opened, and the creaking of a hinge. I was, apparently, deceived, for I examined my walls again as soon as it was light, but the paper which covered them exhibited a smooth surface, and offered no signs of being opened; my doors and windows also were closely shut.

The same evening I found in my night-cap a second letter:

'I shall return in the night between Sunday and Monday if the Chevalier promises me, on the word of a gentleman, that he will make no attempt to detain me. Let him answer me through the same medium.'

Ah! I understand! through the night-cap. The next day my docile messenger was charged with my short dispatch which contained the promise required from me.

The much-wished Sunday arrives! And shortly the night surrounds me with her perfidious shades, that night so remarkable in the history of my life! Jasmin, who had been absent since dinner, returned towards dusk. As soon as he saw me alone, he informed me of the unexpected arrival of Rosambert. The Count had stopped at Luxembourg, from whence he had sent secret despatches to Jasmin; for reasons which he himself would tell me, he could not arrive at Hollirisse until about an hour before midnight, as it was of great consequence that no one should see him enter the house; I was, therefore, earnestly requested to open the little garden gate, precisely at twelve o'clock, with my own hand.

I followed my instructions punctually. M. de Belcourt, angry that I left him sooner than usual, made a remark about it to M. Desprez, with which I was not struck, but by what happened subsequently: Let the convalescent go, said he, I dare say he has some commerce with the spirits, which he does not wish us to know.

Instead of going to my chamber, I slipped gently into the garden. Rosambert was waiting for me at the little gate. Ah! how do you do, my good friend; where is my Sophia? What is become of the Marchioness? Have you any news of her father? Does her husband live still? How is my sister? What do they say of the duel? What think you of the stranger? How do you like my affair with the ghost? Why did you not write to me? How do you do?

A moment's patience, dear Noirval! what vivacity! what eagerness! you put me in mind of the little Chevalier de Faublas, about whom they talk so much in Paris. Let us, in the first place, sit down on this bench, and permit me to make my answers in a little more order than you put your questions. My vigilant emissaries have seen M. du Portail at Paris, and they will follow his footsteps until they have discovered the place of his daughter's retreat, of which they will send us a good account.

Oh! my Sophia! shall I then behold thee again?

Gently, my friend, you shall; do not interrupt me. Madame de B——— is, apparently, retired to one of her country residences, as they can meet with her neither at court nor in the city.—Poor Marchioness, I shall never see thee again!—Perhaps not; do not be grieved at that—the Marquis, whose wound is not deemed mortal, only desires to be cured, that he may go and seek you wherever you are to be found. He vows to pursue you everywhere.—But, Rosambert, have you no idea where she is?—Probably at one of her country seats.—Yes, Madame de B——, but Sophia, I mean?—Ah! in Paris, most probably.—Think you, my friend, that the Marquis will pardon her?—Pardon the Marchioness! Why not? The adventure is an extraordinary one I agree, but the evil is very common. It is only a little noise! Oh! a woman like the Marchioness can make him listen to reason.

Tell me, Rosambert, without flattery, whether you think I can make him restore her to me! What, force the Marquis to give his wife up to you!—No, my friend, it is of my own, and of her father that I speak.—Du Portail! there can be no doubt but they will compel him to give her up.—I shall never see her more! I shall never—never see her more!—On the contrary, since he will be forced to give her up, you will see her.—I was thinking, monsieur, on that unhappy lady—You are always the same, my friend; marriage has not changed you: but let me, in my turn, ask you some questions. In the first place, I see that you are nearly recovered—The hope of shortly seeing my Sophia!—yes! yes! my Sophia!—*and then, that unfortunate lady!*—the Marchioness; I assure you it is not my intention to go in search of her! It is true I sometimes catch myself thinking of her, but it is because—Undoubtedly, Chevalier; I understand you; it is because you cannot help it. A young man of good birth, will, in spite of himself, recollect the kind offices of a young and handsome woman, who first initiated him into the mysteries of Venus? You are eternally jesting, Rosambert!—Tell me, have you, by chance, heard anything of the little Justine?—What! the *fille de chambre* also holds a share of your heart? Ah! that is because you had the pleasure of first instructing her in the rudiments of a Paphian education! But, stop! I think you told me that La Jeunesse had that honour?—Come on, Rosambert, I am wrong, say no more of it.—No, my dear Faublas, let us speak of the spirit.—Ah, yes! how do you like my affair with the spirit? Is it not singular that this woman never speaks a word, and is so wonderfully firm in her resolution? Is it not curious that this little demon should enter my chamber so often, and I cannot tell from whence;—Does she visit you every night, Faublas? No; but I expect her to-night.—So much the better, and we will clear up this pleasant mystery? We shall know—but I amused myself in writing instead of getting my supper, while I was at the inn. I begin to be hungry, Chevalier.—Stop here; I will go and call Jasmin.—What! and make a noise in the house? You must guard against that—stop! I think I have got something in my chaise; I always carry some provisions with me.

He left me; and in a few minutes he brought half of a fowl and a bottle of wine: I have brought two glasses, said he, because I intend you shall sup with me—here, here in this garden, chevalier; we have much to say, and it will not be safe in your chamber. In the first place, let us drink the health of Adelaide, of whom you have only spoken once.—Ah, my dear sister! I love her much, notwithstanding —how is she?—Very well; very well—and grows more charming than ever! I could not resist the inclination of seeing her before I left France. Amiable child! she looks more beautiful in her grief, and pines for the absence of her father, her brother, and her dear Sophia! Let us drink her health, Faublas: let us drink it instantly; I know that it is not fashionable, but we are in the country; and, besides, we are travellers! Stop! eat a morsel; you know I cannot sup alone.—I am delighted to see you, Rosambert: but why stop in the garden? why this mystery?—Because I could not converse with you in private; because the Baron, who has already intercepted my letters to you, would have occupied all my time, and would have desired me to alter the news I bring according to his own wishes.—You are right, Rosambert; and then the spirit! do you think that I should not wish to speak about her?—Come, Faublas, I will give you the health of Sophia.—I have not tasted a drop of wine for this month before; you wish to make me tipsy!—To the health of Sophia! You cannot refuse that, chevalier. Come, drink to Sophia!—Oh, my pretty cousin! it is not the first time you have made me lose my reason! This wine, Rosambert, is uncommonly strong! it affects my head! What think you of the stranger, who, during the ceremony in the cathedral—Faith, I do not know what to say—let us talk of your new mistress—that nocturnal beauty—who loves you with so much discretion. Is she pretty, Faublas?—Beautiful, my friend!—What! a woman who fears daylight! I'll wager she's ugly?—A hundred Louis that she is charming.—Well! I'll take you at your word; but then I must see her.—And then you will inform me—Most willingly: but do you think I can be less curious than yourself. Since you wrote to me the account of your adventure, I have burnt with an ardent desire to develope [sic] the mystery. Permit me to assist you in this experiment: you must go to bed gently, and without a light. You must get into bed quick, and say not a word. I will remain concealed by your bed-side, and am provided with a dark lantern, which will be of importance on this occasion; and, if the spirit is not a sorceress, we will see what kind of a face she has. Therefore, chevalier, let us drink one more health; you have forgot some one.—Ah! yes! the beautiful Marchioness! Oh, my faithful wife! I know well that I should not name her. Come on, then, give me two drops for the Marchioness!—You are jesting, my friend; for so charming a woman you must have it quite full.

This last glass finished me, and I sunk all at once into a delirium of intoxication. The surrounding objects already appeared to me in confusion. I spoke without making myself understood; or rather, I stammered instead of speaking. I presently became dull and stupid: my noisy joy now ceased, and I was overcome by the most invincible sleep. Rosambert, who perceived this, begged me to conduct him to my chamber, but to make no noise, and keep a profound silence. He told Jasmin, who waited my orders in the garden, to retire in the same manner. We went up with no other light than the dark lantern which we left in the passage. As I entered, supported by Rosambert, I came in contact with a sofa, on which he stretched me, to the end, he said, that he might undress me with greater facility. I suffered him to act the part of *valet de chambre*, but he acquitted himself so slowly and awkwardly that before he had finished I sunk into a most profound sleep.

An hour's sleep having dissipated the fumes of the strong wine which had taken away my senses, I was suddenly roused by a loud burst of laughter. At length, cried Rosambert, I am completely revenged; I am willing you shall kill me on the spot, if it is not her! At the same instant I heard a groan, which was followed by a long sigh. I was lying in such a manner on the sofa that I perceived the feeble light of the dark lantern at the bottom of the passage. Prompted instantly both by anxiety and curiosity, I ran into the passage, and entered the apartment abruptly, with the lantern in my hand. I cast the trembling light on the objects before me: what did I see? Alas! even at this day, how can I relate it without a sigh! I saw upon my bed, which he had taken possession of, and in my place, which he had usurped, Rosambert, almost naked, closely embracing, in the most unequivocal position, a woman! Oh! Madame de B——, how beautiful you still appeared to me, although you had fainted. (Vol. II, pp. 167–75).

(9) . . . . if you had a correct notion of what sort of a man M. de Lignolle is, you would know that between him and me nothing has passed exciting joy and pleasure.—What, no pleasure, madam, cried I, but what would you say if I told you how much rapture I feel at your disappointment? What would you say if I announced to you that your kind destiny has conducted an avenger into your apartment?—An avenger?—Yes, you now behold a young man at your feet—one who loves you passionately—who feels every sentiment of tenderness for you, and every degree of admiration for your charms! You are really a young man, and you love me! but perhaps it is not

440

love, exclaimed the Countess; you are here, Mademoiselle de Brumont, but are you really a young man?—My charming Countess, replied I, can have no doubt upon that head. Well, then, said she, avenge my cause; be my avenger—marry me forthwith—I command you—I insist upon it.—My dear Eleanor, replied I, you need not command me—it is the most ardent wish of my soul. The good soul had every reason to be displeased with her husband, but the good man was unintentionally the author of my success. He had actually done so little that every thing remained for me to do, but in enterprises of this description every obstacle only serves to add new fuel to the flame. My courage increased with the difficulties opposed to it, and acquired force from the recollection of past success. A few half-smothered sighs, the forerunners of bliss, announced my approaching triumph, and a mixture of pain and rapture completed the conquest over a young and innocent heart. This triumph was indeed of a most delicious nature, in which the victor, highly pleased with the transports of his conquered antagonist, finds, in communicating pleasure, an additional relish for his own joys. (Vol. III, pp. 65–66.)

(10) I did not, however, indulge the fond hope that my destiny had reserved for me the peculiar privilege of consummating a marriage not my own, while I feel a native instinct for the matrimonial state. (Vol. III, p. 66.)

(11) But now, kind reader, speaking without disguise, would you not wish to be in my place; in the arms of the charming Countess; and in the nuptial bed prepared for another man. I need not tell you that these were the happiest moments of my life, though I may communicate to you the pleasing reveries in which my sportive imagination revelled with uncontrolled delight. (Vol. III, p. 67.)

(12) I soon after awoke my young mistress, and took my place beside her. On opening her eyes, she cast a glance at me, full of more vivacity than tenderness, and I had reason to imagine that the caresses which followed it were not totally disinterested. A few incoherent expressions escaped her, mingled with half-smothered sighs. These symptoms quickly intimated to me that my young pupil was prepared for another lesson, and was secretly wishing to complete her education.

Who, kind reader, could refuse her the favour, if he was still able to bestow it? I therefore recommenced my essays, when a loud knocking resounded at the chamber-door. I quitted my post on this alarm, and was preparing to get out of bed, but the Countess made me a signal to remain where I was, and then enquired with a firm voice, who was at the door?—It is I, replied M. de Lignolle, are you not getting up?—Not yet, sir.—Madam, it is very late.—Yes, but I am busy. —What are you doing? I am composing with Mademoiselle de

Brumont.—I wish I could take part in the lesson.—That cannot be, sir; you are not clever enough; you would hinder us from doing any-thing.—Pray, madam, what are you doing?—I am performing what you will have the credit of—that is, I am finishing a charade.—A charade, indeed; you are in search of the word.—Yes—wait a minute.—I shall find it.

Now, said she, in a whisper to me, this is the moment of complete vengeance and satisfaction. I wish to play him a trick, the recollection of which will amuse me fifty years hence, if I live so long. My dear Flourvac, he has cruelly interrupted our pleasant pursuit.

She said no more, but a glance and a gesture, as well as a tender kiss, conveyed to me an order to resume the exercise so unfeelingly interrupted.

Pleasure rendered me docile and submissive, and I obeyed without any murmur or remonstrance. (Vol. III, pp. 68–9.)

The Trial of William Benbow (1822), as reported in Benbow's *Rambler's Magazine; or, Fashionable Emporium of Polite Literature* (June and August 1822)

(1) *Society for the Suppression of Vice* (1 June, 1822)

It appeared by the public papers on Saturday morning, the 25th of May, that Mr. Adolphus, on the preceding day, moved for a warrant to hold Mr. Benbow to bail, for publishing an obscene libel. The defendant, seeing this, immediately gave notice of bail, which was accepted, and put in the same evening, but neither the warrant nor the form of the recognizance enabled him to ascertain which of his publications had given offence. It was impossible to determine by the newspapers, because they all varied. The Times said it was for five obscene prints; another paper mentioned the 'Rambler's Magazine', and a third, the 'Chevalier de Faublas'. Mr. Benbow has applied to the office of the Clerk of the Peace at Hicks's Hall, for a sight of the indictment, that he might know precisely what the offensive publica-tion was. He was told that it was an obscene libel, and he could not have any further information, without paying for a copy of the indictment, which was very long. This the defendant is not inclined to do, thinking it contrary to the spirit of British jurisprudence, thus to keep a man in ignorance of his imputed crime, to the risk of his continuing to commit it. If a defendant is indicted in the Court of King's Bench, he may read the indictment file at the Crown Office, by paying a shilling; and it does not seem consistent that the petty courts should have the exclusive privilege of being arbitrarily liberal. Of one thing the defendant is certain, viz. that the prosecution is not for obscene prints, as stated in the Times, for he never sold or encouraged such things in his life; but from all he can collect, he has reason to believe it is for the translation he is publishing of the 'Amours, Adventures and Intrigues of the Chevalier de Faublas', a celebrated French Romance, which has been universally read and admired for nearly forty years.

(2)   Vice Society *v.* Benbow (1 August, 1822)
[*As some of our readers in distant parts, may not meet with a full report of the trial, we think it our duty to give them some extracts from Mr. Philips's address to the jury.*]

They were told that the society was composed of honourable men —*most honourable men,* he did not doubt. But how happened it that none of their informations were against rich men? that whoever they had selected, none of their victims were from their own class and station in society? Whatever they might do with respect to others, they had an especial sympathy for the vices of the great. From the time of the establishment of the society to the present, none but poor and humble individuals had been prosecuted by them. Have they indicted any titled libellers?—Have they brought to justice any titled gamesters? Have they suppressed any of those public brothels in St. James's, open to every young man with any thing to lose, and spreading their lures to divest him of fame and fortune? Out of that class have they selected any to bring to the bar of justice? No, gentlemen; it is fathers of families, humble tradesmen, unable to compete with them, that they attack.—They did not warn him of the illegality of his deeds; no benevolent clergyman entered the defendant's shop, expostulated with him on the course he was pursuing, and told him that the law must interfere if he persisted. No, this was a case which required the aid of the secretary Prichard, and the dismissed custom-house officer. Do you hear of their going into the neighbourhood of St. James's, where gaming-houses are public and notorious, and of their indicting them? No; those are frequented by the titled, the wealthy, and the great. Had the gentlemen of the jury heard of any victims from the rich classes? It reminded him of the very old adage, that the laws were constructed like cobwebs, which the great flies could break through with impunity, but which entrapped the little ones.

Gentlemen! who are these vice suppressors, the great supporters of public morals, and the champions of Christianity? They are the worst names that Virtue and Religion could rely on for support. If it were not for their intrusion, many works of immoral tendency would fall still-born from the press. They stimulated persons, careless of their fate, to publish improper books. It was the bounden duty of the gentlemen of the jury to put a stop to these self-elected prosecutors, and to teach them that Englishmen were not to be treated thus with impunity. In the name of God! where were the law officers of the crown? were they so careless of their duty, that they left the scrutiny of these works to the vice society? Was the attorney-general to be accused of pocketing the fees, without performing his duty? Was he either so ignorant or careless, that he knew not his duty? Was the attorney-general a traitor to his trust? These, gentlemen! were the foulest of conspirators: they raked the dying embers of blasphemy and sedition, to fan them into a flame, and to publish them to the wide world.

The learned counsel had adverted to the defendant's removal from the Strand, but he did not tell them why he had removed into Castle-street. The defendant was there in extensive business, when he had the visitation of another somewhat similar gang to this; he was thrown into prison for some months; he was then liberated, without their daring to bring him to trial; and, at the expiration of that period, he found himself with his family in the world, with not a shilling for their support, the profits of his business having been consumed in that time. He was now to be visited with the vengeance of another gang, unless the jury interposed to save him. These were your Christian champions! These were your pretenders to Christianity! It would be well if they opened the sacred volume, and perused it; and they would there learn that it teaches forgiveness—not persecution; and they would there see that the person in whose sacred name they professed to coalesce, never persecuted! Christians!—Pharisees! —Heathens in practice!—Christians only in name! These were your vice suppressors, who had joined their funds to drag to the bar of justice poor men, who, even if acquitted, must be ruined by the enormous expences of the law. Was the poor man the proper victim to contend with them? And let any one read the alleged libels, and say if his was not a vicious and depraved imagination that could find any thing depraved in them. The spider collects poison from the flower that gives honey to the bee! There was scarcely ever a book published in which a depraved mind could not find impure images. The Gospel itself had been charged, by some bad men, with containing heaps of profanation. Was it fair to take isolated passages out of a book, and then call upon them to judge of the whole work? In this way, the Bible might be pronounced to be a heap of obscenity and sedition. Algernon Sidney had lamented this on the scaffold. He protested against parts of his work being brought as evidences of the whole. If any man, said he, were to assert coolly that 'there was no God', he would be instantly set down as a most abominable atheist.

Yet that sentence was in the Bible, But what preceded it? 'The fool hath said in his heart there is no God?'

Mr. Adolphus had mentioned the prints in the *Rambler's Magazine*, yet what would he see there more than a personification of what he had read at school. He wondered what harm could arise from thus expressing in an engraving what was found in the ancients. There was not a vice suppressor but had gloated over it! There was not a reverend prosecutor but what put it into the hands of the children in his care. In old times there was a set of gods, who he dared to say had their vice suppressors. The god Vulcan, a limping ugly old blacksmith, had the shocking presumption to marry Venus, the prettiest of all the goddesses. This Venus, like many ladies of the present day, was fond of a red coat, and Mars, the god of war, presented more attractions to her, than the cross old husband. Vulcan, being apprised of their interviews laid a snare for them, consisting of a net so skilfully constructed, that when he had drawn it round their bed, they could not escape. Then, not content with knowing his own disgrace, he collected the gods that they might also behold them. Just so the vice society search for obscenity, and then publish it to the world. In the whole host of classical books, there was not one from Juvenal downwards but what might be convicted of obscenity. Look at Ovid— look at Horace, that lover of wine and pretty women, and even the chastest poet of all antiquity, was not free from a charge of a more serious description. The other print represented the story of Jupiter and Leda, familiar to every classical reader, and learned in the school books. Jupiter was the prince of the gods, and very fond of pretty women. Finding Leda's husband an obstacle to his amours, he assumed the shape of a swan, and violated Leda while bathing. The bishops, archbishops, and whole host of reverend tithe collectors, were all familiar with the story of Jupiter and Leda, and with Mars and Vulcan. If these stories in classic authors were not to be read, the whole course of education must be changed, and there is not a gem out of the mine of ancient learning that would not be trampled on by these two-legged asses! Mr. Adolphus had alluded to the Latin books slightly, but not one half of the obscenity that was in them was to be found in these. Nay, he would say that there was not a single novel ever published but what might be found to contain passages more offensive than any selected for the jury this day to consider of. As to the song, it was truly ridiculous as a subject of prosecution—and at this moment, there were not less than a hundred of a far more seductive tendency, lying on the music tables of the daughters of the vice suppressors, and they were untouched!

The jet of the inquiry, in the present case, was the intent of the

445

defendant, and the Jury would say whether he had any obscene and indecent motives, when he published a book in sixpenny numbers, the reading of which could be procured for three-halfpence, in any circulating library. They must have recourse to a depraved imagination, to torture them into any thing indecent. What would the vice suppressors say to the exhibitions of paintings and sculptures at Somerset House, where the most modest ladies paid for admission, and for the gratification of their curiosity would patiently endure crowded and heated rooms? Yet in this there was nothing impure. Had the Gentlemen of the Jury visited Carlton Palace, Windsor, or the Marquis of Stafford's, and numerous other collections, where naked statues were seen of the most indecent description? It was easy to make a charge of indecency, but the indecency, if any where, lay in the minds of the prosecutors; they were the quickest at detecting hidden meanings and obscene allusions. The learned counsel had dwelt much upon the circumstance of six stars finishing one of the libels; the next thing, he supposed, would be to indict the firmament and stars for indecency. The defendant must be judged, he said again, by the intent; they would consider that he had already been imprisoned and ruined; they were to see that he had fair play, and that he was not oppressed by any individual. Let him that was not guilty throw the first stone; but let not men whose only virtue was in their purse, assume to themselves a power the law gave them not. In the hands of the Jury he left his client, for they were the only protectors of the poor man against the powerful coalition of the rich.

From *The Merry Muses: A Choice Collection of Favourite Songs gathered from many sources by Robert Burns*. Privately printed (not for sale), 1827[1]

PREFACE

The history of this book is the following:

Robert Burns, fascinated by the simplicity, beauty, and pathetic tenderness of the Songs and Ballads of the peasantry floating around him, set himself to gather them up for preservation. How he accomplished his task, his imperishable works amply show. His researches brought him acquainted with many strange, outspoken ditties;—for gentlemen of antiquarian tastes need not be told that many of the Songs and Rhymes then unprinted were, as Sir Walter Scott says, 'rather high kilted', or, as Burns styles them, 'not quite ladies'

[1] The true date of this edition was not 1827. It was published by John Camden Hotten (1832–73).

reading'. It is the glory of Burns, however, that he improved every song that passed through his hands; purifying it from its licentiousness, and steeping it in the undying hues of his genius. While collecting these 'Auld Sangs', he came across others whose humour was more broad, and language and meaning decidedly free. His antiquarian interest and strong sense of the ludicrous tempted him also to preserve them in manuscript form. In time what he thus collected he was led in a few instances also to imitate, for no other object than to amuse a few of his merry companions in their moments of conviviality.

Accordingly we find him in December, 1793, writing to John McMurdo, Esq., Chamberlain to the Duke of Queensbury (a friend and neighbour of the poet's) 'I think I once mentioned something of a collection of Scots songs I have for some years been making. I send you a perusal of what I have got together. I could not conveniently spare them above five or six days, and five or six glances of them will probably suffice you. A very few of them are my own. When you are tired of them please leave them with Mr. Clint, of the King's Arms. There is not another copy of the collection in the world, and I should be sorry that any unfortunate negligence should deprive me of what has cost me a great deal of pains.

'R.B.'

This collection (including his own few performances) originated in nothing worse than Burns' strong sense of the ludicrous, and although he permitted an intimate prudent crony an occasional peep at the volume, he was very careful of it, and during his lifetime it was seen and known only to a trusted few. After his death the MS. volume having got into a careless hand, a miserable fellow surreptitiously transcribed it and, to the lasting grief of all friends of poor Burns, gave it the honours of the Press.

This note is written therefore to point out Burns' share in this Collection of Merry Songs—a share which was chiefly that of collector, and not that of author; besides, to request of the limited number of antiquarian admirers into whose hands the volume will find its way, that they will be careful of it, and keep it out of the way of 'youth, innocence, and beauty'. To gratify the aforesaid antiquaries, two letters of the Great Poet are now given for the first time, and also an unpublished Poem, from the original manuscript in Burns' own writing.

It is hoped that the reader—be he Puritan or impure-itan—will not be too hard on poor Burns. Remember not the dust specks on his fame, but know him rather as the sweetest and most glorious singer that has yet arisen to charm, and soothe, and strengthen mankind. The age he lived in was different from yours—and if a free spoken ditty of the olden school now and then oozed out, remember that humour in connection with the sexual affections flourished in Greece and Rome ages upon ages ago, and it is not yet extinct in your own country, nor in your own bosom. One of your own Poets but a short time ago bore his share, along with a Rhyming Brother, in the following *jeu d'esprit*, which we are tempted to give:

Poet No. 1 sang:

> Tom went out a Mission—ary,
> Unto the fields of Timbuctoo,
> There he met a Casso—wary,
> Who ate him, and his Hymn-book too.

Thus capped by Poet No. 2:

> Tom and Tim on mischief bent,
> Went to the plains of Timbuctoo,
> They saw three Maidens in a Tent,
> Tom bucked one, and Tim—bucked—two.

The songs which can undoubtedly be assigned to Burns—as well as those of which great doubts exist respecting his connection with them—are placed first in the volume. With those that follow, the reader is assured Burns had nothing whatever to do, though being expressed in the Scottish language inexperienced persons may *therefore* attribute them to him.

A very few copies have been printed, solely for antiquaries; and none of them are for sale.

(2) None of the following Songs, Scottish or otherwise, can claim parentage of Burns. Some of them were in print before he was born, in the chapbooks which formed the popular literature of the times; others had been sung at country fairs, and the free and easies of the period, when he rescued them for his collection.

(3)   *The Mouse's Tail*

> JACK and his master a wager laid
> Of threescore guineas and ten,
> Which of them had the longest p——
> The wager was to win.
> Sing—Fol de rol, &c.

> They measured the length, and eke the breadth
> They measured them round about,
> But Jack he did his master beat
> By four inches and the snout.

448

The maid she went behind the door,
   For which she was to blame,
And when she saw the wager won,
   She ran and told her dame.

The old woman went behind the door,
   To do as she was wont,
And stooping down to piss awee
   A mouse jumped into her——

The old woman cried out to her goodman,
   As loud as she could cry,
'A mouse has run up my whim-wham,
   And without your —— I'll die'.

The old man then laid her on a sack,
   As oft he'd done before,
But he could not reach the mouse's tail,
   By quite four inches and more.

The old man cried out to his man Jack,
   As loud as he could cry,
'A mouse has run up my wife's privates,
   And without your help she'll die'.

'Without you double my wages', said Jack,
   Without you double my price,
Altho' I've got the longest p——,
   My p—— shall hunt no mice'.

'I'll double your wages', said the old man,
   And give thee a hat and a coat,
And if you f—— the mouse out there,
   My dame shall give thee a groat'.

The old man stood on the barn floor,
   With a long broom in his hand,
To knock the mouse all on the head,
   As soon as it should land.

'Then work away, my bonny Jack,
   Of my quim ye need have no doubt,

And if you use your drumstick well,
    You'll turn the mouse about'.

Ride on, ride on, my bonny Jack,
    I think I feel your p——;
Drive on, drive on, don't stop for breath,
    The short strokes will do the trick'.

So Jack he rode, and rode, and rode,
    Till his courage began to flag,
'Tho' your cock it be twelve inches long,
    I don't call this half a shag'.

Jack gave a grunt, a terrible thrust,
    In hopes the groat to win,
'Goodwife, you've got an awful c——
    And that mouse is very far in'.

The prize cock failed, no mouse came out,
    The dame still felt her pain;
The good man, refreshed, went on again,
    And rode with might and main.

He rode and rode, till he fell off,
    The dame still cried for more,
So Jack got up, and bored again,
    Until his great p—— was sore.

The old woman was a cunning dame,
    As well you may believe,
For when these two could f—— her no more,
    She let the mouse out of her sleeve.

TWO POEMS OF THE KIDDERMINSTER CARPET WEAVERS' STRIKE
(1828–9)

[In 1829 Humphrey Price was sent to prison for a year for publishing libels on the master manufacturers of the Kidderminster carpet industry. The poems which follow were two of the libels, published at a time when 1,800 of the 2,000 weavers were said to be on strike. The indictment alleged that in publishing these poems he was 'wickedly and maliciously contriving and intending to encourage the said workmen in their refusal to work for the said Master Manufacturers respectively and to cause it to be understood and believed that the said Master Manufacturers had been guilty of oppression and other improper conduct towards the said workmen in refusing to give them higher wages and in other respects and to excite and stir up enmity and discord between the said Master Manufacturers and their said Workmen and to bring the said Master Manufacturers into public contempt, infamy and disgrace'. There were about fifty master manufacturers involved.]

(1)   *A Kidderminster Weaver's Wife's Dream*

Dearest Husband! hold my head,
I thought that all the town was dead!
To thy dear breast press me with speed,
That I may feel alive indeed.

Yes, yes, I live, now well I know
We've got to meet our latest foe
Well, let him come, he'll only bring
His ruthless dart, he's lost his sting

While on our Saviour we repose.
Come, listen to my sleeping woes
For tho' you dread my dreaming moans
They're softer than our waking groans.

I thought (as just before I said)
That all this populous town was dead!
How it could be I could not tell
But thought we knew it all full well

Had tasted death without its pain
And somehow were alive again!
The sun shone bright yet the summer air
Breath'd on our foreheads soft as fair.

The streets were full of happy people
When lo! upon the old church steeple
A being glorious to behold
(Resplendent all as burnish'd gold,

With purple folded wings, and face
Divinely sweet as God's own grace)
Wav'd high in air his hand of light
And fill'd us with untold delight.

His finger pointed out the road
To an oppressor's[1] rich abode,
Which half reveal'd in shrubb'ry rose,
Perfum'd by every flower that blows.

We saw the spot, much pleas'd, for now
No angry frown lower'd on our brow,
Oppression pass'd was like my dream,
Which is as tho' it ne'er had been.

Delighted with our present lot,
Our present woes all all forgot,
Or just remember'd but to shew
What happiness can spring from woe.

We look'd each other in the face,
Thankful we once had spar'd that place
When stormy passions strongly pent
Had struggled in our breasts for vent.

We hoped too the oppressor's soul,
Shriven of its guilt, had reach'd the goal,
Where Christ stands ready to receive
All who repent and in Him believe.

At this calm moment thro' the air
Clang'd the loud Trumpet heav'nly clear
And notes that spoke articulate sound
Were heard by all the thousands round.

'Woe to the man, however strong,
That builds his house by doing wrong,
Wages inadequate that gives
To the poor men by whom he lives.

'Woe to the man that judges not
The poor and needy's heavy lot,
Woe to the man whose eyes and heart
For covetousness are set apart.

---

[1] The 'oppressor', whose fate is predicted in the poem, was John Broom.

'Shall this man reign because he chose
Himself in cedar to enclose?
Because he said, I now will build
Myself a spacious house and gild

'It for my daughter, wife, or son,
And paint it with vermillion?
No, saith the Lord, were such an one
The signet of my right hand set on,

'Yet in my very injur'd law's defence,
And these poor men's, I'd pluck him thence.'
While these last words from the trumpet sped,
Filling the Heav'n and Earth with dread,

Such scenes before us then arose
I cannot, dare not them disclose.
The thought so fires my dizzy brain
I scarcely feel alive again.

But this I'll say, the house so fair,
And specially the chamber where
The oppressor died, now seem'd to be
The gate of endless misery.

The oppressor's race at last was run
And now his mis'ry had begun.
What horrid sights did us appal!
And his lost soul most horrible!

Awe struck and trembling we hie'd home,
Far otherwise than we had come,
Tho' guarded still by the angel bright,
Who had summon'd us to such a sight,

When you awoke me from my dreams,
Disturb'd no doubt by my sad screams.
But thankful I, dear man, to rest
Thus safely on thy faithful breast.

Tho' miserably oppress'd we are,
The oppressor's fate we shall not share.

Sarah W—d.

(2)   *The Complaint of a Kidderminster Weaver's Wife to her Infant*

1.

Hush thee, my babe! thy feeble cry
Tells me that thou ere long will die.
I'm glad thou hast not liv'd to curse
Our cruel masters. That were worse.

2.

Nor will I curse them, tho' they be
M******** [Murderers] of thyself and me.
Hush thee, my babe, close on my breast,
In death and heav'n we soon shall rest.

3.

Our sorrows soon will cease and we
Meet in a blest eternity.
Thy father too! escap'd the snare
Of oppressors proud, will meet us there.

4.

Hush thee, my babe! thou wilt not live
The living death such wages give
As tyrants offer: Heav'n's thy home,
Tyrants there shall never come.

5.

A few more struggles o'er and then
Vain all the scorn or help of men.
Our death a legacy may be
To our master's late posterity.

6.

On them and on their children dear
Our blood will be: I greatly fear.
O God! forgive them, lest they rue
The deed they now seem bent to do.

7.

Hush thee, my babe! thou wilt not see
Thy mother sink in misery,
Thy father too, all gone his bloom,
And his heart's blood upon the loom.

454

8.

O cruel, cruel, cruel masters!
Dare ye thus mock at our disasters,
See parent, child to frenzy driv'n
And dream yourselves of reaching Heav'n!

9.

Rouse from your slumbers, count the price
Of your own cursed avarice;
And count it well, e'er taught too late
To dread than ours a far worse fate.

Elizabeth.

FROM PERCY BYSSHE SHELLEY, QUEEN MAB

[The following passages are those in respect of which Edward Moxon was convicted of blasphemous libel in 1841.]

(1) They have three words: —well tyrants know their use,
Well pay them for the loan, with usury
Torn from a bleeding world!—God, Hell, and Heaven.
A vengeful, pitiless, and almighty fiend,
Whose mercy is a nickname for the rage
Of tameless tigers hungering for blood.
Hell, a red gulf of everlasting fire,
Where poisonous and undying worms prolong
Eternal misery to those hapless slaves
Whose life has been a penance for its crimes.
And Heaven, a meed for those who dare belie
Their human nature, quake, believe, and cringe
Before the mockeries of earthly power.

(2) Is there a God!—ay, an almighty God,
And vengeful as almighty! Once His voice
Was heard on earth: earth shuddered at the sound;
The fiery-visaged firmament expressed
Abhorrence, and the grave of Nature yawned
To swallow all the dauntless and the good
That dared to hurl defiance at His throne,
Girt as it was with power. None but slaves
Survived,—cold-blooded slaves, who did the work
Of tyrannous omnipotence; whose souls
No honest indignation ever urged

To elevated daring, to one deed
Which gross and sensual self did not pollute.

(3)   A murderer heard
His voice in Egypt, one whose gifts and arts
Had raised him to his eminence in power,
Accomplice of omnipotence in crime,
And confidant of the all-knowing one.
   These were Jehovah's words:

'From an eternity of idleness
I, God, awoke; in seven days' toil made earth
From nothing; rested, and created man:
I placed him in a Paradise, and there
Planted the tree of evil, so that he
Might eat and perish, and My soul procure
Wherewith to sate its malice, and to turn,
Even like a heartless conqueror of the earth,
All misery to My fame.'

(4) The plurality of worlds,—the indefinite immensity of the universe, is a most awful subject of contemplation. He who rightly feels its mystery and grandeur is in no danger of seduction from the falsehoods of religious systems, or of deifying the principle of the universe. It is impossible to believe that the Spirit that pervades this infinite machine begat a son upon the body of a Jewish woman; or is angered at the consequences of that necessity, which is a synonym of itself. All that miserable tale of the Devil, and Eve, and an Intercessor, with the childish mummeries of the God of the Jews, is irreconcilable with the knowledge of the stars. The works of His fingers have borne witness against Him.

THREE 'FLASH CHAUNTS' OF THE MID-NINETEENTH CENTURY
(PUBLISHED BY W. WEST, C. 1850)

(1) From *The Rambler's Flash Songster. Nothing but out and outers, adapted for gentlemen only, and now singing at Offley's, Cider Cellars, Coal Hole, &c.*

Long Tail Jock
A slashing parody on *Long Tail Blue*

I've just dropt in, dear ladies, fair,
I hope it won't you shock,

456

I'll sing you a song, it's not very long,
   It's about my long tail jock.
Just look at my long tail jock,
Oh, how do you like my jock,
I'll sing you a song, it's not very long,
   It's about my long tail jock.

Some niggas tink themselves so big,
   And show dare little cork [sic]
I struts about all the week
   And on Sundays I port my jock.
      Just look at my, &c.

I sailed from wirgenny springs,
   To Gibmutton rock,
And I guess I made the natives stare,
   When they saw my long tail jock.
      Just look at my, &c.

Jim Crow was courting a brown girl,
   And he show'd to her his c—k;
But I guess she let the nigga go,
   When she saw my long tail jock.
      Just look at my, &c.

I went to the City of Washington,
   Of pluck I'd got a good stock;
I stopt at one of Jackson's levees,
   And there show'd my jock.
      Just look at my, &c.

Old Jackson he came up to me,
   And said I much did shock,
All de ladies, that was there,
   With my long tail jock.
      Just look at my, &c.

I thought it time then to be off,
   But dey all round me did flock,
And they pulled me about so very much
   I thought they pull'd off my jock.
      Just look at my, &c.

(2) From *The Flash Chaunter. A slashing, dashing, friskey, and delicious collection of Gentlemen's Songs, now singing at Offley's, Cider Cellars, Coal Hole, &c., &c.*

Of All the Blowens on the Town
A flash parody on *Sally in our Alley*

Of all the blowens on the town,
    There's none like my flash Sally;
By prigs and w—es, she is well known,
    And she lives in S—t-pot Alley.
Her father, he was lag'd for life,
    An out-an-out highwayman;
Her mother, she's a lushington,
    And stone blind drunk all day man.
But blow me if I care a d—n,
    While I have got my Sally,
By prigs and w—es, she is well known,
    And she lives in S—t-pot Alley.

When I'm in quod, she ne'er forgets,
    To bring me good swags, O;
I never can my Sal forsake,
    If I can d—n my rags, O!
So kind a trump she is to me,
    I'll stick close to my Sally;
By all the prigs she is well known,
    And she lives in S—t-pot Alley.

When sessions comes about again,
    O, then I shall be free, sir;
And when I come out, with the string,
    My Sal again, I'll see, sir.
I'll hasten to her snoozing ken,
    Along with my flash Sally,
And on her bed, I'll lay my head,
    Once more in S—t-pot Alley.

(3) From *The Cuckold's Nest of Choice, Flash, Smutty, and Delicious Songs with Rummy Toasts Adapted for Gentlemen only.*

The Slashing Costermonger
A Slummy Smutty Parody on *The Literary Dustman.*
(Singing at all Select Parties, with much Applause.)

Appendix

Some kiddies says my calling's low,
  Acause I wends salt cod, O,
But, 'mongst the blowens, you must know,
  I'm reckoned quite a God, O.
Wegetables I also sells,
  And the vimen, how I loves 'em,
And ven a carrot they buys o' me,
  Two turnips for nothing I gives 'em.
For carrot or cod, no cove, egod,
  Than me can come it stronger,
I'm called by all the mots around,
  The slashing costermonger,
  The rummy costermonger.

I've got a leery moke asides,
  All others he does brown, sirs;
For twenty years or more, indeed,
  I've shown my ass in town, sirs.
Whene'er the blowens twig my ass,
  They feels so devilish funny,
And say, I gives 'em much more cod
  Than any for their money.
    For carrot, &c.

On Sunday I comes it so fine,
  As people does remark, sirs,
I has my ass all nicely vashed,
  And shows it in Hyde Park, sirs.
Of darters I've got two or three,
  To praise them none can cease, sirs,
And, just to show em off, they've got
  A pretty ass a-piece sirs.
    For carrot, &c.

I've made my sons quite gemmen, too,
  And they're such slashing men, sirs,
One on 'em keeps a fencing crib,
  And two a bawdyken, sirs.
My vife she's such a taste refined,
  All hearts she must be vinning,
For ven the turfing trade is bad,
  She gets blunt by cat skinning.
    For carrot, &c.

459

I'm quite a sporting karacter,
    I wisits flashy places,
Last year, my old voman washed my ass,
    An' I vent to Ascot races.
I got jist by the royal booth,
    And there—it is no farce, sirs,
The king, he often bowed at me,
    While the queen looked at my ass, sirs.
        For carrot, &c.

When my son Bill selected forth
    Himself a virtuous bride, sirs,
The morn on vhich they vent to church,
    Of course she lik'd a ride, sirs.
I soon accommodated her,
    Nor left her in the lurch, sirs,
She mounted on my rummy moke,
    And showed my ass in church, sirs.
        For carrot, &c.

So thus, you see, through life I goes,
    As you've seen by my showings,
Respected by the cadgers, and
    Adored by all the blowens;
And ven I'm in the church-yard laid,
    Vich soon may come to pass, sirs,
I vishes that there by my side,
    My friends may lay my ass, sirs.
        For carrot, &c.

FROM THE SATURDAY REVIEW, AUGUST 4 1866. (UNSIGNED ARTICLE
BY JOHN MORLEY.)

Mr. Swinburne's New Poems

IT is mere waste of time, and shows a curiously mistaken conception of human character, to blame an artist of any kind for working at a certain set of subjects rather than at some other set which the critic may happen to prefer. An artist, at all events an artist of such power and individuality as Mr. Swinburne, works as his character compels him. If the character of his genius drives him pretty exclusively in the direction of libidinous song, we may be very sorry, but it is of no use to advise him and to preach to him. What comes of discoursing to a fiery tropical flower of the pleasant fragrance of the rose or the fruitfulness of the fig-tree? Mr. Swinburne is much too stoutly bent on taking his own course to pay any attention to critical monitions as to the duty of the poet, or any warnings of the worse than barrenness of the field in which he has chosen to labour. He is so firmly and avowedly fixed in an attitude of revolt against the current notions of decency and dignity and social duty that to beg of him to become a little more decent, to fly a little less persistently and gleefully to the animal side of human nature, is simply to beg him to be something different from Mr. Swinburne. It is a kind of protest which his whole position makes it impossible for him to receive with anything but laughter and contempt. A rebel of his calibre is not to be brought to a better mind by solemn little sermons on the loyalty which a man owes to virtue. His warmest prayer to the gods is that they should

Come down and redeem us from virtue

His warmest hope for men is that they should change

The lilies and languors of virtue
For the raptures and roses of vice.

It is of no use, therefore, to scold Mr. Swinburne from grovelling down among the nameless shameless abominations which inspire him with such frensied delight. They excite his imagination to its most vigorous efforts, for they seem to him the themes most proper for poetic treatment, and they suggest ideas which, in his opinion, it is highly to be wished that English men and women should brood upon and make their own. He finds that these fleshly things are his strong part, so he sticks to them. Is it wonderful that he should? And at all events he deserves credit for the audacious courage with which he has revealed to the world a mind all aflame with the feverish carnality of a schoolboy over the dirtiest passages in Lemprière. It is not every poet who would ask us all to go hear him tuning his lyre in a stye. [sic] It is not everybody who would care to let the world know that he found the most delicious food for poetic reflection in the practices of the great island of the Ægean, in the habits of Messalina, of Faustina, of Pasiphae. Yet these make up Mr. Swinburne's version of the dreams of fair women, and he would scorn to throw any veil over pictures which kindle, as these do, all the fires of his imagination in their intensest heat and glow. It is not merely 'the noble, the nude, the antique' which he strives to reproduce. If he were a rebel against the fat-headed Philistines and poor-blooded Puritans who insist that all poetry should be such as may be wisely placed in the hands of girls of eighteen, and is fit for the use of Sunday schools, he would have all wise and enlarged readers on his side. But there is an enormous difference between an attempt to revivify among us the grand old pagan conceptions of Joy, and an attempt to glorify all the bestial delights that the subtleness of Greek depravity was able to contrive. It is a good thing to vindicate passion, and the strong and large and rightful pleasures of sense, against the narrow and inhuman tyranny of shrivelled anchorites. It is a very bad and silly thing to try to set up the pleasures of sense in the seat of the reason they have dethroned. And no language is too strong to condemn the mixed vileness and childishness of depicting the spurious passion of a putrescent imagination, the unnamed lusts of sated wantons, as if they were the crown of character and their enjoyment the great glory of human life. The only comfort about the present volume is that such a piece as 'Anactoria' will be unintelligible to a great many people, and so will the fevered folly of 'Hermaphroditus', as well as much else that is nameless and abominable. Perhaps if Mr. Swinburne can a second and a third time find a respectable publisher willing to issue a volume of the same stamp, crammed with pieces which many a professional vendor of filthy prints might blush to sell if he only knew what they meant, English readers will gradually acquire a truly delightful familiarity with these unspeakable foulnesses; and a lover will be able to present to his mistress a copy of Mr. Swinburne's latest verses with a happy confidence that she will have no difficulty in seeing the point of every allusion to Sappho or the pleasing Hermaphroditus, or the embodiment of anything else that is loathsome and horrible. It will be very charming to hear a drawing-room discussion on verses such as these, for example:

> Stray breaths of Sapphic song that blew
> Through Mitylene
> Shook the fierce quivering blood in you
> By night, Faustine.

> The shameless nameless love that makes
> Hell's iron gin
> Shut on you like a trap that breaks
> The soul, Faustine.

> And when your veins were void and dead,
> What ghosts unclean
> Swarmed round the straitened barren bed
> That hid Faustine?

> What sterile growths of sexless root
> Or epicene?

462

What flower of kisses without fruit
Of love, Faustine?

We should be sorry to be guilty of anything so offensive to Mr. Swinburne as we are quite sure an appeal to the morality of all the wisest and the best men would be. The passionate votary of the goddess whom he hails as 'Daughter of Death and Priapus' has got too high for this. But it may be presumed that common sense is not too insulting a standard by which to measure the worth and place of his new volume. Starting from this sufficiently modest point, we may ask him whether there is really nothing in women worth singing about except 'quivering flanks' and 'splendid supple thighs', 'hot sweet throats' and 'hotter hands than fire', and their blood as 'hot wan wine of love'? Is purity to be expunged from the catalogue of desirable qualities? Does a poet show respect to his own genius by gloating, as Mr. Swinburne does, page after page and poem after poem, upon a single subject, and that subject kept steadily in a single light? Are we to believe that having exhausted hot lustfulness, and wearied the reader with a luscious and nauseating iteration of the same fervid scenes and fervid ideas, he has got to the end of his tether? Has he nothing more to say, no further poetic task but to go on again and again about

> The white wealth of thy body made whiter
> By the blushes of amorous blows
> And seamed with sharp lips and fierce fingers
> And branded by kisses that bruise

And to invite Félises to

> Kiss me once hard, as though a flame
> Lay on my lips and made them fire.

Mr. Swinburne's most fanatical admirers must long for something newer than a thousand times repeated talk of

> Stinging lips wherein the hot sweet brine
> That Love was born of burns and foams like wine.

And

> Hands that sting like fire

And of all those women,

463

Swift and white,
And subtly warm and half perverse,
And sweet like sharp soft fruit to bite,
And like a snake's love lithe and fierce.

This stinging and biting, all these 'lithe lascivious regrets', all this
talk of snakes and fire, of blood and wine and brine, of perfumes and
poisons and ashes, grows sickly and oppressive on the senses. Every
picture is hot and garish with this excess of flaming violent colour.
Consider the following two stanzas

From boy's pierced throat and girl's pierced bosom
Drips, reddening round the blood-red blossom,
The slow delicious bright soft blood,
Bathing the spices and the pyre,
Bathing the flowers and fallen fire,
Bathing the blossom by the bud.

Roses whose lips the flame has deadened
Drink till the lapping leaves are reddened
And warm wet inner petals weep;
The flower whereof sick sleep gets leisure,
Barren of balm and purple pleasure,
Fumes with no native steam of sleep.

Or these, from the verses of Dolores, so admirable for their sustained
power and their music, if hateful on other grounds:—

Cold eyelids that hide like a jewel
Hard eyes that grow soft for an hour;
The heavy white limbs and the cruel
Red mouth like a venomous flower;
When these are gone by with their glories,
What shall rest of thee then, what remain,
O mystic and sombre Dolores,
Our Lady of Pain?

* * *

By the ravenous teeth that have smitten
Through the kisses that blossom and bud,
By the lips intertwisted and bitten
Till the foam has a savour of blood,
By the pulse as it rises and falters,
By the hands as they slacken and strain,

464

I adjure thee respond from thine altars,
Our Lady of Pain.

* * *

Thy skin changes country and colour,
And shrivels or swells to a snake's.
Let it brighten and bloat and grow duller,
We know it, the flames and the flakes,
Red brands on it smitten and bitten,
Round skies where a star is a stain,
And the leaves with thy litanies written,
Our Lady of Pain.

* * *

Where are they, Cotytto or Venus,
Astarte or Ashtaroth, where?
Do their hands as we touch come between us?
Is the breath of them hot in thy hair?
From their lips have thy lips taken fever,
With the blood of their bodies grown red?

It was too rashly said, when *Atlanta in Corydon* appeared, that
Mr. Swinburne had drunk deep at the springs of Greek poetry, and
had profoundly conceived and assimilated the divine spirit of Greek
art. *Chastelard* was enough to show that this had been very premature.
But the new volume shows with still greater plainness how far
removed Mr. Swinburne's tone of mind is from that of the Greek
poets. Their most remarkable distinction is their scrupulous moderation and sobriety in colour. Mr. Swinburne riots in the profusion of
colour of the most garish and heated kind. He is like a composer who
should fill his orchestra with trumpets, or a painter who should
exclude every colour but a blaring red, and a green as of sour fruit.
There are not twenty stanzas in the whole book which have the
faintest tincture of soberness. We are in the midst of fire and serpents,
wine and ashes, blood and foam, and a hundred lurid horrors.
Unsparing use of the most violent colours and the most intoxicated
ideas and images is Mr. Swinburne's prime characteristic. Fascinated
as everybody must be by the music of his verse, it is doubtful whether
part of the effect may not be traced to something like a trick of words
and letters, to which he resorts in season and out of season with a
persistency which any sense of artistic moderation must have stayed.
The Greek poets in their most impetuous moods never allowed
themselves to be carried on by the swing of words, instead of by the
steady, though buoyant flow of thoughts. Mr. Swinburne's hunting of

letters, his hunting of the same word, to death is ceaseless. We shall have occasion by and by to quote a long passage in which several lines will be found to illustrate this. Then, again, there is something of a trick in such turns as these:

Came flushed from the full-flushed wave.
Grows dim in thine ears and deep as the deep dim soul of a star.
White rose of the rose-white water, a silver splendour and flame.

There are few pages in the volume where we do not find conceits of this stamp doing duty for thoughts. The Greeks did not wholly disdain them, but they never allowed them to count for more then they were worth. Let anybody who compares Mr. Swinburne to the Greeks read his ode to 'Our Lady of Pain' and then read the well-known scene in the *Antigone* between Antigone and the Chorus, beginning ἔρως ἀνίκατε μάχαν, or any of the famous choruses in the *Agamemnon*, or an ode of Pindar. In the height of all their passion there is an infinite soberness of which Mr. Swinburne has not a conception.

Yet, in spite of its atrocities, the present volume gives new examples of Mr. Swinburne's forcible and vigorous imagination. The 'Hymn to Prosperpine' on the proclamation of the Christian faith in Rome, full as it is of much that many persons may dislike, contains passages of rare vigour:—

All delicate days and pleasant, all spirits and sorrows are cast
Far out with the foam of the present that sweeps to the surf of
    the past:
When beyond the extreme sea-wall, and between the remote
    sea-gates,
Waste water washes and tall ships founder and deep death waits:
Where mighty with deepening sides, clad about with the seas as
    with wings,
And impelled of invisible tides and fulfilled of unspeakable things,
White-eyed and poisonous-finned, shark-toothed and serpentine-
    curled,
Rolls under the whitening wind of the future, the wave of the
    world.
The depths stand naked in sunder behind it, the storms flee away;
In the hollow before it the thunder is taken and snared as a prey;
In its sides is the north-wind bound; and its salt is of all men's
    tears;
With light of ruin, and sound of changes and pulse of years:
With travail of day after day, and with trouble of hour upon hour;

And bitter as blood is the spray; and the crests are as fangs that
   devour;
And its vapour and storm of its steam as the sighing of spirits
   to be;
And its noise as the noise in a dream; and its depth as the roots
   of the sea:
And the height of its heads as the [height] of the utmost stars
   of the air:
And the ends of the earth at the might thereof tremble, and
   time is made bare.

The variety and rapidity and sustention, the revelling in power, are
not more remarkable here than in many other passages, though even
here it is not variety and rapidity of thought. The anapest to which
Mr. Swinburne so habitually resorts is the only foot that suffices for
his never-staying impetuosity. In the 'Song in Time of Revolution'
he employs it appropriately, and with a sweeping force as of the
elements:

The heart of the rulers is sick, and the high-priest covers his head:
For this is the song of the quick that is heard in the ears of the dead.
The poor and the halt and the blind are keen and mighty and fleet:
Like the noise of the blowing of wind is the sound of the noise
   of their feet.

There are, too, sweet and picturesque lines scattered in the midst of
this red fire which the poet tosses to and fro about his verses. Most
of the poems, in his wearisomely iterated phrase, are meant 'to sting
the senses like wine', but to some stray pictures one may apply his
own exquisite phrases on certain of Victor Hugo's songs, which, he
says,

     Fell more soft than dew or snow by night,
       Or wailed as in some flooded cave
     Sobs the strong broken spirit of a wave.

For instance, there is a perfect delicacy and beauty in four lines of the
hendecasyllabics—a metre that is familiar in the Latin line often
found on clocks and sundials, *Horae nam pereunt et imputantur*:—

     When low light was upon the windy reaches
     Where the flower of foam was blown, a lily
     Dropt among the sonorous fruitless furrows
     And green fields of the sea that make no pasture.

Nothing can be more simple and equisite than

For the glass of the years is brittle wherein we gaze for a span

Or than this:

> In deep wet ways by grey old gardens
> Fed with sharp spring the sweet fruit hardens;
>   They know not what fruits wane or grow;
> Red summer burns to the utmost ember;
> They know not, neither can remember,
>   The old years and flowers they used to know.

Or again:

> With stars and sea-winds for her raiment
> Night sinks on the sea.

Up to a certain point, one of the deepest and most really poetical pieces is that called the 'Sundew'. A couple of verses may be quoted to illustrate the graver side of the poet's mind:

> The deep scent of the heather burns
> About it; breathless though it be,
> Bow down and worship; more than we
> Is the least flower whose life returns,
> Least weed renascent in the sea.

>   * * * * *

> You call it sundew: how it grows,
> If with its colour it have [breath],
> If life taste sweet to it, if death
> Pain its soft petal, no man knows:
> Man has no [sight] or sense that saith.

There is no finer effect of poetry than to recall to the minds of men the bounds that have been set to the scope of their sight and sense, to inspire their imaginations with a vivid consciousness of the size and the wonders and the strange remote companionship of the world of force and growth and form outside a man. '*Qui se considérera de la sorte*', said Pascal, '*s'effraiera, sans doute, de se voir comme suspendu dans la masse que la nature lui a donnée entre ses deux abîmes de l'infini et du néant.*' And there are two ways in which a man can treat this affright that seizes his fellows as they catch interrupted glimpses of their position. He can transfigure their baseness of fear into true poetic awe, which shall underlie their lives as a lasting record of solemn rapture. Or else he can jeer and mock at them, like an unclean fiery imp from the pit. Mr. Swinburne does not at all events treat the lot of mankind in the former spirit. In his best mood, he can only brood over 'the exceeding weight of God's intolerable scorn, not to be borne'; he can only ask of us, 'O fools and blind, what seek ye there high up in the air', or 'Will ye beat always at the Gate, ye fools of fate'. If he is not in his best mood he is in his worst—a mood of schoolboy lustfulness. The bottomless pit encompasses us on one side, and stews and bagnios on the other. He is either the vindictive and scornful apostle of a crushing iron-shod despair, or else he is the libidinous laureate of a pack of satyrs. Not all the fervour of his imagination, the beauty of his melody, the splendour of many phrases and pictures, can blind us to the absence of judgment and reason, the reckless contempt for anything like a balance, and the audacious counterfeiting of strong and noble passion by mad intoxicated sensuality. The lurid clouds of lust or of fiery despair and defiance never lift to let us see the pure and peaceful and bounteous kindly aspects of the great landscape of human life. Of enlarged *meditation*, the note of the highest poetry, there is not a trace, and there are too many signs that Mr. Swinburne is without any faculty in that direction. Never have such bountifulness of imagination, such mastery of the music of verse, been yoked with such thinness of contemplation and such poverty of genuinely impassioned thought.

FROM GEORGE MOORE, LITERATURE AT NURSE; OR, CIRCULATING MORALS (PUBLISHER VIZETELLY), 1885.

(1) In 1883, I published a novel called *A Modern Lover*. It met with the approval of the entire press; *The Athenaeum* and *The Spectator* declared emphatically that it was not immoral; but Mr. Mudie told me that two ladies in the country had written to him to say that they disapproved of the book, and on that account he could not circulate it. I answered, 'You are acting in defiance of the opinion of the press—you are taking a high position indeed, and one from which you will probably be overthrown. I, at least, will have done with you; for I shall find a publisher willing to issue my next book at a purchasable price, and so enable me to appeal direct to the public.' Mr. Mudie tried to wheedle, attempted to dissuade me from my rash resolution; he advised me to try another novel in three volumes. Fortunately I disregarded his suggestion, and my next book, *A Mummer's Wife*, was published at the price of six shillings. The result exceeded my expectations, for the book is now in its fourth edition.

(2) Being thus grossly attacked, it has occurred to me to examine the

clothing of some of the dolls passed by our virtuous librarian as being decently attired, and to see for myself if there be not an exciting bit of bosom exhibited here and a naughty view of an ankle shown there; to assure myself, in fact, if all the frocks are modestly set as straight as the title Select Library would lead us to expect.

[Moore proceeds to compare his own novel, *A Mummer's Wife*, with such novels approved by Mudie as Mrs. Campbell Praed's *Nadine*; W. H. Mallock's *A Romance of the Nineteenth Century*, and Robert Buchanan's *Foxglove Manor*.]

(3) Without in the least degree attempting to make an exhaustive list of the books which to my surprise this most virtuous literary trades-men consents to circulate, I may venture to call attention to 'Puck', by Ouida. This is the history of a courtezan through whose arms, in the course of the narrative, innumerable lovers pass. 'Moths', by the same author, tells how a dissolute adventuress sells to her lover the pure white body and soul of her daughter, and how in the end Vera, disgraced and degraded by her ignoble husband, goes off to live with the tenor with whom she fell in love at the beginning of the story. In a book I opened the other day at haphazard, 'Phillida', by Florence Marryat, I find a young lady proposing to a young parson to be his mistress. It is true that the feelings that prompt her are not analysed, but does the cause of morals gain I wonder, by this slightness of treatment?

(4) Instead of being allowed to fight, with and amid, the thoughts and aspirations of men, literature is now rocked to an ignoble rest in the motherly arms of the librarian. That of which he approves is fed with gold; that from which he turns the breast dies like a vagrant's child; while in and out of his voluminous skirts run a motley and monstrous progeny, a callow, a whining, a puking brood of bastard bantlings, a race of Aztecs that disgrace the intelligence of the English nation. Into this nursery none can enter except in baby clothes; and the task of discriminating between a divided skirt and a pair of trousers is performed by the librarian. Deftly his fingers lift skirt and under-skirt, and if the examination prove satisfactory the sometimes decently attired dolls are packed in tin-cornered boxes, and scattered through every drawing-room in the kingdom, to be in rocking-chairs fingered and fondled by the 'young person' until she longs for some newer fashion in literary frills and furbelows. Mudie is the law we labour after; the suffrage of young women we are supposed to gain: the paradise of the English novelist is in the school-room: he is read there or nowhere. And yet it is certain that never in any age or country have writers been asked to write under such restricted conditions; if the same test by which modern writers are judged were applied to their

forefathers, three-fourths of the contents of our libraries would have to be condemned as immoral publications.

(5) The bond of sympathy that should exist between reader and writer is broken—a bond as sacred and as intimate as that which unites the tree to the earth—and those who do not live in communion with the thought of their age are enabled to sell their characterless trash; and a writer who is well known can command as large a sale for a bad book as a good one. The struggle for existence, therefore, no longer exists; the librarian rules the roost; he crows and every chanticleer pitches his note in the same key. He, not the ladies and gentlemen who place their names on the title-pages, is the author of modern English fiction. He models it, fashions it to suit his purpose, and the artistic individualities of his employés count for as little as that of the makers of the pill-boxes in which are sold certain well-known and mildly purgative medicines. And in accordance with his wishes English fiction now consists of either a sentimental misunderstanding, which is happily cleared up in the end, or of singular escapes over the edges of precipices, and miraculous recoveries of one or more of the senses of which the hero was deprived, until the time has come for the author to bring his tale to a close. The novel of observation, of analysis, exists no longer among us. Why? Because the librarian does not feel as safe in circulating a study of life and manners as a tale concerning a lost will.

To analyse, you must have a subject; a religious or sensual passion is as necessary to the realistic novelist as a disease to the physician. The dissection of a healthy subject would not, as a rule, prove interesting, and if the right to probe and comment on humanity's frailties be granted, what becomes of the pretty schoolroom, with its piano tinkling away at the 'Maiden's Prayer', and the water-colour drawings representing mill-wheels and Welsh castles? The British mamma is determined that her daughter shall know nothing of life until she is married; at all events, that if she should learn anything, there should be no proof of her knowledge lying about the place—a book would be a proof; consequently the English novel is made so that it will fit in with the 'Maiden's Prayer' and the water-mill. And as we are a thoroughly practical nation, the work is done thoroughly; root and branch are swept away, and we begin on a fresh basis, just as if Shakespeare and Ben Jonson had never existed. A novelist may say, 'I do not wish to enter into those pretty schoolrooms. I agree with you, my book is not fit reading for young girls; but does this prove that I have written an immoral book?' The librarian answers, 'I cater for the masses, and the masses are young unmarried women who are supposed to know but one side of life. I cannot therefore take your book.' And so it comes to pass that English literature is sacrificed on the altar of Hymen.

But let me not be misunderstood. I would not have it supposed that I am of opinion that literature can be glorified in the Temples of Venus. Were the freedom of speech I ask for to lead to this, we should have done no more than to have substituted one evil for another. There is a middle course, and I think it is this—to write as grown-up men and women talk of life's passions and duties. On one hand there must be no giggling over stories whispered in the corners of rooms; on the other, there must be no mock moral squeamishness about speaking of vice. We must write as our poems, our histories, our biographies are written, and give up once and for ever asking that most silly of all silly questions, 'Can my daughter of eighteen read this book?' Let us renounce the effort to reconcile those two irreconcilable things—art and young girls.

THE PROSECUTION OF HENRY VIZETELLY FOR OBSCENE LIBEL: MAY 1889

[At his second trial, in May 1889, Vizetelly was prosecuted in respect of six novels published during 1885–88

> Paul Bourget, *A Love Crime* (15)
> Guy de Maupassant, *A Woman's Life* (18)
> Guy de Maupassant, *A Ladies' Man* (17)
> Émile Zola, *How Jolly Life Is* (12)
> Émile Zola, *Fat and Thin* (6)
> Émile Zola, *The Rush for the Spoil* (18)
> Émile Zola, *His Excellency Eugène Rougon* (12)
> Émile Zola, *Abbé Mouret's Transgression* (3)

The figures in brackets indicate the number of passages from each translation cited in the schedule to the indictment. The passages which follow here are confined to those cited from *A Woman's Life* (1888) and *Abbé Mouret's Transgression* (1886), though even in the case of these two books it is impossible, for reasons of space, to quote more than a few of the extracts cited in the schedule.]

(1) Guy de Maupassant, *A Woman's Life*
'My pet, I have to perform a very difficult duty which really belongs to your mother; as she refuses to do what she ought, I am obliged to take her place. I do not know how much you already know of the laws of existence; there are some things which are carefully hidden from children, from girls especially, for girls ought to remain

pure-minded and perfectly innocent until the hour their parents place
them in the arms of the man who, henceforth, has the care of their
happiness; it is his duty to raise the veil drawn over the sweet secret of
life. But, if no suspicion of the truth has crossed their minds, girls
are often shocked by the somewhat brutal reality which their dreams
have not revealed to them. Wounded in mind, and even in body, they
refuse to their husband what is accorded to him as an absolute right
by both human and natural laws. I cannot tell you any more, my
darling; but remember this, only this, that you belong entirely to
your husband.' (pp. 55–6).
[This is the first passage from the novel cited in the schedule.]

Jeanne, in her room, was being undressed by Rosalie, whose tears
fell like rain; her trembling hands could not find the strings and pins,
and she certainly seemed a great deal more affected than her mistress.
But Jeanne did not notice her maid's tears; she felt as though she had
entered another world, and was separated from all she had known
and loved. Everything in her life seemed turned upside down; the
strange idea came to her: 'Did she really love her husband?' He
suddenly seemed some stranger she hardly knew. Three months
before she had not even been aware of his existence, and now she was
his wife. How had it happened? Did people always plunge into marriage as they might into some uncovered hole lying in their path?
When she was in her night-dress she slipped into bed, and the cool
sheets made her shiver, and increased the sensation of cold, and sadness and loneliness which had weighed on her mind for two hours.
Rosalie went away still sobbing, and Jeanne lay still, anxiously
awaiting the revelation she had partly guessed, and that her father had
hinted at in confused words—awaiting the unveiling of love's great
secret.
There came three soft knocks at the door, though she had heard
no one come upstairs. She started violently, and made no answer;
there was another knock, and then the door-handle was turned. She
hid her head under the clothes as if a thief had got into her room, and
then came a noise of boots on the boards, and all at once some one
touched the bed. She started again, and gave a little cry; then,
uncovering her head, she saw Julien standing beside the bed, looking
at her with a smile.
'Oh, how you frightened me!' she said.
'Did you not expect me, then?' he asked.
She made no answer, feeling horribly ashamed of being seen in
bed by this man, who looked so grave and correct in his evening dress.
They did not know what to say or do next; they hardly dared to look

at one another, in this decisive hour, on which the intimate happiness of their life depended. Perhaps he vaguely felt what perfect self-possession, what affectionate stratagems are needed not to hurt the modesty, the extreme delicacy of a maiden's heart. He gently took her hand and kissed it; then, kneeling by the bed as he would before an altar, he murmured, in a voice soft as a sigh:

'Will you love me?'

She felt a little reassured, and raised her head, which was covered with a cloud of lace.

'I love you already, dear,' she said, with a smile.

He took his wife's little slender fingers in his mouth, and his voice changed by this living gag, he asked:

'Will you give me a proof of your love?'

The question frightened her again, and, only remembering her father's words, and not quite understanding what she said,

'I am yours, dear,' she answered.

He covered her hand with humid kisses, and, slowly rising, he bent towards her face, which she again began to hide. Suddenly he threw one arm across the bed, winding it around his wife over the clothes, and slipped his other arm under the bolster, which he raised with her head upon it; then he asked, in a low whisper:

'Then you will make room for me beside you?'

She had an instinctive fear, and stammered out: 'Oh, not yet, I entreat you.'

He seemed disappointed and a little hurt; then he went on in a voice that was still pleading, but a little more abrupt:

'Why not now, since we have got to come to it sooner or later?'

She did not like him for saying that, but, perfectly resigned and submissive, she said, for the second time:

'I am yours, dear.'

Then he went quickly into his dressing-room, and she could distinctly hear the rustling of his clothes as he took them off, the jingling of the money in his pockets, the noise his boots made as he let them drop on the floor. All at once he ran across the room in his drawers and socks to put his watch on the mantelpiece; then he returned to the other room, where he moved about a little while longer. Jeanne turned quickly over to the other side and shut her eyes when she heard him coming. She nearly started out of bed when she felt a cold, hairy leg slide against hers, and, distractedly hiding her face in her hands, she moved right to the edge of the bed, almost crying with fear and horror. He took her in his arms, although her back was turned to him, and eagerly kissed her neck, the lace of her night-cap, and the embroidered collar of her night-dress. Filled with a horrible dread, she did not move, and then she felt his strong hands caressing her. She gasped for breath at this brutal touch, and felt an intense longing to escape and hide herself somewhere out of this man's reach. Soon he lay still, and she could feel the warmth of his body against her back. She did not feel so frightened then, and all at once the thought flashed across her mind that she had only to turn round and her lips would touch his.

At last he seemed to get impatient, and, in a sorrowful voice, he said:

'Then you will not be my little wife?'

'Am I not your wife already?' she said, through her hands.

'Come now, my dear, don't try to make a fool of me,' he answered, with a touch of bad temper in his voice.

She felt very sorry when she heard him speak like that, and with a sudden movement she turned towards him to ask his pardon. He passionately seized her in his arms and imprinted burning kisses all over her face and neck. She had taken her hands from her face and lay still, making no response to his efforts, her thoughts so confused that she could understand nothing, until suddenly she felt a sharp pain, and then she began to moan and writhe in his arms.

What happened next? She did not know, for her head was in a whirl. She was conscious of nothing more until she felt him raining grateful kisses on her lips. Then he spoke to her and she had to answer; then he made other attempts, which she repelled with horror, and as she struggled she felt against her chest the thick hair she had already felt against her leg, and she drew back in dismay. Tired at last of entreating her without effect, he lay still on his back; then she could think. She had expected something so different, and this destruction of her hopes, this shattering of her expectations of delight, filled her with despair, and she could only say to herself: 'That, then, is what he calls being his wife; that is it, that is it.'

For a long time she lay thus, feeling very miserable, her eyes wandering over the tapestry on the walls, with its tale of love. As Julien did not speak or move, she slowly turned her head towards him, and then she saw that he was asleep, with his mouth half opened and his face quite calm. Asleep! she could hardly believe it, and it made her feel more indignant, more outraged then his brutal passion had done. How could he sleep on such a night? There was no novelty for him, then, in what had passed between them? She would rather he had struck her, or bruised her with his odious caresses till she had lost consciousness, than that he should have slept. She leant on her elbow, and bent towards him to listen to the breath which sometimes sounded almost like a snore as it passed through his lips.

Daylight came, dim at first, then brighter, then pink, then radiant. Julien opened his eyes, yawned, stretched his arms, looked at his wife, smiled, and asked:

'Have you slept well, dear?'

She noticed with great surprise that he said 'thou' to her now, and she replied:

'Oh, yes; have you?'

'I? Oh, very well indeed,' he answered, turning and kissing her. Then he began to talk, telling her his plans, and using the word 'economy' so often that Jeanne wondered. She listened to him without very well understanding what he said, and, as she looked at him, a thousand thoughts passed rapidly through her mind.

Eight o'clock struck.

'We must get up,' he said; 'we shall look stupid if we stay in bed late to-day;' and he got up first.

When he had finished dressing, he helped his wife in all the little details of her toilet, and would not hear of her calling Rosalie. As he was going out of the room, he stopped to say:

'You know, when we are by ourselves, we can call each other "thee" and "thou," but we had better wait a little while before we talk like that before your parents. It will sound quite natural when we come back after our honeymoon.' And then he went downstairs.

Jeanne did not go down till lunch-time; and the day passed exactly the same as usual, without anything extraordinary happening. There was only an extra man in the house.

[This is the second passage from the novel cited in the schedule.] (pp. 57–61)

They went to a big empty hotel standing at the corner of a vast square, and ordered lunch. When they had finished dessert, Jeanne got up to go and wander about the town, but Julien, taking her in his arms, whispered tenderly in her ear:

'Shall we go upstairs for a little while, my pet?'

'Go upstairs?' she said, with surprise; 'but I'm not at all tired.'

He pressed her to him, 'Don't you understand? For two days—'

She blushed crimson.

'Oh, what would everyone say? what would they think? You could not ask for a bedroom in the middle of the day. Oh, Julien, don't say anything about it now, please don't.'

'Do you think I care what the hotel-people say or think?' he interrupted. 'You'll see what difference they make to me.' And he rang the bell.

She did not say anything more, but sat with downcast eyes, disgusted at her husband's desires, to which she always submitted with a feeling of shame and degradation; her senses were not yet aroused, and her husband treated her as if she shared all his ardours. When the waiter answered the bell, Julien asked him to show them to their room; the waiter, a man of true Corsican type, bearded to the eyes, did not understand, and kept saying that the room would be quite ready by the evening. Julien got out of patience.

'Get it ready at once,' he said. 'The journey has tired us and we want to rest.'

A slight smile crept over the waiter's face, and Jeanne would have liked to run away; when they came downstairs, an hour later, she hardly dared pass the servants, feeling sure that they would whisper and laugh behind her back. She felt vexed with Julien for not understanding her feelings, and wondered at his want of delicacy; it raised a sort of barrier between them, and, for the first time, she understood that two people can never be in perfect sympathy; they may pass through life side by side, seemingly in perfect union, but neither quite understands the other, and every soul must of necessity be for ever lonely. (pp. 66–7).

[This is the third passage from the novel cited in the schedule.]

(2) Émile Zola, *Abbé Mouret's Transgression*
[Three passages from the novel are cited in the schedule, the second and third of which will be reproduced here. The first passage (pp. 198–219) included the whole of Book II, Chapters 14, 15, and 16. Though it is too long to quote in its entirety, it may be interesting to compare paragraphs from this first passage with the subsequent translation done by the publisher's son, E. A. Vizetelly, and issued by Chatto and Windus in 1900.]

Henry Vizetelly, 1886. p. 198.
Then they gazed at the painting in silence. It was stained and decayed with age, and they had not noticed it before. It was an apparition of tender flesh, springing out of the grey wall; a re-embodied wraith, that seemed gradually to assume shape and substance again beneath the influence of the summer heat. It was a woman lying clasped in the embrace of a stag-footed faun. They could plainly distinguish the clinging arms, the melting bosom, the lissom waist of this tall naked girl, taken unawares there on her bed of flowers, strewn for her by young cupids, who, sickle in hand, ever renewed with fresh blossoms her rosy couch. They could see, too, the straining arms of the faun and the throbbing of his panting breast. But, at the other end of the

painting, there was nothing to be seen save the girl's two feet, shooting up into the air like two pink doves.

Chatto and Windus, 1900. p. 174.

They relapsed into silence. From the decayed, faded painting a scene, which they had never before noticed, now showed forth. It was as if the picture had taken shape and substance again beneath the influence of the summer heat. You could see a nymph with arms thrown back and pliant figure on a bed of flowers which had been strewn for her by young cupids, who, sickle in hand, ever added fresh blooms to her rosy couch. And nearer, you could also see a cloven-hoofed fawn [sic] who had surprised her thus.

Henry Vizetelly, 1866. p. 199.

They began to laugh, but their merriment had an unquiet ring about it; and they cast hasty glances at the frisking cupids, who were sporting there in utter nakedness. They went through all the paintings again, impelled by a spirit of something very like bravado, staring at each panel and directing each other's attention to limbs and members which were certainly not there the month before. There were supple backs that bent beneath the clinging pressure of sinewy arms; legs that broke off at the hips; women's breasts clutched in men's embraces; and grasping arms that circled nothing but emptiness. The plaster cupids that sported in the alcove seemed less observant of the restraints of modesty than they had done before; and Albine no longer spoke of them as children at play, and Serge ventured on none of his former hypotheses.

Chatto and Windus, 1900. p. 174.

They began to laugh, but there was a nervous ring about their merriment as they glanced at the nude and frisking cupids which started to life again on all the panels. They no longer took those survivals of voluptuous eighteenth century art to represent mere children at play.

Henry Vizetelly, 1886. pp. 213–14.

The voices were growing more distinct and articulate. The animals in their turn, now cried out to them to love each other. The grasshoppers grew faint with the passion of their songs; the butterflies brushed them with their tiny kisses and pulsating wings. The sparrows indulged themselves in their passing caprices, like amorous Sultans in the midst of their harems. In the clear waters of the streams, the swooning fish brought forth their spawn, and the frogs croaked out their melancholy love-notes, glutting themselves in the hideous embraces of their mysterious passion beneath the dim green of the reeds. From the depths of the forest the nightingales rippled with pearling love-chants, and the stags belled, so mad with concupiscence, that they fell motionless from exhaustion by the side of their almost gutted dams. On the rocky ledges, at the foot of the scanty bushes, the snakes, knotted together in couples, kissed softly; while the spines of the great lizards, brooding over their eggs, quivered with a gentle hum of ecstasy. From every sweet corner, from the sunlit open, from the shades of the foliage, there went up an animal scent, reeking and warm with the universal rut. All this teeming life was in the thrills of procreation. Under every leaf an insect conceived; in every tuft of grass a family was being begotten. The flies, as they skimmed through the air, clinging one to the other, only searched for a settling-place where they might perform the rites of generation. The little specks of invisible life which swarmed through space, the very atoms themselves of matter, were all vibrating with desire, and mingling themselves in pairs. The ground quivered with a voluptuous tremor, and the whole park was one great act of fornication. Then, at last, Albine and Serge understood. Serge spoke not a word, but he strained Albine in his arms more vehemently than ever. The fatality of procreation pressed them round. They yielded to the necessities of the park. The tree whispered into Albine's ear the syllables which mothers murmur softly to brides on their wedding-night.

Albine surrendered herself. Serge possessed her.

The whole garden lost itself with the young couple in a supreme cry of passion. The trunks of the trees swayed and bent, as though impelled by the strength of a mighty wind, the plants broke out into a rapturous sobbing, and the fainting blossoms breathed out their very soul from their gaping lips. In the sky itself the clouds lay faint and motionless in the sun's embrace, radiant with superhuman rapture. The animals, and the trees, and the plants, and the birds, and the rest of Nature's legionaries, who longed and yearned to see these two young people enter into the fulness of living, had triumphed, and the whole park rang with glad applause.

Chatto and Windus, 1900. p. 186.

The voices of Paradou were growing yet more distinct. The animals, in their turn, joined in the universal song of nature. The grasshoppers grew faint with the passion of their chants; the butterflies scattered kisses with their beating wings. The amorous sparrows flew to their mates; the rivers rippled over the loves of the fishes; whilst in the depths of the forest the nightingales sent forth pearly, voluptuous notes, and the stags bellowed their love aloud. Reptiles and insects, every species of invisible life, every atom of matter, the earth itself joined in the great chorus. It was the chorus of love and of nature—the chorus of the whole wild world; and in the very sky the clouds were radiant with rapture, as to those two children Love revealed the Eternity of Life.

[Now follow the second and third of the three passages objected to in 1889. Both were included in the Chatto and Windus edition of *Abbé Mouret's Transgression* in 1900 but E. A. Vizetelly translated them rather more circumspectly than he had done for his father's edition, toning down certain phrases and, in some places, substituting more 'neutral' words. He also expurgated certain passages which had not been cited in the prosecution of 1889 but which might, nonetheless, cause offence.]

Now, there was a velvety bloom upon her lips, and her hips were gracefully rounded, and her breasts billowed out in rich fulness. She was a woman now, with her long oval face that seemed to speak of fecundity. Within her swelling sides vitality slumbered. Her cheeks glowed in the soft perfection of their luscious maturity.

The priest, bathed in the voluptuous atmosphere that seemed to breathe from all this feminine ripeness, felt a torturing pleasure in defying the caresses of her coral lips, the tempting gleam of her eyes, the witching charm of her heaving breasts, and all the intoxicating emanations which seemed to pour from her at every movement. He even pushed his temerity so far as to search out with his gaze those places he had once so hotly kissed, her eyes, her lips, her narrow temples, soft as satin, and her silky gleaming neck. And never, even when he was hanging close clasped in Albine's embrace, had he ever tasted pleasure so sweet as he now felt in thus martyring himself, and looking boldly in the face the love he refused. (p. 279).

For a moment, Albine stood silently gazing at the unhappy man who lay shivering at her feet. Her eyes gleamed with an angry fire. She had flung her arms open, as though she would seize him and strain him to her breast in a wild thrill of desire, but she seemed to be reflecting for an instant, and then she merely took him by the hand. She lifted him to his feet.

'Come!' she said.

She led him away to that giant tree, to the very spot where she had yielded herself up to him and where he had possessed her. It was the same bliss-inspiring shade, the same breathing-trunk as of yore; and the same branches spread themselves widely around, like sheltering and protecting arms. The tree still reared itself aloft, kindly, robust, powerful, and fertile. As on the day of the consummation of their

480

union, the close warmth of a recessed alcove, the glimmer of a summer's night brooding over the naked shoulder of some fair girl, a sob of passionate love breaking upon the voluptuous silence, hung about the clearing as it lay bathed in its dim green light. And in the distance, Le Paradou, in spite of the first chills of autumn, broke out again into its sighing passion. Once more it was turning itself into an accomplice of their love. From the flower-garden, from the orchard, from the meadow-lands, from the forest, from the great rocks, from the spreading heavens, there came a ripple of voluptuous joy, a breeze that bore along with it a dust all pregnant with fecundity. Never had the garden, even on the warmest evenings of the spring-time, been wrapped in such a soft tenderness as on this fair autumn evening, when the plants and trees seemed to be bidding each other good-night ere they sank to sleep. The scent of the ripened branches wafted a thrill of desire through the scanty leaves.

'Do you hear? do you hear?' Albine stammered into Serge's ear, after she had let him slip down into the grass at the foot of the tree.

Serge was weeping.

'You see that Le Paradou is not dead. It is crying out to us to love each other. It is yearning for our union and marriage—Oh, do remember! Clasp me to your heart! Let us belong to each other!'

Serge still continued to weep.

Albine said nothing more. She flung her arms around him in a wild embrace. She pressed her lips to his corpse-like face and tried to warm him into life. But Serge had nothing for her but tears.

After a long silence, Albine spoke again. She was standing over him with an expression of scorn and determination.

'Away with you! Go!' she said in a low voice. (pp. 327–28).

[After pleading guilty to the charges, on his counsel's advice, Vizetelly was sent to prison for three months and the recognizances of £200, which he had given in October 1888, were forfeited.]

From ANNUAL REPORTS OF THE NATIONAL VIGILANCE ASSOCIATION
1888–1910

(1) from the Third Annual Report (1888)

This Association took the strong step, a short time ago, of prosecuting at the Guildhall a cheap edition of Boccaccio's Decameron. Some literary persons were shocked at the idea of prohibiting a standard classic four hundred years old. The Association have no prudish ideas on the subject of literature; they do not for a moment suggest that the Decameron in the original Italian, should not find a place with other medieval literature on the shelves of English libraries. The greater part of it is innocuous enough, if not very interesting, and it has been the custom of English translators and publishers to have regard to the change of manners, and to omit from the English editions the grossest passages. What has now happened is that the literary cheap-jacks who are trying to undersell each other in the filth-market of our large towns have not only reproduced the book with all its original uncleanness, and at the lowest possible price, and advertised the edition, specially as unexpurgated, but have gathered the more bestial portions into a separate pamphlet. It is a direct and intentional appeal to the worst passions. The publishers got frightened, and withdrew the pamphlet. The Association took the unexpurgated shilling edition to the Guildhall; but the worthy Alderman, who boasted that he had read the original both in Italian and French, seems to have been afraid to deal with a classic, and declined either to interfere or to give any reason for not interfering.

Meanwhile Mr. Samuel Smith, M.P., promoter of the recent debate in the House of Commons on the subject, and a warm friend of the Association, undertook a prosecution of three of M. Zola's grossest novels—'La Terre', 'Nana', and 'Potbouille', and having obtained a committal, induced the Government to take up the case. The result is well known. Mr. Vizetelly, the publisher, pleaded guilty, was fined, and undertook to discontinue the publication and destroy his stock. The Association are not letting the matter rest. They find the magistrates timid, but hope to get aid from the police; for it has sometimes been found that the magistrates violate the principles of law by refusing to a private prosecutor what they will grant to the police authorities. There is good reason to hope that the rise of public opinion will ere long bring the magistrates to the level of their duty, and that the great principle of the freedom of the Press may be found to be best safeguarded by protecting it from abuse for the purpose of mere villainy.

There is, however, a large class of indecent publications which cannot pretend to any literary privilege, and the Association have in several recent cases—notably in the case of large shops in Holywell Street—obtained, by means of search warrants, conviction of the publishers and destruction of the papers. Prompt and successful action has also been taken in several cases against the sale of obscene photographs in the streets. (pp. 4–5).

(2) from the Fifth Annual Report (1890)

A large number of copies of one of Guy de Maupassant's novels were recently sold under the hammer by a firm of good standing, who were unaware of the nature of the books. At our suggestion, these were afterwards recalled at some expense, and handed over to our officer for destruction. (p. 22).

(3) from the Sixth Annual Report (1891)

Considerable attention has been paid to indecent publications, and in particular to improper photographs. At the time of the last annual meeting the prosecution of two gentlemen was pending, for the exhibition of certain pictures by Jules Garnier, popularly known as the 'Rabelais Pictures', from the work which they were supposed to illustrate. Indecent and coarse as 'Rabelais' is, the pictures intensified the original. The defendants were found guilty, and sentenced to pay fines and costs, and the pictures were ordered to be returned to France. It is satisfactory to your committee to find that this, which was one of the most important of their prosecutions, was endorsed as well-founded by Sir Peter Edlin, Mr. Vaughan, and the grand and petty juries. (p. 8).

(4) from the Eleventh Annual Report (1896)

In the course of the year a catalogue of indecencies circulated in England has been tracked home to Holland by an officer of the Association, sent over on purpose, and the Dutch Authorities arrested the offender and seized and destroyed his stock.

In a remarkable case, the anonymous owner of a quantity of indecent literature, after communicating with the Society by advertisement, placed his collection in the hands of the Society for destruction, subscribing £20 as an acknowledgement of this assistance to clear his conscience of a mass of perilous stuff. (pp. 5–6.)

Although it was charged upon us by English *littérateurs*, when we first endeavoured to prevent the importation of foreign filth into the English markets, that we were striking a blow at classical literature, we dared to go steadily forward, and to-day there is a healthy concensus of opinion against free trade in obscenity.

In no department of our legal work have we been more successful than in that of the suppression of obscene books and indecent pictures. It is one of our proudest triumphs that it is now much more difficult to obtain either one or the other of these pernicious causes of evil. So risky have our successful prosecutions, and the increased vigilance of the police, made this kind of trade that people who formerly dealt in these wares do not, as they say, think the game is worth the candle. Only very recently, one of our officers was told by the proprietor of a shop, where we had reason to suppose indecent pictures were being clandestinely sold, 'It is no use trying to sell such things now; the officers of the National Vigilance Association are too much on the alert'.

An incident of which any society might congratulate itself was the fact that it was this Association that was selected by the late Lady Burton during her life to destroy a large number of the books of her late husband, which, in her opinion, could not judiciously be read by an indiscriminate public, and in this connection it was our privilege to burn, on one occasion, books to the value of £1,000.

Lady Burton was a strong sympathiser with the work of this Association during her lifetime, and after her death, by her will, it was found that she had appointed, as one of her literary trustees, W. A. Coote, of the National Vigilance Association, who, in conjunction with his co-trustees, is to continue the publication of some of her husband's works; but she forbids anyone to print a single immodest word, and she especially charges her literary trustees not to issue, or allow to be issued, one coarse or indecent word in connection with her late husband's works. Lady Burton's executors are desired, at the cost of her estate, to carry on any proceedings which may be taken at the instance of the Crown, or the police authority, or the National Vigilance Association, or these failing, of the executors themselves, against any person printing or publishing anything objectionable in connection with the works of her late husband. (pp. 24–5).

(5) from the Twenty-Fifth Annual Report (1910)

Another prosecution relates to the sale of 'Balzac's Droll Stories'. Many complaints had been received by the Association concerning the character of this book. It is one which has been fruitful of much harm, and is stocked by vendors of the lowest type. The difficulty has always been that it is regarded by many as a classic.

The case was called on December 29th, and adjourned until January 5th, as we were anxious not to prejudice an independent action by the police against another vendor for the same offence. In the result the man was ordered to pay £5 5s. 0d. costs, and the magistrates ordered the destruction of all the copies of the book. (pp. 17–18).

FROM THE MEMOIRS OF DOLLY MORTON

Philadelphia: Society of Private Bibliophiles, 1904. Strictly limited issue for private subscribers only. [i.e. a novel by 'Hugues Rebell' published by Charles Carrington in Paris.]

Publisher's Notice
Concerning
Foreign Pirates, Private Books,
and
Negro Emancipation

Appendix

The pages of 'Dolly Morton' are not meant for the eyes of 'babes and sucklings'—its tropical descriptions would scorch their weakling sight and unsettle their wavering soul. These private memoirs elucidate certain curious vagaries of the ever-changing human mind which are good to be known, though only by scholars and accredited bibliophiles, who will be careful to place the precious volume on the top shelves of their locked book-case.

A book of this kind can only escape the charge of immorality when kept out of the reach of the multitude by the prohibitiveness of its price and the limited number of the edition. Upon the seared senses of the man of the world or the trained mind of the thinker, it can have no pernicious effect. But if addressed virginibus puerisque and peddled from house to house, it becomes a weapon of the deadliest kind.

The chemist is allowed to dispense poisons under certain conditions; the lawyer, judge, and doctor, to enquire into matters wisely hid from the common ken, and such a work as 'The Memoirs of Dolly Morton' falls, we opine, under the same rules and restrictions.

These are some of the reasons why we decided to issue this fascinating production—a human document in the truest sense.

There are also other reasons of nearly equal importance, but, which concern more particularly the subscribers to this work.

It may not be generally known that shortly after Sir Richard F. Burton brought out 'The Thousand Nights and a Night', a conspiracy was entered into by certain foreign individuals to reprint his work and issue it on the Continent at a lower price, to the great detriment of course, of Burton's original edition. The book had not been copyrighted in England. Hence the danger.

The rumour of the little 'game' en train de cuire came to the translator's ears, and steps were at once taken legally to protect his literary property.

This trick of reprinting privately-issued and uncopyrighted books is often resorted to by unscrupulous dealers in obscenity. Honourable gentlemen of this 'kidney' in Brussels and Amsterdam reprinted the 'Ananga Ranga', 'Kama Sutra', and other books of the Cosmopolis Society directed by Burton and Arbuthnot; and the reprinting goes on, in a similar way, on the clandestine presses of London and Paris.

A work like the present for instance, issued to subscribers at a high price and in a limited number, would, if it were not legally registered, be immediately seized upon by the 'filth vendors', struck off by thousands on common paper and offered at half or quarter the price of the original, with no other object than to turn over money by pandering to the erotic tastes of libertines and debauched men.

Thus a work, issued as a literary curiosity, and because possessing a

485

certain pathological meaning to students, is used as an instrument of shameful gain and degradation, with the result that the bibliophile and subscriber (living at a distance and unsuspecting the fraud), imagines on seeing the advertisement of the bastard reprint (1) that he has been overcharged by his own bookseller. Of course, the reprint more often than not bristles with textual errors from the fact that the literary pirate is absolutely ignorant of the English language, and would never dream of going to the expense of employing a competent proofreader. In fact, in many cases, only half the original text is given—while the full title is preserved—in order further to cut down the expenses of the ignoble and dishonest reproduction. (pp. v–vii).

(1) *The 'reprinters' often copy the very prospectus issued in respect of the original edition, thus adding greater confusion and plausibility to their theft.*

[The Publisher's Notice concludes with some high-minded observations on the history of negro slavery and on its study.]

(2)   CHAPTER XI

A Rabelaisian banquet of nude damsels.—A shocking orgie.—Ten naked waitresses and their bashfulness.—Hot viands and bottom-spanking escapades.—Original racing in the corridors, and the inevitable sequel.

Three months passed, during which period I went through some varied experiences, and saw some curious sights, but if I were to relate everything that occurred, my story would be too long.

However, I will describe one or two of the incidents, just to give you an idea of the sort of man Randolph was.

I have already mentioned the dinner-parties he frequently gave to his male friends, and I have told you that these gatherings were always of a very free and easy sort.

At one of these dinners the proceedings were of a more licentious character than usual. Randolph had invited ten guests, which was the usual number—the parties, including our two selves, never exceeding twelve.

He was very particular on these occasions that all the girls should be nicely dressed, so Dinah used to parade them for my inspection just before the guests arrived. I merely had to see that the girls should be nicely attired outwardly, but Dinah before bringing them to me, had to see that each girl was clean in person, and that she had on fresh underlinen.

On the day of which I am speaking, after my own toilet had been made, I went down to the hall and inspected the girls, finding them all looking clean and smart.

Then I went into the drawing-room where Randolph was lounging on a chair turning over the leaves of a large illustrated book of Rabelais, which he was very fond of reading.

I told him I had seen the girls, and that they were all looking very nice in their black frocks. To my astonishment, he burst out laughing, and said:

'Oh, they won't wear frocks this evening. I have got such a splendid idea from a picture in this old book. I wonder it never struck me before'.

'What is it?' I asked.

'I have just been reading the chapter which tells how Pantagruel and his companions were entertained at a banquet by the Papimanes, and were waited on by a bevy of nude damsels. The dinner to-night shall be a reproduction of the scene described. There are ten men coming, and each man shall be waited on by a naked girl. It will be great fun, and also quite a novel entertainment for my guests'.

Although I was accustomed to his vagaries this new freak horrified me. I should have to sit at the table with ten men, while the same number of women displayed their naked bodies.

The idea was most repugnant to me and I blushed, a thing I had not done for many a day.

'Oh George'! I exclaimed, 'don't do such a thing. It is too shameful'.

'Yes, I will', he said laughing heartily. 'Why Dolly, you are actually blushing! I thought you had got over all your squeamishness by this time'.

'Oh, but this is a particularly horrid idea', I observed. 'And if you are determined to carry it out, don't make me come to table. Just fancy what a dreadful position it would be for me to have to sit among a lot of men, surrounded by naked women. I should not know which way to turn my eyes!'

He again laughed, but there was in his pupils a stern gleam which I had got to know, meaning that he had determined to have his way.

'It does not matter which way you look', he said. 'You are looking very pretty and that's sufficient. You will have to take your place at table as usual, and you must appear to be quite unconscious that the women are naked. None of my guests will insult you by word or glance'.

I still remonstrated, but he sternly told me to shut up, or it would be the worse for me. I held my tongue, for I was afraid of him, knowing him to be a man who would stick at nothing, and it struck me that if I made any more objections he might take it into his head to whip *me*.

487

Sending for Dinah, he told her what he intended to do, and gave her orders to have ten of the young women stripped naked in readiness. He named the ones he wanted, selecting those who had the best figures. Seven of them were quadroons, the other three were octoroons, one of them being Rosa. Dinah received the order, and also some further instructions he gave her, with a perfectly unmoved countenance.

'All right, sah', she said, 'De gals shall be ready'.

She then left the room.

It was nearly seven o'clock, and the guests began to arrive. Some came on horseback, others in buggies, and in a short time the whole party had assembled. All the gentlemen were more or less known to me, and everyone on entering the room shook hands with me in a most polite manner. They were of all ages: the youngest being about twenty-five years of age, while the oldest was upwards of fifty. Most of them were bachelors, but I knew that some of them were married men.

Presently Dinah, looking very smart in her black frock and white cap, made her appearance with a tray of cocktails, and while the guests were imbibing them, Randolph said with a smile on his face:

'I suppose, gentlemen, that most of you have read Rabelais. Those who have perused the book will remember the description of the banquet given to Pantagruel in the island of Papimany. I intend our dinner to-night to be, as nearly as possible, a counterpart of that celebrated banquet. I think I can give you as good fare and as good wine as Homenas gave Pantagruel and his companions. I also think that the 'she-butlers' will please you. They may not be so fair-skinned as were the damsels of Papimany, but in all other respects you will find that the 'waitresses' will answer the description of the ones mentioned in the book. They are 'tight lasses', good-conditioned; comely, waggish, and fit for business'.

The men who had perused Rabelais and knew what was coming, laughed and clapped their hands, but the men who had not read the book looked puzzled. However, knowing Randolph's little ways, they guessed that something funny was going to happen. In a short time, dinner was announced, and then the oldest of the guests, a gentleman named Harrington, who I knew had grown-up daughters, offered me his arm and led me into the brilliantly lighted dining-room. The other men followed, and we took our places at the table, which was beautifully decorated with flowers, and glittering with plate and glass.

Randolph took his place at one end of the table; I faced him at the other end, and five of the guests sat on each side.

When everyone was comfortably settled, Randolph touched a

small handbell beside him, and then the door at the far end of the room was opened. Dinah came in, followed by the ten naked young women with their long black, or dark brown hair flowing loose on their shoulders; each girl, without hesitation, taking up her position behind one of the guests. Dinah had told each waitress where she was to go. They all, without exception, showed signs of bashfulness, for although every one of them had passed through the hands of gentlemen on various occasions, singly in a bedroom, they had never been exposed stark naked before the eyes of a number of people. Some of the girls blushed, the colour showing plainly on their olive cheeks; others cast down their eyes and fidgeted as they stood, while all of them placed their hands over the 'spot' between their legs.

I felt horribly uncomfortable, hot thrills passed over me, and my cheeks grew scarlet. The men smiled, casting amused glances at one another, then they looked with gleaming eyes at the naked girls. Some were slim, and some plump; some tall; some of medium size, and some short; but all of them were pretty and had shapely figures, with firm, round titties and good bottoms, while the brilliant light, shining on their naked bodies, made their smooth, olive-tinted, and in some cases, nearly white skins, glisten. The hair covering the 'spots' was, in all cases, black or dark brown, and one of the quadroons, a plump little girl, nineteen years of age, named Fanny, who had been whipped a couple of days before, still bore on her bottom the pink stripes left by the switch. Rosa was the prettiest of all the girls; she had also the best figure, and she was the lightest in colour; consequently she attracted the most admiration. The dinner was soon in full progress; the girls, directed by Dinah, bustled about bringing in the dishes, changing the plates, and filling the glasses with champagne. Some of them, not being accustomed to waiting at table, were rather awkward, but whenever a girl made a mistake she received from Randolph the next time she came within reach of his arm, a sounding slap on the bottom which made her jump and squeal, and clap her hand to the place.

But no one took the least notice of these little occurrences, the gentlemen continuing to talk and laugh as unconcernedly as if they were quite accustomed to being waited on by naked women, and also to seeing them smacked whenever they made a mistake. But it was a most trying time for me. I sat with my eyes fixed on my plate, and with a very red face, making a pretence of eating, and hardly listening to the conversation of Mr. Harrington, the old gentleman who had taken me into dinner, and who was sitting on my right. He chattered away to me, but I noticed that he kept leering lecherously at Rosa's full bosom and broad bottom, as she tripped gracefully here and there. She had evidently taken his fancy more than any of the other girls, and I felt sure that later on, my pretty maid would be poked by the old satyr. The dinner was a long one, but at last it was over, and the gentlemen settled down to smoke their cigars and sip their coffee, while the conversation turned upon slaves, and the price of cotton.

No improper remarks of any sort were made by the men, but their eyes were frequently turned with lustful looks on the naked girls standing in various attitudes about the room.

When the cigars had been smoked, we all went into the drawing-room, the girls being told to follow. I tried to slip away, but Randolph ordered me to remain. He told his guests to sit down on a row of chairs at the end of the room, and when they had done so, he posed the naked girls in groups in various positions with their arms round each other, some standing, some kneeling, and some lying on their sides at full length, so that their figures could be seen both back and front. These *poses plastiques* greatly pleased the spectators, and they gloated over each lascivious tableau, applauding vigorously; while the girls, utterly astonished at what they were being made to do, gazed timidly at the men with their big, ox-like eyes. At last, Randolph exhausted his ingenuity in inventing fresh tableaux, and I thought he would at least let the girls put on their clothes. But he did not. He had not yet done with their naked bodies.

'Now gentlemen', he said, 'if you will go into the corridor I will let you see young mares' races. Some of them are rather fat, but I daresay I shall be able to make them show their best paces'.

The men, laughing boisterously, trooped out of the room and stationed themselves at intervals on each side of the long broad corridor. The races were to be run in heats, the course being from one end of the corridor to the other and back, twice over. Before starting the girls, Randolph got a long heavy whip, and cracking it in the air, warned them that they had better run as fast as they could. Then as soon as the first lot was off, he took up his position at one side of the corridor half-way down, and as the runners dashed past him in the several heats, he flicked the bottom of any girl who appeared not to be exerting herself, the touch of the whip extracting a shrill cry from the victim, and making her increase her speed, while a red mark instantly showed on her skin where the end of the lash had fallen.

The men grew excited, they laughed, cheered and betted on the girls as they raced up and down the corridor, their long hair flowing loose behind them, their titties undulating and their bottoms swaying.

The final heat was won by a tall, slender octoroon girl, twenty-one years of age, named Jenny.

After the runners had a rest, there was what Randolph called a

'Jockey race'. The five strongest girls had to take on their backs the other five girls, who held on by putting their arms round the necks, and their legs round the loins, of their respective 'mounts'.

This time the course was once up and down the corridor, and heavy bets were laid by the men on the women they fancied.

The signal to start was given, and the race began, the gentlemen whooping and shouting as they watched the extraordinary sight. Five naked women staggering along the corridor as fast as they could, each woman carrying on her back another naked female!

The muscles of the thighs and bottoms of the carriers quivered under the strain, while the legs of the riders, being stretched apart by the position in which they clung to their steeds, the cheeks of their bottoms were slightly separated, so that the spectators could see the hair in the cleft of the thighs. And nearly every one of the bottoms was marked either with the prints of Randolph's fingers, or with the red dot made by the flick of the whip. Two of the girls had both finger-marks and whip-marks, and when all was over only three girls out of the ten had spotless posteriors.

The men's eyes gleamed, their faces were flushed, and I could see that they were all in a state of great sensual excitement. After a close struggle, the race was won by a sturdy young quadroon woman, twenty-five years of age, named Eliza, who had carried the youngest of all the girls, a slightly-built, shapely octoroon named Helen, who was only eighteen years old.

Then we went back to the drawing-room, the girls being allowed to sit down, and Randolph told Dinah to give each of them a glass of wine and water. They were all very thirsty, some of them had tears in their eyes, and one or two were rubbing their bottoms, while the girls who had been carriers were panting for breath; their bosoms heaving tumultuously, and their naked bodies moist with perspiration. As soon as they had recovered their breath, the ten were made to stand in a row with their hands by their sides. Then Randolph said:

'Now, gentlemen, will you each choose a girl, either for a short time, or for the whole night? You can please yourselves'.

The men laughing and joking, began to make their selections, and in cases where two or three wanted the same girl, the matter was settled by tossing up a coin.

Rosa was the favourite, five of the men, including Mr. Harrington, wanting to have her, but finally the old gentleman, as the senior member of the party, was allowed to take her. The selections being made, each man, followed submissively by the naked girl he had chosen, left the apartment and went upstairs to a bedroom.

Randolph and I were left alone.

491

He had been very much pleased with his evening's amusement.

'Oh Dolly', he said laughing, 'what fun it has been! I've never had such a game before. I'll do it again some day or other and when I do, every woman in the house shall strip for the races'.

I did not feel at all mirthfully inclined. I had been wretched and uncomfortable throughout the whole proceedings, moreover the sight of so many bare bottoms, naked bosoms, and uncovered 'spots', had given me a feeling of disgust. A woman is not excited by seeing the nakedness of other women. At any rate I never am.

'I think it was all very horrid and shameful', I observed.

'I don't care what you think', he replied. 'It pleased me, and amused my guests, and that's all I care about. But it has been very exciting work, I am feeling very randy, and my tool is aching from its prolonged erection, so I must take the stiffness out of it at once. I will 'have' you sitting down, so as not to crumple your pretty frock.'

So saying, he seated himself on a chair and let loose his member, which stood straight up with its red tip uncovered.

'Come along now, Dolly, you know what to do'; he said impatiently.

I did know what to do. Turning my back to him, I raised my petticoats above my waist, and pulled open the slit of my drawers as widely as possible, exposing the whole of my bottom; then straddling over his thighs, with a leg on each side of him, I lowered myself down upon his upstanding member, which he guided between my thighs into its place, and the weight of my body forced the weapon up to the hilt in the sheath.

He clasped me round the waist under my clothes, while I, raising myself up and down on my toes, did all the work until the spasm seized me, and I felt the hot torrent inundating my inside. Then I lay back panting against his breast. As soon as I had received all he had to give me at the moment, I got off his lap, pulled my drawers into their place, and shook my petticoats straight, as some of the men might be coming back at any moment. As it was, we got done only just in time, for we had hardly sat down before one of the gentlemen made his appearance, and he was followed at intervals by others, until at last all had re-assembled except three, who had elected to stay all night with their girls. The other lasses, after being poked, had been allowed to go away to their own part of the house. Dinah brought in a tray of liquors and the men refreshed themselves. Then they all sat down to play cards, and I slipped out of the room and went to bed, glad to get away from the men, although not one of them had said an improper word to me during the evening.

It was very late, or to speak more correctly, it was early in the morning, when Randolph came to bed. I was fast asleep, but he soon woke me up by pinching my bottom, and then in a moment or two he was working away at me. As I was very tired and sleepy, I did not respond to his movements in the least, so when he had finished, he said crossly:

'Damn it, Dolly, you lay just like a log of wood. You did not even move your bottom at the finish. What's the matter with you?'

I said there was nothing the matter with me only that I was sleepy. He growled out something uncomplimentary, then turning his back to me, went to sleep, and I speedily did the same.

From REPORT FROM THE JOINT SELECT COMMITTEE ON LOTTERIES AND INDECENT ADVERTISEMENTS, LONDON, 1908.

Chief-Inspector Edward Drew is called in, and Examined as follows:

421. We will take first of all the lotteries?—I am dealing, my Lord, entirely with the indecent part of this Inquiry, Chief-Inspector Walter Dew is dealing with the other part. I have had considerable experience during the last 26 years in the Metropolitan Police, in dealing with matters relating to indecent exhibitions, obscene literature, &c., and I would like to point out the practice which obtains at Scotland Yard when a complaint is received—that an officer is deputed by the Assistant Commissioner to take up the inquiry, and in the case of publishing or selling obscene prints the officer would endeavour to effect a purchase. If successful, and the matter is found to be of an obscene nature, it is at once laid before a Magistrate, who is asked to grant process for the selling, as well as a warrant to search the premises of the seller. I would like here to point out that, in respect to the warrants, the powers of the police are restricted in the case of a search warrant, which can only be executed in the daytime and not on a Sunday, which is not always convenient. It is most essential that both warrants should be executed at the same time, and it would be very useful in practice to the police if this restriction were removed.

422. We have already had a recommendation to that effect, and you wish to support that?—Most decidedly.

423. Have you a *précis* of your evidence?—Yes (*handing the same*). If the case is one in which the matter purchased or seized is of a grossly obscene nature, no difficulty presents itself so far as the police are concerned, except the slow process which has to be gone through in securing the destruction of the matter complained of, to which reference was made by Mr. Muskett.

424. Would you explain to the Committee the difficulties which you

have when such matter is printed and published abroad and sold in this country?—In the case of such matter being printed and published abroad and sold in this country through the post, the only method of dealing with such persons is by proceeding under the Post Office Protection Act, and in dealing with such cases, the police often experience great difficulties indeed, in proof of which I will quote the following case. In January, 1901, a complaint was received by the police from Mr. Ernest Flower, M.P., as to a circular having been received by him through the post at his club in Pall Mall (quite unsolicited), from H. Ashford, of 31, Passage De Harve, Paris. The enclosures were forwarded by us to the Home Office with a view to pressure being brought to bear on the French authorities in respect to the matter. A further complaint was received in February, 1901, from Lord Edward Spencer Churchill, Queensmead, Windsor. This also was referred by us to the Home Office, as we felt we were unable to do anything in the matter. In August, 1901, an anonymous communication was received by us enclosing a circular announcing the offer for sale of obscene books by Monsieur Ashford, 36, Rue de Verneuil, Paris. In January, 1902, Mr. W. S. Caine, M.P., forwarded to us five obscene books, three circulars and a letter which he received from H. Ashford, and which he had written for in order to test the kind of wares sold. These were found to be grossly obscene, and were forwarded by us to the Home Office. In April, 1902, complaints were received by us of advertisements having been received by persons here, the circulars in question having been received wrapped in 'Le Matin' newspaper. The attention of the Post Office authorities was drawn to this ingenious method adopted by Ashford, which was done for the purpose of concealing the contents, and all possible attention was promised in the matter by the post authorities. The complaints continued, however, the postal authorities appearing to be quite unable to cope with the nuisance. According to a communication received by us from the Home Office, in a letter received from the French Embassy, it disclosed the fact that one Ashford died at his home, 36, Rue de Verneuil, Paris, on 28th January, 1902. According to subsequent information received, it was apparent that the same business was being carried on by this man's widow, who, in her communications with persons here, signed herself 'Dolly Ashford'. On 16th April, 1903, a Home Office communication was received by us, in which was a copy of a despatch received at the Foreign Office from His Majesty's Ambassador at Paris, relative to the advertisements sent to England in a copy of 'Le Matin,' and showing that all efforts to trace the offenders made by the French authorities had proved fruitless. After this, complaints ceased for a few months, until

494

March, 1904, when a further complaint was received of circulars having been received from E. S. Ashford, through the post. From inquiry made it was ascertained beyond doubt that the business was then being carried on by 'Dolly Ashford,' the widow of the man who died in Janurary, 1902. In order to test her, an Inspector forwarded, on the 14th April, 1904, from an address at Brixton, an application under the assumed name of Henry Douthwaite, asking to be supplied with a selection from a catalogue which he had received. A reply was received on the 17th April, in which she stated that the books were sent by registered post, that no book sent in this way had ever been seized in the post, and pointing out that if such should occur, ownership should be denied, and a representation made that a mistake had occurred. She also mentioned, in her letter, that she had some real hot photos at 21*s.* per dozen. A reply was sent by the police to this letter, with a promise to do business, and asking if the articles could be received at any other place than the address which the officer had given. On the 22nd, a reply was received by the police, in which she proposed that he should call at her friend's house for the articles, which would be addressed to Monsieur Henry Douthwaite (that is the name the officer assumed), c/o Mrs. Mason, 8, Alfred Road, Union Grove, Wandsworth Road. An order was subsequently sent by the Inspector for six dozen photographs, a certain article described in the catalogue and four books. An arrangement was made for these to be sent to her friend, Mrs. Mason, and that the police should pay her on receipt of same. The price of the above came to a total of £15. On April 9th the police received a communication from her, stating that she had finished sending the parcels (clearly indicating that they had been sent in different parts), and that we would obtain them by calling for them on the next day, at the address of the woman previously given at Wandsworth. She also stated that one of the books was out of print, and that she had substituted another. On that date the Inspector called on Mrs. Mason, and obtained four postal packages, which the Inspector opened in her presence, whereupon Mrs. Mason expressed intense surprise and disgust at the contents, and offered the police every assistance. From subsequent inquiry it was found that she was a highly-respectable woman, and evidently did not know or have any idea of the class of business carried on by Ashford. An information was drawn and laid by the police before Mr. Garrett, at the South-Western Police Court, for process under the Post Office Protection Act (the only Act we could proceed under) against the person Dolly Ashford, in respect of the above-mentioned articles, which were sent through the post, and the Magistrate at once granted a warrant. Since the issue of this warrant no further complaints have been received, and so far as we are concerned, we have heard nothing further from her.

Viscount Llandaff

425. A warrant against whom?—Dolly Ashford, the person we communicated with in Paris.

Mr. H. J. Wilson

426. A warrant in this country?—Yes.

427. For a person in Paris?—Yes, believed to be an Englishwoman, whom, if she came over to this country, we should have a warrant in our possession to arrest, which was the only means we had of doing anything at all.

(The articles are passed round to the different Members of the Committee)
Chairman

428. Are there any other special cases you wish to bring to the notice of the Committee?—Yes, the case of Nicholls. In 1895 complaints were received by the police respecting Sidney Nicholls, a publisher.

429. Would it not be sufficient if you were to state that you had had a number of complaints, without going into the various complaints you receive in the course of each year?—If your lordship pleases. In consequence of those complaints, an application was made to Nicholls, who was then trading as the 'Walpole Press,' at Charing Cross, for books which he was advertising, and which were found to be of a very obscene nature. On that the usual warrant was obtained for holding a search, and the prisoner was arrested, and he was subsequently committed for trial. He, however, absconded (never surrendered to his bail, which was forfeited), and the next we heard of him was in Paris. It was then found that he was sending over a pamphlet, quite unsolicited, to all sorts of persons in this country, and I think it would be as well if I read the pamphlet for the information of your Lordship's Committee. It is headed '27 Place de la Madeleine, Paris, Thursday, the 11th day of April, 1907,' and then follows the name of the gentleman to whom it is addressed, a gentleman holding His Majesty's Commission: 'Dear Sir, an esteemed client of mine, lately deceased, left directions in his will that his trustees were to hand to me a certain sealed box, and that such sealed box, with its contents, were to be *given* to me. This box contained a lot of "private books" and such like things. One of the most noteworthy, undoubtedly, is a copy of "The Pearl," which I beg to offer to you at a bargain price. I enclose herein a somewhat hurriedly typed description of the work for your perusal. The previous owner paid me £20 for these three identical volumes, but as they have now cost

me nothing I shall be quite satisfied if you will pay me £5 for them. Here is an opportunity for you to secure for a mere song a really valuable work which is well worth having. The copy which I am offering you is, of course, second-hand, but in spite of this, it is in excellent condition, perfectly clean as new. The volumes smell somewhat musty, and no wonder, seeing that they have been kept for many years in a safe at a certain well-known London bank! It may be that you will at once snap up this bargain, but in case you do not care to do so, I shall be greatly obliged if you will let me know, for I shall not offer the work to any other person until you have had time to decide whether or not you will take it.—Your obedient and faithful servant, H. S. Nicholls.' Then enclosed with that is a description of the book, which was privately published in monthly parts; the first having appeared in July, 1879, the last in December, 1880.

430. Has that been stopped by the police?—I might mention the steps which were taken with a view of stopping this person. We communicated with the French authorities, pointing out to them that this country was being flooded with pamphlets of that and a similar description, with the result that the Paris police have since written to us informing us that in consequence of our communication the man Nicholls has had an order of expulsion served upon him on the 28th of April last. They say: 'This is the only rigorous measure which can be taken against him, as I have the honour to acquaint you, the French law does not permit of a Frenchman being prosecuted for offences committed abroad.' My Lord, may I mention that in the case of arresting Nicholls no less than about two tons of literature, some of the worst description, were seized and were subsequently destroyed in connection with the charge against Nicholls in this country.

431. That was all printed matter, I suppose?—All printed matter, and some of a very objectionable nature (*some volumes are handed in to the Committee*).

432. Are these a sample of the books?—This is a sample of the enormous quantity of literature which was seized. That was an agent selling it in this country for Nicholls immediately he had absconded to Paris, where he set up a business in his own name. The police were unable to do anything further, except to communicate with the Paris police.

Viscount *Llandaff*.

433. Did he come back to this country?—No, the warrant is still in existence for his arrest whenever he comes back.

Chairman

434. Will you proceed with the next case?—Another case is that of Charles Carrington, a publisher, carrying on business also in Paris.

During the past 14 years he has been a source of considerable annoyance to the police here, by the persistent manner in which he has been carrying on his business through the post in the shape of sending catalogues and books of a very obscene and vulgar character. I would just like at once to call the attention of the Committee to them, so that they may be inspected. I have just selected these two paragraphs as a specimen (*handing in the same*). He was known to be employing agents in this country to whom he was sending the matter in question for distribution, and it was undoubtedly for the purpose of sending them in large quantities in bulk, to be posted in this country to save the expense of being posted abroad, with the result that it was ascertained that one of these agents was residing in London, whereupon a warrant was obtained for his arrest, but before it could be executed he absconded. He was subsequently traced to Folkestone, where he was found to be carrying on the same sort of business, and was prosecuted under the Post Office Protection Act and sentenced to four months' imprisonment. Whilst he was in prison he gave information respecting Carrington, which was communicated to the French authorities through the Foreign Office, and shortly afterwards Carrington was convicted in Paris in connection with the conduct of his business there; but through, so far as we can ascertain, the instrumentality of the 'Paris Vigilance Association.' We were also informed through the Foreign Office that a note had been received from M. Délcasse, the French Minister of Justice, showing that he (the French Minister) did not consider it possible to take fresh proceedings against Carrington, on the ground that the prospectuses sent to this country being in closed envelopes, did not come under the French law of 16th March, 1898. Further representations were, however, made, and a subsequent communication was received from France informing us of Carrington's expulsion in 1901. Even after this, numerous other complaints were received from persons in this country of further indecent literature being received from him through the post, and further representations were made to the authorities, with the result that in May, 1907, a further letter was received from the Paris police, in answer to our complaints respecting Carrington, stating that he had again just been expelled from France. Since that no further complaints have been received respecting him, but there you see he was supposed to have been previously expelled, an order of expulsion having been served on him twice in six years.

Mr. *H. J. Wilson*

435. What was the last date?—The last letter (I will read the letter) is dated Paris, 29th May, 1907, addressed by M. Hamard, Chef du Service du Sûreté, to the Assistant Commissioner at Scotland Yard.

Appendix

'In reply to your letters respecting the man Carrington, bookseller, 13, Rue du Faubourg, Montmartre, I have the honour to inform you that this person has just been expelled from France. It is to be assumed that this will put an end to the acts of which you accuse him. Unfortunately it is possible that he may have imitators, as such deeds are difficult to proceed against in France, when the offence is committed abroad.'

Chairman

436. Is there a further case you wish to state to the Committee?— Yes; the case of Keary. In 1904, complaints were received by the police respecting one C. Keary, a bookseller, carrying on business at 17, Rue du Maubeuge, Paris, sending through the post pamphlets containing pictures of naked women, advertising a book named 'Illustrated Artistic Encyclopedia.' I would like to furnish your Lordships and the Committee with a specimen of the catalogue. It contains photos which the police consider are of an indecent nature, and I would like at this point to inform your Lordship's Committee, what in the opinion of the police is the difference between a photograph of an obscene nude person, and one which might be considered indecent, although not obscene, and that is where the hair is clearly shown on the private parts. That we should consider in this country an obscene photograph on which we could institute proceedings under the Obscene Libels Publication Act (*handing in a book*). You will see on the front page a representation of what we would consider an obscene picture. These books are advertised in different newspapers here, and the attention of the authorities of the General Post Office was called on the 14th November, 1907, with a view to prevent further letters being received in this country in this indiscriminate and unsolicited manner. The Post Office replied that they would take all necessary steps in their power to prevent it. We also wrote to the Paris police on the 7th December last year, with a similar object, and we pointed out to them that photographs of naked women in these circulars showing the hair on their private parts, would be deemed here to be obscene; but the Paris police replied that the circulars complained of would not be considered by them as obscene. I might read a letter that we received as recently as the 29th January this year, from the Chef du Sûreté in Paris to the Assistant Commissioner of Police: 'In returning you the enclosed papers, I have the honour to inform you that the photographs forwarded are not considered as obscene in France. Keary has been warned that dealing in books containing such photographs is prohibited in England, and that he is liable to be prosecuted if he continues the sale.' I venture to say that that will not have a very salutary effect upon him.

437. The police are convinced that there is a very large traffic in this obscene matter, and you have proof of it, I think, in two other cases? —Yes, as to the extent to which it is being carried on in this country. In July, 1900, in consequence of numerous complaints which were received, respecting a person named Edward Avery, carrying on business in Greek Street, Soho, as a bookseller, a visit was made to the premises, and by the adoption of a certain ruse, a certain book of a grossly obscene nature was purchased from the proprietor, Mr. Avery, whereupon an application was made to the Magistrate at Marlborough Street Police Court for the arrest of the seller as well as a warrant to search his premises. It was executed without further delay, and in addition to a large number of already elaborately bound books similar to this (*exhibiting the same*), all of different sizes, and of the most grossly obscene character, there were also found nearly a ton of the letter-press, all printed, wrapped up in separate large parcels, all ready to go to the binders to be bound.

438. That looks a very expensively bound book: Do you know anything about the price?—I think the price of this book would be about £5. They were all of this description, and it is of the most grossly obscene character on that page (*handing in the same*). *This* is an example of another book (*handing in the same*). In addition to the bundles of paper ready to be made into books which I have described, there were found thousands of the grossest and most obscene pictures and photographs that one could well imagine, as well as a number of beautifully carved ivory models showing persons in the act of coition.

439. Could you tell me at all if those books had been printed in England, or printed abroad, and then imported? Could you give me any help about that?—As a rule, my Lord, you generally find proof in these books when they are printed abroad, by the misspelling of different words; but in this case, all the words appear to have been spelt correctly, indicating that they had been printed in this country, and by Englishmen. Where you find books which are printed abroad, you generally find two or three words on the same page misspelt. That is the criterion we use. I ought to mention that Avery was committed for trial at the North London Sessions, where he was represented by counsel, and he pleaded guilty. His counsel pleaded very hard to the Court not to send him to prison, as he had been in business in Soho for 25 years, and this was the first thing that had been found out about him, although he had been carrying on this business for a considerable time. From books that were found on him, it was quite clear he had been trading considerably with the Colonies, and that a number of these books had been sent to the different Colonies. He was sentenced to four months in the second

division. Another case is that described as the 'University Press.' It was a case in which a number of grossly obscene books, purporting to be works of a classical or medical character, were found being circulated from Watford, and as the result of inquiries which were made, a book was obtained, and a warrant was granted both for the search and the arrest; the person was arrested, and there about two tons of literature was again seized. The person who was charged gave certain information to the police, clearly showing that he was only an agent, and in consquence of information which was received from him, the police set to work, and discovered that these books were printed, and the country being practically flooded with them in very large quantities by one De Villiers, alias Dr. Roland, who was found to be carrying on business in the City at Broad Street Buildings, and living down at Cambridge. A book was obtained, a warrant granted for arrest and search of the premises, and five persons, including men and women, were arrested. At the house in Cambridge where De Villiers was living with his wife, and was directing operations with respect to the distribution and circulation of the book, it was found that a part of the house, in anticipation of being raided by the police, contained a sort of secret chamber in the roof. When the police went to make inquiries, although it was certain that he was in the house, he having been seen going towards the house, no trace whatever of him could be seen until some movement was heard up in this room in the roof, which was thereupon burst open, and De Villiers was found concealed. He proved to be a person of German extraction, made a desperate struggle with the police, but was seized, overpowered, and taken to the police station; but before he could be charged, practically within an hour of his arrest, he was seized with a fit of apoplexy, and died. In that case the other persons were proceeded against, and some were punished, others who were found to be simply agents were bound over, and about four tons of this literature was seized. I am unable to show for your inspection any of the identical books in English, but this is a German one, and it was printed in English with these photographs (*exhibiting the same to the Committee*). You see that the first photograph is one we would certainly describe as being obscene. It is written in German, but it is similar to what was printed in English, with these photographs.

Viscount *Llandaff*

440. Could you tell whether the photographs were made in this country?—I cannot say that, but I should think it would be likely that the plates (they are all on plates) might be printed abroad, as De Villiers was a German. He took with him when he died a lot of information which might have been useful to us.

Chairman

441. Have you finished with what you have to say on the University Press?—Yes.

442. We are quite satisfied as to the existence of these things, so that we may perhaps deal with other cases of the same kind, more shortly?
—In certain cases, which may be described as being on the border line, some difficulty is experienced by the police in obtaining process, owing to the difference of opinion prevailing amongst Magistrates as to what is or is not indecent or obscene, and several years ago this difficulty made itself somewhat severely felt by the police in dealing with large numbers of objectionable post-cards, which were being sold throughout the Metropolis. The pernicious and dangerous nature of the traffic in this class of article was ultimately recognised by nearly all the Magistrates, who now appear earnest in their desire to support the police in these prosecutions. I produce for inspection specimen post-cards which have formed the subject of prosecutions. These cases, which are not of a bad character, are usually dealt with by summary process under the Vagrant Act; others are, however, dealt with under the Obscene Publications Act. Some of these post-cards are what are termed trick cards, and here is one:

443. Will you pass it round? (*The witness did so.*)—There are other photographs here which in themselves are of a perfectly innocent character, but when certain parts of the photograph are covered up with the finger, it discloses what is certainly a very obscene photograph (*exhibiting the same to the Committee*).

444. I think we all admit the existence of these things?—As an example of the different views held by certain Magistrates in respect to matters considered indecent or obscene, I quote the following case which recently came under the notice of the police. In April last the Rev. Herbert Williams, St. John's Clergy House, Tooley Street, S.E. complained to the police that he had purchased three books which were being openly and extensively sold by a firm at Duke Street, London Bridge, and which he considered were of a character likely to lead young persons astray. He said that he had shown them to a Magistrate friend of his, who had informed him that they were of such a nature as to bring the seller within the pale of the law.

445. I think we can take this very shortly; the case was laid before the solicitors, I think?—The case was laid before Messrs. Wontner.

446. And an application made to Mr. Rose?—Yes.

447. And the result was that Mr. Rose refused to grant process?—The result was that the Magistrate considered that the book was not obscene, and declined to grant process.

448. Which was naturally a considerable disappointment to the

police; they had no doubt at all as to the character of the books?—
No doubt at all, and the opinion of the legal adviser to the Commissioner was the same. Here is the book (*handing in the same*). I should like to mention for the information of the Committee that these books are being sold in the neighbourhood of London Bridge at from 1*s*. to 2*s*. 3*d*. each.

449. Shall we now deal with the complaints you have received as to quack advertisements relating to female ailments?—If your Lordship pleases. I next refer to the numerous complaints received respecting quack advertisements relating to female ailments, which up till about 1899 were very numerous indeed, owing to the freedom with which they were accepted by all the leading London newspapers. This was, however, checked by a prosecution known as the Madame Frain case, particulars of which might briefly be described as follows. In 1898 action was taken by the Director of Public Prosecutions, and warrants were granted by Mr. Corser at Worship Street Police Court for the arrest of three persons, all of whom were connected with a firm, for unlawfully and maliciously conspiring together to incite Mary Ann Baddams to procure her own miscarriage by taking divers drugs and other noxious things. Mr. Muir was counsel for the Director of Public Prosecutions, and the prisoners were represented by Mr. Cohen, Mr. Abinger, and Mr. Biron. In July, 1899, a further warrant was obtained for the arrest of two other persons connected with this firm. The case was heard before Mr. Cluer, who discharged all the prisoners on the ground that the medicine and pills were found to be harmless. Mr. Muir then, on behalf of the Director of Public Prosecutions, applied to prefer a Bill against all the prisoners under the Vexatious Indictment Act, and this was done. On the 20th November, 1899, the case came on for trial before Mr. Justice Darling at the Central Criminal Court. The prosecution was conducted by the then Attorney-General (Sir R. Webster, Q.C., M.P.), Mr. Sutton (now Mr. Justice Sutton), Mr. (now Sir) Charles Mathews, and Mr. Muir. The prisoner Brown was defended by Mr. C. F. Gill, Q.C., Mr. A. Gill, and Mr. Abinger; Abrahams by Lord Coleridge, Q.C., and Mr. Biron; Fox, Perron, and Cross by Mr. Grain. The trial lasted four days, and all the prisoners were found guilty of conspiring to incite various persons by means of advertisements to procure their own miscarriage and the medical evidence showed that the pills supplied, if taken in excessive quantities, would procure miscarriage, but the medicine was harmless in itself. The sentences on the prisoners were as follows: Brown, 12 months; Abrahams and Fox, nine months each in the second division; Perron and Cross were bound over to appear for judgment if called upon. His Lordship, in sentencing the

prisoners, said that it was a very serious offence, and an illegal, disgusting, nefarious and dangerous business; but the crime had been rendered possible because newspapers accepted advertisements of this illegal business. It should be known that everyone who incited, by whatever means, another to commit a crime, himself committed a crime, and the jury had found, in fact, by their verdict that the advertisements were incitements by the men on whom he had passed sentence, to the crime of abortion. If any of these advertisements or anything like them appeared again, the proprietors, editors and printers of the newspapers making them public would deserve to find themselves, and if any words of his had any effect on the Treasury, they would find themselves, in the dock, and if a jury should find them guilty they would probably receive a more severe sentence than he had passed on these prisoners. Since the conviction of these prisoners, one other advertisement appeared in a Scottish newspaper, in 1903, which emanated from Madame Frain; but the editor was informed of the prosecution of this firm, and no further insertions appeared, and the police have had no further complaints.

450. That prosecution has had a very good effect, I understand?—I would like just to call your Lordships' attention to another case which has just come under the notice of the police. This is a case the police are at present investigating, although I fear at present we shall be helpless to do anything in the matter. It refers to advertisements which appear in a newspaper called 'The Illustrated Police Budget'. It is an advertisement of the ordinary type, 'A word to ladies. Send for Dr. Paterson's famous female pills, which remove irregularities, suppressions, etc., by simple means in a few hours. Recommended by eminent physicians and thousands of ladies, as being the only genuine remedy. 2s. 9d. per box; extra strong 4s. 6d. post free (write or call)'. Then comes the address. In consequence of a certain complaint, a young person has just been seen by the police, and this is the statement she made respecting her visit to this establishment, only a few months ago. She says, after describing herself: 'After learning in December from the doctor that I was pregnant, I saw an advertisement in a paper which, as far as I can remember, said: "Advice to ladies given gratis, either personally or by letter, that they could remove obstructions from whatever cause". One afternoon, about 4 p.m., I went to the shop and there I saw a man behind the counter. I asked for the proprietor. He said, "I am not the proprietor I am his manager". I said, "My menses have stopped, can you give me something to bring them on?—I have not seen anything for 5 months" (or words to that effect). He said, "You must have the strongest pills, which are a guinea a box, they will be sure to bring it on". I paid one

guinea and received from him a box of pills, on the label of which was "Dr. Paterson's female pills". They were silver colour, and there were about 50 of them. I took two each morning and two each night, but I do not remember if the directions were on the box, or if he told me how many to take. The pills purged me very much, and gave me immense pain, but no other effect so far as I know. After taking the pills, I again went to the shop, and I said, "The pills I bought here have not done me any good". He replied, "Well, then, you must be too far gone. Would you like to see the nurse?" I replied, "Yes". He spoke to someone in the back room; a nurse came forward and invited me in. She asked me to undo my jacket, and I did so. At that time I was getting stout, which was noticeable, and which she could see. She said, "Are you sure that" (meaning pregnancy) "is the matter with you?" I said, "Yes, I have been to a doctor". She asked me how long my menses had stopped, and I told her they stopped on 8th July. I then asked her if she could give me something to cause a miscarriage. She said, "I have got what is called electric stays; they run from two to six guineas". She also said, "I can see you are a respectable working girl, and I cannot guarantee they will cure you, but they may". She showed me a pair at two guineas, and I decided to purchase them. As I did not have sufficient money with me to pay for them, I gave her, I think, 24*s.*, and left her my watch as security for the balance. She told me to take off my clothes, and I took off my skirts and petticoats. She then fitted the stays on me, and asked if I felt any life. I said "Yes", but she did not examine me beyond fitting the stays. She said the stays had been made to measure for a lady, but the pills had had the desired effect, and she therefore did not want the stays. I wore the stays, which were strongly boned, but I felt no effect therefrom. I still have the stays. After fitting the stays, she asked me if she could give me some pills or a draught. I said, "Give me the strongest thing you can think of," and she called to the man in the shop. She told him to bring the strongest draught he had. He brought in some black mixture in a dark horn, and I drank it. It tasted bitter, but I cannot describe any other flavour. I left, wearing the stays she had fitted, carrying my stays, which she had wrapped in paper. I was in the place about half an hour altogether. About two days afterwards I suffered immense pain and was purged very much, but beyond this the draught had no effect on my condition. The man who brought me the draught was not the man I saw behind the counter the first day. Early in January I went to the shop again, and saw the nurse. I paid her the 18*s.* and received my watch. The nurse is about' (and she described the nurse). 'The man behind the counter' (and she describes the man behind the counter). 'The man who brought the draught' (and she

505

describes him). 'The silver-coloured pills, produced, are two of those I purchased, and were in the box for which I paid a guinea; the two pink ones are some she gave me to act as an aperient. She also gave me some brown-coloured pills, which she also said would act as an aperient. Neither the pills nor the stays had any effect on my condition, and as I was then six or seven months advanced in pregnancy, the matter continued in its natural way, and I commenced to make preparations for my confinement.' As a matter of fact, she subsequently was confined, and the child is still alive and in the care of some person. I thought your Lordships would like to have a case of that sort, as showing the evil which occurs from visits to shops of this description, and the simple manner in which it is brought about. I might also mention a case that occurred only last year of a man in the neighbourhood of Marylebone who carried on a similar business in pills, and was found to be producing abortion in a wholesale manner, and against whom the police succeeded in obtaining 13 direct cases of abortion. He was sent for trial.

451. Where were those advertisements?—Those were pills, and he advertised from High Street, Marylebone.

452. So that that was the direct consequence of an advertisement?—Undoubtedly, that is the way to attract business. If a person is an abortion monger and wants to set up in business, all he has to do is to advertise pills for females in this manner. There were no less than 13 direct cases of abortion traced to him; the witnesses attended and gave evidence against him. He was convicted and sentenced to 10 years' penal servitude for abortion.

453. The result of this other case of which we have been speaking has been to prevent these newspapers inserting the advertisements?—Yes, that is so far as the London newspapers are concerned.

454. Do you say that the provincial papers are as bad as ever?—I do not say as bad as ever, but they continue to publish them.

455. Would you tell the Committee about the advertisements of preventives?—Another form of advertisement is of the Malthusian kind, in which certain firms are in the habit of sending out to persons advertising the birth of a child in the papers, circulars of a most objectionable character, and in cases where the persons are willing to come forward the police institute proceedings under the Post Office Protection Act. Only as recently as yesterday a case was taken before the Magistrate at Bow Street, who inflicted the maximum penalty. Another is the case of H. Berdott, 7, Stafford Street, and Old Bond Street, London. He had, just previously to the action taken by the police, removed from a fashionable address in Bond Street, and these are the advertisements he sent out which were the subject of the

conviction (*handing in the same*). Another case is the 'Cardinal' Manufacturing Company; these are sent to persons quite unsolicited, who advertise in the newspapers the birth of a child in their family (*handing in specimen advertisement*). I may mention that in cases of this description, where persons come forward, there is no difficulty in obtaining a conviction; but in another case a firm, with a view to evade the law, send out a circular which in itself cannot be described as an indecent circular, but it invites persons to write to the firm for catalogues of goods which it is suggested will be supplied on application, and for which an addressed envelope of the firm is enclosed. Two of the objectionable catalogues were submitted by the police to Messrs. Wontner, their legal advisers, who carefully considered the matter, and they advised that, having regard to the fact that such objectionable and indecent matter was only sent out on application, it would not be safe to risk a prosecution for fear of not being successful.

456. That was a technical point?—Yes.

457. The police in some cases have instituted proceedings under the Vagrant Act?—Yes.

458. With success?—Yes.

459. Would you explain to the Committee exactly what the position is under the Indecent Advertisements Act? It is not an offence, I understand, to place a picture or written matter in the letter-box of any house?—That is so.

460. Although it would be if thrown into the area?—If thrown into the area or into the curtilage of a house it would be an offence, or to send it through the post; but if these advertisements, instead of being sent through the post, had been delivered into the letter-box by a firm employing men for that purpose, we should have been helpless to proceed in the matter at all.

Viscount *Llandaff*

461. What are the words which create the difficulty in the Act?—It does not apply to delivering in the letter-box of a house, it omits to state 'shall not deliver into the letter-box of a house'. It prevents you from throwing it down, on the supposition, I suppose, that the persons it was then intended to prevent carrying on the practice of the distribution of these bills, were in the habit only of throwing them into areas. The delivery of them by messenger appeared to have been lost sight of.

Chairman

462. I think we may now turn to a different class of advertisements, the objectionable paragraphs of an indecent character in certain papers: generally those papers are of a sporting character?—That is so.

463. There has been a case of a prosecution in the newspapers lately?

—Yes. The case I would refer to is that of the 'Favourite', which, after a very short existence, commenced to publish stories of a very suggestive and indecent character (*handing in specimens of the 'Favourite'*). It was not considered advisable to proceed under the Obscene Publications Act, but it was thought advisable to proceed under the Post Office Act in this case. For that purpose the police had to adopt the ruse of sending in an assumed name and address to the publishers, asking them to forward direct to that address by post certain numbers which we intended to take objection to.

464. We have had the details of that before us by a previous witness on another day, so that you may pass from that?—I might mention that immediately after this prosecution the paper ceased to exist, as far as the 'Favourite' is concerned.

465. You wish to refer to the case of 'Judy', I think?—'Judy' differs somewhat from the 'Winning Post' and the 'Favourite'.

466. 'Judy' no longer exists—is that so?—'Judy' no longer exists.

467. I do not think we need go into that, because it has been already done?—If your Lordship pleases. The case of the 'Winning Post' has been referred to also. I have here the papers, which are all marked, and which were the subject of the prosecution (*handing in the same*).

468. You have a copy of an Act of Parliament passed in New South Wales?—Yes.

469. If you can put that in, I think it would be of considerable value. That deals not only with advertisements but with all indecent publications?—Yes (*the New South Wales Act is handed in*).

470. Has your attention been drawn to the Report of the New South Wales Royal Commission?—No. I found this Act which I have just handed in in the course of my search amongst the papers at Scotland Yard, and I thought it would be valuable in case your Lordships were not aware that such an Act was passed in 1900 in New South Wales.

471. It will be of great use to us. We have already heard that the notice of the police has been drawn to the class of public exhibitions including mutoscopes. Have you anything to say in addition to what we have already heard about that? Will you tell us what complaints you have received from persons connected with religious bodies and from the Bishop of Southwark. There have recently been received a number of letters of complaint from different persons as to this class of exhibition, which is promoted by limited companies, who, for the purpose of carrying on these exhibitions, rent in the principal thoroughfares of London, large shops which are in many instances completely gutted. They are then fitted up in the most elaborate manner with a number of machines worked on the automatic principle by the insertion of $\frac{1}{2}d$. or $1d$. in the slot as the case may be. Some of

these machines are of a perfectly inoffensive and unobjectionable character. They are machines containing phonographs and descriptions of songs that the machines play. A number of stereoscopic machines, which are also on view, however, are of a very highly objectionable character, consisting of photographs of women undressing, showing their underclothing, and sitting in certain postures in a highly suggestive manner, also there are some photographs of paintings of perfectly nude women. They cannot be described as being obscene, and if exposed to adults would scarcely be said to be indecent; but as to their being of a demoralising character when exposed to young persons of either sex there can be no two opinions. Upon each machine is exposed to public view a placard on which is printed a seductive title such as 'How shocking!' 'Naughty! Naughty! Naughty!' 'Very spicey', 'Don't miss this', etc., as well as in some cases crude paintings of men and women partly undressed.

472. What did the Magistrate do when the matter was brought to his attention: you say that there was felt to be some difficulty in proceeding?—Yes, it was felt that the pictures were not of such an obscene nature as to warrant application being made for their seizure under the Obscene Publications Act, and the difficulty arose as to how best to procure the pictures; but by going to one of the places which was selected for a prosecution, and which was considered perhaps to be the worst, the proprietor consented to the police taking some of the pictures away as a sample. At the same time he said he considered there was no question about their not being indecent. But upon the Police taking possession of the pictures we were enabled to lay them before the Court, and the Magistrate thereupon granted a summons for keeping an indecent exhibition under the Vagrant Act, which duly came on for hearing. The defendant was represented by counsel, who endeavoured to argue, and did argue, that the pictures were not obscene or indecent in character; but the Magistrate ruled otherwise, and inflicted a penalty of £25 and five guineas costs. After that a very improved tone took place in the rest of the exhibitions throughout London; but nevertheless the character of the exhibition and the manner in which it brings together persons of a very young and humble class must have a very pernicious and harmful effect upon them. I may mention that upon one occasion I myself visited the exhibition that was prosecuted on a Sunday night at the Elephant and Castle, and at the least estimate the number of persons, boys and girls, there was over 300. They were indulging in all sorts of indecent acts among themselves and two were looking round picking out the different machines which bore the most seductive titles and which they thought contained the worst pictures—a boy and girl each spy-

ing on the payment of ½*d*. in the same machine touching one another in an indecent manner, and making use of very indecent language.

473. A very heavy fine was inflicted, I see?—A very heavy fine was inflicted, because it was considered by the Magistrate that the whole place constituted a very indecent exhibition. I would like to say this, that we were fortunate in having a Magistrate who appreciates the great harm done by such exhibitions.

474. There is some fear that you might have difficulty in securing another conviction?—That is what we think, and before we took a case before a different Magistrate in a different district we should have to consider the matter very carefully.

Viscount *Llandaff*

475. Have you ever failed before any Magistrate?—May I point out that this is quite a new character of exhibition in London during the past few years? I may tell you that these houses are not under any control at all, and they are not only established now in London, but I understand they are being established in all the principal towns in the provinces. Heavy prices are being paid for leases of different premises, which are being gutted and fitted up in the same manner as in London. There is no charge made for admission. There is no music played in the place except on the automatic principle, and therefore they do not come within the provisions of the different Acts which regulate places where music and dancing is carried on. They appear to be under no control whatever, whilst they carry on these exhibitions which cannot be said to be obscene or indecent. On Sunday nights they are visited by hundreds and hundreds of the working classes, young and old; and, as no charge is made for admission, no action can be taken under the Lords' Day Observance Act.

476. That really finishes all you have to say to the Committee?—I would like to call your Lordship's attention to a case in which a Malthusian appliance such as that (*exhibiting the same*) was exposed to view in a window at Villiers Street, Strand. That resulted in proceedings being taken under the Vagrant Act, and the proprietor of the shop was sentenced to three months' hard labour. He appealed against the decision, and argued that an appliance of this description did not come within the meaning of the Act. The conviction, however, was upheld at the Sessions. Here is another case which I might call your Lordship's attention to—the 'Police Budget'—which is the paper I referred to in which the young lady saw an advertisement and afterwards went to a certain shop. It may be of interest for your Lordship to understand that in consequence of what was considered an indecent picture in that paper (*exhibiting the same*) a man selling it in the street was arrested under the Police Act, and fined the

maximum penalty which is 40*s*. It was thought better to proceed in that way so as to stop the circulation, the things being sold openly in the street. That had the desired effect, and the proprietor has discontinued publishing what might be considered indecent or obscene having regard to the difficulty he would have in selling them in the street, the majority of such books being sold in the street. I would like also to call your Lordship's attention to a case in which a man was convicted at Bow Street for sending out Malthusian advertisements to persons. Not only was he doing that, but he was sending out books of this description (*exhibiting the same*), and a book which, in the opinion of the adviser of the Commissioner would not be considered of an indecent nature upon which to proceed. I would like to submit these things to the Committee (*handing in the same*). There are other cases similar to those I have already referred to which I could go on multiplying as to which we are in a difficult position not knowing how best to proceed—looking to the present state of the law.

(2) Mr. Robert Standish Siever is called in, and Examined as follows:

1113. As you have called the attention of the Committee to it, the Committee are very glad that you should have an opportunity of speaking to them on the subject of your paper which has been mentioned before them. I dare say you have seen the references which have been made to the 'Winning Post' by one or two witnesses?—Yes.
1114. I am sure the Committee would be very glad to hear anything you wish to say to them with regard to the evidence which has been given?—I thank you, my Lord and the Committee, but my attention was drawn to a report of evidence which was given before the Committee here in which the 'Winning Post' was mentioned, and the evidence was that, after the 'Winning Post' had been prosecuted, which has been the case, certain objectionable paragraphs still appeared in the paper similar to those before the prosecution. This I categorically deny. It is untrue, and on the face of it, if it was so, in my opinion the 'Winning Post' should have been prosecuted again rather than a statement of that kind should be made for the sake of prejudice by the Home Office, with whom we have had some correspondence, which has not been exactly pleasant. It is simply trying to do further harm to the paper. We gave an undertaking before the Magistrate at Bow Street. I may say that such paragraphs as have been even doubtful have been submitted to lawyers of very excellent standing, and, strange to say, I think our lawyers are the same as those who act for the Commissioner of Police.
1115. You are very anxious to impress upon the Committee the fact, if I understand you aright, that there is nothing in the 'Winning

Post' now to which reasonable objection could be made?—No reasonable objection, my Lord, inasmuch as the 'Winning Post' is a sporting paper. I may add that the 'Winning Post' and similar sporting papers are not written with a view to circulating among those who read the 'War Cry'. A paper such as the 'Winning Post' has things in it which you can pick out with a view to proving that the paper is immoral; you could do the same with any other paper. To carry out my suggestion, I have brought with me a paper, the name of which need not be mentioned for publication, and I would submit that here is a most decent picture, perfectly decent, but, if it had appeared in the 'Winning Post', by a stretch of the imagination it would have been said that it was indecent (*handing in the same*). I would say that the evidence given before your Committee to-day has not been unbiassed.

Mr. *Herbert Craig*

1116. Where is the suggestion of indecency there (*referring to the paper just handed in by the Witness*)?—Here (*pointing on the paper*). I should like to add, my Lord, that in some witty paragraphs in my paper a dull mind may only be able to see something indecent. My contention is that the wit overrides everything else.

Chairman

1117. I think perhaps, as you are here, I might draw your attention to your 'Summer Annual' which has been mentioned to us, page 87 (*handing the same to the Witness*)?—I cannot see anything objectionable there (*Mr. H. J. Wilson points out something in the 'Summer Annual'*). That is not in another copy, that is only a blot. If you get another copy you will find that that is only a bad print of one copy.

1118. I am very glad we had the opportunity of asking you about that?—This is the first time I have seen that. It should not have gone into the paper, it is too stupid. I will send you up the original drawing of that, if you like, to-morrow.

1119. I am sure we should be willing to take your word for it?—That is what I have had to suffer sometimes; we have had to suffer because we have been guilty, but we have not been guilty again, and I may say to the Committee while I am here, that the paragraph which we were prosecuted for, and as to which we pleaded guilty, was written by a clergyman.

1120. We will not ask for names?—I will give it to you if you like. The evil mind, my Lord, will turn anything into indecency, while the good mind might turn indecency into something pleasant.

1121. I am sure the Committee were very anxious to give you the opportunity of saying anything you wish. Is there anything further you wish to add?—Nothing further, and I am extremely obliged for the opportunity.

Appendix

Mr. *Herbert Craig*

1122. Was the summer number published before or after the prosecution?—It was published after the prosecution, but it was in the printer's hands before.

Chairman

1123. I suppose you prepare your summer number in the course of the winter before?—Yes, and our winter number is in course of preparation now.

Mr. *Herbert Craig*

1124. Are you prepared to support everything that appears in the 'Summer Annual'?—Yes, as far as I know.

1125. *That* for instance? (*pointing out a verse on a page of the 'Summer Annual'*)—Yes. You can read that with an evil mind, and you can read it the wrong way. If I may be allowed to read it, it is as follows:

'There was a young lady of France,
Who decided to give it a chance,
In the arms of her beau she let herself go,
And now all her sisters are aunts'.

If you wish to say she let herself go, and did something wrong, I say there is a vulgarity there, but it does not suggest that. It suggests that she let herself go, that she was married and did what she liked.

Mr. *H. J. Wilson*

1126. One fact of great art is so to put it as to make it as nasty as you can, so that it is possible to put a different interpretation upon it?—No, the art would be lost if it became nasty.

Mr. *O'Malley*

1127. Do you not think that is calculated to demoralise certain readers of the paper, and to be rather suggestive, and to arouse curiosity, which is undesirable?—No, I should not think it would, because in the first place the people who buy this annual, buy it for the fun; if it had no fun in it, if it was simply what I would call dead lead, then it might be objectionable, but when the wit overrides the *risqué* suggestion, then I think the wit is the only thing that remains.

Mr. *Herbert Craig*

1128. Would it be witty to anybody reading it in other than the evil sense? To anybody reading it in the innocent sense, would it be witty?—I think so; I think, personally speaking, this is a rhyme or a limerick that could be told and very likely is told among people in the ordinary racy way. It is not one a clergyman would take for a text, or anything like that, neither is the volume, it is not printed with that idea, but, if you take up some of our religious papers, they are, if you wish to think so, absolutely blasphemous.

513

Chairman

1129. Have you anything else you wish to say?—I think I might suggest this to the Committee, that where there are papers which really mean to be honest, and do not mean to be vulgar in reality, if they do go over the border line they might get an official hint or letter to say that they ought to be careful. It would do an infinite amount of good.

From THE INDIAN SOCIOLOGIST, AUGUST 1909
INDIAN MARTYRDOM IN ENGLAND

An Example of Heroic Courage and Patriotism
Our Humble Tokens of Appreciation

The name of Madan Lal Dhingra will go down to posterity as that of one who sacrificed his life by remaining faithful to the altar of the ideal. His statement before the magistrate and his final declaration during the trial at the Old Bailey, in London, conspicuous as they both are for their courage, truth, and patriotism, put him on the very highest plane among the liberator heroes in the world's struggle for freedom. Standing alone, and defying the tyranny of piratical Britain on British soil, Dhingra is, as an American friend of vast political experience tells us, one of the most remarkable figures in India's history. What can be more touching and inspiring than the following words he uttered when the death sentence was passed: 'I am proud to have the honour of humbly laying down my humble life for the cause of my country'. Even one of the most rabid English newspapers was compelled to acknowledge the dignity of his demeanour at that fateful moment. The serenity of his bearing, throughout the proceedings in the English Courts, cannot but call forth admiration in the breasts of all who impartially look at everything that transpired at the trial. The declaration of faith, as embodied in his statement, and utterances, regarding the emancipation of his country, will no doubt be circulated among Indian Nationalists as a holy tract, and henceforth let anyone mention Dhingra's name at an independence meeting and the meeting will be on its feet. As will be seen from a letter which appeared in *The Times* of 17 July, and which we reproduce elsewhere, we have already proclaimed Mr. Dhingra to be a martyr in the cause of Indian independence. India owes a debt of gratitude to him, and, as a small token of respect and esteem for the glorious stand he has made by staking his life, we in our humble capacity propose to honour his name by grants of four scholarships similar to those offered and awarded during the early part of this year in connection with the Indian Martyrs' Memorial as originally announced in the December number of the *Indian Sociologist*.

(2) Sedition!

Like cures like! What other remedy has an oppressed and enslaved nation that has been totally disarmed and deprived of the liberty of the Press, freedom of speech, and right of public meeting, besides being liable to imprisonment, without any charge or trial whatever, at the instance of an alien despotism, if it be not its right to resist violence by violence somewhat on the homoeopathic principle—*similia similibus curantur*—or 'Poison is the antidote for poison', as a Sanskrit proverb has it? . . . Voltaire has said that the worse use to which you can put a man is to hang him. The British Government is about to put Dhingra to that use, but denounces his execution of another man. If, therefore, to admit the stoical attitude of Dhingra, is to approve of indiscriminate homicide, surely to approve of the Governmental method is to advocate calculated murder by mercenary hirelings. What right has any man to deny the right of another man to hold a different opinion from the latter but the right of a despot? Beccaria has denounced as barbarous the formal pageantry attendant on the public murder of individuals by Governments. He sees in these cruel formalities of justice a cloak of tyranny; a secret language, a solemn veil, intending to conceal the sword by which we are sacrificed to the insatiable idol of despotism. In the execution of Dhingra that cloak will be publicly worn, that secret language spoken, that solemn veil employed, to conceal the sword of Imperialism by which we are sacrificed to the insatiable idol of modern despotism, whose ministers are Cromer, Curzon, Morley, and Co. Murder, which they would represent to us as an horrible crime, when the murdered is a Government flunkey, we see practised by them without repugnance or remorse, when the murdered is a working man, a nationalist patriot, an Egyptian fellaheen, or a half-starved victim of despotic society's blood-lust.

'SANCTIFIED BIGAMY' from THE LIBERATOR, NOVEMBER 1910

During the year 1890, in the island of Malta, the man who is now the King of England, was united in lawful holy wedlock with the daughter of Sir Michael Culme-Seymour, an Admiral of the British Navy. Of this marriage offspring were born. At the time of that marriage the Duke of Clarence, the eldest brother of the present King was Heir to the Throne. Subsequently the Duke of Clarence died, leaving the present King Heir to the Throne. It is now that we are offered the spectacle of the immorality of the Monarchy in all its sickening beastly monstrosity. In order to obtain the woman of Royal blood for his pretended wife, George Frederick foully abandoned his true wife, the daughter of Sir Michael Culme-

515

Seymour, of the British Navy, and entered into a sham and shameful marriage with the daughter of the Duke of Teck in 1893.

The said George Frederick not having obtained any divorce from his first wife, who, by the common law of England and by the law of the Christian Church, remained, and, if she lives, remains, his true wife, committed the crime of bigamy, and he committed it with the aid and complicity of the prelates of the Anglican Church. This is the sickening and disgusting crime which has been committed by the English Church, which has married one man to two women. Our very Christian King, the Defender of the Faith, has a plurality of wives, just like any Mahomedan Sultan, and they are sanctified by the English Church. The daughter of Sir Michael Culme-Seymour, if she still lives, is by the unchangeable law of the Christian Church, as well as by the common law of England, the rightful Queen of England, and her children are the only rightful heirs to the English Throne.

In discussing this matter by letter with our valued and steadfast friend Edward F. Mylius, of London, we have received from him the following letter:

> I have always understood that the King is above the law and can do no wrong. He may commit murder, rape, arson, or any other crime, yet the law cannot try him. The only way he can be dealt with in this country is by revolution. No one can properly speak of the King acting legally or illegally. We only speak of him acting unconstitutionally or otherwise. It seems to me, therefore, that your article must be directed at the so-called British Constitution, which allows and tolerates a bigamous King to rule over the Empire. The law is not made for the King, but supposedly by the King for his subjects and slaves.

THE SINK OF SOLITUDE (1928)

For themes gigantic verse may well be blank;
(SHAKESPEARE and MILTON take the highest rank)
But duller matters duller treatment need
Now English intellects have gone to seed
So in heroic numbers let us sing
Sad songs of those who make no welkins ring,
Plodding a road of weariness and gloom
Where boredom unalloyed shall be our doom,
In wells of loneliness drink draughts, not deep,
But yet Lethean—since we'll go to sleep
And take a long farewell of pleasant mirth
To cool for ages in most earthy earth.

Sing then, O mundane Muse, of RADCLYFFE HALL
And how she wrote a story that should fall
On souls suburban like a ton of bricks,
Crushing JAMES DOUGLAS and SIR JOYNSON HICKS
And how they wound in the Home Office tape
Another soul suburban, Mister CAPE.
But do not let us seek poetic flights
Nor from the gutter hope to scale the heights,
From JIMMY, JIX, and JONATHAN to cull
Bright interludes where everyone is dull.

The Isles of Greece where burning SAPPHO sung
We analyse in terms of FREUD and JUNG;
Though SAPPHO burned with a peculiar flame
God understands her, we must do the same,
And of such eccentricities we say
' 'Tis true, 'tis pity: she was made that way'.
In a lone hamlet in the Malvern Hills
The LADY ANNA GORDON sits and fills
Her mind for years with thoughts of infant sons,
Pre-natal influence is how it runs.
But even in the best conducted homes
From cruel fact too oft the fancy roams.
The son arrives; the nurse, dull-witted finds
It seems a girl to ill-instructed minds.
Well, well; let's call her STEVE and let it go,
The philosophic father wills it so.
She kicks, she thrives, she grows to man's estate,
For trousers love she feels, for knickers hate.
Alas! the weakness of the human will,
Ladies in trousers must be ladies still.
Her father burns the good electric light
In reading HAVELOCK ELLIS all the night,
But though he masters psychopathic lore
He dies the sole possessor of his store
Exclaiming, as we watch his soul depart
'My lips are sealed. 'Twould break my ANNA'S heart!'
And so the maiden grows to man's estate,
(The sequel will be sad to contemplate).

'Anything once', ANGELA CROSSBY said,
A simple rule that suits an empty head,
As now for STEPHEN she displays her charms

517

And something new attempts in STEPHEN'S arms.
Poor STEPHEN'S heart is lifted to the skies
She decorates herself with shirts and ties,
Buys motorcars, and jewels for her dear,
Thousands of lovers do it every year.
Till ANGELA takes up another scheme
And bursts the bubble of her love's young dream,
Remarking crudely, 'Sorry, STEVE, but see
'Business is business—could you marry me?'
Romance is thus flung whop into the dirt
And STEPHEN seeks to soothe her gaping Hurt.
Greyhounds are drawn to the electric hare
The bus-conductor drawn towards the fare,
Strong men at six are drawn towards the bar
And gallery girls at stage doors seek the star,
So all whom life has laid upon the mat
Inevitably seek a Chelsea flat,
To paint the chimneys or to write a book—
The normal course abnormal STEPHEN took.

And so we follow on the common round
Of novels with a much less novel ground
Paris, then war, danger and noble deeds
For STEPHEN follows where the soldier leads,
Comes peace with victory, and well-earned rest
True love at last makes every hero blest,
For every man a damsel, sometimes two,
And STEPHEN to her happiness won through.
She settles with a kind and gentle she
Whose name is MARY, as it ought to be.
Thus adolescence, lost illusions, flight,
Creative struggles and the sterner fight,
Success, the soul-mate, all the course is run;
A happy ending and our story's done.

But happy endings find no place in Art
A far, far better thing is STEPHEN'S part.
When clouds arise upon domestic joys
The world insists that girls shall not be boys—
Though MARY finds convention all absurd
She weakens from the pressure of the herd,
Unhappy if she stay or if she go
Her loyalties conflicting, hence her woe,

Now once upon a time 'twas pointed out
By someone, who if he were still about
Would take an interest in the present case,
That with mankind it is a commonplace
To find that all men kill the thing they love—
No doubt he thinks so still, although above.
But STEPHEN will preserve an equal mind
And not allow the same for womankind
She finds a man, and though it spoil her life
MARY shall be a mother and a wife,
For love's sweet sake she gives her little all,
And goes to tell the tale to RADCLYFFE HALL.

The tragic story of a woman's grief
Misunderstood, or worldy unbelief—
Beneath the author's hands takes rapid shape
Is finished, typed and sent to Mister CAPE
And after hesitation more or less
It gets a preface and is sent to press.
The way to make a modern novel sell is
To have a preface done by HAVELOCK ELLIS.
The book is published and success seems clear
When sympathetic notices appear.
In praise of RADCLYFFE (Gracious, what a nark!)
The TIMES LIT. SUP. is promptly off the mark
In BOOT'S and MUDIE'S the subscribers stand
Supply falls rapidly below demand,
In London streets the groves of Lesbos bloom—
Man-hatted girls, tweed-coated, light the gloom.
Women in love *now* only love themselves
And men are left (like duller books) on shelves.
For loneliness a recipe is found,
And a pale bud opens on barren ground.

But then at Last JAMES DOUGLAS sees the work;—
While decadents the moral issue shirk
He girds his loins (if any) for the right
Exclaiming 'Onward-Christians-to-the-fight!'
Depress! Repress! Suppress! (Sunday Express)
JAMES DOUGLAS knows what others merely guess—
That woman-interest, sex, and moral ire,
Will set a million readers' veins on fire . . .

Of rhetoric he need not burk a particle
In this week's splurging moral-uplift article.
JIMMY is menaced. He is far from placid.
Ho Ho The Borgias! Who likes prussic acid?
Some women poison with a deadly look,
But RADCYLFFE poisoned JIMMY with a book!
The WELLS OF LONELINESS are far from pure
For poisoned wells JAMES DOUGLAS has a cure,
'Stop up the Well!' Is JIMMY'S urgent call
(Inset: A picture of MISS RADCLYFFE HALL)

In JONATHAN'S office consternation spreads
And while THE MILLION READERS in their beds
Peruse JAMES' Sunday outburst, weep, and sigh;
JO: CAPE sits down to write a long reply.
But all in vain—poor JO: is in a fix,
Among the Million Readers one is JIX.
From JIX to JIMMY deep calls unto deep
For moral sheep will follow moral sheep;
While rapidly the book sells out of stock,
Two great men quiver with a holy shock,
Two men now burst with holy indignation
To save the morals of the British nation.

Two men in Sodom can avert God's spleen:
Two men can keep the British Empire clean:
Two men by filthy books are never flecked
Two *Good* Men—never mind their intellect!
So JOYNSON HICKS to JONATHAN sent a letter
And CAPE withdrew—he ought to have known better!
No more remains to tell of the brave story
Which covered JAMES and JIX with fleeting glory,
Except that MILTON pleading for the Press
Had never read LORD BEAVERBROOK'S 'Express';
Perhaps a certain kind of prejudice
Prevented MILTON reading things so nice
On Sunday as the doings of Society
And chorus-girls and crime. He liked variety.
And so he lustily for Freedom cried
(What *blank* verse he'd have written had he tried
The Areopagitica to revise
To make it fitting for J. Hix' eyes!)

520

But does an Areopagitic cry
To this dull morbid episode apply?
Did SAPPHO sing, did SHAKESPEARE write for us
Beauty obscenely sweetly amorous,
That DOUGLAS might be born, and JOYNSON HICKS,
And RADCLYFFE HALL put CAPE into a fix?
Can Love thus puddled in a lonely well
In which no more than dead leaves ever fell,
Shake nothing more than DOUGLAS in its mud?
Does beauty course no longer in our blood?
Alas, when JIX who cannot understand
The problem shaking (slightly) all the land,
Wrote notes to CAPE, the pathos of the thing
Is that the poor earth once heard SAPPHO sing . . .

(Finis)

COUNT GEOFFREY POTOCKI DE MONTALK, HERE LIES JOHN PENIS
(1932)

To François Vernon

(1) Here lies John Penis
Buried in the Mount of Venus.
He died in tranquil faith
That having vanquished death
HE SHALL RISE up again
And in Joy's Kingdom reign.

(2) Here lies a poet
Who never had a fuck:
Let's hope in heaven
He'll have much better luck!

N.B. *He has since.*—Ed.

(3) *For —— and his girl, on leaving them the key of my room.*
Herewith the key to the heaven between her thighs—
Take it, and in its use be stern and wise.
May Eros leave his fiercest dart in her
And fill her cunt with burning oil and myrrh;
And, not to leave so sweet a thing forlorn,
Apollo give you a stiff splendid horn.
The place is lucky, since the poet's bed
Is hallowed with a bleeding maidenhead.

521

(4) In The Manner of Paul Verlaine

Roman Catholic Poet

The Violin
That in the dark
Speaketh of Sin
In Hagley Park

Recalls how lingers
On the Penis
With lustful fingers
The hand of Venus.

Venus—Shop-girl
Whose elation
Knows how to swirl
The best sensation

Venus y-clept
Whose soft hand full
Stroked as she wept
The beautiful

Cock of the Marquis
Tittle-Dee-Tum
Caressed his carcase
And his bum.

You have undone
His Lordship's pants
And think it fun
So loud he pants

When you tug the tool of
Lord-Tittle-Tum
And your mouth is full of
Lordly come.

O, Marquis, deign
To listen to me
(Not Paul Verlaine)
—My advice is free:

522

Appendix

Don't boast of this shocking
Lewd success
When you are fucking
The Marchioness.

(5) The Song of The Braguette

from the Chiabrena des Pucelles

The wife who sees her man set out for war
From head to heel except his cock-box armed,
Says to him: "Darling for fear you should be harmed
Arm that, that over all the parts I love more."

What? and shall such advice be counted queer?
I say no no: because her greatest fear,
When she saw him in lively mood, was lest
She'd lose the tit-bit that she liked the best.

['The Song of the Braguette' is Count Potocki de Montalk's translation from Rabelais, while 'In the Manner of Paul Verlaine' is what he described as his parody of 'Taille-High-life' in Verlaine's collection *Femmes*.

La galopine
À pleine main
Branle la pine
Au beau gamin.

Edgell Rickwood, according to Count Potocki de Montalk, gave evidence that the parody was a very good version of the original French.]

From THE OBELISK LIST (1938)
60 Francs each

HALF O'CLOCK IN MAYFAIR Princess Paul Troubetzkoy
A vivid picture of the most dissolute aspect of London social life. A series of episodes linked together which bear the hallmark of authenticity in spite of the assurance that they are fiction. For obvious reasons could not be published in England.

DARK REFUGE   Charles Beadle
The effect of hashish on the individual, its annihilation of all conventional taboos, social and sexual. A symphony of lusts and hates, fears and loves. A memorable novel.

523

UNCHARTED SEAS   Eric Ward
The vagaries of sexual passion are the subject of this book by a new and significant writer.

BLACK SPRING   Henry Miller
By the author of *Tropic of Cancer*. A work of genius, saluted as such by the most important authorities.

THE ROCK POOL   Cyril Connolly
2nd edition. Desmond MacCarthy said in his leading article in the *Sunday Times*: 'I have read it twice and shall read it again . . . peremptory, witty . . . worth double the price of an ordinary novel'.

BESSIE COTTER   Wallace Smith
The best story of a prostitute ever written in English. Only existing edition.

STAR AGAINST STAR   Gawen Brownrigg
2nd impression. A new and in many ways better *Well of Loneliness*. 'The fundamentals of passion.' Cyril Connolly in the *New Statesman*.

TROPIC OF CANCER   Henry Miller
The first published novel of a writer of genius. 'A very remarkable book with passages of writing in it as good as any I have seen for a long time.' T. S. Eliot. 'In the first thin rank of contemporary achievements.' Herbert Read.

BOY   James Hanley
Recently suppressed in England. 'Poetic sensuality achieved by nobody since Lawrence.' Richard Aldington.

DAFFODIL   Cecil Barr
A young girl's amorous adventures in the Paris of to-day. In its 14th impression. More copies have been sold than of any other English novel first published in France. *Amour French for Love* and *Bright Pink Youth* are two other amusing and unconventional novels by the same writer.

MY LIFE AND LOVES   Frank Harris
This famous autobiography is now available *complete* in the Obelisk edition, 4 volumes, 60 francs each.

SLEEVELESS ERRAND   Norah James
This brilliant and brutally frank study of London Bohemian society is still strictly banned in England in spite of innumerable protestations. Preface by Edward Garnett.

EASTER SUN   Peter Neagoe
A beautiful story of unbridled passions amongst the peasantry woven about an unforgettable central character, Ileana the Possessed. Recommended by the *Book of the Month Club*. 2nd large edition. By the author of *Storm*.

Appendix

From THE R.P.S. SOUTHERN NEWS NO. 5 (1967)

[In 1967 prosecutions were brought against the publishers of the Racial Preservation Society's *Southern News* and *Midland News*, under the provisions of the Race Relations Act of 1965. The Society describes itself as believing that 'all those people of other races who have entered this overcrowded island should be given the opportunity to return to their own countries and be assisted to build up their own cultures and economies.' The following passages from the *R.P.S. Southern News* are those cited in the prosecution.]

(1) We are far advanced along the road to 1984. That road starts in the class room!

(2) Our Medical Correspondent writes:

'Liberalism' is the modern manifestation of ethno-masochism. This is a strange disease, so strange in fact that it is difficult for the normal, robust, individual to understand its nature or to realise the extent of its corrupting influence.'

Unfortunately in Britain today it is endemic, especially in the spheres of government, politics and administration.

It is a perversion closely akin to all other sexual perversions and it undoubtedly explains the fellow-feeling that 'liberals' have for other deviants such as homo-sexuals.

Ethno-masochism is a self-destructive impulse with an erotic basis. It leads the victim to desire the destruction of his own race, the active promotion of miscegenation or race-mixing being a common symptom of the disease. Other symptoms include a burning desire to see one's own race humiliated and degraded and relishing the downfall of co-racialists overseas.

(3) Strange also that the target for their denunciation should so often be the hapless Irish whose reproductive capacity is, while slightly higher than that of the British mini-family, nowhere near that of the feckless coloured masses who have been allowed to flood into Britain in the last few years.

(4) *Q.* While it is generally accepted that coloured civilisations are inferior to the White and coloured people of inferior intelligence will they not be raised up to our level by improving their standard of life and by education?

A. Most of the leaders of corrupt African states were educated in Britain or European seats of 'higher learning.' Leaders of the obscene conspiracy called Mau Mau, the Congo rapists and those who tortured and mutilated the late Chief Minister of Nigeria, Sir Abubaka Balewa, were exposed to the civilising influence of Western academics

525

or versed in the ethics of Sandhurst military academy. Not much of that influence seems to have rubbed off on them.

In fact education merely imparts a polished veneer. It is possible for an ignorant man to display high intelligence and to be a credit to his nation and his race. Conversely, one can give a fool a good education and the end product is not an intellectual but an educated fool. As you know, this country suffers a surfeit of such people especially in Parliament.

[Four of the defendants in this case were acquitted at Lewes Assizes in March 1968 and proceedings against a fifth defendant were subsequently dropped.]

Index

527

Index

Index

[1] Edited by Swift and, later, Mrs. Manley.
[2] Edited by John and Leigh Hunt.
[3] Edited by F. S. Ellis

Index

Green, T. H., 130; *The Principles of Political Obligation*, 217
Gregory, Francis, *Modest Plea for the Due Regulation of the Press, A*, 36
Grenville, William Wyndham, Lord, 148
Greville, Sabine, 250
Grey, Charles, Lord, 148
Grieves, Charles, 283
Grosse, Justice, 150

Haines, Henry, 55
Haldane, J. B. S., 298
Hale, Sir Matthew, 66, 202
Hall, Joseph, *A Sober Reply to Mr. Higgs's Merry Arguments*, 70
Hall, Radclyffe, *The Well of Loneliness*, 305
Hallam, Henry, *The Constitutional History of England*, 218
Hankey, Frederick, 286
Hanley, James, *Boy*, 306
Hansard, Luke, 104
Harbin, George, *The Hereditary Right of the Crown of England Asserted*, 39
Harding, John, 54
Hardwicke, Lord, *see* Yorke, Philip
Hardy, Thomas, 239, 251, 254, 255, 260, 262; *Far From the Madding Crowd*, 254; *Jude the Obscure*, 254, 302; *Tess of the D'Urbervilles*, 254
Harem Storyteller, The, 287
Harlequin; Prince Cherrytop, 277
Harley, Robert, Earl of Oxford, 50, 51
Harriet Marwood: Governess, 183
Harrington, Lord, 84
Harris, Frank, *My Life and Loves*, 306, 308
Harris's List of Covent-Garden Ladies, 120, 122, 185, 188, 190
Harrison, Thomas, 78
Hart, John Harriott, 145, 147

Hartcupp, 287
Harvey, Daniel, 167
Haslam, C. J., *Letter to the Clergy of all Denominations*, 227
Hastings, Warren, 105
Hawkesworth, John, *The Adventurer*, 88
Hayler, Henry, 289
Headlam, Rev. Stuart, 231
Hegel, Georg Wilhelm Friedrich, 130
'Heller, Marcus van', 314–15; *Nightmare*, 307n.; *Terror*, 307n.
Hennell, Charles, *Inquiry Concerning the Origin of Christianity*, 231
Heptameron of Queen Margaret of Navarre, The, 269
Hetherington, Henry, 227; *The Poor Man's Guardian*, 219, 224
Hey, John, 124
Hey, William, 113
Heywood, John, 16
Hicklin Judgment, The, 193, 241, 264, 303
Hills, Henry, 23
Hilton, Enid, 302
Hirsch, Charles, 271–2, 283
Histoire de Magdelaine Bavent, 305
History and Adventures of a Bedstead, The, 119
Hoadly, Benjamin, 65
Hobbes, Thomas, 69; *Leviathan*, 32
Hodges, James, 115
Hodgkys, John, 11
Hogan, Major Denis, *Major Hogan's Appeal*, 145
Hogg, Alexander, 190
Holloway, Robert, 84, 195
Holstein, Anthony, 190
Holt, Daniel, 138
Holt, F. L., 112, *The Law of Libel*, 191
Holt, Sir John, 77–8, 81
Hotten, John Camden, 245, 253, 261, 270–1, 275, 284, 287

534

537